# Globalisation, Development and Transition

With love, to Jean, Paul and Fiona

# Globalisation, Development and Transition

Conversations with Eminent Economists

Brian Snowdon

*Senior Teaching Fellow, Department of Economics and Finance, Durham University, UK*

**Edward Elgar**

Cheltenham, UK • Northampton, MA, USA

Published by
Edward Elgar Publishing Limited
The Lypiatts
15 Lansdown Road
Cheltenham
Glos GL50 2JA
UK

Edward Elgar Publishing, Inc.
William Pratt House
9 Dewey Court
Northampton
Massachusetts 01060
USA

Paperback edition 2009

A catalogue record for this book
is available from the British Library

**Library of Congress Cataloguing in Publication Data**

Snowdon, Brian.
    Globalisation, development and transition: conversations with eminent economists/Brian Snowdon.
        p.   cm.
    Includes bibliographical references and index.
    1. Entrepreneurship. 2. Globalization. 3. Economic history—
20th century. I. Title. II. Title: Globalization, development and transition.
HF1369.S597      2007
337—dc22

                                                        2006034554

**Mixed Sources**
Product group from well-managed
forests and other controlled sources
www.fsc.org Cert no. SA-COC-1565
© 1996 Forest Stewardship Council

ISBN 978 1 84542 850 1 (cased)
ISBN 978 1 84844 815 5 (paperback)

Printed and bound by MPG Books Group, UK

# Contents

## INTERVIEWS

# Figures

# Tables

# Preface

The twentieth century was a remarkable period of economic and political history. During this era the world witnessed two catastrophic world wars, a 45-year 'cold war', the rise and fall of both fascism and communism, a rapid acceleration in the pace of technological change, a 'Great Depression', 1929–33, that shook the very foundations of the core capitalist economies, the fall and rise of globalisation, the gradual spread of an industrial and demographic revolution that has now influenced the whole world, a significant increase in the number of independent nations, the rise of international terrorism, and, as the century progressed, the eventual spread of democracy to more and more countries. The lasting influence of these events on the evolving international economic and political system of the twenty-first century cannot be overstated.

In writing this book my objective has been to interpret and provide a survey of several of these major issues, each of which has shaped the modern world. In particular, this book focuses on the many controversies relating to the causes and consequences of increasing international economic integration and globalisation, long-run economic growth and development, the rise and fall of the socialist economies, and the problems of transition to capitalism. To shed light on these major issues, the volume contains interviews with eleven leading economists who have each contributed extensively to the literature on international economics, globalisation, economic development, and the economics of socialism and transition.

As I have argued elsewhere (see Snowdon, 2002a, 2002b), economists have much to gain from a greater knowledge of history, in particular economic history. Therefore a major influence that runs throughout the book is the conviction that economists can gain valuable insights concerning important contemporary policy issues from a knowledge of history, and I remain convinced that the study of economic history is much neglected within the modern university education of economists. This is especially the case given the revival of interest and research into the origins of economic growth. Economic historians have developed numerous important insights into the process of economic growth, the influence of institutions and political constraints. Not only does the past provide a gigantic laboratory for testing various hypotheses in economics; history also contains many lessons that can provide useful information for contemporary policy makers, not least those in the developing countries and transition economies. Because the past shapes the present, it must also influence the future. As Claudia Goldin (1995) argues, the 'remnants of the past, which shape the realm of the possible today, are always with us, norms, structures, institutions, and even people'. A knowledge of history helps us to understand how societies and economies change. This is important because contemporary economic historians are primarily interested in the long-run development of economies. Hence they seek to understand the fundamental causes of economic growth, the evolution and impact of institutions, and the historical origins of current economic problems. While history rarely repeats itself exactly, it does offer guidance, broadens our stock of knowledge, highlights what may be important in determining outcomes, and 'enables us to identify and read signals' (Horrell, 2003, p. F186).

My special thanks must go to the distinguished economists featured in this book who, generously, and with good humour, gave their time to enable the completion of interviews, namely: Daron Acemoglu, Alberto Alesina, Padma Desai, William Easterly, Stanley Fischer, János Kornai, Michael Porter, Dani Rodrik, Jeffrey Sachs, Xavier Sala-i-Martin and Jeffrey Williamson. The views and interpretations expressed in Chapters 1–3 are those of the author and do not necessarily reflect the views of the interviewees.

A project such as this involves enormous logistical problems given the geographical distance between the author and all of the interviewees. The University of Northumbria generously funded my travel to the USA on five separate occasions, and also one visit to Budapest. The first interview for this book was with Dani Rodrik, conducted at the American Economic Association Conference in Atlanta, in January 2002. I next interviewed János Kornai, at the Institute for Advanced Study Collegium Budapest, in October 2002. In January 2003 I interviewed Bill Easterly at the Center for Global Development in Washington, DC, and in May 2003 I visited Harvard and MIT to interview Jeffrey Williamson and Daron Acemoglu. During that same trip to the USA I also interviewed Stanley Fischer at Citigroup, New York. In May 2004 I returned to Harvard to interview Alberto Alesina and Michael Porter, and the final set of interviews took place in May 2005 when I visited Columbia University to interview Jeffrey Sachs, Xavier Sala-i-Martin and Padma Desai. I had originally planned to interview Dani Rodrik and Jeffrey Williamson on 12 and 13 September 2001. My flight to the USA on September 11 was diverted, mid-Atlantic, to Amsterdam. If the world was changed dramatically by events in 1914, 1939 and 1989, so too did the world become a different place following the tragic events of September 11, 2001.

The interviewees are all economists whose research and publications have contributed enormously to the modern debate on key issues that will help to shape the course of world history in the twenty-first century, in particular: the impact of globalisation (Fischer, Rodrik, Williamson), ethnic diversity (Alesina, Easterly), the problems of transition from socialism to capitalism (Desai, Fischer, Kornai, Sachs), the shock therapy v. gradualism debate (Desai, Fischer, Kornai, Sachs), the political economy of reform (Acemoglu, Alesina, Desai, Easterly, Fischer, Kornai, Rodrik, Sachs), economic growth and international inequality (Alesina, Easterly, Sala-i-Martin, Williamson), international competitiveness (Porter, Sachs, Sala-i-Martin), the microeconomic foundations of productivity (Porter, Sala-i-Martin), the impact of institutions and geography on growth (Acemoglu, Easterly, Rodrik, Sachs), the importance of macroeconomic stability for sustainable growth (Alesina, Easterly, Fischer, Sala-i-Martin), the development tragedy of sub-Saharan Africa (Easterly, Sachs, Sala-i-Martin), economic integration, the size and break-up of nations, (Alesina), exchange rate regimes and currency unions (Alesina, Fischer), the role of foreign aid (Alesina, Easterly, Sachs), international labour migration (Williamson), political barriers to macroeconomic stability and economic development (Acemoglu, Alesina, Kornai, Desai), the political economy of fiscal policy (Alesina), the natural-resource curse (Sachs, Sala-i-Martin), democracy and development (Acemoglu, Kornai).

I have provided, throughout the text, a large number of references that will enable interested readers to follow up various topics in greater depth. My intended audience includes undergraduate students of economics and the social sciences, as well as graduate students who require a broad introductory survey of the issues discussed in this book. I hope my academic colleagues will also find much to interest them in this volume since the powerful forces of globalisation, growth, development and transition will continue to have an enormous influence on the political and economic landscape of the twenty-first century.

My special thanks go to Caroline Cornish and Alexandra O'Connell at Edward Elgar Publishing Ltd for their superb editorial assistance in the production of this volume.

Finally, my thanks and love to my wife Jean, and (grown-up) children Paul and Fiona. Without their love, encouragement, and support, I could never have completed this project.

# Acknowledgements

The author would like to thank the following who have kindly given their permission to reproduce previously published material, namely:

**NTC Economic & Financial Publishing**, Washington, DC, USA, and Henley-on-Thames, UK, for permission to reproduce large sections of the following articles previously published by the author in the journal *World Economics*:

'Russia at the Crossroads: Padma Desai on Transition, Reform and the "Kamikaze Crew's" Liberal Legacy', *World Economics*, 7(2), April–June, 2006.

'The Enduring Elixir of Economic Growth: Xavier Sala-i-Martin on the Wealth and Poverty of Nations', *World Economics*, 7(1), January–March, 2006.

'A Global Compact to End Poverty: Jeffrey Sachs on Stabilisation, Transition and Weapons of Mass Salvation', *World Economics*, 6(4), October–December, 2005.

'Measuring Progress and Other Tall Stories: From Income to Anthropometrics' (co-authored with Professor John Komlos, University of Munich, Germany), *World Economics*, 6(2), April–June, 2005.

'The Influence of Political Distortions on Economic Performance', *World Economics*, 5(4), October–December, 2004.

'Explaining the "Great Divergence": Daron Acemoglu on How Growth Theorists Rediscovered History and the Importance of Institutions', *World Economics*, 5(2), April–June, 2004.

'Stanley Fischer on the Role of International Institutions in the Twenty-First Century World Economy', *World Economics*, 5(1), January–March, 2004.

'Back to the Future: Jeffrey Williamson on Globalisation in History', *World Economics*, 4(4), October–December, 2003.

'In Search of the Holy Grail: William Easterly on the Elusive Quest for Growth and Development', *World Economics*, 4(3), July–September, 2003.

'From Socialism to Capitalism and Democracy: János Kornai on the Trials of Socialism and Transition', *World Economics*, **4**(1), January–March, 2003.

'Should We Be Globaphobic About Globalisation? Dani Rodrik on the Economic and Political Implications of Increasing International Economic Integration', *World Economics*, **3**(4), October–December, 2002.

**NTC Economic & Financial Publishing**, Washington, DC, USA, and Henley-on-Thames, UK, for permission to reproduce Table 2 from Professor Paul De Grauwe and Filip Camerman, 'Are Multinationals Really Bigger than Nations?', *World Economics*, **4**(2), April–June, 2003.

**The Academy of International Business**, for permission to reproduce the interview with Professor Michael Porter previously published in the March 2006 issue of *The Journal of International Business Studies*, Palgrave Macmillan, Houndmills, Basingstoke, Hampshire, UK.

**The American Economic Association**, Nashville, Tennessee, USA, for permission to reproduce Figure 1 from Professor Robert Fogel's article, 'Catching Up With the Economy', *American Economic Review*, March, 1999.

**Professor Jeffrey G. Williamson**, Harvard University, Cambridge, USA, for permission to reproduce migration data from his paper, 'Poverty Traps, Distance and Diversity: The Migration Connection', Working Paper, Department of Economics, Harvard University; and Table 1 from K.H. O'Rourke and J.G. Williamson, *Globalisation and History: Evolution of the Nineteenth-Century Atlantic Economy*, Cambridge, MA: MIT Press, 1999.

**Professor Kevin H. O'Rourke**, Trinity College, University of Dublin, Ireland, for his permission to reproduce Figure 5 from his paper, 'Europe and the Causes of Globalisation: 1790–2000', published in H. Kierzkowski (ed.), *From Europeanisation of the Globe to the Globalisation of Europe*, London: Palgrave, 2002.

**The International Monetary Fund**, Washington, DC, USA, for permission to reproduce Table 1 from the paper by Professor Stanley Fischer and Ratna Sahay, 'Taking Stock', published in *Finance and Development*, September, 2000.

# 1. The fall and rise of globalisation

> It is hardly possible to overrate the value, in the present low state of human improvement, of placing human beings in contact with persons dissimilar to themselves, and with modes of thought and action unlike those with which they are familiar.
>
> John Stuart Mill (1848, p. 594)

> We cannot take it for granted that the world will continue down the road of globalisation, greater prosperity, and greater democracy. That may be an astonishing thing to say at the end of a century that witnessed the first sustained competition between two clearly defined economic and political systems. The pro-democracy, pro-market, pro-globalisation system won that contest decisively. Nonetheless that system is under attack.
>
> Stanley Fischer (2003, p. 26)

> Globalisation today is not working for many of the world's poor . . . To some, there is an easy answer: Abandon globalisation. That is neither feasible nor desirable . . . The problem is not with globalisation, but how it has been managed.
>
> Joseph Stiglitz (2002a, p. 214)

## 1.1 INTRODUCTION

The twenty-first century will truly mark a new and challenging era for the international political and economic system. During the last quarter of the twentieth century, global economic integration, or in more popular language, 'globalisation', has accelerated. In the long run this trend would seem to be irreversible, even if this is not necessarily the case in the short run. Driving this development have been several important factors, especially (i) the increasing acceptance and influence on public policies of liberal (pro-market) economic ideas, leading to a reduction in trade barriers championed by the General Agreement on Tariffs and Trade (GATT) and the World Trade Organisation (WTO); (ii) technological improvements within the transportation and financial sectors; (iii) the influence of the communications and ICT (information and communication technology) revolution; and (iv) social and cultural convergence driven by individual preferences that favour taking advantage of the increasing opportunities provided by international contact.

*1*

An important lesson of the twentieth century is that increasing and sustainable material prosperity comes from the adoption of market-friendly economic policies combined with a more focused role for the state, not from war, territorial acquisition and plunder. Nevertheless, globalisation, by vastly increasing the volume of cross-border economic transactions, is raising numerous challenges for the world economy as a whole, and enterprises, governments and the major international institutions in particular. The role of the major international institutions is crucial since it is one of their key objectives to provide an enabling political and economic environment that reduces the cross-border transaction costs of mutually beneficial trade (Wolf, 2004a, 2004b).

There were five dominant events of the twentieth century that helped to shape the current international economic system: (i) the uneven spread of the Industrial Revolution and economic growth across the world; (ii) the 'Great Depression' of the 1930s; (iii) the 'Great Inflation' of the 1970s; (iv) the rise and fall of the socialist system; and (v) the fall and rise of international economic integration (globalisation). Many commentators would argue that the latter two formed *the* defining feature of the world economy in the last decade of the twentieth century, even if the world is still very far from the level of international integration that is sometimes implied in popular discussion (Rodrik, 2000a; Glyn, 2004).

While the revival of a more liberal world economy has been the great policy success of the last 50 years, the breakdown of the global economy after 1914, a process accelerated by the Great Depression in the 1930s, also provides a sobering historical reminder of the fragility of the international economic system. The importance of these issues for human welfare cannot be overstated, and in the face of the well-publicised hostility to increasing globalisation from 'anti-globalist' groups there is a need for economists to contribute to the public debate on the costs and benefits of international integration.

## 1.2   GLOBALISATION v. 'GLOBAPHOBIA'

While economists prefer to use the term 'international economic integration' when discussing the growth of overseas economic transactions, the term 'globalisation' is now firmly established in popular discussion of such activities. According to the *Oxford English Dictionary*, the use of the term 'globalisation' emerged in an article in the 5 October 1962 issue of *The Spectator* (see Temin, 1999). But is was not until the early 1980s that the term began to take hold within academia. For example, in Levitt's 1983 *Harvard Business Review* article, 'The Globalisation of Markets', he begins by noting that:

A powerful force drives the world toward a converging commonality, and that force is technology . . . The result is a new commercial reality – the emergence of global markets for standardised consumer products on a previously unimagined scale . . . The globalisation of markets is upon us. (p. 92)

The term globalisation is now firmly established in public discourse, whether it be in the media, or in academic, political and international institutions (Marks et al., 2006). Stanley Fischer (2003, p. 2) notes that

During the 1970s the word 'globalisation' was never mentioned in the pages of the *New York Times*. In the 1980s the word cropped up less than once a week, in the first half of the 1990s less than twice a week – and in the latter half of the decade no more than three times a week. In 2000 there were 514 stories in the paper that made reference to 'globalisation'; there were 364 stories in 2001, and 393 references in 2002. Based on stories in the *New York Times*, the idea of being 'anti-globalisation' was not one that existed before about 1999.

Turning to the Internet, the Google search engine turns up 102 million hits (August 2006) for the word 'globalization' and over 36 million hits for 'globalisation' (Yahoo's search engine yields 25 million and 11.5 million hits respectively).

Although there is no widely agreed definition of globalisation, economists usually think of it as the historical process of increasing international economic integration via reductions in the barriers to trade, and increased capital flows, foreign direct investment, technology and knowledge transfer, and migration. It also embraces political, cultural and environmental dimensions. Despite popular opinion to the contrary, currently the world is only 'partially globalised'. 'Full globalisation' would involve a level of integration where the world economy is as integrated as a single country, and hence where political borders cease to segment markets. In Dani Rodrik's (2004) view, the full unification of markets and complete price convergence are 'quite unfeasible' (see also Temin, 1999; Rodrik, 2000a, 2005a).

One popular measure of globalisation is the 'A.T. Kearney/Foreign Policy Globalisation Index' (KFP). The KFP aims to provide a comprehensive measure of the extent of globalisation across the world by assessing and ranking 62 countries, representing all the major regions, that account for 96 per cent of the world's GDP and 85 per cent of the world's population (http://atkearney.com. See also OECD, 2005, for alternative measures, and Lockwood, 2004, for a critique of the KFP index). The KFP index concentrates on four main dimensions of globalisation:

1. economic integration (trade in goods and services and FDI);
2. technological connectivity (Internet users, hosts and servers);

3. personal contact (tourism, telephone use, international remittances);
4. political engagement (membership and participation in international organisations).

According to the KFP index, in 2005 the top ten countries in terms of global integration were (1) Singapore, (2) Ireland, (3) Switzerland, (4) the USA, (5) the Netherlands, (6) Canada, (7) Denmark, (8) Sweden, (9) Austria, and (10) Finland (the UK was ranked twelfth). The bottom ten countries were (53) Peru, (54) China, (55) Venezuela, (56) Turkey, (57) Brazil, (58) Bangladesh, (59) Egypt, (60) Indonesia, (61) India, and (62) Iran. Russia (ranked 44 in 2004), showed one of the largest declines, having fallen to a rank of 52 in 2005, and has still to complete reforms that will allow entry to the WTO (see Chapter 3 and Desai interview).

As the forces of globalisation increase access to markets, the importance of distance and national boundaries inevitably diminishes, although they are far from eliminated (see Crafts, 2005). Globalisation, by unleashing the powerful forces of competition, has encouraged many firms to restructure their production activities where different parts of the production process are carried out in different geographical locations around the world. Particularly controversial is the phenomenon of 'offshore outsourcing' that has led many non-economists to (wrongly) conclude that globalisation threatens the *general* level of employment in the developed economies (Bhagwati et al., 2004; Blinder, 2006; Mankiw and Swagel, 2006). Therefore, it is not surprising that globalisation, and the challenges posed by the expansion of global capitalism, especially since the fall of the Berlin Wall in 1989, raise strong emotions among participants in the globalisation debate. As Fischer (2003) argues, the debate over globalisation is 'often passionate, and sometimes violent'; consequently, discussions of globalisation invariably focus on numerous emotive issues, including inequality, the impact on wages and employment, poverty, exploitation and child labour, the 'power' of multinational corporations, international labour migration, financial market volatility, environmental degradation, energy supplies and global warming, threats to democracy and the nation-state, fiscal implications, and the future of the welfare state. Many of the fears raised in these debates turn out to be either exaggerated, misplaced or incorrect, while others do have real substance and require urgent attention (the following references give some idea of the breadth of the current globalisation debate: Rodrik, 1997, 1998a, 1999a, 2000a; Burtless et al., 1998; Schultz and Ursprung, 1999; Slaughter, 1999; Gilpin, 2000; Snowdon, 2001a, 2002a; Prakash, 2001; Bhagwati, 2002, 2004a; Calomiris, 2002; Mendoza and Bahadur, 2002; Stiglitz, 2002a; Tanzi, 2002, 2004; Alesina and Spolare, 2003; Deardorff, 2003; Desai, 2003; Fischer, 2003; Baldwin and Winters, 2004; Hamilton, 2004; Henderson,

2004; Panagariya, 2004a; Sutcliffe, 2004; Tanzi, 2004; Williamson, 2004; Wolf, 2004a; Aisbett, 2005; Lackner and Sachs, 2005; Sala-i-Martin, 2006).

At the outset it is important to distinguish between 'anti-globalists' and 'globalisation critics'. 'Anti-globalists' are an extremely heterogeneous group who tend to regard globalisation as a threatening force that is damaging the world economy, in particular the developing countries and poorer groups within developed economies. Many anti-globalists would like to reverse the process of international integration (Bhagwati, 2004b), and their ranks include representation from many labour organisations, environmentalists, anarchists, anti-capitalists, neo-Marxists, anti-Americanism, right-wing extremists, nationalists, religious fundamentalists, politicians and many academics (but notably excluding the vast majority of economists). 'Globalisation critics', notably Nobel Laureate Joseph Stiglitz (2002a, 2004a, 2006) and Dani Rodrik (2000a, 2005a), regard globalisation as a potential engine for increasing world prosperity providing the existing international system, including the International Monetary Fund, the World Bank and the World Trade Organisation, can be substantially reformed, and policies to promote international integration are also accompanied by policies within countries that improve governance and domestic-market-supporting institutions. Even vociferous supporters of globalisation, such as Jagdish Bhagwati, recognise the inherent dangers of 'premature capital market liberalisation' (Bhagwati, 1998a, 1998b) and the need to create institutions and policies that can alleviate the downsides of globalisation. In general, economists believe that the potential benefits of globalisation far outweigh the costs and, as Fischer (2003) concludes, the overall challenge for economists is to help to make 'the global system deliver economic growth more consistently and more equitably, as the best way to further reduce global poverty and inequality'. As Bhagwati (2005) argues, 'Trade enhances growth and growth reduces poverty' (see Dollar and Kraay, 2002a, 2002b, 2004).

While economists generally advocate increasing international integration on the basis that it raises economic welfare in the long run, the historical record shows that globalisation is not irreversible. As the inter-war period demonstrates, the process of international integration can be stopped in its tracks by a 'globalisation backlash' (Williamson, 1998a; James, 1999, 2001; Henderson, 2004).

## 1.3 THE GAINS FROM TRADE AND GOOD GOVERNANCE

Stanley Fischer (2003), in his Ely Lecture to the American Economics Association in January 2003, chose 'Globalisation and its Challenges' as his topic. Fischer used this opportunity to argue that the big challenge facing economists is international global poverty and that the 'surest route to sustained poverty reduction is economic growth'. Since growth is contingent on the adoption of growth-friendly policies, and the evidence strongly supports the positive link between outward orientation of economies and their subsequent economic growth, economists naturally tend to be pro-globalisation although some have questioned the distribution of its costs and benefits (Dowrick and Golley, 2004; Stiglitz and Charlton, 2005; Stiglitz, 2006).

The gains from trade and international integration have long been recognised by economists, and the idea that the gains from trade arise from comparative rather than absolute advantage is one of the most powerful ideas in economics (Budd, 2004). The first coherent statement of the optimistic vision of international integration came from Adam Smith (1776), and was refined and developed by David Ricardo (1817) and John Stuart Mill (1848). Such linkages not only promote static and dynamic efficiency gains, but also the transfer of new ideas which drive technological progress. This is certainly not a new insight. As noted by Mokyr (1994, p. 562), in 1742 David Hume observed that:

> nothing is more favourable to the rise of politeness and learning than a number of neighbouring and independent states, connected together by commerce and policy. The emulation which naturally arises among those neighbouring states is an obvious source of improvement.

International linkages are also likely to facilitate the spread of economic and political freedom as well as reduce the probability of international conflict (Lake, 1992; Dixon, 1994, Bhagwati, 2002; Calomiris, 2002). For example, the most important initial reason for establishing the closer economic ties between France and Germany after the Second World War, which eventually led to the formation of the European Economic Community in 1957, was to provide an important economic incentive that would act as a robust and lasting barrier to future conflict.

Important in the development of economies is the international dimension, and economists generally agree that increased international trade and capital flows have been a major source of rising income per capita in those economies that have pursued outward-oriented development strategies and joined the global economy during the second half of the twentieth century (Bairoch, 1972; Baldwin, 2003; Panagariya, 2004a). It should also be noted that while the classical economists were optimistic about the economic and political benefits of free trade, they also recognised that economic development crucially requires supportive institutions, including good governance, and a coherent market-friendly domestic economic strategy. This is an important theme in the research of Dani Rodrik, who has consistently argued that while there are many economic benefits that can arise from openness, these are only potential benefits, 'to be realised in full only when the complementary policies and institutions are in place domestically' (Rodrik, 1999a). To Rodrik the key fundamentals that need to be in place to foster sustained economic growth are capital accumulation, macroeconomic stability, the development of human resources, technological progress and good governance (ibid.).

While the precise origins of the 'East Asian growth miracle' remain controversial, most economists agree that an essential ingredient of the success of Hong Kong, Singapore, South Korea and Taiwan has been their outward orientation and increased integration into the world economy, together with the development of sound institutions and policies. While Stiglitz is a leading critic of many aspects of globalisation, he is the first to argue that the East Asian miracle was 'largely based on globalisation' (Stiglitz and Yusuf, 2001; Stiglitz, 2004a. See also Rodrik, 1995; Krueger, 1997, 1998; Elson, 2006). Radelet et al. (1997) identify four crucial ingredients for the growth 'miracle' of the Asian Tigers:

1.  they were all in a position where there was substantial potential for 'catch-up' and convergence, having entered the 1960s with low per capita incomes but possessing a relatively educated workforce;
2.  as a group these economies all had relatively favourable geographical characteristics;
3.  the demographic features of these economies were conducive to more rapid growth; and
4.  finally, the overall strategy and economic policies adopted in each case also facilitated the creation of an environment conducive to sustained growth; in particular the high-performing East Asian countries recognised the imperative of joining the world economy through the promotion of labour-intensive manufacturing exports.

The opportunity for further growth remains, although it seems likely that growth rates will be lower than those achieved in the 1960–97 period. This slowdown, in effect, is a measure of the success that Hong Kong, Singapore, Taiwan and South Korea have had in catching up the rich 'Western' economies. During the last 20 years the two 'Asian Giants', China and India, have at last begun to liberalise their economies from the shackles of excessive *dirigisme* and have the potential to repeat the growth miracles witnessed in the East Asian Tiger economies (see Panagariya, 2004b; Branstetter and Lardy, 2006).

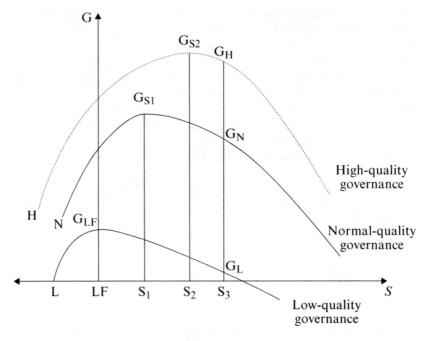

*Source:*   Adapted from Paldam (2003).

*Figure 1.1    State intervention and economic growth*

An important controversy in the debate on the East Asian growth miracle relates to the role of the state (World Bank, 1993, 1997; Rodrik, 1995; Stiglitz, 1996; Stiglitz and Yusuf, 2001; Porter and Sakakibara, 2004). Economists believe that good governance is an important ingredient for sustainable growth, where the characteristics of good governance include the rule of law, rational decision making, accountability and transparency, control of corruption, efficiency, strategic vision, and equity and involvement. The likely relationship between good governance and growth is illustrated in Figure 1.1 (see Paldam, 2003).

Here, the extent of state intervention (S) is measured on the horizontal axis, and the rate of economic growth (G) is measured on the vertical axis. The quality of governance curves, L = Low, N = Normal, and H = High, indicate that different growth outcomes are possible with the same level of state intervention. With low-quality governance a level of intervention of $S_3$ yields a growth rate of $G_L$, a growth rate of $G_N$ with normal-quality governance, and a growth rate of $G_H$ with high-quality governance. In the case of low-quality governance, the growth rate is at a maximum ($G_{LF}$) with *laissez-faire* (LF). In the case of high-quality governance, growth is at a maximum ($G_{S2}$) with a level of state intervention of $S_2$, and with normal-quality governance growth is at a maximum ($G_{S1}$) at a level of state intervention of $S_1$. In all cases growth collapses rapidly at levels of intervention below LF since no economy can function without the establishment of basic institutions such as law and order. This framework perhaps helps to explain why some growth miracles, such as Singapore's, have been associated with significant state intervention, whereas other countries with similar levels of intervention have been growth disasters. As is well documented, the quality of governance on most dimensions in Singapore is very high (see World Bank Governance Indicators, www.worldbank.org).

One area of intervention remains very controversial: the role of protectionism in the early stages of development (Irwin, 1996; Panagariya, 2002; Williamson, 2006a, see Chapter 2). While import substitution industrialisation strategies have generally fallen into disrepute, Greenwald and Stiglitz (2006) have recently restated the case for using a broad-based tariff on industrial products in order to stimulate growth in 'infant economies', citing the successful application of such a strategy in the EEC, Japan, Korea, Taiwan, Singapore, China, and the early history of industrialisation in the USA. While there are inevitable inefficiencies associated with such a strategy, in the Greenwald–Stiglitz model, the dynamic benefits of broad trade restrictions are likely to outweigh the static costs (see also Bruton, 1998; O'Rourke, 2000; Williamson, 2003; Chang, 2002; Stiglitz and Charlton, 2005).

An important stream of thinking among neo-Marxists is the exploitation-via-trade story. This story, in sharp contrast to Adam Smith's classical vision, predicts a trade-induced polarisation between the developed capitalist countries at the 'centre' and underdeveloped countries at the 'periphery' (see Hunt, 1989). The revolutionary policy prescription of this trade impoverishment thesis is that poor underdeveloped countries should withdraw from the capitalist world trading system because to integrate with the world capitalist system is tantamount to economic suicide for low-income countries! However, neither history nor empirical evidence has been kind to this exploitation-via-trade story, although presumably it still carries weight among the anti-capitalist ranks of the anti-globalist demonstrators. However, the East Asian miracle and stagnating experience of closed economies like North Korea are difficult to reconcile with either the centre–periphery thesis or the neo-Marxist story.

Embedded within this story is also the myth that modern multinational corporations (MNCs) are all-powerful given their size which, it is claimed, exceeds that of many developed economies. This result is derived by incorrectly computing the size of MNCs by using sales data, and correctly computing the size of the GDP of countries by using value-added data! This elementary error, highlighted in most first-year undergraduate text-books, grossly inflates the size of MNCs relative to GDP estimates. For example, Anderson and Cavanagh (2000) claim that 'Of the 100 largest economies in the world, 51 are corporations.' By their calculations General Motors (ranked 23) is larger than the Danish economy (ranked 24)! De Grauwe and Camerman (2003), in their critique of Anderson and Cavanagh, show that, measured correctly, General Motors (ranked 53) is actually smaller than the economy of Bangladesh (ranked 51)! Only Wal-Mart Stores (ranked 44) is in the top 50 classified by value-added GDP in 2000 (see Table 1.1). In contrast to popular perceptions, over time 'MNCs have not grown in size relative to the nation-states nor have they become more powerful in the last twenty years' (ibid.).

There is also a contradiction in the claim made by anti-globalists that increasing international integration raises insecurity due to increased competition, while at the same time attacking MNCs as centres of monopoly power! Surely competition *reduces* monopoly power.

## 1.4   WHEN DID GLOBALISATION BEGIN?

While popular discussions and use of the word 'globalisation' are a recent phenomenon, the process of increasing international integration has a long history. As the collaborative research of O'Rourke and Williamson has shown, the assumption made by many journalists, politicians and anti-globalists that globalisation is a modern, late-twentieth-century development is incorrect (see O'Rourke and Williamson, 1999, 2002a, 2002b, 2002c; Williamson, 2002a, 2002b; Frieden, 2006). While the contemporary consequences of globalisation raise many serious issues relating to the design of appropriate political and institutional underpinnings, it is also important to view increasing international integration in its historical context. We are currently witnessing not the first, but the second, age of globalisation, the first age having come to an abrupt end in 1914 (Sachs and Warner, 1995; James, 2001). Jeffrey Williamson's research illustrates how history is particularly relevant to the modern debate on 'globalisation' (see Williamson interview).

Although popular discussion of globalisation has been widespread since the early 1990s, the research of economists and economic historians has convincingly demonstrated that the world economy was reasonably well integrated by 1914, even if the depth of commercial and financial integration was more limited than we observe today (see Baldwin and Martin, 1999; Bordo et al., 1999). On the basis of increasing trade flows, world

*Table 1.1    Countries and corporations classified according to value-added GDP (billion dollars) in 2000*

| | | | | | |
|---|---|---|---|---|---|
| 1 | USA | 9882.8 | 43 | Chile | 70.5 |
| 2 | Japan | 4677.1 | 44 | **Wal-Mart Stores** | 67.7 |
| 3 | Germany | 1870.1 | 45 | Pakistan | 61.6 |
| 4 | United Kingdom | 1413.4 | 46 | Peru | 53.5 |
| 5 | France | 1286.3 | 47 | Algeria | 53.3 |
| 6 | China | 1076.9 | 48 | **Exxon** | 52.6 |
| 7 | Italy | 1068.5 | 49 | Czech Republic | 50.8 |
| 8 | Canada | 689.5 | 50 | New Zealand | 50.0 |
| 9 | Brazil | 595.5 | 51 | Bangladesh | 47.1 |
| 10 | Mexico | 574.5 | 52 | United Arab Emirates | 46.5 |
| 11 | Spain | 555.0 | 53 | **General Motors** | 46.2 |
| 12 | India | 474.3 | 54 | Hungary | 45.6 |
| 13 | Korea, Republic of | 457.2 | 55 | **Ford Motor** | 45.1 |
| 14 | Australia | 394.0 | 56 | **Mitsubishi** | 44.3 |
| 15 | Netherlands | 364.9 | 57 | **Mitsui** | 41.3 |
| 16 | Argentina | 285.0 | 58 | Nigeria | 41.1 |
| 17 | Russia | 251.1 | 59 | **Citigroup** | 39.1 |
| 18 | Switzerland | 240.3 | 60 | **Itochu** | 38.4 |
| 19 | Belgium | 231.0 | 61 | **DaimlerChrysler** | 37.5 |
| 20 | Sweden | 227.4 | 62 | **Royal Dutch/Shell** | 37.3 |
| 21 | Turkey | 199.9 | 63 | **BP** | 37.0 |
| 22 | Austria | 191.0 | 64 | Romania | 36.7 |
| 23 | Hong Kong | 163.3 | 65 | **Nippon T&T** | 36.1 |
| 24 | Poland | 162.2 | 66 | Ukraine | 35.3 |
| 25 | Denmark | 160.8 | 67 | Morocco | 33.5 |
| 26 | Indonesia | 153.3 | 68 | **AXA** | 32.5 |
| 27 | Norway | 149.3 | 69 | **General Electric** | 32.5 |
| 28 | Saudi Arabia | 139.4 | 70 | **Sumitomo** | 31.9 |
| 29 | South Africa | 125.9 | 71 | Vietnam | 31.3 |
| 30 | Thailand | 121.9 | 72 | **Toyota Motor** | 30.4 |
| 31 | Venezuela | 120.5 | 73 | Belarus | 29.9 |
| 32 | Finland | 119.8 | 74 | **Marubeni** | 29.9 |
| 33 | Greece | 112.0 | 75 | Kuwait | 29.7 |
| 34 | Israel | 110.3 | 76 | **Total Fina Elf** | 26.5 |
| 35 | Portugal | 103.9 | 77 | **Enron** | 25.2 |
| 36 | Iran | 99.0 | 78 | **ING Group** | 24.9 |
| 37 | Egypt | 98.7 | 79 | **Allianz Holding** | 24.9 |
| 38 | Ireland | 94.4 | 80 | **E.ON** | 24.3 |
| 39 | Singapore | 92.3 | 81 | **Nippon Life Insurance** | 23.8 |
| 40 | Malaysia | 89.7 | 82 | **Deutsche Bank** | 23.5 |
| 41 | Colombia | 81.3 | 83 | **AT&T** | 23.1 |
| 42 | Philippines | 74.7 | 84 | **Verizon Comm.** | 22.6 |

*Table 1.1*　　(continued)

| 85 | **US Postal Service** | 22.6 | 93 | **Bank of America Corp.** | 20.2 |
|----|------------------------|------|-----|----------------------------|------|
| 86 | Croatia | 22.4 | 94 | **BNP Paribas** | 20.2 |
| 87 | **IBM** | 22.1 | 95 | **Volkswagen** | 19.7 |
| 88 | **CGNU** | 21.5 | 96 | Dominican Republic | 19.7 |
| 89 | **JP Morgan Chase** | 21.0 | 97 | Uruguay | 19.7 |
| 90 | **Carrefour** | 21.0 | 98 | Tunisia | 19.5 |
| 91 | **Crédit Suisse** | 20.8 | 99 | Slovak Republic | 19.1 |
| 92 | **Nissho Iwai** | 20.5 | 100 | **Hitachi** | 19.0 |

*Source:*　　De Grauwe and Camerman (2003).

historians differ on when globalisation began. Temin (2006), in his recent analysis of the early Roman Empire, notes that 'there appears to have been a flourishing wheat market across the Mediterranean area in the early Roman Empire' and that Rome 'gained greatly from being at the hub of an empire and a large trading network'. While not claiming that the economy of the early Roman Empire represented the beginning of globalisation in the modern sense of the term, Temin argues that during this period the areas surrounding the Mediterranean Sea began to specialise according to the principles of comparative advantage and exploit the gains from trade. Other scholars trace the beginnings of globalisation back to the late fifteenth century, when the 'voyages of discovery' by Christopher Columbus (1492), Vasco da Gama (1498) and others opened up the 'New World'. This 'big bang' interpretation sees 1500 as the turning point in history for the world economy (see Frank, 1998).

While historians have tended to use data on trade volumes to measure globalisation, economists prefer to examine data on the convergence of prices of identical goods in separate markets as reliable evidence of market integration. If markets are truly integrated, the prices of identical goods should converge and remaining price gaps will reflect transport costs as well as trade barriers (Findlay and O'Rourke, 2003).

The idea that globalisation began some five hundred years ago is firmly rejected by O'Rourke and Williamson (2002a, 2002b, 2004). Utilising data on commodity price convergence, they demonstate that there is little evidence of global integration of commodity markets before the early nineteenth century. Their evidence shows that a big bang, heralding the first age of globalisation, began in the 1820s rather than the sixteenth century or before, and it was the period from about 1870 up to the First World War that witnessed the most impressive period of globalisation (Estevadeordal et al., 2003). In a recent paper, Kevin O'Rourke (2005, p. 37) also argues

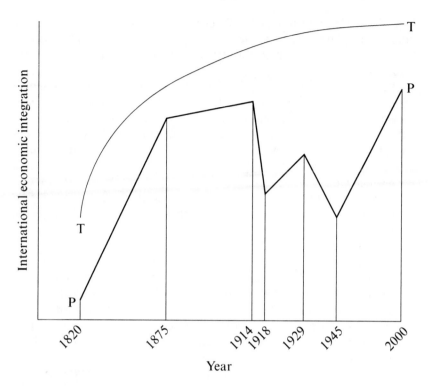

*Source:* O'Rourke (2002).

*Figure 1.2 Globalisation in history*

that, while the 'Revolutionary and Napoleonic Wars' of the period 1793–1815 proved to be a serious impediment to global trade in the short run, ultimately the resolution of those conflicts led to a long period of European peace that 'played a crucial role in modernising the international economy and thus helped to pave the way for the astonishing international integration which was to follow'.

The significant acceleration of global integration during the last quarter of the nineteenth century was driven by the peaceful conditions across Europe and technological developments that significantly lowered the costs of transportation, especially the rapid spread of the railways, the invention of the steamship, and the opening of the Suez Canal in 1869. By 1914, international commodity markets were 'vastly more integrated than they had been in 1750' (Findlay and O'Rourke, 2003).

Following O'Rourke (2002), we can use Figure 1.2 to illustrate the broad pattern of international integration (globalisation) over the period

1820–2000 (Obstfeld and Taylor, 2003, present a stylised view of international capital mobility in modern history that mimics these trends and traces out a similar path to the PP curve in Figure 1.2; see Snowdon, 2002a).

The curve TT represents the maximum feasible level of integration possible over the whole period given the state of technology (e.g. costs of transportation and communication). TT increases throughout the period but at a diminishing rate during the twentieth century. The actual level of integration achieved is given by PP, the location of which is determined by politics and policy. We might refer to the distance between TT and PP as the 'globalisation gap' existing at any point in history, that is, the difference between the level of international economic integration achieved compared to what is technologically feasible. Several points are worth noting:

1.  the globalisation gap is smaller in 1875 than it was in 1820, the year (according to O'Rourke and Williamson) when globalisation begins;
2.  because the years 1820–75 were relatively peaceful for the world economy, technological developments dominate integration trends during this period, politics was influenced by classical free trade philosophy and therefore complemented the pro-globalisation technological developments;
3.  the post-1875 globalisation backlash can be detected by the growing gap between TT and PP in the period 1875–1914, although the growing backlash was not yet strong enough to prevent technological developments from increasing the actual level of integration until 1914;
4.  political developments dominate the globalisation process in the period 1914–45, when war, the Great Depression, protectionism and the political influence of the anti-globalisation backlash led to global disintegration;
5.  since 1945 economic integration has gradually recovered lost ground among the OECD countries (and increasingly, during the last 25 years, also the majority of developing countries), being promoted by international institutions such as the GATT, the WTO, the IMF and the World Bank (Srinivasan, 1999);
6.  since the fall of the Berlin Wall in 1989 the vast majority of former communist countries (and China after 1979) have rejoined the world trading system;
7.  India, since the mid-1980s, has also become a much more open economy and appears to have finally escaped from its 'Hindu rate of growth'.

*Table 1.2   Trade shares, 1870–1987*[1]

| Country | 1870 | 1913 | 1950 | 1973 | 1987 |
|---|---|---|---|---|---|
| Australia | 6.3 | 10.9 | 7.8 | 9.5 | 12.4 |
| Austria | 9.0 | 13.9 | 4.0 | 12.6 | 20.0 |
| Belgium | 7.0 | 17.5 | 13.4 | 40.3 | 52.5 |
| Canada | 12.8 | 12.9 | 13.0 | 19.9 | 23.8 |
| Denmark | 6.6 | 10.1 | 9.3 | 18.2 | 25.8 |
| Finland | 10.5 | 17.0 | 12.7 | 20.5 | 23.0 |
| France | 3.4 | 6.0 | 5.6 | 11.2 | 14.3 |
| Germany | 7.4 | 12.2 | 4.4 | 17.2 | 23.7 |
| Italy | 3.3 | 3.6 | 2.6 | 9.0 | 11.5 |
| Japan | 0.2 | 2.1 | 2.0 | 6.8 | 10.6 |
| Netherlands | 14.6 | 14.5 | 10.2 | 34.1 | 40.9 |
| Norway | 9.3 | 14.6 | 13.5 | 27.4 | 34.0 |
| Sweden | 8.0 | 12.0 | 12.2 | 23.1 | 27.0 |
| Switzerland | 10.4 | 22.3 | 9.8 | 21.3 | 28.9 |
| UK | 10.3 | 14.7 | 9.5 | 11.5 | 15.3 |
| USA | 2.8 | 4.1 | 3.3 | 5.8 | 6.3 |
| Total[2] | 5.9 | 8.2 | 5.2 | 10.3 | 12.8 |

*Notes:*
[1] Merchandise exports as percentage of GDP at 1985 prices.
[2] Average for all 16 countries weighted by country GDP.

*Source:*   O'Rourke and Williamson (1999).

These broad trends can also be detected in the trade and migration data shown in Tables 1.2 and 1.3. In particular, note the declines in trade shares between 1913 and 1950, and also the massive decline in out-migration from Europe and corresponding decline of in-migration into the Western offshoots between the two periods 1870–1913 and 1914–49.

So will the twenty-first century witness the continuing integration of the world economy? Perhaps we can find some answers from history. The research and publications of Jeffrey Williamson convincingly demonstrate just how useful and enlightening the modern approach to economic history can be to contemporary policy makers. In particular his research highlights the relationship between economic history and development economics in an international context. Clearly there is much to learn from historical experience in the modern debate over the costs and benefits of globalisation, and history teaches us that the first age of globalisation went into sharp reversal during the 1914–50 period (Williamson, 2005).

Table 1.3   *Net migration, Western Europe and Western offshoots,*
            *1870–1998*[1]

| Country | 1870–1913 | 1914–49 | 1950–73 | 1974–98 |
|---|---|---|---|---|
| France | 890 000 | −236 000 | 3 630 000 | 1 026 000 |
| Germany | −2 598 000 | −304 000[3] | 7 070 000 | 5 911 000 |
| Italy | −4 459 000 | −1 771 000 | −2 139 000 | 1 617 000 |
| UK | −6 415 000 | −1 405 000[4] | −605 000 | 737 000 |
| **Total Western Europe**[2] | **−13 996 000** | **−3 662 000** | **9 381 000** | **10 898 000** |
| Australia | 885 000 | 673 000 | 2 033 000 | 2 151 000 |
| New Zealand | 290 000 | 138 000 | 247 000 | 87 000 |
| Canada | 861 000 | 207 000 | 2 126 000 | 2 680 000 |
| USA | 15 820 000 | 6 221 000 | 8 257 000 | 16 721 000 |
| **Total Western offshoots** | **17 856 000** | **7 239 000** | **12 663 000** | **21 639 000** |

*Notes:*
[1]  Negative sign indicates net outflow.
[2]  Includes Belgium, Netherlands, Norway, Sweden and Switzerland.
[3]  1922–39.
[4]  Excludes 1939–45.

*Source:*   Adapted from Maddison (2001), Table 3–4.

## 1.5   THE 'GREAT REVERSAL': INTERNATIONAL DISINTEGRATION AND RECOVERY

While the international economy before the First World War was characterised by increasing international economic integration, thereafter, for
over 30 years, the world economy de-globalised as the world's economies
turned inward. This was the period when 'great reversals' in globalisation
took place in the goods, financial and labour markets (Rajan and Zingales,
2003a). The liberal economic order of the late nineteenth century was initially shattered by the catastrophe of the First World War. The consequence, for over 30 years, was economic and political disintegration,
divergence, instability and slower growth. This was especially the case
during the 1929–33 period when, during the Great Depression, the world
economy was sacrificed on a 'cross of gold' (see Eichengreen, 1992;
Snowdon, 2002a). As Figure 1.3 shows, there was a dramatic increase in the
average US tariff rate at the onset of the Great Depression as the
Smoot–Hawley tariff provided protection for both the US industrial and
agricultural sectors. Both Britain and Nazi Germany also moved towards

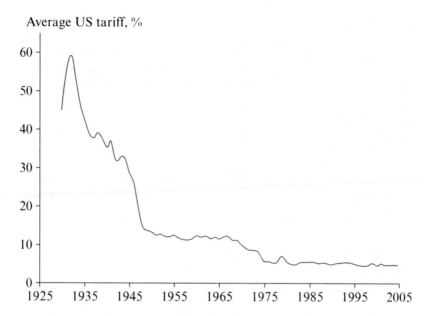

Average US tariff, %

*Source:* *Economic Report of the President*, 2006.

*Figure 1.3    Average US tariff on dutiable goods, 1930–2005*

increased protection. In the twenty-first century the forces of protectionism remain powerful. This will always tend to be the case since politically those who gain from free trade are many but dispersed, whereas the losers are identifiable, vocal and easy to organise (Budd, 2004).

By 1945 the international economic system was in total disarray, and it has taken over 50 years to rebuild the global economic system. In July 1944, representatives from 45 countries met at Bretton Woods in New Hampshire, USA, to discuss the post-war establishment of major international institutions (World Bank, IMF, GATT) whose purpose would be to facilitate international cooperation and increasing international economic integration and development, thereby improving the stability of the world economy. As Table 1.4 shows, today these international institutions comprise the majority of the world's economies and populations.

A major concern of the Bretton Woods delegates was to help prevent a recurrence of the disastrous events and consequences of economic mismanagement that had occurred during the inter-war years. Indeed, as Skidelsky (2005) argues, the Bretton Woods institutions were constructed by 'two market pessimists', John Maynard Keynes and Harry Dexter White, the UK and US Treasury representatives at the conference. According to

*Table 1.4  International institutions and governance, 1945–2006*

| International institution | Date formed | Original membership | Current membership (January 2007) |
| --- | --- | --- | --- |
| United Nations | 1945 | 50 | 192 |
| International Monetary Fund (IMF)[1] | 1945 | 29 | 185 |
| World Bank[2] | 1946 | 38 | 185 |
| General Agreement on Tariffs and Trade (GATT)[3] | 1948 | 23 | – |
| World Trade Organisation (WTO) | 1995 | 112 | 150 |

*Notes:*
[1] Although the IMF began financial operations on 1 March 1947, and came into official existence on 27 December 1945, the Articles of Agreement were negotiated at the Bretton Woods Conference in July 1944.
[2] The World Bank began formal operations on 25 June 1946. The Articles of Agreement were negotiated at the Bretton Woods Conference in July 1944.
[3] GATT was never established as a formal institution but was set up as an interim device which would operate until the establishment of an international trade organisation (ITO). In 1995 this was finally achieved with the establishment of the WTO.

Skidelsky, Keynes believed that the economic and political catastrophe of the Great Depression was the direct result of globalisation 'carried out without adequate macroeconomic management'.

The purpose of GATT was to promote trade liberalisation by encouraging and facilitating the lowering of trade barriers. Since 1995 GATT has been replaced by the World Trade Organisation. As Figure 1.3 illustrates, the average US tariff on dutiable goods for the period 1930–2005 exhibits a dramatic decline since the mid-1930s. Although in the context of the current Doha trade negotiations Stiglitz (2006) has made a strong plea for a non-reciprocal reduction of trade barriers by the rich nations, as Figure 1.4 illustrates, average tariffs in the developing countries, especially sub-Saharan Africa, remain stubbornly high (see Bhagwati, 2005).

Angus Maddison's (2001) recent data indicate that, with the exception of the years 1913–50, the volume of world commodity trade during the period 1870 to 1998 rose faster than world GDP, which itself was growing at rates of 2.11 per cent (1870–1913), 1.85 per cent (1913–50), 4.91 per cent (1950–73) and 3.01 per cent (1973–98). The two world wars and the inter-war slump in economic activity had a severely retarding influence on the pace and process of international integration. Nevertheless, despite this setback, Maddison shows that merchandise exports were 17.2 per cent of

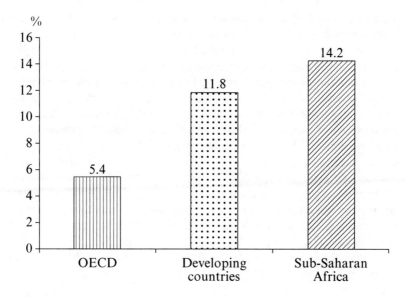

*Source:   Economic Report of the President*, 2006.

*Figure 1.4    Average tariffs across countries*

world GDP in 1998 compared to 4.6 per cent in 1870. However, world trade as a share of world output did not recover to its pre-First World War level until the mid-1970s. Therefore the historical lessons of the period 1914–45 should remind us that the re-emergence of global capitalism (globalisation) since 1950, and especially during the last two decades, should not be viewed as an irreversible process (Wolf, 2003, 2004a, 2004b, 2005). For example, Harold James (2001) provides a sobering historical perspective of how the emerging globally integrated world of the late nineteenth and early twentieth century disintegrated, with catastrophic political and economic consequences. David Henderson (1998, 2001) also rejects the arguments of those who believe that economic liberalism has finally triumphed. Anti-liberal forces have combined to form what he calls a 'new millennium collectivism', and these forces create the risk of an anti-liberal backlash similar to what happened in the early part of the twentieth century. Robert Gilpin (2000, pp. 3–8) also warns:

> At the beginning of the twenty-first century, the increasingly open global economy is threatened . . . Individual nations and powerful groups within nations that believe the world economy functions unfairly and to their disadvantage, or who wish to change the system to benefit themselves to the detriment of others, are an ever present threat to the stability of the system.

Charles Calomiris (2002) has argued that the current historical period should be 'a great time of celebration for advocates of global economic freedom'. But it is not. 'Instead, we are seeing the beginning of a backlash against globalisation.' The continuation of increasing economic integration of the world economy in the twenty-first century faces challenges from international political conflict, war, terrorism, tariffs and quotas, growing inequality, financial crises, unexpected demand and supply shocks, the impact of various domestic economic policies, as well as anti-globalist protesters.

The breakdown of the global economy after 1914, a process accelerated by the Great Depression in the 1930s, provides a sobering historical reminder of the importance of these issues and the need for economists to enlighten public debate on the costs and benefits of international integration and the question of appropriate governance. It is in this context that the research of Dani Rodrik has been particularly important (Rodrik, 1994, 1998a, 1999a, 2000a, 2001a; see also Bhagwati, 2000; Prakash, 2001; Rajan and Bird, 2001; Snowdon, 2001a; Calomiris, 2002; Collier and Dollar, 2002; Irwin, 2002a; Bordo et al., 2003).

## 1.6 FINANCIAL GLOBALISATION

Any rational debate on globalisation must recognise that there are both costs and benefits to the process of increasing international integration. The potential benefits relating to a reduction in trade barriers include the level effects of better resource allocation and increased efficiency in line with the principles of comparative advantage, gains from scale economies and learning by doing, increased product diversity, technology transfer, and reductions in rent-seeking activity associated with trade restriction (Rajan and Bird, 2001). These benefits are well known to economists, relatively uncontroversial, and it is generally accepted that the long-term benefits of trade liberalisation far exceed any short-term adjustment costs. However, when it comes to the liberalisation of international capital markets, economists are much less in agreement about the balance of benefits and costs. As noted earlier, the critics of globalisation include several eminent economists. For example, in his controversial book, *Globalisation and its Discontents*, the 2001 Nobel Laureate in Economics, Joseph Stiglitz, argues that mistaken policies advocated by unreformed international institutions (especially the IMF) present an ever-present threat to the smooth functioning of the international economic system (see also Bhagwati, 1998b; Mishkin, 2005; Stiglitz, 2006).

While financial globalisation is still predominantly confined to the rich developed countries in that international flows of capital are North–North rather than North–South, during the 1980s and 1990s there was a substantial

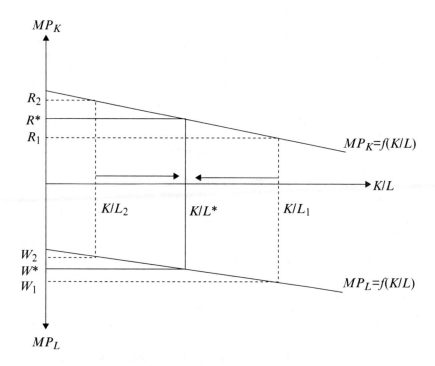

*Figure 1.5   Regional convergence in a neoclassical model*

increase in global financial market integration accompanied by significant growth of capital flows to large sections of the developing world, particularly East Asia (Obstfeld and Taylor, 2004). Moreover, because liberalisation of trade reduces the effectiveness of capital controls and financial repression, the eventual opening of financial markets is inevitable. For example, in economies with financial repression, low real interest rates, which act as an effective tax on saving, encourage capital flight which can be facilitated by the over-invoicing of imports and under-invoicing of exports and transfer pricing (Rajan and Zingales, 2003a). As Aizenman (2002) points out, 'for successful emerging markets that engage in trade integration, financial opening is not a question of if, but of when and how'.

That the flow of international capital to poor countries has not been as substantial as expected (the 'Lucas Paradox') is a surprise from the standpoint of orthodox neoclassical theory (Lucas, 1990). The neoclassical model predicts that in a world of free factor mobility, labour will tend to migrate from poor to rich countries, attracted by higher wages, and capital will tend to migrate to poor countries, attracted by low wages and higher rates of return. Figure 1.5 illustrates the orthodox neoclassical view. Given the assumption of diminishing returns, the marginal product of labour $(MP_L)$ is a positive function of the capital–labour ratio $(K/L)$, and the marginal product of capital $(MP_K)$ is a negative function of the capital–labour ratio. Capital-scarce poor developing countries have low $K/L$ ratios $(K/L_2)$, low wages $(W_2)$ and high rates of return to capital $(R_2)$. In contrast, rich developed countries have high $K/L$ ratios $(K/L_1)$, high wages $(W_1)$, and low rates of return to capital $(R_1)$. Hence, assuming that there are no barriers and restrictions, the international structure of incentives should induce capital and labour to flow in opposite directions until rates of return and wages converge at $R^*$ and $W^*$.

The predictions of the neoclassical theory are challenged by 'cumulative causation' models, inspired by Myrdal (1957), where both capital and labour are likely to flow in one direction, to the rich countries. In Myrdal's model the 'backwash effects' of international integration dominate the beneficial 'spread effects'. Clearly, in countries characterised by political instability, corruption and lack of security of property rights, the risk-adjusted rates of return to capital will be much lower than in the neoclassical model, which assumes away such inconveniences. The neoclassical predictions will also fail in a world of increasing returns and where agglomeration economies are a feature of the real world. In such models, success breeds success and failure breeds failure, and 'path-dependency' effects are important (Krugman and Venables, 1995). As Crafts (2004a) points out, the 'handicaps of distance' and the persistence of suboptimal institutions can have a severe retarding impact on the forces of convergence (see also Crafts, 2005). The research of Hatton and Williamson (2006) also shows that capital tended to follow the mass transatlantic European labour migrations of the late nineteenth century. Nevertheless, where countries have political stability, and have also established good institutions and policies, capital flows from developed to developing countries can be substantial, as demonstrated by the flows to the East Asian economies and China during the last 20 years (for an optimistic assessment of the prospects for international convergence in the twenty-first century, see Lucas, 2000).

## 1.7   THE BENEFITS AND COSTS OF FINANCIAL INTEGRATION

While economists agree that stable and efficient financial markets have significant economic benefits, and that 'sound finance' is a prerequisite in the functioning of any modern economy, the emphasis is on the words *stable* and *efficient*. A well-functioning financial sector is a key ingredient to the long-term success of any economy for a number of reasons. Financial institutions act as intermediaries between lenders and borrowers (entrepreneurs), thereby reducing transaction costs and facilitating the transfer of financial resources to individuals and enterprises that can use them productively for investment purposes, both domestically and internationally. As a result, scarce capital is more efficiently allocated. Financial markets also allow the pooling of risks as well as providing discipline to policy makers who might otherwise follow destructive economic policies such as those that lead to unsustainable budget deficits. The growth of international financial markets allows residents from different countries to achieve these benefits, and this is particularly important to poor developing countries with low capital–labour ratios (Summers, 2000).

Agenor (2003) identifies four main potential benefits from financial openness: (i) international borrowing to facilitate consumption smoothing in response to temporary negative shocks; (ii) an increase in domestic and foreign investment leading to faster economic growth via capital accumulation, the transfer of ideas, and learning by doing; (iii) enhanced macroeconomic stability via an increase in macroeconomic discipline since capital flows are very responsive to 'bad' economic policies; (iv) improvements in the stability and efficiency of the banking system through financial deepening, improved supervision and regulation, and expansion of the range and quality of financial services. Therefore, in theory, capital account liberalisation should have favourable effects on welfare, the efficiency of resource allocation, and long-run economic growth. However, a consensus has emerged that macroeconomic stability is a prerequisite for financial sector liberalisation, and even then should be carried out with extreme caution, especially in developing economies that lack effective institutions.

The impact of financial globalisation on economic growth has been the subject of considerable research in recent years. In terms of the neoclassical growth model, financial liberalisation, by stimulating capital inflows to developing economies, will add resources to domestic saving that will allow for an increase in investment, and faster growth during the period of transitional dynamics (Snowdon and Vane, 2005). In more recent endogenous growth models, which allow for technological gaps between rich and poor countries, capital flows in the form of FDI will lead to beneficial technological spillovers that enhance growth. However, in their recent survey of financial globalisation, Kose et al. (2006) conclude that from macro studies, 'it remains difficult to find robust evidence that financial integration systematically increases growth, once other determinants of growth are controlled for' (see also Rodrik, 1998b; Eichengreen, 2001; Stiglitz, 2000a, 2004a). Research by Arteta et al. (2001) finds that liberalisation of the capital account will tend to have beneficial growth effects providing a country does not have significant macroeconomic imbalances (see also Levine, 1997; Fischer, 1993a; Kaminsky and Schmukler, 2003). An important policy implication from this is that the sequencing of capital account liberalisation is crucial. Furthermore, there may be a complex trade-off between the negative intermediate and positive long-run impact of overall financial liberation (Aizenman, 2002).

While the link between economic growth and FDI is certainly bidirectional, micro studies of the impact of FDI inflows is beginning to produce evidence supporting the beneficial technological spillover effects. FDI acts as a conduit for the transfer of productivity-enhancing knowledge, both organisational and technological (Choudhury and Mavrotas, 2006; Hansen and Rand, 2006). Furthermore, Kose et al. (2006) conclude that the main benefits of financial globalisation are likely to be 'catalytic and indirect'. The growth-enhancing indirect 'potential collateral benefits' of liberalisation include the promotion of greater market discipline on macroeconomic policies, efficiency gains through competition in the financial sector, and pressures that result in improvements in corporate governance. The elimination of capital controls also reduces the power of bureaucrats and the ability of powerful interest groups to engage in unproductive rent-seeking activities (Eichengreen, 2001).

The 1980s and 1990s were characterised by a series of severe financial crises that have brought into focus the downside of financial market liberalisation. There have always been, and there will always be, financial crises as long as there are financial markets, and, as the experience of the Great Depression of the 1930s demonstrates, financial crises are by no means confined to developing economies (Kindleberger, 1978). Financial crises are also heterogeneous, which makes them extremely hard to predict. As the twentieth century drew to a close, the global financial system was reeling from the effects of a series of financial crises during the 1990s, in particular the shock of the East Asian crisis, 1997–98. Bordo et al. (2001) show that while the length and output costs of crises have changed little, their frequency has increased, with a doubling of crisis frequency after 1973 compared to the Bretton Woods period, 1945–73.

As already noted, while the vast majority of economists are staunch advocates of 'free trade', several prominent economists remain highly cautious with repect to full capital market liberalisation (Bhagwati, 1998b; Rodrik, 1998b; Stiglitz, 2000a, 2002b; Basu, 2003). Economists have long recognised that markets can fail due to various problems arising from incomplete markets and imperfect information. This is especially true in financial markets, where reaching decisions about which investment opportunities are more or less profitable involves solving an enormous information problem in a world of uncertainty. In economists' language, a major characteristic of financial markets is that they are permeated by problems of asymmetric information, adverse selection and moral hazard (see Eichengreen et al., 1999; Mishkin, 2001; Lane and Phillips, 2002; Stiglitz, 2002b; Calvo, 2006). So there are clear and significant risks as well as benefits associated with liberalisation of the financial sector. As Lawrence Summers (2000) notes, although like the jet airplane global financial markets have enormous potential to benefit both developed and developing countries, when accidents happen they are highly visible and spectacular. Financial crises also tend to be amplified internationally by the 'fatal attraction' impact of contagion effects driven by trade linkages, common shocks, competitive devaluations, financial linkages, market illiquidity, investors' irrational behaviour driven by 'animal spirits', panic and herding, and reputational externalities (see Kaminsky and Reinhart, 2000; Agenor, 2003). Because information is costly, and therefore necessarily incomplete, the herd-like behaviour of investors during periods of 'positive contagion' (capital inflows) and 'negative contagion' (capital outflows) is generally modelled by economists as being driven by informational gaps among investors that inevitably arise in an increasingly globalised and complex world (Bayoumi et al. 2003). The explosion of information and communication technology (ICT), by increasing financial market linkages, also allows a much greater response of international capital flows to any change in relative rates of return (Agenor, 2003).

Most major financial crises tend to be preceded by a combination of contributory factors, chief of which include financial and banking sector weaknesses, inadequate financial regulation and supervision, pegged exchange rates, macroeconomic imbalances such as inflation and unsustainable fiscal and current account deficits, and large accumulations of short-run debt, often denominated in dollars. In emerging market economies, where debt has been issued and denominated in foreign currencies, the impact of an unanticipated currency depreciation can be devastating to domestic firms and financial institutions. In the case of East Asia the existence of foreign-currency-denominated liabilities also provided a link between the financial crisis and the balance-of-payments crisis (Furman and Stiglitz, 1998; Radelet and Sachs, 1998; Corbett and Vines, 1999; Mishkin, 1999a; Krueger, 2000).

Corbett and Vines (1999) provide a useful framework, illustrated in Figure 1.6, for understanding the simultaneous occurrence in East Asia of both a currency crisis, and a financial crisis, and emphasises the interaction of vulnerability, risk, negative shocks, crisis and collapse.

Vulnerability to a crisis is linked to the macroeconomic policy trilemma problem (see below, section 1.8), combined with a liberalised but

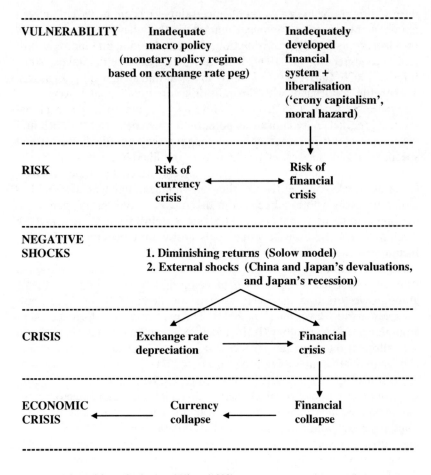

*Source:*    Adapted from Corbett and Vines (1999).

*Figure 1.6    The evolution of a financial and economic crisis*

inadequately developed financial system. In the case of Thailand, because the baht was pegged to the dollar, the attempt by the Thai monetary authorities to dampen the early 1990s boom by raising interest rates led to a flood of capital imports (since dollar interest rates were lower). This created a large stock of unhedged dollar-denominated foreign debt, and this provides the link between the currency and financial crisis that was to follow in 1997. Financial vulnerability was created due to reliance on a 'bank-based financial regime' characterised by implicit guarantees ('crony capitalism') creating a 'moral hazard' problem and excessive high-risk lending. All that was needed to precipitate a crisis was a series of negative shocks. These came in the form of: (i) diminishing returns to capital; (ii) an appreciation of the dollar, hence real exchange rate appreciation, (iii) devaluation of the Chinese yuan in 1994; and (iv) prolonged recession in Japan. In the Corbett and Vines model of the East Asian crisis the series of economic shocks created a currency crisis which then led to a financial crisis and collapse through the impact of 'massive unhedged borrowings of foreign currency'.

What can be done to reduce the vulnerability of the financial sector? Mishkin (2001) defines a financial crisis as a disruption to financial markets so that they are 'unable to efficiently channel funds to those who have the most productive investment opportunities' leading to 'a sharp contraction in economic activity'. He identifies the four main factors that contribute to a financial crisis as, first, a deterioration in financial sector balance sheets, second, a deterioration in non-financial sector balance sheets, third, increases in interest rates, and finally, increases in uncertainty.

In order to reduce the probability of a financial crisis, Mishkin suggests the adoption of the following measures:

1. prudential supervision of the financial sector, including prompt corrective action, a focus on risk management, restrictions on 'connected lending', and providing adequate resources for independent and accountable regulatory authorities;
2. improve accounting standards and disclosure requirements to encourage information and deter excessive risk taking;
3. strengthen the legal and judicial system to enforce property rights and bankruptcy procedures;
4. encourage market-based discipline via the establishment of credit ratings, the entry of foreign banks, and reduction in the role of state-owned financial institutions;
5. allow big corporations to go bankrupt to limit moral hazard;
6. correctly sequence financial liberalisation;
7. provide a stable macroeconomic environment;
8. restrict the build-up of foreign-currency-denominated debt;
9. adopt a more flexible exchange rate regime.

In emerging market economies, where debt has been issued and denominated in foreign currencies, the impact of an unanticipated currency depreciation can be devastating to domestic firms and financial institutions. In the case of East Asia the existence of foreign-currency-denominated liabilities also provided a link between the financial crisis and the balance-of-payments crisis (Krueger, 2000).

## 1.8   EXCHANGE RATE REGIMES AND THE 'OPEN-ECONOMY TRILEMMA'

In a world of capital mobility, many economists, including Fischer, have highlighted the particular dangers of attempting to adopt capital account liberalisation within the context of a 'soft-peg exchange rate regime'. This warning reflects economists' recognition of the constraint imposed on policy by what economists have variously labelled the 'inconsistent trinity', the 'open-economy trilemma' or the 'macroeconomic policy trilemma' (Obstfeld, 1998; Summers, 1999; Mishkin, 1999b; Obstfeld and Taylor, 2003). This trilemma arises if any government attempts to aim for the following three policy goals simultaneously:

(a)  a fixed nominal exchange rate;
(b)  an independent monetary policy aimed mainly at domestic objectives;
(c)  capital market liberalisation.

Any specific governing body can only aim for any two of the above at any one time (the UK experience of the exchange rate mechanism (ERM) membership in 1990–92 provides a graphic demonstration of the 'trilemma' in action, as does the loss of monetary autonomy involved with membership of a monetary union such as EMU). Examples of choices made in response to the open-economy trilemma have included:

1.  the Gold Standard = (a) + (c);
2.  the ERM in Europe = (a) + (c);
3.  a single country within the euro zone = (a) + (c) (a single currency can be viewed as an irrevocably fixed exchange rate regime);
4.  the Bretton Woods system = (a) + (b);
5.  the USA and Japan; and also the UK since 1992 = (b) + (c);
6.  the euro zone = (b) + (c) (see Reinhart and Rogoff, 2004).

Reflecting the trilemma problem, Fischer's (2001a) research confirms that the world does seem to be moving towards a corner (bi-polar) solution with respect to the choice of exchange rate regime, that is, an increase in the percentage of countries having either floating or some form of hard-peg regime (i.e. choices (a) + (c), or (b) + (c). For example, IMF data show that between 1991 and 1998 the proportion of countries with an 'intermediate regime' declined from 62 to 34 per cent. Hard-peg regimes include currency unions, dollarisation and currency boards (Frankel, 1999; Mishkin, 1999a, 1999b; Eichengreen, 2002). Frankel (1999) identifies nine forms of exchange rate arrangement: currency union, dollarisation, currency board, 'truly' fixed exchange rate, adjustable peg, crawling peg, basket peg, target band, managed float and free float (see also Mishkin, 2001; Tavlas, 2003; Reinhart and Rogoff, 2004; Goldstein and Lardy, 2006).

## 1.9 THE ROLE OF THE INTERNATIONAL MONETARY FUND

From September 1994 until August 2001, Stanley Fischer was First Deputy Director at the International Monetary Fund. This change of career, from distinguished 'ivory tower' economist at Massachusetts Institute of Technology (MIT) to a senior management position at the key institution of the international monetary system, significantly increased Fischer's international profile, not least because this period turned out to be a turbulent one for the global economy, with the IMF increasingly playing the role of crisis manager and quasi 'international lender of last resort' (Fischer, 1999a, 1999b, 1999c).

In July 1944, at the Bretton Woods Conference held in New Hampshire, USA, 45 governments agreed on a framework of economic cooperation aimed at avoiding a repeat of the catastrophic events and policies that had created the Great Depression of the 1930s. The outcome of the meeting was the creation of what John Maynard Keynes labelled the 'Bretton Woods twins', the IMF and the International Bank for Reconstruction and Development (IBRD), soon to be more popularly known as the World Bank (see Skidelsky, 2000, for an excellent discussion of Keynes's role in the creation of the Bretton Woods institutions, Skidelsky describes Keynes as 'joint author', with Harry Dexter White, of the Bretton Woods international monetary system).

In December 1945, the International Monetary Fund (IMF) officially came into existence when 29 countries signed its Articles of Agreement (Charter) and it finally began financial operations on 1 March 1947. Today over 2800 employees work for the IMF, recruited from 133 countries, and two-thirds of the professional staff (over 1000) are economists. Currently the IMF has 184 member countries, 96 per cent of the world's total, given that there are 192 member states of the United Nations.

While the main objective of the World Bank is to focus on long-term economic development and poverty reduction issues, Article I of the IMF's Charter sets out the objectives of the Fund as follows:

1.  'to promote international monetary co-operation through a permanent institution which provides the machinery for consultation and collaboration on international monetary problems';

2.  'to facilitate the expansion and balanced growth of world trade, and to contribute thereby to the promotion and maintenance of high employment and real income and to the development of the productive resources of all members as primary objectives of economic policy';
3.  'to promote exchange stability, to maintain orderly exchange arrangements among members, and to avoid competitive devaluations';
4.  'to assist in the establishment of a multilateral system of payments in respect of current transactions between members and in the elimination of foreign exchange restrictions which hamper the growth of world trade';
5.  'to give confidence to members by making the general resources of the Fund temporarily available to them under adequate safeguards, thus providing them with the opportunity to correct maladjustments in their balance of payments without resorting to measures destructive of national or international prosperity';
6.  'in accordance with the above, to shorten the duration and lessen the degree of disequilibrium in the international balance of payments of members'.

In its operations the IMF conducts surveillance, and financial and technical assistance for members. Surveillance activities involve the appraisal of members' economic policies as well as producing analysis of global and regional economic trends and developments. Financial assistance is provided in the form of credits and loans to IMF members who have balance-of-payments problems and who need to implement policies of reform and adjustment. The IMF is neither an aid agency nor a development institution, and lending is temporary and conditional on the policies adopted by the borrowing country. Technical assistance comes in the form of economic expertise and support from the IMF to members, including advice on institution building, monetary and fiscal policy, the collection and analysis of statistical data, and training officials. The IMF's financial resources come from the quota subscriptions of member countries, the size of the quota being in proportion to the size of the member country's economy (for example, the USA currently provides some 17.4 per cent of current total quotas).

## 1.10  GLOBALISATION AND THE IMF: SOME LESSONS FROM THE 1990S

With the expansion of global business, capital flows have increased substantially in recent years, influenced by factors such as high rates of return in recipient countries, technological developments, and the liberalisation of financial markets and international capital transactions. The internationalisation of business activity has created new challenges for the IMF, in particular those associated with the impact of capital market liberalisation and financial crises on the growth prospects of the developing and transition economies (see Krueger, 2000; Summers, 2000; Fischer, 2002; Kose et al., 2006).

The IMF has been severely criticised by several famous economists, notably Joseph Stiglitz, for what they consider to have been its promotion of 'premature' capital market liberalisation and for the way that it handled the East Asian and other economic crises. However, both Stanley Fischer and Kenneth Rogoff have provided a spirited defence of IMF policies. (Rogoff was Chief Economist and Director of Research, International Monetary Fund, 2001–03. Among others, the controversy relating to the role of the IMF has involved Fischer, 1997a, 1997b, 1998a, 1998b; Fischer et al., 1998; Bhagwati, 1998b; Feldstein, 1998; Rodrik, 1998b; Summers, 1999, 2000; Bird, 2000; Meltzer, et al., 2000; Stiglitz, 2000a, 2004b, 2006; Rogoff, 2002, 2003, 2004; Isard, 2005. See also the interviews with Bhagwati and Stiglitz in Snowdon, 2001a, 2001b respectively.)

Stanley Fischer's period of office at the IMF coincided with a very turbulent time for the world economy, with deep economic and financial crises occurring, principally in Latin America, Russia and East Asia. Not surprisingly, the explosive growth of international capital movements and increased frequency of emerging market financial crises during the past decade has placed the international monetary system and its major institutions high on the agenda of policy discussions and analysis among governments, the media, and academic and civil society organisations. In the immediate aftermath of the East Asian economic crisis Fischer (1999c) put forward a list of ten 'tentative' lessons relating to problems of the international monetary system that the IMF would need to confront:

1. predicting an economic crisis is difficult;
2. even when a crisis is anticipated it is hard to get a country to take appropriate action;
3. if the government the IMF is dealing with is divided and weak, it is difficult to get a programme implemented, and, accordingly, 'it is difficult to decide whether to help';
4. the IMF's system of internal governance and accountability is not well understood by IMF members;
5. despite the critics, 'Keynesianism is alive';
6. a strategy of 'going fast on bank restructuring and corporate debt restructuring is much better than regulatory forbearance' (a situation where insolvent institutions are allowed to continue operating);

7.   all the major crises in the last couple of years have involved a fixed or crawling peg exchange rate;
8.   the need to involve the private sector in the solution of international crises is probably the most difficult issue in redesigning the international financial architecture;
9.   'the IMF is here to stay';
10.  'globalisation is here to stay'.

Shortly before leaving the IMF, Fischer (2001b) identified several important priorities for the IMF. In recommending that the Fund should 'refocus' its activities, Fischer articulated the need to give emphasis to strengthening the IMF's research and analysis of global capital markets, reforming the 'international architecture' of the financial system, reducing the 'unduly detailed and restrictive' conditions attached to loans that undermines the sense of 'ownership' of desirable structural policies, and recognising that there is likely to be a trade-off between ownership and programme quality, particularly in low-income developing countries (Bird, 2001; Fischer, 2002). The IMF also needs to continue its dialogue with civil society organisations (CSOs), since they will continue to challenge the IMF on questions relating to working methods, organisation, and their belief that the IMF fails to address important social and political concerns (Dawson and Bhatt, 2001).

   Joseph Stiglitz's (2002a) vociferous critique of the IMF and its economists has received a strong rebuttal from Kenneth Rogoff (2002, 2003). Rogoff (2003) identifies four common criticisms of the IMF:

1.   IMF loan programmes '*impose* harsh fiscal austerity programmes on cash-strapped countries;
2.   IMF loans encourage a significant 'moral hazard' problem;
3.   IMF advice aggravates economic problems in countries in financial crisis;
4.   the IMF has 'irresponsibly pushed' developing countries into premature capital market liberalisation.

Rogoff questions all four of these criticisms; in particular he argues that the austerity critique (1) confuses correlation with causation since the IMF is only called in *after* a country runs into severe financial difficulties. Without IMF loans the situation would involve even greater austerity! Nevertheless, a major task facing the IMF in the twenty-first century is to help build a more robust global financial architecture that not only contributes to greater stability, but also emphasises greater openness, transparency and accountability (see Bird, 2000, 2006; Isard, 2005).

In summarising the measures that countries should adopt in order to reduce the risks of financial instability and promote a positive association between economic growth and financial sector development, Fischer (1993a, 2003) has highlighted the crucial importance of establishing 'a stable macroeconomic environment'. He also emphasises the development of 'a sound regulatory framework'; the reform of inefficient financial institutions (through privatisation and/or foreign competition); 'the removal of discriminatory taxes and other elements of financial repression'; and 'strong corporate governance and the adoption of sound accounting practices'. In such an enabling policy environment Fischer (2003) concludes that 'the potential benefits of well-phased and well-sequenced integration into the global capital markets outweigh the costs'. However, a recent comprehensive study at the IMF reminds us that developing countries should approach financial integration cautiously (Kose et al., 2006).

While financial crises will inevitably recur, the experiences of recent years have led to a much better understanding of such events and it is hoped that emerging market economies now have greater insight into the causes, consequences and policy measures necessary to reduce the frequency and severity of such crises (Feldstein, 2002).

## 1.11 INTERNATIONAL LABOUR MIGRATION

During recent years the issue of international labour migration has re-emerged as a major public policy issue, especially in the UK, where public debate and media coverage relating to asylum seekers, illegal immigrants and the influx of migrants from Eastern Europe following EU enlargement in 2004 reached almost frenzied proportions in the early 2000s (Coleman and Harris, 2003). However, the movement of people has always been a major feature of human development. For thousands of years, humans have migrated, and the geographical movement of people is a major stylised fact of economic development. Since all humans are descended from a common source of ancestors, located in Africa approximately one million years ago, it is clear that the rest of the world must have been populated via a process of slow migration combined with natural growth. As Mussa (2000) notes, the numerous waves of migration throughout history were driven by a combination of changes in transportation technology, human preferences and public policy.

In agrarian societies, where land is obviously a key factor of production, the acquisition of more land through military conquest and consequent forced migration of people made sense to the powerful subjugators.

But in terms of overall human welfare, imperialist strategies produced a negative-sum outcome: the gains of the powerful were offset by the losses inflicted on the defeated. Fortunately, the acceleration of technological change, beginning with the Industrial Revolution, has rendered imperialism redundant as a coherent strategy of economic development. The wealth of a nation in the modern world does not depend on the acquisition of new territories by force. Indeed such a strategy is certainly counterproductive and often disastrous, as both Japan and Germany found out during the period 1933–45. The post-war 'miracle' economic performance of both Germany and Japan confirms how economic progress in the modern world depends crucially on the adoption of coherent economic policies, including those that recognise the key role of mutually beneficial trade. It is hoped that during the twenty-first century nations will improve the living standards of their populations through the adoption of policies that favour production over diversion, trade rather than autarky, and peace rather than conflict and occupation.

Why do people migrate? The main determinants of migration are (1) geographical (floods, earthquakes, the encroachment of deserts, and other natural disasters); (2) political (wars, 'ethnic cleansing', persecution); (3) social (attraction of city amenities, communication factors, education, family ties); (4) demographic (vent for surplus population due to rapid population growth); and (5) economic (real wage and income differentials, employment opportunities, transportation costs). In the absence of geographical and political shocks, by far the most important factors that affect the decision to migrate are economic, and the process of rural–urban migration is central to the classic contributions to the development literature of Arthur Lewis (1954) and Michael Todaro (1969). According to Todaro, the decision to migrate should be viewed as a rational decision, and any potential migrant will weigh up the benefits and costs of migration in order to assess the perceived value of migration given the information available. This applies to the decision to migrate across political boundaries as well as within a single country or region. As noted earlier, within a neoclassical framework, international labour migration can also act as a powerful force for convergence (see Figure 1.5).

Following the theoretical framework developed by Clark et al. (2002), the probability that any individual $i$, living in country $\alpha$, with human capital and skill level of $si$, receiving a wage of $w\alpha$ $(si)$, will migrate $(Mi)$ to country $\beta$ is given by equation (1.1).

$$Mi = \text{Prob } (vi > 0), \quad \text{where } vi = [w\beta \ (si) - w\alpha \ (si)] - \theta$$
$$- c_1 - c_2(q) - \lambda \ (\psi - si) \qquad (1.1)$$

Here, $w\beta$ $(si)$ − $w\alpha$ $(si)$ is the discounted present value of the difference between the income streams received by individual $i$ in country $\beta$ and country $\alpha$; the individual psychic cost of migration given by $\theta$; the direct costs of migration are given by $c_1$, which will vary with distance from destination; $c_2(q)$ represents the waiting-time costs of quantitative restrictions such as migrant quotas; and $\lambda$ $(\psi − si)$ represents the skill-selective immigration policy, where $\psi$ is the benchmark level of required skills, and $\lambda$ is the skill-selectivity of immigration policy. A rise in either $\psi$ or $\lambda$ will raise the costs of migration.

As equation (1.1) suggests, vast differentials in income and employment opportunities combined with reduced costs of migration will greatly increase the probability that any individual in a poor country will migrate from a low-income to a higher-income country. The research of Jeffrey Williamson has led to the accumulation of evidence relating to several of the most important mass migrations in history.

One of the greatest and best-recorded international labour migrations in human history was the mass movement of people from Europe to North and South America and Australasia (the 'New World') between 1820 and 1914. According to Hatton and Williamson (1998), about 55 million Europeans moved to the New World during this hundred-year period and about 60 per cent of these migrants went to the USA (see Figure 1.7). By the late nineteenth century the typical European migrant was a young, unskilled, single male from an urban origin. This was the 'era of free mass migration'. Earlier migrations from Europe to the USA, during the seventeenth and eighteenth centuries, had been a 'mere trickle' by comparison. Only the earlier forced migration of slaves to the Americas comes close in terms of numbers to the free movement of peoples across the Atlantic during the late nineteenth century (see Williamson, 2006b).

As reported in Freeman (2006), the United Nations estimates that in 2000 there were about 175 million people (2.9 per cent of the world's population) who were born outside the country of their current residence compared to 82.5 million in 1970. The USA remains the largest single recipient of immigrants, with 35 million foreign-born citizens that comprised 11.1 per cent of US population in 2000–01, although Australia (23.6), New Zealand (19.5), Canada (17.4) and Sweden (11.3) had higher shares of foreign-born than the USA (see Table 1.5 and Figures 1.7 and 1.8).

Due to the break-up of the Soviet Union, Russia, with 13.3 million immigrants, is the second largest recipient of immigrants, mainly from the former Soviet republics. Germany with 7.3 immigrants is third. The countries with the largest outflow of population are China with 3.5 million, India with 20 million, and the Philippines with 7.0 million. Table 1.6 shows the source area composition of US immigration for the period 1951–2000.

*Table 1.5   Shares of foreign-born in populations, 1870/71–2000/01*

|  | 1870/71 | 1890/91 | 1910/11 | 2000/01 |
|---|---|---|---|---|
| **Europe** | | | | |
| Germany | 0.5 | 0.9 | 1.9 | 8.9 |
| France | 2.0 | 3.0 | 3.0 | 10.0 |
| UK | 0.5 | 0.7 | 0.9 | 4.3 |
| Denmark | 3.0 | 3.3 | 3.1 | 5.8 |
| Norway | 1.6 | 2.4 | 2.3 | 6.3 |
| Sweden | 0.3 | 0.5 | 0.9 | 11.3 |
| **New World** | | | | |
| Australia | 46.5 | 31.8 | 17.1 | 23.6 |
| New Zealand | 63.5 | 41.5 | 30.3 | 19.5 |
| Canada | 16.5 | 13.3 | 22.0 | 17.4 |
| USA | 14.4 | 14.7 | 14.7 | 11.1 |
| Argentina | 12.1 | 25.5 | 29.9 | 5.0 |
| Brazil | 3.9 | 2.5 | 7.3 | n.a. |

*Sources:*   Hatton and Williamson (2005); Williamson (2006c).

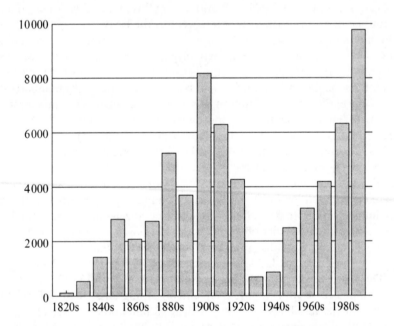

*Sources:*   Mussa (2000); US Department of Commerce, Bureau of the Census.

*Figure 1.7   Total US immigration, thousands per decade, 1820–2000*

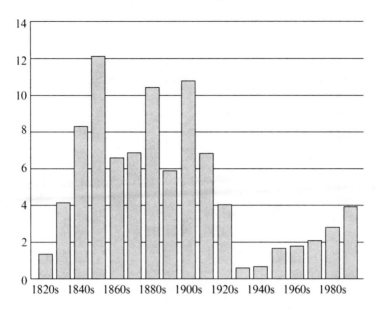

*Sources:* Mussa (2000); US Department of Commerce, Bureau of the Census.

*Figure 1.8*   *US immigration as a percentage of total population,*
*1820–2000*

*Table 1.6*   *Source area composition of US immigration, 1951–2000 (% of*
*total)*

| Region of origin | 1951–60 | 1961–70 | 1971–80 | 1981–90 | 1991–2000 |
|---|---|---|---|---|---|
| Europe | 52.7 | 33.8 | 17.8 | 10.3 | 14.9 |
| West | 47.1 | 30.2 | 14.5 | 7.2 | 5.6 |
| East | 5.6 | 3.6 | 3.3 | 3.1 | 9.4 |
| Asia | 6.1 | 12.9 | 35.3 | 37.3 | 30.7 |
| Americas | 39.6 | 51.7 | 44.1 | 49.3 | 49.3 |
| Canada | 15.0 | 12.4 | 3.8 | 2.1 | 2.1 |
| Mexico | 11.9 | 13.7 | 14.2 | 22.6 | 24.7 |
| Caribbean | 4.9 | 14.2 | 16.5 | 11.9 | 10.8 |
| Central America | 1.8 | 3.1 | 3.0 | 6.4 | 5.8 |
| South America | 3.6 | 7.8 | 6.6 | 6.3 | 5.9 |
| Africa | 0.6 | 0.9 | 1.8 | 2.4 | 3.9 |
| Oceania | 0.5 | 0.8 | 0.9 | 0.6 | 0.6 |
| Total (000s) | 2515 | 3322 | 4493 | 7338 | 9095 |

*Sources:* Hatton and Williamson (2005); Williamson (2006c).

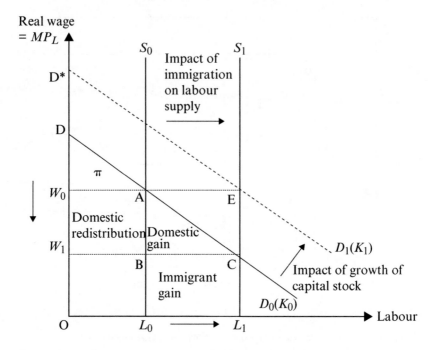

*Figure 1.9    The economic impact of immigration*

The main trends indicate the declining share of immigrants from Western Europe and the increasing importance of immigration from Asia and Mexico.

What will be the likely impact of an increase in immigration on the host economy? According to Borjas (2003, p. 1337), 'the laws of supply and demand have unambiguous implication for how immigration should affect labour market conditions in the short run. The shift in supply lowers the real wage of competing native workers.' Figure 1.9 provides a useful framework for thinking about this question (see Hatton and Williamson, 2005; Freeman, 2006).

The downward-sloping labour demand curves, reflecting the diminishing marginal product of labour ($MP_L$) and a given technology, are represented by $D_0(K_0)$ and $D_1(K_1)$, where $K$ is the amount of capital available to the economy and $K_0 < K_1$. Given the initial supply of labour, $S_0$, the labour market is in equilibrium at point A. The wage of domestic workers before immigration is $W_0$, and employment is $O-L_0$. The area $ODAL_0$ is total output, divided into profits ($\pi$), represented by area $W_0DA$, and wages, represented by area $OW_0AL_0$. The impact of immigration is to increase labour supply from $S_0$ to $S_1$, and, assuming a competitive labour market, the new labour market equilibrium is at point C. Total, output increases by the amount shown by area $L_0ACL_1$. The predicted outcome of immigration is that the equilibrium wage for domestic workers falls to $W_1$, immigrant employment rises by $L_1 - L_0$, area $W_1W_0AB$ represents a redistribution of income from wages to profits, area ABC represents a net domestic gain of output to society (excluding immigrant gains) that accrues to profits, and area $L_0BCL_1$ represents immigrant income (this analysis assumes that the domestic supply of labour is unaffected by the reduction of the equilibrium wage). Following immigration, total output is given by $ODCL_1$, area $DCW_1$ represents total profits, and $OW_1CL_1$ is the share of total output going to wages. The impact of *emigration* can be illustrated using the same framework by reversing the direction of change, although the literature on the 'brain drain' indicates that taking into account remittances and indirect positive feedback effects complicates the welfare implications of emigration (see Commander et al., 2003; Stark, 2005; Sriskandarajah, 2005; Freeman, 2006).

The distributional implications of the above analysis are clear. Employers and immigrants gain and domestic wage earners lose. However, these predictions depend crucially on the assumptions of the model. If the labour market fails to clear, there will be unemployment consequences from immigration. If capital inflows accompany immigrant inflows, then we can expect the labour demand curve to shift from $D_0(K_0)$ to $D_1(K_1)$. In this case the wage remains at $W_0$, total output is now $OD^*EL_1$, domestic wage income remains unaffected, total profits are represented by area $W_0D^*E$, and immigrant income is given by area $L_0AEL_1$. As Hatton and Williamson (2006) observe, 'capital mobility reduces dramatically the effect of immigration on real wages' and the empirical evidence does show that 'migration inflows were typically accompanied by capital inflows in the New World economies'.

Additional complications are introduced into the above analysis if labour is not homogeneous. An inflow of unskilled labour may benefit skilled domestic workers but damage unskilled domestic workers. A more comprehensive analysis would also need to take into account the fiscal implications of immigration. Whether immigrants represent a fiscal burden or fiscal benefit to domestic residents will depend on immigrant wage levels, employment rates and number of dependants. The analysis above also ignores the potential impact that highly skilled immigrants (scientists), with high levels of human capital, are likely to have on stimulating endogenous technological change.

A large number of empirical studies have attempted to identify the impact of immigration on the welfare of domestic residents, in particular wage earners (see Borjas, 1995; Friedberg and Hunt, 1995; Williamson, 2004; Freeman, 2006). As Borjas (2003) observes, the existing studies provide 'a mixed and confusing set of results'. While Borjas (2003) presents evidence that implies that immigration has 'substantially worsened the labour market opportunities faced by many native workers', Friedberg and Hunt (1995) conclude their survey with the following observation: 'Despite the belief that immigrants have a large adverse impact on the wages and employment opportunities of the native-born population, the literature on this question does not provide much support for this conclusion.' Hatton and Williamson (2006), in their historical research, show that 'large-scale immigration has tended to reduce economy-wide real wages, both in the recent and more distant past'. However, the impact on wages of immigration is attenuated in a world of capital mobility, as Figure 1.9 indicates.

Economic theory suggests that the impact of immigration will be to reduce the earnings of substitute factors and raise the earnings of complementary factors such as skilled workers and owners of capital (Freeman, 2006). Given that the impact on profits and on the wages of skilled workers (the latter represent the majority of voters in developed countries) is likely to be positively affected by the immigration, especially in a world of capital mobility, why have immigration policies become more restrictive in most countries compared to the nineteenth century and before? Hatton and Williamson (2006) conclude that this outcome has much to do with the perceived adverse fiscal implications of immigration. Freeman also notes that mass immigration is seen by many host citizens to be 'culturally disruptive' (see Williamson, 2006c, for an analysis how international migration affects ethnic diversity).

Since most of the gains from immigration accrue to the immigrants themselves, for domestic residents to be less hostile to immigration will require a larger share of the gains of immigration to accrue to them. Freeman (2006) therefore suggests that immigrants could be charged admission fees or that immigration permits be auctioned. The revenue from such a scheme would then be used to benefit domestic residents.

## 1.12 THE 'OFFSHORE OUTSOURCING' CONTROVERSY

At a press conference held on 9 February 2004, Gregory Mankiw, Harvard Professor of Economics, and Chairman of the US President's Council of Economic Advisors, discussed the 2004 *Economic Report of the President.* That Report contained the following statement relating to overseas outsourcing: 'When a good or service is produced more cheaply abroad, it makes more sense to import it than to make or provide it domestically.' Responding to questions relating to this section of the Report, Mankiw noted that many more things are now tradable that were not tradable in the past, and that this development was a 'good thing', although governments had a responsibility to respond to the resultant 'dislocations' and help workers to find new jobs (see Mankiw and Swagel, 2006).

None of this is controversial as far as economists are concerned, but Mankiw's response caused a huge furore in the US media and political circles, where his comments were taken as evidence that 'Bush Supports Shift of Jobs Overseas' (*Los Angeles Times*, 10 February 2004). On 11 February, Speaker of the House, Dennis Hastert, expressed Congressional anger at Mankiw's comments, claiming that his ideas had 'failed the basic test of real economics'. As Mankiw and Swagel point out, this episode shows that there is an enormous communications gap between economists and non-economists when it comes to discussions of the purpose and impact of international trade, something that Paul Krugman (1996) has highlighted.

In reality the furore over offshore outsourcing has been blown out of all proportion, especially with respect to the general employment effects. International trade affects the composition of jobs, not the general level of employment, which is determined by macroeconomic policy. High employment levels are possible in both open and autarkic trading systems. In their assessment of what is known about the consequences of offshore outsourcing Mankiw and Swagel (2006) conclude that: (i) the current extent of offshoring is 'modest' relative to the size of the US economy; (ii) in the future more people will be affected by offshoring, and public policy needs to take this into account; (iii) offshoring is correlated with increases in both US employment and investment, not decreases; (iv) while offshore outsourcing creates both winners and losers, as does any structural change, the USA as a whole gains in the long run; (v) the challenge for public policy is not to withdraw from international integration but to decide how best to help those people adversely affected by offshore outsourcing (see also Bhagwati et al., 2004).

Blinder (2006) also reminds us that just as the first Industrial Revolution did not banish agriculture, and the second Industrial Revolution did not banish manufacturing, as economic activities in the rich nations, neither will the third Industrial Revolution involving offshore outsourcing banish service sector employment from rich nations. However, Blinder warns that all revolutions have disruptive impacts, and the main challenge presented by offshore outsourcing is to 'figure out how to educate our children *now* for the jobs that will actually be available to them ten or twenty years from now'.

## 1.13  THE SIZE OF NATIONS

Another important aspect of increasing international integration has been a dramatic rise in the number of nations during the second half of the twentieth century. Since the late 1990s several economists have been using the tools of modern economic analysis to explore the determinants of the size of nations (see Alesina and Spolare, 1997, 2003, 2005, 2007; Alesina, Spolare and Wacziarg, 2000, 2005; Spolare and Wacziarg, 2005). Although historians and other social scientists have studied this issue, economists 'have remained on the sidelines'. Of particular interest to economists is the observation of Alesina, Spolare and Wacziarg (2005) that there has been a dramatic increase in the number of nations since the end of the Second World War as the break-up of colonial empires, followed later by the disintegration of the Soviet Union and Yugoslavia, led to the creation of many new sovereign states. In the case of the break-up of the Soviet Union, one state became 15 (see Chapter 3)!

In 1948 there were 74 countries, 89 in 1950, and 193 in 2001. Alesina, Spolare and Wacziarg (2005) also note that the world 'now comprises a large number of relatively small countries: in 1995, 87 of the countries of the world had a population of less than 5 million, 58 had a population of less than 2.5 million, and 35 less than 500 thousands'. The proliferation of countries has also led to the creation of too many separate currencies (Alesina and Barro, 2002; Alesina, Barro and Tenreyro, 2002). During the second age of globalisation the share of international trade in world GDP has increased dramatically. Can economists help to explain these developments? Alesina, Spolare and Wacziarg (2005) make the following important points:

1.  political borders are made by humans and are not exogenous geographical features;
2.  economists should think of the equilibrium size of nations (measured by total population) 'as emerging from a trade-off between the *benefits* of size and the *costs* of preference heterogeneity in the population';
3.  the main benefits of size are as follows: economies of scale with respect to the production of public goods such as defence, maintenance of law and order, public health etc.; greater safety from foreign aggression; internalisation of cross-regional externalities; better income insurance to regions subject to specific shocks; income transfers of income across regions to achieve greater equity among the overall population; a larger internal market increases the potential for greater specialisation, as noted by Adam Smith;

4. in a world of free trade, country size, as measured by population, is no longer a determinant of market size;
5. it therefore follows that 'the benefits of country size decline as international economic integration increases';
6. the benefits of international economic integration increase the smaller is a country;
7. economic integration and political disintegration are positively correlated;
8. the costs of size include administrative and congestion costs, but much more important are problems associated with the heterogeneity of preferences of individuals which obviously increase with the size of a nation;
9. using ethnolinguistic fractionalisation as a proxy for heterogeneity of preferences, economists have found that ethnic diversity is inversely correlated with economic performance, the quality of governance, and economic and political freedom (see Alesina et al., 2003; Alesina and La Ferrara, 2005); and finally,
10. as international economic integration increases, the trade-off between the benefits of size of a nation and the costs in terms of heterogeneity of preferences shifts in favour of small nations.

This work has important implications for the future of the European Union (EU). EU enlargement clearly increases the heterogeneity of preferences and economic integration lowers the benefits of country size, thereby reducing the costs of independence for small countries. As Alesina, Spolare and Wacziarg (2005) note, 'many have argued that Europe will (and perhaps should) become a collection of regions loosely connected within a European confederation of independent regions'.

Research by economists on the determinants of the size of nations is in its infancy. However, many interesting relationships remain to be explored, including the interconnection between international integration, democracy, the size of nations and international conflict.

## 1.14 GROWTH, PRODUCTIVITY AND INTERNATIONAL COMPETITIVENESS

At the heart of much public discussion about globalisation is the idea that increasing international integration threatens national economic survival unless the 'competitiveness' of the nation can be improved. Unfortunately, as Michael Porter (1990) emphasises, it is 'far from clear what the term "competitive" means when referring to a nation'. While the 'support for free trade is a badge of professional integrity' for economists, the issue of free trade is also where the 'ideas of economists clash particularly with popular perceptions' (Krugman, 1993a, 1993b). The rhetoric of business 'experts', 'policy entrepreneurs', journalist and television pundits, and numerous politicians promotes what Krugman (1996) calls 'Pop Internationalism'. The rhetoric of 'Pop Internationalism' emphasises 'competitiveness' and competition between nations rather than the potential for mutual gains from trade. Given this neo-mercantilist perception, non-economists are always likely to see winners and losers emerging from international trade. Thus, for the policy entrepreneurs, international trade, as an economic activity, tends to be considered in combative terms, as an extension of international rivalry or economic war. But countries are not like giant corporations in competition with each other and 'competitiveness is a meaningless word when applied to national economies' (Krugman, 1996). In the modern globalisation debate Krugman (1994a) has argued that the notion of 'competitiveness' has become a 'dangerous obsession' and refers to the 'rhetoric of competitiveness' popular among business leaders, politicians and the media. This rhetoric mistakenly views each nation as if it were like a giant corporation struggling for survival in the global marketplace. To assume that the EU and the USA are competitors in the same way that Coca-Cola and Pepsi are competitors leads to a neo-mercantilist zero-sum interpretation of the economic consequences of international trade, a view that Adam Smith and David Ricardo discredited in the late eighteenth and early nineteenth century.

In Michael Porter's view, popular definitions of competitiveness frequently highlight and utilise indicators that are 'deeply flawed', such as the movement of exchange rates, balance-of-payments deficits and surpluses, a country's share of world exports, a government's budget balance, the availability of low-cost and abundant labour, natural-resource abundance and the quality of management practices. While 'business leaders are drawn to the market share view' (Porter, 2004), none of these indicators turns out to be meaningful in terms of a nation's competitiveness. Accordingly, 'we must abandon the whole notion of a "competitive nation" as a term having much meaning for economic prosperity' (Porter, 1990).

To provide a meaningful definition of competitiveness Porter (1990) asks two questions: (i) what is the principal economic goal of a nation? and (ii) how can that goal be achieved? Porter argues that the principal goal of a nation 'is to produce a high and rising standard of living for its citizens' and that productivity acts as 'the prime determinant in the long run of a nation's standard of living, for it is the root cause of national per capita income'. In focusing on productivity Porter stresses that:

1. 'competitiveness' remains a concept that is poorly understood;
2. the idea that competitiveness can somehow be measured by a country's share of world exports is 'deeply flawed' and perpetuates the neo-mercantilist zero-sum game view of the gains from trade;
3. true competitiveness is measured by productivity;
4. the productivity of countries is ultimately determined by the productivity performance of their companies;
5. competitiveness is 'rooted in a nation's microeconomic fundamentals', and microeconomic reforms that improve efficiency are crucial for sustained increases in productivity;
6. sound macroeconomic policies, an efficient and trustworthy legal framework and good governance provide the necessary environment within which enterprises can prosper;
7. there are 'distinct roles for government in improving the business environment at the national, state and local levels';
8. rapid productivity growth is also consistent with a clean environment;
9. a successful and productive economy is also one where individuals are free from discrimination, are healthy and well educated.

Given this perspective, the only meaningful definition of the competitiveness of a nation is 'national productivity' performance:

> A rising standard of living depends on the capacity of a nation's firms to achieve high levels of productivity and to increase productivity over time. (Porter, 1990, p. 6)

In seeking to identify the key factors that lay the foundations for sustained productivity growth and economic prosperity, economists need to extend their investigations beyond the narrow confines of the steady-state analysis of orthodox neoclassical growth theory. This implies focusing more research effort on the fundamental determinants of growth, that is, those variables that have an important influence on a country's ability and capacity to accumulate factors of production and invest in the production of knowledge and innovation (see Figure 2.9, Chapter 2). While economists have recently focused their attention on the role of institutions (see interviews with Acemoglu and Rodrik) and the constraints imposed by geography (see Sachs interview), clearly economists also need to highlight the importance of the microeconomic environment facing private enterprise firms and entrepreneurs, whether it be peasant farmers or multinational enterprises. As Michael Porter (2004, p. 19) notes:

> Wealth is actually created in the microeconomic level of the economy, rooted in the sophistication of the operating practices and strategies of companies as well

as the quality of the microeconomic business environment in which a nation's companies compete. Unless these microeconomic capabilities improve, macro-economic, political, legal, and social reforms will not bear fruit.

While the key theoretical and empirical findings from the recent growth literature demonstrate the importance of social capability, property rights, stable, accountable and honest government, trust, law and order and 'good policy', it seems increasingly clear that the 'capitalist growth machine' is driven by a continuous stream of efficiency improvements and innovations reflecting the competitive environment and structure of incentives at the micro level (Sena, 2004).

While macro-level analysis remains important, explaining the wide differences in the growth performance of nations requires closer investigation of the microeconomic underpinnings of productivity. During the last 15 years, Michael Porter has produced a steady stream of research that has made an important contribution to our understanding of the micro determinants of productivity and economic growth (see, for example, Porter, 1990, 1996, 1998, 2000, 2001, 2003, 2004; Porter and Ketels, 2003; Porter and Sakakibara, 2004).

## 1.15  ANALYSING GLOBAL COMPETITIVENESS

In 1971 Professor Klaus Schwab founded the World Economic Forum as a non-governmental organisation (NGO) committed to improving the state of the world. For the last 25 years the flagship publication of World Economic Forum has been the annual *Global Competitiveness Report* (*GCR*). Currently, Professors Klaus Schwab and Michael Porter are co-directors of this project, the objective of which is to provide a detailed assessment of the 'competitiveness' of a large sample of nations. Until recently, the *GCR* analysed the competitiveness of nations using two alternative but complementary approaches. The first approach uses the medium- to long-term macroeconomic-oriented Growth Competitiveness Index (GCI), developed by John McArthur and Jeffrey Sachs (2001). The second approach to measuring competitiveness utilises the Business Competitiveness Index (BCI), developed by Michael Porter, which first appeared in the *GCR 2000* (before the *GCR 2004–05*, the BCI was known as the 'Microeconomic Competitiveness Index'). Both the GCI and the BCI combine hard data with information gleaned from the Executive Opinion Survey of leading business executives and entrepreneurs from over 100 countries. This survey is conducted during the first five months of each year by the World Economic Forum in cooperation with an extensive network of partner institutes (Blanke and Loades, 2004).

In addition to the GCI and BCI, the *GCR 2004–05* introduced a new index of competitiveness developed by Xavier Sala-i-Martin and Elsa Artadi (2004). The new 'Global Competitiveness Index' aims to 'consolidate the World Economic Forum's work into a single index' that reflects the growing need to take into account a more comprehensive set of factors that significantly influence a country's growth performance (see Porter and Sala-i-Martin interviews).

## 1.16   THE GROWTH COMPETITIVENESS INDEX

Theoretical and empirical research by economists on the analysis of economic growth indicates three important 'pillars' that are widely accepted as key factors critical for sustainable economic growth in any country. Therefore the GCI is a composite measure consisting of (1) a macroeconomic environment index (MEI); (2) a state of public institutions index (PII); and (3) a 'technological readiness' index (TI), as illustrated in Figure 1.10.

However, in developing the GCI, McArthur and Sachs emphasise that the weight given to each of these components of the GCI should differ depending on a country's status as either a 'core' or 'non-core' economy. Countries such as the USA, which are technological leaders and are on, or close to, the technological frontier are classified as core economies. In such economies McArthur and Sachs argue that *technological innovation* should be given more weight in the GCI than in non-core economies, such as China, where *technological adoption* is currently more important for sustaining growth via

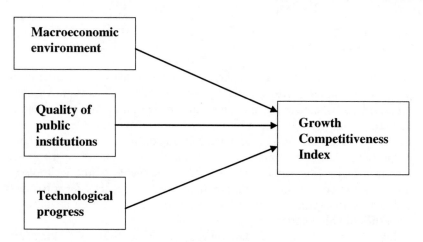

*Figure 1.10    Components of the Growth Competitiveness Index*

a 'catch-up' process (25 core technology-innovating economies are identified and two-thirds are members of the OECD). While Solow's growth model predicts conditional convergence across the world's economies, and explains growth rate differences in terms of 'transitional dynamics', an alternative 'catch-up' hypothesis emphasises the technological gaps that exist between those economies lying behind the innovation frontier and the technologically advanced core economies (Abramovitz, 1986). Whereas in the Solow model the main mechanism leading to differential growth performance in the medium term relates to rates of capital accumulation, in the catch-up model it is the potential for low-income per capita countries to adopt the technology of the more advanced countries that establishes the potential for poor countries to grow more rapidly than rich countries. In other words, there appear to be three potential (proximate) sources of growth of labour productivity:

1.  growth through physical and human capital accumulation, that is, movements along the production frontier;
2.  growth through technological change reflecting shifts of the world production frontier (important for core economies);
3.  growth through technological catch-up involving movement towards the world production frontier (important for non-core economies).

This implies that non-core economies have the opportunity to grow rapidly by moving towards the technological frontier representing 'best-practice' technology (Parente and Prescott, 2000; Kumar and Russell, 2002).

The components and weights of the GCI for core and non-core economies are summarised as follows:

| | |
|---|---|
| Core economies | $GCI = 0.5 (TI) + 0.25 (PII) + 0.25 (MEI)$ |
| Non-core economies | $GCI = 0.33 (TI) + 0.33 (PII) + 0.33 (MEI)$ |

Note that the weight given to macroeconomic stability and the quality of public institutions is also greater for non-core economies than for core economies. It is reasonably assumed that for core economies these fundamentals are largely in place, so that marginal improvements are unlikely to have any dramatic impact on growth rates. In contrast, for many non-core economies, macroeconomic instability and poor-quality institutions remain a major obstacle to growth. The components of the technology index for non-core economies also include a technology transfer sub-index which aims to capture the ability of such economies to adopt technology from the core innovators.

Table 1.7 provides selected data on growth competitiveness rankings for a range of high-, middle- and low-income per capita countries.

*Table 1.7    Selected growth competitiveness rankings and components, 2005–06*

| Country | GCI rank 2005* | GCI rank 2004** | Technology index 2005 | Public institutions index 2005 | Macroeconomic environment index 2005 |
|---|---|---|---|---|---|
| Finland | 1 | 1 | 2 | 5 | 4 |
| USA | 2 | 2 | 1 | 18 | 23 |
| Sweden | 3 | 3 | 4 | 17 | 12 |
| Denmark | 4 | 5 | 5 | 2 | 3 |
| Taiwan | 5 | 4 | 3 | 26 | 17 |
| Singapore | 6 | 7 | 10 | 4 | 1 |
| Japan | 12 | 9 | 8 | 14 | 42 |
| UK | 13 | 11 | 17 | 12 | 18 |
| Germany | 15 | 13 | 16 | 8 | 28 |
| Korea Republic | 17 | 29 | 7 | 42 | 25 |
| Chile | 23 | 22 | 35 | 22 | 15 |
| Malaysia | 24 | 31 | 25 | 29 | 19 |
| Spain | 29 | 23 | 27 | 36 | 24 |
| France | 30 | 27 | 24 | 20 | 27 |
| Thailand | 36 | 34 | 43 | 41 | 26 |
| Hungary | 39 | 39 | 30 | 34 | 63 |
| South Africa | 42 | 41 | 46 | 47 | 31 |
| Italy | 47 | 47 | 44 | 46 | 47 |
| Botswana | 48 | 45 | 76 | 39 | 36 |
| China | 49 | 46 | 64 | 56 | 33 |
| India | 50 | 55 | 55 | 52 | 50 |
| Poland | 51 | 60 | 39 | 64 | 53 |
| Egypt | 53 | 62 | 58 | 53 | 55 |
| Mexico | 55 | 48 | 57 | 71 | 43 |
| Colombia | 57 | 64 | 74 | 49 | 61 |
| Brazil | 65 | 57 | 50 | 70 | 79 |
| Turkey | 66 | 66 | 53 | 61 | 87 |
| Tanzania | 71 | 82 | 86 | 60 | 72 |
| Argentina | 72 | 74 | 59 | 74 | 86 |
| Indonesia | 74 | 69 | 66 | 89 | 64 |
| Russian Fed. | 75 | 70 | 73 | 91 | 58 |
| Pakistan | 83 | 91 | 80 | 103 | 69 |
| Ukraine | 84 | 86 | 85 | 90 | 78 |
| Nigeria | 88 | 93 | 90 | 98 | 76 |
| Kenya | 92 | 78 | 71 | 94 | 106 |
| Bolivia | 101 | 98 | 108 | 84 | 103 |
| Ethiopia | 106 | 101 | 115 | 79 | 108 |

*Table 1.7*   (continued)

| Country | GCI rank 2005* | GCI rank 2004** | Technology index 2005 | Public institutions index 2005 | Macroeconomic environment index 2005 |
|---|---|---|---|---|---|
| Zimbabwe | 109 | 99 | 98 | 80 | 117 |
| Bangladesh | 110 | 102 | 101 | 117 | 83 |
| Chad | 117 | 104 | 117 | 116 | 114 |

*Notes:*
\* Full sample for 2005 = 117 countries.
\*\* Full sample for 2004 = 104 countries.

*Source:*   Adapted from *The Global Competitiveness Report, 2005–06.*

## 1.17   THE BUSINESS COMPETITIVENESS INDEX

Complementary to the GCI is Porter's BCI. Figure 1.11 illustrates Porter's basic framework for thinking about the determinants of productivity and productivity growth. There is wide agreement among economists that the political, legal and social institutions of an economy, combined with macroeconomic stability, create an environment conducive to economic success. However, for that potential success to be realised also requires an economy that is increasingly populated with 'competitive' companies, since 'the productivity of a country is ultimately set by the productivity of its companies'. The competitiveness of companies, in turn, depends on the 'quality of the microeconomic business environment' and the 'sophistication of company operations and strategy'.

Figure 1.12 shows the components of Porter's Business Competitiveness Index. They include Porter's (1990) well-known 'diamond' framework for analysing the quality of the business environment. This in turn consists of four broad determinants of national advantage: (1) factor input conditions; (2) demand conditions; (3) related and supporting industries; and (4) firm strategy, structure and rivalry (see Figure 1.13), which together can be described as 'a mutually reinforcing system' (Porter, 1990).

During the last 15 years Porter has paid special attention to the crucial role played within the diamond framework by the formation of 'clusters', defined as 'geographical concentrations of interconnected companies and institutions in a particular field' (Porter, 1998; see also Porter, 1995, 1996, 2000, 2001, 2003; Porter and Sölvell, 1998). Cluster development improves competitiveness by (1) allowing firms easier access to specialised suppliers, employees and information; (2) increasing firms'

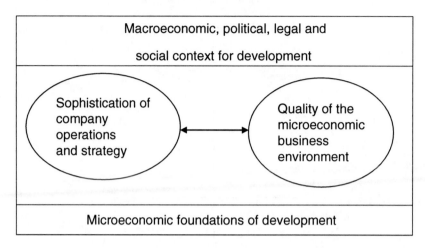

*Source:* Porter (2004).

*Figure 1.11 Determinants of productivity*

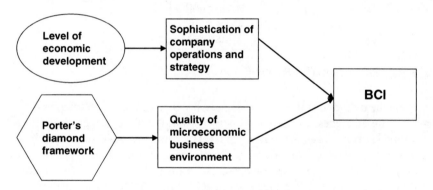

*Source:* Adapted from the *Global Competitiveness Report*, 2004.

*Figure 1.12 Components of the Business Competitiveness Index*

capacity for innovation and productivity growth; and (3) stimulating the formation of new businesses that expand the cluster. Excellent examples of cluster development include: information technology in Silicon Valley, California; financial services in Wall Street, New York and the City of London; wine production in California and Burgundy, France; biotechnology in Boston, USA and Galway, Ireland; aircraft in Seattle, USA; and the numerous tourism clusters throughout the Mediterranean and elsewhere.

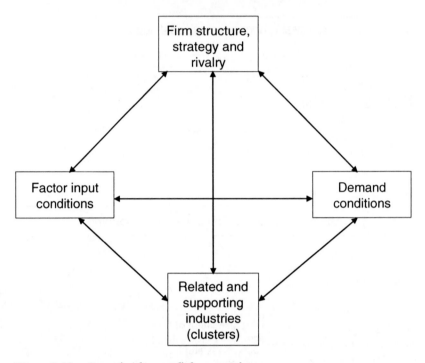

*Figure 1.13    Porter's 'diamond' framework*

As the diamond framework indicates, because 'almost everything matters for competitiveness', improving competitiveness will be 'a marathon not a sprint' (Porter, 2004). Moreover, the level of company sophistication reflects a country's stage of development. Porter distinguishes three types of economy, each of which is characterised by a distinctive stage of competitive development: (1) low-income per capita (GDPpc < $4000) factor-driven economies, where low-cost labour and/or unprocessed natural resources provide the dominant source of competitive advantage; (2) middle-income ($17 000 > GDPpc > $4000) investment-driven economies, where efficiency improvements dominate competitive advantage; and (3) high-income (GDPpc > $17 000) innovation-driven economies, where competitive advantage depends on 'the ability to produce innovative products and services at the global technology frontier'. As Porter (2004, p. 21) argues, 'companies must shift from competing on the basis of inherited endowments (comparative advantages such as low-cost labour or natural resources) to competing on competitive advantage arising from efficient and distinctive products and processes'.

In constructing the BCI, Porter computes sub-index measures of the quality of the microeconomic business environment (QMBE) and sophistication of company operations and strategy (SCOS). The components and weights for the BCI are defined as:

$$BCI = 0.7(QMBE) + 0.3(SCOS)$$

Table 1.8 gives recent BCI rankings for a broad cross-section of countries.

## 1.18   THE GLOBAL COMPETITIVENESS INDEX

As noted in the *Global Competitiveness Report*, the year 2004 represented a transition period because it was decided that subsequent reports would make use of a new single Global Competitiveness Index that consolidates and extends the current dual-track approach involving the construction of the macroeconomic-oriented GCI and the microeconomic-oriented BCI. The more comprehensive Global Competitiveness Index has been developed by Xavier Sala-i-Martin of Columbia University, and Elsa Artadi of Harvard University, in conjunction with the World Economic Forum. In constructing the new 'flagship' Global Competitiveness Index, Sala-i-Martin and Artadi (2004, p. 51) take as their starting point a productivity-based definition of competitiveness similar to Porter's.

> Competitiveness is defined as the set of institutions, policies, and factors that determine the level of productivity. The level of productivity in turn, sets the sustainable *level* of prosperity that can be earned by an economy [and] a more competitive economy is one that is likely to grow at larger rates over the medium to long run.

In other words, productivity as a measure of competitiveness has both static and dynamic elements. However, because the 2003 rank correlation between the GCI and BCI was 95.4 per cent, Sala-i-Martin and Artadi believe that 'the macroeconomic and microeconomic determinants of competitiveness cannot and should not be separated' (see Porter and Sala-i-Martin interviews). Consequently, the new Global Competitiveness Index (GLCI) is based on three basic principles.

*Principle 1* While extensive research indicates that the determinants of productivity are complex, the main influences can be encompassed within 12 'pillars of competitiveness': (i) institutions, (ii) infrastructure, (iii) macroeconomic stability, (iv) personal security, (v) basic human capital, advanced human capital, (vi) goods market efficiency, (vii) labour market efficiency, (viii) financial market efficiency, (ix) technological readiness, (x) openness/market size, (xi) business sophistication and (xii) innovation. In the *GCR 2005–06* the 12 pillars are reduced to nine pillars by combining the three separate market

*Table 1.8*    *Selected business competitiveness indicators and components, 2005–06*

| Country | BCI rank 2005* | BCI rank 2004** | Company operations and strategy, 2005 | Quality of national business environment, 2005 | GDP per capita $PPP, 2004 |
|---|---|---|---|---|---|
| USA | 1 | 1 | 1 | 2 | 39 498 |
| Finland | 2 | 2 | 9 | 1 | 29 305 |
| Germany | 3 | 3 | 2 | 4 | 28 889 |
| Denmark | 4 | 7 | 4 | 3 | 33 089 |
| Singapore | 5 | 10 | 14 | 5 | 26 799 |
| UK | 6 | 6 | 6 | 6 | 28 968 |
| Japan | 8 | 8 | 3 | 10 | 29 906 |
| France | 11 | 12 | 10 | 11 | 27 913 |
| Sweden | 12 | 4 | 7 | 14 | 28 205 |
| Taiwan | 14 | 17 | 13 | 15 | 25 614 |
| Malaysia | 23 | 23 | 24 | 23 | 10 423 |
| Korea Republic | 24 | 24 | 17 | 24 | 21 305 |
| Spain | 25 | 26 | 25 | 26 | 23 627 |
| South Africa | 28 | 25 | 26 | 30 | 10 603 |
| Chile | 29 | 29 | 31 | 29 | 10 869 |
| India | 31 | 30 | 30 | 31 | 3 029 |
| Hungary | 34 | 42 | 40 | 32 | 15 546 |
| Thailand | 37 | 37 | 35 | 37 | 7 901 |
| Italy | 38 | 34 | 28 | 39 | 28 172 |
| Poland | 42 | 57 | 43 | 46 | 12 224 |
| Brazil | 49 | 38 | 32 | 52 | 8 328 |
| Turkey | 51 | 52 | 38 | 51 | 7 503 |
| Botswana | 55 | 62 | 76 | 50 | 10 169 |
| Colombia | 56 | 58 | 49 | 57 | 6 959 |
| China | 57 | 47 | 53 | 58 | 5 642 |
| Indonesia | 59 | 44 | 50 | 59 | 3 622 |
| Mexico | 60 | 55 | 55 | 62 | 9 666 |
| Argentina | 64 | 74 | 52 | 64 | 12 468 |
| Pakistan | 66 | 73 | 68 | 65 | 2 404 |
| Kenya | 68 | 63 | 60 | 69 | 1 075 |
| Egypt | 71 | 66 | 58 | 74 | 4 072 |
| Russian Fed. | 74 | 61 | 77 | 70 | 10 179 |
| Ukraine | 75 | 69 | 71 | 76 | 6 554 |
| Nigeria | 76 | 81 | 65 | 79 | 1 120 |
| Tanzania | 82 | 90 | 93 | 81 | 673 |

*Table 1.8*   (continued)

| Country | BCI rank 2005* | BCI rank 2004** | Company operations and strategy, 2005 | Quality of national business environment, 2005 | GDP per capita $PPP, 2004 |
|---|---|---|---|---|---|
| Zimbabwe | 84 | 82 | 78 | 84 | 2 309 |
| Bangladesh | 100 | 95 | 99 | 101 | 1 875 |
| Ethiopia | 111 | 99 | 113 | 110 | 814 |
| Bolivia | 113 | 101 | 115 | 112 | 2 902 |
| Chad | 116 | – | 116 | 116 | 1 555 |

*Notes:*
* Full sample for 2005 =116 countries.
** Full sample for 2004 =103 countries.

*Source:*   Adapted from *The Global Competitiveness Report, 2005–06.*

efficiency pillars into one pillar entitled 'market efficiency', and by eliminating 'personal security' as a separate category (see Lopez-Claros et al., 2005).

While each pillar is an important contributor to growth in all circumstances, each also plays a major role depending on the stage of development, in one of three broad areas: 'Basic requirements' (BR), 'Efficiency enhancers' (EE), and 'Innovation and sophistication' factors (IF). Figure 1.14 illustrates the structure of the Global Competitiveness Index. The GLCI is therefore a weighted composite index comprising these latter three elements as follows:

$$GLCI = \alpha_1 BR + \alpha_2 EE + \alpha_3 IF, \quad and \; \alpha_1 + \alpha_2 + \alpha_3 \equiv 1$$

*Principle 2* The process of economic development evolves in three stages, namely a factor-driven stage, an efficiency-driven stage, and an innovation-driven stage (Porter, 1990, 2004). The classification of countries, according to stage of development, is based on GDP per capita and the percentage of total exports in the form of primary commodities ($Xp/X$). While basic requirements, efficiency enhancers and innovation factors play a role in all economies, they are given different weights in the construction of the GCLI depending on a country's stage of development. The assignment of weights is as follows:

At the factor-driven stage $\quad \alpha_1 = 0.5, \alpha_2 = 0.4, \alpha_3 = 0.1$
At the efficiency-driven stage $\quad \alpha_1 = 0.4, \alpha_2 = 0.5, \alpha_3 = 0.1$
At the innovation-driven stage $\quad \alpha_1 = 0.3, \alpha_2 = 0.4, \alpha_3 = 0.3$

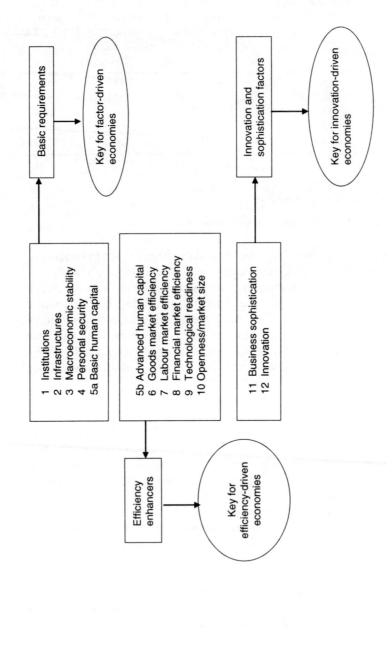

*Source:* Sala-i-Martin and Artadi (2004).

*Figure 1.14   The 12 'pillars' of the Global Competitiveness Index*

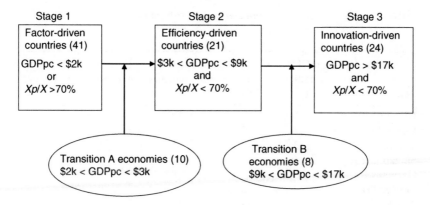

*Figure 1.15    Five stages of development*

*Principle 3* As economies develop they move smoothly from one stage to the next. Therefore, there are two additional groups of 'transition economies' and the weights of the sub-indices 'change smoothly as a country develops'. This overall framework is captured in Figure 1.15, and Table 1.9 provides global competitiveness rankings for a range of countries representing each of the five country groupings.

## 1.19    IMPROVING COMPETITIVENESS IN DEVELOPING COUNTRIES

In its *World Development Report* (2005) the World Bank emphasises the conditions necessary to create a good investment climate in order to stimulate growth and reduce poverty. Using data from Investment Climate Surveys, covering in excess of 26 000 firms from 53 countries, the World Bank (2005) echoes one of Michael Porter's central ideas when it notes that:

> Private firms are at the heart of the development process. Driven by the quest for profits, they invest in new ideas and new facilities that strengthen the foundations of economic growth and prosperity.

Compared to the early post-Second World War period, very few commentators are now enthusiastic supporters of a heavily *dirigiste*, state-oriented development strategy. Following the critiques of public ownership from the public choice and contracting literature, the theoretical case for public ownership based on market imperfections is now largely defunct. There is now

*Table 1.9    Selected global competitiveness rankings and components,*
*            2005–06\**

| Country and stage of development | GCI** rank 2005 | GCI*** rank 2004 | Basic requirements | Efficiency enhancers | Innovation factors |
|---|---|---|---|---|---|
| USA (3) | 1 | 1 | 18 | 1 | 1 |
| Finland (3) | 2 | 2 | 2 | 5 | 5 |
| Denmark (3) | 3 | 3 | 1 | 3 | 7 |
| Singapore (3) | 5 | 7 | 3 | 2 | 14 |
| Germany (3) | 6 | 6 | 8 | 19 | 3 |
| Sweden (3) | 7 | 5 | 7 | 9 | 6 |
| Taiwan (B) | 8 | 11 | 19 | 6 | 8 |
| UK (3) | 9 | 9 | 17 | 4 | 11 |
| Japan (3) | 10 | 10 | 25 | 17 | 2 |
| France (3) | 12 | 17 | 16 | 18 | 9 |
| Korea Republic (B) | 19 | 26 | 20 | 20 | 17 |
| Malaysia (2) | 25 | 23 | 26 | 25 | 25 |
| Chile (2) | 27 | 29 | 24 | 31 | 32 |
| Spain (3) | 28 | 24 | 28 | 27 | 28 |
| Thailand (A) | 33 | 33 | 34 | 41 | 38 |
| Hungary (2) | 35 | 46 | 49 | 30 | 39 |
| Italy (3) | 38 | 56 | 44 | 36 | 30 |
| South Africa (2) | 40 | 36 | 46 | 43 | 29 |
| Poland (2) | 43 | 72 | 57 | 38 | 45 |
| India (1) | 45 | 37 | 65 | 46 | 26 |
| China (1) | 48 | 32 | 45 | 62 | 48 |
| Egypt (1) | 52 | 47 | 53 | 68 | 71 |
| Russian Fed. (2) | 53 | 64 | 60 | 53 | 66 |
| Argentina (2) | 54 | 75 | 62 | 57 | 52 |
| Brazil (2) | 57 | 49 | 77 | 51 | 36 |
| Colombia (A) | 58 | 69 | 63 | 67 | 49 |
| Mexico (2) | 59 | 60 | 55 | 61 | 57 |
| Ukraine (1) | 68 | 73 | 74 | 64 | 60 |
| Indonesia (1) | 69 | 48 | 71 | 74 | 55 |
| Turkey (2) | 71 | 67 | 89 | 54 | 44 |
| Botswana (2) | 72 | 58 | 61 | 69 | 77 |
| Nigeria (1) | 83 | 77 | 78 | 90 | 72 |
| Kenya (1) | 93 | 84 | 108 | 83 | 51 |
| Pakistan (1) | 94 | 87 | 105 | 87 | 63 |
| Bangladesh (1) | 98 | 94 | 95 | 100 | 90 |
| Tanzania (1) | 105 | 97 | 103 | 105 | 88 |
| Zimbabwe (1) | 110 | 101 | 113 | 93 | 87 |

*Table 1.9* (continued)

| Country and stage of development | GCI** rank 2005 | GCI*** rank 2004 | Basic requirements | Efficiency enhancers | Innovation factors |
|---|---|---|---|---|---|
| Ethiopia (1) | 116 | 102 | 115 | 116 | 111 |
| Chad (1) | 117 | 103 | 117 | 117 | 116 |

*Notes:*
\* A = Transition A economy, and B=Transition B economy.
\*\* Full sample for 2005 = 117 countries.
\*\*\* Full sample for 2004 = 104 countries.

*Source:* Adapted from *The Global Competitiveness Report, 2005–06.*

widespread recognition that 'private ownership is the crucial source of incentives to innovate and become efficient' (Shleifer, 1998). Governments are now viewed as playing a crucial role in establishing the conditions necessary for the private sector to flourish (World Bank, 1997; Yergin and Stanislaw, 1999). The developing countries are teeming with potential entrepreneurs who would, in the absence of credit constraints, perverse incentives and regulatory burdens, play a crucial role in the development process.

An emerging consensus rejects the use of industrial policy as a mechanism for 'picking winners', and advocates the use of government policies that encourage competition and technological upgrading, provide necessary public goods and infrastructure, and address serious market failures, including those that arise due to imperfections of information, particularly in financial markets (Stiglitz, 2002b). The bankruptcy of the case for extensive public ownership was also demonstrated by the failure of the 'permit Raj' model of economic development in India and further reinforced by the collapse by 1990 of the Soviet-style central planning system in the Eastern bloc economies (see Chapter 3 and the interviews with Padma Desai and János Kornai). A major lesson is that activities of the state and the market are complementary since markets cannot function without the necessary institutional foundations. Therefore a state's activities should match its capabilities, concentrating on getting the 'fundamentals' right.

Crucial to economic success is the establishment and maintenance of a competitive environment, and it is certainly not the role of government to limit competition. In a recent paper, Porter and Sakakibara (2004) challenge the popular view that Japan's post-war economic miracle was based on a set of institutions and industrial policies that limited competition. Indeed, the evidence shows that the internationally successful Japanese industries were those where 'internal competition was invariably fierce' (see Porter and Takeuchi, 1999; Porter, Takeuchi and Sakakibara, 2000; Porter and Sakakibara, 2001).

While the diversity of development strategies and experience in East Asia is considerable, all the successful 'Tigers' managed to get the fundamentals right, and the increasing openness of these economies proved to be a major source of technology transfer via imports and foreign direct investment (Hernandez, 2004; Keller, 2004). Recent research reconfirms Adam Smith's insight that barriers to competition and free trade are a major retarding influence on efficiency, growth and innovation (see Parente and Prescott, 2000; Panagariya, 2004a; UK Treasury, 2004).

During the last decade a congruence has evolved between the research of Michael Porter and mainstream growth theorists in that there is growing recognition of the importance of microeconomic fundamentals if an environment is to be created that is conducive to sustainable growth. This is particularly noticeable in the recent contributions of Baumol (2002), the OECD (2004), the World Bank (2005), and the development of the World Economic Forum's Global Competitiveness Index by Sala-i-Martin and Artadi (2004).

## 1.20   CONCLUSION

The powerful forces of globalisation have influenced everyone's lives and will continue to do so. While there are costs and benefits to globalisation, unlike anti-globalists, economists tend to be pro-globalisation, recognising that the potential long-run gains are likely to significantly outweigh the short-term costs. However, as happened during the period 1914–50, a globalisation backlash is possible, and this makes it all the more important that globalisation is viewed in historical perspective since the international political and economic disintegration during the inter-war period had catastrophic consequences. While financial crises will inevitably recur, the experiences of recent years have led to a burgeoning of research by economists into such events. It is hoped that emerging market economies now have a much better understanding of the causes, consequences and policy measures necessary to reduce the frequency and severity of such crises as a result of this research.

Because the main driving forces behind increasing international integration are economic, economists must have a key role to play in the contemporary debate on globalisation, not least to counter the many myths that are perpetuated in public discussions. For example, it is poverty that lies behind the employment of child labour, not globalisation. Since both the balance of evidence and economic theory suggest that increasing international integration will promote economic growth, and the latter reduces poverty, globalisation is a potential solution to the problem of child labour, not a cause (Neumayer and De Soysa, 2004). However, the generally benign view of globalisation held by most economists needs to be tempered by recognition that the short-run consequences of globalisation, for some individuals and groups, 'are likely to be extremely painful' (Gomory and Baumol, 2004). Therefore, as Dani Rodrik (2004) argues, 'The relationship between the risks and vulnerabilities created by openness and the demand for social protection is one that requires close attention and political management.'

# 2. Economic development in historical perspective

> All human progress, political, moral, or intellectual, is inseparable from material progression.
>
> Auguste Comte (1896, p. 98)

> Economic growth – meaning a rising standard of living for the clear majority of citizens – more often than not fosters greater opportunity, tolerance of diversity, social mobility, commitment to fairness, and dedication to democracy.
>
> Benjamin Friedman (2005, p. 4)

> To understand where the economy is and how it is evolving one needs to study not only the present but the past.
>
> Robert Fogel (1999, p. 15)

## 2.1  INTRODUCTION

Following the end of the Second World War economists were generally pessimistic about the prospects for sustaining steady economic growth in the developed capitalist market economies, and initiating a 'take-off' of growth in the developing countries. In the USA, influenced by Alvin Hansen (1939), economists worried about the possibility of 'secular stagnation'. The traumatic experience of the 1930s Great Depression also left an enormous shadow, and fears of a return to mass unemployment accompanied the impending demobilisation of over 11 million armed service personnel and the need to reallocate over nine million workers from defence to non-defence sectors (Fogel, 2005). However, once the immediate post-war adjustments were complete, beginning in the 1950s, the USA and other OECD economies had entered what has come to be known as the 'golden age' of growth (Crafts and Toniolo, 1996; Maddison, 2001). The accelerated growth, above the long-run trend associated with the period 1950–70, has been attributed to reductions in the barriers to trade, less macroeconomic volatility relative to the inter-war and earlier periods, the success of the Marshall Plan reconstruction programme in Europe, and opportunities for the European countries and Japan to take advantage of a 'catch-up' growth bonus arising from a backlog of technological developments and the pre-existing technology gap between the USA and other industrial economies (see Abramovitz, 1986; DeLong and Eichengreen, 1993; Maddison, 1995; Toniolo, 1998; Romer, 1999).

In the developing countries, given the history and experiences with colonisation, together with the images forged during the Great Depression, capitalism and markets were viewed with suspicion. As Sachs (1999) comments, most developing countries 'viewed the capitalist countries not as trading partners, but as political and economic predators, former colonial masters who would look for new opportunities of exploitation'. The process of decolonisation, combined with a dual concern about the growing GDP per capita gap between developed and developing countries and the emergence of 'cold war' international politics, led to an increasing interest in the economics of development, within both academia and policy circles. Following the lowering of the 'Iron Curtain' across Eastern Europe in the late 1940s it became the norm to divide the world into three camps; (i) a 'First World', consisting of the relatively prosperous capitalist developed countries; (ii) a 'Second World', which included the Soviet Union, China and other 'socialist' economies; and (iii) a 'Third World', which included the poor developing countries of Africa, Asia and Latin America.

During the late 1950s and 1960s, neo-Malthusian pessimists warned of the dangers of rapid population growth to both the prospects for development in the 'Third World' and the future sustainability of the world economy (Nelson, 1956; Coale and Hoover, 1958; Enke, 1966; Meadows et al., 1972). In retrospect it is now clear the extent to which analysts failed to anticipate the transitory nature of the world's population explosion due to the onset of a worldwide 'demographic transition', the vast potential for raising agricultural productivity, and the enormous potential for rapid growth that existed in Third World countries providing that barriers to development, including those restricting trade, could be removed (Johnson, 1997, 2000; Krueger, 1997; Parente and Prescott, 2000; Lee, 2003). No one seemed to anticipate the 'miracle' Asian growth rates, first experienced in Japan, but later spreading to Hong Kong, Singapore, South Korea and Taiwan, then to Malaysia, Thailand, and Indonesia, and most recently to China and India.

The power and importance of economic growth in raising living standards is perhaps best illustrated by the history of the twentieth century. Despite two devastating world wars, the Great Depression and collapse of international integration during the inter-war period, and the rise and fall of the communist experiment, the majority of the world's population are currently better off than their parents and grandparents in terms of income per capita. While economic growth concentrates narrowly on sustained increases in the flow of goods and services, economic development involves much more and should be conceived of 'as a multidimensional process involving major changes in social structures, popular attitudes and national institutions, as well as the acceleration of economic growth, the reduction of inequality, and the eradication of poverty' (Todaro and Smith, 2003, p. 17; see also Seers, 1972; Sen, 1999a).

There is now strong evidence to suggest that international income per capita differentials were present, although modest, before the onset of the Industrial Revolution (Maddison, 2001; Allen et al., 2005; Hibbs and Olsson, 2005; Landes, 2006). The new empirical growth literature indicates that across the world's economies, income per capita disparities are now large and have grown significantly since the nineteenth century. The data also reveal that growth rate differences between countries across time and space are significant (Pritchett, 1997a). Angus Maddison's (2001) widely used estimates show that during the twentieth century, world real GDP per capita increased faster than at any other time in human history, and this historically unprecedented acceleration of economic growth is the main reason why today the majority of people living in the developed economies enjoy such extraordinarily high living standards, as do the majority of people throughout the world, relative to their ancestors. Overall, the twentieth century was a century of unrivalled increases in prosperity, and life in the higher-income countries has been totally transformed (DeLong, 2000a, 2000b). So there is general agreement among economists that the single most powerful mechanism for generating long-term increases in income per capita is economic growth rather than redistribution of income. It will also act as the main source of divergences in living standards if growth rates differ across the regions and countries of the world.

Over very short time horizons the gains from moderate economic growth are often imperceptible to the beneficiaries, but the gains in the long run are highly visible. It is hardly surprising, then, that for many economists, to understand the causes of economic growth is far more important than gaining a better understanding of business cycles. As Barro and Sala-i-Martin (2003, p. 6) argue, 'If we can learn about government policy options that have even small effects on long-term growth rates, we can contribute much more to improvements in standards of living than has been provided by the entire history of macroeconomic analysis of countercyclical policy and fine tuning.' Although Keynes (1930, pp. 359–61) is normally associated with his work on short-run macroeconomic issues, at the beginning of the Great Depression, the worst business cycle in the history of capitalism, we find him reminding contemporary observers that they should not be blind 'to what is going on under the surface – to the true interpretation of things . . . the power of compound interest over two hundred years is such as to stagger the imagination'.

However, despite this fact, progress across the world has been uneven, and according to Jeffrey Sachs (2005a) there are roughly one billion people in the developing countries who are 'too ill, hungry or destitute even to get on the first rung of the development ladder'. There have been striking examples of development miracles (East Asia), development disappointments (North Africa, the Middle East and South America) and development disasters (sub-Saharan Africa). The progress of some countries has been nothing short of spectacular, while for others progress has been negligible. Yousef (2004), in his assessment of growth and development in the Middle East and North Africa, argues that these regions have 'failed to take advantage of the expansion in world trade and foreign direct investment' during the last 20 years and consequently they are one of the least integrated areas in the global economy (see also Foote et al., 2004; Kuran, 2004; Elbadawi, 2005).

As a result of wide differences of economic performance over time, 'Whether measured by national income, health, or material possessions, the differences in living standards between rich and poor countries in the world today are simply astounding' (Weil, 2005). Poverty and inequality also remain important public policy issues within rich nations (see Hoynes et al., 2006; Smeeding, 2006).

## 2.2  THE 'GREAT ESCAPE'

Angus Maddison's data (see Table 2.1) show that, before the modern era, living standards for the vast majority of the world's population progressed at a glacial pace. This was to change forever as a result of the Industrial Revolution, and nothing in human history compares with the impact that this event has had on the living conditions for the world's population. Although the preconditions necessary to initiate the first Industrial Revolution evolved during the previous millennia, sustained growth of GDP per capita dates from the forces unleashed by this event. While economic historians continue to debate the origins, timing and quantitative aspects of the Industrial Revolution, there is no doubt that during the last 250 years the main consequence has been a distinctive regime change (Easterlin, 1996; Clark, 2003; Sachs, 2005a). As the data in Table 2.1 indicate, an increasing proportion of the world economy finally escaped from the Malthusian dynamics that had previously constrained intensive growth, leading to a new epoch of modern 'promethean' economic growth driven by technological progress (Landes, 1969; Galor and Weil, 2000; Mokyr, 2005a).

In commenting on the power of economic growth, McCloskey (1994, p. 242) reminds us that 'No previous episode of enrichment approaches modern economic growth – not China or Egypt in their primes, not the

Table 2.1 Level[1] and rate of growth[2] of GDP per capita: world, major regions and selected countries, AD 1–2001

| | 1[1] | 1000[1] | 1820[1] | 2001[1] | 1–1000[2] | 1000–1500[2] | 1500–1820[2] | 1820–70[2] | 1870–1913[2] | 1913–50[2] | 1950–73[2] | 1973–2001[2] |
|---|---|---|---|---|---|---|---|---|---|---|---|---|
| Western Europe | 450 | 400 | 1 204 | 19 256 | −0.01 | 0.13 | 0.14 | 0.98 | 1.33 | 0.76 | 4.05 | 1.88 |
| UK | – | – | 1 706 | 20 127 | – | – | 0.27 | 1.26 | 1.01 | 0.93 | 2.42 | 1.86 |
| France | – | – | 1 135 | 21 092 | – | – | 0.14 | 1.01 | 1.45 | 1.12 | 4.04 | 1.71 |
| Germany | – | – | 1 077 | 18 677 | – | – | 0.14 | 1.08 | 1.61 | 0.17 | 5.02 | 1.60 |
| Italy | – | – | 1 117 | 19 040 | – | – | 0.00 | 0.59 | 1.26 | 0.85 | 4.95 | 2.10 |
| Western offshoots[3] | 400 | 400 | 1 202 | 26 943 | 0.00 | 0.00 | 0.34 | 1.41 | 1.81 | 1.56 | 2.45 | 1.84 |
| USA | – | – | 1 257 | 27 948 | – | – | 0.36 | 1.34 | 1.82 | 1.61 | 2.45 | 1.86 |
| Japan | 400 | 425 | 669 | 20 683 | 0.01 | 0.03 | 0.09 | 0.19 | 1.48 | 0.88 | 8.06 | 2.14 |
| Latin America | 400 | 400 | 692 | 5 811 | 0.00 | 0.01 | 0.16 | −0.03 | 1.82 | 1.43 | 2.58 | 0.91 |
| Eastern Europe | 400 | 400 | 683 | 6 027 | 0.00 | 0.04 | 0.10 | 0.63 | 1.39 | 0.60 | 3.81 | 0.68 |

| | | | | | | | | | | | |
|---|---|---|---|---|---|---|---|---|---|---|---|
| Former USSR | 400 | 400 | 688 | 4 626 | 0.00 | 0.04 | 0.10 | 0.63 | 1.06 | 1.76 | 3.35 | −0.96 |
| Asia (excluding Japan) | 450 | 450 | 577 | 3 256 | 0.00 | 0.05 | 0.00 | −0.10 | 0.42 | −0.10 | 2.91 | 3.55 |
| China | 450 | 450 | 600 | 3 583 | 0.00 | 0.06 | 0.00 | −0.25 | 0.10 | −0.62 | 2.86 | 5.32 |
| India | 450 | 450 | 533 | 1 957 | 0.00 | 0.04 | −0.01 | 0.00 | 0.54 | −0.22 | 1.40 | 3.01 |
| Africa | 430 | 425 | 420 | 1 489 | 0.00 | −0.01 | 0.00 | 0.35 | 0.57 | 0.92 | 2.00 | 0.19 |
| World | 445 | 436 | 667 | 6 049 | 0.00 | 0.05 | 0.05 | 0.54 | 1.30 | 0.88 | 2.92 | 1.41 |

*Notes:*
[1] Measured in 1990 Geary–Khamis international (PPP) dollars.
[2] Annual average compound growth %.
[3] USA, Canada, Australia, New Zealand.

*Source:* Adapted from Maddison's tables, http://www.ggdc.net/Maddison.

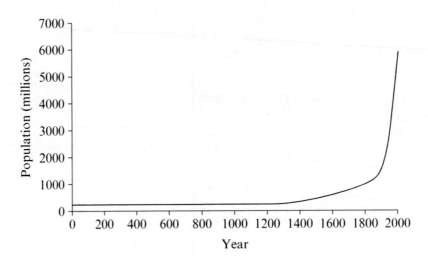

*Source:*   Based on Maddison (2001) data.

*Figure 2.1    World population, 0–2000*

glory of Greece or the grandeur of Rome', and Keynes (1919) observed
that by the end of the twentieth century the 'conveniences, comforts, and
amenities beyond the compass of the richest and most powerful monarchs
of other ages' had become the norm for the vast majority of people living
in the developed countries. In his famous 1930 essay, 'The Economic
Possibilities of Our Grandchildren', Keynes also made the following
important and insightful prediction:

> I would predict that the standard of life in progressive countries one hundred
> years hence will be between four and eight times as high as it is today . . . Thus
> for the first time since his creation man will be faced with his real, his permanent
> problem – how to use his freedom from pressing economic cares, how to occupy
> the leisure, which science and compound interest will have won for him, to live
> wisely and agreeably and well. (pp. 364–7)

In the eighteenth and nineteenth centuries economic growth was largely
confined to a small number of countries, but gradually, modern economic
growth spread from its origins in Great Britain to Western Europe, and initially to 'Western offshoots' (overseas areas settled by European migrants,
Maddison, 2001). As Figures 2.1–2.3 indicate, even though world population has exploded during the last 250 years, average world living standards,
measured by GDP per capita, have shown a marked improvement, and this
achievement is due to the dramatic acceleration of world growth rates of

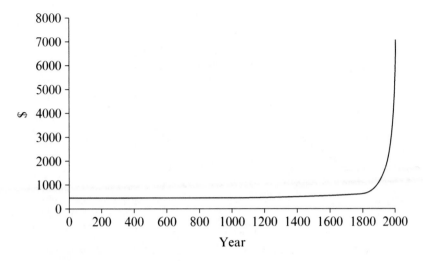

*Source:* Based on Maddison (2001) data.

*Figure 2.2   World per capita GDP, 0–2000*

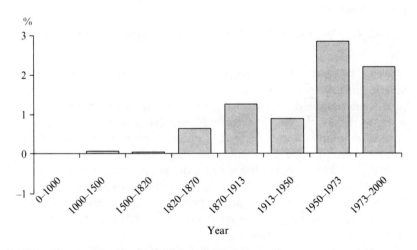

*Source:* Based on Maddison (2001) data.

*Figure 2.3   World per capita GDP growth rates, 0–2000*

per capita GDP. The pessimistic predictions of Malthus and the neo-Malthusians have failed to materialise (concern about overpopulation has now been replaced with concern about sustainability of the environment and global warming. See Stern, 2006; Nordhaus, 2006).

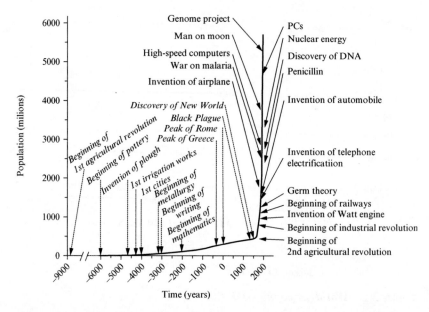

*Source:*   Based on Fogel (1999).

*Figure 2.4*    *The growth of world population and some major events in the history of technology*

Nobel Laureate Robert Fogel, in his Presidential Address to the American Economics Association in 1999, highlighted the impact on the human environment of the 'astounding acceleration of technological progress' during the last 250 years. Figure 2.4 illustrates that there is a close correlation between the growth of world population and the acceleration of technological progress. Not only does technological progress allow the world to support more and more people; the new 'ideas-based' growth theories of Kremer (1993), Romer (1990) and Jones (2002, 2005) also show that a larger world population increases the flow of new ideas which in turn fuels the engine of further technological progress (see Mokyr, 1990, 1998, 2002, 2005a, 2005b).

However, the diffusion of the modern economic growth regime during the last 250 years has been highly uneven and, in some cases, such as sub-Saharan Africa, negligible. The result is a current pattern of income per capita differentials between the richest and poorest countries of the world that almost defies comprehension. For example, recent World Bank data for 208 economies show that in 2004, Luxembourg (rank 1) had a gross national income (GNI) per capita (purchasing power parity – PPP) of $61 220, the USA (rank 2) $39 710, and the UK (rank 13) $31 460. At the other end of the scale, Nigeria (rank 193) had a GNI (PPP) of $930, Ethiopia (rank 200) $810, and Malawi (rank 208) $620! Such huge gaps in living standards are a recent historical phenomenon. Clearly the potential for growth and development has not always been realised outside the 'progressive countries', and the modern era has witnessed large variations in the growth trajectories of different nations (Pritchett, 2000). Moreover, in the developing world many countries have experienced 'start–stop' growth, with periods of growth acceleration followed by growth collapse (Jones and Olken, 2005). The inevitable consequence of these trends has been the emergence of the wide disparities in real per capita incomes observable across the globe as the world entered the new millennium. However, the extent to which these disparities are widening or narrowing remains a matter of considerable controversy among economists (Ravallion, 2003; Milanovic, 2006). For example, Sala-i-Martin's recent research demonstrates that, especially during the last 25 years, significant improvements in living standards via growth have now spread to other heavily populated parts of the world, most significantly to China and India (two countries with a combined population of 2.3 billion people). This is now having a dramatic impact on reducing world poverty and inequality (see Sala-i-Martin, 2002a, 2002b, 2002c, 2006). As everyone now recognises, the main tragedy remains sub-Saharan Africa, and 'there should be no doubt that the worst economic disaster of the twentieth century is the dismal growth performance of the African continent' (Artadi and Sala-i-Martin, 2003).

The importance of economic growth as a basis for improvements in human welfare and poverty reduction cannot be overstated and is confirmed by numerous empirical studies (Dollar and Kraay, 2002a, 2002b). Growth theory also suggests that poor countries have enormous potential for achieving rapid growth and 'catch-up' via capital accumulation and technological progress (Barro and Sala-i-Martin, 2003). Reflecting on the 'Economic Possibilities of Our Grandchildren', Keynes (1930, p. 360) also drew attention to the importance of economic growth:

> From the earliest times of which we have record . . . there was no very great change in the standard of life of the average man living in the civilised centres of the earth . . . This slow rate of progress, or lack of progress, was due to two reasons – to the remarkable absence of important technical improvements and to the failure of capital to accumulate.

There is no better modern demonstration of this observation, relating to the importance of capital accumulation and technological progress, than the experiences of the 'miracle' East Asian economies compared to those of the majority of sub-Saharan African economies during the second half of the twentieth century. The 'miracle' rapid growth of East Asia stands in sharp contrast to the disappointing performance of South America and the 'tragedy' of sub-Saharan Africa (Sachs, 2005a; Elson, 2006).

## 2.3    ALTERNATIVE MEASURES OF 'PROGRESS'

How should progress be measured? Today, economists and economic historians have available to them a rich array of data for a large number of countries on which to base their research (Donovan and Halpern, 2002). Economists certainly recognise that economic development involves much more than growth of real per capita income, and this is reflected in the wide variety of methods used for measuring human progress, both orthodox and unorthodox, including:

1.   real GNP or GDP per capita measured in US dollars;
2.   real GNP or GDP per capita in international dollars, i.e. purchasing power parity (PPP) dollar estimates (Summers and Heston, 1991, 1996; Maddison, 2001; Castles and Henderson, 2005);
3.   combined socio-economic and political indicators (Adelman and Morris, 1967);
4.   the Physical Quality of Life Index, PQLI (Overseas Development Council, 1977; Morris, 1979);
5.   life expectancy and mortality (Hicks and Streeten, 1979; Sen, 1998);
6.   the Human Development Index (United Nations Development Programme, 1990–2007);
7.   a variety of competitiveness indices (Porter et al., 2005; see also Chapter 1);
8.   the Political Freedom Index (Freedom House, 2005; Sen, 1999a);
9.   anthropometrics (Steckel, 1995, 1998);
10.  indicators of 'happiness' (Layard, 2005).

### 2.3.1   Income Measures

Traditionally, the most commonly used measure of development is real GNP or GNI per capita measured in US dollars. GNP is the broadest calculation of a country's national income and measures total value added from both domestic and foreign sources claimed by residents, that is, GNP = GDP + net receipts of factor income from overseas sources. To many economists and economic historians, real GNP or GDP per capita remains the best single measure available for comparing the economic performance of a country over historical periods, or for comparing the performance of different economies (see Jones, E.L., 2002).

For over 300 years economists have analysed the conceptual foundations and methods suggested for measuring the 'standard of living' based on national income data. Nobel Laureate Richard Stone (1986) traces the origins of national income accounting to William Petty's pioneering work on 'political arithmetick' (Vanoli, 2005). However, the most important breakthroughs occurred during the 1930s, in the wake of the Great Depression and the 'Keynesian Revolution', when the modern systems of national income accounts were developed by economists such as Nobel Laureates Simon Kuznets and Richard Stone (Kuznets, 1973; Stone, 1986; Maddison, 2004). The development of systems of national accounts vastly improved the whole basis for empirical economic analysis and the quantitative assessment of questions related to changes in the standard of living.

By the 1950s many of the technical accounting difficulties of calculating national income statistics had been resolved, including the elimination of double counting and adjustments to nominal income and output to take account of inflation. However, comparisons of living standards based on real GNP per capita measured in US dollars give a distorted view because the purchasing power of a US dollar varies considerably across countries and especially between rich and poor countries. In a world of free trade and zero transport costs the 'law of one price', via international commodity arbitrage, would equate the dollar purchasing power of one dollar across all countries. In reality these conditions do not hold and dollar prices vary considerably across countries. In particular, the prices of non-traded services are much lower in poor countries, and this is the main reason why the purchasing power of the dollar is so much higher in developing countries. Because exchange rates are largely determined by the flow of traded goods and international financial flows, they can also be distorted by short-run macroeconomic policies and currency speculation. Therefore, the distortion introduced by using an unadjusted US dollar exchange rate when making international comparisons of living standards leads to an exaggeration of the gap between the estimated per capita incomes of rich countries compared to poor countries. Moreover, the poorer a country is relative to the USA, the greater is the likely extent of any distortion to the unadjusted conversion of per capita GNP. The extent of this distortion is clearly evident in the data contained in Table 2.2.

In order to take account of and correct such distortions, in 1968 the United Nations set up the International Comparisons Programme (ICP), under the direction of Irving Kravis, in order to produce a systematic and consistent set of purchasing power comparisons. This work involved making detailed comparisons of prices across a large sample of countries and ultimately this work led to the production of the celebrated 'Penn World Tables' (Summers and Heston, 1991, 1996). As a result of this research, economists obviously prefer to compare living standards across countries using purchasing power parity (PPP) estimates of real GNP or GDP per capita (see Meier and Rauch, 2005, and Tables 2.1 and 2.2).

While the remarkable achievements of economists' research into national income accounting during the last 60 years have made an outstanding contribution to our understanding of income-based measures of progress, many social scientists believe that real GNP per capita data, even using $PPP estimates, has many shortcomings as a satisfactory welfare measure of progress. Not only are the data unreliable for many developing countries and dictatorships; per capita data also tell us nothing about the distribution of income. Especially since the 1970s, general dissatisfaction with conventional welfare indicators has prompted many scholars to consider alternative perspectives on living standards. For example, Nobel Laureate Amartya Sen introduced the concepts of capabilities and entitlements into the understanding of living standards and this alternative vision has been very influential (see section 2.3.3 below, and Sen, 1981, 1987, 1999a, 1999b; see also Baster, 1972; Kravis et al., 1975, 1982).

### 2.3.2 Beyond Income Measures of Progress: Basic Needs, the PQLI and Life Expectancy

Responding to the need to supplement real GNP per capita when assessing international comparisons of living standards, the US-based Overseas Development Council (1977) proposed the use of a new measure of progress, namely, the Physical Quality of Life Index (PQLI), as a complement to conventional GNP per capita data. As indicated by equation (2.1), the PQLI combines three equally weighted indicators, life expectancy age one (L), infant mortality (IM) and literacy (E) into a simple composite index of development (Morris, 1979).

$$PQLI = \alpha_1 L + \alpha_2 IM + \alpha_3 E, \quad \text{where } \alpha_1 = \alpha_2 = \alpha_3. \qquad (2.1)$$

Table 2.2 includes a selection of Morris's estimates of PQLI for 40 countries (maximum PQLI = 100).

While the PQLI has an attractive simplicity, it was criticised for its arbitrary selection and weighting system, the use of non-comparable data, and the fact that the three independent variables are highly correlated with each other and with per capita income (see Larson and Wilford, 1979; Brodsky and Rodrik, 1981). Moreover, life expectancy measures the quantity of life rather than the quality of life. While in Morris's estimates there are examples where the PQLI ranking differs significantly from the one predicted from per capita income, these cases are atypical and, as indicated

Table 2.2   Selected development indicators, 40 countries, 1870–2003

| Country | GNI per capita[1] ($US) 2003 | GNI per capita[1] ($PPP) 2003 | PQLI[2] early 1970s | Life exp.[3] 2002 | HDI[4] 1870 | HDI[4] 1913 | HDI[4] 1950 | HDI[5] 1975 | HDI[5] 1985 | HDI[5] 2002 |
|---|---|---|---|---|---|---|---|---|---|---|
| USA | 37 610 | 37 610 | 94 | 77 | 0.506 | 0.643 | 0.802 | 0.866 | 0.899 | 0.939 |
| Japan | 34 510 | 28 620 | 96 | 82 | 0.248 | 0.466 | 0.676 | 0.854 | 0.894 | 0.938 |
| Denmark | 33 750 | 31 213 | 96 | 77 | 0.512 | 0.660 | 0.781 | 0.872 | 0.889 | 0.932 |
| Sweden | 28 840 | 26 620 | 97 | 80 | 0.516 | 0.641 | 0.780 | 0.836 | 0.885 | 0.946 |
| UK | 28 350 | 27 650 | 94 | 78 | 0.500 | 0.644 | 0.766 | 0.845 | 0.862 | 0.936 |
| Finland | 27 020 | 27 100 | 94 | 78 | 0.239 | 0.450 | 0.707 | 0.839 | 0.876 | 0.935 |
| Germany | 25 250 | 27 460 | 93 | 78 | 0.463 | 0.614 | 0.744 | 0.860[6] | 0.868 | 0.925 |
| France | 24 770 | 27 460 | 94 | 79 | 0.463 | 0.607 | 0.729 | 0.852 | 0.880 | 0.932 |
| Australia | 21 650 | 28 290 | 93 | 79 | 0.516 | 0.696 | 0.780 | 0.847 | 0.877 | 0.946 |
| Italy | 21 560 | 26 760 | 92 | 79 | 0.268 | 0.485 | 0.668 | 0.841 | 0.865 | 0.920 |
| Singapore | 21 230 | 24 180 | 83 | 78 | – | – | 0.501 | 0.724 | 0.784 | 0.902 |
| Spain | 16 990 | 22 020 | 91 | 79 | 0.301 | 0.421 | 0.627 | 0.836 | 0.867 | 0.922 |
| Korea Rep. | 12 020 | 17 930 | 82 | 75 | – | – | 0.459 | 0.705 | 0.779 | 0.888 |
| Hungary | 6 330 | 13 780 | 91 | 72 | – | 0.507 | 0.695 | 0.777 | 0.807 | 0.848 |
| Mexico | 6 230 | 8 950 | 73 | 73 | – | 0.270 | 0.484 | 0.688 | 0.753 | 0.802 |
| Poland | 5 270 | 11 450 | 91 | 74 | – | – | 0.657 | – | 0.802[7] | 0.850 |
| Chile | 4 390 | 9 810 | 77 | 77 | – | 0.379 | 0.584 | 0.703 | 0.761 | 0.839 |
| Malaysia | 3 780 | 8 940 | 66 | 73 | – | – | 0.407 | 0.614 | 0.693 | 0.793 |
| Argentina | 3 650 | 10 920 | 85 | 74 | – | 0.511 | 0.526 | 0.784 | 0.808 | 0.853 |
| Botswana | 3 430 | 7 960 | 51 | 41 | – | – | 0.253 | 0.503 | 0.633 | 0.589 |
| Turkey | 2 790 | 6 690 | 55 | 70 | – | – | 0.382 | 0.590 | 0.651 | 0.751 |

Table 2.2 (continued)

| Country | GNI per capita[1] ($US) 2003 | GNI per capita[1] ($PPP) 2003 | PQLI[2] early 1970s | Life exp.[3] 2002 | HDI[4] 1870 | HDI[4] 1913 | HDI[4] 1950 | HDI[5] 1975 | HDI[5] 1985 | HDI[5] 2002 |
|---|---|---|---|---|---|---|---|---|---|---|
| South Africa | 2 780 | 10 270 | 53 | 49 | – | – | 0.479 | 0.655 | 0.697 | 0.666 |
| Brazil | 2 710 | 7 480 | 68 | 68 | – | 0.249 | 0.448 | 0.644 | 0.695 | 0.755 |
| Russia | 2 610 | 8 920 | 91[8] | 67 | – | 0.345 | 0.694 | – | 0.813[7] | 0.795 |
| Thailand | 2 190 | 7 450 | 68 | 69 | – | – | 0.388 | 0.613 | 0.676 | 0.768 |
| Colombia | 1 810 | 6 520 | 71 | 72 | – | 0.288 | 0.482 | 0.661 | 0.706 | 0.773 |
| Egypt | 1 390 | 3 940 | 43 | 69 | – | – | 0.291 | 0.438 | 0.539 | 0.653 |
| China | 1 100 | 4 990 | 69 | 71 | – | – | 0.225 | 0.523 | 0.593 | 0.745 |
| Ukraine | 970 | 5 410 | 91 | 70 | – | – | – | – | 0.798[7] | 0.777 |
| Indonesia | 810 | 3 210 | 48 | 67 | – | – | 0.337 | 0.467 | 0.582 | 0.692 |
| Angola | 740 | 1 890 | 16 | 40 | – | – | 0.255 | – | – | 0.381 |
| India | 530 | 2 880 | 43 | 64 | – | – | 0.247 | 0.411 | 0.476 | 0.595 |

| | | | | | | | | | |
|---|---|---|---|---|---|---|---|---|---|
| Zimbabwe | 480 | 2 180 | 46[9] | 34 | – | – | 0.547 | 0.629 | 0.491 |
| Pakistan | 470 | 2 060 | 38 | 61 | – | – | 0.346 | 0.405 | 0.497 |
| Bangladesh | 400 | 1 870 | 20 | 35 | – | – | 0.345 | 0.388 | 0.509 |
| Kenya | 390 | 1 020 | 39 | 45 | – | – | 0.445 | 0.515 | 0.488 |
| Nigeria | 320 | 900 | 25 | 52 | – | 0.194 | 0.324 | 0.401 | 0.466 |
| Tanzania | 290 | 610 | 31 | 44 | – | – | – | 0.413[7] | 0.407 |
| Chad | 250 | 1 100 | 18 | 45 | – | – | 0.206 | 0.301 | 0.379 |
| Ethiopia | 90 | 710 | 20 | 46 | – | – | – | 0.281 | 0.359 |

*Data sources:*
[1] *World Development Report* (World Bank, 2005).
[2] Morris (1979).
[3] *Human Development Report* (UNDP, 2004).
[4] Crafts (2002).
[5] *Human Development Report* (UNDP, 2005).
[6] Data for 1980.
[7] Data for 1990.
[8] Data for USSR.
[9] Data for Rhodesia.

*Table 2.3*    *The Physical Quality of Life Index: five atypical countries,*
*early 1970s\**

| Country | GNP per capita ($)[1] | PQLI[1] |
|---|---|---|
| United Arab Emirates | 14 368   (1) | 34 (112) |
| Kuwait | 13 787   (2) | 74   (62) |
| Qatar | 11 779   (3) | 31 (115) |
| Libya | 4 402 (18) | 45   (93) |
| Saudi Arabia | 3 529 (24) | 29 (119) |

*Notes:*
\* Sample of 150 countries.
[1] Country ranking in parentheses, where 1 = highest and 150 = lowest rank.

*Source:*   Larson and Wilford (1979).

in Table 2.3, comprise a specific group of OPEC oil producers who benefited from the significant oil price hike of the 1970s.

Rather than construct a composite index such as the PQLI, Hicks and Streeten (1979) suggest the use of life expectancy as a single indicator of progress. The rationale for this is linked by Hicks and Streeten to the importance of meeting the 'basic needs' of people in developing countries. Meeting basic needs in developing countries requires that people have access to adequate nutrition, basic education, clean water supply, basic housing, and healthcare. Since the first five of these basic needs can be considered as crucial inputs into the health production function, 'it could be argued that some measure of health, such as life expectancy at birth, would be a simple measure of basic needs. In a sense, life expectancy is a kind of weighted composite of progress in meeting physiological needs'. This view receives supported from Amartya Sen (1998), who also presents a persuasive case for the use of mortality data as an indicator of economic success or failure since such data are 'informationally rich'. Thus mortality data can highlight important problems related to racial and gender inequalities as well as the impact on life expectancy of increasing obesity, alcohol consumption and stress. For example, in their recent study of Russia and the former Soviet Union, Brainerd and Cutler (2005) find that between 1989 and 1994, male life expectancy at birth fell by over six years. While a large residual remains to be explained, Brainerd and Cutler find that increased alcohol consumption and stress are two important contributory factors.

Data on life expectancy are also extremely important in providing an insight into changing living conditions over long historical periods. Wrigley and Schofield (1981) indicate a life expectancy in England of 28.5 years in 1681, 36.6 in 1751, 40.8 in 1831 and 41.3 in 1871. According to Johnson (1997), life expectancy throughout recorded history was 25 years until the middle of the seventeenth century and as late as 1840 life expectancy in high-income countries was 41 years. With the rise of urban living during the nineteenth century, and cities being 'little more than sinkholes of disease and pestilence', life expectancy in the countryside in England and France exceeded that in urban areas by some ten years. Remarkably, life expectancy in Paris as late as 1890 has been estimated to have been as short as 28 years (Johnson, 1997).

The UN *Human Development Report* (2004) indicates that in 2002 the average life expectancy for high-income countries was 78.3 years (UK = 78.1). The lowest life expectancy reported was 46.3 for sub-Saharan Africa, but even here this has improved considerably since the decolonisation period in the late 1950s and early 1960s. An optimistic, if controversial, perspective on sub-Saharan Africa is provided by Sender (1999), who claims that 'there has been a remarkable decline since independence in the risks of death faced by people in this region', even allowing for the impact of AIDS. Furthermore, the child mortality rate has improved significantly since 1960 and female adult literacy rates (95 per cent in 1995) compare very favourably with those in South Asia (36 per cent) and are significantly higher than in Morocco, Egypt and Iraq. So in some very important aspects of human progress the sub-Saharan Africa picture is more complicated and less depressing than is suggested by taking GDP per capita levels and growth rates as the only measuring rod. However, as Figure 2.5 shows, the UN estimates that life expectancy has been falling since the early 1990s due to the AIDS epidemic (for a less pessimistic assessment of the AIDS epidemic in sub-Saharan Africa see Craven et al., 2005). It is also important to note that, with over one-third of the world's population, India and China have improved their life expectancy over the period 1970–2000 from 50.3 to 62.6 and from 63.2 to 69.8 respectively.

In a recent paper, Becker et al. (2003) find that the absence of income convergence across the world is in 'stark contrast with the reduction in inequality after incorporating recent gains in longevity'. Their computed longevity-adjusted income measure ('full income') for 49 countries over the period 1965–95 reveals that low-income countries have grown more in terms of 'full income' than rich countries. This implies considerable longevity convergence. Similarly, Crafts (2003) finds that after making various adjustments to national income accounts, including allowance for lower hours worked and improvements in longevity, 'growth of living standards through the twentieth century was much more rapid than is generally thought' (see also Nordhaus, 2001).

Table 2.4 provides data on life expectancy in India and the UK from 1363 to 1999. While the relative position of India to the UK declined until the middle of the twentieth century, since about the time of independence this divergence has been dramatically reversed.

Life expectancy (years)

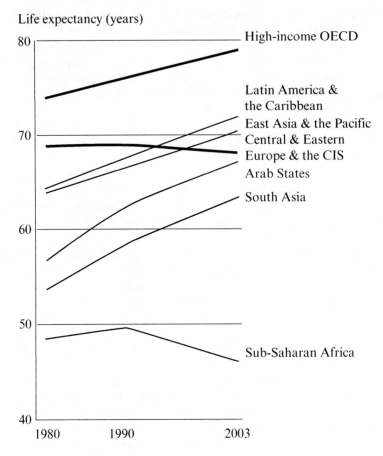

*Source: Human Development Report* (United Nations, 2005).

*Figure 2.5 Recent trends in life expectancy, 1980–2003*

While there remains vast room for improvement, when measuring progress we should not understate the vast improvements in life expectancy that have already been achieved for billions of people around the world (Easterlin, 1996, 1999, 2000; Maddison, 2001; Riley, 2001).

### 2.3.3 The Human Development Index

In 1990, the *Human Development Report*, commissioned and published by the United Nations Development Programme, introduced the Human Development Index (HDI) as a composite measure of human development.

*Table 2.4    Life expectancy: historical estimates for India and the UK,*
*1363–1999*

| Year | India | UK | India/UK % |
|------|-------|------|------------|
| 1363 | 24.0 | 24.3 | 99 |
| 1543 | 24.0 | 33.7 | 71 |
| 1738 | 24.0 | 34.6 | 69 |
| 1813 | 24.0 | 40.8 | 59 |
| 1913 | 24.8 | 53.4 | 46 |
| 1931 | 26.8 | 60.8 | 44 |
| 1950 | 38.7 | 69.2 | 56 |
| 1999 | 63.0 | 77.0 | 82 |

*Source:*    Kenny (2005).

The HDI, inspired by the 'capabilities' approach to development pioneered by Nobel Laureate Amartya Sen, was created as part of the United Nations Development Programme under the leadership of Mahbub ul Haq. From 1989 to 1995, Mahbub ul Haq served as Special Adviser to the UNDP. During this period, along with development economists such as Paul Streeten, Frances Stewart, Amartya Sen and Richard Jolly, he was the chief architect behind the development of the annual *Human Development Reports*.

Rather than concentrating on a commodity-based measure of human welfare, Sen's capabilities approach (1999a) concentrates on 'functionings' in terms of educational attainment and longevity, and views the main goal of development as the 'enhancement of the capability to live a long, healthy, and active life' (Anand and Ravallion, 1993; Haq, 1995; Sen, 1999a, 2000, 2001; Ranis et al., 2000). Since 1990, estimates of the HDI for over 170 of the world's nations have been published in the annual United Nations *Human Development Report*, and these estimates have now been supplemented by three additional indices, namely, the 'Human Poverty Index', the 'Gender-related Development Index', and the 'Gender Empowerment Measure' (see United Nations, 2005).

The HDI is a composite measure of three basic dimension indices of development, namely, real income per capita (PPP US$ = Ypc) adjusted to reflect the assumption of rapidly diminishing marginal utility of income above the world average; longevity as measured by life expectancy at birth (L); and educational attainment (E) captured by the adult literacy rate (weighted 2/3) and the combined gross primary, secondary and tertiary enrolment ratio (weighted 1/3). A 'Dimension Index' (DI) for County $j$ is calculated for each of the above as follows:

$$DI = \frac{\text{actual value for } j - \text{minimum value}}{\text{maximum value} - \text{minimum value}} \qquad (2.2)$$

Therefore, the HDI estimate for any economy ($j$) is a simple weighted average of dimension indices for Ypc$j$, L$j$, and E$j$, as indicated by equation (2.3). Figure 2.6 gives an overview of the construction of the HDI.

$$HDIj = \beta_1(DIYpcj) + \beta_2(DILj) + \beta_3(DIEj), \quad \text{where } \beta_1 = \beta_2 = \beta_3. \qquad (2.3)$$

Although there are serious index number problems in using the HDI as a measure of living standards, and the HDI has come in for a considerable amount of criticism (Srinivasan, 1994; Palazzi and Lauri, 1998; Cahill, 2005), it has nevertheless proved to be a useful additional development indicator, complementing, but not replacing, the traditional 'commodity'-based measures of progress such as income per capita. For example, while there has been unprecedented divergence between the income per capita of the OECD economies and many developing countries, Crafts (1999, 2000, 2004a) has argued that a more optimistic picture of the progress of human welfare emerges if we examine long-run trends in the HDI. As Table 2.2 indicates, the 2002 HDI scores for many poor countries are well ahead of the estimated 1870 HDI scores for the leading countries of that time (current G7 countries) as measured by their per capita income. Compare, for example, the HDI scores of the UK and the USA in 1870 with those of Egypt and India in 2002. Clearly many of the countries listed in Table 2.2 had much lower income per capita in 1975 than in 2000, and yet their HDI scores for 1975 compare very favourably with the 1870 HDI scores of the countries that now comprise the G7 group. Crafts concludes from taking a broader view of progress that it is likely that the growth of living standards since 1870 as measured by real national income per capita is substantially underestimated.

### 2.3.4 Competitiveness Indices

As noted in Chapter 1, Michael Porter (1990) argues that the principal goal of a nation 'is to produce a high and rising standard of living for its citizens' and that productivity acts as 'the prime determinant in the long run of a nations standard of living, for it is the root cause of national per capita income' (see also Lewis, 2004). Since 1971 the World Economic Forum has been producing its annual assessment of the competitiveness of nations in the form of a *Global Competitiveness Report*. Currently three measures of competitiveness are used:

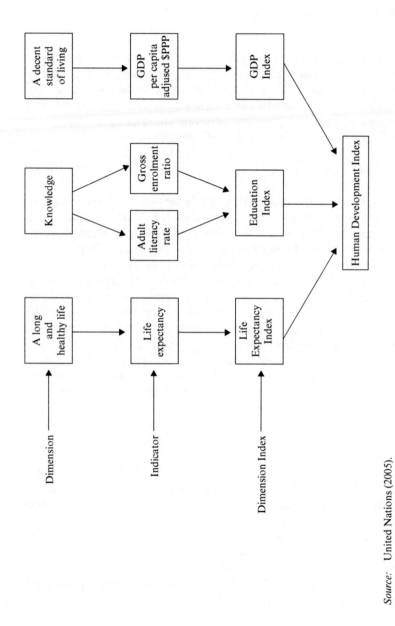

*Source:* United Nations (2005).

*Figure 2.6 Structure and components of the Human Development Index*

1.  the Growth Competitiveness Index, developed by John McArthur and Jeffrey Sachs (2001);
2.  the Business Competitiveness Index (BCI), developed by Michael Porter, which first appeared in the 2000;
3.  the Global Competitiveness Index, developed by Xavier Sala-i-Martin and Elsa Artadi (2004).

Table 2.5 contains rankings data on the three main measures of competitiveness used in the *World Competitiveness Report* as well as data on 'ease of doing business', corruption, and political and economic freedom.

The poorest countries in terms of income per capita display a strong positive correlation between lack of competitiveness and lack of economic and political freedom, and high rates of corruption.

### 2.3.5  Measures of Freedom

Economists are in agreement that a large degree of economic freedom is a prerequisite for sustained increases in prosperity (Friedman, 1962; Barro, 1997; Engerman, 1994). This does not mean that the government does not have an important role to play (World Bank, 1997; Tanzi, 2005); however, the central elements of economic freedom include (i) security of legally acquired property, (ii) personal choice and freedom to trade and conduct voluntary transactions, (iii) freedom from excessive government controls and regulations, and (iv) freedom from government predation via expropriation, confiscatory taxation, or unanticipated inflation (Hanke and Walters, 1997; Gwartney and Lawson, 2003). Table 2.6 contains recent estimates of economic freedom compiled by the Heritage Foundation. According to Freedom House, the world's least free countries in 2005 were Burma, Cuba, Libya, North Korea, Saudia Arabia, Sudan, Syria and Turkmenistan.

For Amartya Sen (1999a) progress is best captured by the extent to which various 'unfreedoms' (political, economic and social) are removed, and the creation of greater individual freedom has both an intrinsic and instrumental importance (see also Dasgupta, 1995; Sen, 1997, 1999b). To Sen (2001), 'Freedom is not only the ultimate end of development, it is also a crucial effective means.' Table 2.5 also provides Freedom House measures of political freedom for 40 countries. It is worth noting that, across the world, there are no examples, nor have there ever been examples, of countries that are politically free (defined as liberal democracy) that do not also have economic freedom (see Friedman, 1962; Barro, 1997; Kornai, 2000a; and Chapter 3). However, while economic freedom is a necessary condition for political freedom, it is by no means sufficient, as is evident from the

Table 2.5  Selected competitiveness, ease of doing business, corruption, and political and economic freedom rankings, 2004–05

| Country | Growth Competitiveness Index[1] 2004–05 | Business Competitiveness Index[2] 2004–05 | Global Competitiveness Index[3] 2004–05 | Ease of Doing Business Index[4] 2005 | Corruption Perceptions Index[5] 2004 | Political Freedom Index[6] 2005 | Economic Freedom Index[7] 2005 |
|---|---|---|---|---|---|---|---|
| Finland | 1 | 2 | 2 | 13 | 9.7 | F | 1.90 |
| USA | 2 | 1 | 1 | 3 | 7.5 | F | 1.85 |
| Sweden | 3 | 4 | 5 | 14 | 9.2 | F | 1.89 |
| Taiwan | 4 | 17 | 11 | 35 | 5.6 | F | 2.29 |
| Denmark | 5 | 7 | 3 | 8 | 9.5 | F | 1.76 |
| Singapore | 7 | 10 | 7 | 2 | 9.3 | PF | 1.60 |
| Japan | 9 | 8 | 10 | 10 | 6.9 | F | 2.46 |
| UK | 11 | 6 | 9 | 9 | 8.6 | F | 1.75 |
| Germany | 13 | 3 | 6 | 19 | 8.2 | F | 2.00 |
| Chile | 22 | 29 | 29 | 25 | 7.4 | F | 1.81 |
| Spain | 23 | 26 | 34 | 30 | 7.1 | F | 2.34 |
| France | 27 | 12 | 17 | 44 | 7.1 | F | 2.63 |
| Korea (S.) | 29 | 24 | 26 | 27 | 4.5 | F | 2.64 |
| Malaysia | 31 | 23 | 23 | 21 | 5.0 | PF | 2.96 |
| Thailand | 34 | 37 | 33 | 20 | 3.6 | F | 2.98 |
| Hungary | 39 | 42 | 46 | 52 | 4.8 | F | 2.40 |
| S. Africa | 41 | 25 | 36 | 28 | 4.6 | F | 2.78 |
| Botswana | 45 | 62 | 58 | 40 | 6.0 | F | 2.44 |
| China | 46 | 47 | 32 | 91 | 3.4 | NF | 3.46 |
| Italy | 47 | 34 | 56 | 70 | 4.8 | F | 2.28 |
| Mexico | 48 | 55 | 60 | 73 | 3.6 | F | 2.89 |

*Table 2.5* (continued)

| Country | Growth Competitiveness Index[1] 2004–05 | Business Competitiveness Index[2] 2004–05 | Global Competitiveness Index[3] 2004–05 | Ease of Doing Business Index[4] 2005 | Corruption Perceptions Index[5] 2004 | Political Freedom Index[6] 2005 | Economic Freedom Index[7] 2005 |
|---|---|---|---|---|---|---|---|
| India | 55 | 30 | 37 | 116 | 2.8 | F | 3.53 |
| Brazil | 57 | 38 | 49 | 119 | 3.9 | F | 3.25 |
| Poland | 60 | 57 | 72 | 54 | 3.5 | F | 2.54 |
| Egypt | 62 | 66 | 47 | 141 | 3.2 | NF | 3.38 |
| Colombia | 64 | 58 | 69 | 66 | 3.8 | PF | 3.21 |
| Turkey | 66 | 52 | 67 | 93 | 3.2 | PF | 3.46 |
| Indonesia | 69 | 44 | 48 | 115 | 2.0 | PF | 3.54 |
| Russia | 70 | 61 | 64 | 79 | 2.8 | NF | 3.56 |
| Argentina | 74 | 74 | 75 | 77 | 2.5 | F | 3.49 |
| Kenya | 78 | 63 | 84 | 68 | 2.1 | PF | 3.28 |
| Tanzania | 82 | 90 | 97 | 140 | 2.8 | PF | 3.41 |
| Ukraine | 86 | 69 | 73 | 124 | 2.2 | PF | 3.21 |

| | | | | | | |
|---|---|---|---|---|---|---|
| Pakistan | 91 | 73 | 87 | 60 | 2.1 | NF | 3.73 |
| Nigeria | 93 | 81 | 77 | 94 | 1.6 | PF | 3.95 |
| Zimbabwe | 99 | 82 | 101 | 126 | 2.3 | NF | 4.36 |
| Ethiopia | 101 | 99 | 102 | 101 | 2.3 | PF | 3.73 |
| Bangladesh | 102 | 95 | 94 | 65 | 1.5 | PF | 3.95 |
| Angola | 103 | 103 | 104 | 135 | 2.0 | NF | 4.48[8] |
| Chad | 104 | 102 | 103 | 152 | 1.7 | NF | 3.38 |

*Sources of data:*

[1] *The Global Competitiveness Report, 2004–2005*, World Economic Forum and Oxford University Press. Full sample of countries = 104.

[2] *The Global Competitiveness Report, 2004–2005*. Full sample of countries = 103.

[3] *The Global Competitiveness Report, 2004–2005*. Full sample of countries = 104.

[4] World Bank data. Full sample of countries = 155.

[5] Transparency International, www.globalcorruptionreport.org. Highest possible score = 10, lowest possible score = 0. Full sample of countries = 146.

[6] Freedom House, http://www.freedomhouse.org. Freedom is measured according to two broad categories, political rights and civil liberties, and reflects data gathered for the period 1 December 2003–November 30, 2004. F = Free, PF = Partly free, NF = Not free.

[7] The Heritage Foundation, http://www.heritage.org. The Heritage Foundation/*Wall Street Journal* Index of Economic Freedom measures freedom utilising 50 independent variables and scores of 1–2 = Free, 2–3 = Mostly free, 3–4 = Mostly unfree, 4–5 = Repressed.

[8] Data for 2000.

experiences of Nazi Germany and many countries in South America and East Asia in the second half of the twentieth century, for example Singapore, South Korea, Chile and Argentina.

## 2.3.6  Anthropometrics

The need for alternative measures of the standard of living is particularly important for economic historians exploring the distant past where conventional estimates cannot be calculated (Steckel, 1995). One important development since the late 1970s has been the use by economic historians of data on stature (height) as a guide to the biological standard of living in the past (Steckel, 1979, 1998; Steckel and Rose, 2002). 'Anthropometric history' is the study of human size as an indicator of how well the human organism fared during childhood and adolescence in its socio-economic and epidemiological environment. Data on the physical stature of a population lay no claim to being a substitute for conventional measures of the standard of living. None the less, physical stature is an important complement, illuminating the extent to which a socio-economic or political system provides an environment – broadly conceived – propitious to the physical growth and longevity of human organisms, so that they can reach their biological growth potential (Komlos and Snowdon, 2005).

Human physical stature is a useful supplementary indicator of wellbeing. With the development of the concept of the 'biological standard of living' as distinct from conventional indicators of well-being, biology is becoming integrated into mainstream economics and economic history (Koepke and Baten, 2005). Height and weight are components, and relatively easily measured indicators, of biological welfare. In addition, we gain hitherto unknown insights of the effect of economic processes on the human organism. Hence anthropometric history emphasizes that wellbeing encompasses much more than the command over goods and services. Rather, it is multidimensional, and height, weight, health in general, and longevity all contribute to it, independently of purchasing power. In many ways, such indices provide a more nuanced view of the impact of dynamic economic processes on the quality of life than income or GDP per capita by itself. Clearly, conventional commodity-based indicators such as GDP per capita are imperfect. Indeed, all indicators are imperfect, but by considering alternative perspectives we can gain a fuller insight into the multidimensional nature of the human experience. Anthropometric indicators are not meant to be substitutes for, but complements to, conventional measures of living standards (see Strauss and Thomas, 1998).

The 'biological standard of living' (measured by physical stature and weight) captures the biologically relevant components of living standards, and indicates generally how well the human organism thrives in its socio-economic environment. Researchers have found that height is a good indicator of the history and nutrition of a population. For example, Fogel (1994, pp. 382–3) reports that 'by current standards, even persons in the top half of the income distribution in Britain during the eighteenth century were stunted and wasted, suffered far more extensively from chronic diseases at young adult and middle ages than is true today, and died 30 years sooner than today'. Sunder (2003) finds that Norway has overcome its 'height deficit' in relation to the USA and attributes this to the influence of the Western European and Scandinavian style welfare states in reducing the impact of spatial inequalities.

The development of anthropometrics has opened up new windows on the ways in which economic processes affected the populations experiencing them, such as the hidden costs of industrialisation and urbanisation. Anthropometrics blends history, economics, biology, medical science and physical anthropology and is now well established, having helped to clarify 'several questions important to economic historians' including those related to 'slavery, mortality, inequality, and living standards during industrialisation' (Steckel, 1998). For example, economic historians have shown that there are many examples of divergences between the biological standard of living, measured by stature, and calculations based on GDP per capita (Komlos, 1996).

Initial research in this vein was influenced by the controversial finding that American slaves were relatively well nourished (Fogel and Engerman, 1974), and was followed up by investigating the height of slaves as an indicator of their nutritional status (Engerman, 1976). The results implied that slaves were well nourished compared to what was previously believed. Indeed, once they reached working age it was found that they were markedly taller than the European lower classes (Figure 2.7), as well as their brethren in Africa (Steckel, 1979). This astounding and controversial finding prompted further research along these lines at a time when there was increased dissatisfaction with relying exclusively on GDP per capita as a welfare indicator.

According to Fogel (1999), during the last 300 years a synergism between technological and physiological improvements has influenced human development in a process now known as 'technophysical evolution'. Fogel notes that

> Technophysical evolution implies that human beings now have so great a degree of control over their environment that they are set apart not only from all other species, but also from all previous generations of Homo Sapiens. This new degree of control has enabled Homo Sapiens to increase its average body size by over 50 per cent, to increase its average longevity by more than 100 per cent, and to improve greatly the robustness and capacity of vital organ systems. (pp. 2–3)

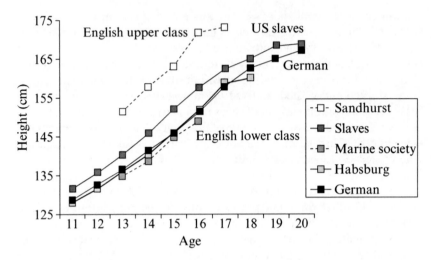

*Sources:* Steckel (1979); Komlos (1987, 1998); Komlos and Coclanis (1997); Komlos and Snowdon (2005).

*Figure 2.7 Height of lower- and upper-class youth during the Industrial Revolution*

### 2.3.7 The Economics of Obesity

While malnutrition is the scourge of poor countries, obesity has become a major problem in many developed countries, particularly during the last quarter-century. It is also becoming a problem in many developing countries, especially China. This has major implications for public health, mortality and the productivity of the labour force. Research into the economics of obesity is now a burgeoning area and there is much concern about the obesity epidemic in the USA and other developed economies, because of its threatening health consequences and economic impact.

From being the tallest in the world until around 1945, Americans have now become, among the OECD countries, the most overweight at the onset of the twenty-first century. As Figure 2.8 indicates, while in 1980 15 per cent of the US population was obese, that is, with a body mass index (BMI) of more than 30 kg/m$^2$, by 2000–02 this had risen to 31 per cent (for a critique of the use of BMI to estimate obesity, see Cawley and Burkhauser, 2006). During the same period the percentage obese in the UK has risen from 7 to 22 per cent. These trends are in sharp contrast to those in Japan, where the percentage obese has risen from only 2 to 3 per cent! Particularly worrying in the USA is the increasing incidence of childhood obesity and in May 2005, former US President (and self-confessed

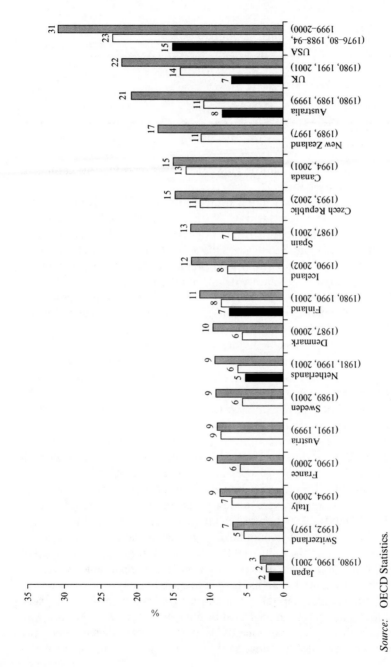

*Source:* OECD Statistics.

*Figure 2.8 Obesity trends in selected developed economies, 1976–2000*

*Table 2.6    Trends in BMI and obesity, persons 18 years and older: USA,*
*             1959–94*

| Period | Body mass index | Percentage obese |
|--------|-----------------|------------------|
| 1959–62 | 24.91 | 12.73 |
| 1971–75 | 25.14 | 13.85 |
| 1976–80 | 25.16 | 13.95 |
| 1988–94 | 26.40 | 21.62 |

*Source:*  Chou et al. (2004).

cheeseburger addict) Bill Clinton announced his support for the campaign to fight childhood obesity.

The health and mortality implications of this obesity epidemic are only just beginning to be fully recognised. With an estimated 300 000 premature deaths per year in the USA attributed to obesity and sedentary lifestyles, the human and economic costs are substantial (for a less pessimistic view on the impact of moderate obesity on premature deaths see Flegal et al., 2005). In comparison, premature deaths associated with tobacco, alcohol and illicit drug use are 400 000, 100 000 and 20 000 respectively (Chou et al., 2004). It is estimated that more Americans are obese than smoke or use illicit drugs. In addition, Americans spend billions of dollars each year on weight reduction products, including memberships of health clubs, which is a sure indication that obesity is generally regarded as welfare reducing. Data on trends in the US BMI and the percentage of US population considered obese are shown in Table 2.6.

Of course it should be remembered that increases in the BMI over the past 200 years represent a major improvement in health given that before the modern era a large proportion of the population in European countries were malnourished. According to Fogel (1994), the average weight of English males around 1790 was about 20 per cent less than current standards. Hence the rise in obesity is a modern phenomenon since before, and for most of the twentieth century, weights were too low to maximise longevity (Cutler et al., 2003). Fogel's (2004a, 2004b) research into health, nutrition and technology confirms that for most of human history chronic malnutrition has been the norm. However, since the Industrial Revolution, enormous improvements in technology and human physiology have facilitated a remarkable increase in human longevity as well as an increase in average body size. These improvements in 'physiological capital' have made a significant contribution to economic growth that has been neglected by mainstream growth theorists.

Although the problem of obesity is part of a worldwide trend, the American obesity rates are now at the top of those obtained in OECD countries (Popkin and Doak, 1998; Philipson, 2001). At the same time, the life expectancy of Americans now lags some five years behind that of Japan, and has also fallen behind levels prevailing in Western Europe (see Table 2.2). Moreover, the US infant mortality rate is the highest in the OECD countries – twice that of Sweden. This is additional evidence that economic prosperity in the USA has not translated into the attainment of a comparably high level of biological well-being relative to other economically advanced countries, in spite of the fact that Americans spend a much larger fraction of their income on health-related services (see Porter and Teisberg, 2006).

In order to implement policies that can reverse the current trend towards increasing obesity it is necessary to understand the underlying causes. Biologically, the cause of weight gain is uncontroversial since weight must increase if more calories are taken in than are expended. Yet we need to know why this is happening among increasing numbers of people. In the case of the USA we do not have a definitive explanation of why the apparent economic prosperity manifests itself in greater-than-average weight but not in greater physical stature of the population; however, several hypotheses have recently been put forward by economists that attempt to explain this rise in obesity.

One explanation is that technological progress has lowered the 'cost of calories and raised the cost of physical activity', with predictable consequences (Philipson, 2001; Lakdawalla et al., 2005). That is, for many people in a post-industrial society, leisure-time exercise (jogging, membership of health clubs) has replaced (paid-for) physical exercise at work. At the same time technological progress, in the form of the development of low-cost convenience foods and the spread of fast-food restaurants, has lowered the labour-intensive time spent on food preparation in the home as well as lowering food prices. Predictably, these developments have contributed to obesity.

Another possible explanation offered by Chou et al. (2004) is that obesity has increased as an unfortunate side-effect of anti-smoking campaigns (including higher real cigarette prices) and clean air legislation, since people who quit smoking tend to put on weight. While a reduction in smoking improves health, rising obesity reduces health. Thus a complex cost–benefit trade-off emerges as an unintended consequence of anti-smoking campaigns. Chou et al. also examine the impact of other factors on obesity such as lower food prices, per capita number of restaurants, education, labour force participation of women, and hours of market work. Their main results indicate that 'these variables have the expected effects on obesity and explain a substantial amount of its trend'.

In their analysis of why Americans have become more obese, Cutler et al. (2003) investigate whether this increased obesity is due to an increase in calorie intake or a decrease in calories expended due to less exercise. They conclude that an increase in calorie intake is more important and attribute this rise in consumption to a 'reduction in the time price of food consumption'. This in turn reflects the 'revolution in the mass preparation of food' that includes vacuum packing, improved preservatives and refrigeration techniques, innovations in food packaging and artificial flavouring, and the increasing use of microwaves (in 1978, only 8 per cent of Americans owned microwave ovens; by 1999 the figure was 83 per cent). As the authors note, 'From 1977 to 1995, total potato consumption increased by about 30 per cent, accounted for almost exclusively by increased consumption of potato chips and French fries.' Moreover, 'most of the increase in calories is from calories consumed during snacks' (grazing). Cutler et al. also argue that we should expect to find that obesity rates are higher in countries that have experienced rapid technological changes in food consumption. Therefore, countries with less regulatory public policies will tend to have more obesity than more regulated economies. Their empirical evidence finds support for this hypothesis.

Another hypothesis, complementary to the explanations discussed above, is that 'an increase in the rate of time preference also contributes to the obesity epidemic' (Komlos et al., 2004). Time preference is a widely used concept in economics; it refers to the rate at which people are willing to trade current benefit for future benefit and is influenced by a variety of social, cultural and psychological factors. Controlling weight requires forgoing current consumption for future health benefits. Exercise, for example, involves the opportunity cost of time as well as possible expenditure on membership of a health and fitness club. The marginal rate of time preference ($\psi$) reflects the degree of 'impatience', that is, the rate an individual is willing to trade current pleasure for future pleasure. Economists use the intertemporal discount rate $[1/(1+ \psi)]$ to calculate the present value of future utility. The greater the impatience of an individual, the higher is the value of $\psi$ and the less that individual values future consumption. According to Komlos et al., the idea that the marginal time preference of Americans has increased and that they are becoming more 'impatient' is supported by several pieces of evidence, including (1) an increase in legal gambling driven by a desire for immediate gratification; (2) a decline in the US personal savings ratio; and (3) a rise in the household debt/disposable income ratio. The authors conclude that 'Both time series and international cross section data indicate that the hypothesis linking obesity and time preference is plausible.'

Yet there are several salient differences between the socio-economic and political systems of the West and Northern European welfare states and the more market-oriented economy of the USA that might eventually provide an alternative solution to the mystery of increasing obesity. For example, Komlos and Bauer (2004) note that socio-economic inequality in America is greater than in Western Europe and has been increasing at the end of the twentieth century. In so far as the lower classes have a higher propensity to obesity, the US social structure might be conducive to it.

### 2.3.8   The Economics of Happiness and Life Satisfaction

The recent literature on 'happiness' has shown how the achievement of a higher GDP per capita is, after all, not an end in itself, but a means to an end, that is, human happiness (see Easterlin, 2001; Layard, 2005). Throughout this chapter it has been assumed that economic growth is important because in the long run it raises living standards in terms of the quantity and quality of goods and services consumed (see Table 2.1). We have also noted that in assessing 'development' and 'progress', it is necessary to complement commodity-based measures (GNP) with indices that take account of important welfare-influencing factors such as health, life expectancy, nutrition, education and infant mortality (see Table 2.2). Recently, economists have been returning to the important question: does the consumption of an ever-increasing quantity of goods and services (affluanza!) actually make people happier? (see Easterlin, 1996, 2001; Frank, 1997; Oswald, 1997; Ng, 1997; Donovan and Halpern, 2002; Frey and Stutzer, 2002a, 2002b, 2002c; Blanchflower and Oswald, 2004; Fritjers et al., 2004; Bruni and Porta, 2005; Layard, 2005; Di Tella and McCulloch, 2006).

It is somewhat ironic that economics, labelled the 'dismal science' by Scottish philosopher Thomas Carlyle, has recently turned its attention to the question of 'happiness'. It was after reading Malthus's pessimistic views on population dynamics that Carlyle gave economics this label. Traditionally economists have assumed that an individual's utility (welfare) is positively related to present and future consumption. The hedonistic utilitarian philosophy of nineteenth-century philosophers Jeremy Bentham and John Stuart Mill emphasised the idea that actions should be judged on the basis of their capacity for generating pleasure (utility) and pain (disutility). On this basis happiness represents a balance of pleasure over pain. Unfortunately, comparing the welfare of different individuals is highly subjective and, following the Hicksian ordinal revolution in microeconomics during the 1930s, economists have generally been hostile to cardinal (absolute) measures of utility and the use of interpersonal comparisons based on what they considered to be a non-measurable concept (Frank, 1997; Ng, 1997). Isidor Edgeworth's idea of a 'hedonometer' for measuring utility remains to be invented! However, in recent years, thanks to the extensive research of psychologists, the measurement of utility has made considerable progress

(Frey and Stutzer, 2002a). For example, in the USA a team of researchers, headed by the Nobel Laureate Daniel Kahneman, plans to launch an new index of 'Well-Being Accounts' to measure people's happiness (Kahneman et al., 1999; Kahneman et al., 2004; Kahneman and Krueger, 2006).

According to Frey and Stutzer (2002a), research on happiness has suggested that it is dependent on three main sets of factors:

1. demographic and personality factors, such as health, age, family, education, gender (Blanchflower and Oswald, 2004, also report evidence that happiness is positively associated with frequency of sexual activity);
2. economic factors, such as income and employment/unemployment (Clark and Oswald, 1994);
3. political factors, such as freedom, participation and democratisation (Sen, 1999a).

Moreover, the main factors cited in surveys as shaping happiness are much the same for the majority of people (Easterlin, 2001). However, Richard Easterlin (1974) was one of the first economists during the modern era to point out that the relationship between income and happiness is puzzling. The Easterlin paradox is that the point-of-time cross-sectional association between income and happiness is positive; that is, within a country, rich people report higher subjective well-being and are generally happier than poor people, and, although there are substantial variations in reported happiness across countries, people in rich countries are on average happier than people in poor countries. At very low levels of income the time-series evidence also shows a positive association between income and subjective well-being (Frank, 1997). In contrast, time-series evidence on the life-cycle pattern of happiness suggests that although income is positively associated with age up until retirement, there appears to be 'no corresponding advance in well-being' (Easterlin, 2001). So the Easterlin paradox is this: 'Why at a point in time are happiness and income positively associated, but over the life cycle there is no relationship?' Easterlin's conjecture is that rising material aspirations over the life cycle offset the impact on well-being of rising income; that is, utility functions shift inversely with material aspirations. Therefore 'Even though rising income means that people can have more goods, the favourable effect of this on welfare is erased by the fact that people want more as they progress trough the life cycle.' This, in turn, is linked to the 'relative income hypothesis'; that is, once individuals escape from high levels of physical deprivation, their subjective well-being is heavily influenced by their relative position in society. As a consequence, as Hirsch (1977) argued, there may be 'social limits to growth' (Frank, 1997). Of course this has long been recognised, as the following quotation from Alfred Marshall (1907, p. 8) indicates:

And the well-to-do classes expend vast sums on things that add little to their happiness and very little to their higher well-being, but which they regard as necessary for their social position.

A related issue is the influence of inequality on happiness. Research by Alesina and Glaeser (2004) confirms that there is much more concern about inequality of income in Europe than there is in the USA (see also Alesina and Fuchs-Schundeln, 2005). Hence support for redistributive policies is much stronger in Europe than it is in the USA. Alesina and Glaeser attribute these differences to greater ethnic heterogeneity in the USA, different beliefs about the causes of poverty, and differences in political institutions that have themselves evolved historically in response to 'the profoundly different geographies and ethnicities of America and Europe' (see Alesina interview).

If rising income per capita among the nations that have managed to overcome severe deprivation with respect to basic needs is not having a dramatic effect on happiness over time, then the whole question of what constitutes a good life remains a key issue for public debate. Nobel Laureate Robert Fogel (1999, p. 13) argues that the 'most intractable forms of poverty are related to the unequal distribution of spiritual (immaterial) resources' and it is these resources, including an individual's thirst for knowledge and ability to envisage opportunities, that have a significant influence on the quality of an individual's lifetime choices and outcomes.

## 2.4  THE BIRTH OF DEVELOPMENT ECONOMICS

The 'old' development economics is associated with the classical economists who from Adam Smith (1776) to John Stuart Mill (1848) were primarily concerned with the long-run issues of growth and development. However, following the 'marginalist revolution' of the 1870s and the birth of neoclassical economics, the attention of the majority of economists was diverted towards the analysis of the static problems associated with efficient resource allocation (it is generally agreed that the publication in 1890 of Alfred Marshall's *Principles of Economics* marks the beginning of neoclassical economics; see Blaug, 1997). During the inter-war period the attention of economists, notably John Maynard Keynes, became focused on the problems facing the advanced capitalist nations during the 1930s as they struggled to cope with the Great Depression. So it is not until the period following the end of the Second World War that the contemporary literature on problems of economic development began to emerge. This was in large measure a response to the perceived sense of political urgency that arose as the former colonies sought to take their place on the escalator of economic growth. The political leaders of the newly independent underdeveloped countries of the Third World actively drew world attention to their development problems. As Meier (1994) recalls, 'An understanding of the forces of development – now meaning growth plus change – was necessary. And the design of appropriate policies to support these forces was essential.' To achieve this objective, the involvement of economists was crucial. And so 'development economics' soon became a distinctive sub-discipline of economics, replacing the earlier study of 'colonial economics' which in the UK 'had catered mainly for those working in, or hoping to enter, the colonial services'.

In the UK the change from studying 'colonial economics' to studying the problems of economic development occurred at Oxford University in 1951–52 with a lecture course entitled 'Introduction to the Economics of Underdevelopment' given by Hla Myint. At Manchester University in the early 1950s, Arthur Lewis also began to teach courses on development economics. In the USA Henry Wallich and Henry Bruton initiated undergraduate and graduate courses in economic development at Yale University in the 1952–54 period, and John Kenneth Galbraith, Robert Baldwin and Gustav Papanek, among others, began lecturing on development economics at Harvard during the early 1950s. This increasing interest also led to the publication of a growing number of journals specialising in development issues. Also significant, following the end of the Second World War, was the establishment of a number of international institutions and specialised agencies concerned directly or indirectly with international economic development and political and economic stability, for example:

1.  the International Bank for Reconstruction and Development (World Bank), 1945;
2.  the International Monetary Fund (IMF), 1945;
3.  the United Nations (UN), 1945;
4.  the General Agreement on Tariffs and Trade (GATT), 1948, since 1995 the World Trade Organisation (WTO);
5.  the Economic Commission for Latin America (ECLA), 1948.

Increasingly, the World Bank has become a very important centre for research and the dissemination of ideas on all aspects of economic development. Prominent senior economists who have worked and influenced the direction of development thinking at the World Bank include Hollis Chenery (1970–82), Anne Krueger (1982–93), Stanley Fischer (1988–90), Michael Bruno (1989–96), Lawrence Summers (1991–93), Joseph Stiglitz (1997–2000), Nicholas Stern (2000–03), and François Bourguignon (2003–).

The World Bank Chief Economist is obviously one of the most influential positions in the economics profession since the role dictates that the person chosen is required to provide intellectual leadership and direction to the World Bank's overall development strategy and research agenda, at national, regional and global levels. The Chief Economist also provides regular advice to the bank's senior management team on economic issues.

In the period following the end of the Second World War, many economists concerned about economic development took the view that the existing corpus of orthodox static neoclassical economic theory was an inadequate vehicle for investigating the daunting dynamic economic problems facing the low-income countries. As a result, during the 1950s, a burgeoning research effort in this area sought to identify a basic theoretical structure from which economists could deduce useful policy recommendations. Beginning with Paul Rosenstein-Rodan's (1943) famous *Economic Journal* paper on 'Problems of Industrialization of Eastern and South-Eastern Europe', the period from 1943 to 1958 became the years of what Krugman (1992) has called 'high development theory'. This was the era of 'big ideas' when several economists developed grand aggregate models echoing the 'magnificent dynamics' of the classical theorists (Meier and Seers, 1984; Hunt, 1989; Pritchett and Lindauer, 2002). Building on earlier work, the research output of economists investigating the problems facing the impoverished countries of the Third World expanded rapidly during the 1950s, with especially influential contributions coming from Raúl Prebisch (1950), Hans Singer (1950), Ragnar Nurkse (1953), Arthur Lewis (1954), Simon Kuznets (1955) Richard Nelson (1956), Walt Rostow (1956), Harvey Leibenstein (1957), Gunnar Myrdal (1957) and Albert O. Hirschman (1958). Also influential during this era was the 'capital fundamentalism' associated with the Harrod–Domar growth model. Indeed, as Easterly (1999, 2001a) has shown, although the Harrod–Domar model is no longer influential among growth theorists, it remains a remarkably resilient influence within major international financial institutions despite strong evidence indicating that the relationship between investment and growth is 'loose and unstable' (see section 2.14 below).

The research of three economists that has contributed directly to a better understanding of the process of economic development has been recognised with the award of a Nobel Prize in Economics to: Simon Kuznets 'for his empirically founded interpretation of economic growth which led to new and deepened insight into the economic and social structure and process of development' (awarded in 1971); and to Arthur Lewis and Theodore Schultz, 'for their pioneering research into economic development with particular consideration of the problems of developing countries' (awarded in 1979).

Although many other Nobel Laureates received their award for research in fields other than development economics, nevertheless, important aspects of their work have provided key insights into major issues relating to economic development. Notable here (research relevant to developing economies and year of award of Nobel Prize in parentheses) are the contributions of Jan Tinbergen (economic planning, 1969); Wassily Leontief (input–output analysis, 1973); Gunnar Myrdal (cumulative causation theory, 1974); Bertil Ohlin (trade theory, 1977); James Buchanan (public choice analysis, 1986); Gary Becker (fertility analysis, 1992); Robert Solow (growth theory, 1987); Douglass North (institutional analysis, 1993); James Mirrlees (project appraisal, 1996); Amartya Sen (capabilities, famines and deprivation, 1998); and Joseph Stiglitz (implications of imperfect information, 2001).

In 2005 Daron Acemoglu received the John Bates Clark Medal from the American Economics Association. This prestigious biannual award is given to the best young US-based economist under the age of 40. Acemoglu's new political-economy research has stimulated work that rethinks the development process, in particular the dynamics of political barriers to development, and the main factors that lead to the persistence of inefficient and damaging policies (see Acemoglu and Johnson, 2005; Acemoglu and Robinson, 2006a).

## 2.5   FROM THE '*DIRIGISTE* CONSENSUS' TO THE 'WASHINGTON CONSENSUS' AND BEYOND

In the development enthusiasm of the 1950s there was widespread acceptance of the view that poor countries were plagued by pervasive market failures. To many development theorists, neoclassical economics seemed most suited to static issues of resource allocation, but of limited relevance when it came to dynamic issues of accumulation, economic growth and development. Since it was naïvely assumed that governments were benevolent social guardians, aiming to maximise social welfare, it seemed obvious, indeed almost self-evident, that a *dirigiste* strategy was the best way of achieving the desired objective of rapid economic growth and the elimination of poverty. It was hoped that enlightened government intervention would be able, via a 'big push', to create a 'virtuous circle' of modernisation breeding modernisation. The economic disasters experienced by the capitalist democracies during the Great Depression of the 1930s also persuaded many economists that severe economic instability might be an inevitable feature of capitalism, and to counter this required an enlightened guiding hand from government.

With distrust of the market mechanism, the association of capitalism and free markets with colonialism and instability, widespread export pessimism, a rose-coloured view of Soviet economic performance distorted by a lack of reliable data, many developing countries, such as India, opted for an inward-looking strategy of import substitution accompanied by an enthusiasm for economic planning which, with the benefit of hindsight, is now hard to comprehend. As a result, policies were typically adopted that combined import controls, public ownership, price controls, overvalued exchange rates, excessive regulation of market activity, neo-Malthusian fertility control policies, and injections of foreign aid to bridge the financing gap between domestic resource availability and the requirements thought necessary to achieve some target rate of growth. In sum, the view that a private-enterprise-dominated system combined with a limited role for government could solve the problem of economic development was widely rejected. This pessimistic view of the role and effectiveness of the price mechanism received further impetus from members of the Latin American 'structuralist school', particularly Raúl Prebisch, first director of the ECLA. The supply and export 'elasticity pessimism' of the structuralists gave encouragement to those advocating inward-looking strategies of import substitution industrialisation. The most extreme trade pessimists were the neo-Marxist-inspired 'dependency school', who advocated that the developing countries should de-link themselves from the international trading system dominated by the powerful capitalist economies. From their perspective the international trading system did not lead to mutual gain; rather it fostered 'unequal exchange' between the capitalist 'centre' and the 'underdeveloped periphery' (see Hunt, 1989). Unfortunately, inspired by many of these ideas, some political leaders engaged in what Pranab Bardhan (1993) refers to as 'iconoclastic excesses' involving 'indiscriminate state intervention', 'autarkism' and a 'preoccupation with blanket market failures'. However, Bardhan recalls how

> As news of the failures and disasters of regulatory and autarkic states in developing countries reached academia and demoralisation set in among this group, orthodox economists made successful inroads in partially recapturing this rebel territory and many a premature obituary of development economics was written.

During the 1970s and 1980s the emphasis on pervasive market failures in developing countries was increasingly challenged, both theoretically and empirically. Many economists, notably Jagdish Bhagwati, Anne Krueger, Peter Bauer, Ian Little, Deepak Lal and Theodore Schultz, reaffirmed the importance of incentives, openness to trade, the dangers of excessive government regulations and the broad failure of aggregate economic planning (for surveys, see Meier and Stiglitz, 2001). The neoliberal reaction to excessively *dirigiste* strategies gained momentum and in 1990 had been given the label 'Washington Consensus' by John Williamson (see Williamson, J., 1990, 2003; Kuczynski and Williamson, 2003). However, according to Stiglitz (2002a), the more extreme advocates of the Washington Consensus, in policy-making circles rather than academia, overreacted to the excesses of the *dirigiste* era and encouraged the adoption of policies in developing countries based on a philosophy of market fundamentalism (see Williamson, J., 2000a, and Fischer interview for an alternative perspective). This overreaction ignored important developments in economic theory that had already undermined the Walrasian framework that underlies orthodox neoclassical economics. In particular, ideas relating to asymmetric information, dynamic externalities and increasing returns to scale, path dependency and multiple equilibria undermined the foundations of mainstream neoclassical faith in the optimality properties of a predominantly *laissez-faire* economy. According to Krugman (1992), these developments breathed new life into the first-generation unconventional ideas of the 'high development theorists' of the 1943–58 period. As Krugman (1995) points out, the emphasis of the early post-war ideas on increasing returns, vicious and virtuous circles, cumulative causation, the strategic complementarity of investment decisions and the possibility of coordination failure 'did in fact identify important possibilities that are neglected in competitive equilibrium models'.

Also important in the recent revival of development economics is the work by Nobel Laureate Joseph Stiglitz and others on imperfect and costly information. By the mid-1980s Stiglitz (1986) was announcing the arrival of 'the new development economics' that identified a whole range of new information-based market failures (e.g. in financial markets) requiring a more extensive role for the state than that identified by the more extreme enthusiasts of the Washington Consensus view. This new thinking has led economists to reconsider the appropriate relationship between the market and the state, to rethink and re-emphasise the importance of incentives and institutions, and to recognise that there is a strong synergy between the market and the state that must be recognised in the design of policy.

## 2.6   GROWTH AND DEVELOPMENT

While everyone agrees that economic growth is not a sufficient condition for economic development, it is certainly a necessary condition. For example, Benjamin Friedman (2005) has provided a recent articulate defence of the 'moral' case for continuing to give economic growth a high priority on the policy agenda because rising material living standards normally foster 'greater opportunity, tolerance of diversity, social mobility, commitment to fairness, and dedication to democracy', whereas little if any progress in meeting these desirable goals is likely in stagnating societies. While economic growth raises material living standards, it also has many disruptive consequences, such as the undermining or destruction of traditional values and cultures, environmental damage, tensions arising from the forces of globalisation, and resource depletion. Friedman reminds us that these 'moral negatives' (costs) need to be compared to the 'moral positives' (benefits) of growth, including its favourable impact on social and economic mobility, tolerance and democracy.

Economists believe that, on balance, the benefits of economic growth far outweigh the costs. Therefore, in order to create an economic system and policy environment that fosters sustainable growth, it is necessary that we better understand the causes of rising GDP per capita. Growth theory attempts to provide the necessary framework for thinking about the causes of economic growth.

Four main waves of growth theory were influential in the second half of the twentieth century and have been central to to discussions of economic development and analysis:

1.  the neo-Keynesian Harrod–Domar model;
2.  the Solow–Swan neoclassical model;
3.  the Romer–Lucas-inspired endogenous growth models;
4.  modern political-economy models, such as those developed by Acemoglu.

The first three approaches emphasise the proximate determinants of growth. Interestingly, in each case the ideas developed represent examples of multiple discovery. The first wave of interest focused on the neo-Keynesian work of Roy Harrod (1939, 1948) and Evsey Domar (1946, 1947). In the mid-1950s the development of the neoclassical growth model by Robert Solow (1956, 1957) and Trevor Swan (1956) stimulated a second more lasting and substantial wave of interest, which, after a period of relative neglect between 1970 and 1986, has been reignited (Mankiw, 1995). The third and most recent wave, initiated by the research of Paul Romer (1986) and Robert Lucas (1988), led to the development of endogenous growth theory, which emerged in response to perceived theoretical and empirical deficiencies associated with the neoclassical model (see Romer, 1994; Barro and Sala-i-Martin, 2003; Snowdon and Vane, 2005).

In the most recent wave of growth theory and empirics, modern political-economy models have been used to investigate the deeper or fundamental determinants of growth. A major problem with formal growth models that focus on the proximate determinants of growth (1–3 above) is that such models ignore the influence of history, the impact of path dependency, ethnolinguistic fractionalisation, and political and economic barriers to reform. In contrast, recent political-economy models of growth focus on the impact on growth of such factors as the quality of governance, the origins of the legal system, ethnic diversity, social cohesion, democracy, trust, corruption and institutions in general (e.g. Fukuyama, 1995; Zak and Knack, 2001; Glaeser and Shleifer, 2002; Landau, 2003; Seabright, 2004; Alesina and Ferrara, 2005; Acemoglu and Robinson, 2006a). Major debates relating to the deeper determinants of growth also consider the relative importance of geographical constraints (Bloom and Sachs, 1998; Sachs, 2005a), the natural-resource curse (Sala-i-Martin and Subramanian, 2003), and the links between international economic integration and growth (Sachs and Warner, 1995; Rodrik, 1995; Bhagwati, 2004a; Wolf, 2004a).

Figure 2.9 provides a suggested framework for thinking about the major proximate and fundamental (deeper) factors that influence the rate of growth. While growth theory and empirical research show that poor countries have enormous potential for catch-up and convergence, these advantages will fail to generate positive results on growth in countries with inadequate growth-supporting institutions (Rodrik, 2003a, 2003b, 2005b).

During the past decade the contribution of William Easterly's research has been very important in improving the understanding of policy makers of what works and what does not work. His numerous papers, including those on the impact of ethnic diversity, the sources of growth, the impact of policy on growth and development, the role of institutions, debt relief and critiques of foreign aid, have made a significant contribution to the development economics literature. Of particular significance is the finding reported by Easterly and Levine (2001) that national policies are 'strongly linked' with economic growth. The design of policies and institutions that can improve human welfare is one of the most important contributions that economists can make, and nowhere is it more important to improve economic performance than in sub-Saharan Africa.

While conventional neoclassical growth theory provides a useful framework for analysing the determinants of output per worker, Jeffrey Sachs has made a major contribution to economists' understanding of the deeper determinants of growth by reminding them of the constraints often imposed by geographical influences, particularly in the case of sub-Saharan Africa. Geography is clearly a major determinant of agricultural productivity, transport costs, health, and the location of exploitable natural resources. Since specialisation and the division of labour depend on the extent of the market, transport costs, as well as economic policy, must play

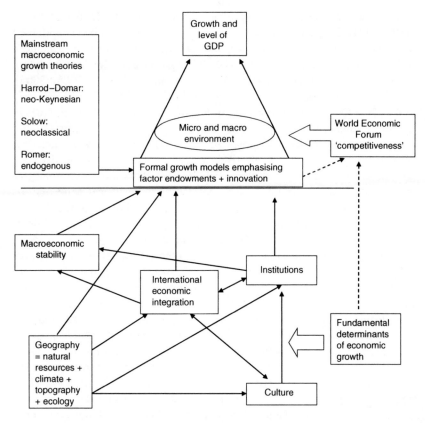

*Source:* Adapted from Snowdon and Vane (2005).

*Figure 2.9   A framework for growth analysis*

a key role in the determination of productivity (Gallup et al., 1999). In reminding economists of the importance of geography, Sachs is following on in the tradition of Adam Smith (1776), who 'gave deep attention to the geographical correlates of growth' as well as the importance of institutions (Yang, 2003).

## 2.7   GROWTH, DEVELOPMENT AND THE ROLE OF INSTITUTIONS

An emphasis on the link between institutions and growth was first clearly articulated by Adam Smith in the eighteenth century and more recently championed during the past 20 years by Nobel Laureate Douglass North (1990, 2004). In the last few years a flood of research has been conducted on the institutional determinants of comparative development and includes notable contributions by Olson (2000), Sokoloff and Engerman (2000), Acemoglu et al. (2001, 2002), Acemoglu and Johnson (2005, 2006); Acemoglu and Robinson (2006a, 2006b); Rodrik (2003a, 2003b), Easterly and Levine (2003), and Grief (2006). We should also note the emphasis in the World Bank report (2002) on *Building Institutions for Markets*, and the United Nations *Human Development Report: Deepening Democracy in a Fragmented World* (2002). Collectively, these important and innovative contributions demonstrate that any satisfactory explanation of comparative cross-country development experience over long historical time periods requires economists to integrate politics and history into their analysis. As a result, once more development economics is a vibrant and exciting field of enquiry attracting some of the best minds in economics.

Moving from the proximate to the fundamental causes of growth naturally shifts the focus of attention to the institutional framework of an economy. There is now widespread acceptance of the idea that 'good' institutions and the incentive structures they establish are an important precondition for successful growth and development. As already noted, the idea that institutions profoundly influence the 'wealth of nations' is by no means a new idea, having first been eloquently expressed by Adam Smith in 1776. However, recent research into the determinants of growth has led to a rediscovery of the quality of governance, legal structures, entrepreneurship, property rights, institutions and incentive structures.

What are the institutions of high-quality growth and what are the main lessons that economists have learned about economic development in the twentieth century that can help poor countries formulate policies in the future? While there is no single model or strategy that is applicable to all countries at all times, there are some basic economic principles that have broad application and should not be ignored. Scully (1988) finds that politically open societies, where resources are allocated predominantly through markets in a stable environment of law and order, and where property rights are secure, grow more rapidly and are more efficient than countries that do not have these characteristics. More recently, Acemoglu (2003a) has identified three key characteristics of 'good' institutions. First, security of property rights 'for a broad cross section of society' is crucial for sustaining incentives to innovate and invest; second, effective constraints on the politically powerful are required to prevent predation; third, equality of opportunity is necessary to encourage broad participation in economic activity. Along similar lines, Dani Rodrik identifies certain desirable 'meta principles' that seem to apply across the globe regardless of history, geography and stage of development (see Rodrik interview). They include the importance of:

1. incentives;
2. security of property rights;
3. contract enforcement and the rule of law;
4. the power of competition;
5. hard budget constraints;
6. macroeconomic and financial stability (low inflation, prudent regulation and fiscal sustainability);
7. targeted redistribution that minimises distortions to incentives.

To a large extent these 'meta principles' are 'institution free' in the sense that they do not imply any fixed set of ideas about appropriate institutional arrangements. In other words, there are many possible models of a mixed economy and in practice the capitalist-market-oriented economies that we observe across the world exhibit a 'diverse range of institutional arrangements'. Every capitalist system consists of an amalgam of public and private institutions and, as the 'new comparative economics' recognises, European, Japanese, East Asian and American forms of capitalism differ (see Dore et al., 1999; Shleifer et al., 2003; Easterly, 2006a). However, as Rodrik (2006) argues, in each case there are firmly in place 'market-sustaining institutions' which he divides into four categories:

1. market-creating institutions (property rights and contract enforcement);
2. market-regulating institutions (regulatory authorities);
3. market-stabilising institutions (monetary, fiscal and financial authorities);
4. market-legitimising institutions ( democracy and social protection).

Given this framework, Rodrik concludes that there is 'no unique correspondence between the *functions* that good institutions perform and the *form* that such institutions take'. There is plenty of room for 'institutional diversity' consistent with meeting the broad 'meta principles'.

## 2.8 ECONOMIC HISTORY AND INSTITUTIONS

Economic history is essentially about the performance of economies over long periods of time and it has a very important contribution to make in helping growth theorists improve their ability to develop a better analytical framework for understanding long-run economic change (North and Thomas, 1973; North, 1989, 1994). The story that emerges from economic history shows that the unsuccessful economies, in terms of achieving sustained growth of living standards, are those that fail to produce a set of enforceable economic rules of the game that promote economic progress. As Douglass North (1991) argues, the 'central issue of economic history and of economic development is to account for the evolution of political and economic institutions that create an economic environment that induces increasing productivity'.

North (1991) defines institutions as 'the humanly devised constraints that structure political, economic and social interaction'. The constraining institutions may be informal (customs, traditions, taboos, conventions, self-imposed codes of conduct involving guilt and shame) and/or formal (laws, contract enforcement, rules, constitutions, property rights). In an ideal world the informal and formal institutions will complement each other. These institutions provide a structure within which repeated human interaction can take place, they support market transactions, they help to transmit information between economic agents and they give people the incentives to engage in productive activities. History is 'largely a story of institutional evolution' and effective institutions 'raise the benefit of co-operative solutions or the costs of defection' (ibid.). History shows that the building of institutions conducive to economic growth and development takes time and also that the process can be halted or reversed by political barriers and conflict (Acemoglu and Robinson, 2000a, 2000b, 2000c, 2001).

A good example demonstrating the importance of institutions for sustained economic growth is provided by the post-Second World War reconstruction of Europe. DeLong and Eichengreen (1993) argue that, 'the Marshall Plan significantly sped western European growth by altering the environment in which economic policy was made' and by providing support to a recovery strategy based on the restoration of a market-based economic system, together with the necessary supporting institutions. DeLong and Eichengreen conclude that the Marshall Plan was 'history's most successful structural adjustment programme'. Eichengreen (1996) also extends the institutional-based explanation of why Europe was able to enjoy a 'golden age' of economic growth in the 25-year period following the implementation of the Marshall Plan. European economic growth during this quarter century was faster than any period either before or since (Maddison, 2001). According to Eichengreen, the foundation for this 'golden age' was a set of domestic and international institutions that 'solved problems of commitment and co-operation that would have otherwise hindered the resumption of growth'.

## 2.9   BANDITS AND KLEPTOCRATS

According to the World Bank (2002), there is a growing body of evidence linking the quality of institutional development to economic growth and efficiency across both time and space. If property rights are the key to reducing transaction costs and the promotion of specialisation and trade, then it should be no surprise to observe that 'almost all of the countries that have enjoyed good economic performance across generations are countries that have stable democratic governments' (Olson, 2000). Whereas good governance and economic prosperity are good bedfellows, autocrats, who are also frequently 'kleptomaniacs', are a high-risk form of investment (Acemoglu et al., 2004). As Easterly (2001a) has highlighted in his analysis of the *Elusive Quest for Growth*, 'governments can kill growth'.

For most of human history the vast majority of the people across the world have been governed by either 'roving bandits' or 'stationary bandits' (Olson, 1993). History provides incontrovertible evidence that benevolent despots are a rare breed and roving bandits (warlords) have little interest in promoting the well-being of the people living within their domain. A territory dominated by competing roving bandits represents a situation of pure anarchy where any form of sustainable economic development is impossible. With no secure property rights there is little incentive for people to produce any more than is necessary for their survival since any surplus will be expropriated by force. Stationary bandits, however, can extract more tax revenue from the territory they dominate if a stable and productive economy can be encouraged and maintained. In this situation despots have an incentive to provide key public goods such as law and order. But property rights can never be fully secure under autocratic forms of governance. History shows that absolutist princes always find it difficult to establish stable dynasties, and this uncertainty relating to succession prevents autocrats from taking a longer-term view of the economy. For example, the monarchy in England between the rule of William the Conqueror (1066) and the 'Glorious Revolution' (1688) was plagued by repeated crises of succession (e.g. the Wars of the Roses). Only in a secure democracy, where representative government is accountable and respectful of individual rights, can we expect to observe an environment created that is conducive to lasting property rights and sustained economic growth.

The general thesis advocated by North and Olson is confirmed by DeLong and Shleifer (1993), who show that those cities in medieval Europe that were under more democratic forms of government were much more productive than those under the autocratic rule of 'princes'. It has also been argued by North that the establishment of a credible and sustainable commitment to the security of property rights in England required the establishment of parliamentary supremacy over the crown. This was achieved following the 'Glorious Revolution' of 1688, which facilitated the gradual establishment of economic institutions conducive to increasing security in property rights (North and Weingast, 1989; North, 1990). The contrasting economic fortunes of the North and South American continents also bear testimony to the consequences of divergent institutional paths for political and economic performance (Engerman and Sokoloff, 2000; Acemoglu et al., 2001, 2002).

## 2.10   BARRIERS TO GROWTH AND DEVELOPMENT

Given that capital and technology can migrate across political boundaries, the persistence of significant differences in the level of output per worker suggest the presence of entrenched barriers to growth and development (Parente and Prescott, 2000; Acemoglu and Robinson, 2000b). An obvious deterrent to the free flow of capital from rich to poor countries arises from the greater economic risk involved in investing in countries characterised by macroeconomic instability, inadequate infrastructure, poor education, ethnic diversity, widespread corruption, excessive regulations, political instability and frequent policy reversals. While the presence of technological backwardness and income per capita gaps creates the potential for catch-up and convergence, Abramovitz (1986) has highlighted the importance of 'social capability' without which countries will not be able to realise their potential. Social capability refers to the various institutional arrangements which set the framework for the conduct of productive economic activities and without which market economies cannot function efficiently. In order to foster high levels of output per worker, social institutions must be developed which protect the output of individual productive units from diversion. Countries with a perverse infrastructure, such as a corrupt bureaucracy, generate rent-seeking activities devoted to the diversion of resources rather than productive activities such as capital accumulation, skills acquisition, and the development of new goods and production techniques (Murphy et al., 1993; Mauro, 1995). In an environment of weak law and contract enforcement, poor protection of property rights, confiscatory taxation and widespread corruption, unproductive profit- (rent-)seeking activities will become endemic and cause immense damage to innovation and other growth-enhancing activities (Baumol, 1990; Tanzi, 1998). Across the world we observe an enormous variation in the quality and performance of government. How well politicians perform their role is closely linked to their accountability to their citizens (Adserà et al., 2003). Unfortunately, in many parts of the world, unaccountable political leaders continue to maintain 'bad' institutions and pursue destructive economic policies. As North (1990) reminds us, 'institutions are not usually created to be socially efficient, but are created to serve the interests of those with bargaining power to create new rules'.

Acemoglu's recent research highlights the importance of 'political barriers to development'. This work focuses on attitudes to change in hierarchical societies. Economists recognise that economic growth is a necessary condition for the elimination of poverty and sustainable increases in living standards. Furthermore, technological change and innovation are key factors in promoting growth. So why do political elites deliberately block the adoption of institutions and policies that would help to eliminate economic backwardness?

Essentially, the political outcome in any country reflects the struggle between elites and the masses over the division of the GDP. Acemoglu and Robinson (2000b, 2001, 2006a) argue that superior institutions and technologies are resisted because they may reduce the political power of the elite (see also Cardwell, 1972; Mokyr, 1994). Acemoglu and Robinson distinguish between *de jure* and *de facto* political power, where the former is determined by formal rules in terms of the electoral systems and constitutions, and the latter is determined by 'brute force', bribery, lobbying and corruption. The persistence of institutions (*hysteresis*) that retard or block economic development will arise even where there is a change of power to a reforming government. The new administration may possess *de jure* power, but the former elite may exercise *de facto* power such that the previous set of institutions persists (this certainly happened in the Southern States of the USA after the Civil War, 1861–65). Many poor countries, especially in sub-Saharan Africa, suffer from the 'iron law of oligarchy', whereby one corrupt elite simply replaces a previous corrupt elite in a never-ending succession of coups or corrupt elections. Even if elected by popular mandate, once the newcomers are in power 'they have no incentive to change the oligarchic structure, and instead use the entrenchment provided by the existing political institutions for their own benefit' (Acemoglu and Robinson, 2006a). The persistence of elites who block progress for the majority of people is determined by the structure of incentives that prevail within the political and economic system. Moreover, the absence of strong institutions allows autocratic rulers to 'adopt political strategies which are highly effective at diffusing any opposition to their regime . . . the kleptocratic ruler intensifies the collective action problem and destroys the coalition against him by bribing the pivotal groups' (Acemoglu et al., 2004). Often financed by natural-resource abundance and foreign aid, kleptocrats follow an effective power-sustaining strategy of 'divide and rule'. In the case of Zaire (now the Democratic Republic of the Congo), with over 200 ethnic groups, Mobutu was able to follow such a strategy from 1965 until he was overthrown in 1997.

Acemoglu's research reinforces the conclusions of Easterly and Levine (1997), who find that ethnic diversity in Africa reduces the rate of economic growth since diverse groups find it more difficult to reach cooperative solutions and scarce resources are wasted because of continuous distributional struggles, of which civil war, 'ethnic cleansing' and genocide are the most extreme manifestations (see Glaeser, 2005; Easterly, Gatti and Kurlat, 2006). Collier's (2001) research also suggests that ethnically diverse societies are 'peculiarly ill suited to dictatorship' and that providing there is not 'ethnic dominance' in the political system, democratic institutions can greatly reduce the potential adverse economic impact of ethnic diversity and the wars of attrition that can take place between competing groups. Where a country lacks 'social cohesion' because of large inequalities in income and ethnic diversity, bad policies are often enacted or maintained because politicians face enormous constraints on their ability to initiate and sustain development-enhancing reforms. The research of Easterly, Ritzen and Woolcock (2006) shows how the extent of social cohesion in a country influences the quality of institutions, which in turn determines the quality of economic policy and economic growth. Easterly (2001b) argues that formal institutions that protect minorities and guarantee freedom from expropriation and contract repudiation can 'constrain the amount of damage that one ethnic group could do to another'. Easterly's research findings show that ethnic diversity does not lower growth or result in worse economic policies providing that good institutions are in place. Good institutions also 'lower the risk of wars and genocides that might otherwise result from ethnic fractionalisation' (see Easterly interview).

## 2.11   SUB-SAHARAN AFRICA'S 'GROWTH TRAGEDY'

The lack of progress in sub-Saharan Africa (see Figure 2.10) is *the* outstanding development failure of the last quarter of the twentieth century and, as is evident from the data in Tables 2.7 and 2.8, sub-Saharan Africa represents the greatest development challenge facing the world in the twenty-first century. This failure has been highlighted even more by the spectacular per capita growth rates achieved in East Asia over the same period (Elson, 2006).

According to Maddison (2001), while the East Asian economies have experienced per capita growth rates of 5.5 per cent in the period 1973–99,

*Figure 2.10    Political map showing countries of sub-Saharan Africa, 2007*

growth in sub-Saharan Africa as a whole over the same period has been negative! Not only has GDP per capita fallen between 1975 and 2000 for 15 out of the 20 most populous sub-Saharan Africa countries; the majority of their HDI scores at the end of the twentieth century lie below the estimated HDI scores for the UK and the USA in 1870 (see Table 2.2). It is therefore easy to agree with World Bank economist Branko Milanovic (2002a, 2002b) when he writes, 'World inequality is a topic whose time has come' (see Sala-i-Martin interview).

Although there is considerable debate about the trend of world inequality, it is broadly accepted that the enormous development gaps that exist at the beginning of the twenty-first century are mainly the result of significant differences in the success of countries in achieving steady and sustained economic growth over the period since the first Industrial Revolution. As the quantity and quality of data relating to the comparative economic performance of nations have become increasingly available, the full extent of

*Table 2.7    Selected development indicators: countries, income groups and world regions*[1]

| Country, income group or region | GNI per capita[1] ($US) 2004 | GNI per capita[1] ($PPP) 2004 | GDP[1] ($PPP millions) 2004 | Population[1] (thousands) 2004 | Human Development Index[2] 2003 |
|---|---|---|---|---|---|
| Low income | 510 | 2260 | 5350327 | 2338083 | 0.593 |
| Middle income | 2190 | 6480 | 19729421 | 3006230 | 0.774 |
| Lower middle income | 1580 | 5640 | 13800110 | 2430310 | NA |
| Upper middle income | 4770 | 10090 | 5968207 | 575920 | NA |
| Low and middle income | 1460 | 4630 | 25070850 | 5334313 | NA |
| High income | 32040 | 30970 | 31004190 | 1000814 | 0.910 |
| East Asia and Pacific | 1280 | 5070 | 9458791 | 1870228 | 0.768 |
| Europe and Central Asia | 3290 | 8360 | 4037790 | 472073 | 0.802[3] |
| Latin America and Caribbean | 3600 | 7660 | 4286169 | 541322 | 0.797 |
| Middle East and North Africa | 2000 | 5760 | 1718585 | 293994 | 0.679[4] |
| South Asia | 590 | 2830 | 4115428 | 1447673 | 0.628 |
| **Sub-Saharan Africa** | **600** | **1850** | **1407349** | **719022** | **0.515** |
| European Monetary Union | 27630 | 27840 | 8638455 | 307446 | NA |
| World | 6280 | 8760 | 55938191 | 6345127 | 0.741 |
| USA | 41400 | 39710 | 11628083 | 293507 | 0.944 |
| UK | 33940 | 31460 | 1832252 | 59405 | 0.939 |
| Japan | 37180 | 30040 | 3774086 | 127764 | 0.943 |
| Germany | 30120 | 27950 | 2325828 | 82631 | 0.930 |
| China | 1290 | 5530 | 7123712 | 1296500 | 0.755 |
| India | 620 | 3100 | 3362960 | 1079721 | 0.602 |

*Notes:*
[1] World Bank data. Country classification by income group: economies are divided according to 2004 GNI per capita, calculated using the World Bank Atlas method. The groups are: low income, $825 or less; lower middle income (**LMI**), $826–$3255; upper middle income (**UMI**), $3256–$10065; and high income, $10066 or more (www.worldbank.org).
[2] United Nations Development Programme classifications. Adapted from the *Human Development Report*, 2005, United Nations (www.undp.org).
[3] Central and Eastern Europe and CIS.
[4] Arab states.

Table 2.8  Selected development indicators, 48 sub-Saharan countries

| Country Classification[1] | GNI per capita[1] ($US) 2004 | GNI per capita[1] ($PPP) 2004 | Population[1] (thousands) 2004 | Life expectancy at birth[1] 2002 | Under 5 mortality rate per thousand 2002[1] | HDI[2] 1985 | HDI[2] 2003 |
|---|---|---|---|---|---|---|---|
| Angola (LMI) | 1030 | 2030 | 13 963 | 47 | 260 | n.a. | 0.445 |
| Benin | 530 | 1 120 | 6 890 | 53 | 151 | 0.362 | 0.431 |
| Botswana (UMI) | 4340 | 8 920 | 1 727 | 38 | 110 | 0.638 | 0.565 |
| Burkino Faso | 360 | 1 220 | 12 387 | 43 | 207 | 0.297 | 0.317 |
| Burundi | 90 | 660 | 7 343 | 42 | 208 | 0.345 | 0.378 |
| Cameroon | 800 | 2 090 | 16 400 | 48 | 166 | 0.505 | 0.497 |
| Cape Verde (LMI) | 1770 | 5 650 | 481 | 69 | 38 | n.a. | 0.721 |
| Central African Rep. | 310 | 1 110 | 3 947 | 42 | 180 | 0.386 | 0.355 |
| Chad | 260 | 1 420 | 8 823 | 48 | 200 | 0.311 | 0.341 |
| Comoros | 530 | 1 840 | 614 | 61 | 79 | 0.498 | 0.547 |
| Congo Dem. Rep. | 120 | 680 | 54 775 | 45 | 205 | 0.431 | 0.385 |
| Congo Republic. | 770 | 750 | 3 855 | 52 | 108 | 0.540 | 0.512 |
| Côte d'Ivoire | 770 | 1 390 | 17 142 | 45 | 191 | 0.448 | 0.420 |
| Equatorial Guinea (UMI) | n.a. | 7 400 | 506 | 52 | 152 | 0.483 | 0.655 |
| Eritrea | 180 | 1 050 | 4 477 | 51 | 80 | n.a. | 0.444 |
| Ethiopia | 110 | 810 | 69 961 | 42 | 171 | 0.291 | 0.367 |
| Gabon (UMI) | 3940 | 5 600 | 1 374 | 53 | 85 | n.a. | 0.635 |
| Gambia | 290 | 1 900 | 1 449 | 53 | 126 | n.a. | 0.470 |
| Ghana | 380 | 2 280 | 21 053 | 55 | 97 | 0.482 | 0.520 |
| Guinea | 460 | 2 130 | 8 073 | 46 | 165 | n.a. | 0.466 |
| Guinea-Bissau | 160 | 690 | 1 533 | 45 | 211 | 0.283 | 0.348 |

Table 2.8 (continued)

| Country Classification[1] | GNI per capita[1] ($US) 2004 | GNI per capita[1] ($PPP) 2004 | Population[1] (thousands) 2004 | Life expectancy at birth[1] 2002 | Under 5 mortality rate per thousand 2002[1] | HDI[2] 1985 | HDI[2] 2003 |
|---|---|---|---|---|---|---|---|
| Kenya | 460 | 1050 | 32447 | 46 | 122 | 0.530 | 0.474 |
| Lesotho | 740 | 3210 | 1809 | 38 | 132 | 0.534 | 0.497 |
| Liberia | 110 | n.a. | 3449 | 47 | 235 | n.a. | n.a. |
| Madagascar | 300 | 830 | 17332 | 55 | 135 | 0.436 | 0.499 |
| Malawi | 170 | 620 | 11182 | 38 | 182 | 0.362 | 0.404 |
| Mali | 360 | 980 | 11937 | 41 | 222 | 0.263 | 0.333 |
| Mauritania | 420 | 2050 | 2906 | 51 | 183 | 0.384 | 0.477 |
| Mauritius (UMI) | 4640 | 11870 | 1234 | 73 | 19 | 0.690 | 0.791 |
| Mayotte (UMI) | n.a. | n.a. | 172 | 60 | n.a. | n.a. | n.a. |
| Mozambique | 250 | 1160 | 19129 | 41 | 205 | 0.287 | 0.379 |
| Namibia (LMI) | 2370 | 6960 | 2033 | 42 | 67 | n.a. | 0.627 |
| Niger | 230 | 830 | 12095 | 46 | 264 | 0.242 | 0.281 |
| Nigeria | 390 | 930 | 139823 | 45 | 201 | 0.386 | 0.453 |
| Rwanda | 220 | 1300 | 8412 | 40 | 203 | 0.401 | 0.450 |
| São Tomé Principe | 370 | n.a. | 161 | 66 | 118 | n.a. | 0.604 |
| Senegal | 670 | 1720 | 10455 | 52 | 138 | 0.375 | 0.458 |
| Seychelles (UMI) | 8090 | 15590 | 85 | 73 | 16 | n.a. | 0.821 |
| Sierra Leone | 200 | 790 | 5436 | 37 | 284 | n.a. | 0.298 |
| Somalia | n.a. | n.a. | 9938 | 47 | 225 | n.a. | n.a. |
| South Africa (UMI) | 3630 | 10960 | 45584 | 46 | 65 | 0.702 | 0.658 |
| Sudan | 530 | 1870 | 34356 | 58 | 94 | 0.396 | 0.512 |

| | | | | | | | |
|---|---|---|---|---|---|---|---|
| *Swaziland ( LMI )* | 1660 | 4 970 | 1 120 | 44 | 149 | 0.584 | 0.498 |
| Tanzania | 330 | 660 | 36 571 | 43 | 165 | n.a. | 0.418 |
| Togo | 380 | 1 690 | 4 966 | 50 | 140 | 0.474 | 0.512 |
| Uganda | 270 | 1 520 | 25 920 | 43 | 141 | 0.412 | 0.508 |
| Zambia | 450 | 890 | 10 547 | 37 | 182 | 0.484 | 0.394 |
| Zimbabwe | 480[3] | 2 180 | 13 151 | 39 | 123 | 0.640 | 0.505 |
| **Sub-Saharan Africa** | **600** | **1 850** | **719 022** | **46** | **174** | **n.a.** | **0.515** |
| World | 6280 | 8 760 | 6 345 127 | 67[4] | 81[4] | n.a. | 0.741 |

*Data sources and notes:*
[1] *Source:* World Bank data (www.worldbank.org). Algeria, Djibouti, Egypt, Libya, Morocco, Tunisia are classified by the World Bank as 'Middle East and North Africa'.
[2] *Source:* *Human Development Report*, 2005, United Nations (www.undp.org).
[3] World Bank data for 2003.
[4] Weighted average.

disparities in terms of levels and growth rates of per capita income has become ever more apparent (the different views on trends in global inequality are reflected in the recent papers by Sala-i-Martin, 2002a, 2002b, 2006; Bourguignon and Morrisson, 2002; and Milanovic, 2003, 2006).

Easterly and Levine (1997) have highlighted sub-Saharan Africa's 'growth tragedy' as the most striking case of development failure relative to the expectations and aspirations present at the time of the decolonisation process. Although it now seems surprising, in 1960 sub-Saharan African countries were generally regarded by many economists as having more growth potential than East Asian countries! But as Easterly and Levine show, 'On average, real per capita GDP did not grow in Africa over the 1965–90 period while, in East Asia and the Pacific, per capita GDP growth was over 5 per cent.' Reflecting the seriousness of 'Africa's growth tragedy', Xavier Sala-i-Martin (2002a, 2000b) concludes his recent papers on global income inequality with the recommendation that economists concerned with international poverty and inequality should focus their attention on Africa because *the* central issue for world inequality is 'how to make Africa grow'. However, in a recent quantitative assessment of Africa's progress towards meeting the 'Millennial Development Goals', Sahn and Stifel (2003) conclude that the 'results are not terribly encouraging for those concerned about raising living standards in Africa'.

Several explanations have been put forward to explain sub-Saharan Africa's relatively poor economic performance (Easterly and Levine, 1997; Bloom and Sachs, 1998; Collier and Gunning, 1999a, 1999b; Herbst, 2000; Bigsten, 2002; Bellows and Miguel, 2006). The 'chief suspects' include:

1.  *adverse external influences and conditions*, including the legacy of colonialism, slavery and cold war politics;
2.  *terms of trade volatility* and heavy dependence on a small number of primary exports;
3.  *damaging economic policies*, including protectionism, regulations, fiscal profligacy, incentives to 'rent-seeking' and 'directly unproductive' behaviour, and excessive public ownership and statism;
4.  *unfavourable demographic factors*, especially rapid population growth;
5.  *disadvantageous geographical factors* – locational disadvantages relating to climate, soils, topography and disease ecology;
6.  *internal political instability* – authoritarianism, corruption, bureaucratic inefficiency, poor governance and lack of accountable democratic institutions;
7.  *ethnic diversity*, absence of trust and lack of social capital;
8.  *lack of adequate physical and social infrastructure*, failure to provide secure property rights and contract enforcement.

A significant factor contributing to sub-Saharan Africa's growth tragedy has been the frequent adoption of economic policies detrimental to long-term sustainable growth and development (Woglin, 1997). Many development disasters in sub-Saharan Africa and elsewhere, including famines, have also been caused by prolonged military conflict and political stability rather than environmental shocks (Sen, 1981; Snowdon, 1985). There also seems little doubt that the majority of African economies marginalised themselves from the world trading system during the 1970s and 1980s and this had a severely retarding impact on their economic progress. By erecting barriers to trade, Africa, by 1990, had become a very hostile environment for capital. Because of its inability to live down the past, adverse 'neighbourhood effects' and 'ignorance' relating to current economic and political conditions, sub-Saharan Africa retains its official rating as 'the most risky region in the world for private investment' (Collier, 1998).

In their influential paper on the impact of ethnic diversity on economic performance in sub-Saharan Africa, Easterly and Levine (1997) provide strong evidence in support of the hypothesis that 'cross-country differences in ethnic diversity explain a substantial part of the cross-country differences in public policies, political instability, and other economic factors associated with long-run growth'. In many ethnically diverse countries that lack credible and stable institutions of conflict management, interest-group polarisation has lead to uncoordinated 'rent-seeking' behaviour and corruption that has strangled the prospects for sustained economic development. To understand the political roots of economic success is a crucial research area for social scientists (see La Porta et al., 1999).

Although there is obviously a great deal of interaction among the various factors that adversely affect economic progress, perhaps the most promising framework for analysing sub-Saharan Africa's growth tragedy is one that focuses on the role of institutions. Many economists are now convinced that the incentive structure created by the institutional environment is the key ingredient that determines the success or failure of countries in their 'elusive quest for growth'. As Robinson (2002) notes, 'The institutional approach to comparative development accounts for economic divergence by positing institutional divergence.'

While Sachs (2005a) agrees that institutions are important, and Table 2.6 suggests that the current political and economic climate in much of sub-Saharan Africa is not conducive to sustained economic growth and poverty reduction, he argues that 'the focus on corruption and governance is exaggerated' and 'Africa's governance is poor because Africa is poor'. Furthermore, according to Sachs, compared to other poor countries with similar quality of governance, growth in sub-Saharan Africa is lower, implying that there must be other important barriers to progress that have been neglected by economists. The chief suspect is 'extraordinarily disadvantageous geography' (Bloom and Sachs, 1998).


## 2.12   FROM 'MARSHALL PLAN' TO MILLENNIUM DEVELOPMENT GOALS

In a historic speech delivered at Harvard University on 5 June 1947, US Secretary of State George C. Marshall set out the basic argument in support of what was to become the 'European Recovery Programme', more popularly known as the 'Marshall Plan'.

> Our policy is directed not against any country or doctrine, but against hunger, poverty, desperation, and chaos. Its purpose should be the revival of a working economy in the world so as to permit the emergence of political and social conditions in which free institutions can exist . . . With foresight, and a willingness on the part of our people to face up to the vast responsibility which history has clearly placed upon our country, the difficulties I have outlined can and will be overcome. (Kunz et al., 1997)

Learning from the disastrous failure of leadership at Versailles in 1919, the post-1947 US aid programme kick-started economic recovery and helped to put Western Europe back on its feet. Described by DeLong and Eichengreen (1993) as 'History's Most Successful Structural Adjustment Programme', the Marshall Plan became 'the model for future foreign aid programmes' (Kunz et al., 1997; the total aid package between April 1948 and June 1951 amounted to $12.5 billion). Of course the conditions prevailing in Western Europe in 1947 at the time of Marshall's speech were very different to those in contemporary sub-Saharan Africa, and the prospects for a similar success for a coordinated international aid programme are very controversial. However, the general principles underlying Marshall's plea for the US population to support the implementation of an enlightened policy against 'hunger, poverty, desperation, and chaos' have been echoed during the last decade in the writings and speeches of Jeffrey Sachs with respect to the measures that he believes are needed to end extreme poverty in the developing world.

Following the *Millennium Development Summit* in 2000, 189 member states of the United Nations unanimously supported the *Millennium Declaration* committing the international community to creating 'an environment – at the national and global levels alike – which is conducive to development and to the elimination of poverty' (http://www.undp.org). The UN Millennium Declaration provides a commitment to freeing the entire human race from extreme poverty. From this declaration emerged the

Millennium Development Goals (MDGs), a set of measurable objectives aimed at halving global poverty by 2015, compared to 1990, that have now been generally accepted as a framework for assessing progress in the developing countries. The MDGs were reaffirmed at the Monterrey (Mexico) Conference on Financing for Development in March 2002, and the World Summit on Sustainable Development at Johannesburg in September 2002. The 'Monterrey Consensus' emphasises the mutual role of both developed and developing countries in achieving the MDGs. As well as recognising the need for more development aid, debt relief and a more open trading system, the 'Monterrey Consensus' also explicitly recognises that 'developing countries have primary responsibility for their own development, and that good governance and a sound development-friendly economic strategy are paramount' (Kofi Annan, Secretary General of the United Nations).

The eight MDGs are as follows:

1. eradicate extreme poverty and hunger;
2. achieve universal primary education;
3. promote gender equality and empower women;
4. reduce child mortality;
5. improve maternal health;
6. combat HIV/AIDS, malaria and other diseases;
7. ensure environmental sustainability;
8. develop a global partnership for development.

While goals 1–7 are directed at reducing poverty in all its manifestations, goal 8 is about establishing the means to achieve poverty alleviation and includes a commitment from the developed countries to reduce trade barriers, provide generous debt relief and substantially increase the flow of aid.

According to Sachs, there is now a 'stark realisation' that 'many of the poorest regions of the world, most notably in sub-Saharan Africa, are far off track to achieve the MDGs' (United Nations, 2005). As Tables 2.7 and 2.8 indicate, sub-Saharan Africa is the region of the world that appears to have the most intractable development problems. Of 59 countries classified by the World Bank as low income, 37 are in sub-Saharan Africa, and of the 48 countries in sub-Saharan Africa, only four are classified as lower middle income (LMI), and seven as upper middle income (UMI). Collectively the 11 LMI and UMI countries have a population of just over 68 million out of the total for sub-Saharan Africa of 719 million. Over 59 million of those in LMI and UMI countries live in either Angola or South Africa, countries not noted for their equitable income distribution. To get some idea of the scale of the sub-Saharan African economy it is interesting to compare

California with sub-Saharan Africa. The 2004 US Bureau of Economic Analysis (http://www.bea.doc.gov) estimates the gross state product of California to have been $1 438 737 million, approximately equivalent to the output of sub-Saharan Africa in total!

## 2.13    2005: A 'PIVOTAL YEAR' IN THE DEVELOPMENT DEBATE?

Given the enormous development task facing sub-Saharan Africa, for economists such as Jeffrey Sachs, 2005 marked a pivotal 'make or break' year in terms of mobilising the international effort to fight extreme poverty (Sachs, 2005b, 2005c, 2005d). Paul Wolfowitz, President of the World Bank, also regards the development problems of sub-Saharan Africa as *the* top priority of the development agenda. Throughout 2005 several major events raised the profile of the sub-Saharan African tragedy, specifically:

1.  January – publication of the findings of the Millennium Development Project (MDP)
2.  March – publication of the Commission for Africa report
3.  March – publication of Jeffrey Sachs's book, *The End of Poverty*
4.  July – G8 Summit at Gleneagles and Live 8 concerts worldwide
5.  September – UN World Summit.

*The Millennium Development Project*   In 2002 the MDP was commissioned by UN Secretary General Kofi Annan, and sponsored by the United Nations Development Programme (www.unmillenniumproject.org). The objective of this independent project, under the directorship of Jeffrey Sachs, was to set out the best strategies and sector-specific proposals for achieving the MDGs by 2015. The MDP consisted of ten thematically oriented task forces involving 300 experts from around the world. The findings and recommendations of the MDP were presented to Kofi Annan on 17 January 2005 in a progress report entitled *Investing in Development: A Practical Plan to Achieve the Millennium Development Goals* (see Sachs et al., 2005). This report is a comprehensive attempt to assess how much progress has been made towards achieving the MDGs and also provides a practical operational framework to help facilitate an investment strategy that will assist the poorest countries to achieve the MDGs by 2015. More specifically, the MDP sets out a detailed plan of action that aims to have the rate of extreme global poverty by 2015, compared to 1990. According to Sachs, the total aid requirements necessary to finance the investments in health, education, infrastructure, sanitation and other key areas is around

$160 billion per year. This is double the current aid budget and represents approximately 0.5 per cent of the combined GNP of the developed donor nations. The estimate of $160 billion per year does not include allowance for other humanitarian projects and, according to Sachs, to meet these obligations, as well as the MDGs, would require assistance amounting to 0.7 per cent of the combined GNP of the rich countries (Sachs, 2005e).

*The Commission for Africa* The Commission for Africa was initiated by UK Prime Minister Tony Blair in February 2004, with the specific aim of 'generating new ideas and action to promote a strong and prosperous Africa' and 'to help deliver implementation of existing international commitments'. In March 2005 the Commission for Africa published its final report entitled *Our Common Interest* (http://www.commissionforafrica. org). This report puts forward the case that the developed world has 'a moral duty – as well as a powerful motive of self interest – to assist Africa'. Much of the argument in the Commission's report echoes Sachs's conjecture that sub-Saharan Africa is caught in a 'vicious circle of poverty' and requires a 'big push' to escape from this poverty trap (for a critique of these ideas see Easterly, 2006a, 2006b).

*The End of Poverty* The main thesis of Jeffrey Sachs's recent book is that extreme poverty around the world can be ended by 2025 and the MDGs can be met by 2015 providing the long-promised modest financial help from rich countries is forthcoming. According to Sachs, this extra assistance, if delivered in a well-formulated cost-effective package of investments, will enable the poorest countries to get their foot on the development ladder. Thereafter, 'the tremendous dynamism of self-sustaining economic growth can take hold'.

*The G8 Summit* Under the chairmanship of Tony Blair, the July 2005 G8 Summit in Gleneagles, Scotland, also focused on the plight of sub-Saharan Africa. The G8 leaders agreed 'a comprehensive plan to support Africa's progress' and to support this plan with 'substantial extra resources which have strong national development plans and are committed to good governance, democracy and transparency'. More specifically, the G8 agreed to double aid to Africa and to eliminate outstanding debts of eligible highly indebted developing countries. According to the Gleneagles *communiqué,* the G8 nations aim to increase assistance to developing countries by around $50 billion per year by 2010 with at least $25 billion of this package allocated to Africa, as well as writing off the debts of the world's poorest countries. The G8 leaders also committed themselves to increasing support for African peacekeeping forces to help 'deter, prevent and resolve conflicts in Africa', and pledged additional resources to finance investment in education and the fight against HIV/AIDS, malaria, tuberculosis and other killer diseases.

*The 2005 UN World Summit*   The 2005 World Summit was the largest gathering of world leaders in history. On 14–16 September, more than 180 heads of state met at the United Nations to forge an action plan for strengthening and reforming the United Nations, promoting international security and human rights, and for achieving the MDGs by 2015. The outcome of the summit was an agreement by world leaders to support a large number of objectives relating to economic development, peace and collective security, human rights and the rule of law, and strengthening the UN. The development objectives include: reaffirmation of a commitment to achieving the MDGs by 2015; reaffirmation of the Monterrey Consensus; promotion of good governance, sound investment-friendly domestic economic policies, more open international trade, increased overseas aid and debt relief; recognition of the 'special needs' of landlocked developing countries; and a number of 'quick-impact initiatives' such as the distribution of anti-malaria bed nets. The '2005 World Summit Outcome' document also recognises the 'special needs of Africa', including the need to increase efforts to 'fully integrate African countries in the international trading system'.

## 2.14   THE FOREIGN AID CONTROVERSY

Recently the foreign aid controversy has been revived by Jeffrey Sachs's (2005a) argument that sub-Saharan Africa is caught in a 'poverty trap', to escape from which needs a 'big push' via a substantial increase in official development assistance (ODA) (see Gupta et al., 2006, for recent data on aid flows). Sachs has also revived the campaign to persuade the rich countries to commit themselves to providing 0.7 per cent of their GNP in official development assistance, a commitment reaffirmed at the 2005 UN World Summit. At the annual World Bank–IMF meeting, 24 September 2005, World Bank President Paul Wolfowitz noted that 'we know that sustained economic growth is essential for development and reducing poverty'. While economists agree that a necessary condition for the elimination of extreme poverty is sustained economic growth (Dollar and Kraay, 2002b, 2004), the idea that an increase in the flow of foreign aid to regions such as sub-Saharan Africa will promote such growth remains controversial. The important debate relating to the effectiveness of foreign aid in promoting growth and development has a long history and is riddled with problems relating to causality, measurement and ideology (see Friedman, M., 1958; Chenery and Strout, 1966; Pearson, 1969; Bauer, 1972; Brandt, 1980; Riddell, 1987, 2007; White, 1992; Cassen et al., 1994; Boone, 1996; World Bank, 1998; Alesina and Dollar, 2000; Alesina and Weder, 2002; Burnside and Dollar, 2000; Easterly, 2001a, 2003a, 2003b, 2004, 2006a; Brautigam and Knack, 2004; Hudson et al., 2004; Easterly et al., 2004; Quibria, 2005; Rajan and Subramanian, 2005a, 2005b; Djankov et al., 2006).

The case for increasing foreign aid in order to stimulate economic growth can be illustrated using the familiar Harrod–Domar growth model (Harrod, 1939, 1948; Domar, 1946, 1947). Within the Harrod–Domar framework the growth of real GDP is assumed to be proportional to the share of investment spending ($I$) in GDP and for an economy to grow, net additions to the capital stock are required. The relationship between the size of the total capital stock ($K$) and total GDP ($Y$) is known as the capital–output ratio ($K/Y = v$), and is assumed to be constant. If we assume that total new investment is determined by total savings ($S$), then the essence of the Harrod–Domar model can be set out as follows. Assume that total saving is some proportion ($s$) of GDP, as shown in equation (2.4):

$$S = sY \qquad (2.4)$$

Since investment spending can be defined as a change of the capital stock (assuming, for simplicity, no depreciation) we have equation (2.5):

$$I = \Delta K \qquad (2.5)$$

Given that we have defined $v = K/Y$, it also follows that $v = \Delta K/\Delta Y$ (the incremental capital–output ratio or ICOR). Since the equality $S = I$ must hold *ex post*, we can write equation (2.6):

$$S = sY = I = \Delta K = v\Delta Y \qquad (2.6)$$

This simplifies to equation (2.7):

$$sY = v\Delta Y \qquad (2.7)$$

Rearranging (2.7), we have (2.8):

$$\Delta Y/Y = G = s/v \qquad (2.8)$$

Here $\Delta Y/Y = Y_t - Y_{t-1}/Y_t$ is the growth rate of GDP. Letting $G = \Delta Y/Y$, we have equation 2.9, the famous Harrod–Domar growth equation:

$$G = s/v \tag{2.9}$$

This simply states that the growth rate ($G$) of GDP is jointly determined by the savings ratio ($s$) divided by the capital–output ratio ($v$). The higher the savings ratio and the lower the capital–output ratio, the faster will an economy grow (allowing for depreciation of the capital stock, $\delta$, the equation becomes $G = s/v - \delta$). Thus it is evident from equation (2.9) that the Harrod–Domar model 'sanctioned the overriding importance of capital accumulation in the quest for enhanced growth' (Shaw, 1992; see also Easterly, 1999, 2001a).

The Harrod–Domar model became tremendously influential in the development economics literature during the third quarter of the twentieth century, and was a key component within the framework of economic planning. The implications of this simple growth model were dramatic and somewhat reassuring, suggesting that the key developmental problem of generating an increase in economic growth could be achieved by simply increasing the resources devoted to capital accumulation. For example, if a developing country desired to achieve a growth rate of per capita income of 2 per cent per annum (i.e. a growth target that would ensure that living standards doubled every 35 years), and population was estimated to be growing at 2 per cent per annum, then economic planners would need to set a target rate of aggregate GDP growth ($G^*$) equal to 4 per cent. If $v = 4$, this implies that $G^*$ can only be achieved with a desired savings ratio ($s^*$) of 0.16, or 16 per cent of GDP (i.e. $G^* v = s^*$). If $s^* > s$, there is a 'savings gap', and planners need to devise policies that can plug this savings gap.

Since the rate of growth in the Harrod–Domar model is positively related to the savings ratio, development economists during the 1950s concentrated their research effort on understanding how to raise private savings ratios in order to enable less-developed economies to 'take off' into 'self-sustained growth' (Lewis, 1954, 1955; Rostow, 1960). Reflecting the contemporary development ideas of the 1950s, government fiscal policy was also seen to have a prominent role to play since budgetary surpluses could (in theory) substitute for private domestic savings. If domestic sources of finance were inadequate to achieve the desired growth target, then foreign aid could fill the 'savings gap' (Riddell, 1987). Aid requirements ($Ar$) would simply be calculated as $s^* - s = Ar$ (Chenery and Strout, 1966) and the growth equation including aid is given by equation (2.10):

$$G = [s + Ar]/v_1 \tag{2.10}$$

However, a major weakness of the Harrod–Domar approach is the assumption of a fixed capital–output ratio. Since the inverse of $v$ is the productivity of investment ($\Phi$), we can rewrite equation (2.9) as follows:

$$G = s\Phi \tag{2.11}$$

Unfortunately, as Bhagwati (1993) observes, the productivity of investment is not given, but reflects the efficiency of the policy framework and the incentive structures within which investment decisions are taken. The weak growth performance of India before the 1980s reflects 'not a disappointing savings performance, but rather a disappointing productivity performance'. Hence the growth–investment relationship turns out to be 'loose and unstable' due to the multiple factors that influence growth (Easterly, 2001a).

The instability of the capital–output ratio was also recognised many years ago by Keith Griffin. According to Griffin (1970), aid inflows are likely to raise the incremental capital–output ratio (lower $\Phi$). This can occur as a result of the politically motivated channelling of aid into large prestigious projects that will 'stand as monuments to the generosity of the donors'. Also, one large aid project is much easier and cheaper for the donors to monitor than a large number of more productive small projects.

Economists soon became aware of a second major flaw in the 'aid requirements' or 'financing gap' model. The model assumed that aid inflows would go into investment one to one. But it soon became apparent that inflows of foreign aid, with the objective of closing the savings gap, did not necessarily boost total savings. Aid does not go into investment one to one. Indeed in many cases inflows of aid led to a reduction of domestic savings together with a decline in the productivity of investment (Griffin, 1970; White, 1992). This is equivalent to a proportion $(\alpha_c)$ of the the aid inflow being consumed; that is, aid is highly fungible. Assuming a constant capital–output ratio, the impact of aid on growth shown in equation (2.10) needs to be modified as indicated in equation (2.12):

$$G = [s + (1 - \alpha_c)Ar]/v_1 \tag{2.12}$$

Clearly, when a proportion of the aid is consumed, the impact of aid on growth is reduced.

Following Griffin (1970), the logic of why a proportion of aid is likely to be consumed is illustrated by Figure 2.11, which shows a conventional neoclassical indifference map combined with budget constraints. The slope of the indifference curves $I_0$ and $I_1$ represents society's (or a government's) time preference over current consumption $(C_t)$ and future consumption $(C_{t+1})$, and the position and slope of the budget line $\beta_0\beta_0$ indicates the combination of current and future consumption that can be achieved with available domestic resources and the rate of return to investment. Let us assume that this economy is initially in a position represented by point A.

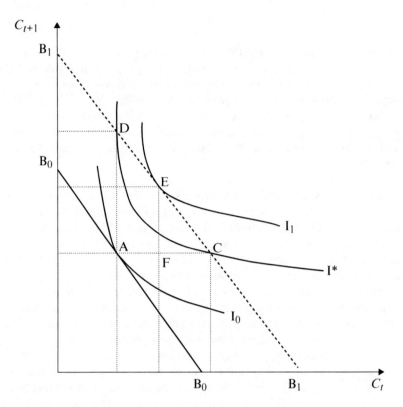

*Figure 2.11   Foreign aid, consumption and investment*

If foreign aid becomes available, we can illustrate this as an outward shift
of the budget line to $\beta_1\beta_1$. In the savings gap model it is assumed that all
these additional resources (AC) will be channelled into investment, leading
to an increase in future consumption. The economy moves to position D.
Therefore, future consumption increases by D – A and current consumption remains unaffected. In contrast, if all the inflow of aid is consumed,
then this economy would be located at point C after the aid inflow. Clearly,
both points D and C are inferior to point E, as indicated by the indifference
map (i.e., any position on I* is inferior to any position on $I_1$). Orthodox
neoclassical theory suggests that the most likely outcome will be that some
of the aid will be consumed (AF) and some of the aid will be invested (FC).
The increase in consumption (AF) is equivalent to a decline in domestic
saving. The return, in terms of future consumption, to the increase in aid
invested is given by FE and the proportion of aid consumed is given by
AF/AC.

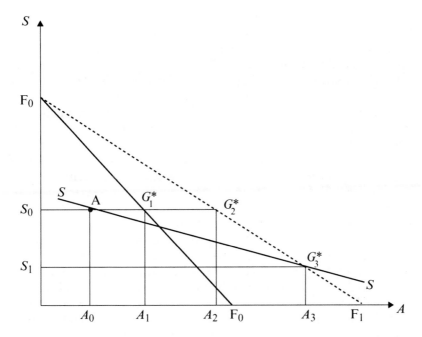

*Figure 2.12   Foreign aid and growth*

According to Griffin (1970), the channels through which an increase in foreign aid can lead to a reduction of domestic savings include (i) a reduction in government savings via a politically popular reduction of taxation; (ii) less effort made in the collection of taxes; (iii) taxes not being raised in line with inflation; (iv) a shift of public expenditure from public investment in infrastructure to public consumption, including higher wages to public employees; and (v) a reduction in the private saving of entrepreneurs as a response to competing projects financed by foreign aid.

Taking into account the adverse impact of aid on the incremental capital–output ratio and domestic savings can illustrate the possible impact on growth of an aid inflow; see Figure 2.12 (see Griffin, 1970). Here, $F_0 F_0$ indicates all the possible combinations of domestic saving ($S$) and foreign aid ($A$) that can produce the desired rate of growth of $G^*$. That is, the vertical intercept equals $G^* v = s^*$. The slope of $F_0 F_0 = -1$, providing that aid inflows have no impact on $v$. If aid inflows increase the value of $v$, then $F_0 F_0$ will be less steep, as illustrated by $F_0 F_1$. The domestic savings function is given by $SS$ and assumes that foreign aid is a partial substitute for domestic saving, so as aid increases, domestic savings fall 'moderately'. If $S_0$ is the initial amount of domestic savings and $A_0$ the initial inflow of foreign aid, then the growth target of $G^*$ will not be achieved; that is, point A lies inside $F_0F_0$. To achieve the target of $G^*$, assuming that all aid is invested (implying a perfectly elastic savings function), then an increase in aid of $A_1 - A_0$ will be required to reach point $G^*_1$. If the productivity of capital declines but domestic savings are unaffected by the aid inflow, then aid requirements will be $A_2 - A_0$ and the growth target will be met at $G^*_2$. However, if as a result of the aid inflow, domestic savings decline and the productivity of capital falls, then an aid inflow of $A_3 - A_0$ is required to achieve the growth target at $G^*_3$, assuming of course that an increase in consumption has no positive impact on growth (this may well be a very dubious assumption in developing countries, where poor health, education and malnutrition have an important negative impact on productivity).

The above 'optimistic' results illustrated in Figure 2.12 imply that foreign aid increases consumption and raises capital accumulation and hence the growth rate. However, the aid requirements necessary to meet the growth target are much higher than suggested by the original savings gap model. Griffin (1970) goes on to argue that a more likely outcome, and one supported by his empirical work, is a situation where aid inflows lead not only to a to a decline in the productivity of investment, but also to a situation where most of the aid is consumed. In Figure 2.12 this would not only imply an outward pivot of the $F_0F_0$ line to $F_0F_1$, but also a much steeper negative savings function. In such a situation the growth target may never be reached. In Griffin's 'pessimistic' case, we have a 'negative resource gap' and a reduction of foreign aid would increase the growth rate! Hence, in the pessimistic version of the Griffin (1970) model, the impact on growth of an increase in foreign aid is negative and is given by equation (2.13):

$$G = [s + (1 - \alpha_c)Ar]/v_2 \qquad (2.13)$$

Where $\alpha_c$ is large and $v_2 > v_1$, $G^*$ can never be achieved via attempts to boost domestic savings with inflows of foreign aid.

## 2.15   AID AND POVERTY TRAPS

The case for increasing foreign aid has recently re-emerged as a major international policy issue and linked to the idea that countries can be trapped in a permanent condition of poverty. That poor countries can be caught in a 'poverty trap' is an old idea in economics dating back at least to the work of Malthus (1798/1909). During the 1950s this idea was revived by Ragnar Nurkse (1953) as the 'vicious circle of poverty' model, and also in the influential paper by Richard Nelson (1956), who developed a model of the 'low level equilibrium trap' to explain persistent poverty. Most recently, Jeffrey Sachs et al. (2004, pp. 121–2) have argued that sub-Saharan Africa is caught in a 'poverty trap':

> tropical Africa, even the well-governed parts, is stuck in a poverty trap, too poor to achieve robust, high levels of economic growth and, in many places, simply too poor to grow at all.

In other words, the neoclassical vision that market forces combined with improved governance can remedy the development problem in many very poor countries is rejected.

Poverty traps (or multiple equilibria) represent self-reinforcing inefficient equilibria and can arise from both market and institutional failure (Azariadis and Stachurski, 2005). One of the best-known poverty-trap mechanisms runs from extreme poverty to low rates of domestic saving, leading to low rates of capital accumulation and low or negative rates of growth of productivity (see Ben-David, 1998). In an open-economy setting, with no restrictions on capital mobility, we should expect to see, *ceteris paribus*, capital flowing from rich to poor countries, attracted by higher potential returns, thereby accelerating the process of capital accumulation. However, poor infrastructure, high rates of corruption and political insta-bility, by lowering the risk-adjusted rate of return to capital, discourages FDI flows. Therefore there is little in Africa's current dynamics that pro-motes an escape from poverty.

Another poverty-trap mechanism arises from the operation of financial markets in poor countries. Credit and insurance markets are plagued by informational imperfections (Stiglitz, 2002b). Risk-averse lenders require collateral before they are willing to make loans and the poor obviously lack assets which they can use as collateral. However, Hernando De Soto (2000) has estimated that 'at least $9.3 trillion' worth of assets in the form of real estate are 'held but not legally owned by the poor in the Third World'. The vast majority of the poor in developing countries 'do not have access to a legal property rights system that represents their assets in a manner that makes them widely transferable and fungible'. The vast potential of this 'dead capital' cannot be activated so long as the conservative legal estab-lishment is more interested in preserving the *status quo* rather than igniting the latent fires of entrepreneurship that remain untapped. 'The cities of the Third World and the former communist countries are teeming with entre-preneurs' (De Soto, 2000). The poor, therefore, remain 'credit constrained' and unable to take advantage of income-generating opportunities that nat-urally emerge in market economies. As Scully (1988) highlights, the 'politi-cal, social, legal, and economic framework of society defines what resources can be owned, who can own them, and how they can be employed'.

Poverty traps also emerge as a result of inefficient institutions that are 'created and perpetuated by those with political power' (Azariadis and Stachurski, 2005; see also Engerman and Sokoloff, 2000; Acemoglu and Robinson, 2006a, 2006b; Graham and Temple, 2006). For example, the current military elite in Burma have little incentive to engage in meaning-ful reforms that would promote development, as such a process would undermine their power and economic status.

Sachs et al. (2004) believe that the solution to sub-Saharan Africa's poverty trap lies in the initiation of a 'big push' on the investment front leading to a 'step' increase in underlying productivity. Given the nature and dynamics of the poverty trap, this big push requires substantial external assistance in the form of foreign aid.

Sachs et al. (2004) utilise modified versions of the Solow neoclassical growth model to support their case for more foreign aid. The Solow (1956, 1957) growth model is built around the neoclassical aggregate pro-duction function equation (2.14) and focuses on the proximate causes of growth:

$$Y = A_t F(K, L) \qquad (2.14)$$

where $Y$ is real output, $K$ is capital, $L$ is the labour input and $A_t$ is a measure of technology (i.e. the way that inputs to the production function can be transformed into output), which is exogenous and taken simply to depend on time. Sometimes, $A_t$ is called 'total factor productivity'. It is important to be clear what the assumption of exogenous technology means in the Solow model. In the neoclassical theory of growth, technology is assumed to be a public good. Applied to the world economy, this means that every country is assumed to share the same stock of knowledge which is freely available to all; that is, all countries have access to the same production function. The aggregate production function given by equation (2.14) is assumed to be 'well behaved', that is, it satisfies the following three 'Inada' conditions (see Inada, 1963; Barro and Sala-i-Martin, 2003). First, for all values of $K > 0$ and $L > 0$, $F(\bullet)$ exhibits positive but diminishing marginal returns with respect to both capital and labour; that is, $\partial F/\partial K > 0$, $\partial^2 F/\partial K^2 < 0$, $\partial F/\partial L > 0$, and $\partial^2 F/\partial L^2 < 0$. Second, the production function exhibits constant returns to scale such that $F(\lambda K, \lambda L) = \lambda Y$; that is, raising inputs by $\lambda$ will also increase aggregate output by $\lambda$. Letting $\lambda = 1/L$ yields $Y/L = A_t F(K/L, 1/L)$. This assumption allows equation (2.14) to be written down in intensive form as equation (2.15), where $y =$ output per worker ($Y/L$) and $k =$ capital per worker ($K/L$):

$$y = A_t f(k), \quad \text{where } f'(k) > 0, \quad \text{and } f''(k) < 0 \text{ for all } k \qquad (2.15)$$

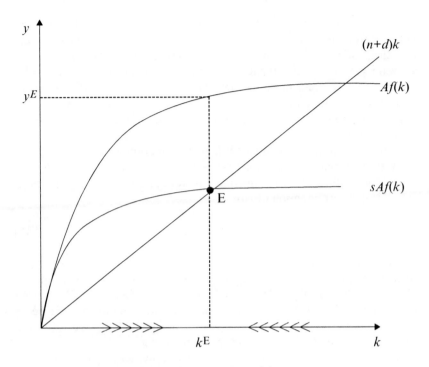

*Figure 2.13   The standard Solow growth model*

Equation (2.15) states that, for a given technology ($A_t$), output per worker is a positive function of the capital–labour ratio and exhibits diminishing returns. The key assumption of constant returns to scale implies that the economy is sufficiently large that any Smithian gains from further division of labour and specialisation have already been exhausted so that the size of the economy, in terms of the labour force, has no influence on output per worker. Third, as the capital–labour ratio approaches infinity ($k \to \infty$), the marginal product of capital ($MPK$) approaches zero; as the capital–labour ratio approaches zero the marginal product of capital tends towards infinity ($MPK \to \infty$).

Figure 2.13 shows an intensive form of the neoclassical aggregate production function that satisfies the above conditions. As the diagram illustrates, for a given technology, any country that increases its capital–labour ratio (more equipment per worker) will have a higher output per worker. However, because of diminishing returns, the impact on output per worker resulting from capital accumulation per worker (capital deepening) will continuously decline. The slope of the production function measures the marginal product of capital, where $MPK = f(k+1) - f(k)$, so in the Solow model, for a given technology, the *MPK* should be much higher in developing economies compared to developed economies (note how in Figure 2.13 the production function *Af(k)* is very steep near the origin). Thus for a given increase in *k*, the impact on *y* will be much greater where capital is relatively scarce, than in economies where capital is relatively abundant. That is, the accumulation of capital should have a much more dramatic impact on labour productivity in developing countries compared to developed countries.

How does capital accumulate? Where *s* = the domestic savings rate, *n* = the rate of population growth, $\delta$ = the rate of depreciation, and *dk/dt* = capital deepening, the fundamental differential equation of the Solow model is given by equation (2.16):

$$dk/dt = sAf(k) - (n + \delta)k \qquad (2.16)$$

The capital-widening term $(n + \delta)k$ indicates the investment (saving) per worker necessary to hold the capital–labour ratio constant (see Snowdon and Vane, 2005). In the Solow model, as long as $sAf(k) > (n + \delta)k$, output per worker will grow. When $sAf(k) = (n + \delta)k$, the economy has reached a steady-state equilibrium, shown as point E in Figure 2.13. In equilibrium capital per worker is $k^E$ and output per worker is $y^E$.

Sachs et al. argue that the neoclassical growth model presented in Figure 2.13 is a special case, and the actual behaviour of an economy at very low levels of output per worker is very different from the one portrayed in the above model in three important ways:

1.  While in the conventional Solow model the *MPK* is nearly infinite at very low levels of the capital–labour ratio, in reality, because production processes require a 'minimum threshold of capital', *MPK* is also low in poor countries. Therefore, without the presence of basic infrastructure (roads, human capital etc.), the productivity of small increments of *k* will be negligible. The Solow model with a minimum capital threshold is illustrated in Figure 2.14. Note that *dk/dt* only becomes positive above point $k^T$, and that at low levels of *k* there are increasing returns to capital accumulation due to a non-convexity in the production function.
2.  As shown in Figure 2.15, when *k* is very low, the saving rate is likely to be low or even negative. Very poor people need to consume all of their income just to survive. With $sAf(k)$ less steep than $(n + \delta)k$ at low levels of *k*; *dk/dt* is again negative below point $k^T$.
3.  A third factor likely to prevent capital accumulation at low levels of *k* is rapid population growth. There is a strong correlation between low

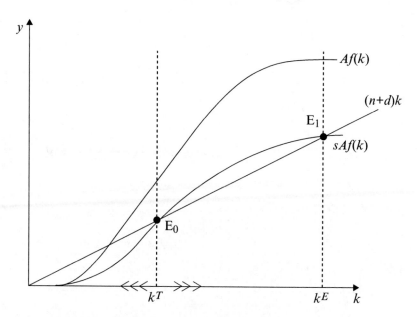

*Figure 2.14 The Solow model with a minimum capital stock threshold*

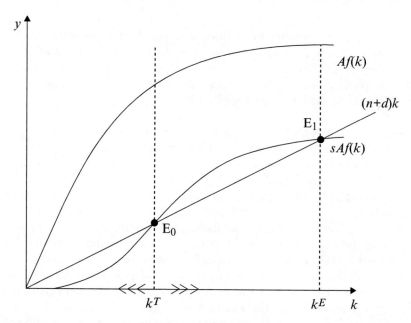

*Figure 2.15 The Solow model with a savings trap*

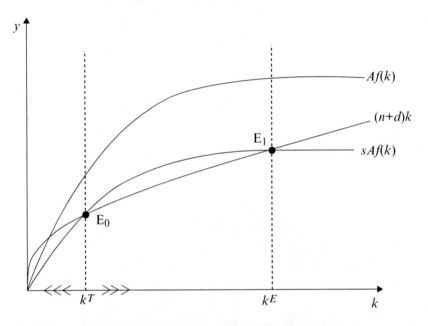

*Figure 2.16    The Solow model with a demographic trap*

income and fertility rates, and poor people, for perfectly rational reasons, aim to have large numbers of children (see Leibenstein, 1974; Lee, 2003). Figure 2.16 illustrates a Solow model with a demographic trap. Note how the $(n+\delta)k$ function is very steep at low levels of $k$. Therefore $dk/dt$ is again negative below $k^T$.

Sachs et al. (2004) believe that in very poor countries the 'capital thresholds, savings traps, and demographic traps' are all likely to interact to produce a powerful 'poverty trap'.

While the arguments of Jeffrey Sachs have provided a rallying point for the pro-aid lobby, many economists remain unconvinced that foreign aid is either necessary or sufficient for successful growth and development. Both Easterly (2006b) and Kraay and Raddatz (2005) find little evidence supporting the existence of poverty traps. In their extensive survey of the poverty trap literature, Azariadis and Stachurski (2005) note that there are a large number of self-reinforcing mechanisms that can interact and potentially cause a poverty trap. Policy shocks will have 'large and permanent effects if one-off interventions can cause the formation of new and better equilibria'. However, they also recognise that engineering such an outcome to achieve more efficient equilibria in practice is very problematic given the perverse influence of the prevailing structure of incentives in many developing countries, together with problems of corruption and the lack of information facing policy makers.

Both Milton Friedman (1958) and Peter Bauer (1972) have been major critics of foreign aid from the liberal free-market perspective. In contrast, neo-Marxists have always argued that foreign aid is a form of neo-imperialism (Hayter, 1971). Even those economists committed to the use of foreign aid accept that the motives of the donors are most often driven by self-interested political foreign policy considerations. For example, Hollis Chenery (1964) openly admitted that 'the main objective of foreign assistance, as of many other tools of foreign policy, is to produce the kind of political and economic environment in the world in which the United States can best pursue its own social goals'. There is also little reason to doubt that the aid policies of the USSR were dictated by political self-interest during the cold war era.

While there is considerable variation in the behaviour of aid donors, the research of Alesina and Dollar (2000) confirms that the criteria for bilateral aid allocations are dominated as much by political and strategic considerations as they are by considerations of economic development. Alesina and Weder (2002) also show that there is no evidence that less corrupt governments receive more foreign aid than more corrupt governments and Svensson (2000) provides evidence that inflows of foreign aid are associated with increased corruption and rent-seeking behaviour (profitable opportunities arising from market distortions), especially in countries where there are competing social groups.

Adding to the critiques of Griffin (1970), and Griffin and Enos (1970), the research of Boone (1996) and Easterly (2003a) suggests that inflows of foreign aid have not raised growth rates in most recipient developing countries. Many economists therefore regard 'capital fundamentalism' and the 'aid-financed investment fetish', which dominated development thinking for much of the period after 1950, as having led policy makers up the wrong path in their 'elusive quest for growth' (King and Levine, 1994; Easterly et al., 2003). Indeed, Easterly (1999), a former World Bank economist, argues that the Harrod–Domar model is far from dead and still continues to exercise considerable influence on economists working within the major international financial institutions even if it died long ago in the academic literature. Easterly shows that economists working at the World Bank, the International Monetary Fund, the Inter-American Bank, the European Bank for Reconstruction and Development, and the International Labour Organisation still frequently employ the Harrod–Domar–Chenery–Strout methodology to calculate the investment and aid requirements needed in order for specific countries to achieve their growth targets. However,

Easterly argues that the evidence that aid flows into investment on a one-for-one basis, and that there is a fixed linear relationship between growth and investment in the short run, is 'soundly rejected'.

## 2.16   FOREIGN AID: A 'WEAPON OF MASS SALVATION'

As is evident from the previous discussion, the use of foreign aid to promote growth and development is a very controversial issue among economists. Radelet et al. (2005) distinguish three broad views on the relationship between foreign aid and economic growth which can be classified as follows: (i) the 'Optimists'; (ii) the 'Pessimists'; and (iii) the 'Conditional Optimists'.

*The Optimists*   Both the Pearson (1969) and Brandt (1980) reports took an optimistic view of the potential for foreign aid to promote growth and development. The idea, based on the Harrod–Domar growth model, that most developing countries are growth constrained due to a 'financing gap' that could most effectively be filled by foreign aid was conventional wisdom among the majority of development economists both within academia and among those working in the key international institutions such as the World Bank and the IMF. This was especially the case during the 1950s and 1960s (see Chenery and Strout, 1966; Easterly, 2006a; Easterly et al., 2003).

*The Pessimists*   Economists such as Milton Friedman (1958) and Peter Bauer (1972) argued that aid fails to increase economic growth, and may even reduce it, because of its adverse influence on the quality of governance and the power of government bureaucracies, the encouragement of wasteful investment projects, corruption, the suppression of local entrepreneurial talent, the undermining of incentives, and the enrichment of entrenched elite groups who have little interest in economic progress. In the early 1970s economists such as Griffin and Enos (1970) also argued that increased aid flows could reduce both public and private sector saving (see Griffin, 1970; White, 1992; Boone, 1996). More recently Easterly has been an eloquent critic of both the theoretical underpinnings of the case for aid as well as the empirical support (Easterly, 2003a). In his review of Jeffrey Sachs's influential book, *The End of Poverty*, Easterly rejects what he refers to as the 'top down', 'mega reform', planned administrative approach to solving the problem of world poverty involving large increases in the flow of foreign aid. Instead, Easterly (2006b) advocates a piecemeal gradualist 'bottom up' approach in the spirit of Edmund Burke and Karl Popper.

However, Easterly does accept that aid *could* be useful in achieving more modest objectives than 'take-offs' into 'self-sustaining growth' *if* incentives structures at ground level were improved and the existing bureaucratic flaws within the international aid agencies could be corrected (Easterly, 2003b, 2006a).

*The Conditional Optimists*   Economists such as Jeffrey Sachs, Joseph Stiglitz, Nicholas Stern, Craig Burnside and David Dollar are conditional optimists who support an aid package directed at those countries that display at least a tolerable level of good governance and a commitment to internationally agreed development objectives. Sachs explicitly recognises that there is little the outside world can do to help a country governed by an elite that has no interest in progress (Sachs, 2005a). The influential study by Burnside and Dollar (2000) concludes that aid can stimulate growth in countries with good policies and institutions but is unlikely to do so other-wise. More recent research by Radelet et al. (2005) distinguishes between three types of aid: (i) aid for disaster and emergency relief; (ii) 'late-impact' aid for health and education projects; and (iii) 'early-impact' aid for infra-structure projects. Obviously there will be a negative statistical relationship between aid for disaster relief and growth, and aid for health and educa-tion projects is only likely to affect growth in the long run. Only 'early-impact' aid is likely to stimulate growth in the short term, and therefore econometric studies that lump all aid flows together and then attempt to identify the impact of aid on growth are inevitably fundamentally flawed. Radelet et al. (2005) conclude that 'while growth in SSA has been disap-pointing, it would have been worse in the absence of this kind [early impact] of aid'. Therefore, for the conditional optimists the 'intense pessimism on aid effectiveness expressed by some analysts appears to be too strong'.

## 2.17   CONCLUSION

At the heart of the global development problem of the twenty-first century is the sub-Saharan Africa growth tragedy. If the majority of sub-Saharan Africa countries are to break free from their poverty, a strategy to raise productivity on a sustainable basis is required since at the heart of extreme poverty is the problem of low productivity. Moreover, as discussed in Chapter 1, the only meaningful definition of the 'competitiveness' of a nation is national productivity performance. Table 2.5 shows the competitiveness rankings for a selection of developed and developing countries from various parts of the globe as well as data on 'ease of doing business', corruption per-ceptions, political freedom and economic freedom. Unsurprisingly, most sub-Saharan African countries are ranked near the bottom in these indicators. For example, the full data set on economic freedom for sub-Saharan Africa shows that out of 42 sub-Saharan African countries, 30 are classified as 'mostly unfree' and one (Zimbabwe) as 'repressed'. Political rights and civil liberties, whilst improving in most of sub-Saharan Africa, are also far from satisfactory.

To overcome many of the constraints on productivity, sub-Saharan Africa will require a sustained programme of investment and improved governance. Accordingly, the 2005 World Bank report, *A Better Investment Climate for Everyone*, highlights the need for governments to improve their countries' 'investment climate' by improving the microeconomic environment in order to increase the opportunities and incentives for enterprises, both domestic and foreign, to invest productively. During the last decade there has been a growing recognition of the importance of improving microeconomic fundamentals, such as reducing transaction costs, risk and barriers to competition, if a good investment climate is to be created that is conducive to sustainable growth and poverty reduction. However, the state has an important role to play, not only in improving the quality of governance, but also in focusing public investment in the key areas of health, education and basic infrastructure. While Sachs rejects inward-looking development strategies based on heavy state involvement, he also emphasises that a major lesson from twentieth-century economic history is that a state's activities should match its capabilities. Following the Ricardian principle of comparative advantage, an effective state will be one that focuses on getting the fundamentals right. Because the activities of the state and the market are complementary, since markets cannot function without the necessary institutional foundations, neither *laissez-faire* nor *dirigisme* are appropriate frameworks for a successful development strategy. 'The idea of a mixed economy is possibly the most valuable heritage that the twentieth century bequeaths to the twenty-first in the realm of economic policy' (Rodrik, 2001a, p. 1). The countries with the most successful economies tend to be those with a strong but focused state (Rodrik, 2001a; see also Krueger, 1990; Sachs, 1999; World Bank, 1997, 2002; Snowdon, 2001b; Stiglitz and Yusuf, 2001; Fukuyama, 2004; Lindert, 2004; Stern et al., 2005; Tanzi, 2005; Snower and Merkl, 2006).

While the 'East Asian miracle' suggests that the key factors contributing to rapid growth and development are the maintenance of macroeconomic stability, a strong but focused government, global economic integration, high rates of productive investment in physical and human capital, and sound public institutions, as Rodrik and Haussman (2003) and Easterly (2006a) argue, economic development is largely a process of 'self-discovery' and the removal of economic and political barriers. Rodrik et al. (2006), in their analysis of growth diagnostics, suggest the following careful gradualist approach to encouraging successful growth and development:

1. identify barriers to growth;
2. select the most important constraints/barriers facing a particular country;
3. identify the optimal sequencing of reforms;
4. implement policies to remove barriers.

The work of Easterly (2001a) has reminded economists of the many wrong turns taken by well-meaning development analysts in the past. This point is also emphasised by Pritchett and Lindauer (2002) in their discussion of the evolution of 'big ideas' in development economics. They conclude as follows:

> Today we stand on the shoulders of giants. But in a non-experimental science like economics, giants face backward, examining the past for hints about the future. The road to development is extremely complex, and the ultimate guide to that path must therefore be more complex than an arrow pointing confidently in one direction.

# 3. The rise and fall of the socialist system and the trials of transition

it is an irrefutable fact that the *existing* (or, heretofore existing) socialism lost the race against the *existing* (or, heretofore existing) capitalism. This is not a value judgement; it is an observable, statistically accountable fact.

János Kornai (2006, p. 211).

it is not sufficient that the state of affairs which we seek to promote should be better than the state of affairs which preceded it; it must be sufficiently better to make up for the evils of the transition.

John Maynard Keynes (quoted in Sidelsky, 1992).

I am not a die hard capitalist. I do not view capitalism as a creed. Much more important to me are freedom, compassion for the poor, respect for the social contract, and equal opportunity. But for the moment, to achieve those goals, capitalism is the only game in town. It is the only system we know that provides us with the tools required to create massive surplus value.

Hernando De Soto (2000, p. 228).

## 3.1 INTRODUCTION

In John Maynard Keynes's undergraduate essay, 'The Political Doctrines of Edmund Burke', written at the beginning of the twentieth century, he endorses the need for exercising extreme caution when the question of radical change is on the political agenda (Skidelsky, 1992). Twice during the twentieth century we have witnessed radical change on such an enormous scale that the outcome inevitably contained many surprises. To many commentators the rise and fall of the socialist system was the defining feature of the world economy during the last century. For example, Kornai (1992a, p. xxi) argues that:

The development and the break-up and decline of the socialist system amount to the most important political and economic phenomena of the twentieth century.

The utopian vision of socialism, held with firm conviction by the Bolshevik revolutionaries in 1917, failed to materialise. Furthermore, as conceived by

Bukharin and Preobrazhensky (1972) in their essay, 'The ABC of Communism', socialism could never have succeeded (Nove and Nuti, 1972; Nove, 1983). However, while many Western Sovietologists, including Abram Bergson and Padma Desai, had commented on the increasingly severe economic problems being encountered by the socialist economies, the timing and speed of the untangling of the great twentieth-century socialist experiment were unexpected. I suspect that many of my generation, who grew up in the era of cold war politics, often momentarily forget that the Soviet Union no longer exists!

Since 1989, a large number of countries have launched themselves into a second great experiment, that of establishing a stable market economy in conjunction with the replacement of communist dictatorship with liberal democracy. This great transition experiment is historically unprecedented. The fall of the Berlin Wall in November 1989 symbolically marked the beginning of an extraordinary historical period of reform, turmoil, success and failure. Just as there was no pre-existing Marxian model of a socialist economy from which the Bolsheviks could draw inspiration in 1917, in 1989 there was no pre-existing theory of the transition process to guide the reformers (Roland, 2001). Neither could the reformers look for guidance to any previous transition experiments on the scale being contemplated. As a result, the strategies and policies adopted by the transition countries have varied considerably across countries, as have the outcomes. Not surprisingly, the great transition experiment immediately became, and has remained, a fertile ground for research and controversy among economists.

In this chapter we will review the legacy of Marx and some of the important events of the twentieth century, leading to the eventual collapse of the great socialist experiment and the subsequent trials of transition, as background to the interviewees' comments on issues relating to the political economy of the transition process (see the interviews with Padma Desai, Stanley Fischer, Jànos Kornai, and Jeffrey Sachs).

## 3.2   THE LEGACY OF MARX

Karl Marx shared Adam Smith's (1776) view that capitalism was a highly productive system and duly credited the bourgeoisie with bringing about the Industrial Revolution. In their *Communist Manifesto* of 1848, Karl Marx and Friedrich Engels conceded that the capitalist bourgeoisie 'has accomplished wonders far surpassing Egyptian pyramids, Roman aqueducts, and Gothic cathedrals' and 'has created more massive and more colossal productive forces than have all preceding generations together'. More recently, Baumol (2002, p. viii) has repackaged this observation:

what is clear to historians and laypersons alike is that capitalism is unique in the extraordinary growth record is has been able to achieve in its recurring industrial revolutions that have produced an outpouring of material wealth unlike anything previously seen in human history.

However, Marx's (1867) analysis and vision of the foundations and long-run dynamics of capitalism led him to the conclusion that this system, driven by the quest for 'surplus value' (profits), was exploitative, and thereby fundamentally flawed, particularly in terms of its distributional consequences and long-term implications for working-class living standards. Building on David Ricardo's (1817) labour theory of value, Marx's analysis identified what he believed to be the key characteristics of the capitalist system: creation of profits (surplus value) through exploitation of the working class (proletariat); the 'anarchy' of the market; destructive competition leading to the concentration of capital into fewer and fewer hands; substitution of capital for labour in the production process; a 'reserve army' of unemployed workers; increasingly severe business cycles; vast inequalities of income and wealth; the inevitable 'immiseration' of the proletariat and, in consequence, social and political revolution leading to socialism, and ultimately communism. The interaction of these forces is illustrated in Figure 3.1.

According to Marx, these forces are endogenous, and hence unavoidable, features of the capitalist system. For example, a significant reserve army of unemployed is necessary under capitalism to help keep wages increases in check, thereby preserving the share of profits in national income, and recurrent business-cycle crises are expressions of the 'fundamental contradictions' of the capitalist system (much later, Michal Kalecki used this insight to formulate a Marxo-Keynesian theory of the political business cycle: see Kalecki, 1943). To Marx, this unacceptable waste of human resources was a key defect of capitalism. Consequently, Marx predicted the inevitable and, to him, welcome collapse of capitalism, driven to destruction by the 'laws of motion' of its own internal contradictions. The destiny of capitalism was chaos and collapse, not Adam Smith's vision of progress and social harmony.

A key prediction derived from Marx's analysis in *Das Kapital* is the impoverishment and immiseration of the proletariat. Although the subsistence wage doctrine was propounded by Marx and Engels in their *Communist Manifesto* (1848), according to Blaug (1997) the notion that Marx continued to pronounce a theory of growing material poverty (absolute impoverishment) of the working class 'is just folklore Marxism'. Although under capitalism the real wages of workers may rise beyond the subsistence level, the quality of life of the proletariat would suffer from the

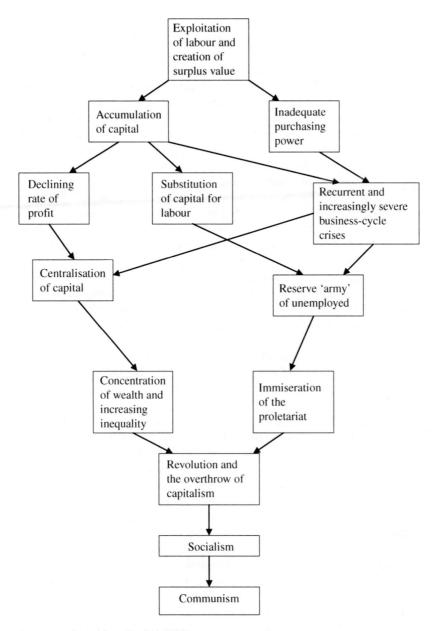

*Source:*   Adapted from Fusfeld (1982).

*Figure 3.1    Marx's theory of capitalist development, crisis and collapse*

growing misery, mental degradation and brutality arising from the constant toil involved with commodity production. Also, with the failure of wages to rise in line with productivity, the relative position of the working class (share of wages in national income) would be eroded.

History has not been kind to either the absolute or relative impoverishment hypotheses. Gregory Clark's (2005) recent research confirms that by 1867, at the time of publication of the first volume of *Das Kapital*, the subsistence wage doctrine was 'increasingly remote from English reality'. Clark estimates that hourly real wages for building workers grew at a rate of 0.9 per cent per year in the period 1820–60, and 1.3 per cent per year between 1800 and 2004 (see also Lindert and Williamson, 1983; Feinstein, 1998). George Boyer (1998) makes a similar point with respect to Marx and Engels and the contents of their highly influential *Communist Manifesto*, published in 1848. Marx and Engels asserted that the real wage of the emerging industrial proletarian was determined by 'the means of subsistence' that workers require 'for maintenance, and for the propagation of his race'. However, as Boyer argues, the *Communist Manifesto* was a 'period piece', a document belonging to the 'hungry 1840s'. It is also a document that reflects Engels's inside knowledge of the Dickensian conditions that characterised the cotton-textile industry of south Lancashire and the 'social and political conditions in Manchester in the 1840s'. According to Boyer, Marx and Engels reached 'overly pessimistic conclusions' about the condition and prospects for the working class in England largely because their ideas were conditioned by the circumstances of the hungry forties and because they 'focussed their attention on the cotton industry', which was particularly badly hit by the depressions of 1841–42 and 1847–48. Marx and Engels were also unable to contemplate the possibility of an increasingly interventionist stance taken by government, reflected in the stream of economic, social and political reforms introduced in the nineteenth century (e.g. the Factory Acts of 1833, 1844, 1847, 1850, 1853, 1867, 1874 and 1878, and the 1867 Reform Act doubled the urban electorate by extending the vote to the higher wage members of the working class; see Boyer, 1998). While 1848 was a year of revolution in many European countries, including Prussia, France, Italy, Austria and Poland, there to it seems that unfavourable short-term economic conditions, the economic crisis of 1845–48 (food shortages and industrial slump) on the Continent, were a more important contributory factor than a surge of radical democratic political ideas (Berger and Spoerer, 2001).

During the twentieth century, sustained economic growth, combined with further social, economic and political reforms, transformed the lives of the 'proletariat' in the mature capitalist economies to an extent that would have greatly surprised Marx (see Table 2.1). Galor and Moav (2006) hypothesise that the demise of the nineteenth century's class structure throughout Europe was 'orchestrated by the capitalists' themselves, who increasingly understood and appreciated the importance of 'Das Human Capital' (skilled labour) in maintaining their profits. Galor and Moav argue that 'the process of capital accumulation gradually intensified the importance of skilled labour in the production process and generated an incentive for investment in human capital' and support for the establishment of publicly funded education.

Along with Joseph Schumpeter (1942), Marx predicted the ultimate demise of capitalism and the triumph of socialism. However, to Marx it was 'self-evident that the socialist order would first take hold in the most highly developed of the capitalist countries' (Kornai, 1992a). On this basis the first communist-led revolutions should have occurred in the leading industrial nations of the late nineteenth and early twentieth century, namely, the USA, Germany, and especially 'England'. For example, we find Marx arguing in 1870 that 'England alone can serve as the lever for a serious economic revolution', because it is 'the only country where the capitalist form . . . now embraces virtually the whole of production . . . It is the only country where the class struggle and the organisation of the working class by trade unions have acquired a certain degree of maturity' (Kornai, 1992a, p. 19). However, the history of the twentieth century confirms that socialism has not been installed as the result of purely internal forces in any developed capitalist country, although several relatively mature capitalist economies in Eastern Europe had socialism imposed on them by the Soviet Union after 1945, for example Czechoslovakia, East Germany, Hungary and Poland. As Kornai (2000a) notes, the transition to socialism is not a spontaneous organic development arising from endogenous forces; rather it is 'imposed on society by the communist party with brutal force, when it gains power'. The first successful communist revolution occurred in Russia in November 1917 (October according to the Russian calendar). At that point Russia was still a predominantly semi-feudal agrarian economy, and certainly could not be reasonably defined as a mature capitalist economy. For example, Davies (1998) notes that on the eve of the First World War the agricultural sector in Russia accounted for over half the national income, and 75 per cent of employment.

Could Russia have taken an alternative path? Following the Stolypin reforms of 1906 and 1910, a spurt of economic development occurred, and, according to Desai (2006a), if 'the war had not intervened and the Bolsheviks had not seized power, the economic momentum and institutional improvements could have continued'. The Imperial government was initially overthrown by the 'bourgeois' revolution of February 1917, and the newly formed provisional government, led by Alexander Kerensky, had liberal-democratic aspirations. The fragile new government also sought to establish a market economy with a strong role for the state in order to complete the industrialisation process. However, the fragile provisional government was overthrown in the Bolshevik-led 'October Revolution' and following the Bolshevik victory in the ensuing Civil War, Russia's fate was sealed for the next 70 years. As Kornai (2006) notes, the creation and eventual expansion of the socialist system represented a major deviation from the main direction of Western history and civilisation which during the twentieth century was towards the expansion of capitalism and democracy.

## 3.3   THE RISE AND FALL OF THE SOCIALIST SYSTEM AND THE SOVIET UNION, 1917–91

There is no question that the Bolshevik revolution, inspired by the ideas of Marx, initiated the 'most important socio-economic experiment of the twentieth century' (Gregory and Harrison, 2005). In the most-quoted passage from the *General Theory*, Keynes (1936, pp. 383–4) argued that 'the ideas of economists and political philosophers, both when they are right and when they are wrong, are more powerful than is commonly understood . . . it is ideas, not vested interests, which are dangerous for good or evil'. There is no better illustration of this point than the impact that Marx's ideas had on the political, social and economic history of the twentieth century. After 1917, the ideas of Marx, in the hands of Marxists, changed the course of world history. In a strong statement Dillon and Wykoff (2002) conclude, the great socialist experiment 'was no more than a tragic detour that contributed nothing positive to humankind's evolution'. Curtois et al. (1999) suggest that communism has been responsible for 100 million deaths worldwide, while for the Soviet Union/Russia, Davies (1998) estimates that population losses, from premature death and the birth deficit resulting from war, famine and oppression, to have been 74 million for the period 1914–45.

Before proceeding further, we need to be clear about what me mean by 'socialist system'. In what follows we adopt Kornai's (2000a) 'parsimonious minimalist' system-specific characterisation of 'the socialist system' where the following main attributes have been historically observed:

1.   the Communist Party (Marxist–Leninist) has undivided political power;
2.   a dominant position for state and quasi-state ownership;
3.   a preponderance of bureaucratic coordination of economic activity;
4.   the 'soft budget constraint syndrome', weak responsiveness to prices and a 'sellers' market';
5.   'chronic' shortages (hidden unemployment and suppressed inflation).

Figure 3.2 illustrates the key characteristics that, according to Kornai, distinguish socialist and capitalist systems, and Table 3.1 indicates that, by 1987, some 34 per cent of the world's population were living in 'socialist' countries, as defined by Kornai. This compares with 22 per cent of the current (2006) world's population living in the five remaining socialist countries (China, Vietnam, Laos, North Korea and Cuba), with China alone accounting for 20 per cent.

As is well known, Marx and Engels left no clear unambiguous blueprint of how to run a socialist system (Nove and Nuti, 1972). Indeed, as Alec Nove (1983) argues, 'Marx had little to say about the economics of socialism'. Kornai (1992a) also writes, 'The bulk of Marx's scientific work was concerned with capitalism; he wrote little about the future socialist society' and only a 'sketchy' blueprint can be compiled from 'scattered remarks'. Therefore, the new revolutionary leadership in Russia, the first socialist country, had to improvise, building a new order on the ruins of a collapsed semi-feudal system (Dillon and Wykoff, 2002).

In the initial period of War Communism, June 1918–March 1921, an attempt was made to launch a command economy with predominantly social ownership of the means of production. During this period the state took control of land, the banking system and trade, and it was decreed that all large- (1918) and small- (1920) scale industry was to be nationalised. However, in response to a profound economic crisis, War Communism was abandoned in 1921. In its place, Lenin launched the New Economic Policy (NEP), which represented a 'temporary strategic retreat from the socialist agenda' and return to a mixed economy (Rosser and Rosser, 2004). The NEP allowed for a limited restoration of markets, although foreign trade and the commanding heights of the economy (large-scale industry and the major banking institutions) remained in the hands of the state (Davies, 1998). Although the NEP provided the framework for 'an impressive recovery' (Desai, 2006a) of the economy, under Stalin's leadership, the NEP was eventually aborted and replaced in 1928 with 'classical socialism' (Kornai, 1992a).

The main elements of the Soviet Union's development strategy were laid out during the 1920s and early 1930s. Throughout the 1920s, as Desai (2006a) notes, great debates 'raged over the issue of an ideal investment strategy' aimed at transforming the Soviet Union into a powerful industrial economy. The so-called 'industrialisation debate' that raged among Bolshevik theorists was actually concerned with how best to extract the agricultural surplus in order to finance industrialisation (Erlich, 1960). On the conservative wing, Nikolai Bukharin argued the case for a 'balanced growth strategy' whereby the agricultural sector would supply industry with the needed raw materials for manufacturing, as well as providing food

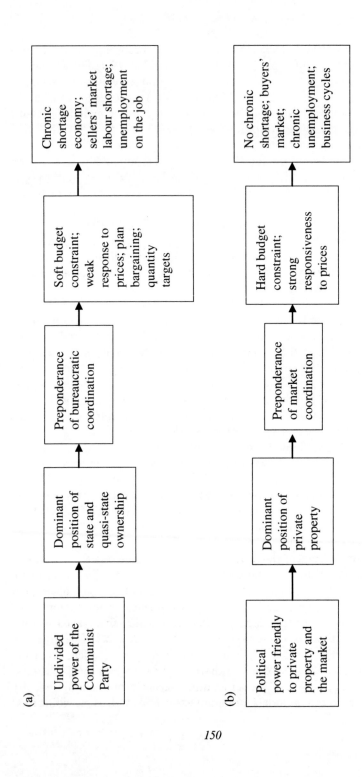

(a)

(b)

*Source:* Adapted from Kornai (2000a).

*Figure 3.2   Stylised model of the socialist (a) and capitalist (b) systems*

*Table 3.1    The socialist countries[1] in 1987*

| Socialist countries 1987 | Year Communist Party attained power | Population (millions) 1986 | Year communist dictatorship ended | Freedom House Index of Political Rights and Civil Liberties[2] 2006 |
|---|---|---|---|---|
| Russia/Soviet Union | 1917 | 281.1 | 1991 | Various[3] |
| Mongolia | 1921 | 2.0 | 1990 | Free |
| Albania | 1944 | 3.0 | 1991 | Partly free |
| Yugoslavia | 1945 | 23.3 | 1992 | Various[4] |
| Bulgaria | 1947 | 9.0 | 1990 | Free |
| Czechoslovakia | 1948 | 15.5 | 1990 | Free[5] |
| Hungary | 1948 | 10.6 | 1989 | Free |
| Poland | 1948 | 37.5 | 1989 | Free |
| Romania | 1948 | 22.9 | 1989 | Free |
| **Korea Dem. Rep.** | **1948** | **20.9** | **Ongoing** | **Not free** |
| **China** | **1949** | **1054** | **Ongoing** | **Not free** |
| Germany Dem. Rep. | 1949 | 16.6 | 1990 | Free |
| Vietnam (North) | 1954 | / | / | / |
| **Vietnam N. & S.** | **1976** | **63.3** | **Ongoing** | **Not free** |
| **Cuba** | **1959** | **10.2** | **Ongoing** | **Not free** |
| Congo | 1963 | 2.0 | 1992 | Partly free |
| Somalia | 1969 | 5.5 | 1991 | Not free |
| South Yemen | 1969 | 2.2 | 1990 | Partly free |
| Benin | 1972 | 4.2 | 1989 | Free |
| Ethiopia | 1974 | 43.5 | 1991 | Partly free |
| Angola | 1975 | 9.0 | 1992 | Not free |
| Kampuchea/Cambodia | 1975 | 7.7 | 1989 | Not free |
| **Laos** | **1975** | **3.7** | **Ongoing** | **Not free** |
| Mozambique | 1975 | 14.2 | 1990 | Partly free |
| Afghanistan | 1978 | 18.6 | 1992 | Partly free |
| Nicaragua | 1979 | 3.4 | 1990 | Partly free |
| All socialist countries | | 1683.9 (34)[6] | | |

*Notes:*
[1] Kornai (1992a) notes that the 'adherents of the Communist party in power never referred to their own system as communist'. Communism refers to 'the unattainable Utopian society of the future, in which all will share in social production according to their needs'.
[2] Freedom in the World 2006, Freedom House, http://www.freedomhouse.org/.
[3] See Table 3.6.
[4] Serbia–Montenegro, free; Slovenia, free; Croatia, free; Bosnia–Herzegovina, partly free; Macedonia, partly free.
[5] Both the Czech and Slovak Republics are classified as free.
[6] Percentage of total world population. Communist states occupied 31 per cent of the world's land area.

*Source:*   The 1987 classification is based on Kornai (1992a).

supplies to the expanding urban population. Agricultural exports would also be a major source of finance for imports of modern machinery. The Bukharin strategy required that the *kulaks* (the conservative 'rich' peasant class created by the Stolypin reforms of 1906) should be encouraged, via market incentives, to increase production. Meanwhile the industrial sector should be encouraged to help agriculture modernise by supplying machinery and fertilisers. Balanced growth implied a 'political alliance' (*smychka*) between the peasants and urban proletariat (see Lavigne, 1995). Opposing Bukharin were a leftist group, led by Leon Trotsky and economist Evgeny Preobrazhensky, who advocated a strategy of 'unbalanced growth' via 'primitive accumulation'. This strategy involved the extraction of agricultural surplus through forced collectivisation of agriculture, taxation and 'non-equivalent exchange', whereby peasants would be required to sell their output for low prices while they would have to pay high prices for industrial goods (Preobrazhensky, 1926; Lavigne, 1995). In effect, collectivisation was to be used as a crude instrument of tax collection (Olson, 2000). Since the *kulaks* would obviously oppose such a collectivisation strategy, their fate was sealed once Stalin threw his support behind the more radical leftist group. The chaos caused by forced collectivisation of agriculture led directly to the man-made famine of 1933 (see also Noland et al., 2001).

The classical command-economy model of 'socialism in one country' had one major objective: rapid catch-up with the major capitalist economies via accelerated economic growth and industrialisation. In 1931, Stalin warned that 'We are fifty or a hundred years behind the advanced countries. We must make good the distance in ten years. Either we do or they will crush us' (see Ofer, 1987). The growth and industrialisation objectives were to be achieved through a series of five-year plans and a newly created Central Planning Board, known as Gosplan, was given the daunting responsibility of formulating and developing each plan. Stalin's strategy gave high priority to the output of producer (capital) and military goods, and implied a trajectory of 'unbalanced growth' (Desai, 2006a).

Recently released archive material relating to the Stalin era (1928–53) of classical socialism provides rich new evidence on the economic arrangements and functioning of a highly centralised command system led by a powerful dictator. In their review and assessment of this new information, Gregory and Harrison (2005) highlight many important insights, including:

1.  confirmation of the extreme overcentralisation of the command system; Stalin was caught in a 'dictator's curse', continually immersed in 'many more economic decisions than he wished';
2.  in the absence of the threat of war, Stalin's obsession was 'to maximise the economy's surplus' (output minus consumption) in order to foster

economic growth and 'super-industrialisation' through accumulation of capital;

3.  while Stalin sought to reduce workers' consumption through coercion, his fear that consumption might fall so low that it would stimulate unrest among the workers led to cyclical instability of investment;

4.  the creation of a surplus stimulated rent-seeking activity and the formation of special interest groups;

5.  Stalin's inability to commit to financial discipline created the 'soft budget constraint syndrome' (Kornai, 1986a); enterprises were not allowed to go bankrupt;

6.  the main flaws of a highly centralised command system became apparent 'almost immediately'; overwhelmed by unreliable distorted information, key decision makers resorted to 'rules of thumb', 'intuition, historical precedent, and common sense';

7.  'the attempt to transform *Homo economicus* into *Homo sovieticus* led to wage equalisation and declining productivity;

8.  Stalin firmly believed that 'a wide range of problems could be solved by force', as exemplified in the collectivisation of agriculture and elimination of the *kulaks*, the criminalisation of work place indiscipline, and extensive use of forced labour;

9.  the design of an efficient coercive system proved to be extremely problematic; ultimately the Gulag system was widely recognised to have failed in its objectives (Harrison, 2002); the new archive documents also show that the Gulag population 'was smaller than observers had previously guessed' and had a 'much higher turnover' of inmates;

10.  Stalin's 'Great Terror' of 1936–38 had a disastrous impact on productivity through its elimination of a 'generation of skilled and knowledgeable managers and technical staff, worsened labour discipline and damaged effort';

11.  the archives illustrate the accuracy of the Mises (1920) – Hayek (1935, 1945) critique of socialism, that central planning would inevitably lead to inefficient decision making due to insurmountable incentive and informational problems (Schroeder, 1991);

12.  despite the enormous limitations of the command system of economic organisation, the Soviet Union also registered several important and impressive achievements, notably: its ability to mobilise scarce resources in order to concentrate on a narrow range of well-defined objectives (Ericson, 1991); rapid (if distorted, costly and forced) industrialisation; significant improvements in the education and health of Soviet citizens; its remarkable ability, after devastating initial setbacks, to mobilise the resources necessary to defeat Nazi Germany in the 'Great Patriotic War', 1941–45; the rise to 'superpower' status after the

Second World War; the creation of 'modern nuclear and aerospace industries', culminating in the launch of the first-ever artificial earth satellite (*Sputnik*) in 1957, and the first manned orbital space flight by Yuri Gagarin in 1961.

Initially the Stalinist system led to rapid economic growth generated by very high rates of capital accumulation and, as Krugman (1994b) reminds us, during the 1950s, and even into the early 1960s, 'Western opinion leaders found themselves both impressed and frightened by the extraordinary growth rates achieved by a set of Eastern economies'. There was continuous serious political and economic debate about if, or even when, the Soviet Union would catch up and overtake the US economy. However, as soon became evident, Soviet growth was largely 'input-driven' and, as orthodox neoclassical growth theory predicts, growth based on accumulation is 'virtually certain' to slow down.

## 3.4   FROM 'GOLDEN AGE' GROWTH TO SLOWDOWN

During the period 1950–73 the world economy witnessed unparalleled rates of growth of per capita GDP. Table 3.2 contains Maddison's (2001) estimates for per capita growth GDP for the period 1820–1998 and, as is clearly evident, the 1950–73 era stands out in comparison to all other historical periods, either before or since. In particular, the growth achievements witnessed in the post-war Western European economy are so impressive that this period has been referred to as the 'golden age' (Crafts and Toniolo, 1996). Although Crafts and Toniolo view the 'golden age' as a 'distinctly European phenomenon', during this same period Japan's growth performance was nothing less than spectacular, and the growth 'miracle' also extended to Latin America, Asia, Africa and the centrally planned economies. Indeed, Ellman and Kontorovich (1992) refer to the 1950s as the 'golden age' of Soviet growth. Mazower (1998) recalls the observation by one Polish economist that 'State socialism was not a good idea badly implemented, but a bad idea which was implemented surprisingly well.' However, after 1973 there was a marked slowdown in growth, with the major OECD economies returning to growth rates more in line with the longer-run trend.

Ofer (1987) surveys estimates of Soviet growth rates of GNP, capital, population, GNP per capita and other key economic indicators. During the period 1928–85, from the beginning of Stalin's strategy of classical socialism until the election of Mikhail Gorbachev, the GNP growth rate of the

*Table 3.2    Growth of per capita GDP, world and major regions, 1820–1998*
         *(annual average compound growth rates)*

| Region | 1820–70 | 1870–1913 | 1913–50 | 1950–73 | 1973–98 |
|---|---|---|---|---|---|
| Western Europe | 0.95 | 1.32 | 0.76 | **4.08** | 1.78 |
| Western offshoots* | 1.42 | 1.81 | 1.55 | **2.44** | 1.94 |
| Japan | 0.19 | 1.48 | 0.89 | **8.05** | 2.34 |
| Asia (excluding Japan) | −0.11 | 0.38 | −0.02 | **2.92** | 3.54 |
| Latin America | 0.10 | 1.81 | 1.42 | **2.52** | 0.99 |
| **Eastern Europe and former USSR** | **0.64** | **1.15** | **1.50** | 3.49 | **−1.10** |
| Africa | 0.12 | 0.64 | 1.02 | **2.07** | 0.01 |
| World | 0.53 | 1.30 | 0.91 | **2.93** | 1.33 |

*Note:*   * USA, Canada, Australia and New Zealand.

*Source:*   Maddison (2001), Table 3-1a.

Soviet Union averaged 4.2 per cent (4.7 per cent excluding the war years 1941–45). During this same period population grew at 1.3 (1.4) per cent, capital at 6.9 (7.5) per cent, and GNP per capita at 3.0 (3.3) per cent. However, Soviet growth of GNP declined sharply over the whole period, from 5.8 per cent in 1928–40, to 2.0 per cent in 1980–85 (per capita growth rates declined from 3.6 to 1.1 per cent). In his report to the 27th Congress of the Communist Party of the Soviet Union (CPSU), Mikhail Gorbachev acknowledged the slowdown in economic growth experienced by the Soviet Union, promising to reverse this trend by introducing new reforms that would bring about a total 'economic and a social reconstruction' of Soviet society through a 'scientific and technological revolution' (Ofer, 1987).

Why was Soviet growth slowing down so dramatically? Neoclassical growth theory gives us some important clues (see Snowdon and Vane, 2005). The growth of output in any economy arises from increases in the inputs of capital and labour, and increases in output per unit of input. In other words, the sources of growth can be traced to the combined influence of accumulation plus increases in efficiency. As the Solow model shows, growth via the accumulation of capital eventually runs into diminishing returns so that sustained economic growth of output per worker can only come from increases in efficiency (innovation and technological progress). Growth accounting research revealed that Soviet growth was based on accumulation with efficiency growth 'unspectacular' to 'nonexistent' (Krugman, 1994b). Indeed, according to Easterly and Fischer (1995), in this respect the Soviet Union was 'the world's most under-achieving economy over the period

1960–89'. The Soviet industrialisation 'miracle' was down to mobilisation of resources ('perspiration rather than inspiration'), but the efficiency gap between the Soviet Union and the USA 'showed no signs of closing'.

While capitalism can be described as a system with low insurance and high incentives, socialism is a system with high insurance with low incentives (Roland, 1994). Given these characteristics, the Soviet growth slow-down was inevitable given its lack of dynamism (Desai, 1986). The eventual outcome of the Soviet model was a rapidly declining growth rate, an almost total absence, outside the defence and space sectors, of innovative activity, a chaotic 'chronic shortage economy' administered by the *nomenklatura* (privileged bureaucratic elite and Communist Party hierachy), a failure of *ex ante* coordination, hidden unemployment, suppressed inflation, the 'soft budget constraint' syndrome, extensive allocative and X-inefficiency, poor-quality products, massive resource waste, risk-averse managers, low worker morale, and increasing alienation, absenteeism and alcoholism (Ericson, 1991; Kornai, 1992a; Dillon and Wykoff, 2002). Kantorovich (1965) estimates that up to one-third of Soviet resources were wasted, and Desai (1986) claims that Russian enterprises were 'plagued' by X-inefficiency (enterprises operating well inside their productive potential).

It was Kornai (1979, 1980) who first introduced the concept of the soft budget constraint into the literature. A decision maker faces a 'hard budget constraint' when there is a 'strict relationship between expenditure and earnings' (see Kornai, 1986a). If an enterprise decision maker expects (with a high probability) to receive financial assistance whenever expenditure exceeds earnings, and this expectation becomes built into their behaviour, then a 'softening' of the budget constraint has occurred. In socialist economies the resources made available to enterprises became unrelated to their performance. This is illustrated in Figure 3.3 where for two goods, A and B, the hard budget constraint is illustrated by $H_1H_1$. If a softening of the budget constraint occurs, then, although the enterprise has experienced a cost overrun, and actual expenditure of $P_1$ is clearly in excess of the original budget, this excess expenditure will be financed from an external source (the state). If in the next period the cost overrun is even greater, indicted by $P_2$ in Figure 3.3, external finance is once again forthcoming and the enterprise is prevented from becoming bankrupt. As a result the actual budget constraint $(S_1S_1)$ becomes 'soft' and tends to drift further away from the original hard budget constraint, $H_1H_1$.

Kornai identifies various ways by which the budget constraint of an enterprise can be softened, namely via soft subsidies, soft taxation, soft credit and soft administered prices. When such practices become embedded within a decision-making system, it becomes impossible to achieve allocative efficiency since 'input–output combinations do not adjust to price

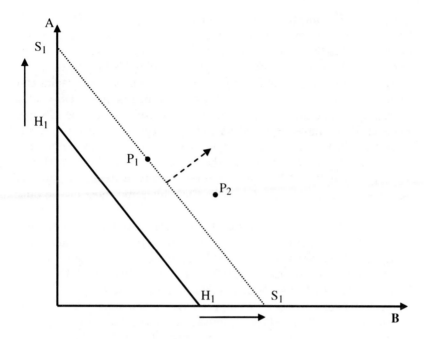

*Source:* Adapted from Kornai (1986a).

*Figure 3.3 A 'softening' of the budget constraint*

signals'. It also leads to increased X-inefficiency (underutilisation of existing resources) since there is little incentive for managers and workers in protected enterprises to maximise effort (Leibenstein, 1966, 1979). In effect,
within a socialist economic system the state takes on the role of a giant
insurance company and, by reducing or eliminating risk, creates the usual
moral hazard problems. As Kornai (1986a) emphasises, 'The soft budget
constraint protects the old production line, the inefficient firm against constructive destruction and thus impedes innovation and development.'
Moreover, this outcome is entirely predictable! To repeat, in Roland's
(1994) words, 'socialism was a regime with low incentives and high insurance' whereas capitalism is a regime 'with more incentives and less insurance'. To foster economic efficiency and the conditions necessary for
sustained economic growth, an economic system requires the steady rede-
ployment of resources from less to more productive uses. Thus bankruptcy,
entrepreneurship, and freedom of entry and exit of firms are key features
of any dynamic economy (Stiglitz, 2000b). Ultimately the inefficiencies and
lack of dynamism of the socialist economies, combined with their suppression of individual freedom, led to their demise.

While no economist predicted the precise timing of the collapse of the Soviet system, the overwhelming inefficiency and increasing economic problems facing the Soviet Union had certainly been recognised for some time by many economic commentators, including Padma Desai (1986, 1987). In 1985, the year that Gorbachev came to power, per capita consumption in the Soviet Union was 28.6 per cent of that in the USA, while per capita consumption in the UK was 65.6 per cent of the US level (Bergson, 1991). Table 3.3 provides selected comparative indictors of development. While Russia's GNI per capita is above the world average, there is a huge gap between Russia and the USA and UK. Russia's Human Development Index (HDI) also deteriorated between 1990 and 2003, and life expectancy in 2003 was lower than in China and most of the other Eastern European economies.

A good measure of the failure of the socialist systems can be easily observed by comparing the historical experiences of similar economies (in terms of size, geography or culture) that have adopted very different institutions and policies (see DeLong, 1992; Fukuyama, 1989, 1992; Dillon and Wykoff, 2002). Table 3.4 contains some suggested international development comparisons over the relevant periods of Communist Party dictatorship (identified in Table 3.1) that come as close as you are ever likely to get in economic analysis to a natural experiment. These natural experiments dramatically illustrate Olson's (1996, 2000) observation that where national borders also mark the boundaries of different public policies and institutions, easily identifiable differentials in economic performance emerge.

## 3.5   WESTERN PERCEPTIONS OF THE SOCIALIST SYSTEM

Mark Mazower (1998) argues that the 'almost universal failure to predict the collapse of communism drove a large nail into the coffin of Western political science'. Given the eventual outcome of the great socialist experiment, in retrospect it seems remarkable that during the 1930s, and at least up until Brezhnev's military suppression of the 'Prague Spring' in 1968, so many Western intellectuals were taken in by the idea of a socialist utopia. For example, after visiting the Soviet Union in 1932, the Fabian socialists, Sidney and Beatrice Webb, produced their *Soviet Communism: A New Civilisation?* (1935), described by Piers Brendon (2000) as 'uncritical' and 'as much the product of senility as gullibility'. Brendon (2000, p. 214) brilliantly captures the extraordinary mood among some intellectuals during the mass unemployment of the Great Depression years of the 1930s:

*Table 3.3*   *Selected key indicators of development: former Soviet Union,*
*Eastern bloc, China, India, UK and USA*

| Country | GNI per capita ($PPP) 2004[1] | GDP per capita growth 2003–04[1] | Population[1] (thousands) 2004 | HDI[2] 1990 | HDI[2] 2003 | Life expectancy[2] 2003 |
|---|---|---|---|---|---|---|
| Russian Fed. | 9 620 | 7.7 | 142 814 | 0.817 | 0.795 | 65.3 |
| Belarus | 6 900 | 11.5 | 9 832 | 0.787 | 0.786 | 68.1 |
| Ukraine | 6 250 | 12.9 | 48 008 | 0.799 | 0.766 | 66.1 |
| Estonia | 13 190 | 6.8 | 1 345 | 0.814 | 0.853 | 71.3 |
| Latvia | 11 850 | 9.4 | 2 303 | 0.799 | 0.836 | 71.6 |
| Lithuania | 12 610 | 7.1 | 3 439 | 0.823 | 0.852 | 72.3 |
| Moldova | 1 930 | 7.8 | 4 218 | 0.739 | 0.671 | 67.7 |
| Georgia | 2 930 | 9.6 | 4 521 | n.a. | 0.732 | 70.5 |
| Armenia | 4 270 | 10.3 | 3 050 | 0.737 | 0.759 | 71.5 |
| Azerbaijan | 3 830 | 10.6 | 8 280 | n.a. | 0.729 | 66.9 |
| Kazakhstan | 6 980 | 8.8 | 14 958 | 0.767 | 0.761 | 63.2 |
| Kyrgyz Rep. | 1 840 | 6.1 | 5 099 | n.a. | 0.702 | 66.8 |
| Tajikistan | 1 150 | 9.4 | 6 430 | 0.696 | 0.652 | 63.6 |
| Turkmenistan | 6 910 | 15.4 | 4 931 | n.a. | 0.738 | 62.4 |
| Uzbekistan | 1 860 | 6.3 | 29 930 | 0.679[4] | 0.694 | 66.5 |
| Poland | 12 640 | 5.4 | 36 160 | 0.803 | 0.858 | 74.3 |
| Czech Rep. | 18 400 | 4.2 | 10 183 | 0.843[4] | 0.874 | 75.6 |
| Slovak Rep. | 14 370 | 5.5 | 5 390 | n.a. | 0.849 | 74.0 |
| Hungary | 15 620 | 4.6 | 10 072 | 0.807 | 0.862 | 72.7 |
| Bulgaria | 7 870 | 6.1 | 7 780 | 0.795 | 0.808 | 72.2 |
| Romania | 8 190 | 7.7 | 21 858 | 0.772 | 0.792 | 71.3 |
| China | 5 530 | 8.8 | 1 296 500 | 0.627 | 0.755 | 71.6 |
| India | 3 100 | 5.4 | 1 079 721 | 0.513 | 0.602 | 63.3 |
| UK | 31 460 | 3.0 | 59 405 | 0.883 | 0.939 | 78.4 |
| USA | 39 710 | 3.4 | 293 507 | 0.916 | 0.944 | 77.4 |
| World | 8 760[3] | 2.9[3] | 6 345 127 | n.a. | 0.741 | 67.1 |

*Notes:*
[1] *World Development Report 2006*, World Bank.
[2] *Human Development Report, 2005*, United Nations.
[3] Weighted average.
[4] Data for 1995.

Westerners failed both to appreciate the deficiencies of the Soviet economy and to understand the nature of Stalin's state. This was partly because disillusionment with capitalism fostered illusions about Communism … It somehow seemed logical to assume that darkness in the west meant light in the east … It was easy to see Depression, unemployment and chaos as the bitter fruit of free

*Table 3.4   Selected 'natural experiments'*

| Capitalist market economies | Socialist economies |
| --- | --- |
| USA 1917–91 | Soviet Union 1917–91 |
| Western Europe 1948–90 | Eastern Europe 1948–90 |
| West Germany 1949–90 | German Dem. Rep. 1949–90 |
| Austria 1948–89 | Hungary 1948–89 |
| Italy 1945–92 | Slovenia 1945–92 |
| Costa Rica 1959–2006 | Cuba 1959–2006 |
| Taiwan/Singapore/Hong Kong 1949–79 | China 1949–79 |
| South Korea 1948–2006 | North Korea 1948–2006 |
| Thailand 1975–2006 | Laos 1975–2006 |
| Malaysia 1975–89 | Cambodia 1975–89 |

enterprise while regarding progress, full employment and the five year plan as the bounty of State Socialism.

In contrast to the Webbs, John Maynard Keynes was never taken in by any socialist utopian propaganda and responded to the crisis of capitalism in the 1930s by putting forward a disillusioned defence, and a persuasive case for reforming capitalism (Robinson, 1975). Despite the prompting of George Bernard Shaw, Keynes remained steadfastly blind to Marx and Marxism, and remained a firm critic of socialist central planning as any kind of proposed solution to the ills of capitalism that were so evident during the 1930s Great Depression. In Keynes's opinion, *Das Kapital* contained nothing but 'dreary out of date academic controversialising' which added up to nothing more than complicated 'hocus pocus'. At one of Keynes's Political Economy Club meetings he admitted to having read Marx in the same spirit as reading a detective story. He had hoped to find some clue to an idea but had never succeeded in doing so (Skidelsky, 1992)! However, in the depths of the Great Depression, even Keynes (1933) was driven to comment that the 'decadent international but individualistic capitalism in the hands of which we now find ourselves after the [First World] war is not a success. It is not intelligent, it is not beautiful, it is not just, it is not virtuous – and it does not deliver the goods. In short, we dislike it, and we are beginning to despise it.' Nevertheless, despite this uncharacteristic outpouring of pessimism, Keynes remained firmly committed to saving capitalism from itself through a process of moderate reforms and the adoption of more enlightened policies of economic management. Keynes's problem was that 'the Capitalist leaders of the City and in Parliament are incapable of distinguishing novel measures for safeguarding Capitalism from what they call Bolshevism' (Keynes,

1930). But, as Skidelsky (1992) documents, Keynes 'rejected socialism as an economic remedy to the ills of laissez-faire. Its doctrines were ideological, obsolete, irrelevant, inimical to wealth creation, and likely to involve gross interferences with individual liberty'. If a revolution came, Keynes would be on the side of the 'educated bourgeoisie'. Keynes (1930) remained convinced that a more enlightened capitalism could be made 'more efficient for attaining economic ends than any alternative system yet in sight'.

## 3.6 ECONOMIC ANALYSIS UNDER SOCIALISM

The architects of the socialist experiment genuinely believed that the inevitable outcome of their rational planned economy would be 'abundance', allowing production to be distributed according to needs. The influential essay by Bukharin and Preobrazhensky, 'The ABC of Communism' (1972), written during the civil war period (1918–20), demonstrates the full naïvety, with respect to economics, of the intellectual leadership of the Communist Party. Bukharin believed that political economy (economics) is the science of an 'unorganised economy' and, therefore, 'the end of capitalist and commodity society signifies the end of political economy' (see Roberts, 1971). Rosa Luxemburg also argued that 'the realisation of socialism will be the end of economics as a science' (Nove and Nuti, 1972).

Ellman and Kontorovich (1992) refer to the 'low level of official economics' during the 1980s. Official economics was engaged in 'apologetics' and was incapable of providing sound advice on policy. Alexeer et al. (1992) show that economics education in the Soviet Union was almost completely divorced from mainstream developments in the West. Students of economics in the Soviet Union were well versed in Marxism and tended to specialise in either 'political economy' or 'mathematical economics', and these two branches of economics exhibited considerable rivalry (see Kornai interview). Typically there was little or no exposure to the theory of the firm, consumer theory, industrial organisation, public finance, public choice, game theory and mainstream macroeconomics. Although Paul Samuelson's best-selling textbook, *Economics*, had been published for the first time in Russian in 1964, very few students read or had access to it. Neither did most students have access to Western economics journals. As a result, the typical Soviet-trained economist did not have the same 'mindset' as the typical Western-trained economist. Surveys conducted by Alexeev et al. confirm that, before 1991, the vast majority of Soviet economists did 'not understand even the basic principles of the workings of markets', having been trained to regard the 'anarchy of the market' as the hallmark of capitalism! Interestingly, with respect to the attitudes of Russian citizens towards the values associated with a capitalist system (e.g. response to financial incentives), Shiller et al. (1991, 1992) show that *Homo economicus* rather than *Homo sovieticus* is alive and well.

As an example of the kind of analysis that was normal in the political-economy field, Alexeev et al. provide an extract from an article published in the 1990 issue of *Voprosy Ekonomiiki* (*Questions of Economics*). Alexeev et al. claim that the form of argument reproduced in the following extract is highly representative of a typical political-economy paper published in this 'flagship' political-economy journal:

> the revolutionary mass proletariat consciousness is characterised by authoritari-anism, hyperideologization, simplification all the way to the primitivization of relations with culture and religious morality, pseudo-rationality based on the primacy of labour relations and theory reduction to a universal form of social community. Finally, the ideal of the factory and the ideal of the proletarian society inhere in the revolutionary mass proletarian consciousness. Historically, initial political and economic post-revolutionary practice was the objectively nec-essary embodiment of this consciousness. . . . (Yevstigneyeva and Yevstigneyeva, 1990)

To any economist educated in the West, this is utterly incomprehensible! Apparently, the paper from which this excerpt is taken contains an analy-sis of *perestroika* and calls for 'a more centralised approach to economic reform while still pursuing political liberalisation' (Alexeev et al., 1992, p. 141).

In Soviet mathematical economics, while the mathematics is often highly sophisticated, there is almost a total absence of Western-style formal behav-ioural modelling. Nevertheless, Leonid Kantorovich was awarded the 1975 Nobel Prize in Economics for his contributions to the theory of optimum allocation of resources, and two other Nobel Laureates, Simon Kuznets and Wassily Leontief, were born in Ukraine and Russia respectively.

## 3.7   FROM *GLASNOST* AND *PERESTROIKA* TO TRANSITION

Following Kruschev's denunciation of Stalin in a 'secret speech' at the 20th Congress of the Communist Party of the Soviet Union (CPSU) in February 1956, Stalinism as an ideology went into decline (however, this did not prevent Khrushchev from brutally suppressing the Hungarian uprising of October 1956). In turn, Nikita Khrushchev's improvised reforming efforts came to an end in 1964 when Leonid Brezhnev began his conservative and 'unimaginative, geriatric' reign as Soviet leader. Following Brezhnev's death in 1982, he was succeeded, in quick succession, by Yuri Andropov (1982–84) then Konstantin Chernenko (1984–85). After the death of Chernenko, Mikhail Gorbachev became General Secretary of the Central Committee of the CPSU on 11 March 1985.

As Padma Desai (2006a) points out, when Gorbachev came to power he inherited a 'poisoned chalice'. The legacy of Russian history as a tsarist autocracy, followed by 70 years of Soviet communism, had created 'daunting challenges' from three main directions:

1.  an economy in severe crisis;
2.  the Soviet-controlled economies of Eastern and Central Europe were becoming more restive and potentially volatile;
3.  an increasingly fragile Soviet Union held together by an authoritarian ideology enforced from Moscow (Desai, 1997a).

Adding to these enormous problems was the Soviet Union's ongoing and costly involvement (since 1979) in Afghanistan, and in April 1986, the explosions at the Chernobyl nuclear power plant created a human and environmental catastrophe.

In 1987 Gorbachev attempted to initiate fundamental improvements in the Soviet economy with his strategy of *glasnost* (openness), *perestroika* (restructuring and reform), and *demokratizatsiya* (democratisation). However, as Desai (2006a) shows, Gorbachev remained convinced that the Soviet model could be reformed without bringing down the whole system. For example, Gorbachev (1987, p. 36) set out his intentions as follows:

> I would like to point out once again that we are conducting all our reforms in accordance with the socialist choice. We are looking within socialism rather than outside it for the answers to all the questions that arise . . . Those who hope that we shall move away from the socialist path will be greatly disappointed. Every part of our program of perestroika . . . is fully based on the principle of more socialism and more democracy.

While Gorbachev's position was extremely naïve, he played a key, if unintentional, role in the eventual transformation of the Soviet Union. This role is highlighted by Sergei Rogov, who observes (quoted in Desai, 2005a, 2006a):

> Gorbachev is a unique leader in Russian history because he initiated changes at a time when it was possible simply to continue . . . Until Gorbachev, the majority of Soviet citizens never thought of alternative arrangements. His changes prompted people to start thinking of the possibility of a totally different system.

> That was a revolutionary move. People began searching for an ideal transparent system because they knew that the Soviet system was a big lie.

Once Gorbachev had opened the floodgates, the process of change became unstoppable. As De Tocqueville once so insightfully observed (see Mazower, 1998, p. 367):

> Patiently endured so long as it seemed beyond redress, a grievance comes to appear intolerable once the possibility of removing it crosses men's minds.

Embarking on a programme of economic reform can prove to be a 'dangerous' moment for any government in that it 'could prove to be their undoing' (Krueger, 2005).

## 3.8   THE POLITICAL ECONOMY OF TRANSITION

In his survey of 'Soviet Economic Growth: 1928–1985', Ofer (1987) concludes by assessing the prospects for reform using a classification of strategies derived from Berliner (1983) and Colton (1986). The possible strategies available to the Soviet Union when Gorbachev took over the reigns of power were perceived to be:

1.   revert to the reactionary model of classical socialism; attempt to improve the planning system and increase the use of coercion;
2.   move towards a moderate model; modify the existing planning regime to facilitate more dynamism, flexibility and entrepreneurship, and allow limited expansion of the private sector;
3.   adopt a 'radical' reform model; decentralise by converting the system from central planning to 'market socialism'.

The reactionary model (strategy 1) required a return to excessive coercion, and that was no longer a viable option, even if the old system, with increasing creaks and groans, could have stumbled on for a few more years. Gorbachev chose not to go down this road and by 1987 had committed himself to the more moderate reform model (strategy 2). With respect to this choice of strategy, Murphy et al. (1992) offer a critique of partial economic reform, arguing that the economic collapse of the Soviet Union in the late 1980s to early 1990s was in large part due to the reform-induced destruction of 'traditional coordination mechanisms' without the provision of a viable alternative in terms of working markets. Thus 'partial reform contributed to the collapse of output'. A similar criticism of

Gorbachev's reform strategy is made by Ellman and Kontorovich (1992), who argue that the immediate causes of the economic collapse 'were the actions of the leadership itself, its destabilising institutional changes and economic policies'. Furthermore:

> The incompetence of the leadership, which was very marked in 1985–90, reflects the fact that although well meaning, they simply did not understand economic policy. Their belief in the reformability of the system led them to think that reforms would make things better. They did not consider the possibility that the system was brittle and that if sharply attacked would simply disintegrate.

Hence Gorbachev's reforms demolished the prevailing economic system, which, while far from optimal, at least functioned in a rudimentary way. Whilst the ultimate decline of the economy was inevitable in the long run, and rooted in system characteristics, the immediate cause, according to Ellman and Kontorovich, reflected the 'unintended consequences' of Gorbachev's partial reform programme.

Ericson (1991) and Kornai (1992a) are also critical of further reforms as a viable solution to the economic decline of the socialist economies. The Soviet-type economy is a 'system', and the 'treadmill' of reforms (1965, 1967, 1972, 1976, 1979, 1982) all failed to deal with the fundamental problem, which was the socialist system itself. Indeed the frequency of failed reform attempts is itself compelling evidence that the system is 'not reformable' (Nuti, 1988). Harrison (2002) also argues that a cycle of reforms and counter-reforms under socialism tends to harm a dictator's reputation and undermine regime credibility, thereby making it increasingly difficult to attain a high-output equilibrium.

In the Ericson–Kornai analysis, the only strategy that had the potential to work is the very one that did not enter Gorbachev's mindset, namely, abandon the socialist model altogether, set out a strategy of transition to a capitalist market economy, and bring to an end the Communist Party's political dictatorship. In Ericson's view, such a strategy could not hope to be smooth given the scale of the task. A period of 'serious economic deterioration' seemed inevitable, and no 'soft landing' for the Soviet Union, or any other industrialised socialist economy, appeared to be possible. The great socialist experiment was turning out to be the 'longest road from capitalism to capitalism' (Nuti, 1988). A truly radical strategy involved destruction of the old institutions, and the only real debate was over how quickly this should be done (the 'gradualism v. shock therapy debate').

But what of strategy 3, 'market socialism'? Was there not a 'third way'?

## 3.9   A THIRD WAY: IS MARKET SOCIALISM FEASIBLE?

The feasibility of 'market socialism' has remained a controversial issue among economists since the protracted 'socialist calculation' debate of the first half of the twentieth century (see Mises, 1920; Taylor, 1929; Dickinson, 1933; Dobb, 1933; Robbins, 1933; Lerner, 1934; Hayek, 1935, 1940, 1945; Lange, 1936, 1937; Bergson, 1967; Roberts, 1971; Vaughn, 1980; Nove, 1983). This debate received a temporary new lease of life with the collapse of the socialist economic system in 1989 (see Lavoie, 1985; Kornai, 1990a, 1990b, 1992a; Bardhan and Roemer, 1992, 1993, 1994; Shleifer and Vishny, 1994; Stiglitz, 1994; Caldwell, 1997).

Before the contribution of Mises, the Austrian economist, Friedrich von Weiser had been one of the first to recognise that every economic system, regardless of its political ideology, must face up to the resource allocation problem (see Rima, 1986). Whilst aware of the resource allocation problem, neither Marx nor Engels seriously considered a solution to this issue under a socialist system (Lange and Taylor, 1938). Indeed the resource allocation problem was not seriously discussed by socialists until the 1930s. The essence of the 1930s 'socialist calculation' debate revolved around the question: is it possible, in principle and practice, to organise an efficient working economy without the use of free markets and without capital and land being under private ownership? In other words, is a rational allocation of resources achievable in a socialist state? Mises, Hayek and Robbins said no; Taylor, Dickinson, Langer and Lerner said yes.

Mises (1920) had been provoked into making the opening contribution to this debate after hearing of a proposal, by philosopher and sociologist Otto Neurath, that wartime central planning should be carried over into the peacetime organisation of economies. Neurath envisaged a moneyless economy organised as one gigantic enterprise where inputs and outputs would be calculated in purely physical terms (see Caldwell, 1997). The naïve utterances of the utopian socialists (Bukharin and Preobrazhensky), who denied the importance of resource scarcity and advocated the need for a moneyless economy, also reinforced the Mises critique (see Nove, 1983).

The 'bourgeois theory of socialism' (Schumpeter, 1942) envisaged in this debate (bearing no resemblance to the practice of socialism that had actually emerged in the Soviet Union) is one which allowed free consumer choice and free choice of occupation by workers, but where there is no free market for capital goods. Mises argued that this form of socialism 'is the abolition of a rational economy' since 'where there is no free market there is no pricing mechanism' and 'without a pricing mechanism, there is no economic calculation'. Without private ownership of the means of production, exchange relations between production goods (capital goods) cannot be established. Where production goods never become the object of market exchange, no calculation of their relative scarcities is possible and enterprise managers will be 'left groping in the dark'. To Mises a rational solution to the resource allocation problem in a socialist economy was not even feasible in principle. Thus a socialist revolution does not banish the laws of economics and the same principles that form the basis of rational resource allocation decisions in a free market must also be taken into account in a socialist system.

During the late 1920s and throughout the 1930s, Taylor (1929), Dickinson (1933), Lerner (1934) and Lange (1936, 1937) attempted to refute the Mises critique by building on the seminal paper by Barone (1908), and developing a static neoclassical general equilibrium model of socialism. The new breed of socialist writers admired the efficiency properties of the model of perfect competition but, at the same time, were critical of real-world capitalism because it did not measure up to this ideal. In particular, Lange was well aware of the adverse impact on efficiency of monopoly power. However, while Lange believed that only under a socialist system could the worst aspects of monopoly be avoided, the Austrian writers attributed permanent monopoly power to anti-capitalist forces, especially government interventionist policies (see Persky, 1991). In contrast, market socialist writers believed that their proposals would not only enable a socialist system to achieve efficient resource allocation, but would also allow for a more equitable distribution of income and elimination of the many imperfections associated with capitalist market economies, such as monopoly power, externalities and business cycles.

The claim that rational calculation was possible in a socialist system was made by Taylor and Dickinson on the basis that, at least theoretically, any economy can be described by a set of Walrasian simultaneous equations, as suggested by Barone. Whereas these equations are solved by the invisible hand of the market in a capitalist system, under socialism this task would fall to the central planning authorities. Hayek and Robbins denied that such a solution was possible in practice given the mass of data needed and the complexity of repeatedly solving hundreds of thousands of simultaneous equations. Not even modern-day computing power could overcome such difficulties.

In the most thorough statement of the solution to the resource allocation problem under socialism, Lange (1936, 1937), building on the ideas of Barone, Taylor and Dickinson, put forward his 'competitive solution' (Bergson, 1967). In Lange's scheme, managers of enterprises would be required to follow two rules. First, they should choose the combination of inputs that minimises costs of production. Second, they should choose the scale of output where price equals marginal cost (Lerner, 1934). Beginning with provisional, historically given prices, the Central Planning Board performs the function of the market, arriving at the correct set of accounting prices by a process of 'trial and error'. Where there is excess demand of producer or consumer goods, prices would be increased. Where there is excess supply of producer or consumer goods, prices would be reduced. Lange therefore claimed that not only was rational calculation under socialism theoretically possible; it was also possible in practice. The problem of solving innumerable equations appeared to have been circumvented. Indeed it was claimed that a Central Planning Board could outperform the free market!

In hindsight the naivety of the market socialists in adopting the Walrasian general equilibrium framework in order to defend the rationality of socialist calculation seems 'positively laughable'. In Mark Blaug's (1993) view, 'Only those drunk on perfectly competitive, static equilibrium theory could have swallowed such nonsense' and, as one who swallowed this 'nonsense' as a student in the 1950s, Blaug castigates himself for his 'own dim-wittedness'. It is also worth noting that Lange proposed a transition strategy to market socialism from capitalism that today would be labelled as 'big bang' or 'shock therapy'. How such a strategy could be achieved while maintaining the political freedoms associated with liberal democracy remains a mystery.

There are two enormous problems with Lange's 'competitive solution'. First, the critiques of Mises, Robbins and Hayek are much more robust than the market socialists appreciated and showed that even if socialism was possible in principle, it could never be made to work efficiently in practice using the trial-and-error method. Second, the clear intention of the Marxist socialists (Lenin, Bukharin, Preobrazhensky and others) was to replace, not mimic, the market (see Dobb, 1940; Eremin, 1970; Roberts, 1971).

Hayek (1935, 1940) rejected Lange's claim of the practical feasibility of rational socialist calculation. The use, by the market socialist writers, of the static Walrasian general equilibrium framework to establish the practical feasibility of rational socialist calculation was misguided and revealed a simplistic view of the functioning of markets (Caldwell, 1997). In contrast to the static model adopted by the market socialists, in a real-world dynamic setting the relative price structure is constantly in flux as demand and supply conditions change. Therefore entrepreneurs, when making their key decisions, must pay attention to anticipated future prices. Furthermore, without private property rights and appropriate incentives, the managers of socialist enterprises would be extremely unlikely to perform their tasks as well as managers operating within a capitalist market system. Only in a genuinely competitive market can entrepreneurs hope to acquire the knowledge of least-cost production processes. In a world of dispersed knowledge, market-determined prices convey information to producers and consumers. No Central Planning Board could ever hope to effectively simulate this decentralised process. As Caldwell (1997) observes, the 'competitive–entrepreneurial process for the discovery, and coordination of knowledge, has become the central theme of Austrian thought'.

A second problem with the 1930s analysis of the market socialists is their failure to address the criticism that their model had nothing to do with the idea of socialist planning as envisaged by the Marxists. Roberts (1971) reminds the market socialists that socialism is a system that intends to '*replace* a system of market relations with a system of planning'. For Marx, the alienation of the proletariat arises from market–exchange relationships; therefore socialism requires an organising principle different from market exchange. According to Eremin (1970), the idea of market socialism is 'a definite anti-Marxist concept' and Dobb (1940) succinctly captures this position when he emphasises that 'Either planning means overriding the autonomy of separate decisions or it apparently means nothing at all.' Thus the defence of socialist efficiency by Taylor, Dickinson, Lerner and Lange, utilising the tools of orthodox neoclassical theory, misses the point. Market socialism is a system that 'no socialist ever believed in, place hopes in, or fought for' (Roberts, 1971). The informational critique of Hayek is thus doubly reinforced in a bureaucratic centrally planned system as it emerged in practice in the Soviet Union from 1928. Such a system could not hope to produce static and dynamic efficiency. In addition, such a system was incompatible with individual freedom and liberal democracy (Hayek, 1944, 1988; Friedman, M., 1962; Caldwell, 1997; Kornai, 2000a, 2006).

The modern revival of the debate on market socialism was short-lived. The case for market socialism presented by Bardhan and Roemer (1992, 1993, 1994) failed to influence the reformers in the transition economies. The critique by Shleifer and Vishny (1994) that under all forms of market socialism 'the state ultimately controls firms, and hence politicians' objectives must determine resource allocation' appears irrefutable and devastating. Moreover, Kornai's critique was well known to the Russian reformers. As Yegor Gaidar comments (Yergin and Stanislaw, 1999, p. 281), Kornai 'was the most influential on all of us in the 1980s . . . He focused on the practical mechanisms of socialism. His analysis of the economy of shortage in the early 1980s, had a great impact on all of us. He was addressing our problems. We knew all his books.'

While the demise of the socialist planned economies may not represent the 'end of history' (Fukuyama, 1992) with respect to the modern operation of capitalist market economies, the role of government remains crucial. As Rajan and Zingales (2003b) observe, 'The right position is the Goldilocks position ... neither too little nor too much of government is best for markets.' Nobel Laureate Joseph Stiglitz argues that the 'ideological debates should be over; there should be agreement that while markets are at the centre of the economy, governments must play an important role. The issue is one of balance, and *where that balance is may depend on the country, the capacity of its government, the institutional development of its markets*' (Snowdon, 2001b, emphasis added).

Along similar lines, but in a very different age, Keynes (1926, p. 313) argued:

> Perhaps the chief task of economists at this hour is to distinguish afresh the Agenda of Government from the Non-Agenda; and the companion task of politics is to devise forms of government within a democracy which shall be capable of accomplishing the Agenda.

Reflecting this vision, the World Bank's annual *World Development Report* for 1997, *The State in a Changing World*, concentrates on issues relating to the balance between government and the market. The predominant modern view is that governments need to be strong, but focused on the areas where they have a comparative advantage. 'History has repeatedly shown that good government is not a luxury but a vital necessity. Without an effective state, sustainable development, both economic and social, is impossible' (World Bank, 1997).

In terms of Figure 3.4, a states capacity to function well will be greatly enhanced by being located in Quadrant I, whereas the socialist systems are typically located in Quadrant II. Within Fukuyama's (2004) framework we can view the idealised transition from socialism (S) to capitalism (C) as a shift from Quadrant II to Quadrant I; that is, to reduce the scope of state activities while maintaining (or even increasing) the strength of state institutions. Fukuyama argues that the influence of the 'Washington Consensus' (WC) represented a 'perfectly sensible' package of policy measures that were intended to facilitate this desirable change. Unfortunately, in the adjustment process many countries also reduced the strength as well as the scope of their state institutions, so they ended up in Quadrant III rather than Quadrant I.

## 3.10　ALTERNATIVE PATHS OF TRANSITION: THE SHOCK THERAPY V. GRADUALISM DEBATE

While the transition to socialism did not arise from organic development, Kornai (2000a) argues that the transition from socialism to capitalism can

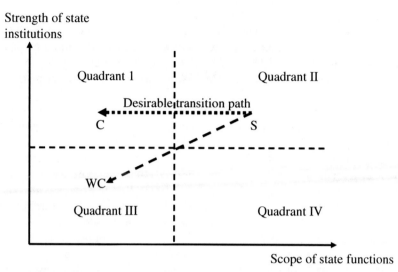

Strength of state
institutions

Quadrant 1

Quadrant II

Desirable transition path

C

S

WC

Quadrant III

Quadrant IV

Scope of state functions

*Source:* Adapted from Fukuyama (2004).

*Figure 3.4   The state capacity matrix*

occur naturally because there is no need to impose capitalism on society, and the simple removal of administrative barriers is sufficient to stimulate 'vigorous' development in the private sector. However, the spontaneous emergence of capitalism and markets can be accelerated if the state plays an active enabling role. Therefore a key issue in the process of reform is the choice of transition strategy and the supporting role of government.

As noted earlier, a truly radical reform strategy implies the quick replacement of the old bureaucratic socialist system and establishment of market-friendly policies and institutions. In 1989, when the Berlin Wall fell, there was no established theory that policy makers could refer to with respect to easing the process of transition from socialism to capitalism. An important debate emerged among the reformers and their economic advisers over how this transition was to be achieved. This emerging debate has often been characterised as one between supporters of a 'big bang' or 'shock therapy' approach (Lipton and Sachs, 1990a; Balcerowicz, 1994a, 1994b; Woo, 1994; Aslund, 1995, 2002), and supporters of a more gradualist approach to reform (Murrell, 1991, 1993, 1995, 2006; Lau et al., 2000; Stiglitz, 2000b, 2002a; Dewatripont and Roland, 1992, 1995; Roland, 1994, 2001, 2002).

The 'shock therapy' or 'big bang' approach to transition derived its name from the economic reform package initiated in Poland on 1 January 1990. Roland (2001) links the shock therapy approach to the Washington Consensus and the gradualist approach to an incrementalist evolutionary–institutionalist perspective. While Murrell (1991) refers to the shock therapy approach as 'neoclassical', Marangos (2002, 2005) distinguishes between a neoclassical shock therapy model and a neoclassical gradualist model. Easterly (2006a) views shock therapy as the straightforward application of IMF–World Bank structural adjustment policies.

Lipton and Sachs (1990a, 1990b) are usually cited as the authors who provided one of the first coherent statements of the economic and political logic supporting the case for 'a rapid and comprehensive process of transition'. The case for a big bang strategy is founded on the argument that partial reforms are unlikely to work; indeed, they are more likely to contribute to disorganisation (Murphy et al., 1992). Because reforms are complementary, they need to be introduced quickly as a comprehensive package. Shock therapists also base their case on the idea that reformers need to take advantage of a political 'window of opportunity', 'honeymoon period', or 'period of exceptional politics'. Reformers need to implement radical change while the forces of resistance are relatively weak and the new government has the support and goodwill of the majority of the people (Balcerowicz, 1994a, 1994b; Desai, 2006a).

Since a market economy cannot function efficiently without a proper structure of relative prices, Lipton and Sachs provide a strong case for rapid price deregulation, including a move to a convertible currency. Given that socialist economies typically suffer from excess demand (a shortage economy with suppressed inflation), the deregulation of prices inevitably leads to a burst of inflation. Clearly, in the case of a transition economy that starts out with severe macroeconomic imbalances, stabilisation has to be an important priority. So price deregulation must be accompanied by a programme of fiscal and monetary stabilisation. In the short run this policy package is almost certain to lead to a reduction of growth and rising unemployment. However, with respect to the programme of microeconomic reforms, it should be noted that Lipton and Sachs (1990a) explicitly recognise that privatisation is a process that will probably take many years to complete. Figure 3.5 indicates a stylised representation of the likely path followed by a transition economy from growth crisis to price liberalisation and stabilisation, to renewed growth following successful structural reforms.

Those economists who support the gradualist strategy, influenced by Hayek's (1944, 1945) critique of top–down societal engineering, and the conservative political philosophy of Karl Popper (1971), emphasise the uncertainties and ignorance created by implementing a rapid comprehensive programme of reform and are much more sanguine about the outcome of partial reforms (Roland, 2001). They regard the shock therapists as favouring a top–down, technocratic, utopian social engineering approach that

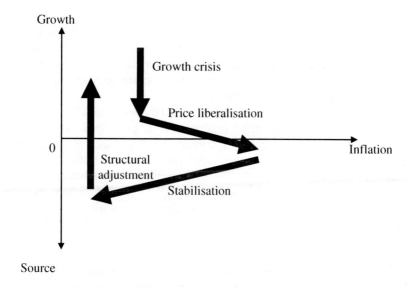

Source

*Source:* Adapted from Bruno (1993).

*Figure 3.5 Stylised representation of crisis, adjustment and reform*

underestimates the potential for creating an institutional void and an *ex post* political backlash (Murrell, 1993). Stiglitz (2000b) is highly sceptical of the shock therapy approach since such a strategy is based on conventional neo-classical economics and consequently underestimates the importance of (i) informational imperfections, including those that arise in the context of corporate governance; (ii) the importance of social and organisational capital; and (iii) the necessary legal and institutional infrastructure which is a key prerequisite for an effective market economy. Easterly (2006a), a former advocate of shock therapy in the early 1990s, has recently confessed that 'Economists like me were slow on the uptake, in that it took us a decade of failure to convince us that top–down imposition of markets did not work.'

Dewatripont and Roland (1992) and Roland (2002) emphasise the attractiveness of a gradualist strategy in circumstances where, due to the 'heterogeneity in the distribution of losses', the 'political acceptance of full and immediate reforms involves costly compensation'. Roland (1994, 2002) also highlights the advantages gained by the sequencing of reforms in a gradualist strategy whereby 'demonstrated successes' create a constituency for further reform. In the case of privatisation, Roland stresses the need to proceed slowly and to give priority to privatising first those enterprises where favourable outcomes are most likely. Gradualists also advocate the need to nurture the development of the key institutional foundations of capitalism attuned to the specific conditions of each transition economy (Roland, 2001; Beek and Laeven, 2006; Bromley and Yao, 2006). In successful economies, the key institutional structures that support a market economy have evolved over a long historical period in an organic process. To assume that such institutions can be transplanted quickly into former socialist states is at best a very 'bad bet'.

Gradualists typically cite the case of China's growth miracle as evidence of the advantages of adopting a gradualist strategy (Roland, 2001, 2002). Although Kornai (2006) is highly critical of China's lack of democracy, Fogel (2006) believes that China's rapid growth can continue for another generation and is unlikely to be undermined by political instability. However, with respect to the gradualist v. shock therapy debate, as Woo (1994) points out, the different outcomes that we have witnessed in China and Russia are mainly the result of differences in economic structure rather than the economic strategies adopted. China after 1979 represents the classic problem of development, highlighted by Arthur Lewis (1954), involving the need to adjust from a low-productivity economy, dominated by agriculture with surplus labour, to an economy that absorbs surplus (rural) labour into an expanding (urban) industrial sector. The problem facing Russia and the other Eastern European transition economies in 1990 was quite different. Here the process of transition is dominated by an adjustment problem in an already industrialised economy, whereby resources must be reallocated from inefficient uncompetitive enterprises to newly emerging competitive enterprises. Woo argues that 'economic development is easier than economic adjustment both practically and politically' (see Sachs interview, and Sachs and Woo, 1994, 1997). Moreover, Prasad and Rajan (2006) believe that the time has come for China to overhaul and 'modernise' its growth paradigm as the pressures from international integration reveal the deficiencies of the existing strategy.

The gradualism v. shock therapy debate focuses on the risks and rewards likely to emerge with each approach. However, as the World Bank (1996) highlights, it is important to recognise that the historically determined initial economic and political circumstances of each economy engaged in the transition process will have a major impact on the range of reform policies and outcomes available to it. Fischer and Gelb (1991) also stress that the particular reform path that a country follows will depend on several key factors, in particular: (i) the state of the economy at the beginning of the transition process; (ii) the tolerance of the population for the inevitable disruption that the reform process will create; and (iii) the political situation in each transition country.

Figure 3.6 illustrates a stylised 'prototype' reform programme suggested by Fischer and Gelb (1991) that would be suitable for a representative

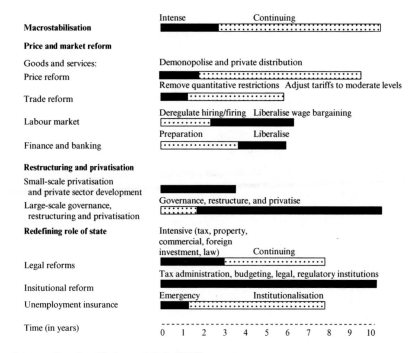

Macrostabilisation — Intense / Continuing

Price and market reform

Goods and services:
Price reform — Demonopolise and private distribution

Trade reform — Remove quantitative restrictions  Adjust tariffs to moderate levels

Labour market — Deregulate hiring/firing  Liberalise wage bargaining

Finance and banking — Preparation / Liberalise

Restructuring and privatisation

Small-scale privatisation
  and private sector development

Large-scale governance,
  restructuring and privatisation — Governance, restructure, and privatise

Redefining role of state

Legal reforms — Intensive (tax, property, commercial, foreign investment, law) / Continuing

Insitutional reform — Tax administration, budgeting, legal, regulatory institutions

Unemployment insurance — Emergency / Institutionalisation

Time (in years): 0 1 2 3 4 5 6 7 8 9 10

*Source:* Based on Fischer and Gelb (1991).

*Figure 3.6   Transition strategy: the phasing of reform*

Eastern European transition economy such as Poland or the former Czechoslovakia. According to the Fischer–Gelb framework, transition policies are best thought of as groups of complementary policy reforms being introduced sequentially. Inevitably some reforms need to be introduced rapidly while others are best introduced gradually. As Figure 3.6 illustrates, any crude gradualism v. big bang distinction oversimplifies the complications involved in the process of transition (see interviews with Fischer and Sachs).

## 3.11   THE POLITICAL ECONOMY OF REFORM

Following Dillon and Wykoff (2002), we can use Figure 3.7 to illustrate one of the problems facing any reforming government. Effective reforms take time to work, and the initial effect of radical reform often leads to a deterioration of the overall economic situation before the benefits of the reforms have time to 'kick in'. In a fledgling democracy it can, therefore, be very difficult for reforming politicians to survive the transition phase (from

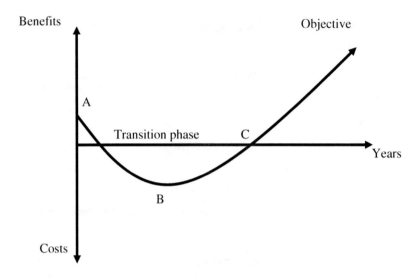

*Source:*   Adapted from Dillon and Wykoff (2002).

*Figure 3.7    The political economy of reform: the 'no gain without pain'
                model*

point A, through B, to point C) unless sufficient numbers of the population
become winners, or can perceive the longer-term gains from the reforms. As
Kornai (2006) has recently argued, during the transition period, false illusions, impatience and nostalgia can quickly emerge and act as impediments
to further reforms. Rodrik (1996, p. 10) also argues that 'Good economics
does often turn out to be good politics, but only eventually. Policies that
work do become popular, but the time lag can often be long enough for the
relationship not to be exploitable by would-be reformers.'

The transition experiences of the 1990s certainly confirm Ericson's
(1991) analysis discussed earlier. As Campos and Corcelli (2002) show, for
the transition economies of Eastern Europe and the former Soviet Union,
the 1990s witnessed a dramatic initial fall in GDP, shrinkage of the capital
stock, massive labour reallocation, a reorientation of trade, extensive
restructuring, the destruction of old institutions, and significant transition
costs in the form of unemployment, increased mortality rates, and
increased poverty and inequality (Kornai, 1994; World Bank, 1996;
Blanchard and Kremer, 1997; Havrylyshyn, 2001; Svejnar, 2002). The most
dramatic feature of the early transition period was the large measured
decline in GDP (Kornai, 1994; Ellman, 1994; Campos and Corcelli, 2002).

Table 3.5 illustrates the extent of the initial output decline in 25 transition
economies during the period 1989–99. While most economists attribute the

*Table 3.5*    *Output performance, transition economies, 1989–99*

| Transition economy | Cumulative output decline to lowest level $(1989=100)^1$ | Year in which output was lowest[1] | Simple average of output growth since lowest level (%) | Ratio of output in 1999 to output in TT–1[1] |
|---|---|---|---|---|
| Albania | 39.9 | 1992 | 6.6 | 1.03 |
| Armenia | 65.1 | 1993 | 5.4 | 0.56 |
| Azerbaijan | 63.1 | 1995 | 5.9 | 0.53 |
| Belarus | 36.9 | 1995 | 6.0 | 0.83 |
| Bulgaria | 36.9 | 1997 | 3.0 | 0.74 |
| Croatia | 37.6 | 1993 | 2.2 | 0.80 |
| Czech Republic | 15.4 | 1992 | 1.7 | 0.95 |
| Estonia | 36.5 | 1994 | 3.2 | 0.87 |
| Georgia | 76.6 | 1994 | 5.8 | 0.46 |
| Hungary | 18.1 | 1993 | 3.1 | 0.99 |
| Kazakhstan | 40.2 | 1998 | 1.7 | 0.70 |
| Kyrgyz Republic | 50.5 | 1995 | 4.1 | 0.68 |
| Latvia | 52.8 | 1993 | 2.6 | 0.64 |
| Lithuania | 40.8 | 1994 | 3.0 | 0.70 |
| Macedonia, former Yugoslav Republic of | 45.6 | 1995 | 2.0 | 0.59 |
| Moldova | 69.2 | 1999 | n.a. | 0.38 |
| Poland | 13.7 | 1991 | 5.1 | 1.28 |
| Romania | 26.6 | 1992 | 0.0 | 0.80 |
| Russia | 46.5 | 1998 | 3.2 | 0.59 |
| Slovak Republic | 24.7 | 1993 | 4.9 | 1.01 |
| Slovenia | 20.4 | 1992 | 3.8 | 1.05 |
| Tajikistan | 74.0 | 1996 | 3.7 | 0.46 |
| Turkmenistan | 49.6 | 1997 | 10.5 | 0.66 |
| Ukraine | 64.5 | 1999 | n.a. | 0.41 |
| Uzbekistan | 14.4 | 1995 | 3.1 | 0.93 |
| CEE[2] | 27.9 | 1992 | 3.2 | 0.90 |
| Baltics[2] | 43.4 | 1994 | 3.0 | 0.70 |
| Other former Soviet Union[2] | 54.2 | 1995 | 4.9 | 0.60 |

*Notes:*
[1] Output decline from 1989 to the year in which output was the lowest. For countries in which output has not begun to grow, 1999 is taken as the year of minimum output. Output is real GDP measured on an annual average basis. TT–1 denotes one year before transition began.
[2] CEE refers to the following Central and Eastern European countries: Albania, Bulgaria, Croatia, Czech Republic, Hungary, former Yugoslav Republic of Macedonia, Poland, Romania, Slovak Republic and Slovenia. Baltics refers to Estonia, Latvia and Lithuania. Other former Soviet Union refers to Armenia, Azerbaijan, Belarus, Georgia, Kazakhstan, Kyrgyz Republic, Moldova, Russia, Tajikistan, Turkmenistan, Ukraine and Uzbekistan. Simple average for values and mode for years.
n.a.: not applicable.

*Source:*   Fischer and Sahay (2000a).

initial decline in GDP to a combination of aggregate demand and supply shocks, Aslund (2001, 2002) and Shleifer and Treisman (2005) argue that Russia's GDP decline was significantly smaller than officially reported by the 'deeply flawed' official statistics containing 'monumental statistical biases'. Therefore the fall in measured GDP was much larger than the fall in actual GDP. Aslund attributes this to several factors, including: (i) the incorrect use of 1989 instead of 1991 as the base year for measuring the GDP decline; (ii) the overreporting of output (to meet targets) under communism; (iii) the underreporting of output (to avoid taxes) under capitalism; (iv) the tremendous expansion, after 1991, of the unofficial underground economy; (v) unwanted and poor quality of output ('sheer waste') under communism; and (vi) the elimination of value detraction. According to Aslund (2001), the 'alleged misery of post-communist transformation is primarily the delayed revelation of the true costs of communism'. Moreover, the correlation between the strength of reforms and economic recovery, measured by the ratio of 1995 GDP to 1989 GDP, is much more pronounced using revised GDP estimates compared to the official data.

While the transition economies have now recovered from most of these initial shocks, in Russia the outcome of the privatisation process has left an enormous political and economic scar (see the Desai and Sachs interviews). It is generally agreed that the main motivation leading to greater privatisation around the world has been the well-documented inefficiency of state enterprises. These efficiency losses arise from managerial distortions introduced by continuous political interference, incentive problems, the soft budget constraint syndrome, lack of transparency and accountability, and lack of competition. Economists have long recognised that for success, privatisation requires much more than just a transfer of ownership. What is required is a strategy of what Zinnes et al. (2001) call 'deep privatisation', that is, a change of ownership that is supported by the introduction of new institutions that 'address agency issues, hardening of budget constraints, market competition, and depoliticisation of firms' objectives, as well as developing institutions and a regulatory framework to support them'.

There has been considerable disagreement on how best to manage and implement the privatisation process. Early in this debate Kornai (1990c) warned that it is 'impossible to privatise in a big bang', so privatisation should be 'looked upon as a problem of social transformation and therefore necessarily as an evolutionary process'. Figure 3.8 illustrates a stylised gradualist path of privatisation during the transition process as a socialist economy, dominated by state sector output, is transformed into a capitalist market economy dominated by private sector output.

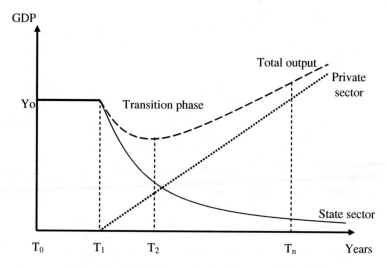

*Figure 3.8*   *Stylised path of state, private and total output during transition*

In the case of Russia, Kornai's warning was not heeded. As a result, for many Russians the outcome of privatisation and the emergence of the oligarchs has adversely tainted the image of capitalism, markets and liberal democracy. Privatisation also remains an issue that continues to attract extensive attention, controversy and criticism from a large number of economists (Aslund, 1995; Boycko et al., 1995, 1996; Desai, 1995a; Meggison and Netter, 2001; Zinnes et al., 2001; Djankof and Murrell, 2002; Stiglitz, 2002a; Ellerman, 2003; Hoff and Stiglitz, 2004; Stiglitz and Hoff, 2005; Guriev and Rachinsky, 2005; Guriev and Meggison, 2006; Godoy and Stiglitz, 2006).

In a recent paper, Rajan and Zingales (2006) argue that the failure in many instances of capitalism and markets to capture the hearts and minds of people is that true free market capitalism with supporting institutions (including a strong but focused government) is not established. Instead, a distorted version takes root and adversely influences perceptions. Because powerful market forces in a competitive capitalist system will undermine privilege and power, and provide opportunities for upward social mobility, it will tend to be opposed by existing elites. In the case of Russia, the powerful elites (oligarchs) who acquired early access to valuable assets in a limited market setting are now using their power to limit market access and competition, and the introduction of effective corporate governance systems. Hoff and Stiglitz (2004) have explored this theme in relation to the case of the corrupt 'robber baron' Russian privatisation process arguing that those oligarchs who have 'stolen' valuable assets act as a barrier to the emergence of a market friendly legal regime. Roland (2001, p. 41) eloquently describes the outcome of the Russian privatisation strategy as follows:

> the Russian experience shows the downside of the Washington Consensus view because of the neglect of uncertainty. A window of opportunity was used to implement mass privatisation and this has been done so as to create irreversibility of reform, but the relative irreversibility thus created has locked the Russian economy in an inefficient situation where interest groups, who gained most from mass privatisation (the famous oligarchs), have become so powerful as to block further reform such as tax reform, government reform, stronger law enforcement, and stronger security of property rights.

This outcome, described by Ellerman (2003) as 'the Mother of all Debacles', is in sharp contrast to the predictions of the Boycko et al. theory of privatisation (1995). In their model, a large-scale big bang privatisation strategy creates 'an economically and politically powerful lobby' advocating market-supporting institutional reform, including the rule of law. Unfortunately, the 'market bolshevism' (Reddaway and Glinsky, 2001) approach to privatisation, by transferring property rights before the establishment of the rule of law, has created a class of economic agents 'whose entrepreneurial efforts are directed towards theft and who oppose legal reform' (Stiglitz and Hoff, 2005). Godoy and Stiglitz (2006) also find evidence that rapid privatisation is negatively associated with economic growth in transition economies.

In a different context, Keynes (1933), writing about the Bolshevik transition in the Soviet Union, from semi-feudal economy to a highly centralised socialist planned economy, commented as follows (cited by Ellerman, 2003, p. 7):

> We have a fearful example in Russia today of the evils of insane and unnecessary haste. The sacrifices and losses of transition will be vastly greater if the pace is forced . . . For it is of the nature of economic processes to be rooted in time. A rapid transition will involve so much pure destruction of wealth that the new state of affairs will be, at first, far worse than the old, and the grand experiment will be discredited.

Following the break-up of the Soviet Union, in December 1991 Boris Yeltsin became the first President of the Russian Federation. According to Desai (2006a), Yeltsin's primary goals were 'to end the authoritarian Communist political system and the planned economy – not to reform them, but to finish them'. As Yeltsin himself recalls (interviewed in the *Moscow News*, October 2003):

What was needed was a kamikaze crew that would step into the line of fire and forge ahead, however strong the general discontent might be . . . I had to pick a team that would go up in flames but remain in history.

Table 3.6 provides data on freedom and other measures of the business and investment climate in the former Soviet Union, Eastern bloc countries, China, India, the UK and the USA. In terms of Figure 3.7, Russia would appear to be somewhere near point C. It seems that Boris Yeltsin's objective, that Russia must aim to become a well-established, stable market economy, committed to liberal democracy, has yet to be achieved. Russia's 'Great Transformation' remains incomplete (see also Lopez-Carlos, 2005).

## 3.12  CONCLUSION

With respect to achieving a stable liberal democracy, Kornai (2000a) reminds us that there are certain minimum conditions for a 'workable democracy':

1.  a government can be dismissed peacefully by regular, open, transparent and competitive electoral procedures;
2.  no political party or ideology has a monopoly of power backed up by state force;
3.  political freedoms are guaranteed and include freedom of expression and association.

It is also the case that there has never been a democracy in history 'whose economy has not been dominated by private ownership and market co-ordination', that is, economic freedom (Friedman, M., 1962). However, while there are no examples in history of socialist democracies (as defined above), economic freedom is a necessary condition for democracy, not a sufficient condition, as exemplified by the many examples of dictatorships in predominantly capitalist systems, for example Nazi Germany, Fascist Spain, and in East Asia and Latin America. Moreover, Guriev and Rachinsky (2005) note that since a majority of Russian citizens regard the property rights of the oligarchs as illegitimate, this creates 'a fundamental problem for building a democratic and prosperous Russia'. Nevertheless, in Padma Desai's view, Russia has made 'considerable progress' during the last 15 years and remains 'rather optimistic' about Russia's future, despite several 'troubling negative features' (see Desai interview).

In the case of the other European transition economies, Kornai (2006) provides a relatively sanguine assessment of the 'Great Transformation in

Table 3.6 Freedom, and business and investment climate indicators: former Soviet Union, Eastern bloc, China, India, UK and USA

| Country | Global Competitiveness Index[1] 2005 | Ease of doing business index[2] 2004 | Corruption perceptions index[3] 2005 | Economic freedom index[4] 2006 | Political freedom index[5] 2006 |
|---|---|---|---|---|---|
| Russian Fed. | 53 | 79 | 2.4 (126) | 122 | Not free[6] |
| Belarus | n.a. | 106 | 2.6 (107) | 151 | Not free |
| Ukraine | 68 | 124 | 2.6 (107) | 99 | Free |
| Estonia | 26 | 16 | 6.4 (27) | 7 | Free |
| Latvia | 39 | 26 | 4.2 (51) | 39 | Free |
| Lithuania | 34 | 15 | 4.8 (44) | 23 | Free |
| Moldova | 89 | 83 | 2.9 (88) | 83 | Partly free |
| Georgia | 86 | 100 | 2.3 (130) | 68 | Partly free |
| Armenia | 81 | 46 | 2.9 (88) | 27 | Partly free |
| Azerbaijan | 62 | 98 | 2.2 (137) | 123 | Not free |
| Kazakhstan | 51 | 86 | 2.6 (107) | 113 | Not free |
| Kyrgyz Rep. | 104 | 84 | 2.3 (130) | 71 | Partly free |
| Tajikistan | 92 | n.a. | 2.1 (144) | 137 | Not free |
| Turkmenistan | n.a. | n.a. | 1.8 (155) | 148 | Not free |
| Uzbekistan | n.a. | 138 | 2.2 (137) | 144 | Not free |
| Poland | 43 | 54 | 3.4 (70) | 41 | Free |
| Czech Rep. | 29 | 41 | 4.3 (47) | 21 | Free |
| Slovak Rep. | 36 | 37 | 4.3 (47) | 34 | Free |
| Hungary | 35 | 52 | 5.0 (40) | 40 | Free |
| Bulgaria | 61 | 62 | 4.0 (55) | 64 | Free |
| Romania | 67 | 78 | 3.0 (85) | 92 | Free |

| | | | | | |
|---|---|---|---|---|---|
| China | 48 | 91 | 3.2 (78) | 111 | Not free |
| India | 45 | 116 | 2.9 (88) | 121 | Free |
| UK | 9 | 9 | 8.6 (11) | 5 | Free |
| USA | 1 | 3 | 7.6 (17) | 9 | Free |

*Notes:*

1 *World Competitiveness Report, 2005–06*, World Economic Forum, http://www.weforum.org/. Data for 117 countries.

2 *Doing Business in 2006*, World Bank, http://www.doingbusiness.org/. Data available for 155 countries.

3 *Global Corruption Report, 2005*, Transparency International, http://www.transparency.org/. Data available for 159 countries. Scores range from 10 (highly clean) to 0 (highly corrupt). Ranking in parentheses.

4 *Index of Economic Freedom, 2005*, Ranking of 157 countries, Heritage Foundation. http://www.heritage.org/Research/.

5 *Freedom in the World, 2006*, Freedom House, http://www.freedomhouse.org/.

6 Freedom House note that 'Under the leadership of President Vladimir Putin, Russia's governance has taken a sharp turn toward more highly concentrated rule. The Kremlin's tightening grip has increasingly marginalized key societal institutions, including the press, the judiciary, and civil society.'

Central Eastern Europe' (CEE). In the context of world history the changes that have taken place in Estonia, Latvia, Lithuania, the Czech and Slovak Republics, Hungary, Poland and Slovenia (former socialist countries that became EU members on 1 May 2004) are without precedent. The 'Great Transformation' of this region between 1989 and 2006 comprises six major characteristics that are unique compared to other major transformations in world history (such as Russia after 1917, China after 1949, and West Germany after 1945):

1.  the changes redirected the CEE region back on track with respect to the main path of 'Western civilisation' in the *economic sphere*, that is, in the direction of a capitalist market economic system;
2.  the changes redirected the CEE region back on track with respect to the main path of 'Western civilisation' in the *political sphere*, that is, towards liberal democracy and recognition of human rights;
3.  the transformation was complete in all spheres, political, economic, legal and societal stratification;
4.  the transformation has been accomplished without violence;
5.  the transformation was peaceful in the sense that it was not preceded by war and forced on the CEE by occupation;
6.  the transformation has taken place with 'incredible speed'.

By way of comparison, while China's transformation in the economic sphere has been remarkable, in the political sphere, the monopoly power of the Communist Party remains intact. Furthermore, change has not been free from violence, as demonstrated by the 'iron fist' suppression of student demonstrators in 1989. The pace of economic transformation in China has also been much slower than in the CEE region.

Kornai is fully aware of the 'grief and disappointment' felt by many citizens in the CEE region with respect to the changes that have taken place, and also recognises that capitalism is 'not a very likeable system', especially with respect to inequality and unemployment. However, Kornai remains convinced that, on balance, the recent and ongoing changes that have taken place in the CEE region amount to 'an unparalleled success story', not least because the establishment of economic freedom is 'an indispensable precondition for a functioning democracy'. In the economic sphere, over the long run, the imperfections of capitalism pale into insignificance compared to the inefficiencies of the socialist economies as they operated in practice during the twentieth century. In the political sphere, while liberal democracy has many deficiencies, it is difficult not to agree with Winston Churchill, who famously remarked in a Parliamentary debate on 11 November 1947 (Lindert, 2003, p. 1):

No one pretends that democracy is perfect or all-wise. Indeed it has been said that democracy is the worst form of Government except all those other forms that have been tried from time to time.

Relating Churchill's observation to an assessment of the great socialist experiment of the twentieth century is easy if we simply substitute into the above quotation the words 'capitalism' for democracy, and 'economic system' for Government.

Interviews

# Daron Acemoglu[1]

Daron Acemoglu is currently the Charles P. Kindleberger Professor of Applied Economics at the Massachusetts Institute of Technology. He completed his undergraduate education at the University of York (1989), UK, and his MSc (1990) and PhD (1992) degrees at the London School of Economics. Before joining MIT in 1993, he was a lecturer in economics at the London School of Economics, 1992–93, and from 1997 to 2004 he was Pentti Kouri Associate Professor of Economics, then Professor of Economics at MIT.

Professor Acemoglu is a Research Associate of both the National Bureau of Economic Research and the Centre for Economic Policy Research, a research affiliate of the Centre for Economic Performance at the London School of Economics, editor of the *Review of Economics and Statistics*, and a member of the editorial board of the *Journal of Economic Growth* and the *Quarterly Journal of Economics*. He became a member of The Canadian Institute for Advanced Research (CIAR)'s Economic Growth and Policy Program in January 2000, and is now participating in the Institute's two-year research initiative on economic growth and institutions.

Professor Acemoglu has received numerous awards and prizes for his research, including three National Science Foundations Grants, the Sherwin Rosen Award for outstanding contributions to labour economics from the

*189*

Society of Labour Economics, and the prestigious John Bates Clark Medal, awarded biannually by the American Economics Association to 'that American economist under the age of forty who is adjudged to have made a significant contribution to economic thought and knowledge'.

Professor Acemoglu's research interests lie in the areas of income and wage inequality; human capital and training; economic growth; technical change; search theory; and political economy. His recent work has focused on the political economy of development, political and economic transitions, and institutional and technical change. Professor Acemoglu and his co-authors have made highly influential and innovative contributions to the debate relating to the 'deeper' institutional determinants of economic growth and the role of political distortions as barriers to progress. To date he has authored/co-authored over 50 papers, published in leading academic journals. His new book, *Economic Origins of Dictatorship and Democracy* (co-authored with James Robinson), was published by Cambridge University Press in March 2006.[2]

In the interview that follows I discuss with Professor Acemoglu several key issues relating to the key role played by 'good' and 'bad' institutions in determining the economic performance of countries.


## BACKGROUND INFORMATION

*I understand from reading your CV that you were educated at the University of York and the LSE in the UK. What attracted you to study economics? Did anyone or anything in particular inspire your interest?*
What inspired me to become an economist is, by a strange coincidence, exactly the same as what I am working on right now. I became interested in politics and economic development, both from a historical perspective and from the point of view of trying to understand what was happening to poor countries around the world. This was when I was a high school student in Turkey. I started to read a lot of historical literature and also the Marxist and dependency school literature. That was very appealing at the time and I was drawn into economics because I wanted to know more. When I first went to York I began to study politics and economics because I believed that both disciplines were necessary in order to understand development problems. After about six months or so I found that I was becoming increasingly drawn towards economics. Undergraduate politics can be a lot of fun but I found it a little bit frustrating because there was little sense of what was right and what was wrong. The ideas were more open. That is not a shortcoming *per se* but at that time I wanted answers. When my professors disagreed with my arguments I could not understand

why. So I switched to economics. Within economics I was slowly drawn towards the more macro topics like unemployment and growth. But I never lost my interest in development and political-economy issues. That was always there in the background. After a while I started revisiting these topics.

*Were there any particular economists who influenced you?*
There is no one person who has influenced me throughout my career but there have been specific people at certain points in time. Although I found their work difficult at the time, I was influenced by the formal and rigorous approaches of Kenneth Arrow, Gerard Debreu and Paul Samuelson. Later, when I turned to labour economics and human capital, Gary Becker was a major figure. When I started working on political economy the work of Bob Bates influenced me enormously.[3]


## ECONOMIC HISTORY

*In many of your recent papers economic history plays a key role in your investigations. We can discuss some of these papers later.[4] Meanwhile, in more general terms, what role do you see for economic history in the education of an economist? To me it seems unfortunate that over the last 30 years economic history has been increasingly neglected in the education of economics students, especially at graduate level.[5]*
Yes, I agree that economic history has a very important role. At the end of the day economics is both a theoretical and an empirical discipline, and economic history provides a very large data set. Maybe we cannot find the millions of observations in micro data sets, but for particular events, such as what initiates the growth process or what causes countries to stagnate, I think that economic history is the prime source of data. We can see through history how different societies have organised themselves politically and economically, and how they have performed through time. For example, we can learn a great deal about the role of institutions in the process of growth and development by researching the different colonial experiences of Africa, Asia and Latin America, compared with what happened in the so-called 'Western offshoots', the USA, Canada, and Australia and New Zealand.[6] If I were to make a conjecture I would say that economic history could be made much more interesting to graduate students if it were more integrated with economic theory. Unfortunately many graduate students have their hands full in learning the techniques needed to get through the core economics courses and asking them to also study economic history in narrative form is unappealing. If economic history were used to help

students understand certain theories it would be much more popular. It also provides ammunition for future research topics.

## GROWTH THEORY

*Economic growth is a necessary but not sufficient requirement for sustained economic development. What are the main findings to have come out of recent theoretical developments in growth theory that may be useful to the developing countries?*

One important insight that has emerged from recent research, that will not be of much immediate or direct use to developing countries, is that economists are now thinking much more deeply about technological change. Since most poor countries do not produce their own technologies, but borrow and adopt technology from the rich countries of the world, this development will not be of immediate direct benefit. However, once we start to think more carefully about technological progress, this opens up the way for a more systematic study of technology adoption and this is very important for the dynamics of development. This is an area where both theory and empirics are deficient. Economists need to understand better the factors lying behind decisions to adopt new technologies. A second issue, and this came with the development of endogenous growth theory, is the attempt by economists to model growth processes together with structural change. If you look at the standard Solow growth model, or simple endogenous growth models, they do not take into account that as economies grow there are also changes in how life is organised, how the economy is organised, where people live, and how they enter into different types of contract. On the other hand, if you look at the development economics literature, especially that produced during the 1960s and 1970s, its full of issues like structural change and rural–urban migration.[7] Economists are now beginning to combine the two types of insight. This new growth and development literature is very important and is producing many useful insights.

*Taking up your comment about technology, in a couple of recent co-authored papers you have been modelling how a country's distance from the technology frontier impacts on its innovative activities.[8] What impact does this distance have on innovation?*

Our model suggests that as an economy nears the world technology frontier the equilibrium organisation of firms changes. Firms that are vertically integrated need to allocate time to both production and innovation. Because this creates managerial overload, the rate of innovation is adversely affected. Therefore it is sensible for such firms to engage in the outsourcing of some of their production activities. For countries close to the technology frontier, the selection of highly skilled managers is crucial · for innovative success. In contrast, developing countries far from the technology frontier are best advised to pursue an investment-based strategy. It is important that these countries do not switch to an innovation-based strategy too soon.[9] Institutions and policies that encourage investment-based strategies may be required until such countries are in a position to switch to putting greater emphasis on innovation activities. However, there is always a danger that vested interests and powerful producer groups may resist attempts to switch strategies when the time is appropriate.

*In your recent paper, 'Technical Change, Inequality and the Labour Market' (2002), you survey the implications of technological change for the labour market in the USA. What were the main findings of your research for that paper?*
I documented, like others before me, that for the past 60 years the returns to education have risen as well as the supply of educated workers. This implies that technological change over this period has been skill-biased, and this bias seems to have accelerated during the last 20 years. This contrasts with the nineteenth century, when technological change appears to have been skill-replacing.

*One of the most prominent recent debates among economists interested in growth and development is the one related to the impact of trade regimes on economic growth.[10] Do more open economies grow faster than more inward-looking economies? Economists are well versed in the static gains from trade. However, there is much more controversy concerning the mechanisms and extent of the dynamic gains, or growth effects, of trade and openness. What is your assessment of these issues?*
Economists have accumulated a large number of theories in this area. The static gains from trade are well documented in both the Ricardian comparative advantage and the Hecksher–Ohlin factor proportions models. The dynamic impact of trade on growth is linked to ideas about endogenous technological change, market size, factor price incentive effects, the impact on efficiency of greater competitive pressures, and the free flow of ideas. Coming from Turkey, I am well aware of the importance and beneficial impact of increasing competition though greater openness as a means of raising the productivity of inefficient firms. There are also models that highlight what the dynamic costs of free trade could be. If, after opening up to trade, a country specialises in sectors that have low 'learning by doing', then it will experience slow growth. For example, the historical experience of

China and India in the nineteenth century exhibits de-industrialisation followed by slow growth. Despite these caveats, my overall view is that trade is
good for growth although there are many theoretical and empirical loose
ends that need tying up. For example, economists are now exploring the
interaction between trade and institutions. Having good institutions, both
political and economic, is very important if a country is to successfully reap
the static and dynamic gains from trade.[11] There are many examples of
countries with abundant natural resources to trade that fail to develop successfully due to the competition for rents among powerful and unaccountable elite groups. So there are some interesting theoretical and empirical
issues that need exploration when thinking about why some countries like
South Korea have done so well by opening up while others like Nigeria have
made little progress despite substantial oil resources. Another example is
Botswana, which has used its natural resources productively while many of
its resource-rich neighbours have not.[12]

## GROWTH IN HISTORY

*While the Solow and Romer growth models concentrate on the proximate
determinants of growth, namely human and physical capital, and technology,
your recent research is digging into economic and political history to find the
'deeper' or 'fundamental' sources of economic growth. Once you start doing
this you confront what I would like to call 'the onion problem'. As you pull
back each layer of history you find yet more puzzles and have to pull back
more and more layers of the historical onion. For example, in trying to identify the origins of the Industrial Revolution and subsequent 'Great
Divergence', just how far back do economists need to go with their research?*[13]
I like the analogy of the onion (*laughter*). How far should we go back?
There is no limit, but for any particular problem that you are investigating
there is usually some specific time frame relevant to your investigation. For
example, to understand post-war growth in Western Europe it is important
to understand the institutions and policies of the countries that you are
investigating. Because those institutions evolved historically, you need to
trace their origins. How far back do we need to go? One investigator might
be happy to go back to the development of those institutions in the nineteenth century; others will want to dig deeper to earlier periods. In my own
work I have investigated the countries that were colonised by the Europeans
because they provide a unique sample where institutions were shaped to an
important degree by the intervention of the European colonists. In this case
it makes a lot of sense to go back to the sixteenth century because that is
when the natural experiment of colonisation began.[14] Someone else might

want to ask the question 'Why did the Europeans colonise Latin America and North America rather than the Chinese, West African's or some other nation or group?' To answer that question you have to peel back another layer of the onion and investigate even earlier periods of history. Jared Diamond (1998), in his book, *Guns, Germs and Steel*, went all the way back to the Neolithic revolution to find answers to these kinds of question.

*As you go further back you inevitably have to deal with the role that religion and culture play in influencing economic activity. Economists such as Deepak Lal and David Landes clearly think that culture is important. Recently Robert Barro and Rachel McCleary have produced some interesting papers investigating the connection between religion and economic growth.*[15] *How important is culture in determining the economic performance of nations?*
I certainly do not share the view of some economists that culture is unimportant. However, I just don't know how important it is. There is a danger of using culture as a label to cover a whole host of things that are not easily explained. Research into how religion shapes individual attitudes is important. But religion is only part of culture. The north and south of Italy have the same religion but there are significant cultural differences. There has been some interesting work done by Luigi Guiso, Paola Sapienza and Luigi Zingales looking at survey data on attitudes.[16] Questions were asked of various racial and religious groups about their motivations, trust and willingness to cheat on contracts etc. Robert Barro and Rachel McCleary have also recently investigated the impact of religion on economic growth at the cross-country, aggregate level. I think the investigations at the micro level are more informative because at the aggregate level you are always wary that some other factor correlated with religion is influencing your results. The same problem exists to a lesser extent at the micro level because there are economic differences in the USA between different religious groups.

## GROWTH AND INSTITUTIONS

*Institutions are clearly an important factor in the process of growth and development.*[17] *But how can economists measure the influence of institutions?*
If you had asked me that about ten years ago I would have said that I think institutions are important but we lack convincing evidence about how much and in what way they matter. In the mid-1990s, Knack and Keefer attempted to find evidence on the importance of institutions by looking at the correlation between institutions and economic outcomes.[18] But here you run into the same problem I mentioned before, namely, the problem of correlation and causation. There are many other things correlated with

economic outcomes as well as institutions. How can we determine which are the important factors? One way to make progress is to adopt the methodology that Simon Johnson, James Robinson and I used to investigate the importance of institutions. Try to find plausibly exogenous sources of variations in institutions and try to find out if they lead to the type of effects that we conjecture. In other words, try to identify examples of natural experiments in history. We argue that the colonisation of the globe by the Europeans after 1500 provides such an experiment because colonisation led to the transformation of institutions in the colonies.

*Taking up your point about natural experiments in history, many economists, in particular Nobel Laureate Douglass North, have argued that the Industrial Revolution occurred first in England because of the establishment of institutions favourable to economic progress following the 'Glorious Revolution' of 1688.[19] But we are back to the onion problem. Even if we accept this hypothesis we are still left with questions such as 'Why did these events and institutional changes develop first in England and not elsewhere?' and 'What do economists and economic historians mean when they talk about institutions?' To make further progress using the institutional explanation of economic outcomes, it seems to me that economists need to spell out more clearly what they mean by institutions. In your recent paper with Simon Johnson, 'Unbundling Institutions', you attempt to start dealing with this kind of question.[20] Can you explain what that paper is about?*

You are quite right to point out that there is a growing number of economists who accept the broad outlines of North's emphasis on the role institutions. So the motivation for writing the 'Unbundling Institutions' paper is that we believe that economists have not yet pinned down any consistent or coherent definition of institutions. The kind of research that Simon Johnson, Jim Robinson and I did earlier looked at the historical sources of variation in economic performance. We investigated the colonisation of the Americas and found that different types of colonisation experiences produce significantly different outcomes. For example, different colonisation strategies influenced how the political system was organised and evolved. This in turn had consequences for property rights. In the Caribbean economies most people were slaves with no economic and political rights. They were denied access to education. In sharp contrast, in the northeast of the USA there evolved a smallholder society with diffused political and property rights. However, while some economists stress property rights, others emphasise the legal system and associated institutions. Simon Johnson and I attempt to 'unbundle' the broad cluster of institutions that support private contracts, which we call 'contracting institutions', and institutions that constrain predatory behaviour by governments or powerful elite groups, which we refer to as 'property rights institutions'. We proxy property rights institutions using risk of expropriation measures developed by Political Risk Services together with Polity IV's measure of constraints on the executive.[21] We proxy for contracting institutions by using data on legal formalism developed by Andrei Shleifer and his co-researchers.[22] The extent of legal formalism provides evidence relating to the costs of enforcing contracts. Shleifer et al. show that many countries have been influenced by the French civil law tradition, which emphasises legal codes and formal rules. Other countries were influenced by the English common law tradition, which is less formal and involves broader legal principles. Shleifer argues that the civil law approach makes the legal process slower and more inefficient, thus corresponding to worse contracting institutions. So using these two sources of variation within the sample of former European colonies, we attempt to distinguish the separate roles of property rights institutions and contracting institutions.

*What is the relative impact on economic performance of 'contracting institutions' compared to 'property rights institutions'?*
We found that those countries, such as the USA, that developed greater constraints on their politicians have had a much better record of economic performance as measured by growth rates, investment rates and income per capita. This confirms the importance of property rights institutions. Where the power of elites goes unchecked there is little hope of credibly protecting property rights. We also find that the impact of contracting institutions is less important. Contracting institutions affect the way that you conduct business deals but seem to have little impact on the big issues like growth. For economic growth it is the political institutions that influence property rights that really seem to matter.

## INSTITUTIONS AND GEOGRAPHY

*Your co-authored papers on the 'Colonial Origins of Comparative Development' and 'Reversal of Fortune' have had an enormous impact on the ideas about economic growth and development of both economists and economic historians.[23] Those papers challenge the arguments put forward by Jeffrey Sachs that emphasise the role that geographical factors play in determining economic outcomes. Sachs believes that economists have neglected the impact that geography has on economies and their development. This is especially the case when it comes to explaining sub-Saharan Africa's growth tragedy.[24] Have economists who are interested in explaining growth and development neglected the influence of geography?*

First let me say that I think Jeffrey Sachs has done some very important research that has highlighted the importance of geography. Others before Sachs have argued along similar lines, including major figures such as Gunnar Myrdal, Alfred Marshall and Adam Smith. It is true that the economics profession during the 1970s, 1980s and 1990s did act and write as if geographical characteristics were unrelated and unimportant for economic development. So Jeffrey Sachs is quite right to remind economists of the first-order fact that if you look at economic development across the world's economies there is a clear correlation between latitude and income per capita. This is an undeniable and significant fact. But what is the cause of this correlation? Have geographical influences actually *caused* the low income per capita that we observe in the more tropical areas of the world? Do the physical, climatic and ecological characteristics of countries within the tropics cause their relatively poor economic growth performance? I certainly don't think that they do. But the correlation between geographical characteristics and economic performance is there for all to see and we need to account for that correlation if we are to challenge the 'geography determines development' view.

*How has your 'historical' research supported the 'institutional approach' to explaining economic development?*
The line that we have pushed is that geography doesn't have a significant *direct effect* on growth. What we are observing when we note this important correlation between geography and income per capita is the outcome of a particular path of historical development. That history must take account of the impact of European colonisation on the subsequent economic performance of the colonies. In 1500 the Aztecs and Incas had relatively rich civilisations. The North American continent was much less developed than Central and South America. Today the USA, Canada, Australia and New Zealand have a much higher standard of living than the average for Latin America. The key fact is that the Europeans colonised large parts of the world but the colonisation process differed substantially across these colonies. Where the climate was more similar to Europe, and hence favourable to Europeans, the colonisers established permanent settlements. These colonies were further away from the equator. In these colonies the settlers established institutions that are conducive to economic growth. Those institutions protected private property and provided important constraints on government power. In contrast, the more tropical areas, which were richer at the time of colonisation than the areas climatically favourable for settlement, experienced a very different extractive form of colonisation strategy. These areas were often densely populated, reflecting that they were relatively prosperous. So rather than establish permanent

settlements, the colonisers forced these populations to work for them and in this way exploited the resources of the colony. This led to the establishment of a very different set of extractive institutions than the ones we find evolving in the North American colonies. So what we observe today, when we look at the correlation between geography and development, is the long-term consequences of these different institutional paths of development. Furthermore, the institutions established during the colonisation period have persisted to the present day. If the geography hypothesis was right, then you would expect the areas that were prosperous in 1500 to have stayed prosperous because their physical environment has not changed over 500 years. But North and South America have experienced a 'reversal of fortune' in terms of living standards during this period of history.

*Does this mean that geography does not matter?*
Certainly not. Geography must have some influence in a direct way. We observe the prevalence of malaria in tropical sub-Saharan Africa and this is clearly a geographical feature linked to climate. But the prevalence of malaria is also an economic issue in the sense that if the countries in sub-Saharan Africa were richer they could invest more resources in public health and eradicate malaria. They have not done so because they lack the resources. Our 'colonial origins' and 'reversal of fortune' story sets out the interaction between geography and institutional development. Europeans settled in the places that were healthier for them to do so. There are two important points that we emphasise with respect to the geography versus institutions issue, especially in the 'Reversal of Fortune' paper. First, the argument that currently there is a direct and significant causal connection between geography and income per capita is very weak. For example, look at countries like Nigeria or Haiti. There is very little evidence to show that these countries have low income per capita because their geography is directly preventing them from achieving economic growth. Once you take into account the impact of their institutional development there is not much left to explain. If we go back to around 1500, before these countries had their institutional experiment, Nigeria was actually richer than North America, whichever way you may want to measure it. Nigeria was more densely populated and it was more urbanised than North America. The second important point relates to the fact that there is an important and undeniable interaction between geography and institutions. During the last 500 years something different happened across the sample of countries that we examined, leading to their current economic positions. But this does not show that there is a *deterministic* link between geography and income and that the low-income countries are geographically disadvantaged. Our argument is that geography has an important *indirect impact* on income via its

influence on colonisation strategies and subsequent institutional development. So the important influence on current outcomes is through the historical interaction between geography and institutional development. To
make the same point another way, suppose that the Aztecs, instead of the
Europeans, had colonised the world. The Aztecs were susceptible to smallpox, so they would have been very reluctant to set up permanent settlements in Europe. They would have preferred to settle in more tropical areas!
They would have been more attracted to settling in Africa, and perhaps set
up more extractive institutions in Western Europe. Naturally, I am not suggesting that the Aztecs could have done so given their level of development
relative to European civilisation, but just trying to point out how different
the cross-country patterns of institutional development, and consequently
economic development, would have been in that case.

*Marxist historians and dependency theorists have also blamed colonialism for
the underdevelopment of large parts of the global economy.*[25] *So is capitalism
to blame for underdevelopment?*
The essence of our story is that the countries of North America and
Australasia experienced a different form of capitalism compared to much
of Latin America, sub-Saharan Africa and Asia. So the 'reversal of
fortune' was caused by the wrong type of capitalism rather than too much
capitalism.

*In order to conduct your empirical investigation you obviously need data on
living standards over a long historical time period. How did you overcome data
problems in your research?*
While we lack accurate income per capita data, in our research we use existing urbanisation and population density data as proxies for living standards. Urban societies and large population densities can only be
supported if agricultural productivity increases. So there tends to be a
strong positive correlation between urbanisation and income per capita.

## ATLANTIC TRADE AND INSTITUTIONAL DEVELOPMENT

*In your co-authored paper 'The Rise of Europe: Atlantic Trade, Institutional
Change and Economic Growth'*[26] *you argue that the economic rise of Western
Europe is closely linked to Atlantic trade and colonialism in both a direct and
an indirect way. The stimulus to capitalist development provided by Atlantic
trade led to 'a historically unprecedented period of sustained growth' that
created perhaps the 'First Great Divergence' in living standards between*

*Western Europe and the rest of the world. How did Atlantic trade interact with institutional development leading to an acceleration of economic growth?*
Our theory suggests that trade, working through either the usual Ricardian or Hecksher–Ohlin mechanisms or other channels, affects the distribution of income. This in turn influenced and changed the distribution of political power which then brought about institutional change. In our 'Atlantic Trade' paper we focus on the case where trade benefited the merchant classes who as a group sought to escape the arbitrary political and economic rule of the monarchy. In the British case we argue that this was a powerful force that led to the kind of institutional changes that were conducive to growth. The large profits earned by the bourgeoisie from expanding trade meant that this group had the power to demand institutional reforms that increased protection of property rights. We find no evidence of differential growth among the Atlantic traders before 1500 but find convincing evidence showing that the expansion of the European economies between 1500 and about 1850 is being driven mainly by the rise of those nations engaged in Atlantic trade. Atlantic ports also grow much faster than Mediterranean ports. However, we also detect that there is an important interaction between initial institutional development, *circa* 1500, and subsequent economic development. Both Britain and the Netherlands with relatively non-absolutist initial institutions do much better in terms of benefiting from Atlantic trade than countries such as Spain and Portugal, where absolutist monarchies tended to monopolise international trade. Venice and Genoa also did less well than Western Europe given their limited access to Atlantic trade.

*Does this mean that trade will always lead to better institutions?*
Definitely not! It only leads to better institutions when it benefits the people who are then willing and able to lobby and pressurise for institutional change. On the other hand, if increasing foreign trade raises only the incomes of those groups who prefer the *status quo* of 'bad' institutions that preserve the power of narrow interest groups, then trade will not in all likelihood lead to positive institutional change and sustained economic growth. For example, look at the Caribbean case. Here we observe a plantation economy that could not exist without international trade. These economies specialised in the production of sugar for export using slave labour. The plantation owners used their wealth to finance military power to preserve the *status quo* and forcefully put down any attempt to initiate political change. If these economies had been closed to trade, then the whole economic basis of the political power of the elite would have collapsed and with it the political system which supported the institution of slavery. So we need to note that trade does not always guarantee the development of good institutions.

*There seems to be a link here with some recent research highlighting the 'curse of natural resources'. Many countries that have valuable, abundant and tradable natural resources have developed an unrepresentative institutional framework that enables powerful sectional interests to exploit those natural resources for their own financial benefit.*[27]

Yes, natural resources often do turn out to be a curse on development when a country has the wrong institutions. Jim, Simon and I wrote a paper about Botswana for Dani Rodrik's edited volume, *In Search of Prosperity: Analytic Narratives on Economic Growth.*[28] Botswana is very interesting because it has been the fastest-growing country, in terms of income per capita, in the world for over 30 years. Between 1965 and 1998 Botswana experienced an annual rate of economic growth averaging 7.7 per cent. As a result Botswana's income per capita of $5796 (PPP) is almost four times the average for sub-Saharan Africa! How has Botswana achieved this outcome? Is it because Botswana has diamonds? But, as you say, many other resource-rich countries, such as Iraq, the Democratic Republic of the Congo (formerly, until 1997, Zaire), Nigeria, Angola and Sierra Leone, have lots of natural resources but have failed to develop successfully.

*Why is this the case?*

It seems that the presence of natural resources opens up the possibility for rent-seeking behaviour, corruption and tyrannical dictatorships. But for resource-rich countries that can get their act together, the prospects for growth and development are excellent, as Botswana has demonstrated. Botswana is a landlocked country where about 85 per cent of the country is arid. So although Botswana did not begin its post-colonial development with favourable conditions, it subsequently achieved outstanding growth because it adopted sound economic policies. It used the income from diamond exports to invest in education and to build up an efficient and relatively non-corrupt meritocratic civil service. The short answer to why Botswana prospered is therefore that they adopted the right policies and provided a secure environment for both domestic and foreign investors. The longer answer is more complicated. The reason why Botswana could adopt relatively good policies is probably related to its pre-colonial tribal institutions which were more participatory than most others in sub-Saharan Africa, to the fact that the British did not really set up a colony there, to the fact that the major producers in society, the cattle owners, were in favour of relatively secure property rights, and to a lot of good luck, especially in having good and relatively honest politicians. In brief, natural resources are not a natural curse. In fact, natural resources provide the opportunity for development, but they also create serious political-economy challenges, especially in preventing various social groups fighting to become the beneficiaries of the rents from natural resources. As a result, while Botswana managed to grow fast partly thanks to the diamonds, many of the resource-rich countries of sub-Saharan Africa have failed to take advantage of these resources to promote sustained development and have instead suffered severe civil wars and ethnic conflicts. Countries like Japan, Singapore and Hong Kong have also demonstrated how economic success can be achieved even when natural resources are not available from the domestic economy. It seems that natural-resource abundance is neither necessary nor sufficient for the development of specific countries.

## INEQUALITY AND GROWTH

*During the 1950s and 1960s it was generally believed that income inequality within developing countries would be conducive to growth. It was assumed that inequality would produce higher savings and investment, and, given the emphasis placed on capital accumulation in the growth and development models of that era, economic growth would naturally follow as a result of high rates of accumulation. During the last decade there has been a change in thinking on this issue. Several economists have begun to emphasise the adverse impact of inequality on growth.[29] How would you interpret the evidence on the relationship between growth and inequality?*

There has been both a reversal of the 1950s conventional wisdom on this and also, as you might expect in economics, subsequent critiques of that reversal. The current state of play on the nature of this relationship between inequality and growth revolves around how you interpret the available cross-country data. But there are so many things going on in these data that it is hard to identify cause and effect. The problem is compounded in this case because the data are very questionable. Most recent research relies on the Deininger and Squire World Bank data sets on inequality.[30] Unfortunately the quality of these data is not very good. But, for what it is worth, contrary to the earlier assumptions and theories, the available evidence is unambiguous. If you look at the correlations between growth and initial levels of inequality over a period of 30 years, there is a negative correlation. That negative relationship does not survive for shorter time periods. A paper by Kristin Forbes shows that once you look at the relationship between inequality and growth during shorter time periods and controlling for country fixed effects, what you find is a positive relationship, not a negative one.[31] A more recent paper by Banerjee and Duflo, on the other hand, argues that the relationship is between the growth rate and net changes in inequality, with changes inequality in any direction (up or down) associated with declines in growth.[32] In short, there are many different patterns you can see in the data!

The other problem is that we do not really have a clear idea of what the intervening channel is for this relationship. The earlier capital fundamentalist models in the 1950s saw a channel running from high inequality to high savings and investment, and hence higher growth. The new wave of models, such as the models developed by Alberto Alesina and Dani Rodrik, and Persson and Tabellini, have a political-economy flavour.[33] These authors apply the median voter theorem to their growth model and present a channel of adverse causation running from high inequality to higher taxation and lower saving. These authors find a negative correlation between inequality and growth in the data. But when researchers took a closer look at the data to confirm these channels, they found that more unequal societies do not redistribute or tax more than more equal societies! So other channels were proposed. For example, more unequal societies may be less able or willing to invest in education and this lowers their growth rate. That seems a plausible story to me but given the fragility of the empirical data we must be careful in inferring too much. I think the relationship between the political economy of a country and inequality is interesting, though I hesitate to jump to conclusions based on existing data.

*Is there any way to reconcile the two stories in a coherent way?*
One way of linking the 'old inequality is good for growth' story with the newer stories that 'inequality is bad for growth' is as follows. Think of a model where, in the early stages of development, giving resources and political power to the same group leads to higher rates of investment. But suppose also that in a dynamic world these people who are rich and powerful are no longer the ones who can take advantage of the changing economic opportunities. The entrenched groups with political power become an unproductive oligarchy resistant to change. They utilise their economic and political power to block the entry of new, more dynamic groups of people. This reverses the relationship between inequality and growth. The high-inequality countries are those that begin to stagnate. Of course this is conjecture squared (*laughter*). But it is a story that is consistent with the history of the Caribbean economy. In the seventeenth and eighteenth centuries we find that the Caribbean economies are doing very well by focusing narrowly on producing sugar for export. It is a highly inhumane and unequal economic system but the political elite with all the economic and political power concentrate on maximising the production of sugar. They do this very effectively despite inefficiencies and the extremely inhumane treatment of their slave workers. But when we come to the industrial age, a new breed of entrepreneurs is required to seize the new opportunities becoming available. The plantation owners are not interested in these new opportunities created by the Industrial Revolution. They have no incentive to educate their workforce and invest in the future.

# GLOBAL INEQUALITY

*There has been a flood of recent research on trends in global inequality. This research has led some economists to proclaim that world inequality has peaked and is now declining. Others challenge this conclusion. How do you read the evidence and are you optimistic that the twenty-first century will witness increasing convergence between the world's economies?*[34]

I am very optimistic on the possibilities for convergence. I believe that there will be a tendency for the worst type of poverty to be reduced, even if this process is slow and there are occasional setbacks. If what we have recently seen in India and China is repeated elsewhere, then the prospects for substantial reductions in poverty and inequality are good and we will witness considerable progress in the twenty-first century.[35] Is the gap between the richest and the poorest people in the world likely to narrow? I do think this is likely. Do I agree with some of the recent research that concludes that there has already been a significant narrowing of world inequality in the last 30 years? No, I do not believe that there is a strong case for this interpretation of the data. But neither am I convinced that inequality has increased during this period. The first reason for my indecision on this is that there is a big discrepancy in what the data show from national accounts and what researchers find in the micro data. The methodology of several studies is to take the data from national accounts and then combine these with Gini coefficients or the Deininger and Squire World Bank data relating to the quintile income shares of the population. Both sets of data are suspect. National accounts data are the best source of data that we have for measuring economic growth, and over long periods of time they are fairly good indicators. But when countries are undergoing structural change it is quite possible that national accounts data can exaggerate growth. For example, there is quite a lot of evidence suggesting that the rate of growth in China has been overstated. In both China and India, many activities that were previously done within households and have now been transferred to the market will show up as higher GDP growth. When we then look at details of individual income in survey data collected over four- or five-year intervals, we also find income growth but not at rates consistent with the national income accounts. Second, the data used to measure inequality are wholly unreliable. We have really no idea what inequality was like before these economies began to experience large structural changes. Again, the micro data suggest bigger rises in inequality than the World Bank data sets indicate. There are some students here at MIT who are working on Chinese inequality and their research shows that there has been an enormous increase in inequality. We need to dig deeper and produce much better data before we can reach firm conclusions on the current state of world inequality and recent trends in inequality. So my conclusion is that this research is very important, but at the moment the findings are at best suggestive.

*Jeffrey Williamson has reminded us that the first era of globalisation in the period 1870–1914 was brought to a halt by a 'global backlash' as well as the impact of the First World War and its consequences. Huntington has also talked about 'the clash of civilisations'.*[36] *Globalisation is often associated with the exercise of US power in many anti-globalist circles and this also fuels the potential for a backlash. Some even blame the USA for the current levels of world inequality. Do you fear the potential consequences for world economic progress of these developments?*

I don't like to engage in too much speculation; however, yes, I do fear the possibility of these developments. For example, we do see anti-globalisation demonstrations against the IMF and WTO as well as widespread anti-Americanism around much of the world, especially the Middle East. My best guess is that these forces will slow down globalisation but not reverse the process unless some unforeseen world crisis emerges of similar proportion to what happened in the 1930s with the Great Depression. I am convinced that globalisation is a strong force leading to improvement in institutions. Globalisation facilitates an increasing flow of ideas and international integration pressurises countries to adopt arrangements that act as a basis for encouraging further institutional change. No country can aim to trade effectively with the rest of the world and hope to progress without having a well-functioning legal system that protects not only domestic traders but also foreign traders. Countries like Iraq, Iran and Saudi Arabia have been able to maintain non-democratic regimes because of their oil revenues. These revenues finance the capacity of these types of regime to maintain their political and economic power. For most other countries, including large countries such as India and China, globalisation has been a positive force in their progress.

## THE POLITICAL ECONOMY OF GROWTH

*It is becoming increasingly clear from economists' research that institutional failures frequently prevent a country from adopting the most productive technologies. Some economists have suggested an 'economic losers' hypothesis' whereby powerful interest groups resist the adoption of new technology in order to protect their economic rents.*[37] *In one of your recent co-authored papers you advocate a 'political losers' hypothesis' as a more important explanation of why there emerge institutional barriers to development.*[38] *Why are political losers a more important barrier to development than economic losers?*

First of all, empirically there are few examples where economic losers have been able to block economic progress except maybe in the short run. For example, in England during the Industrial Revolution, the Luddites were unsuccessful in their attempts to resist the consequences of technological change. Second, economic losers need to have political power if they are effectively to block change. So this leads me to believe that the impact of economic change on the structure of political power will be a key determinant of whether technological progress will be blocked by an existing elite.

*How would you relate this argument to the case of England during the Industrial Revolution? Why didn't the politically powerful landed interests block the forces of industrialisation which ultimately weakened their political power?*
In England, the landed interests did not attempt to block industrialisation. Why did they not resist change? Because they felt that their political power was relatively secure. Despite the political reforms that extended the franchise in England in 1832, 1867 and 1884, the landed interests were protected by the House of Lords.

*Economists know what the broad requirements are that are needed for economic growth – or rather they at least know what not to do! In several recent papers you have analysed the main elements within the political dynamics of situations where countries continue to choose what everyone knows to be disastrous policies.[39] Since policies and institutions seem to be 'first-order' determinants of the economic performance of countries, why don't governments learn from their mistakes and switch to better policies?*
There are countries that persist with dysfunctional institutions and policies over many years and not always with the same person at the political helm. There are many countries where one disastrous dictator is replaced with another dictator who then proceeds to maintain the same failing policies and institutions. Often the new dictator turns out to be even worse and more incompetent than their predecessor! Lessons do not seem to be learned. The post-colonial experience of countries like the Democratic Republic of the Congo and Nigeria comes to mind. This process is repeated, decade after decade.

*What explains the persistent and repeated adoption and maintenance of inefficient institutions and proven bad policies? This is clearly one of the most important contemporary questions in political economy. Do you have any clear answers to this question?*
No. But I do have a sense of where the answer may lie. In economic theory the 'Coase Theorem' maintains that in the presence of well-defined property

rights and zero transaction costs, agents will achieve an efficient output-maximising result via contracting. This result holds irrespective of who owns particular assets. Recently I have discussed what I call the 'Political Coase Theorem', which suggests that there are strong political and economic forces that will push countries towards the adoption of policies and institutions that are optimal from society's point of view.[40] However, the applicability of the Political Coase Theorem is limited because of inherent commitment problems linked to political power. Powerful political groups that control the state will lack credibility in writing intertemporal contracts with the rest of society that promise reforms that will improve economic performance but weaken the power of the elite and also redistribute income to poorer groups. This has led me to emphasise two factors that are important in explaining the persistence of inefficient policies and institutions: the first relates to distributional conflict, and the second to problems associated with commitment. If we are going to have a rational choice explanation, that is, one that does not assume that these dysfunctional political leaders are irrational and ideologically blind to reason, then we have to assume that while the policies of these apparently dysfunctional political leaders are disastrous for the country as a whole, those same policies do produce immense benefits for the leaders and the groups that they might represent. This is what I mean by distributional conflict. Take the case of Mobutu in Zaire.[41] Clearly his policies were disastrous for Zaire. The economy shrank at about 2 per cent per year for about 30 years. But Mobutu himself accumulated a great deal of power and wealth. These issues raise some very interesting theoretical questions about how ideology and self-interest interact. Did Mobutu really believe that his policies would benefit Zaire in general? I doubt it.

*What about the rest of sub-Saharan political leaders, were they also simply looking after their own self-interest and wealth?*
Kleptocratic regimes have appeared all over the world. The regimes of Idi Amin in Uganda, the Somozas in Nicaragua, the Dominican Republic under Trujillo, the Duvaliers in Haiti, the Philippines under Marcos, and Liberia under Charles Taylor are all good examples of kleptocractic political regimes. In each case these administrations ruined the economy of the country, while small groups and individuals prospered. They all implemented highly inefficient economic policies, expropriated the wealth of their citizens and engaged in conspicuous consumption. But there are some political leaders who have adopted disastrous economic policies, not because they seek to accumulate wealth, but because they get themselves into an ideological dynamic where they actually think that these policies will promote growth and development. Julius Nyrere of Tanzania comes to mind as a leader who approached economics wearing an ideological blindfold but who

did not appear to have been motivated by a desire to accumulate personal wealth.

*An obvious question that emerges from this would seem to be: why don't the rest of society, who are losing out and suffering from bad policies, overthrow the self-interested dictator and install a new government committed to better development policies?*

Although dictators may have military power on their side, it is still the case that if the rest of society organises against a dictator then they cannot maintain their position. Clearly there must be some free-rider problems here and issues of divide and rule that allow dictators to remain in power for so long. The divide-and-rule strategy is made possible by institutional weaknesses. For example, dictators often use ethnic divisions within a country to divide and weaken the power base of the opposition.[42] Groups that threaten the power of the kleptocrat are also more likely to be taxed heavily than other groups. Research indicates that kleptocratic policies are more likely to arise in countries that have natural resources and receive foreign aid. These resources are then exploited to provide rents for the kleptocrat, who can then use them to buy off opposition groups.

*Why don't powerful dictators adopt efficient policies that will maximise income, then redistribute the gains to themselves?*

There is no guarantee that when a dictator adopts better policies the gains will only go to groups friendly to the dictator. Maybe opposition groups will also benefit. Suppose a dictator is backed by landowning interests, but a change in policies will mainly benefit merchants and industrialists who have traditionally opposed this particular dictator. The dictator could tax these groups. Is there anything preventing such action? These are the types of question that we need to answer when trying to understand the persistence of inefficient, dictatorial and corrupt political regimes.

*Are you finding any plausible answers to these kinds of question?*

One conjecture that I have been working on is as follows. While at first it is possible to tax groups that benefit from economic change, very soon the forces that a dictator unleashes by implementing reforms may overwhelm them. Industrialisation increases the economic power of groups who oppose the dictator and eventually these groups may become powerful enough to oppose the taxes or even overthrow the dictator.

*We seem to be in need of a convincing theory of political transitions.[43] How are some societies able to move successfully from dictatorship to democracy while others fail, often repeatedly?*

In recent work with James Robinson we have constructed a model where the political elite have an incentive to block change where they fear what we call 'a political replacement effect'. The political power of a non-democratic elite will often be threatened by technological change and economic progress. This makes them unwilling to initiate desirable reforms. They may even block progress deliberately to maintain their political power.[44] Our model predicts that elites are more likely to support reforms and progress when there is a high degree of political competition, or when the elite is highly entrenched.

*Can you explain why this is the case?*
An entrenched elite feels secure and does not feel threatened by reforms. Since a more productive reformed economy will raise the rents of the entrenched elite groups without reducing their political power, they are willing to support industrialisation and technological change. In the case where there is intense political competition, the elite is prepared to innovate to avoid being replaced completely. Those elites that are partly entrenched but also face some competition turn out to be the ones most opposed to change.

*Can you give some examples from historical experience?*
In Russia the elite had a lot to lose from change and the tsar blocked reforms. A similar scenario applies in the case of the Austria-Hungarian elites of the Habsburg Empire. In the UK the elite groups, in the face of political competition, were prepared to extend the franchise. This was a strategic decision to reduce the risk of social unrest and revolution.[45] In Germany the landed aristocracy felt secure and the *Junkers* formed a coalition with the emerging industrialists. In nineteenth-century Japan the power of the Tokugawa shogunate, a coalition of landowning groups, was shattered by the external threat posed by the activities of the UK and the USA in Asia. After the Meiji restoration in 1868, Japan began a process of defensive modernisation. In the USA the political environment, especially following the War of Independence from Britain, was highly competitive. This competition promoted institutional change and industrialisation.

# DEMOCRACY AND DEVELOPMENT

*Leading on from what you have just said, how important was the establishment of the US Constitution in the 1780s as a key element in the successful economic development of the US economy? The arguments developed by economists such as Douglass North and Mancur Olson highlight the importance of establishing credible constraints that encourage the establishment of non-predatory governments if private entrepreneurs are to respond to market opportunities and incentives.*[46] *Is democracy and good governance a major determinant of sustained development?*

Ultimately that must be so. But the issues here are very complex, especially in the short run. While labels are a good way of clarifying your thinking, the problem here is that the word democracy can mean many different things. The US Constitution does prevent power from residing in the hands of small groups, be they an economic group or a political group. And, in the long run, democracy is the only way of preserving such a diffusion of power. This has undoubtedly been essential for America's success. Any system that is non-democratic is not going to be able to have a credible and sustainable diffusion of political power.

*In sub-Saharan Africa, the colonial experience with democracy has been very disappointing. Why is this the case?*

All the African countries that were part of the British and French empires had terrible institutions before they became independent. After independence they became democratic and one might assume that this was a move in the right direction. However, in some ways it made their institutions worse. Why? Most of these countries had no tradition of democracy. They had no history of constraining the arbitrary use of power, so when opportunistic governments were elected they began to redistribute resources to their supporters. Even worse, they soon realised that the only way that they could remain in power was by engaging in very destructive patron–client relationships. Take the case of Ghana, a country that many people, in the late 1950s and early 1960s, thought had excellent development prospects. After independence the less productive urban centres were politically powerful compared to the more productive, but less politically powerful, rural areas. As a result taxes were levied on the cocoa producers and the tax revenue was used to benefit the powerful urban elites. This was how government after government sought to maintain their political power. This behaviour destroyed the productive rural economy. So in the case of Ghana, democracy became associated with bad policies. Where there are possibilities for one group to hijack democracy, the outcome can be disastrous for economic policy and political liberty. Take also the case of democracy in Islamic countries. Suppose there is a free election and the outcome is the formation of a popular Islamic government. This is a democratic outcome. But what if the Islamic government then bans opposition parties? Sustainable democracy is then extinguished. These are important issues for countries like Iraq, Iran and Algeria. Look also at the case of Singapore, South Korea and Malaysia. These countries were not democratic but for a long time they operated with a system that led to successful economic development.

*Why has democracy been so durable in the USA and Western Europe and so insecure and unstable in places like Latin America?*

A crucial determinant of political instability is the extent of inequality.[47] Where there are large inequalities in the distribution of income, the politically powerful rich elite have strong incentives to resist democratisation because democracy increases the power of the poor and leads to redistribution. So Latin American inequality is a key determinant of the political instability of that region. This relates back to the history of Latin America and the colonial origins of the extractive state that we discussed earlier.[48]

## CURRENT RESEARCH

*In addition to your work in macroeconomics and labour markets, what are your current research priorities in relation to the areas that we have been talking about?*

There are two areas where I feel that I need to do much more work. The first area where I would like to have a better understanding relates to questions such as: when and how do bad policies get adopted? Why do bad institutions persist? Take a country like Haiti that became independent in 1804. Haiti still has dysfunctional institutions and continuous political instability after 200 years of independence. Is this a coincidence, or a result of cultural and political factors? We need to develop a theory that explains what makes certain elite groups powerful and also anti-developmental in their choice of policies. In answering questions like this I feel that I am only touching the tip of an enormous iceberg (*laughter*). A second area that interests me is to carry out political economy analysis at a more micro level. We need to look at and understand what goes on within countries because that is where a lot of politics is decided. We need to go to the level of local politics because in large countries like India, China and Brazil, different things are going on in different states and regions. I would like to know much more about how the different histories of these regions impacts on their local politics and institutions. I am also co-authoring a new book with James Robinson entitled *Economic Origins of Dictatorship and Democracy*.[49]

## NOTES

1.  I interviewed Professor Acemoglu in his office at MIT on 16 May 2003.
2.  Details of Professor Acemoglu's publications can be found at: http://econ-www.mit.edu/faculty/index.htm?prof_id=acemoglu.
3.  See Bates (1981, 1989, 2001, 2004).

4. See, for example, Acemoglu and Zilibotti (1997); Acemoglu and Robinson (2000a); Acemoglu et al. (2001, 2002, 2003a, 2003b, 2005a, 2005b, 2005c); Acemoglu (2003a). See also the recent papers by Galor and Weil (2000); Galor and Moav (2002, 2006); Galor and Omer (2002); and Galor and Mountford (2006).
5. Snowdon (2002a, 2002b).
6. Maddison (2001).
7. Todaro and Smith (2003).
8. See Acemoglu et al. (2006).
9. See Chapter 1, sections 1.14 and 1.15.
10. See Panagariya (2004a), and Dani Rodrik interview.
11. Acemoglu and Johnson, and Robinson (2005a).
12. Sachs and Warner (1995, 1999, 2001); Acemoglu et al. (2003b); Sala-i-Martin and Subramanian (2003).
13. Pomeranz (2000).
14. Acemoglu et al. (2001, 2002).
15. Temin (1997); Landes (1998); Lal (1999); Barro and McCleary (2003, 2005, 2006); Noland (2003).
16. Guiso et al. (2003, 2006).
17. World Bank (2002); Jütting (2003); Rodrik (2003a, 2003b); Rodrik et al. (2004).
18. Knack and Keefer (1995, 1997).
19. See, for example, North (1989, 1990, 1991, 1994); North and Weingast (1989).
20. Acemoglu and Johnson (2005).
21. See www.prsonline.com. On the 'Polity IV Project' see Marshall and Jaggers (2000).
22. Glaeser and Shleifer (2002); Djankov et al. (2002).
23. Acemoglu et al. (2001, 2002).
24. Easterly and Levine (1997, 2003); Bloom and Sachs (1998); Gallup et al. (1999); Sachs and McArthur (2001); Artadi and Sala-i-Martin (2003); Rodrik (2003a, 2003b); Sachs (2003a, 2003b); Yang (2003).
25. See, for example, Frank (1978).
26. Acemoglu et al. (2005a).
27. Collier (2003); Eifert et al. (2003).
28. Acemoglu et al. (2003b); Rodrik (2003a).
29. Alesina and Perotti (1994); Benabou (1996); Aghion et al. (1999); Barro (2000); Galor and Moav (2002); Glaeser et al. (2003).
30. Deininger and Squire (1996).
31. Forbes (2000).
32. Banerjee and Duflo (2003).
33. Alesina and Rodrik (1994); Persson and Tabellini (1994).
34. See Bhalla (2002); Bourguignon and Morrisson (2002); Sala-i-Martin (2002a, 2002b, 2006); Acemoglu (2002, 2003b); Acemoglu and Ventura (2002); Milanovic (2006).
35. See Lucas (2000) for some optimistic projections.
36. Williamson, J.G. (1998a); Huntington (1996).
37. See, for example, Parente and Prescott (2000).
38. Acemoglu and Robinson (2000b).
39. Acemoglu and Robinson (2000a, 2000b, 2000c, 2001).
40. Acemoglu (2003c).
41. Acemoglu, Johnson and Verdier (2004).
42. Easterly (2001b).
43. Acemoglu and Robinson (2001).
44. Acemoglu and Robinson (2000a, 2000b).
45. Acemoglu and Robinson (2006a).
46. North (1990); Olson (1993, 1996, 2000).
47. Alesina et al. (1996).
48. See also Engerman and Sokoloff (2000).
49. Acemoglu and Robinson (2006a).

# Alberto Alesina[1]

Alberto Alesina received his undergraduate education in economics at Università Bocconi in Milan before completing his Masters (1985) and PhD (1986) degrees at Harvard University. Since 1986 he has held the following professional positions: Postdoctoral Fellow, then Assistant Professor of Economics and Political Economy, Carnegie Mellon University (1986–88); Assistant Professor of Economics and Government at Harvard University (1988–90); Paul Stack Associate Professor of Political Economy, Harvard University (1991–93); Professor of Economics and Government, Harvard University (1993–2003); Nathanial Ropes Professor of Political Economics, and Chair of the Department of Economics, Harvard University (2003–2006).

Professor Alesina has been the recipient of numerous honours, awards and research grants, was Olin Fellow at the NBER (1989–90), Visiting Professor at MIT (1998–99) and IGIER–Bocconi (2002–03). He is also a Research Fellow at the Centre for Economic Policy Research (1987–present), Research Associate at the NBER (1993–present), Research Associate at the Centre for International Development at Harvard (2000–present), a senior associate at the Harvard Centre for European Studies (1994–present) and Weatherhead Centre for International Affairs (1997–present), and Faculty Associate at the Centre for Basic Research in the Social Sciences at Harvard (2003–present). Professor Alesina has been a consultant to the World Bank (1991–92), the

Italian Treasury (1996–97), and an academic visitor at numerous institutions including the IMF and the Kiel Institute for World Economics. He was a co-editor for the journals *Economics and Politics* (1991–94), and the *Quarterly Journal of Economics*, (1998–2004), and is also an associate editor for several other prestigious journals, including the *Journal of Economic Growth* (1994–present) and the *European Economic Review* (1992–present). Since 1987, over 80 of his influential papers have been published in leading academic journals, and to date he has also co-authored and edited ten books.[2] His most recent book, *Europe: A Wake Up Call* (co-authored with Francesco Giavazzi), was published in 2006.

The relationship between the economy and the political system has always attracted the interest of economists since it is obvious that politics will influence the choice of economic policies and consequently economic performance. During the last 30 years, research into the various forms of interaction between politics and economic performance has become a major growth area. Professor Alesina has made major contributions to this field of research activity, in terms of both theoretical analysis and empirical investigation. A major feature of Alesina's research is its originality. Both he and his co-researchers have repeatedly made imaginative use of the tools of modern economic analysis to explore a wide range of important and controversial contemporary issues. The burgeoning field of 'new political economy' makes specific use of the modern technical apparatus of economic analysis, including game theory, to investigate numerous key public policy issues such as business cycles, the conduct and implementation of stabilisation policies,[3] the relationship between dictatorship, democracy, inequality and economic growth, the origin of persistent budget deficits, international integration and the size of nations, and the impact of ethnic diversity on economic performance.

In the interview that follows, Professor Alesina gives his views on several important contemporary issues, including, politics and the business cycle, budget deficits, currency unions, the European Union, the size of nations, economic growth, inequality, democracy, foreign aid, ethnic fractionalisation, and the welfare state in the USA and Europe.

## BACKGROUND INFORMATION

*In your work you have always emphasised the interaction of political and economic forces in order to provide greater insights into key public policy issues. What or who influenced you to pursue this line of thinking in your research?*
There was no particular person who early on influenced me to take this direction. The most important influence was growing up in Italy. Going to

university there led to a view that an understanding of political forces was critically important for understanding how an economy functions. At that time, in the late 1970s, students in Italy were eating and breathing politics. There were many intense political debates going on and I was a very interested participant. My undergraduate supervisor was Mario Monti, currently a member of the European Commission responsible for competition, who was very involved in the political–economic debate in Italy. He wrote many newspaper articles and I learned from him how economics was interesting, not as an abstract science, but as a way of influencing economic policy.

*You then left Italy and came here to Harvard.*
When I first came to Harvard in 1982, for a couple of years I was immersed in studying economic theory, math, econometrics, and the other tools used by economists. But when I started to work on my thesis my interest in the linkages between politics and economic policy resurfaced. This was about the time that Robert Barro was writing his seminal papers relating to the time inconsistency issue in monetary policy, first introduced to the economics literature by Finn Kydland and Edward Prescott.[4] That whole literature was very influential for me. One of my supervisors was Jeffery Sachs, who at that time was getting heavily involved with providing policy advice to various countries. From his practical experiences he also emphasised to me just how important an understanding of political forces is in influencing economic policy decisions.[5]

*Is this when your interest in political business cycles began?*
Yes, and I wrote my PhD thesis on this issue.


# POLITICS AND THE BUSINESS CYCLE

*You have described your work as 'new political economy'. How does this differ from the 'old political economy'? Was the rational expectations revolution the dividing line that separates your work from that of 'political business cycle' theory contained in the 1975 seminal paper by William Nordhaus?*
I would not classify the Nordhaus paper on political business cycles as something fundamentally different to the work in this area in the late 1980s. The connections are much stronger than the differences. The main differences between the older tradition of political economy that I associate with James Buchanan and the public choice school, and what has been called the new political economy, is not so much the subject matter or the nature of the results; rather it is that the older tradition has always been on

the sideline of mainstream economics whereas the new political economy is part of the mainstream. James Buchanan was always reluctant to use the standard tools of economics in his work and on the other side economists were not ready to open their minds to the fact that politics was important. There was a definite schism. What the new political economy has done is to reduce this schism. Mainstream economists now have a much greater appreciation of the importance of taking into account the influence of political factors into their analysis.[6] Those economists researching in the new political economy field now use the same tools and methodology as those working in the mainstream. While the Nordhaus paper created a lot of interest, it did not generate a burst of work in political economy. That came in the late 1980s. Since then there has been an explosion of research in this area.[7]

*Allan Drazen has recently reviewed a quarter-century of the political business cycle literature.*[8] *His review concluded by arguing that 'monetary surprises are an unconvincing driving force for political cycles, either opportunistic or partisan; research should concentrate on fiscal policy as the driving force, especially for opportunistic cycles. Political monetary cycles are more likely the effect of accommodation of fiscal impulses, that is, are passive while fiscal policy is active in trying to affect election outcomes.' What is your view of Drazen's conclusion?*
I think that paper gives the wrong overall impression. It is not necessary to choose between one view or the other on the causes of political business cycles. I don't think it is particularly interesting whether or not it is fiscal or monetary policy that is being used opportunistically by politicians. It is possible that politicians will use both. In some countries fiscal manipulations may predominate; in other countries monetary manipulations may predominate. There is also evidence that governments that manipulate fiscal policy in election years may alienate voters.[9] However, it is true that most recent papers that I have seen on the political business cycle issue have focused on fiscal policy. So I do not deny the importance of fiscal policy, but there is evidence for both fiscal and monetary distortions of policy. Having said that, if I were to review the literature on the political business cycle I would not try to present the research findings in this way.[10]

*How would you approach such a survey?*
I see the main issues in the political business cycle literature to be related to whether or not voters behave rationally, the significance of opportunistic behaviour versus partisan behaviour, the link between electoral systems and the business cycle, the impact of central bank independence on the opportunistic and partisan behaviour of politicians, and the extent of

political distortions to policy making in developed versus developing countries. To me these are some of the more important research issues. In his
survey paper Drazen offers his AFMP model [active fiscal passive monetary policy] in order to address some of the problems associated with earlier
models such as the partisan monetary surprise model. However, it seems
unlikely that opportunistic models will find strong empirical support from
US data because the USA has a well-informed media and a large degree of
central bank independence.[11]

*Your rational partisan theory suggests that left-of-centre governments are
likely to have a problem in establishing their anti-inflation credibility when
they get elected.[12] In Britain this is of particular interest because as soon as
the 'new' Labour government was elected in May 1997, the Chancellor,
Gordon Brown, hit the ground running by announcing that the Bank of
England would be given 'operational independence' in the conduct of monetary policy. I understand that Gordon Brown's former economic adviser, Ed
Balls, was a student here at Harvard in the late 1980s. It is tempting to believe
that it was your ideas, carried to Downing Street via Ed Balls, that played a
significant part in the Chancellor's decision.[13]*
Ed Balls was not directly my student but I did know him and he was certainly aware of my work. I think the work that has been done on central
bank independence has been very influential and I have contributed to that
literature.[14] I agree with the inference of your question that the Labour
Party did make the Bank of England independent to strengthen their anti-
inflation credibility.[15] This line of research linking anti-inflation credibility
with central bank independence has in general been very influential.[16] As I
recall, when Chancellor Brown announced that the Bank of England would
be given operational independence, he explicitly identified the need for
monetary policy to be free from political influences as a major factor
influencing the decision.[17] Today, few economists disagree with the idea of
giving the central bank a certain amount of independence, although controversy still remains over the optimal degree of independence.

## THE POLITICAL ECONOMY OF BUDGET DEFICITS

*During the mid-to-late 1990s you produced a number of important papers on
the problem of excessive budget deficits in OECD economies.[18] In those co-
authored papers, with Roberto Perotti and others, you made it clear that
reducing budget deficits would involve making difficult and unpopular decisions because sustainable reductions in deficits require cuts in government
spending in politically sensitive areas. Your influential 1991 paper with Allan*

*Drazen, 'Why are Stabilisations Delayed?', also highlights the 'war of attrition' problem that inevitably occurs when different groups in society attempt to escape bearing the burden of adjustment that accompanies a programme of deficit reduction. Looking back, what are your reflections on that body of research?*

Modesty aside, I think it was some of my most successful work. The paper with Allan is certainly one of my most cited papers. That paper helps to rationalise why the path of policy during a crisis often appears to be completely crazy. Everybody knows that sooner or later tough decisions will have to be made and that the longer the decisions are delayed, the tougher will be the outcome. And yet we observe countries where governments continue with non-sustainable policies that lead to the excessive accumulation of public debt and severe inflation. While an efficient social planner would stabilise immediately, in societies populated by heterogeneous groups, conflict arises over who should bear the burden of adjustment. This is what leads to the costly delay of the required stabilisation policies. Stabilisation is eventually implemented when one group becomes visibly stronger than the other and the weaker group ends up bearing the increased tax burden.

The work on fiscal adjustments captured the attention of policy makers at the IMF and OECD. What we found with that research was that successful fiscal adjustment, that is, adjustments that can be sustained, are those that cut spending rather than raise taxes, and significant cuts in spending can only be achieved by reducing politically sensitive items that tend to grow automatically, such as public transfers, social security and public sector wages. This is the bad news. The other result that we found, which is the good news, is that if you make this kind of effective fiscal adjustment there is a good chance that the cuts will not produce a recession as a traditional textbook Keynesian model might predict. Contrary to popular opinion, the macroeconomic environment does not necessarily deteriorate as a result of a fiscal adjustment. The most famous example is Ireland, where following the late 1980s fiscal adjustment economic growth took off. In neoclassical models a permanent cut in government consumption should lead to a rise in private consumption because the reduction in future tax liabilities increases the wealth of the private sector. A successful fiscal consolidation is also likely to lead to a reduction in interest rates due to a reduction in default and inflation risk. So effective fiscal adjustments can be expansionary.

*Some economists have argued that budget surpluses are undesirable because they present a great temptation for governments to expand spending and the size of government. Budget deficits, in contrast, act as a constraint on government spending. Do you agree with this argument?*

That is an interesting question because I am currently writing a paper with Guido Tabellini that addresses this very issue.[19] There is certainly some substance to this argument, particularly for non-OECD countries where mismanagement and corruption are more of a problem. One observation that is now commonly accepted is that fiscal policy in a lot of non-OECD countries is procyclical, so when there is a boom in the economy, and a consequent budget surplus, spending increases. In recessions, spending is cut. This is the exact opposite of what should be happening to stabilise the economy.

*In the* Financial Times *earlier this week there was a leading article discussing Italy's current fiscal position.[20] The article points out that Italy's fiscal position is probably the most serious in the European Union and that Italy has slow growth, rising unemployment, inflexible labour markets and a loss of competitiveness. Moreover, having joined the single currency, Italy has lost independence with respect to its monetary and exchange rate policy. This is a pretty depressing summary of Italy's current economic situation. As an Italian, what are your thoughts on this assessment?*

Although I have not seen this particular article I agree with the general summary that you provide. Italy does have all the problems that you highlight from this article. The Silvio Berlusconi government is a right-wing government but has not yet introduced the necessary reforms. One problem is that the 'social right' in Italy has many of the same preferences as the 'social left' and is very reluctant to accept any kind of cuts to spending, or the reform of pensions, and wants to preserve the over-protective labour market legislation. It certainly has little interest in market liberalisation. Another problem for Berlusconi is that he has been involved with personal problems involving conflicts of interest for a long time. Italy desperately needs a more pro-market economic policy based on the usual changes involving a serious tax cut, supply-side reforms, market liberalisation in both the goods and labour market, and control of government spending. The education system also needs reforming. Having said all that, I am not so sure that Germany is in any better shape than Italy at the moment, although Italy does have some problems that other countries do not have, such as the disparity of living standards between the north and the south, a significant tax evasion problem, and an administration that is not as efficient as in other EU countries.

## CURRENCY UNIONS AND THE EUROPEAN UNION

*In your recent publications on currency unions you argue that since 1947 the increasing integration of international markets would imply 'that the optimal number of currencies would tend to decrease, rather than more than double as it has'.*[21] *Why are there too many currencies in 2004?*

In 1945 there were 76 countries and 65 separate currencies. Now there over 190 countries in the world and over 160 different currencies. Either there were too few currencies in 1945 or there are too many now unless we think that every country needs to have its own currency. There is no economic rationale for believing that there needs to be a one-to-one relationship between the number of countries and the number of currencies. So there appear to be too many currencies and that is the starting point of our recent research in this area. An increase in the number of countries increases the volume of international transactions and this should increases the attractiveness of currency unions. So the number of currencies should rise disproportionately with the number of countries. As Robert Mundell showed many years ago in pioneering work on optimal currency areas, political borders and currency boundaries should not always coincide.[22] That there are so many currencies across the world economy must reflect the importance governments attach to maintaining a symbol of monetary autonomy.

*What are the main costs and benefits of a currency union?*
The main benefits of currency unions result from lower transaction costs of trading in goods and services, and, as the recent research of Jeffrey Frankel and Andrew Rose shows, common currencies do stimulate bilateral trade and also boost overall trade, leading to gains in output and consumption.[23] Research has also shown that 'border effects' are significant. For example, trade between Canadian provinces is much greater than between a Canadian province and a neighbouring US state across the border.[24] These border effects are large even without explicit trade restrictions. Where there are different currencies across borders it appears that this acts as a restriction on trade flows. Currency unions also commit member countries to greater monetary stability. This is especially beneficial to countries that have a history of monetary indiscipline. These benefits need to be compared to the loss of monetary sovereignty and the implications of this for the use of independent monetary policy to target specific domestic shocks within member countries. The European Central Bank does not use monetary policy to deal with specific shocks that may affect any single member country. Rather, its mandate is to target European shocks.

*Who gains the most from the formation of currency unions, small countries or large countries?*
Our research shows that small open economies gain the most from the formation of a currency union, especially if they trade a lot with one big

partner. Countries that have difficulty maintaining a credible low inflation policy also gain from joining a currency union. Such countries gain credibility by eliminating domestic monetary policy. El Salvador, for example, has dollarised, and gained a lot. Countries that have the largest co-movements of GDP and prices with a potential anchor currency will have much less to lose from a loss of monetary independence.

*The early research on optimal currency areas highlighted the relevant issues that needed to be considered when a particular group of countries is considering the formation of a currency union or fixed exchange rate system. It was Nobel Laureate Robert Mundell who pioneered the analysis of which countries or which groups of countries represent an 'optimal currency area'.[25] In his seminal paper, Mundell asked the question: 'What is the appropriate domain of a currency area?' Do you think that the European Union is an optimal currency area?*

If you read what economists were writing six months before the euro came into place, it was all quite negative on economic grounds. The introduction of the euro seems to have worked reasonably well. It is certainly true that some of Mundell's conditions are not satisfied. If we believe that labour mobility is a fundamental precondition for a successful currency union, then there would be few currency unions. So there are other factors that must compensate for this deficiency. These include the gains from trade, financial integration and greater competition. It remains to be seen whether or not the euro will be a long-term success. However, we should not forget that the introduction of the euro is also seen as an important step towards political integration. That really worries me. The European currency union is fine but I do not want to see EMU used as an excuse to coordinate taxes and labour laws, and eventually everything else. That is a very slippery slope to get on.

*One particular problem for UK entry into the EMU is that the UK's business cycle is currently out of line with the major countries in the euro area. Some writers have suggested that business cycles will harmonise endogenously as countries respond to a common monetary policy.[26] Is that a plausible argument?*

Yes, to a certain extent. With a single monetary policy there is bound to be some harmonisation of the business cycle across the economies of the euro area. Increased trade should increase the co-movements of output and prices. But research into this issue has not provided a clear answer. Theoretically the answer depends on the extent of inter-industry trade versus intra-industry trade, with the latter more likely to lead to more co-movements as trade increases following the formation of a currency union.

In the former case, heightened specialisation is likely to lower co-movements since a specific shock to an industry then becomes a country-specific shock. Since intra-industry trade is more important in rich countries I suspect that ten years from now we will read a lot of papers that show that business cycle harmonisation has taken place. The lack of perfect business-cycle synchronisation creates potential costs from the formation of a currency union, and these costs have to be weighed against the benefits of such a union, which include reduced transaction costs and the gains from increased trade and greater competition. That said, I think the reluctance of the UK to enter EMU has much more to do with the fear that it will mark an important step towards European political integration, rather than technical monetary policy considerations.

*According to Hugh Rockoff, it took something like 150 years for the USA to become an optimal currency area.[27] Surely this is not good news for euro enthusiasts?*
Although I have not read that particular paper I would be wary of transferring the experiences of the USA 200 years ago to Europe today.

*In your 2002 paper with Robert Barro and Silvana Tenreyro on 'Optimal Currency Areas' you argue that although there exist well-defined euro and dollar currency areas, there is no well-defined yen currency area. Why is this the case?*
In that paper we considered the dollar, the euro and the yen as three potential anchor currencies. We identified which countries were correlated in business-cycle terms with each of the USA, the EU and Japan. We also looked at the trading links of various countries with the USA, the EU and Japan. We found that there was a fairly well-defined group of countries that traded a lot with the USA and were reasonably well correlated to the US business cycle. The same is true in the case of Europe. But as far as Japan is concerned we found that there are very few countries that trade mostly with Japan and are also in line with Japan's business cycle. In fact the Japanese business cycle over the last 30 years does not appear to have been correlated much with that of any other country. At the moment there is a lot of discussion about the possibility of an East Asian currency union but it is unlikely that this will involve the adoption of the yen. Rather it will likely involve the introduction of a new currency, as was the case with the euro.

*The EU changed profoundly on 1 May 2004, with the entry of ten new members. In your recent papers on the EU you have argued that the policy-making institutions of the EU have now extended their domain well beyond the original mission of establishing a free market zone with a common external trade policy.*[28] *Is there a danger that the EU has now become too large and hence a potentially unwieldy international organisation?*

The general theme of these papers is to review the evolution of European integration and the allocation of powers between European institutions. There is a well-established literature in economics related to the issue of fiscal federalism that discusses what different levels of government should be doing.[29] That literature generated a set of criteria that can be used to determine what policies are appropriate at different levels of government. In our recent papers we have tried to apply the same principles to the EU. What are the appropriate tasks for the various layers of government within the EU? Empirically, we find that the allocation of tasks in the EU is the outcome of conflict between different bureaucracies fighting with each other in order to maintain their prestige and influence rather than a rational allocation. Currently the EU has a complex web of institutions that have overlapping jurisdictions. This has led to a distinct lack of clarity in the allocation of powers across the major EU institutions. As a result the European Commission does a lot of things that duplicate activities, or does lots of things that it shouldn't really be doing at all. Conversely, there are many things that the Commission should be doing that it is not doing. If you think of the EU as a federal state, which I don't think it should be, then foreign policy is clearly something that should be coordinated at the highest level. Yet it seems highly unlikely that such a coordinated foreign policy will happen any time soon. In other areas such as regulation, social protection and agriculture, EU involvement is over-expanded and there is far too much involvement. In short, the EU is heavily involved in too many areas where economies of scale are low and the heterogeneity of preferences among citizens is high. The result is a significant difference between the desirable compared to the actual allocation of policy responsibilities among EU institutions. The ongoing debate on what the functions of the EU should be is very important, not least because of the enlargement of the EU. There are certainly inconsistencies between both enlarging and deepening the scope of the EU.[30]

## THE SIZE OF NATIONS

*Much of your recent research has focused on the economic determinants of the size of nations, where size is measured by total population.*[31] *How much does size matter for economic success?*

If you look at the five largest countries in the world in terms of population, that is, China, India, the USA, Indonesia and Brazil, only the USA has a high per capita income. We also find that many of the richest countries in the world have populations below the world median, which is about 6 million people. These small countries also have some of the fastest growth rates of per capita income. Of course not all small countries are rich, but Singapore, with a population of 3 million, shows just how much a small country can prosper by being integrated into the world economy.

*To what extent is the size of a country determined by geography?*
Political borders are made by people and are not exogenous geographical features.

*To most non-economists the determination of the size of nations has to do with politics. Your research provides a coherent explanation of the determination of the size of nations based on economic analysis. What are the main benefits and costs associated with the size of a nation?*
It is best to think of the equilibrium size of countries as the outcome of a trade-off between the benefits of size versus the costs of preference heterogeneity, which inevitably increase with population size. One of the main benefits of size is national security. There are clear economies of scale linked to military spending. Even if you are a small country you can take advantage of size by belonging to a military alliance with a large country, but it is unlikely that as a junior partner you will be able to determine policy. So size matters for security. A second benefit relates to economies of scale in the production of certain public goods. For example, a small country may find it difficult to develop a good university system. A third benefit of size is mutual insurance. If you live in a particular region of a large country, and that region suffers a recession, then there are likely to be transfers from other regions that can stabilise the regional economy.[32] Fourth, in a world of trade restrictions there are economies of scale coming as a result of having a large internal market. In contrast, in a world of free trade a country can be small and trade with the whole world. So this last benefit of size becomes less important as the world economy becomes more open and globalised. The importance of market size as a determinant of the limits of specialisation and productivity growth was recognised early on by Adam Smith in *The Wealth of Nations*. As far as the costs of size are concerned, the most significant one that we emphasise is that a large country is likely to be very diverse in terms of culture, preferences, ethnicity and religion. This makes it much more difficult to govern because of the heterogeneity of preferences. Larger countries may also experience increasing administrative and congestion costs.

*Given that the benefits of size fall as international economic integration increases, should we therefore expect to see, in a more globalised world, more countries?*

Yes, the optimal size of a country will be smaller in a world economy with freer trade. Increasing trade openness shifts the balance of benefits and costs so that small countries can prosper. This is why political disintegration and economic integration are correlated. Country size is endogenous to several important economic factors.

*There is evidence that a more democratic world would almost certainly be a more peaceful world.*[33] *Some writers argue that globalisation has a positive effect on the spread of democratic political institutions.*[34] *Does this imply that international economic integration and globalisation will lead to a more peaceful world?*
I think so. Think about two countries that may go to war with each other. If they have significant economic ties, then a war will be very costly in economic terms. So economic integration acts as a disincentive to conflict between two countries. The evidence also strongly supports the idea that democracies do not tend to go to war with each other. Whether democracies do not go to war with each other because they are democracies or because democracies are more open to trade remains to be determined. So democratisation, globalisation and peace should go together. So there is great potential for small countries to prosper. Although the world in 2004 does not look very peaceful, I would attribute much of that to the fact that there remain many non-democratic countries that are also not very open.

# ECONOMIC GROWTH, INEQUALITY, DEMOCRACY AND AID

*Another research area where you have been a participant is the nature of the relationship between economic growth and inequality.*[35] *The old view that dominated thinking in the early development economics literature was that inequality is good for growth because the rich tend to have a high propensity to save and capital accumulation was viewed as the key driver of economic growth. This thinking came out of the influential Lewis and Harrod–Domar growth models.*[36] *The modern view, supported by your research, suggests that inequality may be detrimental to growth. Why should inequality be bad for growth?*
The modern literature emphasises a variety of channels. For example, credit market imperfections reduce the ability of the poor to invest in human capital, inequality creates socio-political instability, thereby increasing uncertainty and reducing investment. Inequality is also likely to promote redistributive policies that introduce tax distortions and damage work effort and entrepreneurship. It is fair to say that there is also not much empirical evidence to support the proposition that more inequality leads to

more growth. The evidence that less inequality leads to more growth is certainly stronger. While the whole issue is complicated because the relationship between inequality and growth may be different at different levels of income, most people now seem to agree that too much inequality may be counterproductive in terms of growth for poor countries but not for rich countries. The main controversy is over the mechanism that links inequality to slower growth. Economists don't fully understand this link.

*What about the relationship between economic growth and democracy? Does democracy promote growth?*
The relationship between democracy and growth is very controversial but I do not think that there is any strong positive empirical relationship running from democracy to economic growth. The rich countries of the world are certainly more democratic, but that does not prove any causation. We have also seen excellent growth performance from some dictatorships in East Asia and dreadful growth performance from dictatorships in sub-Saharan Africa. Having said this, my view is that if you put yourself behind a veil of ignorance and ask whether you would like to live in a dictatorship or a democracy, most people will choose democracy. Good dictators are rare and if you get a bad dictator you are in really big trouble. So while democracies have various problems, they are a much more attractive proposition than having a bad dictator. Having a benevolent dictator might be acceptable but there are not many of those around, and what if they turn 'bad'?[37]

*In a recent paper, Daron Acemoglu and his co-authors argue that in countries where initial political institutions placed checks on the absolute power of the monarchy, the growth of Atlantic trade in the period after 1500 led to further empowerment of the merchant groups and changes in institutions that favourably affected the protection of their property rights.[38] These changes were crucial to the acceleration of economic growth in the more democratic European states such as Britain compared to the more absolutist states such as Spain.*
I am not convinced that the link between Atlantic trade, democracy and growth is so strong. There is certainly a link between Atlantic trade and growth, but that link does not necessarily run though the democracy channel. Looking at more recent times, the fact is that if you run a regression on data for the last 30 years on democracy and growth performance you find no relationship. I find the Barro–Lipset story that increasing prosperity promotes democracy to be more convincing.[39] The case of England in the seventeenth century, highlighted by Douglass North, Daron Acemoglu and others, may be correct, but during the last 30 years the evidence on a positive link between democracy and growth is weak. The

correlation between the protection of property rights and economic growth is far from perfect.

*Many papers have been written in recent years on the issue of convergence and divergence of living standards across the economies of the world. For example, Robert Lucas is an optimist on convergence while Nick Crafts and Tony Venables are much less sanguine.[40] Drawing on the new economic geography and new institutional economic history literature, Crafts fears that 'the handicaps of distance and the persistence of sub-optimal institutions will act to dilute this process' of convergence. What do you think are the prospects for convergence in the twenty-first century?*

Although I am reluctant to make a prediction on such a big issue, my feeling is that Robert Lucas is right. I am especially optimistic for India, China and Eastern Europe. I certainly agree that the case of sub-Saharan Africa is a major problem, but with this exception I am very optimistic that other regions of the world will experience significant catch-up during this century, especially if global economic integration continues to increase.[41]

*Much attention in economic growth research has recently focused on what Dani Rodrik has called the 'deeper determinants of growth'.[42] These deeper determinants include the impact of institutions, geography and culture. Jeffrey Sachs has criticised economists for their neglect of geography in their explanations of international differences in the level and growth rate of per capita income.[43] Do you agree with Sachs that economists have for too long neglected the impact of geography on the economic performance of nations?*

I think that geography is very important. I know Jeff very well and when he wants to make a point he tends to exaggerate. Sometimes it almost sounds as if he is saying that geography is all that matters. It certainly matters, but how much is the interesting question. Jeff is certainly right in criticising economists for underestimating geographical influences for a long time. There are some aspects of geography that are endogenous. Jeff makes a big issue about whether or not a country is landlocked. But, as we discussed earlier, that is a question of politics, not of geography. That is why wars have often been fought – to gain access to the sea and trading routes.

*Jeffrey Sachs has also been a vociferous champion of the role of foreign aid in promoting development.[44] Your recent papers on foreign aid, along with those of Bill Easterly, are highly critical of placing such high faith in the role of foreign aid in promoting growth and economic development.[45] Why has aid had such disappointing and often counterproductive results?*

Jeff Sachs has taken on the role of advocating an increase in resource transfers from rich to poor countries. In my view he underestimates the waste and corruption generated by aid transfers. For Sachs to be more convincing he should be more up front about how to deal with the corruption problem. Jeff Sachs argues that the sub-Saharan tragedy is mostly about adverse geography rather than bad governance and destructive policies. I think that this is an over-simplistic view and ignores too much the extensive failure of governments on that continent. Political instability has been a major constraint on economic progress and I do not believe that providing more foreign aid in that kind of environment is sensible. To take a very small but revealing example, a friend of mine got married and collected money from wedding guests to donate to some charitable foundation in Africa in order to build a school. We heard later that a local warlord had stolen all the money, so my donation is now probably financing the purchase of weapons, drugs or prostitutes! The evidence shows that the way that aid is dispersed has a lot to do with political links between the donor and recipient. The only exceptions to this are the aid dispersions from the Northern European countries such as Norway and Sweden. With a lack of colonial history and few political links they can do a much better job at allocating their aid resources.

## ETHNIC FRACTIONALISATION

*Another burgeoning research area is investigating the impact of ethnic diversity on the economic performance of nations, regions and cities. You have contributed several important papers to this issue.*[46] *What are the costs and benefits of ethnic diversity?*
I am currently writing a survey article on ethnic fractionalisation for a forthcoming issue of the *Journal of Economic Literature*. I find this to be a fascinating subject. The potential benefits arise from variety of production while the costs come from increased problems linked to difficulty in agreeing the provision of public goods and public policies. For example, on the costs side there is mounting empirical evidence that supports the hypothesis that in more ethnically diverse localities in the USA, the provision of public goods is less efficient, trust is less, and economic success, measured by growth of city size, is inferior.[47]

*Why does ethnic fractionalisation so often lead to negative rather than positive outcomes?*
For a variety of reasons, having to do with individual psychology, culture, language and history, different ethnic groups have difficulty understanding each other, sometimes to the extent that they hate each other. There is evidence that trust does not travel well across racial groups.[48] So a lot of political conflict around the world has an ethnic dimension to it. Recent

well-known examples include the conflicts in Bosnia, Kosovo, the Caucasus region of the former Soviet Union, Rwanda and the Sudan. There is a lot of evidence that ethnic fractionalisation causes huge problems in some countries, such as many in sub-Saharan Africa.[49] On the other hand the USA and Switzerland are countries that have very successful economies even though they have a high degree of ethnic and/or linguistic fractionalisation. Of course there are examples of ethnic conflict in the USA in the form of racial problems in the inner city. And yet New York and Los Angeles, both of which have very high ethnic fractionalisation, have very successful economies and lead the way in the arts. So when ethnic diversity works well it becomes a very creative melting pot. When it works very badly we get, in the extreme, cases like Rwanda and Bosnia. In Africa they seem to be getting the worst consequences from high ethnic diversity whereas in the USA, in the main, we see some of the best consequences. There is now a large literature on the impact of ethnic fragmentation on government activities, the quality of institutions and economic outcomes. I suspect that this whole area of research is going to be absolutely critical over the next few years and beyond. Ethnic diversity also has implications for the size of countries. As we discussed earlier, heterogeneous preferences, which increase with country size and the extent of ethnic diversity, make it more difficult to implement common policies. Hence the break-up of a country often has an ethnic dimension.

*Paul Collier suggests that democracy is much better than dictatorship in resolving conflict for countries that have high ethnic diversity.[50] Do you agree?*
Collier's idea is that minorities feel more represented in democratic systems and therefore less oppressed than they would under dictatorship. The problem with this line of argument is that democracy is highly correlated with the level of income per capita. So it is hard to say for certain that it is democracy that helps a country cope with ethnic diversity, or the fact that rich countries are more capable and have more resources to solve or prevent ethnic conflict.

## THE WELFARE STATE IN THE USA AND EUROPE

*In an interesting paper you ask the following question: 'Why Doesn't the US Have a European Style Welfare State?'[51] The USA and Europe clearly have a very different approach to the welfare state. How do you explain this?*
This issue is also the subject of my new co-authored book with Edward Glaeser, *Fighting Poverty in the US and Europe*.[52] In that book we conclude that purely economic explanations leave the investigator almost

empty-handed. We find that the most important reasons for the difference relate to the nature of the political institutions in the USA compared to Europe, together with American ethnic heterogeneity. These differences lie deep in their respective histories and culture. The USA has a majoritarian rather than proportional system of representation, federalism and numerous checks and balances. These institutions favour the forces of conservatism. More generous welfare states are associated with political systems that allow proportional representation. The US Constitution was drawn up by men of property who were determined to prevent a predatory state from confiscating their property. Therefore the political left in the USA has always found it very hard to make any progress and have influence on policy outcomes.

*Why did the US develop this way?*
One reason is linked to ethnic diversity. Income differences are correlated with racial fragmentation, with the average income per capita of whites being higher than blacks and Hispanics. The white majority have never supported the development of a welfare state that would redistribute income to racial minorities. Ethnic and racial fractionalisation in the USA made it virtually impossible to build up the Marxist idea of class consciousness and that is one major reason why a socialist or communist party never materialised in the USA.[53] If you were an Irish worker in Boston you felt Irish before you felt any working-class solidarity with an Italian worker. With the exception of the Civil War, the USA has been a very stable country politically. Another part of the story relates to the perception by others of the poor. While 70 per cent of Americans think that the poor are lazy, in contrast, 70 per cent of Europeans think that the poor are unlucky and deserve help. The typical American feels that they live in a very mobile society, while Europeans feel much less upwardly mobile. So the key differences relate to political institutions, ethnic diversity and attitudes to poverty.

*You also have a paper that discusses the relationship between happiness and inequality.[54] Again it seems that Europeans and Americans are different.*
That paper is part of the same story. In that research we found that individuals tend to be less happy when inequality is high. However, Americans are much more tolerant of inequality than Europeans because if a person is poor, it is largely perceived to be their own fault and even if you are poor today you could very well be rich tomorrow. Europeans view inequality as much more stable. If you are poor today you are also likely to be poor for ever. Thus in Europe the poor and the political left are much more unhappy about inequality than their counterparts in the USA. Perceptions of social mobility do influence preferences for redistribution. Where people perceive that they can move up the income ladder through their own efforts they are

more tolerant of inequality. Given these different perceptions it is not surprising that, in general, European citizens are more in favour of redistributive policies than US citizens, and the evidence shows that European fiscal systems are more progressive, and their welfare states more generous than in the USA.

## CURRENT RESEARCH

*What are your current research priorities?*
I will have a very hard time answering this question because I never really know what I am doing until after I have done it *(laughter)*. Nevertheless, here goes. Currently I am working on 'endogenous constitutions'. A vast literature takes, for instance, electoral rules as exogenous and examines their effect on the politico-economic environment. But the latter itself determines who will write constitutions and who will benefit from them. Another area that I am pursuing is a better understanding of when and why policymakers delegate functions to relatively independent bureaucrats. Why, when central banks are independent, do politicians keep a firm grip on every aspect of fiscal policy? I am also continuing my work on fiscal policy. In particular, I am interested in explaining why, in so many middle-income countries, fiscal policy is procyclical, that is, it has the opposite properties that it should have. Also, I continue to be interested in the question of why different countries follow such different policies in terms of welfare and distribution.[55]

## NOTES

1.  I interviewed Professor Alesina in his office at the Department of Economics, Harvard University, on 28 May, 2004.
2.  Details of Professor Alesina's publications can be found at http://post.economics.harvard.edu/faculty/alesina/alesina.html.
3.  See Alesina, Roubini and Cohen (1997); Drazen (2000a, 2000b); Gärtner (2000); Hibbs (2001).
4.  See Kydland and Prescott (1977); Barro and Gordon (1983a, 1983b); Snowdon and Vane (2005).
5.  See Alesina and Sachs (1988).
6.  See, for example, the recent contributions of Daron Acemoglu.
7.  See Alesina (1994, 1995); Alesina and Rosenthal (1995); Alesina, Roubini and Cohen (1997).
8.  Drazen (2000a). See also Drazen (2000b); Alesina (2000a).
9.  See Alesina, Perotti and Tavares (1998).
10. See Snowdon and Vane (2005) for an extended interview with Professor Alesina on the issue of political business cycles.
11. See Alesina and Roubini (1992); Alesina, Cohen and Roubini (1992, 1993).

12. See Alesina (1987, 1988, 1989).
13. See Snowdon (1997); Snowdon and Vane (2005).
14. Alesina and Summers (1993); Alesina and Gatti (1995).
15. See Alesina and Tabellini (1988).
16. See Eijffinger (2002a, 2002b) for recent surveys.
17. In introducing 'The New Monetary Policy Framework' for the UK economy on 6 May 1997, which established 'operational independence' for the Bank of England, Chancellor Gordon Brown (1997), in an official statement, provided the following rationale for the government's strategy (emphasis added): 'We will only build a fully credible framework for monetary policy if the long-term needs of the economy, not short-term political considerations guide monetary decision-making. *We must remove the suspicion that short-term party political considerations are influencing the setting of interest rates.*'
18. See Alesina and Perotti (1995, 1996a, 1996b, 1997a); Alesina and Ardagna (1998); Alesina, Perotti and Tavares (1998); Alesina (2000b).
19. Alesina and Tabellini (2007).
20. *Financial Times*, Tuesday, 25 May 2004.
21. See Alesina and Barro (2001, 2002); Alesina, Barro and Tenreyro (2002).
22. See Mundell (1961).
23. See Frankel and Rose (2002).
24. See McCallum (1995).
25. Mundell (1961).
26. See Frankel and Rose (1998, 2002).
27. Rockoff (2000). See also Bordo (2004).
28. See Alesina and Perotti (2004); Alesina, Angeloni and Shucknecht (2005).
29. For a recent survey, see Oates (1999).
30. See Alesina, Angeloni and Etro (2005).
31. See Alesina and Spolare (1997, 2003, 2005, 2007); Alesina, Spolare and Warcziarg (2000, 2005).
32. See Alesina and Perotti (1998).
33. See Lake (1992); Dixon (1994).
34. See Bhagwati (2004a); Wolf (2004a).
35. See Alesina and Perotti (1994, 1996c); Alesina and Rodrik (1994); Alesina et al. (1996).
36. See Snowdon and Vane (2005).
37. See Daron Acemoglu interview.
38. See Acemoglu, Johnson, and Robinson (2005a).
39. See Barro (1997, 1999); Lipset (1959).
40. Lucas (2000); Crafts and Venables (2002); Crafts (2004b, 2005).
41. See Artadi and Sala-i-Martin (2003).
42. See Rodrik (2003a). Rodrik et al. (2004).
43. Sachs (2003a).
44. See Sachs et al. (2004); Sachs (2005a), and interview with Jeffrey Sachs.
45. See Alesina and Dollar (2000); Alesina and Weder (2002); Easterly (2001a, 2003a); Brumm (2003).
46. See Alesina et al. (2003) and Alesina and La Ferrara (2002, 2005).
47. See Alesina, Baqir and Easterly (1999).
48. See Alesina and La Ferrara (2002); Glaeser (2005).
49. See Easterly and Levine (1997).
50. Collier (2001). See also Easterly (2001b).
51. Alesina, Glaeser and Sacerdote (2001). See also Alesina and Perotti (1997b).
52. Alesina and Glaeser (2004).
53. See Lipset and Marks (2000).
54. Alesina, Di Tella and MacCulloch (2001).
55. Many of Professor Alesina's current working papers are available on his webpage at Harvard, http://post.economics.harvard.edu/faculty/alesina/alesina.html.

# Padma Desai[1]

Professor Padma Desai is widely recognised as one of the world's leading authorities on the Soviet/Russian economy. Born in India, she was educated at Bombay University before completing her PhD in economics at Harvard University (1955–60). Since 1957 she has been a Teaching Fellow at Harvard (1957–59); Associate Professor of Economics, Delhi School of Economics (1959–68); Research Associate, Harvard Russian Centre (1968–80); a visiting research associate at Columbia (1967), MIT (1971) and Berkeley (1974) Universities; and Professor of Economics at Columbia University (1980–92). Since 1992, she has been the Gladys and Roland Harriman Professor of Comparative Economic Systems at Columbia University, where she is also Director of the Centre for Transition Economies. Professor Desai has acted as US Treasury Advisor to the Finance Ministry of the Russian Federation (1995), is a member of the Council on Foreign Relations and, in 2001, was President of the Association of Comparative Economic Studies.

Professor Desai's publications include 11 books, and numerous articles in scholarly and professional journals, as well as regular contributions to the *Wall Street Journal*, *New York Times* and *Financial Times*.[2] Her most recent book, *Conversations on Russia: Reform from Yeltsin to Putin* (2006a), is a unique account of the reasons for the collapse of the Soviet Union, and the subsequent trials and tribulations of the Russian reform programme as it evolved during the 1990s.[3]

# BACKGROUND INFORMATION

*How did your interest in economics emerge when you were a student in Bombay in the early 1950s? Was it the enormous economic development issues facing the newly independent India that captured your imagination?*

Actually it was a bit of a quirky decision on my part. It was not a considered decision at all. My father, who was a graduate of Cambridge University, was a professor teaching English literature in the local college. My elder sister had already followed in his footsteps and studied English literature as her choice, so my father suggested that I should do something different. I had hoped that some day I would become a professor and a writer chasing ideas and resolving practical problems. So I thought: why not economics? It seemed like a useful and relevant subject and it would enable me to pursue a writing and teaching career. I don't think that I was worried about Indian poverty at that stage of my life.

*For your PhD in economics you went to Harvard.*

Yes. In those days many young Indian students went to England for their university education, supported by their parents.[4] But my father said that he could not afford to send me to England and I was fortunate enough to win a fellowship enabling me to go to Harvard. That is how I ended up there rather than England for my PhD. After getting my doctorate, on my way back to India, I went via Oxford to visit Jagdish [Bhagwati], whom I had met while he was at MIT in 1957. He told me that he was going to introduce me to three knights, namely, Sir John Hicks, Sir Roy Harrod and Sir Donald MacDougall.[5] Wow, I was impressed (*laughter*)! Lady MacDougall said to me, 'You are the first Indian woman that I have met who has been educated in the United States.'

*When you were a young student, who were the people who had the most influence on your thinking and academic development?*

The main influence on me came from my mathematics teachers, both at my school and in college. I had fabulous mathematics teachers and it was a discipline that bowled me over. I was totally enamoured of it. In particular I loved its logical structure, its precision and systematic unfolding. I like to think that this has been the underpinning of my scholarly work as an economist.[6] I wanted to be a mathematician but in my sophomore year in college I ruined one of my examinations and as a result lost my confidence. But I mastered it enough to have an adequate background to pursue economics which, as you know, has over the years become increasingly mathematical.

*When did your interest in the Soviet Union begin?*

As a youngster, I devoured Constance Garnett's translations of Dostoevsky and Tolstoy, and took one of those rash teenage decisions to read them in the original. Russians often ask me why I study Russia. When I say 'because of Dostoevsky', they seem puzzled. 'But he is so disturbing', one of them said. 'That is exactly why', was my response. When at Harvard in 1955–59 doing my PhD I also studied Russian in the university's famous Slavic department. It's complicated but has a precise grammatical structure that fascinated me. But of course, I became an economist. I had also a personal reason for pursuing the study of the Soviet economy and I am happy to talk about it. In 1967, Jagdish and I published a joint book titled *India: Planning for Industrialisation*, which became a best-seller.[7] At that time we were not married, but writing that book with Jagdish almost pushed our non-marriage onto the rocks (*laughter*). I wanted to develop my own field of expertise that I hoped would be an area of darkness for him. So when we returned to the USA in 1968, I decided to give up my interest in development economics and joined the Harvard Russian Centre as a research associate.

## PLANNING AND INDIA'S ECONOMIC DEVELOPMENT

*After it had become independent from British colonial rule, socialist ideas undoubtedly influenced India's political leaders and hence its economic policies. India adopted a* dirigiste *development strategy. To what extent were India's political leaders, such as Nehru, influenced by the apparent success of the Soviet model of development?*
I like to think that India's policies were more influenced by Nehru's Fabian ideas which he learned when he was a student at Cambridge University. His view was that the state should play a major role, not only in economic policy making, but also in the ownership of some means of production, in particular the key heavy industrial sectors. So I think that Fabianism was a more important influence on his socialist commitment than the Soviet experiment.[8] Of course, the Soviet model was the earliest socialist example on the ground. He was well aware of Soviet accomplishments in science, education and public health, and he was undoubtedly impressed by this. The first Indian five-year plan, covering the period 1951–56, had a heavy industry orientation and the planning model which was formulated by Nehru's advisers and policy makers was based on the idea that India should have its own steel mills and heavy engineering plants. The first Soviet five-year plan, the *Fel'dman Plan*, as it is known, also gave emphasis to the development of heavy industry and the production goods sector.[9]

*The economic catastrophe that hit the capitalist world during the Great Depression of the 1930s led to a loss of faith in markets. Given this experience, and the dreadful political fallout, some academics began to contemplate the possibility that a strongly* dirigiste *strategy, even central planning, might offer a better alternative to capitalism and markets, especially for poor developing countries. Did you ever develop an enthusiasm for the idea of central planning?*

I was never an admirer of central planning. I was in my early twenties when I arrived at Harvard, and I like to think that I have a solid American education. I was never bitten by the socialist bug. The formulation of my thinking during this key period was dominated by the ideas of Adam Smith, David Ricardo, the Utilitarian philosophers, and the Scottish Enlightenment. But I did formulate a planning model because it was an attractive topic for my PhD thesis at that time, and I was very fortunate to have Wassily Leontief as my teacher.[10] I managed to put together some data and came up with solid results and got my PhD degree. But I was never attracted to socialism or socialist planning out of any conviction.

*Did Marx ever capture your interest? Much later you did edit a book on Marx.[11]*

I did read Marx but the book that made a tremendous impact on me when I first came to Harvard was Max Weber's *The Protestant Ethic and the Spirit of Capitalism.*[12] So I never developed a socialist way of thinking, like a planner.

*I know that Jagdish has been very critical of India's 'licence Raj' style of import-substitution-led industrialisation.[13] At what point did you become disillusioned with this style of development strategy?*

It was about the time of the 1967 book that we wrote together.[14] That book was very critical of Nehru's socialist policies that had degenerated into excessive state intervention and regulation. The organised industrial sector was shackled by the so-called 'licence Raj'. The foreign trade sector was also severely constrained by quotas. The whole strategy led to excessive bureaucratisation of economic management so far as the industrial sector was concerned. Our critique was way before the present Prime Minister, Manmohan Singh, introduced reforms in 1991.[15] I remember around that time, when Manmohan Singh visited New York, he even referred to our book.

*India has now taken off with respect to its economic growth, although there is controversy about whether the acceleration of growth began during the 1980s rather than post-1991.[16] Are you optimistic that India is now on a path of sustained growth?*

When I go to India now I see enormous confidence among journalists, politicians and business groups. When you travel in the cities you are aware of enormous energy. People are on the move and the country is clearly on the up. We no longer hear talk about 'the Hindu rate of growth'. I teach a course in emerging market economies here at Columbia and we look at comparisons between China and India.[17] When you look at the data you find that the Chinese investment rate is around 45–50 per cent of GDP, and the growth rate is around 10 per cent per annum. In India, the investment rate is around 25 per cent of GDP, and the growth rate is 6–7 per cent. So if you were to measure the efficiency with which investment resources are utilised, then these numbers suggest that India is doing quite well compared to China.[18]

There is also a growing demographic problem in China. In the rich developed countries and former communist countries, we are witnessing a demographic dilemma involving below-replacement levels of fertility and an increase in the age structure of the population.[19] China is also becoming a country with an ageing population *before* it has become rich. As a consequence of its one-child policy, China has a low and falling rate of population growth, an ageing population, and the ratio of workers to retirees is declining.[20] This is bringing the old age security and pension system into trouble as it is in many rich and former communist countries. India, by contrast, has different demographics. In India, the ratio of young workers to retirees is quite favourable to future growth. The age structure should be favourable to savings, which will boost investment and growth.[21]

Again, after 1991 India did open up and industry was liberalised and deregulated. Firms were increasingly exposed to the rigours of competition, both domestic and international. On a personal level, the biggest and most amazing change for me is that, when I visit India, relatives no longer ask me to bring things from the USA (*laughter*). Everything is now available in India. I think that India is now quite a competitive liberal economy, certainly compared to what it used to be.

*One of the remarkable things about India since gaining independence in 1947 is that, unlike many other countries following decolonisation, especially in sub-Saharan Africa and Latin America, it has successfully retained its democratic institutions.[22] How do you explain India's success in maintaining its democracy?*
I often think about this. India for thousands of years has had its own traditional ways of sorting out issues, not only within the family, but also in the wider community and beyond. Of course, these tradition-bound institutions were hierarchical and lacked the legal underpinning of the modern Anglo-Saxon variety, but they were capable of sorting out various societal issues. I also believe, although not many of my Indian friends agree, that

the British did provide and leave liberal aspirations in the form of a parliamentary system, a law-based state and the English language.

*But this was also true in the former British colonies in sub-Saharan Africa, and the establishment of sustainable democracy there has been a major problem since the late 1950s.*
Yes, and this is where the traditional methods and institutions in India have been so important. Indian culture, while diverse, complex and hierarchical, facilitates problem solving via give and take. Although there are 15 major languages in India, Hinduism is an important glue for the majority of Indians, and this cuts across languages, customs and regional differences. This has helped to keep the country together.

## THE SOVIET ECONOMY

*The Soviet economy and political system ultimately failed and disintegrated in 1991. If Ludwig von Mises and Friedrich von Hayek were still alive they would probably say 'I told you so!' While in the nineteenth century Karl Marx predicted that capitalism would lead to economic chaos and political revolution, during the 1920s and 1930s Mises and Hayek predicted that the irrationality of the Soviet style of economic organisation, based on central planning, would ultimately lead to chaos and fail.[23] The Austrian critique was ultimately validated by events.*
It was, and the young Russian reformers whom I have interviewed were definitely influenced by the ideas of Hayek and also of Milton Friedman.[24] The Soviet system was incredibly over-planned and over-administered. Every production and service sector unit was given quotas and prices. They were even allocated targets with respect to technological innovation. The managers and workers hardly had any initiative left. I think the best description of this system is the one that observes 'We pretend to work and they pretend to pay us' (*laughter*). The incentive systems were completely distorted.[25] The 'cold war' competition between the Soviet Union and the USA, which became very pronounced during the Reagan Presidency, also absorbed huge amounts of valuable resources, often the best resources, into the military sector. This ultimately squeezed the output of consumer goods such that the standard of living of the people in the Soviet Union was not improving. Workers were becoming increasingly alienated from the system. There was also massive corruption that allowed the Communist Party bureaucrats to have many privileges denied to the ordinary Soviet citizen. This also led to resentment. When Mikhail Gorbachev became General Secretary of the Communist Party in March 1985, he realised that the

system was not working and needed to be changed.[26] So began the period of *perestroika* (restructuring) and *glasnost* (openness).

*The end of the socialist system in Eastern Europe and the Soviet Union seemed to come both unexpectedly and very quickly, beginning with the fall of the Berlin Wall in 1989. While some economists did predict big problems for the system and its eventual downfall, nobody seems to have anticipated the timing of the collapse. I don't recall any commentators saying in 1988–89, 'The economic and political system of the Soviet bloc is about to collapse.' In 1987, your book entitled* The Soviet Economy: Problems and Prospects *was published. When you were preparing that book did you ever imagine that within four years the whole system would come crashing down?*

That book was a collection of my econometric essays. I remember I had a model, reproduced in that book, that used CIA data to project Soviet growth rates for the 1980s. Those predictions were for negative growth! So as early as the late 1970s, when I wrote that particular essay, I was predicting negative economic growth. Other scholars of the Soviet economy, such as Abram Bergson, also noted the growth retardation.[27] The slowdown of growth reflected the combined effect of diminishing returns to massive capital accumulation and low rates of technological change and innovation.[28] Also important were the high levels of allocative inefficiency that characterised centrally planned economies. The economic loss from resource misallocation in the Soviet economy, calculated by me (with my co-author Ricardo Martin), was enormous.[29] At the plant level, the lack of competition, either domestic or from imports, also generated high levels of X-inefficiency.[30] Enterprises failed to maximise productivity and minimise costs in the sheltered markets of the Soviet Union. The absence of innovative activity was also inevitable given the lack of incentives. Soviet enterprises faced 'soft budget constraints' as described by János Kornai.[31] Thus there was little incentive to economise on the use of resources in a world where the bankruptcy of an enterprise was not a real possibility.

Unfortunately, as the Soviet Union began to disintegrate we observed the emergence of instant experts on the Soviet system. This was very frustrating for serious scholars – among them myself – having spent some 40 years of research analysing the Soviet system. Numerous politicians and journalists were quick to make their ill-informed pronouncements and analysis while the real experts were drowned out. As an economist I had been saying for years that the Soviet economy was in serious trouble.[32] But as for predicting the precise timing of the collapse, and the way the system fell apart, I don't think that was possible.

For me the most important riddle and unanswered question relating to the way the system fell apart is: why did the military sit on the sidelines and watch the collapse? In my interview book, Boris Nemtsov, the young pioneering market reformer in the Yeltsin government, remarked that Soviet military generals, unlike their Latin American counterparts, did not have political ambitions. Remarkably, the massive changes that occurred happened with virtually no loss of life. There was of course the titanic power struggle between Yeltsin and Gorbachev. But once Ukraine decided by referendum, in late 1991, that it no longer wanted to remain part of the former Soviet Union, there was no way that the Union could be maintained. Boris Yelsin quickly recognised this.

Some fascinating observations emerged in my recent interviews with eminent Russian and Western policy makers.[33] Very interesting were the comments by Richard Pipes, who was Ronald Reagan's National Security Advisor on Eastern European and Soviet affairs in 1981–82, and was an eminent historian at Harvard. Citing from his book, *The Formation of the Soviet Union*, published in the mid-1950s, he points out that a strange dichotomy existed in the Soviet Union, where you had a very centralised political union which was ruled by the monolithic Communist Party of the Soviet Union, combined with an autonomous recognition of the various nationalities within the Soviet Union.[34] Pipes argued that if ever something went seriously wrong at the centre, then the whole system would collapse because the union was so artificial and held together by force. So Pipes, very early on, recognised the possibility of a dissolution of the Soviet Union. But to name the precise timing of collapse, even by scholars who regularly studied the Soviet system, was not possible.

*In 1987 Gorbachev's book was published, entitled* Perestroika: New Thinking for Our Country and the World. *To me, as an economist, this is a very confused book because Gorbachev did not seem to understand that trying to reform the system was doomed because, as Kornai has argued, it was the system that was the problem.*[35] *Gorbachev took it for granted that the Communist Party would maintain its control of political power. The collapse came as a great shock to him. So Gorbachev was obviously important in accepting that the system needed changing, and he played a pivotal role. However, he never seemed to grasp, until later, that the whole system had to go. Is that how you interpret what happened in the late 1980s?*
Yes, I think your interpretation is right. Of course, Gorbachev introduced changes. It was Gorbachev who liberated Eastern Europe from Soviet control and initiated the 'winds of change' in the Soviet Union. Essentially he was wanting to decentralise arrangements because the system was run from the top down by a monolithic party. He wanted to introduce more democracy *within* the Communist Party election procedures. But he never thought in terms of a Western-style democratic multi-party system. So far as

economic understanding is concerned, Gorbachev did not have a clue about how market systems actually function. In a sense he was an intellectual prisoner of his socialist background. In his *Perestroika* book he talks about 'socialist competition', 'socialist efficiency' and 'socialist incentives' without ever acknowledging that you cannot have genuine incentives without also having private property ownership. When pressed about how far he was prepared to go in allowing for private property he provided answers such as: 'Maybe people can own a truck for transportation.' This was about as far as he would commit. He certainly did not want to be seen as the leader taking the Soviet Union away from socialism and towards Jeremy Bentham or Milton Friedman's corner (*laughter*). To Gorbachev, socialism was an article of faith that he was unwilling to give up.[36] He also believed that something could be retrieved from the revolutionary past and that Stalinism was an aberration that could be cleaned from the system. I don't think that he ever gave up on the legitimacy of the Bolshevik Revolution.

*What is Gorbachev's position now? Have you talked to him about these events? With the benefit of hindsight, does he admit the errors in his previous thinking?*
I have not talked to him since the late 1990s but he still blames Yeltsin for the break-up of the Soviet Union. When he talks about this period he gives the impression that he believes that the Soviet Union could have been preserved as a voluntary confederation of the constituent republics. He seriously believes that this was a realistic possibility.[37] When I interviewed him in the late 1990s I could not record the interview as it was done in a hurry. I said to him that I thought his biggest mistake was not to have gone over the heads of the party bosses in early 1990 and held a presidential election because at that time he was the most popular leader in the Soviet Union, ahead of Yeltsin, and even ahead of Andrei Sakharov. That way he could have attained legitimacy. He does now admit that not holding a popular presidential election was a mistake.

*In a controversial article, published in 1994, Paul Krugman noted that during the 1950s many Western observers of the Soviet Union had concluded that Soviet central planning might be brutal, but it did a very good job of promoting industrial growth, so much so that it was feared that the Soviet Union was rapidly catching up the USA in terms of economic power. This view was reinforced by the memorable comment made in 1956 by Nikita Khrushchev: 'We will bury you.'[38] I interpret this statement as implying that in Khrushchev's view, the Soviet Union, as an economy, would eventually surpass the economic power of the Western nations, especially the USA. What is perhaps remarkable, especially during the 1950s, was that a great number of intellectuals were*

*taken in by the propaganda emanating from the Soviet Union and other social-*
*ist economies. For example, in the case of North Korea the famous Cambridge*
*economist, Joan Robinson, was certainly taken in by socialist propaganda.*[39]
*I recall going to a lecture on the 'Cultural Revolution in China', given by Joan*
*Robinson at Leicester University in 1970. In that lecture she gave unreserved*
*praise for the achievements of the 'Cultural Revolution' which we now know*
*to have had a catastrophic impact on China's economy. What do we really*
*know about the true economic performance of the Soviet Union during the*
*post-Second World War period?*[40] *Were the statistics always massaged?*

So far as the statistics are concerned, it was more a case of how the national income was calculated rather than deliberate falsification.[41] For example, double counting was a problem in calculations of Soviet GDP. As every student of economics should know, you should not add together steel output and machines' output if the steel has already been used up in producing the machines. Much more of a problem was what was being produced. The planners were unable to get the system to produce the goods and services that people actually wanted. In a decentralised market system consumer sovereignty prevails. Producers respond to consumer demand as indicated by their spending patterns, subject to earning a profit. But in the Soviet planned economy bureaucrats had to decide what to produce. Here they immediately ran into the information problem identified by Hayek.[42] How could planners possibly know what the Soviet citizens wanted? At one point the Soviet Union was the largest producer of shoes. And yet it also had the largest inventory of shoes because factories were turning out shoes that the people did not want. Major and sustained shortages and surpluses of goods were a permanent feature of centrally planned economies, and inevitably so. Demand and supply were frequently out of line with each other. Clearly these are symptoms of a very inefficient economic system.

*Another feature of the Soviet economic system was the lack of technological*
*progress and innovation outside the military sector. In William Baumol's most*
*recent book he highlights the outstanding growth achievements of the capi-*
*talist system, driven by a constant desire for innovation and new ideas.*[43] *Even*
*Karl Marx and Friedrich Engels recognised this positive achievement of cap-*
*italism.*[44] *The lack of innovation and technological progress also contributed*
*to the eventual collapse of the Soviet economic system.*

Yes, even the technological targets were handed down to the factory managers by the planners. Managers lacked incentives at the plant level to take risks by thinking about developing new products and processes. There were no incentives for research and development. Plant managers did not have the funding or any incentive structures in place to take the initiative with respect to innovative activities. In contrast, in the military there were strict performance criteria in place in terms of producing a jet fighter, for example. Failure to perform in the military sector could have serious consequences, including being sent out to Siberia. The military sector also received the best resources and materials available, including scarce human capital resources. That kind of arrangement could not be replicated for the entire Soviet economy. As a result, the rate of growth of technological change in Soviet industry was low compared to that experienced in Western market economies.

## THE ECONOMICS OF TRANSITION

*An important debate relating to the problems facing the transition economies is the one concerning whether such economies should adopt a strategy of 'shock therapy' or 'gradualism' in their path from socialist central planning to market economy. In your writing you come down in favour of the gradualist approach.[45] When I raised this question with Jeffrey Sachs, your colleague here at Columbia, he argued that 'the distinction drawn between big bang and gradualism is a gross oversimplification of the whole question of the pace and sequencing of reform'.[46] He takes the view that the very nature of the transition problem requires that some measures be taken quickly, such as currency convertibility, while other changes, including privatisation, will take much longer. How do you now view this debate?*

I don't agree with Jeffrey on this issue. For quite a number of years I did carry on a public debate with him whenever and wherever I got the opportunity, in both the news media and in professional journals.[47] I see the main difference between the two strategies as follows. In Russia the main focus of shock therapy was on, for example, how speedily you can cut back on the budget deficit by removing subsidies to industries and by reducing government procurement of military items. In early 1992, when Yegor Gaidar became the acting Prime Minister in charge of the whole programme of reform, the 1991 deficit had been estimated by the IMF to be about 17 per cent of GDP. This is very high, so a major issue was how expenditures could be cut back. In the very first quarter of 1992 the budget deficit was planned to be brought down to zero. This was a pie-in-the-sky component of shock therapy. Another was the decontrol of prices and making the ruble convertible by removing exchange controls. Trade was to be liberalised and the whole Gosplan planning mechanism was to be dismantled. A major stumbling block to this whole demolition enterprise was the communists in the legislature who were hell bent on opposing the programme because they could see that the aim of the reform strategy was to bring down the whole communist planned system by cutting back the role of government.

*What about the political economy argument that many of these changes needed to be implemented quickly because, as is normally the case with a reforming government, there is a window of opportunity to do things while the former powerful groups who will oppose reform are relatively weak and the new government also has a honeymoon period with the people? A strategy of gradualism would give time to the forces opposing transition to regroup and block the reforms.*

The window-of-opportunity argument, which is essentially a political and psychological argument, was borrowed from the successful Polish experiment led by Leszek Balcerowicz.[48] The Polish experiment was successful because, after ten years of the Solidarity-led movement against General Jaruzelski, the public was ready to accept the radical changes. For example, Solidarity accepted that the reforms would, in the short run, imply a cut in real wages. However, such was the faith in the reform programme that, after the zloty was made convertible on current account, within a few months the Central Bank of Poland accumulated substantial dollar reserves as Poles converted their holdings of dollars into zlotys. But the same arguments do not apply to Russia. In 1991 and early 1992 Yeltsin was very popular, but was he so popular that the general public and Communist Party would go along with him? Ultimately they didn't. By August of 1992 inflation was accelerating and the Russian Central Bank was printing currency to match the deficit in the budget. By the end of 1992 inflation was running at an annual rate of about 2400 per cent.

The debates in those days focused on whether or not shock therapy was tried at all. Some argued that shock therapy was not tried and, had it actually been implemented, it would have succeeded. Ultimately the question is: what did Yeltsin's reformers accomplish? I believe that reformers such as Yegor Gaidar, Anatoly Chubais, Boris Nemtsov and Sergei Dubinin did accomplish one major task, which was to demolish the communist planned system. Theirs was more a demolition project than a creative one.

*But did they succeed in putting in place a successful and stable market system?* Not yet, because this is where market-supporting institutions are so important for the successful operation of a market economy. These institutions include, among others, a properly functioning central bank, an effective judicial system, rule-bound financial institutions and a sophisticated stock market. It takes time to establish these institutions. In a *Moscow News* interview, in October 2003, Yeltsin said that what he had wanted from the outset was a kamikaze crew that would 'step into the line of fire and forge ahead, however strong the discontent might be'. He needed a team that would 'go up in flames but remain in history'. Because the Yeltsin team was very technocratic in its approach, this ultimately led to its demise in the political arena. Unlike Gorbachev, however, Yeltsin did not want to reform or change the system; he wanted the system to be overturned. That he certainly accomplished.

## RUSSIAN PRIVATISATION

*The Russian privatisation programme has been heavily criticised, probably more than any other aspect of the reforms.*[49] *What went wrong?*
Russian privatisation took place in two stages. The first stage occurred between late 1992 and mid-1994. In October 1992 vouchers worth 10 000 rubles each were distributed to every man, woman and child in Russia, and could be used to buy shares in any enterprise that was to be privatised. The aim was to establish broad-based asset ownership in Russian capitalism. That programme was decidedly motivated by the desire to keep the reform momentum alive. So voucher-based privatisation had a political purpose and was popular.[50] Owners of the vouchers thought that they were going to become instant capitalists, and wealthy as a result. In April 1993 Yeltsin organised a country-wide referendum that asked the population if they supported the president. Yes, was the answer. They were also asked if they were in favour of the president's reforms. Again the answer was yes. So the voucher privatisation programme was meant to keep the pro-market reforms on track because by this time inflation was beginning to shoot up and macroeconomic stabilisation was failing. But the voucher privatisation was done very hurriedly and people did not understand what they were putting their vouchers into. To them the enterprises to be privatised were just 'black boxes'. Many pensioners and poorer Russians sold their vouchers for cash to domestic middlemen and foreign companies. Another problem was that if you lived in Moscow there was no way that you could put your voucher into an enterprise in Vladivostok because there was no established electronic means of conducting such transactions.

In the second phase, which dates from 1995 to early 1996, the federal government needed cash to meet its budget deficit targets. The people who were later to be called Russia's oligarchs quickly offered to provide the cash provided the government gave these oligarchs, as collateral, stocks in some of Russia's best companies. Because the government could not repay these loans, the 'loans for shares' phase of the privatisation programme handed the oligarchs state shares in Russian companies. For example, the oligarchs captured the valuable oil and nickel companies. Part of the deal between the government and the oligarchs was also for them to support Yeltsin's re-election as president, thereby preventing the election of Gennadii Zyuganov, the communist leader. In early 1996 Yeltsin's popularity ranking had fallen considerably, Chubais took over the election campaign and Yeltsin was elected. If you talk with the reformers they all say: 'If Zyuganov had been elected in 1996, where would Russia be now, what would have been the consequences for the course of Russian history? The events of 1996 ensured that the communists would never rule Russia again.' So for the reformers, 1996 was a key turning point because the 'loans for shares' scheme, for all its deficiencies, kept the reform movement alive. However, the way privatisation was achieved ultimately led to the Russian people becoming totally disillusioned with the reform process. Their view was: here are these valuable assets, which under Stalin we had all built with our blood, sweat and tears, and jointly owned, yet now these same assets are controlled by a few corrupt oligarchs.

*Where did the oligarchs get the financial resources to lend to the government?* This is an issue that is not fully understood. The cash originated in Gorbachev's days and pre-dates the Yeltsin reforms. Under Gorbachev there were modest reforms, but the price controls were still firmly in place. But if you had the drive and money-making ambition, and you also had the right contacts, for example, with communist bosses and company managers, you could buy oil and minerals at the controlled prices and export these valuable items at world prices, and deposit the dollar earnings in an offshore bank. So the financial resources were in place and once the opportunity came under Yeltsin, in late 1995 and early 1996, the oligarchs seized it with both hands.[51]

*In your co-authored book with Todd Idson,* Work Without Wages: Russia's Non-payment Crisis, *you investigated the wage payment crisis in Russia.[52] How did that problem arise and how was it resolved?*
The problem had its origins in the dislocation caused by the reform process.[53] Both the government and enterprises found that their balance sheets had gone haywire. The supply lines and client relationships had broken down. After 1991, when Russia began its path of transition to becoming a market economy, a lack of budget discipline, a breakdown of contractual obligations in both the public and private sectors, and failure to enforce laws led to the pervasive non-payment of wages. Enterprises found that their earnings did not match their payment obligations, in terms of both wages and taxes. We had a massive data set of 17 000 household members who had been repeatedly interviewed about the non-payment of wages and the scale and the duration of non-payment. We had a treasure trove of information. So it seemed like a good opportunity to investigate a whole bunch of interesting microeconomic questions using this database. For example, from a microeconomic perspective, we were interested in

questions such as: how does a factory manager decide from which group of workers to withhold payments? Are there some coherent criteria governing that decision? How often were wage payments held back, and for how long? How did families cope and survive without regular wage payments? Did they sell assets, engage in home production, or borrow from relatives? We were also interested to know if the workers who were denied payment fell into poverty. Answering that particular question requires a rigorous methodology. Our econometric analysis shows that the answer to that question is yes.

I presented our evidence in Moscow to an audience that included many sociologists and political scientists, and I had a hard time because they insisted that everyone in Russia was feeling poor whereas I was interested in detecting differential impoverishing outcomes between those who were denied wages and those who were not. In that book, we, as economists, were interested in building models and in assessing the empirical evidence relating to the patterns of non-payment across various demographic groups, defined by age, education, gender, occupation, industries and regions. With the economy reviving and growing, and the rise in oil prices, the non-payment problem is no longer an issue.

## THE 1998 CRISIS

*In August 1998, the Russian government was forced to devalue the ruble, default on domestic debt obligations and place a moratorium on payments to foreign creditors. What were the main factors that led to this meltdown?*
My paper in the *American Economic Review*, May 2000, looks at this issue.[54] There I argue that the ruble collapse resulted from both exogenous and domestic factors. The two main exogenous factors were, first, the influence of the collapse of the East Asian currencies, which began with the Thai baht in August 1997. Nervous foreign investors also dumped their ruble-denominated assets.[55] Second, the decline in oil and non-ferrous metal prices that began in late 1997 had a large impact on Russian foreign exchange earnings. The price of oil fell from $23 to $11 per barrel in early 1998. The current-account balance in 1998 turned negative to the tune of $5 billion from an annual surplus of about $4–6 billion for the previous three years. This also led to a non-resident flight from government short-term bills, and the ruble collapse could not be prevented even with interest rates rising to 150 per cent by June 1998.

On the domestic front macroeconomic stabilisation policies involving a slowing down of money supply growth rates had led to a considerable reduction of inflation to about 1 per cent per month by September 1997.

However, there were fundamental weaknesses on the fiscal side that made the Russian economy vulnerable to a large external shock. The federal budget deficit remained high, about 7–8 per cent of GDP during 1995–97. As I argue in my paper, I do not believe that an earlier devaluation would have helped avoid the default and moratorium on payments to foreign creditors. Given the lack of timely and adequate support from the IMF, I believe that the introduction of temporary exchange controls would have been a less damaging option.[56] Unfortunately, the IMF and the US Treasury did not support that option, although they later conceded that under certain circumstances such controls had a justifiable rationale.

## RUSSIA 2005: A NORMAL MIDDLE-INCOME COUNTRY?

*In the Symposium on Russia, in the Winter 2005 issue of the* Journal of Economic Perspectives, *Andrei Shleifer and Daniel Treisman claim that, based on a variety of economic and political data, Russia can now be regarded as a 'typical middle-income capitalist democracy'. Their argument is that during the 1990s, Russia underwent an extraordinary transformation 'from a communist dictatorship to multi-party democracy', 'from centrally planned economy to market economy' and from 'belligerent adversary of the West to a cooperative partner'. Therefore the common perception that Russia is a disastrous failure is far from reality. Its problems are ones that are common among middle-income developing countries such as Brazil or Mexico or Malaysia or Croatia. Also, when the USA was a developing country in the late nineteenth century, it had its own set of oligarchs, such as J.P. Morgan and J.D. Rockefeller, who came to be known as the 'robber barons'. Do you accept this argument?*

I think cross-country comparisons raise tricky conceptual and measurement issues. Besides, Russia's triple transformation from a communist dictatorship to a multi-party democracy, from a centrally planned economy to a market system and from a belligerent adversary to a cooperative partner of the West will proceed in a haphazard, imperfect fashion. For example, some people argue that there is a reversal under Putin on progress in the triple transitions. So the analyst runs the risk of having to revise his or her judgement about the progress on each count and compare it with a comparison economy.

As for the oligarchs, they emerged in Russia because of the profitable opportunities that arose in a weak legal and overly political environment. You could argue that they would arise in any country, given the circumstances and incentives that emerged in Russia during the 1990s.[57] But I am reminded of an observation made by the communist leader, Zyuganov. He said that at least the American 'robber barons' kept their wealth in their own country and contributed to its subsequent economic development, whereas the Russian oligarchs plundered and looted their country of its most valuable resources and then deposited a large portion of their vast fortunes abroad.

## PROSPECTS FOR THE RUSSIAN ECONOMY[58]

*What have been the main achievements of the Russian economy during recent years?*
The Russian economy emerged from the financial collapse and debt default of August 1998 with robust GDP growth in 2000 accompanied by solid macroeconomic health and reduction in household poverty. During the five-year stretch from 2000 to 2004, the Russian economy improved remarkably on several fronts. The GDP growth rate, averaging 6 to 7 per cent annually, placed Russia among the fastest-growing global economies behind China and India. Government finances improved steadily over the period. The Moscow stock exchange rose by 8 per cent in 2004, demonstrating a positive portfolio investment environment. At the same time, foreign direct investment flows rose from $6.8 billion in 2003 to $9.4 billion in 2004.

*That is the good news. What is the bad news? In what areas does Russia have the most catching up to do?*
There are troubling negative features continuing into 2006 that fall into four main categories. Although the relative share of the poor has steadily come down from its highest point at 30 per cent to a current World Bank estimate of 17.8 per cent, they remain deprived even by Russian standards. The poverty line is currently defined at monthly wages of 2451 rubles or 88 dollars. Again, the income gap is widening, with the top 10 per cent of wage earners making nearly 15 times those in the bottom 10 per cent in 2004, in contrast to the norm of less than five in developed countries. Putin's agenda of economic growth in the interest of poverty reduction faces arduous challenges from a comparative perspective. Russia's per capita GDP is only about one-quarter that of the USA.

A second problem facing Russia is that monopolies continue to dominate the economy to the exclusion of middle-level and small businesses. Monopolies in the energy, metals, banking and railroad sectors dominate the economy as they did in the past. A mere 23 businesses control one-third of output and one-sixth of employment in Russian industry. According to the latest Forbes listing, Russia has 27 billionaires, third in global rank after

Germany with 57. The related concentration of ownership threatens the tax authorities' ability to raise revenue and the judiciary's clout in handling corporate misdeeds. Until anti-monopoly and anti-trust laws are successfully implemented, Russian big business will continue to exercise inordinate political influence. Again, small businesses have a minor role in employment and output creation, reflecting a long-term historical feature. The number of small businesses employing no more than 100 workers rose by 10 per cent in 2004 to 946 000 by September 2004. However, businesses of this size generated only 10 to 12 per cent of Russian GDP (in contrast to 50 to 60 per cent in developed market economies) and provided employment to 19 per cent of the workforce (in contrast to almost 70 per cent in some European economies). At the same time, regional and local regulations and meddlesome bureaucrats, as in the days of the tsars and the Soviet-era communists, stifle the small business environment.

A third problem is that the resurgent economy, buoyed by vast export earnings from the oil, energy and metals sectors, is unbalanced. Russian infrastructure is crumbling. The transportation and railroad rolling stock, the ports and bridges, the electric power generators and turbines of Soviet days need to be replaced with massive investments. The strong ruble has put the Russian manufacturing sector at a disadvantage because the ruble buys more items denominated in weaker foreign currencies and attracts imports.[59] At the same time, the Central Bank's emission of rubles, in exchange for its acquisition of foreign exchange, has added to inflationary pressures. In fact, lowering the annual inflation rate from its current 10–12 per cent and moderating the real appreciation of the ruble are the twin policy challenges facing the Central Bank, and Putin has singled out inflation control as one of the top governmental priorities.

A final negative feature of the Russian economy is linked with the Yukos prosecution and the associated excessive tax claims. Have they damaged the investment climate irretrievably? The Yukos trial, the escalating tax demands, and the enhanced role for majority-owned Russian companies in the energy sector have evidently combined to dent domestic and foreign investor confidence. Will foreign investors, especially the super majors, step into Russia's energy sector in a minority role? The Russian energy sector badly needs new technologies and management expertise which foreign private investors can supply only if the rules of engagement are stable, predictable and transparent. Lacking such rule-based participation of foreign private investors, Gazprom, converted into a 51 per cent state-owned behemoth, will remain a corruption-prone, bureaucratized black box.

*Russia is also faced with a demographic crisis that will have damaging consequences for the long-term growth prospects of the economy. This is a problem facing many high-income, as well as transition, economies, notably Japan and China. Russia is unlike Western Europe, where a history of immigration has partially compensated for the decline in the natural population growth. Can the natural decline in Russia's population be countered by immigration?*

The numbers warn of a looming catastrophe. Russia's population declined by 1.8 million in 2003–04 to 145 million by the end of 2004. The net inflow of immigrants in 2004 was a mere 40 000, in contrast to 840 000 in 1994. The current contraction of population, the fourth since 1913, differs significantly from the previous three, which were caused by extreme social shocks – the First World War and the Civil War; famine,[60] the repressions and purges of the 1930s; and the Second World War. By contrast, the current loss is conditioned by stable changes in the demographic behaviour of Russians. That is why one should not expect that it will be transitional and that a positive natural growth in population will be re-established in the near future, leading to an increase in the number of the country's residents. The Russian population will continue to decline in the future. All demographers agree on this prognosis. At the same time, the high mortality rate, which can be traced to 'external causes' such as alcoholism, accidents and suicide, cannot be countered by merely refurbishing the antiquated health system.[61]

In my interview[62] with Anatoly Vishnevsky, Russia's leading demographer, he provided me with the following estimates:

> In order to keep the population at 146 million people, the count at the turn of the current century, Russia would need to accept, on average, over 700 000 migrants on a net basis and gradually increase the inflow to 1.2–1.3 million by 2035.

Russians, however, do not support an active strategy for encouraging migrants, even Russian immigrants from the neighbouring states. Indeed, the fear of job loss from outsiders, including Russians, is reflected in Russia's citizenship law. It is so strict that few of the 20 million Russians left in the surrounding states would qualify for a Russian passport. In the long run, however, this diaspora could provide a solid source for arresting the decline in natural population growth.

Not surprisingly, public reaction to migrants from China and the Caucasus region tends to be xenophobic. That too cannot be remedied right away. Russians have limited experience of dealing with problems of cultural assimilation facing immigrants or of assessing their contribution to the economy. A recent poll taken on 23 May 2005 of 1600 representative respondents bears out their negative reaction: 63 per cent believed that immigrants contributed to crime and corruption; 40 per cent desired stricter immigration laws; 60 per cent believed that they take away jobs from local workers. The influx of Chinese migrants, especially in the Far Eastern province of Russia, poses a special problem. In his interview Richard Pipes reminded me that the phrase 'yellow peril' was coined in the late nineteenth century by the philosopher Vladimir Solovyov, who referred to the Chinese as the yellow hordes. However, I believe these fears to be exaggerated. Most Chinese immigrants enter Russia on a temporary basis and official policy remains pragmatic.

*An important aspect of transition has been the reintegration of the Soviet bloc and China into the world trading and financial system.*[63] *How integrated is the Russian economy with the rest of the world?*
The ruble is now traded openly. It is almost freely convertible. The trade participation, measured by the share of imports and exports as a proportion of GDP, has steadily increased. But Russia's importance in the world economy comes about mainly because of its energy resources of gas and oil. It is now a bigger oil exporter than Saudi Arabia. It supplies significant exports of natural gas to European countries. For example, I think Germany receives up to 25 per cent of its gas from Russia.

## US–RUSSIAN INTERNATIONAL RELATIONS

*What shape do you expect Russian–US relations to take in the future?*
Everything considered, current US–Russian relations have reached a stalemate if not a dead end. By contrast, the shared interests under the Reagan–Gorbachev and Clinton–Yeltsin presidencies transformed the bilateral negotiations into an energetic joint enterprise. At present, US–Russian relations, despite shared concerns over a number of issues, have been overtaken by marked inertia and mounting opposition to Putin's political consolidation. These relations have entered a different phase marked by converging interests and conflicting pressures. With the end of the cold war, the demise of the Soviet Union, and the near oblivion of the Communist Party, the superpower ideological and military confrontations on a global scale seem to have receded into the past. These have been replaced by US–Russian intrusive foreign policy manoeuvres in the new independent states in Russia's neighbourhood. These interests diverged in Ukraine and Georgia, but mostly converged in Kyrgyzstan and Uzbekistan, thereby testing the judgements and tactical skills of policy makers. Russia, however, has become economically stronger, politically more stable and diplomatically more visible. As a result, the greater Russian assertiveness under Putin has made the bilateral dialogue and decision making slow and at times contentious, because Russian input has become relevant and, on occasion, indispensable.

*In the international arena, what are the major areas of common concern between the USA and Russia?*

Terrorism control, non-proliferation of nuclear and weapons of mass destruction, and advancing US–Russian nuclear parity are the major areas of common concern. Occasionally, the negotiations tend to involve several countries around the world. The European Union, and later Russia, stepped forward in helping the USA counter Iran's presumed plans for converting reactor fuel into nuclear material. Six negotiators, including the USA and Russia, are engaged in forestalling North Korea's programme of further advancing its nuclear capability. A UN conference on nuclear non-proliferation in late May 2005 failed to produce an agreement. In view of their massive nuclear arsenals and the rivalry surrounding the bilateral nuclear parity issue, neither the USA nor Russia, the participants insisted, could serve as exemplars of nuclear non-proliferation around the globe. Nevertheless, while the current problems will at times pull in many participants, their ongoing resolution will be driven by US and Russian security interests. In this context, the new fly in the ointment is whether the consolidation of political authority by Putin will revive the mistrust of the cold war days and intensify US moves to contain potential Russian adventurism in its neighbourhood. Even the more tractable trade issues run the risk of being defined in terms of political rather than economic parameters. Despite this caveat, the give and take will be driven by the mutual concern for terrorism control, which ranks at the top of US–Russian cooperation.

*To what extent does Russia still feel threatened militarily by the USA?*

The exaggerated perception of external threat and the overreaction to safe-guard Russian security by developing advanced weapons systems are often associated in Russian views with the defeat and humiliation following the dissolution of the Soviet Union. From a historical perspective, every defeat on the battlefield after the Crimean War of 1854–56, the Russo-Japanese War of 1904–05 and the two world wars was followed by a military build-up and a determination to start anew. Putin's characterisation of the dissolution of the Soviet Union as 'the greatest geopolitical disaster of the twentieth century' also symbolized this subjective Russian viewing of the defeat, loss and humiliation associated with the event to his deliberate exclusion of reference to the repression imposed by Soviet rule inside the Soviet Union and outside. However, with the protective nuclear umbrella in place, Putin's operational mode consists in stabilising Russian interests by accepting the *fait accompli* when inevitable; sorting out border disputes; and promoting bilateral economic interests, rather than flexing military muscle. In any case, he does not have the numbers. The size of the armed forces has declined from 4 million at its height to a little over 1 million. Its upkeep is poor and its morale is low. The Russian economy, despite its recent upbeat performance, has a lot of catching up to do. The line of least resistance reflects Putin's pragmatic assessment of these limitations.

*What issues emerge with respect to Russia's accession to WTO membership, which requires US bilateral support?*

Russian entry into the WTO has taken the overtones of a contentious political issue as a result of mounting opposition in the US Congress associated with Putin's illiberal measures. It is doubtful if Russia's entry into the World Trade Organisation, which requires US–Russian bilateral agreement and abolition of the Jackson–Vanik[64] Amendment by Congress, will move forward in 2006. Prior to the politicisation of the issue, the major bilateral bone of contention was US demands for intellectual property rights (IPR) protection in Russia and the free entry of US banks and insurance companies in Russia. While the Duma has passed an IPR law, its implementation is weak. Piracy of foreign films, CDs, DVDs, drugs and pharmaceuticals in Russian markets is widespread. According to Russian specialists, however, such violations pale before the brazen piracy practices in China, already a WTO member. Besides, with each negotiating phase, Russia is being put to stricter standards. For example, Russian negotiators regard the demands that Russia scale back its protective regime for its agriculture as unfair. Not only because the USA and EU subsidise their agriculture, but because agricultural protection automatically declined substantially over the decade of the 1990s as Russia's federal budget suffered massive deficits.

WTO membership for Russia would be useful in creating psychological confidence at various levels. Foreign investors know that a WTO member must follow internationally accepted norms and rules. They may not be stringent but a member country has accepted established codes of conduct in foreign trade, global finance and the like. It may not produce tangible results right away but outside investors feel that a WTO member will not suddenly go off a policy track. From that perspective, it is useful.

## THE POLITICAL FUTURE OF RUSSIA

*In assessing the future prospects of Russia, opinions vary from optimism to pessimism. For example, in Gerard Roland's recent assessment, 'The Russian Economy in 2005', he concludes that the short-term prospects are good but the 'long term picture is less rosy'.[65] On the political front, Richard Pipes reminds us that 'Russia is a deeply conservative nation' and that although critics accuse President Putin of turning Russia into a one-party state, polls indicate that 'the anti-democratic, anti-libertarian actions of the current administration are*

*not being inflicted on the Russian people but are actually supported by them'.*[66]
*In your* Wall Street Journal *article, 'Give Putin a Break', you conclude as*
*follows: 'Despite the consolidating impetus under Mr. Putin, aimed at the*
*effective governance of a vast and chaotic country, full-fledged liberal arrange-*
*ments can be expected ultimately to prevail in Russia.'*[67] *A similar conclusion*
*appears in your recent* Journal of Economic Perspectives *article where you*
*conclude by saying: 'In managing the end of Communism, the Yeltsin team*
*went up in flames. But despite the consolidating impetus under Putin, its liberal*
*legacy will ultimately prevail.' What are the prospects for the survival of a*
*liberal political order in Russia? Are you optimistic?*

I am rather optimistic. Russia is moving toward a capitalist system with a
large degree of private ownership, and yes, there has been considerable economic progress during the last 15 years, especially following the recent rise in
oil prices.[68] However, the Russian system still needs to have more robust institutional underpinnings with respect to property rights, and the financial and
judicial system. This will take time. As for Putin, his background is KGB and
he firmly believes in a strong state.[69] But he is a pragmatist rather than an ideologue. He is determined to keep Russia's interests at the forefront. There is
no reason why the USA and Russia cannot work together, and I do think that
Russia needs to look to the West. In this context, Jack Matlock's book is
interesting.[70] He argues that during the Gorbachev–Reagan era the USA and
Soviet Union worked very well together. Bill Clinton and Boris Yeltsin also
had a good personal relationship. He preferred working with Yeltsin drunk
to working with any other Russian politician sober (*laughter*).

*What is your interpretation of the pessimistic scenario about Russia's future*
*that recently seems to have gained prominence?*[71]

The pessimistic scenario is that Putin will increasingly consolidate his authority over the political arrangements and take Russia back to an illiberal system.
This seems to be the burden of much of the criticism in the Western media
today. I feel it is based on excessive pessimism and ignores the solid changes
that Russia has experienced. In the view of former Prime Minister Mikhail
Kasyanov and Central Bank chairman Sergei Dubinin, Russia and Russians
have changed. Yegor Gaidar, who launched the reforms in 1992, remains
wary of Putin's democratic credentials but does not 'believe in the emergence
of non-democratic regimes in countries with educated, urban populations'
such as Russia's. Since the adoption of the Constitution in 1993, Russia has
had four parliamentary and three presidential elections. The reform momentum has slackened but the reform issues, among them reining in corruption
and slashing the bureaucracy, redesigning the pension and Soviet-era welfare
systems and restructuring the monopolies, are daunting challenges and time-
consuming endeavours under the best of circumstances.

The Russian voters may not have fully matured but their middle-of-the-road responses to public opinion polls seem to rule out either extreme of the restoration of fast-paced reforms or an excessive tilt to further authoritarianism. Outside attempts at forcing the former to thwart the latter will have to contend with the Russian electorate's rejection of rapid-fire economic changes and their preference for steady economic benefits in the currently resurgent economy. As for Putin's grooming of a successor of his choice, incumbent leaders around the world exercise that prerogative. Yeltsin chose Putin because, as he declares in his interview, Putin was not a 'maximalist' and could act as a stabiliser by reining in the post-Yeltsin political disorder and public discontent.

Of course, the Russian scene changes continuously and throws up new problems. So trying to crystal-gaze into the future is a bit like shooting a moving target. Despite that challenge, I continue to be optimistic about the future prospects of Russia's evolution to a liberal order. In managing the end of Soviet communism, the Yeltsin team went up in flames, but it earned its place in history for implanting the powerful ideas of democracy and markets in an inhospitable environment. Viewed in the context of the historical antecedents, it is a monumental achievement. Despite the consolidating impetus under Putin, the kamikaze crew's liberal legacy will ultimately prevail because Russians are changing. I think Russia will eventually embrace liberal values and gain economic stability. But unlike Europe and Japan, it will have geopolitical interests in its neighbourhood, along its southern borders, and in the Far East.

While subscribing to American values, Russia's leaders might choose to define their interests independently. A fully democratic Russia would always find it difficult to be a 'junior partner' to the USA. In my view, the future does not guarantee a bilateral identification of shared values and interests. The USA will remain an economic and military frontrunner, but sorting out the geopolitical issues with a reconstructed Russia will keep US leadership fully engaged in demanding win–lose dialogues and 'verify-but-trust' decision making.

## CURRENT RESEARCH

*What are your current research interests?*
I am engaged in working up rigorous empirical models for answering two policy issues that confront the Russian policy makers. The first arises from the presumed damage to the Russian manufacturing sector associated with a strong ruble led by energy exports: does the continuing real appreciation of the ruble damage the competitiveness of Russian manufacturing? If the

answer from the model is yes, the ruble appreciation needs to be reined in.[72] The second issue is related to the escalating taxation of oil export earnings. Do these 'punitive' tax rates curb investment by oil companies? If the answer is yes, the escalating tax rates associated with rising oil prices need to be lowered. These dual policy exercises will keep me busy for a while.

## NOTES

1. I interviewed Professor Desai in her office at Columbia University on 5 May 2005.
2. Details of Professor Desai's publications can be found on her personal webpage: http://www.columbia.edu/cu/economics/faculty/current/pd5.html.
3. The interviewees are: Yegor Gaidar (acting Prime Minister for one year under President Yeltsin), Anatoly Chubais (architect of Russian privatisation), Boris Nemtsov (a liberal pro-market politician), Grigory Yavlinsky (liberal academic economist), Sergei Rogov (Director of Moscow's Institute of US and Canada Studies), Nodari Simonia (Director of the Moscow-based Institute for International Economy and International Relations), Sergei Dubinin (former Chairman of the Central Bank of Russia), Oleg Vyugin (Central Bank of Russia Deputy Chairman), Boris Jordan (investment banker), Mikhail Kasyanov (Prime Minister, 2000–04), Anatoly Vishnevsky (Director of the Centre for Demography and Human Ecology), Strobe Talbott (US Deputy Secretary of State, 1994–2001), Jack Matlock (former US Ambassador to the Soviet Union, 1987–91), Richard Pipes (Emeritus Professor of History at Harvard, and National Security Adviser to President Reagan), Martin Malia (Emeritus Professor of History at Berkeley) and George Soros (renowned financier and philanthropist).
4. Many outstanding Indian economists were students at Cambridge University, for example, the 1998 Nobel Laureate in Economics, Amartya Sen, India's current Prime Minister, Manmohan Singh, and the world's leading authority on international trade, Jagdish Bhagwati. Jawaharlal Nehru, India's first Prime Minister following independence in August 1947, was also a graduate of Cambridge University.
5. Sir John Hicks (1904–89), Drummond Professor of Economics at Oxford University, 1952–65, was one of the most influential economists of the twentieth century, and was awarded the Nobel Prize (jointly with Kenneth Arrow) in 1972 for his 'pioneering contributions to general economic equilibrium theory and welfare theory'. Sir Roy Harrod (1900–78) taught economics at Oxford University between 1924 and his retirement in 1967. He is best remembered for his development of the Harrod–Domar growth model, which became a central idea in the post-war economic development literature, and, according to Easterly (1999), still has an important influence in the World Bank. Sir Donald MacDougall (1912–2004), fellow of Nuffield College, Oxford, was Head of the Government Economic Service, and Chief Economic Adviser to the Treasury, 1969–73.
6. Desai's (2005b) research philosophy is 'rigorous analysis combined with reliable information and sensible conclusions based on their interaction'.
7. Bhagwati and Desai (1970, 2nd edition).
8. Bhagwati and Desai (1975, p. 218) note that Mahatma Gandhi was attracted to the Marxist idea of a classless society, but he totally rejected the violent means of achieving a socialist system. He was also highly critical of the Bolshevik obsession with industrialisation and the suppression of individualism.
9. Fel'dman's 'first theorem' of growth is that the rate of growth is a positive function of the $Kp/Kc$ ratio, where $Kp$ is the capital stock in the production goods sector, and $Kc$ is the capital stock in the consumer goods sector. See Ellman (1989).
10. See Desai (1961, 1963). Wassily Leontief was awarded the Nobel Prize in Economics in 1973 'for the development of the input–output method and for its application to important economic problems', in particular economic planning.

11. Desai (1983).
12. Weber (1904).
13. See, for example, Bhagwati (1993); Snowdon (2001a). See also Desai (1969).
14. Bhagwati and Desai (1970).
15. Manmohan Singh was Finance Minister in Prime Minister Narasimha Rao's government between 1991 and 1996.
16. See Sachs and Bajpai (2001); Ahluwalia (2002); DeLong (2003); Panagariya (2004b); Kochhar et al. (2006); Rodrik and Subramanian (2006).
17. See Desai (1975a). For a recent comparison of the growth and reform experience of India and China, see Tseng and Cowan (2005).
18. Using the Harrod–Domar growth equation of $G = s/v$, where $G$ = the rate of growth of GDP, $s$ = the savings ratio, and $v$ = the incremental capital output ratio (ICOR), a back-of-the-envelope calculation suggests that the productivity of investment is higher in India than China, i.e. ICOR India < ICOR China.
19. See Lee (2003); Morgan (2003).
20. China's 'one-child policy' was adopted in 1979.
21. Deepak Lal (2005) argues that if India continues with its reform programme, it 'could overtake China', and the 'race between the two Asian giants is set to be the most dramatic event of this century'.
22. As Yergin and Stanislaw (1999, p. 218) observe, 'India's commitment to democracy stands as one of the great achievements of the second half of the twentieth century. Its free elections, independent judiciary, free press, and free speech were in marked contrast to political realities in much of the rest of the developing world which succumbed for long periods to dictatorship, ethnic wars, and political fission.'
23. Marx (1867); Mises (1920); Hayek (1935); Vaughn (1980); Nove (1983). See János Kornai interview.
24. Sergei Rogov, Director of Moscow's Institute of USA and Canada Studies, and a former proponent of Gorbachev-style reforms, observes that 'The so-called Yeltsin liberals went for the right wing conservative ideology of the US as an alternative to a communist planned economy. They exchanged Marxism–Leninism for Friedmanism'. See Desai (2005a, 2006a).
25. See Gregory and Harrison (2005) for an excellent survey of recent research on the Soviet economy that uses new evidence from archive material. See also Kornai (1992a).
26. See Gorbachev (1987).
27. Bergson (1978). See also Desai (1986, 1987).
28. As Krugman (1994b) notes, the 'alarmist belief' in the Soviet economic miracle failed to recognise that the high growth rates were more the result of 'perspiration' rather than 'inspiration', and, since such growth was 'input-driven' was 'virtually certain to slow down'.
29. See Desai and Martin (1983).
30. The concept of X-inefficiency was developed by Harvey Leibenstein in the mid-1960s and refers to the technical inefficiency that arises when firms and economies 'do not operate on an outerbound production possibility surface consistent with their resources' (Leibenstein, 1966, p. 24).
31. See Kornai (1986a); Kornai et al. (2003).
32. See Desai (1975b, 1976, 1979), and Desai and Martin (1983), for quantitative analyses of Russia's increasing problems with efficiency and growth.
33. Desai (2005a, 2006a).
34. See Pipes (1954).
35. See Kornai interview.
36. See Desai (1990, 2005a).
37. See also Desai (1997a).
38. Nikita Khrushchev (First Secretary of the Communist Party of the Soviet Union, 1953–64) famously used an expression generally translated as 'We will bury you!', while addressing Western ambassadors at a reception in Moscow in November 1956.
39. See Robinson (1975).
40. See Ofer (1987); Bergson (1991).

41. Desai (1973).
42. See Hayek (1945).
43. See Baumol (2002).
44. Karl Marx and Friedrich Engels, in their *Communist Manifesto* of 1848, observed that 'the bourgeoisie has created more massive and more colossal productive forces than have all preceding generations together'.
45. Other eminent economists who support the gradualist approach to transition include János Kornai (1997a), Gerard Roland (2001, 2002), and Nobel Laureate Joseph Stiglitz (2002a). See also Murrell (1991, 1993, 1995).
46. See interview with Jeffrey Sachs.
47. See Desai (1994a, 1994b, 1995b, 1996, 1997b).
48. See Balcerowicz (1994a, 1994b).
49. See Boycko et al. (1995); Desai (1995a, 1999a); Hoff and Stiglitz (2004); Stiglitz and Hoff (2005); Godoy and Stiglitz (2006).
50. Biais and Perotti (2002) use the term 'Machiavellian privatisation' for a strategic privatisation policy aimed at building up support for right-wing (pro-market) political parties.
51. See Goldman (2003); Guriev and Rachinsky (2005).
52. See Desai and Idson (2000).
53. See Blanchard and Kremer (1997) for an analysis of the 'disorganisation' caused by transition.
54. See also Desai (1998).
55. See Desai (2003).
56. See Rodrik (1998b).
57. See Guriev and Rachinsky (2005). For a superb analysis of the allocation of entrepreneurial talent in alternative institutional settings, see Baumol (1990, 2002).
58. The final part of this interview was completed by correspondence in January–February (2006).
59. See Desai (2006b).
60. See Ellman (2000).
61. See Brainerd and Cutler (2005).
62. Desai (2006a).
63. See Desai (1999b).
64. This amendment to the 1974 Trade Act denies favourable US trade relations to specific countries with non-market economies and restricted emigration. Russia no longer fits the profile, but Congress has not revoked the Amendment.
65. Roland (2005).
66. See Pipes (2004).
67. Desai (2005c).
68. See Shleifer and Treisman (2005).
69. According to Boris Nemtsov, a liberal, pro-market politician, Putin wants a healthy market economy but 'unfortunately he doesn't believe that Russia needs a democracy too. It is difficult to explain to someone with a KGB background that there is a connection between democracy and competitive markets' (quoted in Desai, 2005a). For a classic statement of the link between political and economic freedom, see Friedman M. (1962).
70. See Matlock (2005). Jack Matlock was US Ambassador to Moscow during the Gorbachev–Reagan era.
71. Freedom House, in their publication, *Countries at the Crossroads 2005: A Survey of Democratic Governance*, include Russia as one of 60 key countries that are at a 'crossroads' in determining their political future. http://www.freedomhouse.org/. See also Aslund (2005).
72. See Desai (2006b).

# William Easterly[1]

William Easterly is a leading economist in the field of economic growth and development. After completing his PhD in economics at MIT in 1985 he joined the World Bank, where he remained for 16 years, becoming a senior adviser in the Research Department of the Macroeconomics and Growth Division in 1989. After leaving the World Bank in 2001, Professor Easterly carried out research at the Institute for International Economics (IIE) and the Centre for Global Development (CGD) in Washington DC. Since January 2003, he has been teaching and researching at New York University, where he is currently Professor of Economics.

Having conducted extensive research in the field of economic growth and development, Professor Easterly has broad knowledge and expertise on the problems facing developing countries. While working at the World Bank he travelled extensively in Africa, Latin America and Asia, and is therefore well placed to comment on the key issues and debates surrounding the question of how best to promote increased well-being in the poor countries of the world. In this debate Professor Easterly has become a leading critic of foreign aid as an effective solution to complex development problems.

In almost two decades of research, Professor Easterly has published numerous scholarly articles in the leading economics journals,[2] and his recent books, *The Elusive Quest for Growth: Economists' Adventures and Misadventures in the Tropics* (2001a), and *The White Man's Burden: Why the West's Efforts to Aid the Rest Have Done So Much Ill and So Little Good* (2006a), have received widespread critical acclaim.[3]

## BACKGROUND INFORMATION

*What first got you interested in economics?*
I liked the combination of mathematics, which I have always liked, with attention to important social problems. Economics is the only field that brings together social concerns with mathematical rigour.

*Were there any particular people, ideas, or books that influenced your thinking and inspired you?*
Before I knew much about economics I read some of John Kenneth Galbraith's books. Later I soon realised I would have to unlearn much of this (*laughter*). Paul Samuelson was a definite influence, being a key figure in the development of the mathematical approach to economics. As an undergraduate I also liked the work of William Baumol. He had a great book, *Economic Theory and Operations Analysis*, that taught me a lot of mathematical economics.

*It is clear from reading your recent book,* The Elusive Quest for Growth: Economists' Adventures and Misadventures in the Tropics, *that you have a deep and genuine concern for the problems facing the developing countries. As you indicate at the beginning of your book, your main motivation for working in the field of economic development comes from an acute awareness of the vast differences in the living conditions of those people who live in rich countries compared to those who live in poor countries. Where did your interest and concern for development issues first originate?*
My interest started when I was very young because I lived in Ghana for a year (1969–70) when I was 12 years old. My father had a Fulbright Professorship to teach at a university in Ghana. So that experience awakened me to development problems even at that early age. Much later, when I was in Graduate School at MIT, many of my friends were from developing countries, especially Latin America. The graduate programme at MIT had a huge number of Chileans, Mexicans and Argentineans, and I hung out a lot with them and as a result became interested in what was going on in their countries. I ended up spending a year at a university in Mexico, arranged by one of my friends.

*As an economist, what is it that you feel you can contribute most to the problems facing the poor countries of the world?*

Recently it has been to debunk the many myths that have too easily been accepted by the development establishment. Of course that role is necessarily limited because it is important to come up with constructive answers to the development issues that are in urgent need of solution. But for progress to occur, the mistaken approaches have to be cleared out of the way. After the Second World War many economists sought to discover the means by which the poor underdeveloped countries of the world countries of the world could transform themselves into developed countries. Many times new formulas for growth and development were advocated that turned out to be fundamentally flawed. In my research I have tried to make clear how misguided some of the past panaceas have turned out to be. Unfortunately, some of those flawed ideas are still influential in some policy circles.

## THE BIRTH OF 'DEVELOPMENT ECONOMICS'

*Why did it take until the second half of the twentieth century for economists to become seriously interested in development issues?*
Well, for a long time there was a lot of pseudo science that was explicitly racist. From this perspective there was nothing to explain because it was simply assumed that other races and civilisations were inherently inferior to the 'Western' civilisations, the great white man in the north. This despicable racist attitude was, unfortunately, the common view throughout most of European history. It was only when the decolonisation process began in the post-Second World War period, together with the reaction to the Nazi Holocaust, that these kinds of view began to wane and the minds of people were opened up to non-racist explanations of the wide development gaps that existed across the world.

*What about the influence of the cold war? Surely this also played an important role since the 'Third World', as it was called in those days, inevitably became an ideological battleground between communism and capitalism championed by the Soviet Union and the USA respectively.*
Yes, the cold war was a very important reason for the Western governments to become increasingly interested in developing countries. We should not exaggerate the altruism of the West towards the developing world. The break-up of colonialism after the end of the Second World War was followed by a period of post-colonial manipulation of the developing countries for strategic geopolitical reasons. The USA and the Soviet Union both wanted to gather allies among the newly emerging independent former colonies and other developing countries. As Henry Kissinger said in 1975,

'If we cannot hold on to Luanda, how can the Europeans trust us to defend Europe?' It seems unbelievable today that Luanda was at one time seen as the front line in the cold war against the Soviets! (*laughter*) The cold war certainly influenced a lot of foreign policy decisions of the European countries, the USA and the Soviet bloc towards the developing countries. It certainly influenced, and continues to influence, the allocation of foreign aid.[4]

## 'CAPITAL FUNDAMENTALISM' AND FOREIGN AID

*You have already said that one important role that economists can play is to debunk the large number of development myths that have emerged in the literature in the last half century. You do this very effectively in* The Elusive Quest, *where you identify five development myths. Let us look at each of the myths that you identify. First and foremost you attack what has been called by Robert King and Ross Levine 'capital fundamentalism'.[5] In the 1950s the development literature was dominated by models that emphasised the key role of capital accumulation for economic growth and development. These models were associated with some great economists such as Arthur Lewis, Walt Rostow, Roy Harrod and Evsey Domar.[6] In turn, capital fundamentalism also provided a framework for believing that foreign aid for investment projects could help raise the growth rates of poor countries. Given the many disappointments with this 'elixir', should we conclude that while capital accumulation is not a 'sufficient' condition for economic growth, it is in some sense a 'necessary' condition since rich countries do have large capital–labour ratios?*

That kind of statement, about necessary and sufficient conditions, is made a lot but I don't think it gets it quite right. In the short to medium run, over which most of us are doing the analysis, capital accumulation is not even necessary. There are countries that have experienced rapid growth without at the same time experiencing rapid capital accumulation. But capital accumulation is necessary in the long run. You are not going to see an advanced, highly developed economy that does not have high capital–labour ratios. However, what people want to know is: how do we get growth to increase in the short to medium run, say over the next ten or 15 years? That is a very long horizon for any politician (*laughter*). The answer that used to be given to that question, and is still given today by a lot of development economists, is: 'increase investment'. That is still seen to be the magic lever that will raise growth rates. Maybe some will admit that this will need to be complemented by good economic policies in other areas, but they will still see investment as the key ingredient for growth. The empirical evidence just does not support that conclusion. Rather, the evidence points to something else, the so-called 'Solow residual' that accounts for most of the growth.[7] That something else that is so important for growth has to do with incentives, institutions, efficiency, and not with the physical amount of capital accumulation.

*The findings in your recent paper with Ross Levine, which support this conclusion, seem to challenge the evidence presented in Alwyn Young's well-known papers on the Asian Tigers.[8] Young's account of the experience of Singapore in particular emphasises the crucial role played by human and physical capital accumulation in the growth process.[9] In your paper with Levine you argue that 'the residual rather than factor accumulation accounts for most of the income and growth differences across nations'.*

Alwyn Young's papers are really doing something different. Its not an empirical study of whether capital accumulation matters and he was not testing empirically the hypothesis that capital accumulation is associated with faster growth. He carried out an accounting exercise for some countries that grew rapidly and then investigated how much of that rapid growth could be accounted for by capital accumulation. In the case of Singapore it seems that capital accumulation accounts for nearly all of its growth in per capita output. What Young does not say is that there are a number of countries scattered throughout Africa and the Middle East that also had rapid capital accumulation like Singapore but did not have rapid growth. So when you do a statistical test to see if capital accumulation explains a lot of growth across a wider sample of countries, you do not see strong evidence supporting the hypothesis implied by Young's view. Even Young's East Asian accounting exercise has been questioned, and in my view successfully undermined, by some recent research by a bright young economist now at Princeton. Chang-tai Hsieh's doctoral dissertation re-examined Young's work on the Asian Tigers and he used an alternative method where he looked at what was going on with wages and the rate of return to capital.[10] Hsieh pointed out that if a lot of the growth in Singapore or the Asian Tigers in general was due to physical and human capital accumulation, then we should have seen falling rates of return to both types of capital. But as Hsieh's research shows, we do not see that. So even limiting the analysis to Singapore, Hsieh's results raise doubt about Young's conclusions.

*Does it make a difference if we distinguish between countries where capital accumulation is mainly carried out by the private sector compared to countries where capital accumulation is largely state led, as it was in the former Soviet Union?*

Even private investment is not a panacea for growth. If you carry out statistical tests on sub-Saharan African country data, and look at the relationship between private investment and per capita growth, the only country where you find a strong association is Botswana, which has experienced both high growth and high rates of private investment. Take out Botswana from your sample and there is no association between the rate of private investment and growth in sub-Saharan Africa. What that seems to tell us is that private investment can also end up being wasted when the institutional environment provides bad incentives for efficiency, for productivity, for adopting modern technology, and for training workers properly. So not even private investment is either a necessary or sufficient condition for growth in the short and medium run where the right incentives are absent.

*What about the research findings of Bradford DeLong and Lawrence Summers, which showed a strong association between equipment investment and economic growth?*[11]
That was an interesting lead at the time, that equipment investment might act as a leading edge in an economy. There might be a technology story here in that it is the technology embodied in the new equipment that is important. But again the DeLong–Summers study identified a very long-run association. In the short to medium run you do not find that even equipment investment is a very strong predictor of growth.

*While many anti-globalist groups attack foreign direct investment (FDI), most economists argue that FDI has an important role to play in helping to improve the growth performance of developing countries. If, as you argue, the importance of capital accumulation has been grossly overstated in the development literature, does this mean that the optimism with respect to FDI is also misplaced, or are their other benefits from FDI?*
FDI is a whole package of things in addition to just capital accumulation. FDI also brings in foreign technology and new ideas, as emphasised by Paul Romer.[12] The experience of Bangladesh provides a good example. A Korean firm in the garment industry, the Daewoo Corporation, invested in Bangladesh in 1979, signing a collaborative agreement with a local Bangladeshi firm, Desh Garments Ltd. The Korean firm took 130 Desh workers to Korea for training in Daewoo's Pusan plant. The managers and workers of Desh Ltd learned too well. After a year the Desh workers cancelled the agreement with Daewoo and started their own garment-exporting business. During the 1980s many of the Desh workers left to form their own garment-exporting businesses. So today we find that Bangladesh has a multi-billion-dollar garment-exporting industry. That's the kind of technological seed that can be planted by FDI. This story shows how investment in knowledge leaks. Ideas are non-rival. It is difficult for knowledge to be retained by the original investor.

*The belief that capital accumulation was the key to growth and development also gave rise to the view that if developing countries did not have enough resources to invest to achieve their growth targets, then the 'savings gap' could be plugged by foreign aid. Economists such as Milton Friedman and Peter Bauer argued against that view and it would appear that economists are now much less sanguine about what foreign aid flows can achieve.[13] You identify foreign aid, tied to the idea of capital fundamentalism, as one of your development myths. Are aid flows more about politics and foreign policy than economic development?*

Aid flows are certainly explained very well by foreign policy considerations. In an interesting paper, Alesina and Dollar use the percentage of time the recipient of aid votes with the donor at the United Nations to identify the foreign policy influence of foreign aid. There is also evidence that IMF lending is influenced by the same variable.[14] The enthusiasm for foreign aid is closely associated with the simple predictions of the Harrod–Domar growth model that GDP growth will be proportional to the share of investment expenditure in GDP. Combining this idea with the idea that developing countries had a savings or financing gap led to the conclusion that, first, aid could fill the gap, and second, that more investment would lead to higher growth.[15] As I discuss in *The Elusive Quest*, neither of these conclusions has turned out to be right. Take the case of Zambia, where there is no evidence that increased investment led to growth. Futhermore, as aid to Zambia increased, rates of investment actually went down!

*One of the main criticisms made about foreign aid is that the evidence seems to indicate that these funds flow just as much to corrupt and inefficient governments as they do to less corrupt and more effective governments.[16] In your book you argue that 'aid should respond to the level of policy performance already achieved and not as much on proposed changes in policy'. In this way you say that 'we could at last get donors' and governments' incentives aligned for growth'. While the logic of this is fine, the key issue is how such a recommendation is likely to work out in practice. It is difficult not to believe that foreign policy interests will always override and get in the way of optimal strategies.*

I agree that it is very hard to fight against the foreign policy tide. We are seeing this again now with the war on terrorism. Aid is going to places like Central Asia where many countries are dominated by corrupt autocrats and are far from being pro-development. But one can only hope that, to the extent that there is some altruistic motivation driving some donors, they will be influenced by rational efficiency considerations. For too long we have seen examples where countries play a successful game where they switch from bad policies to good policies for just long enough to receive more aid, only to revert back to bad policies after receiving more aid.

*Would you be an advocate of increased aid flows if you thought that these resources would in future be allocated on grounds of economic efficiency rather than politics? The recent paper by Craig Burnside and David Dollar provides evidence that aid has a positive impact on economic growth for countries that have good economic policies and little effect in countries that are known to have poor policies.*[17]

Unfortunately it is not as simple as that because the aid allocation issue is not the only problem. The other big problem relates to the aid institutions themselves, the big bureaucracies. A long time ago Milton Friedman pointed out that if you spend your own money on yourself, you care a lot about how much you spend and how you spend it. If you spend someone else's money on somebody else you care little how much is spent or how it is spent. Although Milton Friedman has often been portrayed as some kind of right-wing ideologue, he was in fact drawing attention to a very real and difficult problem that has to be faced. Under these circumstances, even if aid was allocated more to pro-growth governments, we would still have to worry about how the aid donors design their own bloated bureaucracies. We should also remember that the intended customers of the aid industry are the poor people in developing countries. Unfortunately they have little or no voice! They have no voice in their own government, never mind having any kind of voice with the aid donors. Surprisingly, there is far too little emphasis on evaluation of aid donations. Do they actually benefit the poor? We need more *ex post* evaluations of what worked and what didn't.

## EDUCATION AND KNOWLEDGE

*Another panacea for growth that emerged in the development literature, particularly after 1960, was the need for more education and human capital formation. Claudia Goldin has argued that much of the economic success of the US economy in the twentieth century can be attributed to human capital accumulation.*[18] *You also place much emphasis on the importance of knowledge in your work on economic development. So why has the expansion of schooling in the developing countries yielded disappointing results?*

Knowledge is a key ingredient for growth but the problem is that educational spending has not always created knowledge. There was a large increase in schooling in developing countries after 1960. But for increases in schooling and education to create knowledge, a set of institutions and incentives needs to be in place to ensure that you have well-trained, highly motivated teachers. You also need highly motivated students and parents. Students have to want to acquire knowledge. Teachers need to know that rewards and promotions will be based on merit rather than political patronage. In Pakistan, for example, a survey found that the teachers were frequently only slightly better educated than their students. In sub-Saharan Africa you often find situations where educated kids have little confidence that a skilled job will be available to them after they have completed their studies. In such situations the incentive to invest in your own education is obviously reduced. Schooling pays off when government policies establish incentives for growth rather than redistribution. So greater knowledge and an educated mind is a wonderful thing but the actual herding of kids into classrooms will not always accomplish these objectives. Many sub-Saharan countries such as Ghana, Mozambique and Zambia had rapid growth of human capital in the 1960s, 1970s and 1980s, yet were nevertheless growth disasters. Lant Pritchett's study for the World Bank could not find any positive correlation between growth in output per worker and growth in human capital.[19]

## NEO-MALTHUSIAN PESSIMISM

*During the 1950–80 period, conventional wisdom supported the need for developing countries to adopt policies to limit fertility. To the neo-Mathusians, rapid population growth is a major impediment to economic growth and, in the most extreme statements, even poses a threat to the future survival of the human race.[20] Concern over population growth even led the Chinese government in 1982–83 to impose a draconian policy of one child per family, a policy that is still in place. Can such drastic infringements of human rights ever be justified in the interests of economic growth?*
I think China's one-child policy cannot be justified on either moral or economic grounds. To have an authoritarian government tell you how many children you can have is appalling. This policy is not justified on economic grounds because the neo-Malthusian population alarmists have really been proved to be wrong by the experience of development. We have seen exploding populations but we have not seen the outcomes predicted by the alarmists, outcomes such as widespread famine and increased mortality. People have children because they want to have children. They will also limit their family size when they believe it to be in their own interests to do so. Children are viewed as a desirable good; we have three ourselves, I like them very much and I am glad that nobody ordered us to have just one (*laughter*). I always found it an insulting view of human potential to say that an extra mouth to feed would simply decrease the amount available to everyone else. Each new person is potentially a productive human being who can create more output. A pair of hands and a brain come with each extra mouth. The evidence is also clear that there is a negative relationship between per capita income and population growth. Higher incomes lead to

a demographic revolution as birth rates fall, showing that development itself is the most powerful contraceptive. Over the very long run we can see that the more people there are, the more ideas there are, and ideas drive technological change.[21]

*So would you agree with the argument that China's real problem, before adopting this draconian one-child policy, was not so much too rapid population growth, but a failing economic system that was unable to support a growing population? The 'Great Leap Forward' (1958–62) and 'Cultural Revolution' (1966–69), initiated by Mao Zedong were economic development disasters.*

Yes, exactly. A healthy and vibrant economy can support a rapidly growing population, as US economic history shows. The turning point for China was not the adoption of the one-child-per-family policy but the adoption of economic reforms around 1978 after the death of Mao in 1976.

## POLICY REFORM

*In your paper 'The Lost Decades', you document the following puzzle.[22] Why have so many developing countries grown more slowly in the 1980–98 period than the 1960–79 period despite various policy reforms taking many developing countries closer to the so-called 'Washington Consensus' position? Washington Consensus policies are supposed to be good for growth. Did structural adjustment fail?*

There are two broken links in the chain that went from structural adjustment lending by the World Bank and IMF to the developing countries. First, that lending was supposed to promote policy reform and second, those policies adopted were supposed to promote economic growth. In reality both of those links were either weak or broken. In many countries policy reform did not take hold. And where policy reform did take hold it was largely independent of the number of adjustment loans received from the international financial institutions and so those institutions do not get any credit for that. Where we do see structural reform happening we do not see the growth response that was expected. So in the 1980s and 1990s there was a lot of reform going on but growth was lower than that experienced in the 1960s and 1970s, which were supposed to be the bad old days preceding neoliberalism. This was undoubtedly a blow to the optimism surrounding the Washington Consensus.

*In Joseph Stiglitz's recent book* Globalization and its Discontents *he provides an extensive critique of many of the policies advocated by the IMF towards developing countries and the transition economies. He has also been a vociferous critic of the 'Washington Consensus'.*[23] *So it is not just anticapitalist and anti-globalisation demonstrators who are attacking the major international financial institutions; their policies are also under attack from a highly respected Nobel Prizewinning economist. Do you share Stiglitz's concerns and criticisms?*

I think Joe Stiglitz goes a little too far and is in danger of throwing out the baby with the bath water. There are some principles of sound economic management that most economists would agree with. Countries will get into trouble if they have macroeconomic instability arising from high budget deficits leading to the high accumulations of public debt. Look at Argentina! Stiglitz seems to advocate a kind of demand stimulus based on Keynesianism that is not entirely always appropriate to many of these crisis situations. He was probably right in the case of East Asia where the crisis did not originate from mismanagement on the fiscal side. But in most crisis situations elsewhere in the world the problem very often has its origin in excessive budget deficits, not because the crisis country needs more Keynesian demand stimulation. So I think the East Asian case is the exception rather than the rule.

## DEVELOPING COUNTRIES' DEBT RELIEF

*The Jubilee 2000 campaign called for forgiveness of all debt accumulated by developing countries. This campaign is supported by one of the world's leading economists, Jeffrey Sachs, as well as high-profile individuals such as Bono from the rock group U2. In your research on the debt issue you conclude that 'debt forgiveness grants aid to those recipients that have proven their ability to misuse that aid. Debt relief is futile for countries with unchanged government behaviour.'*[24] *Would you support Michael Kremer's idea that odious debt should be forgiven?*[25]

I think where Michael Kremer is very imaginative about this is to say that lenders should be made aware in advance that lending to some governments may involve future cancellation of their 'odious debt'. The incentive properties of such an arrangement are much better than to announce that a debt is odious after the fact. After the fact you can always make the argument that the current government is better than the previous government. But what would it mean to say that your government is better than that of Mobutu? Remember the repayment of debt was intended to be a useful way to deliver resources to developing countries. The repaid debt provides resources that can be channelled to other poor countries. Too often the debt problem is portrayed as rich countries sucking resources out of poor developing countries. That is not how it was set up to work. Official debt was set up to be a revolving fund where resources were to be recycled to other developing countries or even for new projects to the same developing countries. If you forgive debt in a haphazard unlimited way, then you will eventually destroy the effectiveness of the revolving fund. Now it is certainly true that the lenders should be held accountable for making some of their dumb decisions about lending. For example, when so much money poured into French West Africa before the devaluation of the CFA (Central French African) franc, this was clearly an unsustainable situation. The IMF and the World Bank also have a lot to answer for in their lending to dictators like Mobutu and Suharto. Some people are right to draw attention to this. But we must not destroy the effectiveness of the debt instrument by granting ever more favourable terms for debt relief. There is a perverse incentive effect here as countries may borrow in anticipation of debt forgiveness. They may also delay much-needed reform waiting for the best deal. For countries where the government has a high discount rate, where the present is all-important compared to the future, debt relief is likely to encourage asset decumulation and new borrowing. In other words, debt forgiveness is futile for countries that have unchanged long-run savings preferences. So although those who advocate debt relief do so with good intentions to help the poor, if such policies delay the adoption of reforms needed for growth, then it will be the poor who suffer.

## GROWTH THEORY AND EMPIRICS

*Economists' concern with the causes of economic growth results from their knowledge that it is sustained growth of real income per capita, rather than redistribution, that, in the long run, predominantly determines living standards. In the* Elusive Quest *you make clear early in the book that recent empirical research at the World Bank supports the view that faster economic growth is strongly associated with fast poverty reduction.*[26]
It certainly spreads down to the poor in the long run. The most important factor in deciding whether or not a person is rich or poor is where they were born. If you are fortunate enough to be born into a country that has experienced sustained growth over the past two centuries, then you will most probably be rich compared to other people around the world. If you are born in a country that has stagnated over the past two centuries, then you are likely to be poor. So poverty reduction is closely linked to long-run growth. But we should not exaggerate the connection in the short run. In the short run there are all kinds of winners and losers during the process of economic growth. There can be periods when the poor lose out even though

the economy is growing rapidly. It should also be noted that improvements in a developing country's quality-of-life indicators will also depend on global socio-economic progress as well as domestic growth. For example, improvements and breakthroughs in medical technology made in the developed countries often benefit poor countries.

*Turning to theoretical issues relating to growth, how useful is the Solow growth model in helping us analyse issues relating to economic growth and development? Greg Mankiw seems to think that an augmented Solow model can explain a great deal of what we observe with respect to income per capita differentials across nations.*[27]

There is a lot of irony here because Robert Solow himself would say that his model should not have been applied the way it has been applied to explain income differences across countries. Solow had in mind the long-run experience of the USA. The only time he applied his theory to a particular historical episode is when he applied it to the USA in the first half of the twentieth century. I don't think he would ever have argued that his model could be used to explain the gigantic income differences across countries. I don't think he would go along with Greg Mankiw, David Romer and David Weil, who argue their case based on the assumption of a common technology across countries.[28] Their augmented Solow growth model is used to show that income differences can be explained by differences in savings propensities. But, after all, it was Solow himself who was the originator of the idea that investment does not matter for growth but only for levels of output per worker. He showed that capital accumulation could not in the very long run be the main driver of per capita income growth. Solow showed how it was technology or the residual that ultimately drives growth. In a recent paper with Ross Levine we suggest that the stylised facts of economic growth are more consistent with theories of economic growth that emphasise the role of productivity growth and technology than theories that concentrate on factor accumulation.[29] Currently Solow also expresses a great deal of sympathy for theories that attempt to show how technological progress can be made endogenous to the model. Theories that concentrate on innovation and adoption of foreign technology are important here.[30]

*Since the mid-1980s there has been a flood of research on the issue of convergence. Are the poor countries catching up with the rich or is there, to use Lant Pritchett's words, 'Divergence Bigtime'?*[31] *Some recent contributions from economists such as Robert Lucas and Edward Prescott and Stephen Parente seem to imply an optimistic scenario for twenty-first-century convergence providing the barriers to development can be removed.*[32] *Are you as optimistic about the prospects for convergence in the twenty-first century as Lucas?*

No, because economic development is a lot more difficult and complicated than can be captured in a simple model. Economic development is not just about the diffusion of technology and capital from the rich to the poor countries. In the process of development there are a whole lot of collective action problems that cannot be solved by individuals. They have to solved by the state or by groups acting in concert. Take a basic issue like contracts. How are you going to have inflows of FDI and technology if you cannot even enforce a contract between two businessmen? What good is it going to do me to adapt a foreign technology if I have no confidence that my input suppliers are going to deliver the goods that I signed the contract for? Things are really much tougher in the trenches than within the confines of theoretical models of growth. There are a lot of institutional problems that have to be solved for growth to spread. Now it is true that we have witnessed very rapid growth in China during the last 20 years, and to a lesser extent in India more recently. I think that is where a lot of the optimism is coming from because together they contain more than a third of humanity. But we need to remember that before the 1980s India and China were not great success stories. And this worries me because success stories do not always persist in being success stories. Everyone used to bemoan the Indian 'Hindu' rate of growth. We still do not fully understand how that rate of growth began picking up in the 1980s even before economic reforms started to influence events. China's growth experience is easier to explain in terms of the advent of economic reforms initiated after 1979. But there remain a lot of unresolved problems in China and it is still very unclear which way that country will go. China still has a very authoritarian government, a lot of corruption, and is still very far from having the institutional requirements that are needed in the long run to sustain progress.[33]

*Another feature of the growth literature during the past 15 years or so has been the development of endogenous growth models. In* The Elusive Quest *you emphasise the importance of virtuous circles and increasing returns, suggesting that you are a fan of endogenous growth models. Are you enthusiastic about this line of thought?*

Yes I am. The virtuous circle idea is helpful in explaining why we do see such huge disparities in per capita incomes across the world. It is not because some people are inherently low-productivity workers. It is not because the poor people in the world have inferior cultures relative to the rich people of the world. It is really because there are what economists call multiple equilibria. When everyone around you is doing the right thing, then you are also more likely to do the right thing for economic development. So you can get virtuous circles forming where everyone does the right thing and skills complement each other. But you can also get vicious circles where everyone is doing the wrong thing. Getting into a virtuous circle might require some specific government intervention in the creation of knowledge.

*Another recent controversy that has attracted many contributions has been the trade–growth debate. Do more open economies grow faster than more closed economies?*

The record of the past few decades suggests that massive interference with international trade usually brings pretty bad results. In my view inward-oriented industrialisation strategies have not done well in the long run. Having said that, we should not look upon free trade as a panacea for development. Again the basic problem is that free trade will be of limited benefit if you do not have well-established property rights. You need other things in place to fully take advantage and benefit from trade, for example, good institutions such as the rule of law, enforcement of contracts, low corruption, and accountability of government to its citizens.

*There is a consensus among economists that high and variable inflation is damaging to growth. There is less agreement on the economic costs of low and stable inflation. So why do governments in their inflation-targeting strategies make statements that low inflation will be good for growth when research by economists has not established strong links between low inflation and economic growth?*[34]

Well, inflation may have level (efficiency) effects even if, at low levels, it does not have significant growth effects. And we know from surveys and experience that people do not like inflation. People feel that inflation threatens their financial security. It creates uncertainty for business decisions. It messes up accounting procedures. Economists prefer to allow people's preferences to be sovereign and people have shown that they don't like inflation. There is also evidence to show that the poor suffer more from inflation than the rich.[35]

# SUB-SAHARAN AFRICA: ETHNIC DIVERSITY, GEOGRAPHY AND CULTURE

*Sub-Saharan Africa is generally recognised as the least successful part of the developing world. Recent explanations have emphasised geographical influences, ethnic diversity and the lack of democracy. In particular, your 1997 paper with Ross Levine emphasises the impact of ethnic diversity on economic performance. To what extent has this problem been inherited from the colonial experience of sub-Saharan Africa?*

Yes, there is some responsibility resting with the colonial powers who drew the political boundaries in sub-Saharan Africa, ignoring the pre-existing ethnic divisions.[36] The colonial powers also added to the ethnic tensions by often favouring one particular ethnic group over another. For example, some people have suggested that the Hutu–Tutsi divide was mainly created by the Belgian colonialists. Unfortunately we cannot change the history of Africa so we have to take the world as it is, and that includes ethnic divisions and strife. We cannot progress matters by wishing such divisions did not exist when they do. Instead we should concentrate on identifying the institutional arrangements that are likely to mitigate the adverse consequences of ethnic diversity.

*What has recent research concluded about the impact of ethnic diversity on the economic performance of nations?*
Research has shown that ethnolinguistic fractionalisation has adversely affected sub-Saharan economic performance. It certainly helps to explain a great deal of the political instability in that continent. Ethnically divided countries are more likely to experience social and political conflict through internal wars of attrition. Ethnically diverse nations seem to suffer more from the impact of external shocks. Foreign aid is more likely to find its way into unproductive and corrupt activities. Even in the USA, research has found that there is a link between ethnic diversity and bloated government payrolls. Ethnic diversity also lowers trust and makes it more difficult to build social capital. However, on the positive side, research does seem to show that better institutions can help to manage ethnic conflict.[37] By adopting better institutional arrangements that guarantee property rights, provide a more efficient non-corrupt bureaucracy, and more democratic accountability of government, the adverse effects of ethnic diversity can be reduced. The hope is that, as democracy and other good institutions spread, these problems associated with ethnic diversity will diminish.

*Is there a strong link between ethnic diversity and the incidence of genocide?*
Yes. State-sponsored killings are frequently associated with the degree of ethnic diversity. Between 1960 and 1990 there were 16 incidents that can be classified as genocide. In every case ethnic divisions played a key role.[38] However, research shows that ethnically diverse countries that also have high institutional quality, such as Canada, Malaysia and Thailand, do not experience genocides. So it is crucial for countries with high ethnic diversity to develop good institutions of conflict management.

*Are you persuaded by the arguments of David Bloom and Jeffrey Sachs relating to the importance of geography in explaining sub-Saharan Africa's relatively poor economic performance?*[39]

No, I am not convinced by this line of argument. I think the best refutation of the geography argument has been provided by Daron Acemoglu, Simon Johnson and James Robinson in their recent papers.[40] They show how a few centuries ago the tropical parts of the world were relatively rich and productive areas. The Europeans were jousting for control of those areas precisely because they were so productive. There is a story that after the Seven Years War in the eighteenth century, the British furiously debated among themselves whether they should trade Canada to France for the small island of Guadeloupe (*laughter*). Because things have changed so drastically since then, countries that were relatively rich around the sixteenth century are now relatively poor. Acemoglu et al. make a pretty convincing case that it is the change in institutions rather than geography which explains the 'reversal of fortune' between the tropics and the now developed countries.[41]

*You have taken up this theme in your most recent paper with Ross Levine where you test the geography, institutions and policy views as explanations of cross-country variations in economic development. What are the main findings from that research?[42]*
We find that the kind of arguments that some people put forward about the importance of geography all seem to work through institutions. For example, the historical process shows that where there is a low-mortality disease environment in temperate latitudes we see the spread of smallholdings and family farms. With that we see the diffusion of democracy and property rights, and the control of corruption. Historically we have seen that good institutions for growth have tended to evolve in certain geographic environments. That is where all of the explanatory power of geography comes from. We cannot deny the fact that most of the countries near the equator today have much lower per capita incomes than countries in the more temperate latitudes. But the reason for this seems to be entirely due to institutional developments resulting from accidents of history. Many countries that endured colonisation and the slave trade were left without good institutions conducive to growth and development.

*I notice that Robert Barro has recently co-authored a research paper investigating the link between religion and economic performance.[43] Do you find explanations of comparative development based on cultural differences convincing?*
The culture arguments suffer from the way that they are used as *ex post* rationalisations of whoever is successful or unsuccessful at a particular moment in time. If you think of culture as a very long-run historical tradition, then there are immediate problems. If you go back over the last

thousand years we find China ahead of Europe as the world economic leader, only to see it fall back. Then we find Max Weber arguing in his book *The Protestant Ethic and the Spirit of Capitalism* that Confucianism was inimical to the development of capitalism because it encouraged people to look down on merchants.[44] Then, when the Asian Tigers experienced their growth miracles, the Confucian ethic argument was reversed and used by some commentators to explain East Asia's success. I am suspicious when arguments like this get moved around so easily. Similar lines of argument are now being forwarded about the adverse impact of Islam on economic performance. But if we go back in history we see the Ottoman Empire and the great Islamic civilisations of northern India and the Middle East. These civilisations were ahead of those in Europe in terms of technology and science until the last few centuries. So if you think of culture as being a very long-run fixed characteristic of certain parts of the world, then it does not do very well at predicting economic performance and the various shifts and reversals of fortune that we have observed in history.

## SOCIAL CAPITAL, DEMOCRACY AND TRANSITION

*In recent years the concept of 'social capital' has been receiving considerable attention from researchers across the social sciences. For example Professor János Kornai and his colleagues have an interesting research project under way entitled 'Honesty and Trust in the Light of Post-Socialist Transition', centred at the Collegium Budapest, Institute for Advanced Study.[45] How important is 'social capital' for successful economic development?*

Social capital is a term used as shorthand for a set of social relationships that a producer has. Economists have increasingly come to realise that production is really a social activity. That is why you see the concentration of particular products, professions or ethnic groups in certain locations. These concentrations develop because of the presence of social networks that facilitate the diffusion of knowledge and expertise within certain localities. Why, for example, are there great French chefs? It is not due to the French culture of religion. It is just that there is tradition of cooking within France that has been disseminated within families and from one French person to another. The social capital preserves the French comparative advantage in cuisine. We find the same applies to the Swiss with watches. I was recently travelling in Ethiopia where there is a small ethnic group that dominates the markets in Addis Ababa because it has a family tradition of being merchants. One generation passes on knowledge to the next generation. You can also use kin groups when the society-wide institutions fail to establish trust. It is easier to trust people within your kin network than people outside that group because if you cross members of your kin group you know that you will be ostracised. So kinship networks help to provide social capital when national government institutions are seen to be ineffective.

*Dani Rodrik (2001a) has suggested that 'The idea of a mixed economy is possibly the most valuable heritage that the twentieth century bequeaths to the twenty-first in the realm of economic policy.' Jagdish Bhagwati argues that democracy and markets are essential ingredients for the establishment of prosperity. In a previous interview with Joseph Stiglitz he commented that 'the idea that you need a dictatorship in order to generate good economic growth is just plain wrong. As time has evolved we can now see a variety of reasons why democracy is both good for poverty and economic growth'.*[46] *These are conclusions that you also support in your published work.*

Yes. Democracy plus free markets combined with effective public services is an attractive combination. But there are many variations on this theme across societies. I don't think you can make sweeping statements about government being bad or good because it really depends on the incentives that government actors face in each society. If a society has a great civil service tradition where people are promoted on the basis of merit, and if governments are accountable to their citizens, then governments may be able to perform certain tasks much better than markets. If those conditions are absent, then governments are likely to perform badly. To create the right incentives to generate sustained private sector growth you need democratic institutions that protect property rights and individual freedom. In undemocratic polarised societies, especially ones that are ethnically diverse, a lack of trust makes it very difficult to build social capital. Societies that are ethnically more homogeneous tend to have higher levels of trust and social capital. Research indicates that ethnic diversity has a much greater negative impact on economic performance when institutions are poor. This is one important explanation of the poor economic performance of sub-Saharan Africa.

*In your 1995 paper co-authored with Stanley Fischer you analysed the contributing factors to the Soviet economic decline over the 1960–89 period. What is your broad assessment of the transition process since 1990?*

As far as the transition economies are concerned, in retrospect it seems as if the transition could have been handled better. The collapse of output was dramatic. To some extent this was inevitable given that you had inefficient bureaucrats organising the production of shoddy goods. Once people had a choice, they were always going to stop buying those goods and production in those sectors was bound to collapse. Output from the new private sector was never going to be able to expand fast enough to compensate for the fall in output from the old declining sectors. It was naïve of economists to think that all you needed to do was to organise price liberalisation and private property and these former socialist economies would simply take off as immediately successful capitalist economies. When people have been operating within a framework of poor and inefficient institutions for a long time you cannot expect them to adapt immediately to a new set of capitalist institutions, even assuming those institutions can be quickly and effectively established. It takes time for people to become entrepreneurs and to feel secure about their property rights.

## THE TWENTY-FIRST CENTURY

*In his controversial book,* The Clash of Civilisations, *Samuel Huntington argues that 'In the post-Cold War world, for the first time in history, global politics has become multi-polar and multi-civilisational . . . In this new world the most pervasive, important, and dangerous conflicts will not be between social classes, rich and poor, or other economically defined groups, but between peoples belonging to different cultural identities.'*[47] *How much of this idea would you go along with?*
As far as the clash of civilisations is concerned I find Huntington's argument to be a gross oversimplification of the world we live in. Islam is incredibly diverse and encompasses Indonesia, Bangladesh, Pakistan, the Middle East and North Africa. These are all vastly different societies. The idea that these countries form one homogeneous group who must inevitably clash with the USA and Europeans I find highly questionable. The 'clash' part of Huntington's book may be right, but not clash between civilisations. This is a ludicrous simplification. We have always had clashes between human societies and we would be naïve to think that these will steadily go away just because communism collapsed in 1989. So I do not agree with the fault lines that Huntington identifies.

*Are you optimistic about development prospects in the twenty-first century?*
I think the idea that economies follow a path that can be described by rigid stages should be thrown out of the window. There is no deterministic path towards a more advanced stage of development, however you define advanced. Each society and civilisation has to find its own way, make its own compromises, learn from its own mistakes and the mistakes of others. In the old days people tended to envisage that every economy, as it developed, would eventually become like a little USA. That is definitely not going to happen. Despite the growth of the world economy, increasing international integration and globalisation, countries will continue to make

different choices about their form and role of government, their laws, the extent of consumerism and so on. So I would expect there to remain a lot of diversity at the end of the twenty-first century.

*Do you think that we really do learn from history?*
Yes, but very slowly (*laughter*).


## NOTES

1.  I interviewed Professor Easterly on 3 January 2003 in his office at the Centre for Global Development, Washington, DC.
2.  For details consult Professor Easterly's personal webpage, http://www.nyu.edu/fas/institute/dri/Easterly/index.html.
3.  See, for example, Wacziarg (2002); Sen (2006).
4.  See Alesina and Dollar (2000).
5.  See King and Levine (1994).
6.  The models associated with these economists are discussed in Todaro and Smith (2003).
7.  In growth accounting exercises the 'Solow residual' measures the growth in total factor productivity, calculated as the percentage change in output minus the percentage change in weighted factor inputs.
8.  Easterly and Levine (2001).
9.  See, for example, Young (1995).
10.  Hsieh (1999).
11.  See DeLong and Summers (1993).
12.  See Romer (1990, 1993).
13.  See Friedman, M. (1958); Bauer (1972).
14.  See Alesina and Dollar (2000); Thacker (1999).
15.  See Chenery and Strout (1966).
16.  Alesina and Weder (2002). See also Easterly (2006a, 2007).
17.  Burnside and Dollar (2000).
18.  Goldin (2001).
19.  Pritchett (1997b).
20.  See Ehrlich (1968).
21.  See Jones (2001, 2005).
22.  Easterly (2001b).
23.  See Stiglitz (2002a); Snowdon (2002a).
24.  See Easterly (2002a).
25.  See Kremer and Jayachandran (2006). 'Odious debt' is defined as debt accumulated by dictatorial rulers who borrow without the consent of the people and who use the borrowed funds for personal gain and/or to repress the population. Examples would include Somoza (Nicaragua), Duvalier (Haiti), Marcos (Philippines), Mobutu (Zaire), and Abacha (Nigeria).
26.  For example, Dollar and Kraay (2002a, 2002b).
27.  Mankiw (1995).
28.  Mankiw et al. (1992).
29.  Easterly and Levine (2001).
30.  See Solow (2002).
31.  Pritchett (1997a).
32.  Lucas (2000); Parente and Prescott (2000).
33.  See Rodrik (2003a).
34.  For example, see Temple (2000).

282     *Interviews*

35.  See Easterly and Fischer (2001).
36.  For an excellent discussion of African political geography, see Herbst (2000).
37.  For discussions of these various issues see Rodrik (1999b); Alesina, Baqir and Easterly (1999); Collier (2001); Easterly (2001c).
38.  See Glaeser (2005).
39.  Bloom and Sachs (1998).
40.  See Acemoglu, Johnson and Robinson (2001, 2002).
41.  See also the recent response to his critics by Sachs (2003a).
42.  Easterly and Levine (2003). See also Easterly (2001d, 2002b).
43.  See Barro and McCleary (2006).
44.  Weber (1904).
45.  See Kornai interview. See also Dasgupta and Serageldin (2000).
46.  See Rodrik (2001a); Bhagwati (1998a); Snowdon (2001b, 2002a).
47.  Huntington (1996).

# Stanley Fischer[1]

Stanley Fischer's career has been dominated by his association with the prestigious Department of Economics at MIT and his work at the World Bank and the IMF.[2] He graduated from the London School of Economics (1962–66) with BSc Econ. and MSc Econ. degrees before completing his PhD at MIT in 1969. In addition to the numerous consultancy positions, fellowships and honours he has received,[3] the main highlights of Professor Fischer's distinguished academic career include: 1969–70, Postdoctoral Fellow, University of Chicago; 1970–73, Assistant Professor of Economics, University of Chicago; 1973–77, Associate Professor of Economics, MIT; 1977–92, Professor of Economics, MIT; 1992–95, Killian Class of 1926 Professor, MIT; 1993–94, Head of Department of Economics, MIT; 1986–94, editor of the National Bureau of Economic Research *Macroeconomics Annual*; 1988–90, Vice President, Development Economics, and Chief Economist, World Bank; 1993–94, Member of Academic Advisory Council, Congressional Budget Office; 1994, Adjunct Senior Fellow, Council on Foreign Relations; 1995, Vice President, American Economics Association; 1994–2001, First Deputy Director, International Monetary Fund (IMF); 2001–02, Special Advisor to the Managing Director, IMF; 2002–05, President of Citigroup International, and Vice Chairman of Citigroup. Since May 2005, Professor Fischer has been Governor of the Bank of Israel.

Professor Fischer has authored/co-authored some 13 books and over 200 papers in professional journals.[4] His research has covered a wide range of issues, but he is best known for his expertise in macroeconomics, where his principal contributions have focused on the analysis of the actual and potential roles of activist stabilisation policy, the costs of inflation, rules v. discretion in the role and conduct of monetary policy, and, more recently, the international monetary system, the economics of growth, development and transition, and globalisation issues.[5]

Throughout his professional career Fischer has been guided by a firm belief that 'ivory tower' economists have 'an important social role to play . . . through teaching and research' and through 'participation in public life' via the media, consultancy, and as policy advisers. On leaving the IMF Fischer emphasised the importance of his academic background to his work as an applied economist and policy maker, noting that 'Much of what one learns in academic life is essential in dealing with the technical problems that come up in the IMF.'[6]

In the interview that follows I discuss with Professor Fischer several important issues relating to the contemporary world economy including problems of stabilisation, inflation and growth, the economics and politics of transition, exchange rate regimes, the IMF, the East Asian crisis, and globalisation and economic development.

## BACKGROUND INFORMATION

*Before coming to Citigroup you spent your life working as a professional economist in academia and also in two of the world's most important and influential international institutions, the World Bank and the International Monetary Fund (IMF). How does working as an economist in these important institutions differ from working as a professor at MIT?*

The biggest change in moving from academia to a policy job is that, as a policy maker, after considering all the arguments you have to make up your mind on an issue, and come down on one side or the other. As an academic, when considering an issue I could identify the pluses and minuses and conclude on the need for more research to resolve difficult questions. But when you have to recommend action you have at some point to get off the fence and decide – taking into account the gaps and imperfections in your knowledge.

*In your role as Vice President, Development Economics and Chief Economist at the World Bank and First Deputy Director at the IMF, you were in positions of considerable power and influence. Obviously, decisions taken at the World Bank and the IMF have a profound influence on the lives of millions of people around the world. As you have just said, at some point you had to make decisions. Did you ever feel that the onus of responsibility of making or participating in those decisions was sometimes becoming too much of a burden?*

You are constantly aware of the responsibility, but you have to get on and make the decisions that have to be made. Or, as Michel Camdessus, the Managing Director of the IMF, would say on those occasions, 'We must do our job.' It helped in making those decisions to know that the Executive Board of the IMF, on which all the member country governments are represented, would have to approve every decision – so that ultimately one was asking what would be acceptable to the member governments.

The couple of years following the start of the East Asian crisis was a period of high tension, and I remember feeling, somewhere around March–April 1999 when the situation in Brazil finally began to improve, that a physical burden that had been present since July 1997 was lifting. But I don't want to exaggerate, because the policy makers in the crisis countries who had to make policy decisions were under much greater pressure.

*What is your role here at Citigroup and to what extent do you use your training as an economist?*

I have a variety of roles, the most important of which is probably country risk management, which means deciding on the scale and scope of our activities in different countries. My economics training is essential in this area, as is the knowledge of particular countries that I gained while at the IMF. I also spend time talking to and working with my colleagues who are active in the markets, where much of the finance that I studied as an academic helps a great deal. I also used economics all the time at the IMF, though you never knew which particular piece of economic analysis you would be using next. Of course, the basic economic tool was the Mundell–Fleming model and its updates.[7] But quite often I would find myself in situations that reminded me of some game-theory article that I had read, and could better understand the context in which I was interacting with colleagues or officials in a member country.

Without a solid training in economics it would be virtually impossible to figure out what is going on within national economies and across the international economy. The whole experience of working as an applied economist is fascinating and drives home what a great intellectual discipline ours is.

# INFLATION, GROWTH AND STABILISATION POLICY

*The last time we talked, in February 1993, we mainly discussed the state of macroeconomics.*[8] *How would you assess the current macroeconomic state of the world economy? At the moment we can see the continuing depressed deflationary state of the Japanese economy, sluggish growth in the European Union, talk of deflation in Germany and uncertainty about the direction of the US economy. Paul Krugman has warned about the 'return of Depression economics' and articles about the threat of deflation are appearing with increasing frequency in academic journals and the news media.*[9] *Is deflation something that we should really worry about?*

We are talking now in May 2003 when the cyclical situation is not very good in continental Europe, there is uncertainty about whether US growth will really accelerate in the second half of the year, and the situation in Japan has been dismal for a long time. Considering that these are the world's three biggest economies, the outlook is pretty difficult. Deflation is obviously a concern in Japan. But I don't believe it needs to be a concern in the USA or Germany, particularly because our monetary policy has been very expansionary. For the German economy to begin to grow in a sustainable way, it is also necessary for that country to undertake a set of well-understood but politically difficult structural reforms.

*Although in your 1993 paper, 'The Role of Macroeconomic Factors in Growth', you present evidence that inflation has negative effects on economic growth, economists have not really produced convincing systematic evidence that variations of inflation at the low end have significant effects on real variables such as growth and employment.*[10] *Many economists have argued against aiming for a target of zero inflation on the basis that such a target would entail a strong risk of deflation.*[11]

Deflation has generally been bad for growth, although there have been important episodes – for instance in the USA in the last quarter of the nineteenth century – where deflation was accompanied by economic growth. I don't believe the long-run Phillips curve is vertical all the way down to zero inflation, both for reasons set out in the 1996 paper by Akerlof, Dickens and Perry, that emphasizes the difficulty of relative price and wage adjustments, and because the lower bound of zero on the nominal interest rate presents a serious problem for monetary policy when the maintenance of full employment demands a very low or negative real interest rate.

There is also a considerable literature on the relationship between growth and inflation at low rates of inflation. Michael Bruno and Bill Easterly have done work that suggests that at inflation rates below 40 per cent per annum, inflation is not bad for growth.[12] Later work suggests that the breakpoint in the negative relationship between inflation and economic growth as the inflation rate declines occurs at single-digit inflation rates, with considerable uncertainty about the location of the turning point.

*Your recent co-authored paper on hyperinflation in the* Journal of Economic Literature *makes it abundantly clear that hyperinflation and high inflation have damaging real effects on an economy.*[13]

Hyperinflation, defined as inflation exceeding 50 per cent per month, is very destructive of economic performance, as is ongoing moderate to chronic inflation. In that paper we also show that hyperinflation is mainly a modern phenomenon, a result of the invention of paper money. It has also generally been associated with wars and their aftermaths, and the break-up of empires. Between 1947 and 1984 there were no hyperinflations and there have been only seven hyperinflations in market economies since 1987. All transition economies experienced at least one episode of inflation in excess of 25 per cent and most had inflation episodes exceeding 400 per cent. The data confirm that there is a strong correlation between monetary growth and inflation in both the long run and the short run. So inflations can be ended by monetary contraction. But the key question is: what drives monetary growth in the first place? There is quite strong evidence to show that for high-inflation economies there is a close short-run link between fiscal imbalance, monetary growth and inflation.

*There has been a lot of criticism of the European Central Bank with respect to the conduct of monetary policy. Many economists believe that the ECB has been too conservative and too concerned about inflation rather than the dangers of deflation and recession. Similar criticisms have been made about the Bank of Japan. Some economists, such as Lars Svensson, and also Mervyn King, who will become the new Governor of the Bank of England in June this year, argue for a flexible approach to inflation targeting, giving due consideration to real instability as well as inflation.*[14] *Are you in favour of 'flexible inflation targeting' as practised by the Bank of England and the US Fed?*

The Bank of England has a formal inflation target whereas the US Fed does not. The Bank of England's conduct of monetary policy in recent years has been very good. I do support flexible inflation targeting, provided we underline the word flexible. This means paying attention to the business cycle as well as to inflation. The way the Bank of England does this is to target future inflation, inflation forecast targeting, rather than current inflation. I would also emphasise the symmetric nature of an inflation target. To have inflation below the target is just as bad as having inflation above target. So I am in favour of symmetrical, flexible inflation targeting.

For understandable reasons, the ECB has given a lot of weight to the need to establish its anti-inflation credentials or credibility. But they have been slow in cutting interest rates in response to economic weakness; that could have been done more rapidly, paying more attention to slow growth in the heart of Europe. However, I also accept the ECB argument that few of Germany's problems would be resolved by lower interest rates. Germany has some deep-seated structural problems that should be tackled.

*In your 2001 paper with Bill Easterly, published in the* Journal of Money, Credit, and Banking, *you argue that low inflation helps the poor. What is the mechanism whereby low inflation benefits the poor?*
Many people, me included, used to reject the idea that inflation is a regressive tax. But when you look at low-income, high-inflation economies, Brazil in 1994 is the best example, you do see that the poor benefited when inflation was reduced. The mechanisms have to do with wages and the financial sector. As a financial tax, inflation hits the poor because they hold more cash relative to their income than the rich, and by and large they are not debtors. They are not going to benefit from inflation on the borrowing side, but they are going to get hit on their assets, namely cash holdings. The rich are more likely to have access to financial instruments that allow them to hedge against inflation. Also the poor depend more on minimum wages and state-determined income payments that are not always indexed to protect against the effects of inflation.

In the paper with Bill Easterly that you mention, we presented evidence drawn from an international poll of over 30 000 respondents from 38 countries. This evidence shows that the poor themselves are more strongly averse to inflation than those with higher incomes. Included in our sample of countries were rich developed countries and poor developing countries as well as transition economies. Our data also indicate that high inflation tends to reduce the income share of the lowest 20 per cent of the population. So politically, fighting inflation is more popular than I used to think when I started studying these issues at MIT in the mid-1970s.

*Since we last talked, the area of macroeconomics that has really taken off is growth theory and empirics. Have developments in this area of macroeconomics over the last decade provided any key insights that will be useful in promoting sustained economic growth in the developing countries?*
Economic growth is a complicated process. There are not a lot of ideas in the new growth theories that were not around in some loose sense before. There have always been those who have argued that investment in technology, R&D and education are the keys to promoting faster economic growth. The problem was to figure out how to formalise such ideas within

a coherent analytical framework rather than leaving them as broad insights. So the achievement of the new growth theorists has been to formalise many of these intuitive ideas. In doing that, for instance through the focus on economies of scale, technology transfer, the role of the financial sector and the creation of human capital, economists working in this area helped to concentrate the minds of the profession on these issues.

Getting the new ideas to the influential policy makers in the developing countries would certainly help them concentrate on what matters for growth. In thinking about the impact of the new growth theory, I recall a remark made by Paul Samuelson about macroeconomic forecasting: he said that he would rather have Bob Solow's forecasts than those of an econometric model, *but* that he would rather have Bob Solow with access to an econometric model than Bob Solow without such access. It's the same here. There are smart policy makers all over the world who you would rather trust to set policy than some freshly minted graduate student armed with the latest set of models. But it would be even better if the policy maker had an understanding of the latest ideas and research in economics. This certainly applies to the new developments in growth theory and empirics.

With respect to the developing countries, the evidence is persuasive that poverty reduction occurs fastest where there has been rapid growth, and also that openness to the international economy is a necessary though not sufficient condition for sustained growth.[15]


## THE ECONOMICS OF TRANSITION

*A major feature of the transition process across all the former Eastern bloc is the decline in real GDP. In a recent paper Campos and Coricelli state that 'the defining stylised fact of the first ten years of transition from central planning to market economies is the massive output fall'.[16] This decline in output, or at least the scale of the output decline, seems to have taken everybody by surprise.*

Back in 1990 when the transition process started it was generally recognised that GDP would fall as a result of stabilisation policies, resource realloca- tion and the disorganisation that would inevitably come with such large- scale change. However, the extent of the decline in GDP was larger than anyone expected and there was a large output decline in all the transition economies in the former Soviet Union, Eastern Europe and the Baltic States. Some economists argue that the output decline would be much less if output were measured correctly.[17] I'm sure the output decline has been significantly exaggerated by the data we use, but I don't know how large the exaggeration is. Even according to the official data, most of the countries that suffered a decline of GDP were experiencing growth by 1999, although only a few had recovered and surpassed their pre-transition levels.

*In 1991 you wrote a paper with Alan Gelb published in the* Journal of Economic Perspectives, *entitled 'The Process of Socialist Economic Transformation'.*[18] *In that paper you included a chart where you mapped out the desirable sequencing of reforms and desirable policy actions. Looking back at over a decade of transition, how do you now view the phasing that you mapped out in those early years? Do you think that you highlighted the right priorities given what has happened subsequently?*

I think the priorities identified in that chart were basically correct. In particular the chart did not neglect the need for institutional development. It included both institutional reform and the need to develop the legal and regulatory framework. A frequent criticism of the standard approach to transition is that it did not give enough emphasis to institutional change. That's not right because, as the chart shows, institutional reform was not neglected. Rather it was widely recognised from the beginning that the creation of a successful market economy would require a supporting institutional infrastructure that included legal reforms, new accounting and governance procedures, the creation of financial institutions and a credible fiscal system.

The real problem was not that this element was overlooked but that efforts at institutional reform were not as successful as we had hoped. What would I say differently after a decade plus? It would be to acknowledge that the process of reform has been much more difficult than most economists expected. Putting in place new institutions is no easy task. A vast amount of technical assistance about various aspects of institution building was provided to the transition economies, including advice from private sector organizations, for example from the American Bar Association on legal reform. But to change institutions effectively after decades of communism turned out to be a very slow process.

*Was it possible in the early 1990s to foresee which of the transition economies would have the greatest difficulties in switching to a capitalist market economy? Was it obvious early on that Russia was going to be more of a problem than Poland or Hungary?*

We thought it likely from the beginning that the European countries that had become communist after the Second World War and were more 'Western' to begin with were more likely to succeed more quickly than the former Soviet Union. And indeed the countries that have performed best in the transition process tend to be those closest to Western Europe, that spent the least time under communist rule, and that were more economically advanced when they began the transition process.

The case of Hungary, which had started the transition in the 1960s, looked promising from the start.[19] One of the surprises was the Czech Republic, which did much better than anticipated, at least early on in the transition process. The determination of the Baltic countries to join Europe certainly helped their transition.

The complexity of the Russian transition may have been underestimated, although it was clear to everyone that this was the country where the communist power apparatus was the most powerful and entrenched. There is still discussion over whether more Western financial assistance and a more sympathetic understanding of Russia's needs would have eased their transition process. That would probably have had a positive effect, but would not have been decisive. For it was Russia where the stakes were greatest because of its natural resources, and Russia where the necessary political changes were likely to be the most difficult given its long history of communism and highly centralised economic coordination. After the 1996 elections there were powerful vested interests whose actions prevented Russia from pushing ahead with its reform programme.

*A very controversial debate among those working on transition issues relates to the arguments over the desirability of adopting a 'big bang shock therapy' strategy versus the adoption of a more 'gradualist' process of transition.[20] In a co-authored article published in* Finance and Development *you argue that 'the best performers are countries that were the most committed to reform at the start and that have carried out reforms rapidly and consistently'.[21] This would seem to put you in the shock therapy camp, along with economists like Andrei Shleifer and Jeffrey Sachs. Is it political economy considerations that decide which is the best strategy? For example, a major consideration in the case of Russia was fear of the communists regaining political control before the reforms were implemented. Was it a case of there being only a brief window of opportunity to get reforms under way and it had to be done quickly?*

In Poland, which was the first country to undertake rapid reforms, the strategy was certainly very controversial in the period 1989–93, although by 1994 people could see that the strategy was working and the controversy began to die down. There the political argument was made explicitly by Poland's former Minister of Finance, Leszek Balcerowicz, that there was a window of opportunity, a period of 'extraordinary politics', and that the reformers needed to seize the moment.[22] Given that the first transition era government was followed by a more left-wing government after democratic elections, I guess he was proved right.

It was very similar in the Russian case. The reformers there, particularly Yegor Gaidar and Anatoly Chubais, explicitly aimed to make it impossible for the communists to come back. Price controls were dismantled immediately after the inauguration of the first Russian government at the end of 1991, and this was probably the biggest shock the economy experienced – but within a few months markets were beginning to respond to price signals. Probably the most controversial of all policies in Russia was the 1996 loans-for-shares privatisation scheme. This was clearly election related. The reformers wanted to reduce state ownership as fast as possible in case there was a change of government in 1996.

Could one conceive of a different process of transition with a powerful government controlling it all? Theoretically, that was a possibility. However, at the practical level the history of the Soviet Union suggests it was not a real option. Several attempts at gradual reform had been tried since 1962 without much success. *Perestroika* itself was an attempt at gradual reform – and it failed. So I do not think there were a lot of options to do it differently at the grand strategic level, though no doubt many of the specific decisions could have been better, and better executed.[23]

*Many of the critics of the Russian transition process frequently use China as an example of successful transition via gradualism. Is this a completely unrealistic comparison to make?*
The Chinese route, of having a strong state in charge for a long period of transformation, was not an option for Russia given the weakness of the Russian state by 1990. In addition, there were important differences between the structures of the Chinese and Russian economies. In the early 1990s, at the start of Russia's transition process, the industrial sector in Russia was much bigger relative to the size of the economy than was that of China in 1978. Russia's transformation problem in 1990 was not to create an industrial sector but to transform and restructure the existing sector and make it more efficient.

In 1978, China's main problem was to make agriculture more efficient, and it did that through a form of shock therapy, with very rapid transformation. Between 1978 and 1981 China completely changed the agrarian system, moving from collective farming to a system that allowed individuals to manage their own land, even though they didn't own the land. The initial success of that very rapid change allowed China to pursue more gradual policies in the industrial sector. China was following a path like that in the classic Lewis model of economic development, with surplus labour being drawn from the agricultural sector to the expanding industrial sector.[24] So comparisons are difficult to make.

But China has still to deal with some problems that Russia resolved through its rapid privatisation programme; in particular the Chinese state-owned enterprise sector is still very large, still losing money, and because many firms cannot service loans, still creating massive problems in the financial sector. The conventional wisdom may even be changing: there was an interesting article a while back in the Sunday edition of the *New York Times* asking whether Russia had got it right compared to China because Russia has gone through the difficult process of political transition, and has privatised to a much greater extent.

*So are you optimistic about the future of Russia?*
Yes, there are a lot of encouraging signs there. Some say that the faster growth is only because of oil, but an oil economy is difficult to manage, and many countries that have relied on oil or other abundant natural resources have failed to produce sustained growth.[25] The Russian economy is now much more stable than it was before the crisis, and is making steady progress on corporate governance and in setting a stable macroeconomic framework and policies. But many microeconomic reforms remain to be made, including in the natural-resource sectors, and there are concerns about maintenance of press freedom and civil liberties.

None the less, I am optimistic about the ongoing process of change in Russia. There is also a generational aspect to the transition process. We are now over ten years into transition and there are many Russians in their late twenties and early thirties who see living in a market economy as a normal way of life. And there is a whole generation coming through who cannot remember communism or were not even born before it collapsed.

# EXCHANGE RATE REGIMES AND CURRENCY UNIONS

*In your paper 'Exchange Rate Regimes: Is the Bipolar View Correct?', you argue that there has been an increasing trend towards the adoption of either hard pegs or floating exchange rate regimes and that this trend is likely to continue.[26] Is that still your view?*
During the 1990s we witnessed a series of capital-market-related crises, namely those in Britain, 1992; Europe in 1992 and 1993, Mexico, 1994; East Asia, 1997; Russia and Brazil, 1998; and Argentina and Turkey in 2000. These crises demonstrated what economists call the problem of the 'impossible trinity'; that is, you cannot have simultaneously a soft pegged exchange rate regime, a liberalised capital account, and at the same time operate an independent monetary policy dedicated to domestic objectives. In a world of free capital mobility, if you adopt a soft pegged exchange rate, then monetary policy must be targeted at maintenance of the exchange rate. But with capital mobility a soft peg regime is vulnerable to speculative

attack.[27] It has accordingly proved difficult for monetary authorities to credibly commit to a soft peg.

Each of the crises I mentioned was related in some way to a pegged exchange rate regime. The bipolar solution of choosing either hard pegs or letting a currency float was therefore seen by many economists and policy makers to be preferable to various forms of soft peg exchange rate regime. Hard pegs include the adoption of currency boards, dollarisation and currency unions. I am not sure that I should have used the word 'bipolar' in that paper because what I regard as a flexible exchange rate or floating regime is not the same as a free float. By floating I mean a situation where the authorities are not committed to defending any particular exchange rate. Intermediate regimes between these two do not seem to be sustainable.[28]

When I wrote that paper I was still at the IMF and had to choose my words very carefully. If I were to refine that paper from where it was two years ago I would say – particularly after the collapse of the Argentine peg – that we are less likely to see currency boards in the future, and that we are likely rather to see more cases of straightforward dollarisation. We will see more countries getting rid of their currencies and there will be more currency unions.[29] On the other hand we will see very few soft peg regimes. I think that we will still see lots of currencies where there is intervention but not in the sense of holding to a particular rate plus or minus a few per cent.

*You said that there will be more currency unions in the future. Hugh Rockoff has two interesting papers pointing out that it took the USA about 150 years to become an optimal currency area.[30] The US currency union was set up in 1788, but it was not until the 1930s that institutional changes were implemented that addressed the problems caused by regional shocks within the US economy.[31] Whatever else one thinks about European Monetary Union, I think everyone agrees that the European Union countries do not comprise an optimal currency area in the way it was originally defined and set out by Robert Mundell.[32] Are you a euro enthusiast?*

I am generally in favour of the euro. We need to remember that it is not only an economic enterprise, but also and importantly a political enterprise. I find persuasive the argument made by Jeffrey Frankel and Andrew Rose, that what becomes an optimal currency area is affected by the currency arrangements.[33] The creation of the 'Single Market' after 1992, combined with the adoption of the euro, will drive the members of EMU more and more towards becoming an optimal currency area.

As countries overcome their nationalism, more and more good things will result from EMU. Sitting here in the heart of a major financial centre I am surprised at the extent to which the financial authorities of European countries are still playing nationalistic games, but I don't think that will continue.

With respect to the depressed situation of the German economy, they would benefit in the short run from having more exchange rate and interest rate flexibility. But that is not the fundamental issue about the German economy, nor does it say much about the ECB, for it is unlikely that the Bundesbank would have pursued any different policies than the ECB. Rather, every time in the last 15 years that Germany has shown signs of growth, even before the Deutschmark disappeared, the growth would be cut off by increased inflationary pressure on wages. This indicates the need for a more flexible labour market.

*Another controversial area in international economics relates to the issue of capital market liberalisation. Some eminent economists, notably Jagdish Bhagwati, Dani Rodrik and Joseph Stiglitz, have questioned the wisdom of 'premature' capital market liberalisation in emerging economies.*[34] *What is your response to this whole debate over capital controls versus liberalisation?* This is a debate where there is more heat than light, and the excessive use of straw men by the critics of the IMF. Capital controls can enable a country to have both a pegged exchange rate and an independent monetary policy. Under the Bretton Woods system most of the industrialised countries kept capital controls in place until the 1970s. If countries have capital controls they certainly shouldn't lift them until their banking and financial systems are in reasonable shape and any major macroeconomic imbalances are removed. There are clearly desirable preconditions that need to be met before liberalising capital markets, and if they are not met it is possible to have premature financial market liberalisation and premature lifting of capital controls.

In 1997, when the issue of amending the IMF Articles of Agreement to make the promotion of capital account liberalisation a goal of the Fund was on the agenda, I supported it.[35] I take the view that it is the goal of most countries to integrate themselves into global capital markets because the benefits of such integration outweigh the costs. But at the IMF we emphasised the *orderly* liberalisation of the capital account. Having controls on short-term capital inflows may be reasonable under some circumstances. Having controls on FDI flows and other longer-term flows is generally counterproductive. It is striking that very few countries have gone back to using capital controls, despite everything that has been said by Jagdish Bhagwati, Joe Stiglitz, Dani Rodrik and others.

When at the IMF I discussed the possible use of capital controls at various stages of different crises with the people who were in positions to make decisions on implementing controls. Some officials from Latin

American countries said that they simply did not want to impose controls. They had done so in the 1980s and it caused a mess, didn't work and led to increased corruption. Capital controls are very pernicious in terms of fostering corruption, creating economic inefficiencies and continuing attempts to circumvent the controls. Having said all that, it is important to recognise that there are market failures in this area. If I were heading a central bank I would want a very good information system, like the Brazilians have, on what capital flows are coming into and out of the country.

## THE IMF

*Have the objectives of the IMF remained the same as they were when that institution was set up in 1945?*
Article I of the IMF's Articles of Agreement sets out the purposes of the Fund. They were written in 1944 and have remained essentially unchanged and valid despite all the changes that have taken place in the international financial system.

The IMF has many roles in addition to acting as a lender of last resort to countries with balance-of-payments problems.[36] The IMF provides advice and technical assistance to member countries, undertakes surveillance of world economic conditions and promotes the adoption of good economic policies.

However, the framework and environment within which the IMF is operating has changed a great deal over the years. You could also say that the IMF has gone from being an institution that primarily helped European and Latin American countries in the early post-war years, to being much more global and dealing less with what are now the developed countries. That is in large part due to the end of the Bretton Woods adjustable peg exchange rate regime. There has been a host of shocks that have affected the industrialised economies in the 30 years since 1973 that, if we still had pegged exchange rates, would probably have produced crises requiring the involvement of the IMF.

*What is the nature of the relationship between the major international institutions, the IMF, World Bank and the World Trade Organisation (WTO)? The* Meltzer Commission Report *argues that the functions of the World Bank and the IMF now seriously overlap.*[37]
The IMF remains fundamentally a macroeconomic institution with expertise in monetary, financial, exchange rate and fiscal policy. But there is a 'Catch 22' situation for the IMF in defining its mandate very narrowly. That became clear in the East Asian crisis, when the IMF was accused of

ignoring unemployment and the need to strengthen the social safety net in its programmes, and at the same time was also accused of stepping on the World Bank's toes by trying to deal with these problems.

There is a need for a clear division of labour and one can be drawn in most areas. But there are always going to be areas of overlap, such as the financial sector. In this area the World Bank and the Fund can work very well together, and have done so.

I disagree with the standard criticism of the IMF that says that the Fund should get out of the poor countries, even though I had made that criticism myself before I went to the Fund. I do not accept that argument because poor countries also have macroeconomic problems, and those are the province of the IMF; poor countries should be full members of the IMF with access to its resources. The World Bank should be dealing with the microstructural problems of the poor countries and with their overall development strategies.

As a result of pressure to cooperate better, especially from the British, the development of the Poverty Reduction and Growth Facility (PRGF) and the Poverty Reduction and Strategy Paper (PRSP) provide vehicles for better cooperation between the two institutions and the developing countries.[38] I don't see the IMF, particularly under the direction of Horst Kohler, wanting to interfere too much in the World Bank's sphere. But the IMF has not agreed, and should not agree, that the poor developing countries are somebody else's problem.

The IMF cooperates to some extent with the WTO. From time to time there are discussions on trying to figure out how to do more together. The Fund does cooperate and liaise with the WTO on the liberalisation of trade. There have been suggestions that the IMF should provide more funds to help the process of trade liberalisation. We need to think more about the relationship between the IMF and the WTO.

## EAST ASIAN CRISIS

*The East Asian crisis, beginning in 1997, brought a great deal of criticism down on the IMF, in particular with respect to the policies recommended by the IMF to the affected countries to deal with the crisis. There are several explanations of the causes of that crisis. Some economists blame the crisis on deep-seated structural problems within the crisis countries; others put it down to market failure within the financial sector.[39] What is your explanation of that particular crisis?*
I believe it was due to both the factors that you mention. There were very large short-term capital flows into these countries that were premised on

the assumption that their exchange rates were unlikely to change very much. Some countries, including Thailand and Korea in particular, had encouraged short-term capital inflows. The crisis countries also had very inefficient financial systems, which were vulnerable to capital account difficulties or weaknesses in the economy.

Then came the events that led investors to reappraise the situation with respect to capital inflows. Once the outflows began, they exposed the weakness of the financial system.

There was also mismanagement, although that could not be said at the time. The Thais and Koreans made the mistake of running their reserves down almost to zero before turning to the outside world for help. They decided to defend the exchange rate at all costs. If exchange rates had been more flexible, financial systems stronger, and had short-term capital inflows been discouraged, these crises need not have happened.

The country that was hit hardest relative to its previous performance was Indonesia. They had run reasonable macroeconomic policies but had problems both of corruption and massive inefficiencies in the financial system. When these weaknesses were combined with an open capital account (it had been open since the early 1970s), Indonesia became extraordinarily vulnerable to a reversal of sentiment. I remember getting nervous about Indonesia when I was there in 1996. There were well over 200 banks in Indonesia at that point, and it was clear that they were not all very good ones. Many were politically connected, and that was part of the problem.

It was common to say that the financial sector is crucial for successful economic development even before these crises in the 1990. The experience of the East Asian crisis confirmed just how destructive a rotten financial system can be for the stability of an economy.

*Was the East Asian crisis foreseen in any way by the IMF?*
Certainly the depth and precise timing of the crisis was not foreseen. But in the case of Thailand, we were concerned about the likelihood of a crisis from late 1996 onwards. We did a lot to try to make the Thais aware of the danger and to head it off by having a more flexible exchange rate. However, they did not listen to us. Once the Thai crisis broke there was contagion to other East Asian economies and the markets overreacted. With respect to Korea, while one part of the Fund pointed out weaknesses of their financial system, another part of the Fund continued to be impressed with the underlying dynamism of the economy. On balance we did not think they were likely to have a crisis.

There was a lot of concern about the financial sector in Indonesia, but perhaps an underestimation of just how vulnerable that sector was and how delicate the political situation was. I believe that had President Suharto resigned from power in the early 1990s he would have gone down in history as a great leader who had set Indonesia on the road to sustained growth. If he had managed to engineer a democratic transition at that time things would probably have turned out differently. Now people remember him for corruption. Well, he was corrupt, but he was also the leader who had produced a period of sustained growth that massively reduced poverty. When dealing with him I was always aware of both sides of his leadership.

*How do you react to the criticism that the IMF recommended inappropriate 'Hooverite' anti-Keynesian policies during the East Asian crisis that depressed aggregate demand and made the situation worse, deepening the recessionary impact of the financial crisis?*[40]

That argument has several components. First, that the tightening of fiscal policy was mistaken. That view was correct, and that is why the IMF quickly reversed that policy in Thailand by the end of 1997 and in Korea by the beginning of 1998. So I do not think that the initial fiscal mistake had a big impact on what happened later. Incidentally, it was difficult to persuade the authorities to run bigger deficits and in at least two countries the authorities wanted to run a tighter fiscal policy than that recommended by the IMF.

Second, the criticism of monetary policy was not correct. There were two things going on in those economies. You had people and firms who were heavily indebted in dollars. As the exchange rate fell, more and more dollar debtors were put into severe difficulty. On the other hand, if you raised the interest rate you created difficulties for debtors in domestic currency. There was a trade-off between raising rates and allowing the currency to continue depreciating, and it would have been a mistake to just let the exchange rate go because that would have produced both difficulties for those indebted in dollars and high inflation.

It has also been argued that there would have been more confidence if interest rates had not been raised, and the currency would therefore have been stronger. That is nonsense. The currencies were collapsing precisely during the period when the central banks were sitting by doing nothing, not raising interest rates and not reacting to the crisis in any way, and just letting the reserves pour out. This inaction did not reassure the markets.

There is a theoretical possibility that interest rates can become so high as to be counterproductive in stabilising the exchange rate. I do not believe that happened in East Asia. In Korea there was a period for a couple of months when the real interest rate was high. In Indonesia the real interest rate was typically negative, at worst 20 per cent for a month or two. At the IMF we went through the arguments carefully and rejected the idea of not raising interest rates. We argued that a short period of interest rate tightening was necessary in order to stabilise the currency, after which interest rates would be reduced to more normal levels. And that is what happened.

## GLOBALISATION AND ECONOMIC DEVELOPMENT

*Bill Easterly's recent book,* The Elusive Quest for Growth: Economists' Adventures and Misadventures in the Tropics, *highlights the various elixirs that have been recommended by economists in the post-1950 period in order to promote growth in the developing countries.*[41] *The so-called 'Washington Consensus' policies could be regarded as yet another elixir for growth. Do you still have faith in Washington Consensus policies?*
Yes, I still have faith in the set of policies originally described in John Williamson's publication back in 1990 that was unfortunately described as the Washington Consensus. John Williamson himself has said that his biggest mistake was to call his classification of policies the Washington Consensus because it was at that time a global consensus.

John Williamson is certainly not a 'let free markets rip' kind of economist. Anyone who actually reads his original contribution would agree that his formulation contains the essence of a set of necessary conditions for economic success.[42] These are sensible policies that countries should implement because they are good for stability, economic growth and the social welfare of citizens. The recommended policies do not include freeing up short-run capital movements but they do advocate encouraging FDI; they include maintaining positive but moderate real interest rates, tax reform, privatisation and deregulation, a reasonable budgetary position, and exchange rates that are not overvalued.

Williamson also emphasises the desirability of increasing the outward orientation of developing economies. I remain firmly convinced that export orientation and integration into the world economy are essential elements for economic success.[43]

The original Washington Consensus consists of common-sense policies that should be part of any country's growth strategy. In a recent publication edited by Kuczynski and Williamson, called *After the Washington Consensus,* John Williamson has added to his original formulation.[44] For example, he gives greater emphasis to trying to make the economy more resilient to crises, and higher priority to the provision of a social safety net.

In sum, I fundamentally believe that the Washington Consensus policies lie at the heart of a set of sensible economic policies that countries should implement if they want to promote sustained growth. Of course, at the practical level, some of the Washington Consensus recommendations are politically hard to achieve, such as maintaining a reasonable fiscal balance.

*There have been many papers in the last couple of years devoted to examin-
ing trends in world inequality, with disagreement frequently depending on how
inequality is measured.*[45] *You also made the relationship between globalisation and economic development a central theme in your Richard T. Ely lecture
to the American Economics Association in January 2003.*[46] *Do you think that
we are likely to witness greater convergence or divergence in world inequality
during the twenty-first century?*

It's very difficult to forecast what is going to happen to inequality in the
twenty-first century (*laughter*). Our first-order concern should be to reduce
world poverty, and reductions in poverty may or may not be accompanied
by reductions in inequality. For instance, poverty in China has been massively reduced in the last 20 years despite an increase in inequality. Several
hundred million people have been lifted out of poverty although some have
been left behind so far. Other things equal, we should strive to reduce
inequality. But what China has achieved in the last two decades is still
miraculous, and positive.

The evidence for the global economy shows that the *proportion* of people
living in poverty, those living on less than $1 a day, has been falling quite
fast, while the *absolute numbers* of poor have decreased marginally or
increased somewhat. The decline in the global poverty rate is hardly surprising given the recent growth rates experienced in the world's two most
populous countries, China and India. Increasingly, and unfortunately, we
are seeing the global poverty problem concentrating in sub-Saharan Africa.

In terms of inequality among nations, after some 400 years of increasing inequality between the per capita incomes of nations, we do now seem
to be witnessing a slowdown or reversal of this trend.

Looking forward, it is difficult not to think we are heading for difficult
times. Terrorism is a major threat and old alliances that brought stability
may be breaking up. However, given reasonable economic stability, I think
that the world's poor will get richer and global inequality will decline.
Those countries that are far behind the technological frontier have the
capacity to grow very rapidly given favourable circumstances and institutions, and a willingness to embrace the global economy. Some countries in
sub-Saharan Africa have shown that they can achieve sustainable growth
and I believe that the international community has a responsibility to
provide an external environment that will help African countries achieve
their potential.[47] Meanwhile, countries that are already at the frontier, such
as the USA, can only grow at an annual rate of about 2 or 3 per cent per
capita.

*There have been several interesting papers produced lately on the role of
foreign aid in promoting growth and development. According to Burnside and*

*Dollar, aid seems to work best when injected into countries that have good policies.*[48] *However, there seems little evidence to show that aid gets allocated mainly to non-corrupt governments who are following 'good' policies.*[49] *Do you think that foreign aid will have an increasing role in the future, given its disappointing record?*

Until the last year or two, the proportion of foreign aid in donor GDP has been decreasing, despite the stated commitment by donor governments to raise their contributions to 0.7 per cent of GDP by 2015. I would like to see the share of aid increasing, but I do not expect that, even though people like Jeffrey Sachs keep on making a powerful case that the very poorest countries should receive large amounts of aid to improve their health and education systems.[50]

It is very difficult to figure out how aid should be allocated. One school of thought contends that foreign aid should be given only to governments pursuing good policies. But there is also a humanitarian element to consider. This consideration points to some aid being allocated towards the poorest and least successful countries. Often these are the countries with the most corrupt governments. If we could find an effective way of getting the aid to the people who actually need it, life would be a lot easier.

I have wrestled for a long time with this kind of problem. In the case of Zaire [now the Democratic Republic of the Congo] the rulers were totally corrupt. Should we ignore the plight of the poor in that country because of this? That would certainly suggest relying more on NGOs, who should be better at providing aid directly to the poor. But with regard to governments, one has to ask whether refusing to give aid to such countries led to desirable political change. Eventually I decided that if it was possible to ameliorate the conditions of the poor, then there was some point to providing aid even to such countries.

## THE FUTURE

*What do you see as your own future? Do you miss life in academia?*

One of the great things about living in the USA is that you do not have to think very far ahead because something interesting always comes along. The two things I miss most about academic life are the outstanding colleagues and outstanding graduate students at MIT. Graduate students at MIT were always ready to tackle new and exciting problems, and it was great to talk to them and offer some help and advice – although often they could manage very well on their own. There is nothing like that anywhere else that I have been. I also enormously enjoyed working with colleagues at the IMF.

In my new life here in the private sector there is so much to learn that is new. I have been extraordinarily lucky to embark at my fairly mature age (*laughter*) on a new career where I feel that I am learning something new every day. I don't know what will come next, but it has been great fun so far.

## NOTES

1. I interviewed Professor Fischer in his Office at Citigroup, New York City, USA, on 13 May 2003.
2. Three Nobel Laureates in Economics, Paul Samuelson, Robert Solow and the late Franco Modigliani, have been long-term residents at MIT, and numerous graduate students from the Department of Economics are now among the most influential figures in the economics profession, for example George Akerlof, Ben Bernanke, Jagdish Bhagwati, Olivier Blanchard, Alan Blinder, Paul Krugman, Greg Mankiw, Kenneth Rogoff, Andrei Shleifer and Joseph Stiglitz, to name only a few.
3. For example, Professor Fischer is a Guggenheim Fellow, a Fellow of the Econometric Society and the American Academy of Arts and Sciences, and has been a Visiting Scholar at the Hoover Institution and the Hebrew University, Jerusalem.
4. Details of Professor Fischer's publications can be found on his personal webpage, http://www.bankisrael.gov.il/abeng/nagid_now_full_eng.htm. Among his books are three of the best-selling student textbooks in economics at the principles, intermediate and graduate level respectively. See Begg (2003); Dornbusch et al. (2004); and Blanchard and Fischer (1989).
5. See, for example, Fischer (1977, 1980, 1988, 1990, 1991, 1993a, 1995a, 1995b, 1996a, 1999a, 2001a, 2003, 2004, 2006); Cooper and Fischer (1973); Barro and Fischer (1976); Fischer and Modigliani (1978); Fischer et al. (1988).
6. See Stanley Fischer's IMF 'Farewell Dinner Speech', 29 August 2001 (www.imf.org).
7. See Dornbusch et al. (2004).
8. See Fischer (1994). See also Rolnick (1999) and Prescott (2006).
9. For example, see Krugman (1998, 1999a); DeLong (1999); Kumar (2003).
10. See, for example, Temple (2000); Kirshner (2001). See also Brown (2001).
11. See Bernanke et al. (1999) and the interview with Ben Bernanke (currently Chair of the Board of Governors of the US Federal Reserve System) in Snowdon (2002a).
12. See Bruno and Easterly (1998).
13. Fischer, Sahay, and Vegh (2002). See also Fischer and Modigliani (1978); Fischer (1993a, 1996a); Edwards (1994).
14. King (1997a, 1997b); Svensson (2000).
15. See Dollar and Kraay (2002a, 2002b, 2004).
16. Campos and Coricelli (2002). See also Fischer (1993b, 1996c, 2001c, 2001d); Easterly and Fischer (1995); Blanchard (1996); Fischer, Sahay and Vegh (1996); Havrylyshyn (2001).
17. For example, Aslund (2001).
18. See Fischer and Gelb (1991), Fischer and Sahay (2000a, 2000b); and Figure 3.6.
19. See Kornai interview.
20. See Murrell (1995); Marangos (2002); Ellerman (2003).
21. See Fischer and Sahay (2000a, 2000b); Fischer (2001c).
22. See Balcerowicz (1994a, 1994b).
23. For a critique of the Russian privatisation process see Stiglitz (2002a); Ellerman (2003); Goldman (2003).
24. See Lewis (1954).
25. Sachs and Warner (2001) provide evidence of a 'curse of natural resources', that is, countries with abundant natural resources tend to grow more slowly than resource-poor countries. See also Fischer (2001d).

26.  Fischer (2001a).
27.  See Fischer (2002)
28.  For a defence of the 'intermediate' exchange rate option see Williamson, J. (2000b).
29.  See Alesina and Barro (2001, 2002).
30.  Rockoff (2000).
31.  These measures included federal fiscal transfers and bank deposit insurance.
32.  See Demirbas (2002).
33.  Frankel and Rose (2002). See also Alesina, Barro and Tenreyro (2002).
34.  See Bhagwati (1998b); Rodrik (1998b); Stiglitz (2000a, 2002a); Snowdon (2002a).
35.  See Fischer (1997a, 1998a); Fischer et al. (1998).
36.  See Fischer (1999a, 1999b); Citrin and Fischer (2000).
37.  See Feldstein (1998); Fischer (1998b); Krueger (1998); Stiglitz (1999); Bird (2000, 2001, 2006); Meltzer (2000); Meltzer et al. (2000); Caballero (2003); Fischer et al. (2003).
38.  See www.imf.org, for details.
39.  See Nixon and Walters et al. (1999).
40.  See Snowdon (2001b); Stiglitz (2002a); Rogoff (2002, 2003).
41.  Easterly (2001a).
42.  See Williamson's discussion of the Washington Consensus on his webpage at the Institute for International Economics, www.iie.com, and Williamson, J. (1990, 2003, 2005).
43.  See Baldwin (2000, 2003) for surveys.
44.  Kuczynski and Williamson (2003).
45.  See Bhalla (2002); Bourguignon and Morrison (2002); Sala-i-Martin (2002a, 2002b, 2006); Milanovic (2003).
46.  Fischer (2003).
47.  See Fischer, Khan and Hernandez-Cata (1998); Artadi and Sala-i-Martin (2003).
48.  Burnside and Dollar (2000). For a critique of the Burnside and Dollar paper, see Easterly, Levine and Roodman (2004).
49.  See Alesina and Dollar (2000); Alesina and Weder (2002).
50.  For example, Sachs (2005a).

# János Kornai[1]

János Kornai is generally regarded as the world's leading scholar on socialist economic systems. To date, Professor Kornai is the author/coauthor/editor of 18 books and over 100 academic papers, most of which have been concerned with providing a comprehensive analysis of various aspects of the operation and reform of socialist economies. Reflecting the worldwide interest in his work, many of his papers and books have been translated into other languages; for example, his book *The Road to a Free Economy*, 1990, has been translated into 16 languages!

In addition to the numerous prizes and honours he has received, the main highlights of Professor Kornai's distinguished academic career include: 1955–58, Research Fellow, Institute of Economics, Hungarian Academy of Sciences; 1958–63, Head of Economics Research Department, Institute of Textile Industry; 1963–67, Head of Research Department, Computing Centre, Hungarian Academy of Sciences; 1967–91, Research Professor, Institute of Economics, Hungarian Academy of Sciences; 1964, Visiting Professor of Economics at the London School of Economics; 1966, Sussex University; 1968, 1972–73, Stanford University; 1970, the Cowles Foundation, Yale University; 1972, Princeton University; 1976–77, Stockholm University; 1983–84, Institute of Advanced Study, Princeton; 1984–85, Harvard University; 1972–77, Vice Chairman, Committee for Development Planning, United Nations; 1978, President of the Econometric Society;

1987, President of the European Economic Association; 1986–2002, Professor of Economics, 2002 to date, Professor Emeritus, Harvard University; 1989–94, Member of Scientific Advisory Council, European Bank for Reconstruction and Development; 1995–2001, Member of Board, Hungarian Central Bank; 1992 to date, Permanent Fellow, Collegium Budapest, Institute for Advanced Study, Budapest.

In almost 50 years as a professional economist, Professor Kornai's principal interests and contributions have been directed towards questions relating to the analysis of comparative economic systems, quantitative aspects of the planning process in socialist economies, the political economy of reform under socialism, the economics of shortage and the 'soft budget constraint', the economics of post-socialist transition to capitalism, various issues relating to reform of the welfare state and, most recently, research into 'honesty and trust' in transition economies. In addition to pioneering the use of mathematical programming and two-tier planning in the Hungarian planning process, in his book *Anti-Equilibrium* (1971) he also provided a penetrating critique of neoclassical Walrasian general equilibrium theory that typically dominates mainstream 'Western' economic analysis. In this case, Kornai's insightful critique contributed to providing a framework for the development of a non-Walrasian style of analysis, stimulating new approaches to the analysis of practical real-world problems.

In the interview that follows I discuss with Professor Kornai the evolution of his thinking on the political economy of the socialist system, its characteristics, reform, transition and future.

## EARLY LIFE

*You were born in 1928 and so you were a teenager during the Second World War. What were your early life experiences during this traumatic period of history?*

My father was a lawyer and I had two brothers and a sister. I went to primary school and high school at an excellent German-speaking school and so grew up bilingual, speaking Hungarian and German. My first real interests as a young teenager were in literature, philosophy and history. My interest in economics came much later. My family was Jewish and we were very assimilated. But the fact that I was Jewish had a strong impact on my life because Jews were persecuted; there were anti-Jewish discriminatory laws in Hungary at that time. Then of course came the German military occupation of Hungary in 1944, which amplified that persecution to the extreme.

*So when the Soviet army finally drove the Nazis out of Budapest in February 1945, after a long siege, this must have come as a great relief to you. The Soviet army were your liberators.*

Those were terrible times with horrible, brutal events taking place. Our lives were in permanent danger and many people around me were killed or died, not only Jews, but many others who hated and opposed the Nazi regime. So yes, for us, the Russians were looked upon as liberators in 1944–45.

*When did you first get the opportunity to continue your education at University?*

I finished high school in 1945 after the change of political regime and it was then that I became a student at the Pázmány Péter University of Budapest. I registered for an undergraduate programme in history and philosophy but I was not a very diligent student (*laughter*). At that time I became rather active in the Youth Movement of the Left and was only nominally a student, although I did pass my exams. Then, in 1947, I became a journalist on the main communist newspaper, *Szabad Nép*. Although I was very young I was appointed to ever higher positions on the newspaper, so there came a point when I gave up my university studies. I started my graduate studies much later and was admitted without having first completed an undergraduate course. It was at the newspaper that I became very much interested in economic affairs. At that time I was really enthusiastic about socialism. Initially I was very much in favour of the new system of socialist economic planning. I became the economic editor of the newspaper and was becoming more and more involved and fascinated in trying to understand what was going on in the Hungarian economy. I had access to important statistical data, which others didn't have, so I was getting an insider's view of how the system operated. So this was the real beginning of my studying and understanding the economics of socialism. In a sense I was getting much more insight into how the system actually worked than a university student might acquire from just reading books.

*What brought your career in journalism to an end?*

It ended because of a series of political events. The sequence began in 1953, the year that Stalin died. There began a relaxation of the rigid Stalinist regime. In Hungary we had a new prime minister, Imre Nagy.[2] Back in 1953 he was a very different prime minister from his predecessor, Mátyás Rákosi, who was the Stalinist dictator of Hungary. Nagy began to liberalise the regime, encouraging greater production of consumer goods and relaxation of the collectivisation of agriculture. As a result of these changes there developed tremendous in-fighting within the party between those supporting Nagy and Rákosi, respectively. Very early on I supported Imre Nagy

and published a long review in the newspaper praising his book, a volume
of his collected essays. In the editorial office of the newspaper there was
strong protest against Stalinism. What made the situation particularly
interesting was that the protest came from people who still regarded themselves communists, but wanted a different type of socialism. I suppose to a
Western observer this period in Hungary might be likened to the 'Prague
Spring' of 1968. We wanted socialism with a human face and a more democratic style of government. The so-called reformists did not form an anti-
socialist movement. I myself and my friends were personally active in
promoting reform at meetings during this period. Unfortunately, in
February 1955 Nagy lost the contest with Rákosi. The leading members of
the reformist group at *Szabad Nép* were fired by a Politburo decree. Luckily
Stalin was gone and we were not sent to a Gulag or executed. As it happened, by 1955, and for a few years before, I had wanted to leave journalism anyway but I had been prevented from doing so. By then I had already
been a part-time graduate student for two years at the Academy of Sciences
and had passed various exams. The official name for the qualification that
I was studying for, following the Soviet terminology, was Candidate of
Science. This is more or less equivalent to the Doctor of Philosophy degree
in the West. Having been fired from the newspaper gave me the opportunity to concentrate on my studies, and I joined the Institute of Economics
of the Hungarian Academy of Sciences as a Junior Research Fellow. In
spite of the drastic fall in my earnings – I earned about a third of my salary
as a journalist – I was glad to work in a research environment. So 1955
marked the start of my professional academic career. I had begun to think
about my thesis while I was still working at the newspaper, but I actually
worked on it and finished it after my dismissal, in 1956.

*What did you write your thesis on?*
My dissertation for my Candidate of Science degree was eventually
published in 1957. The English version, entitled *Overcentralization*, was published by Oxford University Press in the UK in 1959. This was my first
appearance as an author in the West. The book reflects my naïve but honest
belief at that time that the socialist system could be reformed. I thought then
that replacing bureaucratic coordination with market coordination would,
without making any changes in the political structures, suffice to improve the
system. Later I realised that 'market socialism' could never work.

*During all of this came the Hungarian uprising of 1956. How did that momen-
tous event affect you?*
When the uprising of 1956 broke out, I was, so to speak, already mentally
prepared. The transformation of my own thinking had already started in

1954 with my earlier disappointment with the way things had turned out. I was commissioned by one of Imre Nagy's deputies to write an economic programme for the new government. So for many days after 23 October I worked on this. The idea was for Imre Nagy to take the new proposals to Parliament and present the ideas in a speech. But there was no speech and no Parliament as the uprising was short-lived; it was suppressed and defeated. Before 1956 I was a member of the Communist Party, but after the uprising I turned my back on the party and never returned. Not only did I leave the Communist Party; I also emphatically declared that I was no longer a Marxist or a Leninist.

## OVERCENTRALIZATION IN ECONOMIC ADMINISTRATION

*You have already mentioned that your thesis formed the basis of your first book,* Overcentralization, *which is a critique of the classical socialist model of central planning. How were you able to publish this critique in the aftermath of the failed 1956 uprising?*

I actually wrote the book in 1955 and 1956, before the October revolution, and published it after the revolution. In the period immediately following the revolution the government of János Kádár was preoccupied with consolidating power and suppressing resistance. So they were not concerned about or did not pay much attention to what was going on in academic publishing. There was a courageous publisher who brought out my book in Hungarian in 1957. I pointed out in the preface to *Overcentralization* that I had written it before 23 October 1956, and that if my arguments were valid before the events in October, they were also valid later. While many people changed their ideas, I did not. The manuscript was smuggled out of Hungary and arrived in Oxford, England, where it drew the attention of John Hicks. As far as I know it was Hicks who recommended my book to Oxford University Press, and they published an English translation of it in 1959. *Overcentralization* was the first critical book on central planning from an insider, and that is why it attracted attention in the West. From then on there was a bifurcation of the story of that book. In Hungary it was heavily attacked, even by my own boss at the Institute of Economics, who labelled it 'revisionist'. Later on I was called a traitor to socialism, which was a very harsh accusation. At the same time the book received high praise in the Western press. It was favourably reviewed in the *Manchester Guardian* and *The Times*. It also got long appreciative reviews by economists in several of the leading Western academic journals. So it was praise in the West and condemnation in the East (*laughter*). A Communist Party investigation at the Institute of Economics led to the decision to fire me, together with my friend András Nagy, who expressed similar views on various occasions. In those months and years many of my friends were arrested and tried, and one was sentenced to death and executed. Some of my friends emigrated.

*So by publishing this book you were not only risking your career, you were also risking your personal safety.*
This was a period of great uncertainty. There was no way to tell whether Stalinism would be resurrected in its extreme form or replaced by a milder form of repression. As is known in retrospect, Stalinism was not restored, but immediately after the failed revolution of 1956 nobody knew that would be the outcome. So it was a dangerous period. The reprisals were extremely brutal after 1956. Three hundred and fifty people were executed for political reasons. That's a huge number. It exceeds the total number of executions that took place following the defeat of the anti-Habsburg revolution in 1849, the Hungarian Communist revolution in 1919, plus those sentenced to death in the 1945 anti-Nazi trials in Hungary.


## INTELLECTUAL INFLUENCES

*How exposed were you in the 1950s to Western economic ideas? Did you have access to such work and were you at liberty to study 'bourgeois' economic analysis?*
The main obstacle had nothing to do with not being allowed to read such material because if I had been eager to read it I could somehow have gained access to it. The main problem is that so long as someone is a strong believer in Marxism, he does not feel compelled to read anything else. A committed communist believes that Western bourgeois economists simply do not understand the true nature of capitalism, unlike Karl Marx did in *Capital*.[3] Marxists believe themselves to be beholders of the truth. This feeling comes from within. You are completely committed from the start to one specific interpretation or vision of capitalism and markets. It's about as close to dogmatic religious fervour as one can get. A devoted believer in one particular religion will rarely convert a believer in another religion. Certain ideas are regarded as axiomatic and they are not to be questioned. Once you accept the axioms of Marxism, the rest follows naturally. My eagerness to read the work of Western economists started with my disappointment with Marxism–Leninism and the Communist Party. That more or less coincided with the beginning of my graduate studies. Once my own axiomatic belief in Marxist political economy had collapsed I began to search for and read books by the hundred. Initially I read more in politics than in

economics. After the defeat of the revolution and especially after I had been fired from my job, I had plenty of time to read and educate myself. It was a period of rigorous self-training. I had long discussions with mathematicians and computer scientists. I worked with a brilliant mathematician, Tamás Lipták, with whom I later co-authored some papers.[4] He helped enormously with my understanding of mathematics.

*When you started to read the mainstream literature on economics, who impressed you the most?*
My first guide was a very good book on the history of economic thought written by Farkas Heller (1943), a Hungarian university professor before the war. His book gave me a good guideline for selection. Then, very early on, I read Oskar Lange's *Economic Theory of Socialism*.[5] This interested me very much and immediately exposed me to ideas and analysis concerned with market socialism and reforming a socialist planned economy. Then I read a very good three-volume German textbook by Erich Schneider, followed by Paul Samuelson's famous principles textbook, *Economics*. I also read his *Foundations of Economic Analysis*. I then moved on to Gottfried Haberler's book *The Theory of International Trade* and Joseph Schumpeter's books, *Capitalism, Socialism and Democracy* and *Theory of Economic Development*. I got my introduction to Keynes from Paul Samuelson and Erich Schneider, who were early converts to Keynesianism. Later on, when I was working on linear programming and head of the Economics Research Department at the Computing Centre of the Hungarian Academy of Sciences (1963–67) I used the book by Robert Dorfman, Paul Samuelson and Robert Solow, *Linear Programming and Economic Analysis* (1958). I became deeply influenced by neoclassical economics in this period.[6]

My first trip outside the Eastern bloc was to a conference at Cambridge University in 1963. It was Edmond Malinvaud and Tjalling Koopmans who invited me, and I made a lot of useful contacts and friends at that conference. In 1968 I visited Stanford on invitation from Kenneth Arrow. This was when I was working on a critique of general equilibrium theory and I received helpful and supportive comments from both Arrow and Koopmans.

*What about the writings of the Austrian school, for example Ludwig von Mises and Friedrich von Hayek?[7] They were the earliest critics of central planning and the socialist form of economic organisation. When did you first come across their critiques?*
I read their work in the mid-1960s, much later than Lange's. Hayek had a strong impact on my thinking. He showed that all economic systems must

make efficient use of information. Certainly, it's a great advantage of decentralised market systems that information is created and utilised efficiently. In bureaucratic systems it may not always be possible or in the interest of agents to transmit information efficiently. Marx and committed Marxists thought planning would be a relatively easy task that would rescue the world from the chaos created by markets. Hayek's work showed how this ran counter to reality.

*In all of your work, but particularly your 1992 book* The Socialist System, *you prefer to call the centrally controlled economies we are discussing 'socialist' economies rather than 'communist' economies. Does this relate to some intellectual influence from Marx?*
I don't think so. You will notice that the subtitle of my 1992 book *The Socialist System* is *The Political Economy of Communism*. I prefer to use the term socialist economy because that is what the political leaders of these countries called their system. They did not refer to their system as a communist economic system. According to Marxist–Leninist ideology, communism that provides everyone according to their needs represents a later stage of development. If you talked to a communist in a socialist country, say, in the 1970s, he would say that we have not yet arrived at communism; we are still at the earlier stage, socialism. It was Western commentators who tended to use the term 'communist system' or just simply 'communism' when referring to these economies. In the Eastern bloc they always talked about 'socialist camp', 'socialist system' and 'socialist economy'. In my book *The Socialist System* I make it clear from the outset that I wanted to examine only those countries that were under the control of a Communist Party.

## MATHEMATICAL MODELLING

*Much of your early professional work as an economist was concerned with designing mathematical models to help make the planning system work better.[8] What motivated you to follow that line of interest and, looking back, how do you now view that work?*
To understand my motivation, first of all you have to go back to the context, to the political and social environment at that time. My *Overcentralization* book was empirical and based mainly on my interviews with enterprise managers. It analysed how the system worked in practice. I wanted to continue my investigation to write a second volume. But after 4 November 1956 came the period of harsh repression and I'd been fired from my job. I realised it would be impossible, given the new political climate, to

repeat my earlier success in getting *Overcentralization* published. I did not want or intend to write books and papers praising the unreformed social- ist system because I wanted to convey the truth. But it was no longer pos- sible to write a critical book about the system: after 1956 this route was closed. So I had to look for another outlet for my work, and that's where the inspiration for my formal technical work on mathematical model build- ing came from. I was also motivated by my declaration of no longer being a Marxist. This was more than a political statement or protest; it was also an intellectual conviction. However, I did not want to enter into a polemi- cal debate about fundamental theoretical issues. That was not possible. Having abandoned Marxism, I had to write in a different language that made it clear to the reader that the writer was a non-Marxist. I wanted to publish work that did not use the language or vocabulary of Marxism. The use of mathematics had a strong educational purpose. It was not only a method to help me arrive at coherent propositions and results. It was also a way of enabling me to depart from Marxism without stirring up a loud protest from the authorities. This is very different from what happened for example in Soviet economics, where economists continued to use a Marxian language. I was trying to smuggle genuine economics into my writing in a way that would still be publishable. My choice was: do I want to write illegal or legal material? I chose the latter and therefore had to write in a way that would not provoke the authorities. Many years later the leading Hungarian economics journal published an interesting study on citations in the Hungarian economic literature.[9] It looked at the number of references to Kornai, to Western scholars and to Marx, Engels and Lenin. In this study there is a diagram showing that I gradually became the most often cited author in Hungary. Also, the growing number of references to my work was strongly correlated with citations from Western writers. I reg- ularly cited Western sources and so did quite a few other Hungarian authors. At the same time reference to the work of Marx, Engels and Lenin went down. For me, mathematics was primarily a tool to contribute to the re-education and re-orientation of Hungarian economics.

*But surely your work also had a clear objective: to improve the planning system.*
Yes, of course. In all of my writing I took the view that my point of depar- ture was that we have a plan anyway – that is given, at least for now. So is there anything we can do to make the plan somewhat more consistent and improve some of the indicators? But in fact I considered this work much more a learning process than an undertaking to improve planning. In ret- rospect I think it proved to be a good education for those participating in the project. In the mid-1960s I led a team of 200 economists working on

mathematical planning. Later many of the participants in the project became leading figures in the field of research and teaching. Ultimately my experience with mathematical modelling also taught me that planning does not, and cannot, meet its targets. I learned the hard way about the vital importance of having good information and incentives. I learned that from my research for the *Overcentralization* book and again from my work on mathematical planning. So I learned my Hayek from the real world rather than from a book (*laughter*).

*How does the incentive structure within the planning apparatus distort the development of reasonably consistent plans?*
Within the planning mechanism there are incentives but they are perverse incentives. At the lower end of the planning hierarchy the planners are almost compelled to lie to their superiors. The people further up the hierarchy also have to lie to their superiors and to the people at the lower level. To achieve your plan targets you need to convince those higher up in the hierarchy that you need more resources; otherwise you may produce less than the plan target. There is bargaining for resources. If everyone had perfect information and unselfishly served the common purpose of maximising an agreed welfare function, planning might work all right. But since all these assumptions are invalid, the theorems on optimal planning based on them are untenable. By the way, some of these assumptions correspond to those made by Oskar Lange in his analysis of socialism in the 'debate on socialist calculation'.[10] That is why I have always been very critical of his theory as a basis for talking about a practical form of market socialism. Just as no perfect Walrasian equilibrium can be achieved in the real world of a market economy because of the lack of perfect competition, no perfect plan can be created in the real world of socialism. I did write a book on mathematical planning (Kornai, 1967) but I never claimed that it was possible to compute an 'optimal' central plan.

*Is this the line of thinking that led to your book* Anti-Equilibrium, *first published in 1971?*
It certainly was one of my motivations. By 1968 I had become acutely aware of the problems connected to the practical implementation of planning that we have already discussed. I felt that I had to go back to the foundations of general equilibrium theory and study Arrow and Debreu (1954). The result of that investigation was my book, *Anti-Equilibrium*, which is a critique of Walrasian general equilibrium theory and an attempt to work out an alternative analytical framework bringing in elements from information theory, disequilibrium economics, management and organisation theory. Walrasian analysis dominated the foundations of Western main-

stream thinking, and I felt that it prevented economists from dealing effectively with problems of the real world. Many of the directions I was moving towards in *Anti-Equilibrium* have now been explored, for example work on asymmetric information, non-price signals, disequilibrium states, conflicts and bargaining.

## CLASSICAL SOCIALISM AND THE ECONOMICS OF SHORTAGE

*In your book* The Socialist System *(1992a) you distinguish 'classical socialism' from 'reform socialism' and 'postsocialist transition'. What are the key features of the classical socialist system?*
Classical socialism is probably best exemplified as the type of system that operated under Stalin and was mimicked elsewhere in several Eastern European, Asian and African countries. This system, although repressive and very inefficient, was coherent. A key feature of classical socialism is a political structure where the Communist Party has a complete monopoly of power and there is no accepted competition between rival ideologies. Growth through investment was seen to be the main economic objective not least because it was important to catch up with the Western economies. There is almost complete elimination of capitalist property relations as state ownership dominates the economy. The entire banking system is state owned and the scope for any private property is extremely limited. The main coordination mechanism is carried out by a centralised bureaucracy whose task is to produce and implement a plan for the economy. There is direct bureaucratic control of employment, prices and wages.

*Your published work, especially in the 1970s and 1980s, builds on the theme that socialist economies suffer from endemic and widespread shortages.[11] In particular, your 1980 book* Economics of Shortage *received a great deal of international attention. What are the main elements of your argument in that book that made it so influential?*
The central idea of this book is that shortages in socialist economies are severely dysfunctional. In socialist economies shortages are all-pervasive; they are everywhere. Shortages are painful, welfare diminishing and a tormenting phenomenon for people living in these economies. Standing in queues for hours, week after week, year after year, is humiliating. It is difficult to comprehend, for people living in the West who have never experienced such things, how, as an individual, you feel powerless, at the mercy of the producer and the seller. There is no consumer sovereignty. So you buy whatever is available on a particular day. And you frequently buy as

much as possible of some goods when they do become available because
there is always uncertainty about future supplies. The people living under
socialism were trapped in a sellers' market. I felt that it was much more
important to highlight the phenomena of shortage than to continue writing
about the technical details of planning. The main message of the book was
that the shortages are systemic. They do not arise because a planner somewhere made a mistake which could be rectified in the future with some
adjustment to demand or supply. My discussions with Western scholars
inevitably ended up with their referring to Marshall's demand and supply
diagram. If the price is below equilibrium there is a shortage: demand
exceeds supply. From this the self-evident solution is to allow prices to rise,
which will stimulate supply and reduce demand. Once the price is right the
problem is solved. But the logic of this argument belongs to a capitalist
market economy where agents respond to profit and price signals. My
empirical counter-argument was that in spite of frequent price increases in
a socialist economy, widespread shortages remain. The adjustment of
prices simply does not make them disappear. They are recurrent and
endemic. That argument made a very strong impression; it struck a chord.
I talked to many people all over Eastern Europe and the feedback that I got
from those conversations was that after having read that book people
looked at socialism in a different way. *Economics of Shortage* did well all
over Eastern Europe and when it was published in China it sold over
100 000 copies. I believe it acted as a catalyst for thinking about system
failure.

*Was* Economics of Shortage *therefore seen as a very radical book?*
Before this book many people believed that the system could somehow be
corrected and improved by partial adjustments. They thought that
maybe some reform could put things right and the faults could somehow
be patched over. *Economics of Shortage* convinced many people that the
problems were incurable. So I like to think of this book as revolutionary,
not because it mobilised people for an uprising but because it suggested
clearly that reform would never be enough. To solve the problem you need
to change the whole system. In that sense it was a good preparation for the
events of 1989. I think this was well understood by many fellow economists
in the Eastern bloc, as well as many political scientists and sociologists in
the West. But somehow quite a few of my economist colleagues in the West
just could not see that. They were still getting excited by reading Oskar
Lange and thinking about the possibility of creating some form of market
socialism. Socialism without centralisation still captured the imagination.[12]
They were less excited about the shortage issue, which is what everyone
living in socialist economies cared about. People suffered from distressing

housing shortages. They could not get a telephone for years, or the food that they wanted. This is what bothered and really mattered to them.

## THE SOFT BUDGET CONSTRAINT

*You also introduced the concept of the 'soft budget constraint' in* Economics of Shortage *as well as in your* Econometrica *paper published earlier in 1979. This concept certainly did raise interest and excitement among Western economists and has been incredibly influential because of its broad applicability. How does this concept fit into the broad theme of shortages under socialism?*
The existence of persistent endemic shortages has many reasons. It is a multi-causal phenomenon and *Economics of Shortage* provides an overview of these causes. Certainly, the soft budget constraint is not the ultimate but a very important intermediate cause of shortage. It is apparent in the socialist economic system, and coupled with a few other conditions it creates runaway demand and pervasive shortages. In addition to its role in explaining shortages, the soft budget constraint turns out to be a workable concept *per se*. The soft budget constraint syndrome appears in other economic systems as well. So it is worthwhile to look at the soft budget constraint as a general phenomenon that can usefully be applied to many other situations as well as help us understand certain problems that characterise socialist systems. There is now a huge literature on the subject, several hundred articles discuss it in a variety of contexts and a number of interesting models have been developed. The Dewatripont–Maskin model played a pioneering role and is now well known in this field. I have just completed a survey on the subject co-authored by Eric Maskin and Gerard Roland. This paper presents an updated survey of the literature on the soft budget constraint.[13]

*You imply that in a socialist system the soft budget constraint problem is unavoidable. Could you explain why?*
Let me first clarify what I understand and mean by the terminology 'socialist system'. By socialism I do not mean Western-style social democratic systems. For example, I would never refer to the Swedish economic system as socialism. We must also exclude the UK under Labour governments in the post-war period. As we discussed earlier, in my definition a socialist system is an economy where political power is in the hands of a single party, the Communist Party. In this politico-economic setting state ownership is the dominant form of ownership. If you have state ownership, then those in possession of the political control will always be reluctant to let an enterprise fail. It is, so to speak, not part of their mindset. They are not playing a competitive economy game that emphasises prices and profits. Why

should they play this game? They are not interested in achieving profit max-
imisation. They play by their own rules. So state ownership is the most
important cause of the soft budget constraint. Even in a capitalist system
it is only on rare occasions that state-owned enterprises are allowed to fail.
There is also concern for the unemployment consequences of allowing a
large state-owned enterprise to fail. Socialist systems are driven by the
desire for expansion, so the idea of voluntarily shutting down existing
capacity just because an enterprise is unprofitable is anathema to
Communist Party officials. Profitability is not taken seriously as an important indicator that key decision makers should be concerned about. They
are much more interested in growth rates.

*So would you say that the threat that an enterprise may go bankrupt is virtu-
ally zero?*
Bankruptcy is never a real threat. In classical socialism, enterprises could
be confident that they would receive assistance from the state to overcome
a financial crisis. Even chronic loss makers are bailed out on a regular basis.
The financial assistance comes in a variety of forms, such as soft subsidies,
bargaining over taxation, soft administrative pricing and easy credit.
Bankruptcy belongs to the world of hard budget constraints.

## REFORM AND THE 'SOCIALIST SYSTEM': WAS THERE A THIRD WAY?

*Twelve years ago you were the first economist to offer a comprehensive set of
proposals for post-socialist transition. In your book* The Road to a Free
Economy *you claim very forcefully that there is no third or middle way for
socialist economies. The idea of market socialism is a non-starter. You make
the same point in your* Journal of Economic Perspectives *paper published
about the same time.*[14] *Why did you become so convinced that there was no
third way, no form of market socialism that the Eastern bloc economies could
embrace after 1989?*
First of all it is important to make clear that this debate about a third way
is not connected to such debates that have been taking place in social democratic systems. Those debates are really about what the proper role for government is in a liberal democratic capitalist market economy. Everyone
accepts that the government has an important role to play in any economy,
and there is a legitimate debate about where the borders of the state should
lie.[15] Debate about the possibility of a third way in the context of the socialist systems involved different issues. To make this clear, let us talk about the
many proposals for a third way in socialist systems, including those put

forward in 1987 by Mikhail Gorbachev. First we need to go back and remind ourselves about the characteristics of what I like to call the classical socialist system. What are the foundations of this system? There are three layers. The first and most important one is the monopoly rule of the Communist Party. The second one is state ownership. The third one is reliance on bureaucratic coordination instead of market coordination. Society is permeated by discipline enforced by the centralised control of careers. Any promotion is decided by the Communist Party. To climb up a career ladder you must please the party machine. The Communist Party is the integrating force of society. The dominance of the Communist Party, party discipline and political repression are absolutely crucial for the system to function. To use Albert Hirschman's terminology, there is virtually no *exit* for enterprises in socialist economies; employees and consumers also have little opportunity to exercise *voice*.[16] Workers are always supervised by the *nomenklatura*, by the party apparatus. Now if you really understand how the socialist system operates, being based on these three layers just discussed, it should be clear that you cannot make adjustments by replacing bureaucratic coordination with some other mechanism to create 'market socialism'. But this is exactly what all the naïve reformers like Gorbachev thought was possible. No search for a third form of ownership and coordination mechanism will allow you to escape from the tough choices that have to be made. All these three layers of the foundation have to be changed! Otherwise you end up with a confused and incoherent system, or, at best, 'goulash communism'. Trying to reform socialist economies makes you fall between two stools. This is what happened to the Gorbachev-type reforms. This is not to say that a reformed socialism is not more flexible than classical socialism, and that those socialist countries that had introduced the greatest number of reforms were not better prepared for 1989. But the Gorbachev-style reforms exposed all the cracks in the system. They allowed people to see that it was the system itself that posed the problem.[17]

*One type of response that is often heard from some 'anti-capitalists' is that the systems that operated in the former Soviet Union and Eastern bloc economies were 'not real socialism' or 'not real communism'. These critics of capitalism then go on to argue that the Soviet system was just 'state capitalism'. They then proceed as if there were some utopian form of socialist system that could be established rather than accepting the need for transition to capitalism. How do you respond to this line of thinking, which I am sure you have come across?*

I like to think about reality rather than dream of utopian forms of socialism. Just look at the historical realities. What has socialism been like in reality? The twentieth century witnessed a contest between two long-lasting,

grand types of system: centrally controlled socialism dominated by a communist party and various forms of capitalism. There is no third system.
Market socialism is an unrealisable dream. However, the debates on market
socialism and the attempts to reform the classical socialist system paved the
way for and played a crucial role in preparing these economies for the important changes taking place after 1989. That preparation for transformation
was important. So I do not join those who belittle Gorbachev and the many
other reformers in an arrogant style. They played a very important role, even
though in many cases they did not fully understand what they were doing.

*So in effect reformers such as Mikhail Gorbachev let the cat out of the bag.*
Exactly. And that is also true for many periods of enlightenment in history.
Reformers provide a catalyst for change. The socialist reformers contributed to the erosion of the foundations of classical socialism, to which I
have already referred. Those fundamental layers were well established and
very rigid. Someone had to start chipping away at them before more profound changes could be made. Some erosion and loosening in the political
sphere was needed, and this is where Gorbachev played a crucial role. This
is why I believe that Gorbachev should be recognised as a towering figure
of this period, or indeed of the twentieth century. Although some of his
ideas proved unworkable, he at least knew things had to change, unlike previous Soviet leaders such as Leonid Brezhnev. Although he had no idea
where the reform process would lead to, he understood that the Soviet
Union had to move away from its existing economic organisation. So I have
great respect for Gorbachev for creating the opportunity for change.

## TRIALS OF TRANSITION

*Gerard Roland, in his paper 'Ten Years After: Transition and Economics',*
*points out that, and I quote, 'When the Berlin Wall fell unexpectedly, there*
*was indeed no pre-existing theory of transition.*[18] *We had no pre-existing*
*theory of the effects of political constraints on transition strategies, the effects*
*of liberalisation in socialist economies with no pre-existing markets, how to*
*privatise socialist enterprises given the legacies left by socialism, and how to*
*harden budget constraints and achieve efficient restructuring.' This is some-*
*what surprising and gives the impression that no one expected the socialist*
*systems to implode like they did and when they did. Economists were not pre-*
*pared for this epoch-making historical event. How do you explain this?*
That is a very good and legitimate question to ask, given the huge importance of what happened in 1989 and since. These issues simply didn't
feature in public discourse before 1989. The speed of collapse was quite

unforeseeable. It came as a great and unexpected shock. Of course, those of us who had written about reform were convinced that sooner or later the system would have to change. We hoped for that to happen and were sure that it would come some day. But nobody predicted that it would happen in 1989. In that sense it was a surprise. Maybe there are some exceptions that I do not know about, but it was certainly not a dominant feature of intellectual discussions in either the West or the East. Change was expected to come, but later and with a much longer period of transition. Consider just one example. At the first Solidarity roundtable meeting in Poland a certain number of seats were reserved for the Communist Party to take after the election. They regarded it as self-evident that even if the election went 100 per cent for Solidarity, the Communist Party would still be allocated a certain number of seats. Nobody was thinking in terms of allocating seats simply on the basis of votes. These events should teach us to be modest about our predictions and forecasts. History has a habit of providing big surprises. Sometimes change is gradual, occurs step by step. Other times it accelerates, taking everyone by surprise. We know this from the study of business cycles. Panic can suddenly hit financial markets. Such explosive events have occurred repeatedly. Just look at what happened in East Asia in the late 1990s. Extrapolation from a curve is always a risk. After the initial surprise of 1989, the speed of change was not so unexpected for me because, having lived through the events of October 1956 in Hungary I had learnt that things can change a lot in just one day. What happens on Wednesday can be very different from what happened on Tuesday. In three days everything can turn upside down.

*Do you agree with Francis Fukuyama's thesis that we have witnessed the 'end of history' with the demise of the great socialist experiment of the twentieth century?*[19]
I have to admit I never understood what he really wanted to say with that astonishing announcement. On the one hand, the great twentieth-century socialist experiment is not over. What will happen in China, that vast country? What kind of system will it turn into, after being a more or less standard socialist system in the initial period, and how much longer will the transformation take? There is no excluding the possibility of China's transformation requiring a whole period of history.

Who knows what the future has in store, what new, hitherto unknown social formations will come into being, for instance through the influence of the technical revolution in information and communications? The term 'historical' means a great many things to me, among others the birth, transformation and demise of systems, to use the concept in the sense that my book *The Socialist System* employs it. History goes on.

*One interesting development that has come out of the debate on transition is*
*that, in studying the problems of moving from socialism to capitalism, econ-*
*omists are also learning to understand better and appreciate the importance*
*of institutions and how, for markets and capitalism to work reasonably well,*
*there are specific institutional prerequisites. Many Western economists who*
*have lived and worked all of their lives in capitalist market economies take for*
*granted many of these institutions that support the workings of markets. The*
*institutions that reduce transaction costs, protect property rights, encourage*
*trust, and provide law and order are crucial ingredients of successful market*
*economies. Would you go along with that interpretation?*

Yes, I would. I'd add further thoughts to that, the first of a more personal
nature. Right from the start of my research career, I always gave precedence
to describing the institutions associated with the system I was examining,
and understanding and analysing how they operate. That is what I did in
*Overcentralization*. The main message of *Shortage* was that the chronic
shortage apparent in the communist economy was caused not by mistakes
of economic policy, but by the institutions present in the system. Analysis
of the system's institutions runs all through my book *The Socialist System*.
Many other works have discussed separately some institution or other or a
narrower ensemble of institutions, such as the political structure, the legal
system, property relations and suchlike. My book was an attempt to present
the institutions as a coherent system, showing how they were built one upon
the other and how affinity and cohesion developed among them – for as
long as that cohesion lasts and does not break down. Now that this question has come up, I would add that I am sorry there was little professional
recognition of this methodology, because I think it is an essential and characteristic feature of the book. This system-centred approach is, in my view,
crucial for understanding how the communist order could survive for so
long and how it came about that it collapsed eventually in 26 countries.

Analysis of institutions, separately and joined together in a system, was
also emphasised strongly in my works about the post-socialist transition. I
was influenced to think in this way by many other written sources and by my
own experiences as a researcher. I have to say that unfortunately I did not
know Douglass North's work at the time I was writing *Overcentralization*,
the *Economics of Shortage* or *The Socialist System*.[20] That is why I did not
link my ideas to his, and did not cite his works. Later, when the North school
of modern institutionalism suddenly became fashionable, there were many
who did not even notice how closely related my work was to institutionalism, not in its terminology, but in its methodology, its approach to the reality
of society. I am sorry that it turned out that way.

While emphasising the kinship, I would also like to point out differences.
I am arguing here less with North than with some of his slightly one-sided

and over-enthusiastic followers. The understanding of institutions (and, if need be, alteration of them) is extremely important. It is necessary, but normally not sufficient in itself. Attention cannot be concentrated exclusively on institutional change. This we experienced, precisely in the period of the transition, sometimes in quite a bitter way. A splendid new institution is created, following strictly the most refined Western pattern, and it just does not want to work in the way we would expect. It won't because it is abused, for instance, by the autocratic political will and it cannot be supervised by a political sphere still insufficiently cultured and lacking in democratic traditions. The transformation of society is a very broad and comprehensive process in which the transformation of institutions, the disappearance of old ones and the appearance of new, is just one, albeit essential, component. However, it does not preclude the influence of other factors, such as culture, tradition, the personalities of the occupants of important positions, etc.

*Focusing on the economic aspects of transition, how do you account for the variation in performance across transition economies?*
The transition of the economies in Eastern Europe, so far, has been more successful than in Russia. There are several reasons for this and I could not single out one in particular. The Soviet Union had a longer history of communism than Eastern Europe, 70 years rather than 40. The Eastern bloc has more organic linkages to Western Europe than the Soviet Union. It was much more problematic for Russia to feel close to Europe than for countries like Hungary, Poland and Czechoslovakia. These countries had always felt that they were part of Europe, with more family ties, and cultural and commercial linkages. Geographically these countries are also closer to the industrial hub of Europe and the main markets centred around Frankfurt, London, Paris, Milan and Zurich. That is always an advantage. Also important is the fact that Eastern Europe has always had more exposure to reformist ideas in both the political and economic spheres. There was more experimentation with reforms in some of these economies. Another key influence on success or failure comes from the responsibilities and quality of personal leadership. Who made more and who made fewer mistakes in designing the transition strategy? I think the Russian leadership made many of the wrong choices. We should also consider policy mistakes made by the West in their relationship with the transition economies.

*Did some of the advice coming from Western-based economists turn out to be misguided?*
Yes. My main criticism relates to the way that privatisation was carried out, the way that ownership was changed.[21] I preferred a more 'organic' strategy

of bottom–up development of the private sector. Russia was too much concerned with privatising the run-down state enterprises. It is important to allow new enterprises to emerge spontaneously, including small and medium-sized business enterprises. It is crucial to foster a new business ethos where Schumpeterian creative destruction and entrepreneurship become the norm. Vibrant productive entrepreneurship is a crucial engine of economic progress and I don't think it was given enough emphasis in Russia or by the Western advisers.[22] The advisers also neglected to emphasise the importance of establishing secure institutions to protect the legal framework of business activity.[23] Western advisers would mention this at the end of a report, but with too little emphasis being paid to it. After 1989 the Holy Trinity of the 'Washington Consensus', namely privatisation, liberalisation and stabilisation, dominated the thinking of many reformers and advisers. There was not enough emphasis and discussion given to the importance of creating law enforcement and hardening the budget constraint. Then there is the neglected problem of tax collection. Under the socialist system no fiscal problem existed. There was a monobank and taxes were automatically collected by it directly from the enterprises. There was no question of tax evasion. Once the payment of taxes ceased to be automatic, many stopped paying and serious fiscal troubles emerged.[24] Also neglected was the position of the welfare state in post-socialist economies.[25] Under socialism a premature welfare state was created out of all proportion to resource constraints and fiscal capacity. With the shock of transition and problems with tax collection, economists need to give more attention to the necessity of reforming the welfare state. So many Western 'experts' had to learn quickly how to widen their thinking beyond just economic theory and the concerns of the 'Washington Consensus' to be able to provide relevant and useful advice.

*In your recent paper, 'Ten Years After "The Road to a Free Economy": The Author's Self Evaluation', you conclude by saying that the gradualism v. shock therapy debates of the early 1990s involved a 'false dichotomy'.*[26] *What exactly did you mean by that?*
I have a number of problems with this dichotomy. One is that the transformation is a very complex process and the speeds of its several components necessarily differ very strongly. Some regulations can be introduced very quickly. But there's no way of creating by fiat a new private sector built up out of a hundred thousand new start-ups. The stock exchange can be opened soon enough, but diverting capital into joint-stock-company form is a very slow process. Averaging the speed of post-socialist transformation is as meaningless a concept as arriving, for instance, at an average speed of movement in a big city, including the pedestrians, cyclists, private cars, lorries and

underground railways. If the features of the transformation are examined one by one, different criteria appear for deciding what speed is best for each.

I have an aversion to placing a decision about speed in the foreground of the debate. There are many other questions to decide. For instance, there are economic, legal, moral and political criteria to apply to developing the private sector. People can form their own opinion, bearing these in mind. And once we have chosen according to these criteria, then come the implications of speed. If we feel it is important for a broad entrepreneurial stratum to emerge and for foreign capital to participate willingly in investment, it is clear that we cannot achieve this hey-presto with one decisive piece of legislation.

*In that same self-evaluation paper you mention in a footnote that you turned down all invitations to be an adviser to governments of transition economies but that you considered yourself to be an adviser 'in the broader sense' of conducting and publishing research and making policy recommendations as an outsider. Why did you turn down those invitations to be an adviser on the inside?*
I would like to make it plain that in my view, those serving as advisers to democratic governments, ministries and parties are performing an honourable and important task. However, it has to be acknowledged that people who undertake such functions will have to be loyal to those they are advising. If advisers disagree with something, they can convey their criticisms behind closed doors, but they cannot make their remarks public. They have to pay full attention to the political-cum-tactical criteria that guide the actions of the person they are advising.

For me, these are constraints that I cannot accept. I would like to retain my full intellectual and political independence. I normally publish my positions. If the government, some minister or some other political personage asks for my opinion or calls for my advice, I am at his or her service under suitable conditions. Such conversations have taken place on more than one occasion. Still, I think it is one thing to give *ad hoc* advice that does not commit the person presenting his opinion to giving loyal service to the statesman or parliamentarian being advised, and another to undertake a formalised, official job as an 'adviser'.

*One of the big surprises to economists in the 1990s was the depth and duration of the recessions that occurred in the former socialist economies during the initial phase of transition.[27] The enormous transformations taking place were bound to create disorganisation for a period, and Blanchard and Kremer have attempted to explain the fall in output in these terms.[28] Was the severity of the recessions that were experienced also a surprise to you?*
Yes, absolutely. I did not expect such large falls in output. Disorganisation is certainly one of the reasons. There was for a period an institutional

vacuum. The old institutions disappeared without there being adequate replacement. The new institutions had still to be created.

## CAPITALISM, SOCIALISM AND DEMOCRACY

*How have the people in Hungary and the rest of the transition economies reacted to the profound political and economic changes that have taken place?*
I am more appreciative about the changes than many of my fellow citizens in Hungary and the other transition countries. The man in the street, the average citizen of the country, is usually not grateful to history; he is rather inclined to look at the darker side of events. Many citizens are disappointed with the results of change. That is because most people had unreal expectations about what could be achieved quickly. They believed that once the switch from socialism to capitalism had taken place, everybody would be lifted out of poverty and into high standards of living almost overnight. So there is a high degree of dissatisfaction in the transition countries.

*Do you include Hungary among the countries where there is dissatisfaction?*
Yes, I do. The gap between expectations and reality was just too large. I think the Hungarians were expecting even more than people in some of the other transition countries. As one who has spent half of his life studying the field of 'comparative economic systems', I had much less expectation about what could be achieved quickly. I think I understand how capitalism and socialism function, so I am not disappointed. As an economist I know that you cannot expect a sudden jump in the standard of living to Western levels. Productivity has to rise, and this takes time. I also know that capitalism is far from being a perfect system. In the Churchillian sense it is better than any of the not very good alternatives. Although capitalism still has many faults, such as excessive income inequality and recurrent problems with unemployment, nobody has yet invented a better economic system. There was some inequality under socialism but less than under capitalism. The inequality is now more conspicuous because some individuals make a lot of money and it is highly visible. What I really value about the changes after 1989 is that we now have democracy and freedom of speech. That is extremely important.[29] The political situation now is incomparable with the situation as it was under the rule of the Communist Party. In the economy there is now much more flexibility, much more entrepreneurship and initiative coming through. This is a great achievement. We have got rid of the endemic shortages.[30] It is as if many people have already forgotten what it used to be like before 1989. Seeing that the shops are full, they complain that they cannot afford to buy the goods on offer. I understand how

they feel, but as an economist who spent a lot of time on analysing chronic shortages I can see profound improvements compared to the way things used to be. The hope is that these improvements will continue and then everyone will begin to feel the benefits of the change of system. My view is that the changes led us in the right direction and the long-run prospects are promising. Initially, the shock of change had a negative impact on production, which painfully worsened the economic situation of many people. We also have troubles linked to widespread dishonesty and corruption. But I believe the worst is over. From the broader perspective the positive achievements have been much more important.

*Looking back over the political and economic events since 1989, how would you assess what has happened on the road from socialism to capitalism? What have you learned about the determinants of success?*
Before I can answer that I need to know how you define success.

*I guess most economists would define success as when a transition economy finally gets into a situation where markets work well, leading to sustainable growth of income per capita.*
I prefer not to have such an exclusive indicator. In my mind there are at least two equally relevant success indicators. The first is freedom; the second is material well-being. If you look only at GDP per capita, you have only half of the picture. You must consider both. In fact, in my subjective judgement, freedom is more important. I cannot say that China is more successful than Russia. China has been more successful on one of these measures, the growth rate of GDP, but much less successful in establishing greater freedom. China's success with GDP growth is in part due to the maintenance of stability in the country. In this stable political framework, with the dominance of the Communist Party, they have achieved high rates of economic growth. But they have paid a precious price for that. In China the political regime is extremely oppressive and there is no political liberty or freedom of speech. So I do not regard China as a shining example just because it has been successful in economic growth. In making comparisons you have to refer back to your basic beliefs and philosophy. Having experienced political repression for many years, I attach great importance to freedom. I cannot say, for me as a Hungarian or for you as a UK citizen, freedom is important but that for the people in China it does not really matter; let them be content with their higher growth rate of GDP per capita. That is hypocritical. If you really think that freedom of speech is not important, then go and try your luck in a faster-growing economy under the dictatorship of a Communist Party. So I am not prepared to ignore the political side of change. While Russia is certainly not consistently democratic, it is

certainly no longer ruled by a single party. There is political rivalry and election, and there is much more freedom of speech than in China. It is not a mature democracy, but it's a vast improvement on how things used to be.

*I take your point. Again those of us who have lived all our lives in democracies tend to take these freedoms for granted. Related to this general issue of freedom and democracy, in your paper in the* Journal of Economic Perspectives, *'What the Change of System from Socialism to Capitalism Does and Does Not Mean', you argue that 'capitalism is a necessary condition of democracy . . . There has been no country with a democratic political sphere, past or present, whose economy has not been dominated by private ownership and market co-ordination.'*[31] *Why is capitalism necessary, although not sufficient, for democracy?*

First let me be clear about what I mean by democracy. I follow Schumpeter's definition of democracy as a system that exhibits certain minimal conditions, namely, that governments can be peacefully changed on a regular basis by electoral methods; that no single party or ideology has a monopoly of power; there is a competitive multi-party system; and there is freedom of expression and the press. So by those criteria you cannot find one single example of a democratic socialist state. Not one. As far as I am concerned that settles the issue until someone can show me an example to the contrary. Empirically there is no argument. Capitalism is not a *sufficient* condition for democracy because there have been capitalist systems with dictatorial political regimes, for example, pre-war Italy and Germany, and there are many post-war examples in Southern Europe, Africa, Latin America and East Asia. But there is also a logic to why capitalism is *necessary* for democracy. This has to do with the ownership question. For democracy you need freedom of the individual. People must be free to speak out, and that is not possible in a society where individuals are in all respects dependent on and at the mercy of their employer, which in a socialist system is predominantly the state. Again, to use Hirschman's terminology, there is no exit. You need genuine decentralisation of ownership and power for democracy to develop; otherwise you are subject to common central commands. There is nothing wrong in having a certain share of public ownership, a genuine mixed economy. But to have the economy dominated by a monopoly or predominance of state ownership is incompatible with democracy. For real democracy there must be a predominance of private ownership.

*Since 1979 China has been freeing up its economy in a gradualist way and the private sector has been allowed to expand. Given that this trend is expected to continue, what are the prospects for democracy in China?*

At some point, sooner or later, the communists will have to give up their monopoly of power. But we don't know when and we don't know how this will happen. My guess is that it will occur through a transformation of the Communist Party itself. Although the Communist Party retains the same name, it does change over time. Today's Chinese Communist Party is different from the time of Mao's. The same happened in Eastern Europe in the 1980s. Transformations can take place in the thinking of the Chinese Communist Party. Also, once you begin to allow the private sector to grow, sooner or later the business community will desire political representation. So I am, in that sense, optimistic for the very long-run situation in China.

## EUROPEAN UNION ENLARGEMENT

*How important is it for the former socialist countries of Eastern Europe to be accepted as members of the European Union?*
It poses a dilemma that Hungary, and the other Eastern European economies, have only recently broken free from the dominance of the Soviet empire and achieved national sovereignty. Joining the European Union will involve handing over a large measure of that sovereignty. That is a hard decision to make. There are trade-offs, costs and benefits. But on the whole I give it strong support because I think the benefits of membership will out-weigh the costs over the longer term. There are nationalistic movements in each Eastern European country that oppose membership. I am convinced that being a member of the EU will exert some discipline on the former socialist economies, both from the economic and the political aspects. This comes back again to my concern for freedom and democracy. I am not pre-pared to assess the merits of membership simply on the impact of such a move on GDP growth and economic efficiency. My main objection to com-munism was not that it led to a poor growth performance and economic inefficiency, although these features were of course important drawbacks of the socialist economies. My main objection was against the political system and all that it implied. I firmly believe that EU membership will provide greater protection of human rights, including the rights of the minority populations in the former socialist countries, and will also give more support to democratic institutions.

## CURRENT RESEARCH

*Your current research interest is focused on the project 'Honesty and Trust in the Light of Post-Socialist Transition', centred here at the Collegium*

*Budapest, Institute for Advanced Study. What is the motivation behind this broad research agenda and what are its main objectives?*
The motivation comes from the experiences we have had in transition economies. I mentioned before that many people are disappointed, and the level of dissatisfaction is much greater than can be explained by simply looking at the GDP performance of the transition economies. There has been an explosion of corruption and dishonesty. People feel that they cannot rely on other people's word. There is a problem of trust. Under socialism the institutions of government became discredited and as a result cheating on the state became acceptable. People would only trust close family and friends. And then came the dramatic events of 1989–90, bringing about political upheaval. While political and economic institutions changed relatively fast, the evolution of new social norms takes longer.

*How is the project progressing?*
This particular project developed from my collaboration with Professor Susan Rose-Ackerman of Yale University.[32] Beginning with a preliminary planning workshop in May 2001, we have since organised a series of conferences based on the interests of the participants. Our aim was to form a 'focus group' by bringing together scholars from across the academic spectrum to carry out this work. Much of the research is interdisciplinary, reflecting the fact that we have scholars participating from political science, sociology, philosophy, law and economics. These scholars come from all over the world, including the former Eastern European socialist economies and Russia, but also from the USA, Mexico, Scandinavia, Western Europe and Canada. We organised the project around three major themes, all of which derive from problems connected to political legitimacy and institutional quality. The first theme is: how can we create a trustworthy state? Here we are interested in questions such as: what are the main causes of bureaucratic corruption and what can be done to reduce it? How can we use the law to reduce dishonesty and corruption? What system of incentives can be designed to encourage public officials to go about their duties in an efficient and competent manner? How can we increase accountability and transparency in government? The second theme relates to formal and informal cooperation. The research here looks at issues such as law enforcement, informal contacts, reputation, organised crime, state capture and networking. It is desirable in the post-socialist economies for business enterprises to develop norms of behaviour based on trust and reputation. What are the rules of the game when politicians get involved with business and vice versa? How impartial is the state? These are all important public policy issues for the transition economies. Our third theme relates to the value that we place on honesty and trust. For example, how important is honesty and

trust in successfully building a credible democracy? How has the legacy of socialism influenced people's behaviour? Do different groups within a country behave differently? We have organised three workshops around these three themes and have just had the first related to 'Creating a Trustworthy State'. Papers were given on many of the topics I have just referred to. We have another workshop focusing on 'Formal and Informal Cooperation' to be held in November 2002, and a third workshop on 'The Value and Price of Honesty and Trust' in December 2002.[33] The current project will conclude with the publication of a book containing our research findings. The hope is that the participants will also continue their collaboration in these important questions into the future.

## THE FUTURE

*How optimistic are you about the future for the transition economies of Eastern Europe?*
I am optimistic for the medium and long term, but I am making no predictions about the short term. Too many unexpected things can happen in the short run. As economists we see this all the time. I do hope that the worst of the adjustment is over. I look forward to continuing our integration into Europe. The cultural history of Eastern Europe has always been linked to Western Europe. We are by geography and history tied closely with the rest of Europe. Historically, Eastern Europe has produced many great writers, scientists and composers.

*And, might I add, many great economists.*

## NOTES

1. I interviewed Professor Kornai in his office at the Collegium Budapest, Institute for Advanced Study, on 25 October 2002.
2. Imre Nagy was removed from power in 1955, became prime minister again in October 1956, and after the defeat of the revolution and his overthrow, he became a martyr when he was executed in 1958.
3. Marx (1867).
4. Kornai and Lipták (1962, 1965).
5. Lange and Taylor (1938).
6. Schneider (1956); Samuelson (1947, 1948); Haberler (1936); Schumpeter (1942); Dorfman et al. (1958).
7. See Hayek (1935).
8. See, for example, Kornai (1965, 1967, 1969, 1970); Kornai and Martos (1973); Kornai and Simonovits (1977).
9. Such and Tóth (1989).

10.   See Vaughn (1980); Stiglitz (1994).
11.   For example, see Kornai (1976, 1982); Kornai and Weibull (1978, 1983).
12.   See, for example Nove (1983); Bardhan and Roemer (1993).
13.   Dewatripont and Maskin (1995); Kornai et al. (2003). See also Kornai (1986a, 1993, 1998a, 1998b, 2001).
14.   Kornai (1990a, 1990b).
15.   See Snowdon (2001b, 2002a).
16.   Hirschman (1970).
17.   On reforms see Kornai (1981, 1986b, 1990a, 1990b, 1997a).
18.   Roland (2001).
19.   Fukuyama (1989, 1992).
20.   See, for example, North (1990); Snowdon (2002a).
21.   See Kornai (1992b, 2000b, 2000c); Djankov and Murrell (2002); Stiglitz (2002a).
22.   See Baumol (2002), for an excellent discussion of the importance of entrepreneurship.
23.   See Roland (2001); Hoff and Stiglitz (2004).
24.   See Kornai (1992c).
25.   See Kornai (1997b, 1997c).
26.   Kornai (2000b). See also Marangos (2002).
27.   See Kornai (1992d, 1994); Campos and Coricelli (2002).
28.   Blanchard and Kremer (1997).
29.   See Kornai (1988).
30.   See Kornai (1995).
31.   Kornai (2000a).
32.   See Rose-Ackerman (2001).
33.   Details of these workshops can be found at www.colbud.hu/honesty-trust/.

# Michael Porter[1]

Professor Porter graduated in 1969 from Princeton University with a BSE, high honours, in aerospace and mechanical engineering, before completing an MBA with distinction (1971), and a PhD in Business Economics (1973) at Harvard Business School. For over 30 years Professor Michael Porter has pioneered the use of economic analysis to investigate important issues relating to 'competitiveness' at the firm, industry and national level. During this period Professor Porter has authored/co-authored/edited 17 books and over 90 academic papers, as well as making numerous contributions to the business press, acting as a consultant, and providing expert testimony to governments.[2] He is widely regarded as one of the world's leading authorities on the competitive strategy of enterprises, the competitiveness and economic development of nations, states and regions, and the application of competitive analysis to a variety of key social problems, including those linked to the environment, healthcare and philanthropy.

Currently Professor Porter is the Bishop William Lawrence University Professor at Harvard Business School (HBS). A 'university professorship' is the highest professional recognition that can be bestowed to a Harvard faculty member, and he is only the fourth faculty member from HBS to earn this distinction.

In June 2001, Harvard University announced the establishment of the Institute for Strategy and Competitiveness (ISC). This new interdisciplinary

*333*

research institute, based at HBS, is headed by Michael Porter and focuses research on the implications of competitive forces for company strategy, assessing the competitiveness of nations, regions and cities, and investigating the impact of competitive capitalism on society and social progress. The ISC also serves as a major international centre for management education and innovative curriculum development. Since its foundation, under Porter's direction, the ISC has produced a continuous stream of publications, including over 100 'National Competitiveness Profiles' for the World Economic Forum's annual *Global Competitiveness Report*, the production of 'Regional Cluster Maps' that detail the structure and composition of state, regional and urban economies in the USA, and developing an extensive database on 'Company and Industry Financial Performance' for every public company in the USA.

In the interview that follows I discuss with Professor Porter his work and ideas relating to the microeconomic foundations of global competitiveness and economic development.

## THE ROLE OF ECONOMIC ANALYSIS IN BUSINESS SCHOOL RESEARCH

*On your appointment to the position of 'University Professor', Kim Clark, the Dean of Harvard Business School, paid tribute to you as a 'pioneer in using economic principles to solve important problems in competitiveness'. How important was your economics training to your later work?*
It was fundamental to my work. I see my basic discipline as economics and I see myself as an economist. There are certain economic fundamentals that influence everything else and my principal initial contribution was taking some knowledge of industrial economics and for the first time bringing that perspective into the business strategy field.[3] So I have always tried to bridge two fields. I have taken economic theory and concepts and applied them in a productive way in more practical settings.

*When it came to the issue of competitiveness, what was it that economists were missing in their analysis?*
When I came to looking at competitiveness I found that there was virtually nothing in the economics literature that addressed the micro aspects of competitiveness. I wanted to find a *framework* that would better capture the full complexity of competition. The *Competitive Advantage of Nations* book was a six-year effort involving research teams in ten different countries because we had to create massive amounts of primary data. My aspiration has always been to create a dialogue in order to bring from economics some

analytical rigour into management thinking, but also to bring to economics a deeper understanding about the nature and deeper reality of competition.

## COMPETITION AS A UNIFYING THEME

*You have contributed to a wide variety of fields, including strategy, competition and competitiveness, industrial economics, innovation, the economic development of nations, regions and cities, corporate philanthropy and environmental issues. Is there a common theme that connects your thinking on each of these issues?*
There certainly is. The core of all of my work is to establish a deep and sophisticated understanding of the nature of competition in individual markets. How do firms compete in markets? How do they develop strategies? How do they gain competitive advantage? So that initial core of work was really about firm-level competition. I didn't even utter the word government or locational factors. Those issues were not even on the radar at that time. Then I got exposed, almost by accident, to the issue of national competitiveness. I was appointed by President Reagan to a commission investigating the competitiveness of the USA. I immediately started to scratch my head because there is no simple translation between the competitiveness of a firm and the competitiveness of an economy. Drawing analogies between the competitiveness of firms and the competitiveness of nations involves a fallacy of composition that causes tremendous confusion. So when I started mulling this over and over in my mind it became clear to me that in order to understand the competitiveness of nations it would be necessary to adopt a bottom–up or microeconomic approach. My work started with the question: how do firms compete? That led me to the 'cluster' and 'diamond' concepts, and a very granular and close-in view of the business environment. This approach is complementary to the more traditional top–down approach to economic development which emphasises factors such as institutional development, trade liberalisation, privatisation and macroeconomic stabilisation. In the same way the work on regions and inner cities is a derivative of the work on nations.[4] It turns out that you can take the same theory and apply it to nations, regions and cities, providing you make some important conceptual adjustments.

## COMPETITIVENESS AND PRODUCTIVITY

*As you have pointed out, the word competitiveness leads to much confusion and misunderstanding between academics and non-academics (media, politicians*

*and business executives). You also stress that it is important to distinguish
between competitiveness from a firm's point of view and competitiveness from
a nation's point of view. Trade between nations is a positive-sum game whereas
competition between rival firms is a zero-sum game. The UK is not in competition with China in the same way that Coke is in competition with Pepsi. In
your work on the competitiveness of nations, regions and cities, you focus on
productivity as the key to understanding competitiveness.[5] Why is productivity the key to the competitiveness of nations?*

I agree that this confusion between the competitiveness of firms and
nations is widespread. When you look at a firm you need to remember that,
barring restrictions, it can operate, produce and sell in any market. Its
measure or scorecard of competitiveness is market share and profitability.
In contrast, when you start to look at location, I argue, and believe very
strongly, that the true metric of competitiveness is the productivity of the
resources utilised in that location. Take for example a company making
shoes in Massachusetts that is gaining market share, but is only paying its
workers 50 cents per hour wages. The low wage makes it competitive in
selling shoes but is not boosting the prosperity of Massachusetts, which
would like to have high wages. So if you are trying to understand what
creates the prosperity of a location, you have to see that there is a different
scorecard that you need to use compared to when you are trying to assess
the success of a company. Obviously companies and locations are linked
because companies have to operate in geographical locations. There has to
be a synthesis. But fundamentally you have to see that there are two
definitions of victory and that the competitiveness of locations is not a
zero-sum game. For a firm operating in a marketplace, its gain in market
share is some other firm's loss of market share. When you think about competing across locations, the situation is different. China competes with the
USA only in an indirect sense in terms of whether or not it can support and
attract productive activity. Nations compete in providing a platform for
operating at high levels of productivity, and therefore attracting and retaining an ample investment in those activities that support high returns to
capital and high wages. This is a very big issue and one of the great problems in discussing economic development is confusion about what is meant
by competitiveness. As I mentioned earlier, we see the same problem in discussions on the meaning of strategy. Economists make it worse in some
cases when they say things like 'Wages fell or the currency value declined,
making a country more competitive'. That does not map with prosperity
because a fall in wages makes people poorer. Falling wages are not a
measure of competitiveness but rather a sign of lack of competitiveness. So
I find that my number one job when I am working with a state, region or
country is to get everybody on board as to the meaning of competitiveness

and what are the goals that we are trying to achieve. In the case of a company it is return on invested capital; in a region or country it is productivity measured by value, not in the narrow sense of volume.

*You have argued, and I quote, that 'National prosperity is strongly affected by competitiveness, which is the productivity with which a nation uses its human, capital, and natural resources. Competitiveness is rooted in a nation's microeconomic fundamentals, manifested in the sophistication of its companies and the quality of its microeconomic business environment . . . The central challenge to the world economy is now microeconomic reform.'[6] What are the important microeconomic reforms that are needed in order to boost productivity and prosperity?*

First of all I want to make it clear that it is important to acknowledge that there are some overarching areas of context that can make it easier or harder to influence productivity. I am referring here to the need for macroeconomic stability, and sound political and legal institutions. If these are not in place, then the risk aversion of investors increases and you cannot increase productivity without a commitment to invest. So context is important. However, while the right context is *necessary*, it is not *sufficient* to raise productivity. A country might have the most stable macroeconomy in the world and a well-functioning and accountable democratic political system, but that will not in itself guarantee prosperity. In modelling the microeconomic influences on productivity we emphasize that the ultimate determinant of the productivity of the economy is the productivity of the firms within that economy. When I say firms I mean both local firms and also units of multinationals that may be located in a particular country. It is the output per unit of labour and capital that is going to determine the prosperity of a nation. I sometimes make economists angry by pointing out that only firms can create wealth, and governments, NGOs and universities cannot create wealth. Only firms can create wealth when they create a product or service that they can produce efficiently and sell at a price higher than the cost of production, thereby making a profit. What allows firms to be productive is the sophistication of the firms themselves and how they compete, and also the business environment within which the firms compete. That is where the 'diamond theory' comes in.[7] This theory tries to look at the immediate business environment that is surrounding and influencing the competition process. The factors illustrated by the diamond influence the conditions that will have a fundamental impact on the productive potential of firms, namely, factor input conditions, demand conditions, the context of firm strategy and rivalry, and the availability of related and supporting industries. The process of economic development is about improving that diamond so that firms can achieve successively higher levels of achievement and productivity.

*Do the main challenges of economic development change as a country grows?*
Yes, the challenges of economic development do evolve as you ratchet up
that process. Economic development is a sequential process. At low levels
of around $1000 GDP per capita, the constraints on productivity often
revolve around problems with the infrastructure. When you get to $15 000
GDP per capita you need the institutional and incentive structure to create
original best-in-the-world innovations. Therefore the microeconomic economic challenge is constantly evolving. The stages of competitive development involve moving from being a factor-driven economy to becoming an
investment-driven economy, and finally to becoming an innovation-driven
economy.

*One of your economist colleagues here at Harvard, Alberto Alesina, has
recently produced some interesting collaborative work on the economic determinants of the size of nations.*[8] *Increasing globalisation and trade liberalisation reduces the advantages of a particular region belonging to a large nation
in order to gain scale economies and other advantages of a large internal
market. Small nations are more economically viable in a globalised world and
the number of countries has increased from 74 in 1945 to 193 in 2004! What
are your thoughts on the implications of this line of research?*
This is an interesting line of research. One of the points that I made in *The
Competitive Advantage of Nations*, and many times since, is that there is
what I call a 'location paradox'. You would think that, in an increasingly
globalised world, open international markets and the free flow and
exchange of information, ideas and resources, location would become less
important. Therefore virtually any economic activity can be carried out in
any location, within reason. My argument is that in the global economy, so
long as you have the clusters, the critical mass, a particular field of business
activity can be extremely efficient and productive. This does not require a
large local market; you just need a very high quality local market.
Empirically, if you look at case studies of the countries that have done well,
there is a lot of evidence showing that many small countries have done very
well by integrating themselves into the global economy. Singapore is a
classic example. Also, if you look at the large countries that are successful,
you find that one of the important reasons for that success is that those
countries effectively make themselves into several small countries by
devolving a lot of initiative and authority down to the local regional level.
One of the big themes in our work on competitiveness and economic development here at the Institute is the importance of multiple levels of geography. The classical view was that the large nation state was the key unit for
thinking about competitiveness. Now we understand that national and
international factors are important, but a lot of the real action is going on

in relatively small units. So I am very much in agreement with that general line of research.

*Economists emphasise 'comparative advantage' when they explain trade patterns whereas in your 1990 book* The Competitive Advantage of Nations *you emphasise 'competitive advantage'. In your 1995 co-authored paper, 'Green and Competitive', you say that 'Today, globalization is making the notion of comparative advantage obsolete.' Why is this the case?*
Basically I argue that traditional trade theory, based around the idea of comparative advantage, focuses on a country's factor endowments of land, labour and capital. But this is not what is driving the current patterns of trade between nations. The most obvious limitation of the traditional theory is with respect to capital. You no longer need your own domestic supply of capital. If Estonia or Poland offer a profitable economic opportunity, they can get all the capital they need from the international capital markets. With respect to labour, it is not so much the *quantity* of labour that affects your competitiveness in a given field, rather it is specialisation and the quality of labour that is important. So it is crucial to recognise that the advantages arise less from inputs in the conventional sense, and more from technology and the efficiency with which those inputs are utilised. I argue that the efficient utilisation of inputs is fundamentally affected by location and proximity. As the globalisation process evolves, what we see is more subdividing and specialisation of clusters. Ten or 20 years ago there would be a semiconductor cluster in the USA and another in Japan. The one in Japan was heavily skewed towards memory chips whereas the one in the USA was skewed towards microprocessors. Now what you see is a cluster specialising in a narrow set of activities, based around manufacturing, for example. If there are 20 manufacturing plants, you do not see these scattered across 20 different countries. They tend to be in a cluster in one location. So the specialisation process is intensifying and we find that even a small economic region can become a world player. But this cannot be done with one firm; you need the cluster, the critical mass that gives the externalities and efficiency gains. It is much more efficient for components, machines and back-up services to be all in the same location. We now see the outsourcing of more products that used to be bundled into the vertically integrated firm. I was recently at a board meeting of a company that is the world leader in computer-aided design software. Here we are just beginning to see some outsourcing of development activities rather than manufacturing. We estimate that only about 30 per cent of the development work can be outsourced, but even that is a big change from zero. So instead of having all the R&D people in the design cluster, we are also going to have design support clusters based elsewhere, maybe in India or China, for

example. So we are witnessing an increasing subdividing and specialisation of clusters. Instead of having three or four significant clusters in the world, we now have ten or more. There is an inexorable process whereby economic efficiency and productivity rule. The more trade barriers there are in the world, the more other factors rule rather than productivity, factors such as the size of the local market, military issues and political ties. Because productivity now rules, we see more specialisation and more clusters.

## GEOGRAPHY AND CLUSTERS

*In your work on economic development you have highlighted the importance of 'clusters' and external economies.[9] In economics, several economists have recently began to emphasise the neglected role of geography. For example, the work of Paul Krugman and Jeffrey Sachs has been very important in this revival of interest.[10] To what extent is there a link between your research on economic development and this line of research in economics?*
Paul Krugman visited our group here at Harvard in the second half of the 1980s and I give him a manuscript copy of *The Competitive Advantage of Nations*. He was quite intrigued with it and I think it did have some influence on his thinking with respect to introducing a geographical dimension to trade theory. Of course, Jeffrey Sachs and I already work very closely together on the preparation of the *Global Competitiveness Report*. You are right in saying that there is a growing awareness of the influence of various dimensions of geography on the work going on in economics. The other area that is undergoing a revitalisation is regional science. There is a long tradition to this perspective. For example, there is a beautiful chapter in Alfred Marshall's *Principles of Economics* about the importance of geography in the competitive process.[11] But this kind of thinking was later squeezed out by the neoclassical tradition that has dominated economics since Marshall. I hope that the new geographical perspective can be reintegrated into mainstream economics. In my work I try to bring some new focus to this work by emphasising the micro dimensions to competitiveness. I think that this view has become widely accepted. Most practitioners working in the field of economic development now recognize that the big missing link was the microeconomic and business side of the equation. Getting the context right is only part of the story. The microeconomic perspective involves focusing on how the quality of the business environment influences competitiveness.

*Where does the idea of clusters fit into this story?*
The idea of clusters is a derivative of the diamond theory and refers to geographically concentrated groups of interconnected firms and associated

institutions in a similar field. If you believe that the four elements of the diamond theory are important, then you would expect to observe clusters because they represent an efficient productive structure within which firms can operate. I think there is now widespread acceptance of the whole notion of cluster-based development, and recent research has placed increasing emphasis on the importance of clustering as an important driver of innovation and competitiveness. As we speak there are literally thousands of cluster initiatives around the world. In the USA we have numerous examples that include microelectronics and biotechnology in Silicon Valley, the auto industry in Detroit, financial services in New York, the aircraft industry in Seattle and the Hollywood entertainment cluster.[12] The real challenge that we now face in the economic development field is not so much at the conceptual level; rather it is the challenge of process. By that I mean the following: how can we actually organize societies and communities in order to create change? We have a good idea of what policy levers to put in place but it's actually getting the job done that is the problem. This problem has to be confronted in democracies where you have multiple levels of government and where you have a decentralised private sector. Clusters influence competitiveness in several ways. The geographical concentration of firms allows more efficient access to specialised suppliers, information and workforce. Opportunities for innovation are easier to perceive within clusters. Take the case of the Boston life sciences cluster. In the Boston area the presence of world-class research universities such as Harvard and MIT, teaching hospitals and biotech companies provide an excellent environment conducive to the rapid development of new ideas. Clusters also reduce barriers to entry given that new firms have access to an established pool of resources. A major challenge for any economy is to upgrade the sophistication of its clusters towards more advanced high-value activities.

## THE ROLE OF GOVERNMENT

*You have argued against economic strategies that rely too heavily on government involvement. But the Asian Tigers, Singapore, Taiwan and South Korea, as well as Japan, employed economic development strategies involving significant government interference. However, in the case of Japan you argue that Japanese government intervention is the cause of failure, not success.[13] The new World Bank position on the role of government argues for a 'significant but focused role' for government.[14] Where do you stand on this issue?*

Governments have a crucial role to play in establishing macroeconomic stability and providing stable political, legal and social institutions. However, given these prerequisites for prosperity, we need to look to the microeconomic level, to the sophistication of firms and the quality of their microeconomic environment. Governments should act as a catalyst, helping companies to improve their competitive position. With respect to East Asian development, the country that I know best is Japan, and my co-authored book *Can Japan Compete?* really grew out of the competitiveness of nations work.[15] Even back in the 1980s I was sceptical about the Chalmers Johnson industrial policy perspective of Japan's success where the government is regarded as having played a key role in forging Japan's economic miracle.[16]

*Popular explanations of Japan's recent economic problems have tended to focus on the collapse of the bubble economy, over-regulation, and the mismanagement of macroeconomic policy. You argue that the problems run much deeper.[17]*

Yes, I developed a different view by coming to this issue from a more microeconomic perspective. Macroeconomic issues are important but they do not tell the whole story. The problem is deep seated and rooted in microeconomic inefficiencies linked to distortions to the competitive process. My recent paper on Japan, co-authored with Mariko Sakakibara, puts our book on Japan into the context of the broader literature.[18] The research on Japan was striking because it proved beyond a shadow of a doubt that the accepted wisdom that it was government policy that was mainly responsible for Japan's competitiveness was deeply flawed in almost every dimension. That is not to say that the Japanese government didn't do some useful things. But they certainly did not do the useful things that were being articulated as being representative of the successful industrial policy model of Japan. We found that those industries where those practices were prevalent were the ones that were basically failures. In those industries where government policies led to the restriction of competition we find a lack of international success. The successful Japanese industries turn out to be those where internal competition is robust. So the Japanese did not find a new, more successful form of capitalism. Our research confirms the positive association between vigorous competition and rising productivity and economic success. There is more debate about South Korea, Taiwan and some of the other East Asian countries. In those countries, in many cases, the government was playing a fairly aggressive role in directing economic activity. But in both South Korea and Taiwan there were also very powerful micro, diamond-type factors that were also at work. In my view it was these factors, rather than government direction, that played the dominant role in their success. Let us take the case of South Korea. One of the central core concepts in the *Competitiveness of Nations* and subsequent work is the fundamental importance of local rivalry, that is, the need to have multiple competitors co-located fighting head to head locally. In South Korea in almost all the important industries we had the chaebol, and each chaebol had a representation in every major industry. The same kind of thing happened in Japan. Yes, the Korean government had a role in the overall story and tried to do a lot of what it considered to be useful intervention in the economy. But in each area of intervention there was also intense competition which, in my view, was a far more important stimulus to economic success. Given my faith in competition, I am a strong believer in the need for governments to provide strong anti-trust enforcement with the objective of enhancing the productivity growth of firms.

## THE GLOBAL COMPETITIVENESS REPORT

*You are involved with the production of* The Global Competitiveness Report, *which provides an annual ranking of nations according to their 'competitiveness'.*[19] *The report makes use of two measures, the 'Business Competitiveness Index' and the 'Growth Competitiveness Index'. What is the rationale behind these two indicators?*
The first indicator, the Business Competitiveness Index, is logically prior to the second, and focuses on the current level of sustained productivity that can be achieved. The Business Competitiveness Index, which we used to call the Microeconomic Competitiveness Index, captures the determinants of the level of GDP per capita and hence a country's standard of living. In this case you need to have information about the broad set of factors that influence the productive potential of an economy such as the sophistication of company operations and strategy, and the quality of the microeconomic environment. The second indicator, the Growth Competitiveness Index, developed by Jeffrey Sachs and John McArthur, tries to capture the dynamism of an economy.[20] We want to know if a particular country has in place the conditions and requirements that will allow it to move rapidly up the international competitiveness rankings. So growth competitiveness focuses on factors such as investment rates and rates of technological change, both of which respond positively to the stability of the macroeconomic environment and the quality of public institutions. It is my assertion that you need to look at both indices, although there is a lot of pressure to roll these two concepts together to produce a single index. Although both indices are highly correlated, there are many productive and prosperous countries that lack dynamism and vice versa. In the 2003–04 Report Chad, Haiti and Angola come out as the three lowest-ranked countries in both the BCI and the GCI. Finland, the USA, Sweden and Denmark come out in

the first four positions in both the BCI and the GCI. However, there are countries that are ranked higher by the GCI than the BCI, and include Taiwan, Portugal and Botswana. There are also countries that are ranked higher by the BCI than the GCI, for example France, Germany, Italy and the UK. So if you have a two-by-two matrix there will be countries in every cell. So I think that combining these two measures would suppress useful information. I am now working on this problem with Xavier Sala-i-Martin of Columbia University. In fact there is an imminent conference on this very issue. Xavier is thinking about how to combine these two indices while I favour retaining them as separate but complementary measures of competitiveness.

*What are the major changes that appear to be taking place in the global ranking of 'competitiveness'?*
Since I have been involved with *The Global Competitiveness Report*, we have seen the increasing success of Scandinavian countries, Sweden, Denmark and Finland, and the stagnation of Japan. Finland is ranked first in both the Growth Competitiveness Index and the Business Competitiveness Index. On the innovation side we are beginning to see many more countries that have developed the capacity for innovation, while the USA has recently experienced a slowdown of innovation rates. The East Asian economies, in particular South Korea, Singapore and Taiwan, continue to do well, while in Latin America economic performance has been extremely disappointing, with the exception of El Salvador and Chile. In the Middle East, Jordan, and to a lesser extent Turkey, have shown dramatic improvement in the quality of public institutions. In sub-Saharan Africa, with the exception of Botswana, there is very little progress. Botswana enjoys the highest ranking in sub-Saharan Africa for the quality of its public institutions and macroeconomic environment although it lags behind South Africa in technology. We are beginning to see some encouraging progress in some of the former Soviet Union transition economies, particularly in the Baltic States. Again, this in part reflects the importance of their geographical location. It is much easier for them to integrate with nearby European Union economies than the economies that are located much further east. For example, it is increasing integration with Finland and Sweden that is driving Estonia's economy.

*Is it an interest in the actual ranking of countries and changes in those league tables that attracts your involvement with this research?*
The main reason that I am involved with *The Global Competitiveness Report* is not so much that I am interested in the actual rankings of countries; rather, I am interested in the data. If you accept the micro view of competitiveness that I advocate, then you very quickly come to understand

that there are many dimensions of the environment of a country that affect competitiveness. There are not one or two, but hundreds of important factors. The schools matter, the roads and infrastructure matter, investment and technology matter, macroeconomic and political stability matters, clusters matter and so on. For many of those factors it is almost inconceivable that you can get rigorous and consistent international data. During the competitiveness-of-nations body of research, except for some work we did with trade statistics, we could never do any empirical testing. Instead we looked at massive numbers of in-depth case studies of countries, regions and clusters. It was from these studies that the theoretical framework evolved. What *The Global Competitiveness Report* data have allowed us to do is to begin serious statistical analysis, for example, on demand conditions. A lot of people argue that local demand conditions are irrelevant in a global economy because countries have access to the global market. In the dynamic cluster-based view of economic development the local market remains important and we need data to confirm this view. We also need additional country data so that we can do a better job of benchmarking and comparing country performance.

## GLOBAL ECONOMIC LEADERSHIP AND THE US ECONOMY

*The USA has been the dominant economy in the world throughout the twentieth century. Towards the end of the 1980s many commentators were pronouncing the demise of the US economy relative to the performance of Japan and the European Union. For example, Lester Thurow of MIT wrote* Head to Head, *where he presented a very pessimistic scenario with respect to US economic performance compared to Japan and the European Union.[21] This has to go down in publishing terms as very bad timing because during the 1990s the Japanese economy stagnated while several major European economies, in particular France, Germany and Italy, experienced high unemployment and very disappointing growth performance. In contrast, after recovering from the 1991 recession, US economic performance for a decade was spectacular, with Robert Gordon even referring to the US economy as the 'Goldilocks' economy.[22] In a recent paper Nick Crafts of the London School of Economics argues that the major European economies are no longer catching up with the USA.[23] Do you think that the USA can maintain its position as the dominant world economy throughout the twenty-first century given the well-documented rise of countries like China and India?*

I think that the USA is likely to sustain its position as the single leading economy for quite some time to come. I think that Japan has had a severe setback although there are unmistakable signs that it is now recovering. There is no question that China is on a very robust path, with spectacular rates of economic growth, although we must remember that it is still building up from a very low level. When we look at patenting per capita in China it is still only something like 0.2 patents per million people, whereas in the USA it is something like three or four hundred per million. China's biggest wild card is its political future, which remains problematic. Also, many of the investments currently being made are not likely to earn a good return as many of them have been based on faith in China's large and growing internal market. India is a more difficult case because its political structure and system is more complex in terms of policies. India's economy is still riddled with distortions and inefficiencies although they have made considerable progress since the reform programme began. But taking all things into consideration, I still see the USA as a very dynamic and innovative economy. The big strength of the USA is its resilience and its ability to deal with problems. When some problem arises in the USA, once it is perceived as a problem, it is dealt with. The 'Savings and Loans Crisis' is a good example of this when restructuring and write-offs soon had the industry on its feet again. The contrast here with Japan is striking, where delay and indecision characterises their approach to a crisis in the hope that it will somehow go away.

*What are the main challenges facing the US economy?*
The big problem facing the USA is the human resource situation. At the university and science and technology level, things are great, even if the USA inevitably will be less dominant in the future, given the catch-up effect. The USA has a tremendous infrastructure and talent at this level.[24] The US population is also very computer literate. However, the average worker is not necessarily much better than the average worker in India or China. Looking to the future, the USA is not graduating enough engineers and there are not enough new people going into science and technology. During the last ten years there has been a massive effort to improve the public schools system. Unthinkable revolutionary things have begun to happen. For example, in Massachusetts, the most liberal state, every kid has to pass a test to get out of high school. In the old days no competency was required. It was a case of 'You have been here long enough, off you go!' (*laughter*). But to deal effectively with this problem will take not a couple of years but decades. The level of technological dominance enjoyed by the USA has allowed us to paper over this issue, but in an increasingly competitive and globalised world, this problem will be increasingly exposed in terms of reduced competitiveness. I attended a board meeting recently of a big manufacturing company that produces very sophisticated software packages for the oil industry, allowing them to make complicated designs that can be

electronically tested. There is a specific test that can be taken to measure your competency as an engineer in using this technology, and one of the directors commented that his Houston engineers were scoring around 25 whereas the engineers located in Bangalore were scoring around 90! That is worrisome. Now of course those Bangalore engineers are only a tiny fraction of India's workforce but with a population of one billion that will still amount to a lot of people. The USA has also got itself into a tangle on diversity, and the proliferation of lawsuits, not to mention geopolitical issues such as the war on terrorism. But on balance, taking everything into consideration, I think that the USA is going to remain quite competitive and dynamic for the foreseeable future.

*Earlier this year Greg Mankiw was heavily criticised for arguing that outsourcing was probably a plus for the US economy in the long run. His comments provoked an outburst of criticism from both Democrats and Republicans, concerned about the number of jobs lost since the president took office. Do you agree with Mankiw on the impact of outsourcing?*
There are two types of outsourcing, one that reflects true economic efficiencies and another that reflects failures and flaws in the US economy. For example, we have a mediocre education system. There are no more engineering graduates today than there were five years ago despite the increasing technological intensity of the US economy. So we are losing some jobs because we do not have an adequate supply of highly skilled people in the right areas. Therefore we have to make sure that the outsourcing is efficiency generating rather than a reflection of failures and distortions that have been generated within the USA. From a political point of view there are also better ways of making the point that Greg Mankiw was trying to articulate. He is a very bright guy and I have a lot of respect for him so I hope he learns from this experience and it will all soon be forgotten. When Larry Summers was the World Bank chief economist he once made a suggestion about exporting pollution to the developing countries which created a huge adverse reaction. But he went on to be Chief Secretary to the US Treasury Department and is now President of Harvard. So you can recover from such experiences (*laughter*).

*What about Europe?*
European economic performance has been a big disappointment, with a few exceptions, mainly on the fringes.

*Do you include the UK as one of your exceptions?*
Yes, I believe that the UK has had a remarkable turnaround, although there is a question about how to sustain the progress.[25] I think there is a

dynamism and willingness to try new things that makes Britain a refreshing place to visit. In fact all the dynamism seems to be located on the periphery, in the Scandinavian countries, the UK and several of the accession countries. There seems to be a lot more going on in the UK than in the other major economies of Europe such as Germany and France, which are in a mess. But the UK now faces the challenge of transforming itself into an economy that produces high-value products and services. The evidence indicates that UK companies are not allocating sufficient resources to innovation and modern managerial practices. In the study that Christian Ketels and I did for the DTI [Department of Trade and Industry] we identified six priority areas that we considered crucial for the enhancement of UK competitiveness. These were increased public investment, including education, transport infrastructure and building up scientific and technological capacity; improvements in competition policy; cluster development, a strengthening of the regional focus of policy; the development of new institutions that facilitate private sector led development; and a redirection of company strategies towards an emphasis on innovation and the development and production of high-value goods and services. The recent success of the UK had much to do with the introduction of market-based reforms during the past 25 years. The UK now needs a new approach that will upgrade its competitiveness based on innovation.

## CULTURE AND ECONOMIC PERFORMANCE

*You have a recent interesting paper on the impact of culture entitled 'Attitudes, Values, Beliefs and the Microeconomics of Prosperity'.*[26] *The impact of culture on economic performance and business practices has always provoked great controversy.*[27] *What role does culture play in the determination of economic 'progress'?*

I think that economic culture is very heavily derived from the incentives and reality that people face. For example, the Japanese are legendary for being very energy efficient. But that behaviour has more to do with the pricing signals and strict energy efficiency standards that the Japanese face than it has to do with Japanese culture. In other words, culture reflects context. I am therefore fairly optimistic that culture can be changed because it is not inherent but learned, and because culture derives from what is rewarded in society. Therefore, changing the rules will lead to a change in culture. If you live in a society where rent-seeking behaviour is rewarded, then you will inevitably see such behaviour becoming widespread. But this does not mean that the population of this country is inherently unproductive because of culture.[28]

*Going back to the case of China, it seems clear that their move from being an increasingly productive society to becoming an increasingly innovative society will involve a significant cultural leap.*

Yes, but you could say the same thing about Japan. I did a video conference recently with Beijing University. They are one of the affiliates that teaches my competitiveness course. I was very impressed with the questions that the students raised, so it is clear that China has immense potential.

## THE ROLE OF 'BUSINESS INTELLECTUALS'

*You are widely recognised as one of the world's leading 'business intellectuals' in rankings that include both academics and practitioners. It is also clear that you care about how people think and how they behave. Is influencing thinking the most important role that 'business intellectuals' fulfil?*

I firmly believe that my fundamental role is to create ideas and to change the way that people think. My fundamental goal is to change the framework, to change the perspective of the way that people look at a problem. Most things in life are driven by ideas. In my case I am not writing and addressing my work primarily to the academic community and literature. I see my main role as aiming to change practice, whether it be the practice of government officials setting economic policy or business leaders setting company strategy. This is deeply embedded in me after being here at Harvard Business School for so many years. I always felt that I had to engage in practice.

*How does this philosophy work out?*

Usually the way it works is that I will do some thinking and some research, then I will go and try it out in real company or a city, region or country. It's a kind of iterative process. I try to use any ideas that I develop. That is very important to me. I also want to speak to my fellow academics and shape the way they write and think because communication with other scholars is a very important way of disseminating ideas. But the biggest test of my work always comes when I ask myself the question: does this idea really connect and resonate when we confront actual practice? Here at Harvard Business School we are encouraged and rewarded for taking this approach whereas at many other business schools the natural focus is on publishing papers primarily for the academic community. Having said all this, I have written many such papers myself and indeed I am back writing articles for economics journals as I did at the start of my career. I have three or four in the pipeline and I love doing that work. Some of my best days are those when I feel that I have completed some work that scholars will value. But in order to achieve that, particularly given the way that I attack problems, I feel that there has to be a connection with actual practice.

*Is this vision shared by your colleagues?*
It is often very difficult to persuade younger members of the Faculty that it is changing the world that is important rather than just communicating with fellow academics with scholarly articles. There is a tremendous pressure in US academia to publish scholarly papers and usually it is quite difficult to break away from the existing structure of that literature and develop ideas that are orthogonal to the mainstream. This makes it more difficult to achieve true innovation.

*What is your secret for developing innovative ideas?*
I think real innovation in ideas requires the bridging of different disciplines. I see my work as integrative. This is what I was trying to do with my early work on strategy and competitiveness. People on the strategy side thought I had landed from Mars, and even economists thought my work was a little Martian (*laughter*). It is important that the universities create the right structure and environment to facilitate innovative thinking. Here at Harvard we have tried really hard to encourage innovative thinking and we are very proud of what has been achieved during the last 25 years. We have some outstanding scholars here now, such as Robert Merton, whereas before the 1980s Harvard Business School was associated with the case study approach.

## NOTES

1.  I (together with Professor George Stonehouse of Northumbria University) interviewed Professor Porter in his office at the Institute for Strategy and Competitiveness at Harvard Business School, on 27 May 2004.
2.  Details of Professor Porter's publications can be found at on his personal homepage at www.isc.hbs.edu.
3.  Porter (1980).
4.  See Porter (1994, 1995). See also Porter and Teisberg (2006) for an innovative analysis of healthcare provision based on competition.
5.  See, for example, Porter (1990, 2003).
6.  See Porter (2004, 2005).
7.  See Porter (1990).
8.  See Alesina and Spolare (2003).
9.  Porter (1990, 1998).
10. See Krugman (1997); Sachs (2003a).
11. Marshall (1890).
12. See Porter (2003).
13. Porter and Takeuchi (1999).
14. World Bank (1997).

15. Porter, Takeuchi and Sakakibara (2000).
16. See Johnson (1982).
17. Porter and Takeuchi (1999).
18. Porter and Sakakibara (2004). See also Porter and Sakakibara (2001).
19. Porter et al. (2004); Porter, Schwab, and Lopez-Claros (2005).
20. See Porter *et al.*, (2001).
21. Thurow (1992).
22. See Gordon (1998).
23. Crafts (2004b).
24. See Porter, Stern and Furman (2002).
25. See Porter and Ketels (2003).
26. Porter (2000).
27. See, for example, Temin (1997).
28. See Baumol (2002).

# Dani Rodrik[1]

Dani Rodrik is currently (since 1996) the Rafiq Hariri Professor of International Political Economy at the John F. Kennedy School of Government, Harvard University. After graduating in 1979 with an AB degree from Phi College, he then completed his MPA and PhD in economics at Princeton University in 1981 and 1985 respectively. From 1985 to 1992 he was Assistant (1985–89) then Associate Professor (1989–92) of Public Policy at the J.F. Kennedy School of Government at Harvard University. From 1992 until 1996 he was Professor of Economics and International Affairs at Columbia University.

To date he is the author/co-author and editor of 14 books as well as over 100 academic papers.[2] Professor Rodrik has been awarded numerous prestigious research grants, and is affiliated to the National Bureau of Economic Research, the Centre for Economic Policy Research, the Centre for Global Development, the Institute for International Economics and the Council on Foreign Relations.

Professor Rodrik is best known for his work on economic growth and development, international economics, trade policy, globalisation, the institutional foundations of economic development, and the political economy of economic policy reform. Much of his recent research has been concerned with the limits and consequences of international economic integration (globalisation) for economic growth and development. In the

interview that follows Professor Rodrik gives his views on several important contemporary issues relating to the international economy. On several
of these issues Professor Rodrik challenges the mainstream view of economists and major international institutions such as the World Bank and
the IMF, in particular with respect to the nature of the relationship
between the 'openness' of an economy and its prospects for economic
development.

## BACKGROUND INFORMATION

*How did you develop your interest in economics?*
I was born in a developing country and so I grew up with questions such
as: why do different countries have such varied levels of well being and
wealth? Why is it that some countries grow much faster than others? So
finding answers to those types of questions was a very long-standing
curiosity that first crystallised when I was still in high school. But it took
me a while to find my way to economics, and my initial interests were more
directed towards political science and history. However, once I made my
mind up to follow an academic career and study for a PhD, I decided that
I would rather do economics than political science. I looked at a copy of
the *American Economic Review* and the *American Political Science Review*
and I realised that after I had completed my PhD in economics I would still
be able to read the *APSR* but that if I did a PhD in politics I was not sure
if I would be able to read the *AER* (*laughter*).

*Were there any particular economists, papers or books that influenced the
development of your thinking? In particular, what led to your interest in issues
relating to economic growth, trade and development?*
International economics has a tremendously rich tradition. Not only is it
analytically very rigorous; it has also been more stylish than other areas of
economics. If you look at some of the greatest expositors of international
economics, such as Carlos Diaz-Alejandro and Albert Hirschman, these
were certainly two economists whom I greatly admired and they both had
gifts and qualities that I wanted to emulate. They were analytically very rigorous, they wrote extremely well and were therefore able to reach a wide
audience. Being widely read, they were also good at being able to work
across disciplines. This is something I really admire although it has not been
very common in economics.

## MEASURING PROGRESS IN DEVELOPMENT

*The first of your papers that I read, many years ago, was 'Indicators of Development and Data Availability: The Case of the Physical Quality of Life Index'.[3] Clearly much of your work has a common focus relating to the issue of economic development and how countries can best improve their living standards. We therefore need to measure progress, and there are now several composite indicators used for this purpose in addition to the conventional index of real income per capita. What are your views on how we can best measure development?*

It really depends on what your objective is. You would be ill advised to focus exclusively on GDP per capita or its growth as the only indicator that matters. There are other indicators of social and human development, broader gauges of the capacity of individuals to live their lives as they would like to live them. That is extremely important. On the other hand, I think for a lot of the work that we do as economists, if we have to focus on one measure, then the level and growth of real GDP per capita remains *the* key indicator. I am not one of those detractors of GDP per capita as a useful summary statistic in measuring development.

*But are you sympathetic to the views of economists like Amartya Sen[4] who define development as a 'process of expanding the real freedoms that people enjoy'?*

Oh yes, absolutely. Ultimately that is what development is about. However, even Sen would agree that an increased command over material goods is among the things that will contribute the most to that objective.

*In terms of economic progress, the twentieth century has witnessed many development miracles, notably the experience of the East Asian 'Tiger' economies since the early 1960s. But there have also been many development disappointments and disasters, most notably in sub-Saharan Africa. However, the overall impression of twentieth-century economic development across the world's economies, coming from recent papers by Nick Crafts, Bradford DeLong and Richard Easterlin,[5] is that we have witnessed remarkable progress in the last 100 years. Is that also your impression of the twentieth century?*

Yes, absolutely, especially the second half of the twentieth century. Our memories are short. For example, a great many of my students tend not to look back beyond the 1980s when looking at development experience. When I tell my students from Latin America that in the period 1950–80 all but three Latin American countries grew faster than they actually did in the 1990s, the latter being a period of relatively high growth following the debacle of the 1980s, or that a dozen countries in sub-Saharan Africa grew extremely rapidly until the late 1970s, they think I am making this up (*laughter*). Many of them have never been told how much progress was made all over the developing world during the first three decades after the Second World War. And it was not just progress in terms of income per capita growth. Social indicators such as life expectancy, education and infant mortality also showed significant improvement.

## THE REVIVAL OF GROWTH ANALYSIS

*A major feature of the economics literature during the last 15 years or so has been the increase in papers and books written about economic growth.[6] Given this burgeoning literature, what progress do you see on the theoretical side?*
On the theoretical side we now have a much finer vocabulary. What economists have developed during the last two decades is a series of conceptual boxes that we can relate experience to. This is a very useful exercise and it is now normal to refer to the Solow growth model, endogenous growth models, R&D models, models with externalities, models with learning-by-doing, and so on. This theoretical development has been very useful in terms of broadening our ability to talk about issues that are clearly critical for long-term development and in ways that do not force us to turn our back on neoclassical economics. Earlier, neoclassical economics did not have many good tools to deal with questions related to long-term growth. That has been a useful reconciliation. I don't think theory teaches us anything about the real world. But it does give us a way of making sense of the real world and analysing it in a manageable way.

*Your research has frequently focused on the political economy aspects of growth and development. Of particular interest is your work with Alberto Alesina on the relationship between inequality and growth. Recently, several papers have focused on the interaction between income inequality and economic growth, and it does seem to be an important issue when trying to understand what we observe, and have observed, in the economic performance of Latin America.[7] How do you interpret the recent research findings in this area?*
There has been an important transformation in our understanding of the empirical relationship between inequality and growth. If you were to ask development economists about this issue, even as late as the 1980s, a majority would probably tell you that a relatively high degree of inequality might be more conducive to growth. So if there was a relationship, it was a positive one between inequality and subsequent growth. A lot of the ideas were

driven by the older development models where richer individuals were assumed to have a higher propensity to save and therefore you need concentration of wealth in order to drive growth. The highly influential classical surplus labour model of Arthur Lewis made increased inequality in the early stages of growth a corollary of the development process.[8] Following my paper with Alberto Alesina, and a parallel paper by Torsten Persson and Guido Tabellini, this presumption has been reversed.[9] To the extent that there is a relationship, I think that there are now many more economists who are prepared to argue that there is a negative relationship between inequality and growth. Empirically there has been a clear shift.

*But why is inequality bad for growth? What are the mechanisms that are likely to produce a negative relationship?*
The argument in the Alesina–Rodrik paper was a political one. Greater inequality sets off an economically damaging tug-of-war for redistribution. Other papers in this line of analysis have made other arguments. Greater inequality makes it harder to build up human capital in the presence of financing constraints. Greater inequality prevents the building up of high-quality, representative institutions – since the elite have more to lose by sharing power.

*There is now an enormous literature relating to the issue of convergence. This interest was sparked in particular by the publication of the papers of Moses Abramovitz, William Baumol and Paul Romer. Some economists are much more optimistic than others on the catch-up prospects for developing countries. For example, the recent paper by Robert Lucas suggests that by the end of the twenty-first century we are likely to observe a significant reduction in world income inequality. In their recent book Stephen Parente and Edward Prescott argue that many countries are poor because they erect 'barriers to riches', and these are designed to protect certain vested interests. If these barriers were dismantled the whole world would soon be rich.[10] Are you an optimist with respect to the prospects for international income convergence?*
I think a major feature of the twentieth century has been the great heterogeneity of experience, and this heterogeneity has increased tremendously in the last few decades. So we have witnessed countries that are converging very rapidly, such as the East Asian Tiger economies, and others that are retrogressing, particularly in sub-Saharan Africa. Some of the latter have never been in a catch-up process, but others, such as many Latin American countries, did very well for a number of decades but have been diverging more recently. Most strikingly, China and (to a lesser extent) India have been doing very well since the early 1980s. The key task is to figure out more precisely what underlies this heterogeneity. I am very sceptical of single-theory

or single-cause explanations of convergence phenomena. If you look at some of the highly optimistic convergence scenarios you will find that they are based on very crude social theory that says that all that matters, in a world where technology is (apparently) common to all countries, is property rights. I see this as being simple-minded. A lot of what we have learned tells us that development is much more difficult than the optimistic scenario would have us believe.

*The post-colonial development record of sub-Saharan Africa is generally regarded as one of disappointment and failure, and is several cases the word 'disaster' might be more appropriate. Paul Collier and William Easterly have recently drawn attention to the issue of ethnic diversity as a potential source of conflict and shown how this can inhibit economic progress. You have also drawn attention to social conflict and how it impacts on growth and economic performance. Other economists, notably Jeffrey Sachs, emphasise sub-Saharan Africa's unfavourable physical environment, its climate and geography as a major retarding factor.[11] When you look at sub-Saharan Africa what do you conclude about the major factors retarding economic growth in that region?*

I think it's always a combination of factors but the question is: what is your preferred entry point? Where do you start when trying to fix things? My entry point is very much an institutional one: trying to fix institutions. This includes property rights, but it goes beyond that. What is crucial is to create an environment conducive to private investment and entrepreneurial activity. In many sub-Saharan African countries you could fix property rights all you want but by itself this would not be enough. Sub-Saharan Africa is obviously a very high-risk environment for investment so there is a need to build solid institutions of economic management, public–private collaboration, and democratic governance and participation. This is what allows ethnic diversity to be managed, public health systems to be developed and geographical disadvantages to be overcome.

*In your 1995 paper, 'Getting Interventions Right: How South Korea and Taiwan Grew Rich', you downplay the emphasis given to export orientation by other economists and emphasise instead the importance of increased investment as an explanation of the growth take-off that took place in those two economies in the early 1960s. In William Easterly's recent book,* The Elusive Quest for Growth, *he presents a very persuasive attack on what King and Levine refer to as 'capital fundamentalism'.[12] How do you reconcile your views in your 1995 paper with Easterly's scepticism of the importance of higher investment for higher growth? There are many examples of countries where high investment rates have not led to high growth rates.*

There are parts of that argument that are quite misleading. It is true that in the short run there is not a very strong relationship between investment and growth. If you were to look on a year-to-year basis you would not be able to observe much of a relationship between investment rates and growth rates. But if you were to look at the data on a long-term basis, or over periods of 15 to 20 years, you would find a clear association between countries that have grown very fast and those that have high investment rates. With respect to well-known examples such as the former Soviet Union, we need to take into account that the investment decisions were not made by the private sector so I do not think that particular example detracts from the association found in those countries where investment decisions are predominantly market based. And of course the establishment of a cross-country association does not mean that there will not be exceptions. There is always a scatter around the regression line. But if we are asking whether it true that countries that have grown fast over long periods of time have also tended to have high investment rates compared to countries experiencing slow growth rates, then the answer to that question is surely, on average, yes. There are also separate debates in the literature about lines of causation and also about how best to encourage high investment rates. To some extent I think that Easterly is overreacting to the capital fundamentalism that prevailed in large parts of the development community where for a time everything was seen in terms of physical investment. But that should not cloud the fact there is a basic long-term association between investment rates and economic growth.


## POLICY REFORM AND THE 'WASHINGTON CONSENSUS'

*In your 1996 paper in the* Journal of Economic Literature, *'Understanding Economic Policy Reform', you discuss the 'Washington Consensus'. What now remains of the Washington Consensus? Do you agree with Joseph Stiglitz that we are now in the 'post-Washington Consensus' era?*[13]

I am not exactly sure what Stiglitz means by the 'post-Washington Consensus' but I think I know what has happened to the 'Washington Consensus'. There has been layer upon layer of different requirements and reforms being imposed on developing countries as the impact of each layer has proved to be disappointing on its own. So the situation that we have right now is that the 'Washington Consensus' has grown from John Williamson's original ten items to about 30 items.[14] It has become an impossibly demanding agenda for institutional transformation. When you look at what is on this agenda, it goes well beyond privatisation, deregulation, liberalisation and openness to trade. It now entails the adoption of a whole set of institutional reforms related to public governance, labour markets, banking and finance etc. Essentially it has become the end point of development rather than a useful starting point. The items on the augmented 'Washington Consensus' are things that societies achieve after they have become rich rather than things they need to do to get there. So it has pretty much lost all prescriptive value. At least the original 'Washington Consensus' had ten items that you could understand. Right or wrong, they were things that you could do. But now, as far as I am concerned, it has lost all operational significance. Intellectually it is probably doing more harm than good right now in the sense that it is not providing policy makers with a clear sense of priorities and is focusing too much on best-practice institutions and imported blue-prints as opposed to the need to develop domestic institutional strengths. It also puts too much emphasis on achieving rapid integration with the world economy as a way of achieving technological and institutional change. In my opinion the augmented 'Washington Consensus' is not a useful guide for economic development.

*Why are policy reforms that are generally recognised and accepted as necessary for economic progress so often resisted for so long?[15] It almost seems to be the case that some countries need to experience a major crisis before they can finally be persuaded, or have no other option, to move onto a genuine path of effective policy reform.*
Well it depends on what kind of reforms that you have in mind. I think the 'Washington Consensus' perspective on reform is resisted because it offers a very uncertain set of benefits to society. It is only to some economists that the augmented 'Washington Consensus' provides a clear programme for improvement that will benefit everybody. It is not at all clear to the average person on the street. In fact with hindsight we might argue that the person on the street was right in being suspicious about the benefits of these policies and it was the economists advocating these policies who were wrong (*laughter*). So if we are talking about a wholesale set of institutional reforms of the kind embodied in the augmented 'Washington Consensus', then you don't have to think too hard about why people resist such a programme of reform. These reforms are not well grounded in the reality of how transformation actually takes place. On the other hand, if you are talking about some of the most successful reforms in the developing world in recent decades, they have not been wholesale but incremental. In fact they have been extremely gradual in many cases. The striking empirical fact of the last two decades is that when you look at the countries that have had the highest increase in their sustainable growth rates they are countries that at the outset did not undertake a huge amount of policy reform and institutional transformation. For

example, take a country like India that began to grow much faster in the early to mid-1980s compared to the previous two or three decades. You will be hard pressed to identify a single decisive break with the past in terms of the institutional setting and policies. Or take the more striking case, in terms of what happened to economic growth, of China since 1978–79. Of course in terms of institutions China has evolved tremendously in the last two decades. But if you look at what were the specific reforms that are responsible for this huge increase in growth since the late 1970s you don't find a very large-scale institutional transformation. Instead you find very gradual, small-scale changes in the nature of incentives moving towards allowing market prices to be established at the margin, allowing much greater autonomy for households in the rural areas, allowing private production in township and village enterprises, and establishing special economic zones.[16] If these had not worked, the 'Washington Consensus' economists would have said: 'Of course they didn't work . . . they didn't do enough.' But once these small-scale transformations begin to work you can get into a virtuous circle where further reform and economic growth feed on each other. And so the scale of institutional transformation gradually increases. But the idea that in order to have a significant increase in economic growth you need to undertake wholesale institutional transformation of the type that is envisaged with the augmented 'Washington Consensus' is empirically false. And just as well, because such transformations would be impossible to achieve for any country in a short time scale.

## TRADE, OPENNESS AND GROWTH

*In your recent paper with Anna Maria Mayda,[17] using a cross-country data set containing information on attitudes to trade, you investigate why some individuals and countries are more protectionist than others. What did you find from that study?*
The key thing that we learned is that individuals' attitudes towards trade and trade restrictions are driven in equal part by economic self-interest and by other values that don't relate necessarily that much to economics and self-interest. The key issue that economists as a whole, and trade economists in particular, need to consider and take into account is that people's attitudes to trade issues are driven by both these very different sets of factors. Opposition to trade by those who fear losing their jobs because of competitive imports is easy to understand. More complex are the set of values relating to people's sense of community, how people see themselves in relationship to their neighbourhood and community, to people's sense of nationalism and patriotism, to people's perception of how well national

institutions are performing. This second set of factors has a very powerful influence and it is a mistake to think that you can easily change the public's opposition or doubts about the benefits of free trade. Equally, it is a mistake to think that you can change the nature of the debate about globalisation simply by having economists promising that the losers from greater international integration can be compensated. If the concerns of the public are not fundamentally about economics, that kind of response will not get you very far. You have to deal with people's genuine concerns about globalisation by taking into account these issues relating to values and attachments.

*Jagdish Bhagwati continues to champion the case for free trade as a crucial positive component in the battle against world poverty.*[18] *What is your interpretation of the theoretical and empirical arguments in the trade–development debate?*
The comparative advantage argument demonstrating the mutual gains from trade is of course very well established among economists. In terms of efficiency (or 'level') effects it is quite clear what the underlying structure of the argument is and what is necessary for these positive gains from trade to materialise. Few economists have done more than Bhagwati himself to clarify the restrictive assumptions that are necessary for the mutual gains from free trade to be realised. In particular, he has clarified the wide variety of circumstances that can generate perverse results. So at the level of theory there is no disagreement, and the arguments are very well understood among economists. The main controversies relate to empirical questions (how large are the gains, and is there a determinate relation between trade liberalisation and economic growth?) and to issues of policy choice and priorities (how important is rapid, deep trade liberalisation? Should it drive the rest of the reform agenda?). Disagreements arise over how you read the evidence. Do you read the evidence as telling us that the economic effects of trade liberalisation are so overwhelming and strong that trade liberalisation has to be given top priority in a country's development strategy? In some cases the evidence is interpreted as suggesting that trade liberalisation should be *the* strategy . . . period! But how do you weigh the adjustment costs, the distributional consequences, or fiscal impacts of trade liberalisation against the efficiency gains? The liberalisation of trade usually leads to efficiency gains, the so-called level effects, but these gains frequently come with a tremendous amount of redistribution of income. The redistribution of income may not always move in a normatively desirable way, so how are you going to balance the efficiency gains against the adverse distributional effects? How are you going to prioritise when governments have scarce administrative, human and political capital? How are you going to decide

on your priorities in the efforts that must be made in harmonising your institutions, incentives and systems with the WTO regime? There are many other claims on scarce administrative resources, so how do you decide when trade reform should have greater priority than other important development goals, economic and non-economic? So these are some of the empirical and policy questions where I have disagreements with the enthusiastic advocates of trade reform.

*In your co-authored paper with Francisco Rodriguez you have been involved in a controversial debate with Bhagwati, Srinivasan and other economists about the growth effects of moving towards a more open economy.*[19] *In the trade–growth debate, Bhagwati does not seem to think much of evidence based on endless cross-country regressions but prefers to put more faith in the findings gleaned from detailed country studies. How do you respond to the economists who claim that more outward-oriented economies grow faster and that the causation runs from greater openness to faster economic growth?*

First of all I am in complete agreement that in empirical work there needs to be a healthy balance between case studies and cross-country regression analysis. I would not dismiss regression analysis in the same way that Jagdish often does. Evidence from country studies that is not borne out by careful cross-national analysis ought to be taken with a grain of salt. On the other hand I think that any regression results that are not supported by careful case studies are not worth very much. So my approach is one of balance because I believe that you need both kinds of analysis, and this is reflected in my own research, where I have done a bit of both. I have carried out country studies as well as cross-country regression work. The interesting thing about the country studies, on which Bhagwati and many others rely when they say that openness promotes growth, is that their findings, when you look at them carefully, often differ from the overviews or summaries presented by the editors. In fact, my own study on South Korea and Taiwan drew heavily on the South Korea volume in the 1978 Bhagwati–Krueger NBER series.[20] If you read the actual South Korea study in this series you would come out with a somewhat different conclusion than the one you would get if you read only the summaries provided by Bhagwati and Krueger. I think the country studies in the NBER series, or in the 1970 Little, Scitovsky and Scott OECD studies, which were also influential, are very important and valuable, but the underlying country evidence is actually a lot more nuanced and open to diverse interpretations. In the actual country studies you find a lot of interesting things that are quite inconsistent with the conclusions drawn about the impact of lower trade barriers having a predictable and systematic positive impact on growth. The actual studies do not show that.

*What about the link between outward orientation and faster economic growth provided by endogenous growth models that emphasise ideas and knowledge accumulation? It is argued that knowledge accumulation is more rapid in open economies and this is an important reason why they grow faster.[21] More open economies are not only open to goods and capital but also to the greater inflow of knowledge and ideas.*

That's absolutely right. The fact that you have a whole stock of technology and ideas out there which is much more advanced and you do not have to develop on your own significantly increases the potential for growth of a developing economy. This is an important way that openness can help, by providing access to this stock of productivity-improving ideas and technology. But you need to combine access to these ideas with a domestic capacity to make effective use of them. There is no such thing as off-the-shelf technology. All successful cases of transfer of technology involve a process of adaptation to the domestic conditions of the receiving country. If you look at the case-study literature on the transfer of technology between countries, the one clear conclusion that comes out of that research is that all such projects involve domestic investment to make the foreign technology useful under local conditions. If you do not do that, if you simply rely on imported blueprints, then what you find is that the productivity which the new technology is capable of will be a fraction of that achieved in the donor country. This was true in the nineteenth century when British firms from Lancashire exported textile machinery to India. In this case they had to send their own skilled workers and management to set up the textile plants in India. Yet these plants in India, which had exactly the same machines and technology as those in Lancashire, had only half the productivity (as studies by Greg Clark have shown).[22] This was also true during the 1950s, 1960s and 1970s, as technology was transferred to countries such as South Korea and Taiwan. If these countries had not invested in their own workers, entrepreneurs and technological capacities, they would have been unable to fully benefit from the inflow of new ideas, knowledge and technology. Just lowering barriers at the border and waiting and hoping for foreign technology to implant itself in the domestic economy is unlikely to prove a successful strategy. So it is important to appreciate that technology has many tacit elements. Technology cannot simply be written down as a blueprint and handed to somebody else. Making technology work, learning about tacit elements and absorbing it into a new environment, requires that entrepreneurs are prepared to undertake a commitment to invest. So the key question becomes: how are you going to organise your strategy? On the one hand you are going to open up to the external world of new ideas and technology. On the other hand you will need to build an environment that will stimulate your own domestic entrepreneurs to adopt/adapt the new technologies. Successful cases in the past have often involved letting your entrepreneurs work behind protective barriers – provide them with a period of assured profits so that they have the incentive to adopt the new technologies because very often these projects will have highly uncertain returns. So the process is more complicated than is often portrayed in conventional arguments. Countries should not close themselves off to the world of ideas, but neither does it make sense simply to remove barriers and hope for a miracle to happen.

*What is your response to the claim made by David Dollar and Art Kraay that 'increased trade has strongly encouraged growth and poverty reduction and has contributed to narrowing the gaps between rich and poor worldwide'?*[23]
These papers by Dollar and Kraay have served to confuse rather than clarify matters. What does 'increased trade' mean as a causal driver of growth and poverty reduction? Policy makers do not have levers called 'increase/reduce exports' – they have to work with policy instruments such as tariffs or WTO membership. If the claim is that countries that have pursued more open trade policies, and thereby have increased their trade/GDP ratios more than others, have also done better in terms of growth and poverty reduction, this is patently false, and anyone who looks closely at the Dollar–Kraay work will realise that these authors fall well short of making such an argument. What to make of countries like China and Vietnam that have increased their trade ratios tremendously despite (and perhaps because) of highly restrictive trade policies? At the end of the day, the most that you can take out of the Dollar–Kraay work is that countries that have done well over the last two decades have also experienced rising trade/GDP ratios. This is as useful as knowing that countries that have grown fast have also, say, increased the share of the tertiary sector in GDP – and as useful from a policy perspective. I certainly haven't heard any arguments recently about how the tertiary sector is a driver of growth and poverty reduction!

*Do you think that outward orientation is a more important component of a development strategy for small countries rather than large countries?*
In a strictly accounting sense that has got to be true but I do not think that the size of a country has very important operational implications. It might to the extent that a country like Brazil may decide that it has the capacity to produce steel and that it will make sense to protect the steel industry for a while. On the other hand, if you are talking about a country like Mauritius, such a strategy would be much more costly as the market size is so small. But in general I do not find size of country a very helpful distinction in deciding on the optimal development strategy.

*As a committed multilateralist, Bhagwati is highly critical of preferential trade agreements, free trade areas and the rise of regionalism. Freer trade is not the same thing as free trade. According to World Bank data the move to regionalism has become a headlong rush during the last decade. The 'explosive proliferation' of preferential trading agreements has created what Bhagwati has labelled the 'spaghetti bowl' problem.*[24] *What are your views on the trend towards increasing regionalism in the world economy?*

Well, first of all we have the European Union, which, on the whole, I believe to be a shining example of success as far as regionalism is concerned. The role of regionalism in my view is to enable deeper integration among like-minded countries with relatively common historical trajectories and institutional preferences. Such countries can move much more rapidly towards deeper economic integration. The larger membership of the WTO will never be able to agree on a very large project of institutional harmonisation at least as long as the process is semi-democratic. This has a cost in that the degree of economic integration that you are going to get compared to a truly multilateral system is going to remain relatively limited. The size of the market is limited by the reach of national jurisdictions, and if you do not enlarge the jurisdiction or harmonise institutions, then you are not going to proceed very far down the road of economic integration. The reason why the European market is so much more integrated today in terms of goods, services and capital is because it has gone down a path of jurisdictional–legal–institutional harmonisation that is much more ambitious than we have seen anywhere else in the world. I do not think that kind of integration would have been possible among countries that do not have a common historical experience and a similar income per capita. So you need a world where you do allow countries who want to go down the regional path to do so. In that sense regionalism can be a positive force.

## CAPITAL MARKET LIBERALISATION

*Many economists, including Jagdish Bhagwati and Joseph Stiglitz, have been highly critical of capital account liberalisation in developing countries. You have also asked the question, 'Who Needs Capital Account Convertibility?'.*[25] *Along with Furman and Stiglitz and Radelett and Sachs you have discussed the potential destabilising role of short-term capital flows, particularly in emerging markets and the case of the 1997–98 East Asian economic crisis.*[26] *What lessons have been learned?*

Empirically the issue seems clear, although I am not sure we understand it theoretically. Maybe I should say that on the theoretical front the reasons for market failure are overdetermined in the sense that economists know of numerous reasons why financial markets do not always work that well. It took a long time for nation states and national governments to figure out how to tame their financial systems. If you read the economic history of Western Europe in Charles Kindleberger's book, *Manias, Panics and Crashes*, he notes that about every ten years there was a financial crash.[27] So the phenomenon of boom and bust is nothing new and has been a recurring problem in financial markets throughout history. What has happened in a domestic setting is that institutions have developed to help make financial instability a less frequent phenomenon and reduce the costs of such instability when it happens. So we have, for example, lender-of-last-resort facilities, deposit insurance and financial regulators. These are key institutions that help to prevent financial institutions from taking too much risk. The problem is that these kinds of institutions do not exist in the international arena. The counterparts in the international sphere are just mockeries of the real thing. So the international financial system does not have a regulatory superstructure of governance. In an environment where this interacts with poor domestic governance in many developing countries you get a very volatile mix. This is one area where there has been a tremendous transformation in even orthodox views. Even Stan Fischer and Larry Summers would no longer disagree, I think, that capital market liberalisation proceeded too rapidly in many developing countries, particularly in the area of short-term capital flows.

*With respect to the choice of exchange rate regime, Stanley Fischer has drawn attention to the fact that since the early 1990s an increasing number of countries have moved to the adoption of either hard pegs or a floating exchange rate.[28] Is that trend inevitable?*
That view presumes a world where the conduct of macroeconomic policy is subject to the unchanged constraint of full capital mobility. I do not think this a useful way of thinking about macroeconomic policy. Macroeconomic policy entails making choices along many dimensions, including the degree of capital mobility considered to be optimal. Fischer's statement about the bipolar trend in exchange rate regimes is correct given full capital account convertibility. But I do not see why you should take full capital account convertibility as a given. For many countries, less-than-full mobility will make more sense, and that opens up alternative avenues for the exchange rate regime.

## GLOBALISATION AND GLOBAPHOBIA

*Globalisation has a wide variety of meanings, but to economists it involves increasing international economic integration, reductions in the barriers to*

*trade, increasing capital flows and foreign direct investment, technology trans-*
*fer, labour migration, and also embraces wider political, cultural and envi-*
*ronmental dimensions. You have made numerous contributions to the*
*globalisation debate.*[29] *Is increasing globalisation a threat or an opportunity*
*to the world economy?*
In terms of labour migration we are now living in a world where mobility
is much more restricted compared to the nineteenth century. It is important
to remind ourselves of that fact. In the globalisation debate many commentators talk about globalisation as if it were a single phenomenon when
in fact, as you point out, it has many dimensions. You could imagine a
world where labour flows are unrestricted but where capital flows are highly
regulated. The distributional implications of this world would be very
different from what we have now. The debate on globalisation is sometimes
portrayed as being one between pro-globalists and anti-globalists. I do not
find that portrayal to be very meaningful or helpful. The more intelligent
opponents are not arguing against globalisation *per se* but against the existing form of globalisation. This is the debate that we ought to be having.
What kind of world do we want? Where and in what areas would we like
there to be more globalisation by having more relaxed rules and fewer regulations? Where do we need better governance?

*In your* Journal of Economic Perspectives *paper, 'How Far Will International*
*Economic Integration Go?', you introduce the idea of 'the political trilemma*
*of the world economy'.*[30] *You argue that we can have at most any two of the*
*following: mass politics, the nation state, and international economic integra-*
*tion. What prevents us having all three simultaneously?*
What has just happened in Argentina is a good illustration of the trilemma.
The reason why national sovereignty interferes with full global integration
is that it imposes transaction costs when goods, services and capital move
across borders. With regard to international capital flows, the transactions
costs arise from the possibility that sovereign entities might renege on their
debt and this inhibits the possibility of full capital market integration. You
cannot sanction a recalcitrant sovereign state in the same way that you can
sanction a debtor in a domestic court because the nation state is a sovereign entity with its own jurisdiction. This creates significant transactions
costs that prevent full capital market integration. In principle you could
imagine a nation state that viewed its objectives as the expansion of the
interests of capital and was unresponsive to domestic political forces. In
that case you would be able to sustain a high level of capital market
integration by ignoring domestic mass politics. The cost of economic integration is that you cannot have mass democracy at home. This is what
Tom Friedman meant when he said this is already what we have because

essentially all politics is reduced to a choice between Pepsi and Coke.[31] There are no other flavours left anymore because the demands of the international financial speculators do not allow any government to move beyond the boundaries of Pepsi versus Coke. If they did, they would be immediately punished by capital outflows. What is interesting is that Argentina appeared for a while to be the precise illustration of that point. If you look at economic policy in Argentina in the 1990s, no government tried harder than Argentina's to endear itself to world capital markets. The economic policies looked like Pepsi versus Coke because there was no difference between the political parties. What is interesting is that it turns out that even if the top political leadership is following this particular agenda, democratic politics still casts a very large shadow over international capital flows. In the end, Argentina's interest rates rose as perceptions of the risks of default increased. It wasn't that international capital markets thought that de la Rua or Cavallo would willingly default; it was the fear that their domestic political constituencies would eventually say 'no' to debt service at usurious interest rates. In fact that's what happened and in the face of mass rallies and protests both Cavallo and de la Rua eventually had to resign. So the real lesson is that even when you think that the real choice is limited to that between Pepsi and Coke it turns out that as long as you have some semblance of democratic politics you will continue to face the trilemma, and you will be unable to combine a democratic nation state with full capital market integration.

*Paul Krugman has argued that 'The raw fact is that every successful example of economic development this past century – every case of a poor nation that worked its way up to a more or less decent, or at least dramatically better standard of living – has taken place via globalisation'.[32] Do you agree with that argument?*

It is difficult to know what to make of this kind of statement. It is like saying no country has successfully developed without having experienced technological progress. It is probably correct at some level but when Krugman makes that kind of statement, what does he actually mean? What use is such a statement to policy makers? How can we turn this statement into something that has operational meaning? Suppose what we observe is that no country becomes rich without experiencing, say, a very large increase in its export to GDP ratio (statements like Krugman's are often based on such an observation). What does that mean? As I already mentioned in connection with the Dollar–Kraay work, we also know that no country becomes rich without its tertiary sector expanding – but we do not draw policy conclusions from that. We certainly do not go around telling governments to squeeze other sectors of their economy and to subsidise their services because all rich countries have a very large service sector! Suppose instead that when Krugman says that no country has developed for a long period of time without globalising, what he means is that no country has successfully developed without lowering its barriers to trade and capital flows. But this would be entirely false. Very few countries have successfully developed starting with low barriers to trade. Almost all countries have started out with very high barriers to trade, including most critically, of course, the USA during the latter part of the nineteenth century as it caught up with Britain.[33] With regard to capital flows, ditto. So what are we to make of a statement like that? I understand the motivation behind such statements in the current environment. But muddying the waters cannot be the right way to take on the loony fringe of the anti-globalisers.

*How optimistic are you about the future of the world economy in the twenty-first century, especially after the events of 11 September? Do you foresee a globalisation backlash?*
On balance I am more worried than optimistic. I think the medium-term effect of September 11 is more than likely to make the USA more insular and withdrawn. It may become less willing to carry the burden of global public goods. So from that standpoint I see a world where there are a number of risks. I see Latin America having completely lost its way. I see a situation in Africa where things seem to be going from bad to worse. In comparison, a few Asian countries continue to do rather well. So it does not build up to a picture where we can be reasonably confident that we will see a world economy that can provide prosperity for a majority of the world's economies.

*The World Bank, the IMF and the WTO have all come in for heavy criticism from the anti-globalisation movement. Among economists, Nobel Laureate Joseph Stiglitz is also a very influential critic of the 'Washington Consensus' and IMF policies. In recent years Barry Eichengreen and other economists have discussed the need for a 'new international financial architecture'.[34] In your view, what major changes to the international economic architecture are needed and what ought these international institutions be doing to help create a more stable and prosperous world?*
In a sense, international institutions have been victims of their own success. As long as these institutions operated under the premise that international economic rules served the needs of domestic economic management – rather than vice versa – the world economy did fine. That was the secret of the Bretton Woods regime's success. Since the 1980s, the emphasis has been reversed, and national economic policies have been reoriented in the

direction of 'deep' integration. Hence we have moved from the GATT's shallow integration agenda to an ever-expanding set of trade agreements that reach beyond the border. We have created a new set of international codes and standards so as to make the world safe for international capital flows. I think we need to redress this balance. We need to provide more autonomy for national democracies to devise their own development strategies. We need an architecture that is more permissive of deviation from the fad of the day in the international institutions.

## DEMOCRACY, GROWTH AND DEVELOPMENT

*The relationship between democracy, economic growth and development has stimulated a lot of research interest in recent years.*[35] *Although much empirical work has been carried out, the theoretical foundations of the link between democracy and economic growth remain weak. Is democracy good for economic growth?*

The relationship between democracy and long-term growth is generally ambiguous. So I do not think that there is a strong systematic relationship between greater political freedoms and economic growth in the long run. However, there is something that we have learned about the relationship between democracy and growth that is not sufficiently appreciated. There is strong negative relationship between democracy and economic volatility/instability. More democratic countries tend to exhibit much lower volatility and greater stability in their growth rates than less democratic countries. While more democratic countries do not necessarily produce higher growth rates on average, they do produce much more predictable, more stable and less volatile growth rates. So if you look at the question of economic performance as a package – involving both growth and stability – from a purely instrumental standpoint, ignoring the intrinsic value of democracy, you would still want to go with democracy. So democracy is better for economic performance not because democracy produces higher growth rates on average but because democracy produces much less instability on average. That is clearly established in the data. I think it is easier to construct a theoretical argument for why there ought to be a link on the volatility side than why there ought to be a link on the growth rate side. I have discussed this in a couple of papers and I think that one important argument has to do with the virtue of regular transfer of power in democracies.[36] If as a politician I know that you are going to succeed me, I have an incentive not to expropriate you because you will have the opportunity to do the same to me when you have power. There is a long-term equilibrium strategy favouring compromise and cooperation rather than extremist outcomes involving conflict and expropriation, as often happens in authoritarian regimes. If you are an authoritarian leader and you don't know when somebody else will come and expropriate you, then your best strategy is to exploit everyone while you have a chance and while you have the power. There is also the argument made a long time ago by John Stuart Mill that if you are in a deliberative process, then you tend to appreciate where the other side is coming from. You understand that their opposition to your views may not be simply motivated by ill will but may be based on some genuine concerns. So the process of democratic participation leads to moderation because you see how other people are thinking. Therefore democracy will tend to produce moderate rather than extreme policies and outcomes. Democracies may also be much better at aggregating information. After all, policy makers are not omniscient, they do not and cannot know everything. It is important that policy makers be able to aggregate information from the local level to see how policies may work out, and this is much easier to achieve with democratic institutions where there are more mechanisms for undertaking such tasks and making better decisions. If you are going to adopt policies that are going to hurt some people very badly, then it is better to be aware of this beforehand rather than after the fact. This helps to prevent bad decisions from being taken. So there are lots of arguments that you can construct to explain why there is this link between democracy and greater stability.

## DEVELOPMENT LESSONS OF THE TWENTIETH CENTURY

*There have been many fashions in the development literature in the last 50 years, including development planning, import substitution, capital fundamentalism, foreign aid, outward orientation and the 'Washington Consensus'. What are the main lessons that economists have learned about economic development in the twentieth century that can help poor countries formulate policies in the future?*

I would say that we have learned some meta principles that apply equally well to all countries regardless of history, geography and stage of development. These are principles that all countries have to take on board. They include the importance of incentives, the power of competition, the importance of hard budget constraints, the importance of property rights, the importance of sound money and fiscal sustainability. But what we have also learned is that these meta principles provide only limited guidance to policy makers in terms of institutional design. In fact, these principles come 'institution free' in the sense that they do not imply any fixed set of ideas about appropriate institutional arrangements. The great mistake that the augmented 'Washington Consensus' makes is to attach specific institutional blueprints to these meta principles. We end up providing institutional recommendations to countries where they are unlikely to work. Yes, everybody responds to incentives and hard budget constraints, and property rights matter wherever you are in the world. But the key issue is how to put these principles into operation. We have learned from the Chinese experience that even something so basic as property rights is sometimes best provided via highly unconventional institutional forms – look at the household responsibility system, or the township and village enterprises. We have learned that each country has to find its own institutional solutions to implement these meta principles. For this reason the institutional paths that we observe will exhibit a great deal of heterogeneity across countries. The sooner economists stop recommending cookie-cutter institutional approaches all over the world, the better. And the sooner we can encourage and empower policy makers in developing county to look at their own problems through their own lenses, rather than through the lenses of Washington or Cambridge, Massachusetts, the better.[37]

## CURRENT RESEARCH

*What are you currently working on?*
There are several ideas that I am excited about right now. One is the question of how you develop industrial competence in a world where technology transfer has this tacit element that I mentioned before. Technology cannot just be pulled off the shelf and imported like a blueprint. You have to develop the capacity to absorb new ideas and technology. When you think about this issue it becomes clear that the initial entrepreneur who figures out, for example, that Pakistan can produce soccer balls very cheaply and sell them to the rest of the world, can only capture a fraction of the huge value created. This is due to the competitive entry that follows as imitators are attracted into the market and excess profits are quickly and easily competed away. So this is a situation that I think is highly endemic to problems of industrial transformation in developing countries. The initial entrepreneur bears the large investment costs associated with developing and putting into operation the new idea, but others can easily join in later without bearing the initial costs. As a result, in this kind of setting, entrepreneurial activity in non-traditional areas may be severely underprovided. What does this imply for government policy with respect to the provision of incentives? This is one set of issues that I am currently working on.[38]

# NOTES

1. I interviewed Professor Rodrik at the American Economics Association Conference held in Atlanta, Georgia, USA, in January 2002.
2. Details of Professor Rodrik's publications and many of his papers can be found on his homepage at Harvard, www.ksg.harvard.edu/rodrik/.
3. See Morris (1979); Brodsky and Rodrik (1981). The PQLI is a composite development indicator combining, with equal weight, infant mortality, literacy and life expectancy.
4. Sen (1999a, 1999b, 2001).
5. Crafts (1999, 2000); DeLong (2000b); Easterlin (2000).
6. For example, see Temple (1999); Jones (2001).
7. See Alesina and Rodrik (1994); Benabou (1996); Barro (2000); Sokoloff and Engerman (2000).
8. Lewis (1954).
9. Alesina and Rodrik (1994); Persson and Tabellini (1994).
10. See Abramovitz (1986); Baumol (1986); Romer (1986); Lucas (2000); Parente and Prescott (2000). See also the recent more optimistic findings on convergence presented by Sala-i-Martin (2002a, 2002b, 2006).
11. See Easterly and Levine (1997); Bloom and Sachs (1998); Collier and Gunning (1999a, 1999b); Rodrik (1999a, 1999b); Collier (2001); Easterly (2001a).
12. King and Levine (1994); Easterly (2001a).
13. See Stiglitz (1998); Snowdon (2001b, 2002a).
14. Williamson, J. (1990).
15. See Rodrik (1993).
16. See Rodrik (2003a).
17. Rodrik and Mayda (2005).
18. See Bhagwati (1998a, 2000, 2002); Snowdon (2001a); Panagariya (2002).
19. See Balassa (1989); Dollar (1992); Edwards (1993, 1998); Sachs and Warner (1995); Harrison (1996); Krueger (1998); Frankel and Romer (1999); Baldwin (2000); Rodriguez and Rodrik (2000); Bhagwati and Srinivasan (2001, 2002); Irwin (2002b).
20. See Rodrik (1995); Bhagwati (1978); Krueger (1978).
21. See Romer (1990, 1993, 1994, 1999); Grossman and Helpman (1991); Rivera-Batiz and Romer (1991a, 1991b); Ben-David and Loewy (1998).
22. See Clark and Wolcott (1999).
23. Dollar and Kraay (2004).
24. Bhagwati (2002).
25. Rodrik (1998b).
26. See Bhagwati (1998b); Furman and Stiglitz (1998); Radelet and Sachs (1998); Rodrik and Velasco (1999); Stiglitz (2000a, 2002a); Kaplan and Rodrik (2001).
27. Kindleberger (1978).
28. Fischer (2001a).
29. See Rodrik (1997, 1998a, 1998c, 1999a, 2000a, 2001a, 2001b).
30. Rodrik (2000a).
31. Friedman, T.L. (1999).
32. Krugman (1999c).
33. For a critique of this view see Irwin (2002b).
34. Eichengreen (1999); Snowdon (2000).
35. See Barro (1996, 1997, 1999); Rodrik (1999d, 2000b, 2000c); Bhagwati (1998a); Olson (2000); Rodrik and Wacziarg (2005).
36. See Rodrik (1999b, 1999c, 2000c).
37. See Rodrik (2000b, 2001a, 2003a, 2003b, 2006); Rodrik and Mukland (2005).
38. Rodrik (2005b).

# Jeffrey Sachs[1]

Jeffrey Sachs received his BA, *summa cum laude*, from Harvard College in 1976, and his MA and PhD degrees from Harvard University, in 1978 and 1980 respectively. Professor Sachs is one of the world's leading economists and is internationally renowned for his research, especially in the fields of monetary economics and international economic development. He is the author/co-author and editor of numerous books and hundreds of academic papers.[2] Professor Sachs joined the Harvard faculty as Assistant Professor in 1980, was promoted to Associate Professor in 1982, then Professor in 1983. He spent over 20 years teaching and researching at Harvard University, where he became Director of the Centre for International Development and Galen L. Stone Professor of International Trade. In 2002 Sachs moved to Columbia University to take up the post as Director of the prestigious Earth Institute,[3] where he is also Quetelet Professor of Sustainable Development and Professor of Health Policy and Management. Currently he is a 'Special Advisor' on the Millennium Development Goals to United Nations Secretary General Kofi Annan and is Director of the UN Millennium Project. Previously, he has been a consultant to several international institutions, including the IMF, the World Bank, the OECD, the World Health Organization, and the United Nations Development Programme. During the last 30 years he has also been an economic adviser to many governments in Latin America, Eastern Europe, the former Soviet Union, Asia and Africa.

In this interview I discuss with Professor Sachs his work over the past 30 years relating to macroeconomic stabilisation, the economics of transition, and several important issues in the field of international economic development, especially as it relates to the sub-Saharan growth tragedy. This key humanitarian issue received enormous coverage in the media, especially throughout 2005, highlighted in particular at the G8 meetings in Gleneagles and worldwide Live 8 Concerts in early July, and the UN World Summit in September.

## BACKGROUND INFORMATION

*How and why did you become an economist?*
I started out in this line of activity 33 years ago as a freshman at Harvard College and quickly fell in love with economics. I think this was because I came to economics, not so much out of an interest in the tools and techniques, although these are important and intriguing, but because of the big important issues with which economics is concerned. As soon as I started travelling and seeing other parts of the world, seeing the various ways that societies are organised, even at a young age I started to ask myself big questions. What works? Why is there a communist world and a capitalist world? What helps societies achieve internal peace and cohesion, and material well-being? Why are some developing countries failing to achieve satisfactory progress? What makes for good public policy? These are the sorts of questions that got me engaged with economics very early on. I am still looking for answers to many of these types of questions today and this makes economics endlessly captivating.

*Were there any particular economists, events or ideas that influenced you during this early period?*
Yes, one particular experience did have a big effect on my thinking. I decided to visit a pen-pal in East Berlin at the end of high school. My exposure for a week to socialist society was a big eye-opener. I was absolutely befuddled by the experience (*laughter*). It also made me realise just how little I actually knew about my own country. During that whole week I was besieged with questions from young East Germans. Why do you have unemployment in the USA when we do not? Why do you have poor people and inequality in the USA? I could not challenge or give satisfactory answers to these questions about my own country! I did not even know what the facts were or what the appropriate framework was to think about those kinds of questions. At the end of that trip I was taken to a tourist store to spend my East German marks and I spotted some books. One was

*Historical and Dialectical Materialism* by Karl Marx, which I bought, took home with me, and tried to make sense of. By the time I got back to the USA, and was preparing to go off to Harvard, I had been assigned, as fresh-man reading, Joseph Schumpeter's classic work, *Capitalism, Socialism, and Democracy.*[4] I remember being mesmerised by the ideas in that book, and also not understanding much of it. But at the same time I could see that these were issues that I really wanted to understand. By the time I began my studies at Harvard I was already overflowing with questions about eco-nomics. I continue to be fascinated by economics and regard being an econ-omist a remarkably challenging and satisfying profession.

## EARLY WORK

*It is very evident from reading your book,* The End of Poverty, *as well as some of your early papers, that you have a great interest in history, in particular economic history.*[5] *In your 1999 paper, 'Twentieth-Century Political Economy: A Brief History of Global Capitalism', you argue that for the first 25 years or so after the Second World War, it is evident that the wrong lessons had been learned about the Great Depression. In particular you say that Keynes was mistaken to argue that such massive instability is inherent to the capitalist system. As a consequence you say that Keynes's* General Theory of Employment, Interest, and Money *helped to propagate the view that the 'Great Depression was a general situation of market economies rather than a one time fluke of grotesque proportions'.*[6] *In what ways did Keynes's disillu-sioned vision of laissez-faire capitalism influence post-war ideas, in particular those relating to economic development?*
My education at Harvard left me with a tremendous admiration for Keynes and I still regard him as the greatest political economist of the twentieth century, and perhaps the greatest clinical economist of all time, in terms of his ability to read most situations. Like Keynes, I believe that governments have an important role to play in market economies. However, I think one of the most interesting observations about John Maynard Keynes was made by Friedrich von Hayek, whose ideas, unlike those of Keynes, I do not tend to follow. Hayek said that one of Keynes's really important mis-takes was to call his masterwork the 'General Theory' rather than 'A Tract for Our Times'. That is quite an important and astute observation because the Great Depression was, *sui generis*, the largest disruption that industrial societies have experienced since the start of the Industrial Revolution. Thank goodness it has never been repeated. Therefore it was probably not fitting for there to be a '*General*' theory about such a unique event result-ing from a confluence of extraordinary events that led to a severe crisis of

capitalism during the 1930s. Although Keynes did more than anybody else to analyse this event, several important lessons were *not* learned and unfortunately had an adverse influence on policy choices made in many developing countries. For example, in his 1933 lecture, 'National Self Sufficiency', Keynes clearly had lost faith in free trade.[7] It reflected a loss of nerve that is completely understandable given the circumstances of that period. However, unfortunately the loss of faith in free trade continued after the Second World War and experimentation with protectionism and import substitution-led industrialisation strategies became widespread, especially among developing countries, with very debilitating effects. Even darker lessons were mis-learned with respect to the relative merits of socialism versus capitalist market organisation. The example of the Great Depression was used not only to make the sensible case for stabilisation policy; it was also used, though not by Keynes himself, to support arguments in favour of state ownership on a massive scale. So this calamitous event, which was the result of a confluence of historical processes after the First World War, especially the inability of the Gold Standard to support the international economic system, was taken much more generally as an indictment of trade, markets and capitalism.[8] This inevitably led to a tremendous amount of mischief and misunderstanding that took a long time to rectify.

*During the 1970s the problem of stagflation dominated economists' attention, and the poor macroeconomic performance of many of the leading economies during the 1970s and early 1980s contributed to a growing disillusionment with interventionist policies in general. It was towards the end of this period of instability that your 1985 co-authored book with Michael Bruno, the* Economics of World-wide Stagflation, *was published.[9] Looking back, what perspective do you now have on the macroeconomic instability of the 1970s?*
Three things happened in the early to mid-1970s that are still not easy to disentangle. First, there was the collapse of the Bretton Woods exchange rate system, which represented a huge monetary shock because the dollar could no longer serve as the stable anchor for the international monetary system given the high inflation in the USA. As the Bretton Woods system collapsed there was a huge explosion of monetary growth and high inflation in many of the industrial economies. Second, there was a sharp decline of productivity growth that lasted for 20 years. The productivity slowdown was not understood then and it is still not fully understood now. Third, there were the OPEC oil price shocks of 1973–74 and 1979 and what that meant for the world economy. My research during those years was focused on trying to understand something about the balance of impact of those three forces. The book with Michael Bruno gave a great deal of attention to the supply

shocks. In a sense our treatment was not Keynesian because we put emphasis on shifts of the aggregate supply curve rather than shifts of the aggregate demand curve. I think in that book we made some headway in understanding the impact of supply shocks. Neither we, nor anybody else, understood the significant change in productivity trends that turned out to be reasonably long term. For me, another important feature of that whole period was the growing emphasis among economists of the influence of comparative institutions. My 1980 PhD dissertation at Harvard focused on how labour markets in Europe and the USA had reacted differently to those supply shocks. I became fascinated by differences in institutions as a basis for explaining differential economic performance. This in turn raised my awareness of the historical, political and social roots of different institutions. So this period for me was one where I was trying to broaden the range of issues that macroeconomics deals with, including paying more attention to the impact of supply shocks and the role of institutional design.

*At that point, did you anticipate that you would broaden your analytical approach even further to take into account the impact on economic performance of such factors as geography, climate and disease?*
For me this period was the very beginning of my appreciation of how location influences economic outcomes and why a single model can never be satisfactory for comparing the performance of different economies. It began with my research on labour markets, but in more recent years I have focused increasingly on physical geography and ecology. In my own mind I can see the relation of my current work with that in the early 1980s. In trying to account for comparative economic performance I find that the connecting thread in my research is the emphasis given to the structural characteristics of economies.

## BOLIVIA 1985

*In 1984–85 Bolivia experienced a serious hyperinflation. You were invited to Bolivia to offer advice on how to bring to an end this hyperinflation and duly arrived in La Paz in July 1985.[10] In offering advice to the Bolivian government, and in drawing up a draft plan of action, how and to what extent were you influenced by the Keynesian, monetarist and new classical contributions to the macroeconomics literature?*
When I think back, it is amazing how I compartmentalised this challenge. Of course I knew Bolivia was poor, but I did not at that time think of myself as a development economist or one concerned with long-run growth issues. Rather, I saw myself as a macroeconomist who was technically equipped to

offer advice on situations of extreme monetary instability, in this case a hyperinflation which over two years had reached about 24 000 per cent. For such episodes monetary theory must be at the centre of any coherent analysis. So my main reference points related to the monetarist work of Milton Friedman and Philip Cagan. Also crucial was the wonderful essay by Thomas Sargent, 'The Ends of Four Big Hyperinflations', which I took with me to La Paz.[11] Sargent, who is usually thought of as a rational expectations new classical macroeconomist, showed how hyperinflations can be stopped very quickly. But the work of Keynes, in his *Economic Consequences of the Peace* and *Tract on Monetary Reform*, also greatly influenced my thinking.[12] In 1919 Keynes had emphasised how the debt burden imposed on Germany at Versailles could undermine the chances, not only of Germany's economic recovery, but also the recovery of Europe as a whole.

*What were the essential elements in your recommended strategy?*
Initially my focus was on the short-term question: how do you end this hyperinflation? Since the proximate cause of any hyperinflation is excessive monetary growth, that obviously had to be the starting point in my approach to drawing up a strategy. Excessive monetary growth usually has its origins in persistent government fiscal deficits. In Bolivia's case we agreed on a package of fiscal measures combined with an increase in the price of oil that was specifically aimed at increasing the flow of government revenue. The programme was initiated at the end of August 1985 and within a week the hyperinflation was over. In 1985 the Bolivian government was bankrupt and unable to service its foreign debts. I also helped to organise a strategy of debt cancellation. There is one other important point that I want to make relating to my Bolivian experience. The more I get involved with practical matters, the greater is my disenchantment with academic economics for not having a real feel for what the crucial issues are. Many economists have a tendency to get into debates which are not, in my experience, about the relevant issues. For example, I remember my frustration relating to the Bolivian situation when, some three years later, following the successful stabilisation programme, several economists began attributing slow economic growth in Bolivia to the chosen exchange rate policy. This was so unrealistic. Did those economists critical of the strategy have any knowledge of the geographical constraints facing Bolivia? Here is a land-locked country, half of which is 12 000 feet up in the Andes and half is in tropical lowlands, facing very high transportation costs. While altitude does not affect monetary theory and the analysis of hyperinflation, it certainly impacts on the potential for economic development and growth. While Adam Smith in his *Wealth of Nations* was well aware of the constraints imposed by geography on a country's ability to integrate with the

rest of the world, modern economists were quick to offer advice that largely ignored these geographical realities.[13] So after that experience I began to seriously question the quality of academic analysis (*laughter*).

## THE ECONOMICS OF TRANSITION: POLAND, RUSSIA AND CHINA

*In the late 1980s and early 1990s you became heavily involved with problems of transition, acting as an economic adviser in both Poland and Russia during this period.*[14] *Did your work in Bolivia prepare you in any way for this enormously difficult task?*

Yes, my work in Bolivia had forced me to think about longer-term issues in ways that I had not anticipated. I began to think about the underlying causes of poverty and economic development, and about the implications of Bolivia's geography, given its position as a landlocked mountainous country. I also started to think about the role of globalisation in economic development because it was impossible to think about Bolivia's longer-term prospects without taking into consideration its links with the outside world. During the 1980s the liberalisation of trade, which I fully support, was becoming a big issue. Although I had not gone to Bolivia to look at longer-term development issues, by acting as an adviser to the head of Bolivia's economic team, who was interested in broad-based liberalisation, it was inevitable that I would get engaged with very practical questions to do with globalisation, although we were not using that terminology back then. So by the time I was invited to Poland, in April 1989, I started to have a real sense that the essential issue for Poland was how it was going to relate to the rest of the world. In Bolivia you could not ignore the geographical realities that it was a landlocked mountainous economy that had historically been a relatively closed society. In Poland it was a case of reconnecting the Polish economy with the rest of Europe. I immediately likened the situation in Poland in 1989 to that of Spain *circa* 1955 in terms of land mass, size of population, distance from the centre of the European Union, GDP per capita, and its predominantly Catholic religion. In 1989 Poland was also returning to Europe after being in the Soviet sphere for 40 years, while Spain in 1976 was returning to Europe after 40 years, of fascist dictatorship under Franco. But while Spain after 1976 had been quickly reintegrated into the mainstream of European cultural, political and economic life, Poland had been artificially kept apart. So I began to see that the Polish revolution was about reconnecting with Europe just as post-Franco Spain had reconnected with Europe after 1976. My advice was therefore tailored to this reality.

*To what extent has the focus on 'gradualism v. shock therapy' offered an accurate summary of the two broad paths available to the former communist economies in their objective of creating a viable capitalist market economy?*
When I got involved with policy advice in Poland, all of a sudden every discussion began to be framed in terms of the shock therapy v. gradualism dichotomy. This really surprised me because this is almost entirely an academic debate, and I have to say that I use those words in the pejorative sense (*laughter*). The distinction drawn between big bang and gradualism is a gross oversimplification of the whole question of the pace and sequencing of reform. Clearly some of the measures that I was recommending needed to be done quickly. The real 'shock therapy' was the idea that you could move quickly to currency convertibility rather than over a ten-year period, as happened in post-Second World War Western Europe with the European Payments Union. I advised a quick move to currency convertibility because it was necessary to re-engage Poland with the international trading system. The zloty was devalued and unified with the black market rate, and then pegged to the dollar, and the new peg was successfully defended by a 1 billion dollar zloty stabilisation fund.[15] Other important matters, such as privatisation, were obviously going to take a long time. I remember the first document that I prepared on this suggested that privatisation would be a five-to-ten-year, rather than an overnight, process. Other changes, such as Poland's whole mode of thinking and organisation, moving from a communist structure to a market economy structure, were going to take much longer, 20 or more years. So I agree that there were debates on these matters, but I have always regarded labels such as 'big bang', 'shock therapy' and 'gradualism' as totally misleading. Indeed, the labels struck me as odd. The one real innovation about speed that I introduced was the idea of quick currency convertibility. That move was a great success and played a crucial role in helping Poland engage in trade, fill up the empty shelves in the shops, and stimulate private-sector-led economic growth. I believe that none of us knew much about how best to plan for privatisation on a massive scale. Actual Polish experience proved to be better than any theory, by far.

*Do you think that from a historical perspective Poland's reforms will be viewed as highly successful?*
In 1989 Poland was not only in chaos but felt to be in chaos by the Poles themselves. Most visibly the shops were empty. There were profound concerns about whether the country could even hold together, whether there would be civil war, even whether there would be starvation. Solidarity, the leading political authority in the country, was very reluctant to take power early on. That's how much fear there was, and many commentators thought that the whole situation was uncontrollable. Actual results vindicate the

strategy adopted, with some important innovations and political economy successes. For example, my recommendations in negotiating a big cancellation of Poland's debt as well as the idea of establishing the 1 billion dollar zloty stabilisation fund were a success. The privatisation process turned out to be unlike anything any of us expected, with some hits and some misses, but was much better than the disastrous privatisation strategy in Russia.[16] So I think the Polish transition has on the whole been very successful. Basically Poland got reconnected to Western Europe. On the other hand, those Poles aged over 45 in 1990, who had been trained for life in a socialist economy, never found a happy or comfortable footing in the new market economy. This is one of the most unfortunate legacies of a half-century of disastrous economic management under a communist system.

*Some critics argued that institutional reform was neglected in the reform strategies recommended to transition economies. How do you react to this line of criticism?*
I sometimes find it very frustrating to listen to academics talking about these issues. I am constantly asked, 'Don't you know that countries need institutions and the rule of law?' To me this is obvious and apparent to anyone with their eyes open. I was, and I am, well aware of the importance of institutions and the rule of law. It's all in Adam Smith! But an economic adviser has to be concerned with practical steps about how to proceed in real historical circumstances.[17]

*The Russian privatisation has deservedly received a bad press. What went wrong?*
First let me emphasise and repeat what I believed *should* have happened before I discuss what *actually* happened. Those are two very different things. I favoured a very quick privatisation in Russia of the non-resource sector of the economy. So this privatisation strategy would specifically *exclude* the oil, gas, diamonds, nickel and other raw material sectors. These sectors were all vital contributors of tax revenue to the public finances of Russia. Indeed they were the main flow of income for the state, and these revenues financed the pension and healthcare systems. On the technical side I did not think that these sectors were an important priority for privatisation because I believed that these vast enterprises could be successfully managed within a state ownership framework, as they are in many other parts of the world. So what I recommended for privatisation were the smaller enterprises such as the garment factories, the umbrella factories, the clock factories, the raincoat factories and so forth. These smaller enterprises should be privatised through schemes such as vouchers or worker–management buyouts. I thought it was very important to get some

private ownership fairly early on. The outcome of that part of the privatisation process was disappointing and did not work out very well. Some of
the things that I recommended were done, but overall I was not too
impressed with the results. But the privatisation of the energy and raw
material sectors was an utter disaster. There was a massive political and
corrupt grab of the real sources of cash flow and wealth in the economy.
The oil, gas and diamonds sectors should never have been in the frame for
privatisation and I was staunchly against this from the beginning. The
voucher and management buyout ideas were certainly not appropriate for
these high-value sectors. I knew from my experience in Bolivia and many
other countries that these sectors were the core of Russia's public finance.
In 1995, some 18 months after I had left as an adviser, the government
implemented the disastrous privatisation strategy that in reality amounted
to the organised theft, by a group of oligarchs, of the energy and mineral
sectors. This strategy consisted of a set of policies that were obviously
corrupt at the time. An amoral elite acting in a country that lacked any
organised opposition or civil society seized this easy opportunity to steal
valuable natural resources, and there was a lot to steal! Although I was no
longer directly involved day to day with Russia, I obviously still knew a lot
of what was going on and I recall making vociferous complaints to the
IMF, the World Bank and the US Treasury about the corrupt grab of valuable assets that was happening in Russia. Basically the US government and
other Western powers were not interested because they thought that this
action would somehow help strengthen the position of Boris Yeltsin. To me
it looked more like the putting into practice of Proudhon's famous dictum,
'Property is theft'. In Russia the oligarchs had taken this literally.

*What do you say to those who took the view that it did not really matter who
gets the assets so long as they end up privately owned and in the long run things
will work themselves out?*
I regard that position as sheer nonsense and could only appeal to people
who do not appreciate the fact that societies are held together by ethical
standards, by legitimacy, by a sense of fairness and basic political standards. The bottom line is this. The situation in Russia was very complex. It
was not simply four times Poland in terms of scale. It was much more complicated because of the sharp internal divisions and lack of international
support. The voucher privatisation that I supported early on was a
muddled affair but not disastrous because not too much of a problem can
result for the Russian economy if the privatisation of a raincoat factory
does not go to plan. And it is hard to know what realistic alternatives there
were at that time. When you are sitting there and there are some 30 000
enterprises without any management guidance available because the Soviet

Union no longer exists, it is very difficult to know the best way forward. The key point is that there is no excuse for what happened in 1995. You do not give away billions of dollars worth of oil and gas assets to a small group of oligarchs and expect a good outcome. Russia is still having to grapple with the consequences of that strategy. For example, who does one side with in the recent tension between President Putin and the oligarchs? It's an awful choice.

*As an adviser you must have been very frustrated by what you were witness-ing in Russia during this period.*
Absolutely. For a lot of reasons that I discuss in *The End of Poverty*, almost nothing that I said was actually applied in the first two years because the domestic political situation in Russia was horrendously more complex than in Poland. Also, the Western international community, particularly the USA, was considerably more hostile towards Russia on geopolitical grounds that I did not agree with. My hope that a 'grand bargain' would be struck between Russia and the USA, that the USA would provide financial help to cushion the hardships that would result in the short term provided Russia accelerated its reforms, never materialised in the amount needed. The USA was simply not interested in helping Russia in the same way that it had helped Poland. My previous experience as an adviser in Bolivia and Poland had taught me that when a country is in a desperate economic crisis, both dramatic internal reforms and outside aid is needed to have any chance of success. Keynes had seen this clearly in the case of Germany after the punitive Versailles Treaty in 1919. Unfortunately the US government was blind to this reality after the collapse of the Soviet Union in December 1991. This was very frustrating given the high risks involved with such a strategy.

*What important lessons as an adviser did this whole Russian episode teach you?*
I have learned one very important lesson from this whole episode. The lesson is that no matter what one actually says and recommends, it will be the outcomes that are attributed to you. Whether your actual advice was followed, or completely ignored and followed in its antithesis, does not seem to matter. So when these enterprises were stolen by the oligarchs, many people said to me, 'How could you let that happen?' In reality, the pri-vatisation strategy was the polar opposite of what I had actually advised. So there is still much confusion on this matter. Let me take this opportu-nity to put it on the record that I have made a lot of recommendations in recent years for controlling malaria. If these recommendations are not taken up I do not want to end up being blamed for malaria in Africa![18]

*At what point did you decide to end your role as an economic adviser to Russia?*

I acted as an economic adviser to Russia for two years, 1992–93, and resigned at the end of 1993. In fact in 1993 I only stayed on at the request of the finance minister because I could already tell from my experience in 1992 that the complex political economy problems of the Russian situation were way beyond those I had been dealing with in Poland. The sheer scale of the problems, the thousand-year political legacy of autocratic rule, the 75-year legacy of rigid central planning, the lack of any civil society, and the geographical, cultural and linguistic diversity of Russia, all meant that there were going to be no easy options in the transition process. Virtually everything in Russia needed an overhaul. But, at the same time, I also firmly believe that in life you should try to do your best even when you know that the odds of success are sometimes not great. The idea is to help if you can, and that's what I was doing in Russia in 1992–93. When I left at the end of 1993 the young talented reformers led by Yegor Gaidar had been thrown out and Victor Chernomyrdin, a dull Soviet-era apparatchik, whom I did not trust, for very good reasons, had become Gaidar's successor.

*In a recent paper, published in 2005, Andrei Shleifer and Daniel Treisman argue that the commonly held view that Russia is a disastrous and threatening failure as a transition economy is incorrect. The reality, they argue, is that Russia has successfully been transformed from a communist dictatorship to a multi-party democracy, and from a centrally planned economy to a capitalist market-based economy, in a relatively short period of time. Therefore they conclude that Russia is now a typical middle-income capitalist economy, and many of its characteristics, including corruption levels, are normal for its stage of development. Do you agree with this assessment?*

No, I do not. I witnessed first hand the good orderly reform strategy in Poland. Even though there was chaos at first, Poland eventually experienced continuing rising living standards, including improving health conditions, without the system falling apart and the legitimacy of the political order being brought into disrepute. That is what I consider to be a successful reform strategy. In my view Russia did not have a successful decade of reform. Life expectancy fell sharply, anxiety and stress levels were extremely high, and corruption was massive. I suppose one can take the Olympian view that history sorts all of these things out, that Russia is now growing and is a market economy. But I think that the standards of economics should be a lot higher than that. As an adviser you are there to help reduce the transition costs. If you simply take the view that everything will be allright in the long run, then you are not saying very much. By now I have seen a lot of successful reform and I have also observed unsuccessful cases, as in Russia and Yugoslavia. In the case of Yugoslavia we saw a massive social, political and economic failure induced by the most irresponsible vitriolic demagogy and appeal to violence that I have seen close up. These cases are failures. Russia may in the end, as Boris Yeltsin always hoped, become a normal democratic market economy. But that in no way absolves responsibility for what happened during the 1990s, which to my mind was not economics at its finest. I do not hold myself accountable because the chosen strategy was not what I advised, and I would not present the Russian example as a case of successful reform. Having said all that, the worst did not happen. Many thought there would be civil war. There has been much violence, for example in Chechnya, but there have also been successes. But I cannot help thinking that Russian society could have been happier, healthier and more prosperous today if a sounder economic strategy had been applied and supported internationally. The responsibilities for why that did not happen are extremely complex. So although I am cautiously optimistic about the future, I would not call Russia a successful example of transition based on what actually happened during the 1990s.

*A popular misconception among many transition commentators is that China after 1978 chose a superior gradualist path of reform compared to Russia, the implication being that Russia should have learned from this and imitated China's successful strategy. But surely such comparisons are extremely naïve given the huge structural differences that existed between these two countries at the start of their reform process. So, in reality, the Chinese transition strategy was never going to be a viable option for Russia.*
That's right, but what is also not widely appreciated is the fact that Gorbachev had already tried gradualism between 1985 and 1990. It failed! Hungary's attempt at gradual reforms, the so-called 'goulash socialism', also failed even earlier.[19] Anyone who wants to assess the options available to China and Russia in 1978 and 1991 respectively must take the following facts into account.[20] In 1978 China was still a predominantly agricultural economy with about 80 per cent of the population living in rural areas. Therefore the structure of the Chinese economy in 1978 was more like the structure of the Russian economy before 1914. In China only 20 per cent of the population worked in state-owned enterprises in urban areas. Conversely, in Russia virtually all of the working population were employed in state-owned enterprises. China implemented a 'big bang' liberalisation of the large communally owned agricultural sector in the late 1970s. This really was shock therapy! This significantly boosted agricultural output and also allowed many workers to migrate to the special economic zones along the coast that were to become the engine of labour-intensive export-led growth. Taking advantage of its 'backwardness', China followed a path of nor-

mal economic development as surplus labour transferred from the low-productivity rural sector to the high-productivity emerging industrial sector.[21] So China used a 'two-track' strategy of shock therapy in agriculture and gradual reform in the relatively small state-owned enterprises sector. In Russia there was no large non-state sector to be liberalised. Soviet-style agriculture was large scale and capital intensive. Unlike China, Russia had an enormous, heavily subsidised, state-owned industrial sector in need of liberalisation. So in almost every respect the reform strategy in Russia was going to be much more complicated and conflictual. The unavoidable problem for Russia was how to implement massive structural adjustment rather than initiate normal economic development. I have also argued that China's experimental institutions, such as the 'household responsibility system', 'land leasehold', 'township and village enterprises', 'special economic zones' and 'liberalised state-owned enterprises', represent a half-way house in terms of institutional development resulting from ideological differences within the Chinese political leadership. I expect those institutions to evolve and change so that they eventually converge towards those in other successful East Asian capitalist market economies.[22] So the Chinese strategy was never a viable option for the former communist economies of Eastern Europe and the Soviet Union. Remember also, unlike Russia, the Chinese have yet to accomplish the perhaps more difficult task of political liberalisation.

## THE INFLUENCE OF GEOGRAPHY AND INSTITUTIONS

*You have been involved in a long debate in the literature concerned with the deeper, more fundamental determinants of economic growth and development.[23] This debate has focused on the relative importance of geography v. institutions. As you have already stressed earlier, economists have for too long neglected the influence on growth and development of geographical factors such as climate, location and topography. But there are cases where institutional differences clearly dominate, such as North and South Korea and East and West Germany, where very different living standards are observed alongside very similar geographical features. How do these cases fit into your argument?*

There is no question that institutional differences are definitely the most important factor in explaining the gaps in living standards between North and South Korea, and also those gaps that were generated between East and West Germany during the cold war period. They also explain the differences in lots of other cases, such as Austria and Hungary. But institutions are not the most important factor in explaining the gaps between Mali and France, Ethiopia and the USA, and Tanzania and the UK. This is not an argument about geographical determinism because many things contribute to the economic development outcomes on our planet. The idea that there is a single-factor explanation which can satisfactorily account for the pattern of world development amounts to a preposterous misunderstanding of complex systems. The idea that explanations of economic development can be reduced to one variable is one of the shocking trivialisations of this field that has occurred in recent years. I find this more and more amazing the more I find out about the world, and it highlights the fact that economic analysis can too often become detached from reality. To pose such a question as: what determines economic growth and development, geography or institutions? Seems to me ridiculous! Economic progress is affected by geography, *and* institutions *and* geopolitics *and* policies *and* history *and* accident. A large number of complex forces will shape a complex system. Economic development is about complex adaptive evolving systems; that's what we are dealing with. So there are many determinants of the performance of complex systems. The fact that people don't choose to live in the Sahara desert, but do live on the river plains of the Nile or the Ganges in vast numbers is not because of differences in governance. It's because in one place you can't grow food and in the others you can. The fact that people in the majority of mountainous landlocked regions all over the world tend to be more isolated and find it very difficult or near impossible to engage in international trade, and attract foreign direct investment, is not because of governance; it's because of transport costs.[24] Economics and economists need to understand that there are physical realities in this world, not just social systems. Physical realities shape how production processes work, what transportation costs are, how communications work, what diseases occur, what population densities occur, how many people can be sustained, where cities are located, how they trade with one another and so on. Adam Smith understood all of this very clearly, and his book is about geography as well as market institutions. Most economists seem to forget or ignore this. Smith never claimed that economic progress was just about free trade and markets. He also described the implications of being landlocked compared to being located on, or near, the coast. I just don't understand our field when it ignores these obviously important and well-established factors that influence the world and regional patterns of development that we observe. Practitioners dealing with regional development, transportation and public health issues know all about the importance of geography. Why has it been a lot more difficult to develop western China than it has been to stimulate development in coastal China?[25] Why, in spite of its huge land resources, does economic activity in the USA congregate predominantly in coastal regions?[26] It's mainly geography!

*There are two main strands in the geography of economic development literature. One strand, associated mainly with the work of economists such as Paul Krugman and Tony Venables,[27] highlights increasing returns and cumulative causation types of influences in the spirit of Gunnar Myrdal and Nicholas Kaldor.[28] I think that Michael Porter's work on clusters and competitiveness can also be linked to this line of thinking.[29] In the other strand, which you are associated with, emphasis is placed on the direct impact of physical geography, climate and ecology.[30] In what ways can the two approaches be linked?*

Paul Krugman follows a long tradition that begins by asking: if we start out by observing a geographical area that is a large, undifferentiated, homogeneous plain, where economic activity can take place, are there reasons why clustering will occur? And there are good economic reasons, such as agglomeration economies and increasing returns to scale, why firms and people may choose to live close together. Krugman's models are simply massive amplifiers of what the initial conditions and geography have already done to disadvantage some places relative to others. In Krugman's models, human and physical capital leaves disadvantaged places rather than accumulating and contributing to development. This literature can explain how you can get trapped if you are isolated and operate at insufficient scale. In such a situation you can generate cumulative outcomes where success breeds success, and failure breeds failure. In a lot of Krugman's models he starts out with two locations, A and B. If A gets an initial advantage, then, as a result of cumulative processes, B disappears from view. I am saying pretty much the same thing but I start out from a different perspective, which is the reality that the world is not a homogeneous undifferentiated plain. There are seas, rivers, plains, mountains, valleys and deserts. There are cold, wet, dry and hot climates. There are places where malaria thrives and places where malaria is not transmitted. In my view, extremely difficult geography can lead to poverty traps where the poverty is so extreme that a fight for survival is a day-to-day occurrence. This is what I have witnessed first hand when I have been in rain-fed, inland, tropical sub-Saharan Africa. The confluence of barriers to development there is huge. Enormous transport costs, a massive disease burden, the fragility of agriculture, a drought-prone climate and lack of irrigation are the realities. To me that adds up to a disaster. I believe that these geographical influences are important in shaping the pattern of world history and development, and of our current circumstances. How could they not be influential? I don't think that anyone would disagree that in the pre-industrial era there were good reasons why civilisations grew up on river plains. There were good reasons why the Egyptians lived alongside the Nile rather than in the desert. It had nothing to do with governance; it was to do with the practicalities of growing food. But somehow economists' models have become too divorced from the physical realities in which they are placed. Maybe sitting writing a textbook in a university in the USA, an advanced urban economy where transportation problems have to a large extent been overcome in relative terms by the advance of technology, we can justify writing down production functions that include technology, capital and labour, but that ignore natural resources and the physical environment. But if you actually go to poor countries, where the vast majority of the people are living off the land, growing food for their own consumption, relying on inadequate rainfall, fighting the ravages of malaria on a day-to-day basis, where biomass is the only source of energy, then the physical ecology becomes a profoundly important shaper of life.

*So by giving prominence to geographical factors in your explanation of poverty traps, as you mentioned earlier, you are not advocating a new form of geographical determinism.*
I am not a geographical determinist. The main point that I make in *The End of Poverty* and in previous work is that even when you identify geographically related causes of poverty, this does not mean that you are advocating geographical determinism. The essence of what we have learned from the experience of the developed world is that there are investments that can, to an important extent, alleviate or even eventually overcome these circumstances. At least we know how to take measures that could keep millions more people alive and healthy. With a real effort we can help these unfortunate countries have some chance of development for themselves and even more for future generations. In my view the essence of a poverty trap is the following: you find yourself in an extraordinary situation, you can see what needs to be done in terms of the investment requirements, but you cannot afford to make those investments. This is not geographical determinism. What I am saying is that physical geography in a variety of manifestations is shaping circumstances and that geography must be taken into account in the design and financing of public policy. The poorest countries of the world need a positive response from the rich nations to help them face those geographical challenges and escape from their poverty traps.

*As a student at Harvard, were you ever made aware of the importance of these geographical influences on growth and development?*
No. During my training as an economist at Harvard no one ever mentioned or seriously discussed the possibility that geography might impact on economic performance. None of this was evident to me when I started out on

my research into development issues. This was not an intellectual pursuit where I began by saying that geography was really important. I was working for three years in Bolivia before I realised that I should take more account of Bolivia's geography, that it was an isolated mountainous economy. Thank goodness monetary policy works at 12 000 feet; otherwise the stabilisation plan would have failed (*laughter*). I just had not thought about what the significance was of an economy being in a geographical situation like Bolivia. But now I have seen the world as it is from the perspective of more than 100 countries. I have seen terrorist-occupied highlands, I have seen tropical lowlands, I have seen deserts, temperate climates and the tundra. Basically, with this 20-year experience, especially having worked in the low-income world where the physical boundaries of life are so incredibly powerful in shaping survival, the non-homogeneous aspects of the world strike me as being fundamentally important. There are places in the world that have truly difficult physical environments. Countries such as Afghanistan, Mali and Bolivia come to mind. The fact that these countries are impoverished is no accident, and to blame their situation on institutions alone seems to me to be preposterous. It represents a real misunderstanding of what this is all about.

*What about the case of Botswana, a country that is frequently hailed as a success story because of its successful policies and institutions?*
The geography v. institutions debate reaches ludicrous extremes at times. In one of Dani Rodrik's edited volumes[31] the case of Botswana is used as if it was some sort of proof against the geography hypothesis. Botswana is a landlocked tropical country, but also has good governance and a relatively low level of corruption, and is a peaceful society. It has had very successful growth and is one of the few success stories in sub-Saharan Africa. To me this example illustrates how our profession has lost its basic diagnostics. Botswana was basically a hunter–gatherer society in the Kalahari Desert until diamonds were discovered and exploited. Without the diamonds there is mass poverty. The discovery of diamonds made Botswana. It is also true that many other countries with diamonds have ended up with civil war. So Botswana had good governance and diamonds which helped it reach a per capita income of about $3000. It did not prevent it from becoming the global epicentre of the world AIDS pandemic. Botswana has become the highest AIDS-prevalence country in the entire world. This is clearly geography and institutions interacting. The desire to find single causes of complex phenomena is simply bewildering to me.

*In several papers you have investigated another aspect of development related to geographical factors, namely the 'natural-resource curse'. It has been observed that many countries that are richly endowed with natural resources fail to develop or grow as successfully as other countries that have few natural resources.[32] What are the main reasons for this curse?*

The evidence in favour of the natural-resource curse is quite strong, particularly in countries such as Venezuela and Nigeria. Resource abundance, contrary to what might be expected, seems to be an important determinant of economic failure. Explanations include crowding-out mechanisms via positive wealth shocks from the natural-resource sector that in turn drives up the prices of non-traded goods. This feeds into wage and other input costs, and squeezes the profitability of traded manufacturing activities. The decline in manufacturing then leads to slower export-led growth. Other explanations focus on the political-economy determinants of the rent-seeking behaviour and corruption stimulated by the opportunities for rapid enrichment that vast oil revenues offer, especially in non-democratic states where politicians are much less accountable.

## SUB-SAHARAN AFRICA'S POVERTY TRAP

*The tragedy of sub-Saharan Africa's poverty is now at the centre of international attention and debate.[33] In your 2004 co-authored paper, 'Ending Africa's Poverty Trap', you argue that tropical Africa is 'simply too poor to grow at all' and that what is needed is a 'big push' in order to break this poverty trap. When you set out your theory of Africa's poverty trap the analysis and language remind me very much of the early development literature of the 1940s and 1950s when Ragnar Nurkse and Richard Nelson popularised the idea of a 'vicious circle of poverty' and a 'low-level equilibrium trap'; Harvey Leibenstein also talked of a 'critical minimum effort'; Walt Rostow famously invoked the idea of 'preconditions' for a 'take-off' into 'self-sustaining growth', and Paul Rosenstein-Rodan advocated that a 'big push' is necessary if the poor countries are to get the process of economic growth started.[34] What leads you to the conclusion that a 'big push' is necessary to get growth started?*

You are exactly right about the link with the earlier development literature. In 1956 Richard Nelson published his great paper on poverty traps at the same time that Robert Solow published his seminal paper on neoclassical growth theory.[35] To me, economic theory is about having tools to understand the range of possible diagnostics. Theory alone, in almost all cases, does not allow us to identify the nature of the world. It reminds us of the range of possibilities. So there are a lot of poverty trap theories such as Nurkse's idea of a vicious circle of poverty, Nelson's demographic trap model, Murphy, Shleifer and Vishny's increasing returns–big push type model, and Ben-David's low saving rate in subsistence economy model.[36] What I try to do in my work is help to choose which among these various theories can help us understand the situation in tropical Africa. Clearly the USA is not stuck in a poverty trap and these types of model do not apply to the developed countries of the world. I don't think Argentina is stuck in a poverty trap. It is certainly stuck, but not because of a poverty trap. But Rwanda *is* stuck in a poverty trap and for most sub-Saharan African countries nothing short of a massive coordinated development effort, a big push, is needed if sustained poverty reduction and the achievement of the Millennium Development Goals is to be realised within an acceptable time horizon. The conventional Solow model is not an appropriate tool of analysis for poverty trap situations.

*What are the deficiencies of the Solow growth model in these situations of extreme impoverishment?*
Typically economists begin by setting out the basic Solow model and then introduce the Inada conditions, which say that the marginal product of capital becomes infinite at low levels of capital per worker.[37] That makes the curves in the familiar Solow diagram just the right shape so that you do not get a trap.[38] Remarkably, it took me 20 years to realise the implications of that innocently slipped-in mathematical condition. I have visited lots of impoverished places and I am absolutely convinced that the marginal product of capital is not infinite! For small investments it is more likely to be zero because if a village is 100 kilometres in the hinterland, and you pave the first kilometre of road, it doesn't get you very far. Some minimum threshold of physical and human capital is necessary before modern production can begin. So I am prepared to believe that there are indivisibilities, increasing returns to scale and very low marginal productivities to capital in impoverished environments. This problem is compounded by savings behaviour at subsistence levels of income. Only when households can meet their basic needs will they begin to save. Furthermore, population growth increases as incomes rise from very low levels. A combination of the need for a minimum capital threshold together with savings and population traps can cause a serious poverty trap. So let us all make a greater effort to understand that our economic theories give us a menu of possibilities rather than definitive answers. Unfortunately, the standard way of teaching the subject of economic growth does not help. The conventional Solow model works reasonably well in describing the growth experience of developed countries, but has an unjustified inbuilt optimism with respect to the prospects of convergence for very poor countries.

# THE ROLE OF FOREIGN AID

*An explicit theme in your* End of Poverty *book, and other recent work, is the crucial need for an increase in aid if we are really serious about ending the tragedy of poverty in sub-Saharan Africa and other impoverished parts of the world. Beginning with the success of the Marshall Plan, the foreign aid debate has a long history in the development literature and there are many economists who are highly sceptical of the idea that sustained economic development can be effectively promoted by injections of aid. Over the last 50 years these include Milton Friedman, Peter Bauer, and more recently William Easterly, who describes the foreign aid lobby as a 'cartel of good intentions'.[39] In the recent debate many critics of foreign aid point to the poor governance and corruption problems that seem to pervade sub-Saharan Africa. In their view any increase in aid flows are likely to be wasted or be appropriated by kleptocrats.[40] What do you say to these critics and what role can foreign aid play in a solution to the poverty trap in sub-Saharan Africa?*

I think two issues are important here. First, do the impoverished countries really need foreign aid to help them accomplish their development goals? Yes they do! During the United Nations Millennium Summit in 2000, the heads of state of 147 countries adopted the Millennium Development Goals with quantitative targets for 2015. With current aid flows, sub-Saharan Africa is clearly not going to meet those targets.[41] Second, if aid is necessary, is it also sufficient? No, aid needs to be combined with other important measures, including improved governance and trade reform in the developed countries. On the first question, if you subscribe to the basic Solow growth model and its recent variants, you can take the view that every country in the world can develop and grow because there is no such thing as a poverty trap. Countries that are failing to develop must be doing something wrong, so they should correct those problems and get on with it. That view has become a very dominant view of the development problem, especially from a 'Washington Consensus' perspective over the last 25 years.[42] I think this perspective is absolutely wrong and that is the key point that I have been trying to get over in recent years. It is not simply that impoverished places have only themselves to blame. Their particular circumstances matter, including geographical constraints. The formal implications of this perspective, as a matter for theory and practice, are that if countries are really caught in a poverty trap and aren't simply suffering because of bad governance, then the idea of external help becomes a logical corollary. If impoverished countries cannot break out of the trap by their own efforts, then either the people of these countries will be left to suffer and die, or they can be helped. So the case for foreign assistance is based on an analysis of the sources of poverty that does not accept that failure to develop and grow is for the most part self-inflicted and can be cured by a few lectures on how to improve governance. The problem is more structural, with identifiable causes. This is why I am interested in promoting a 'green revolution' in Africa, help to control malaria, and help to overcome economic isolation by investing in infrastructure developments. So that's the underlying philosophical base that links the aid debate to our earlier discussion about geography and development.

*What are the main objections to these ideas?*
The objections come in two forms. One goes under the fancy name of 'Dutch disease'-type arguments. That is, too much help is bad for your health. There are many variants of this argument, most of which I regard as simply wrong. Second, there is the real issue of agency, because there is a problem of responsibility attached to aid inflows. How do you ensure that the extra resources made available turn into the kind of investments that are growth-promoting and poverty-reducing rather than fuelling the consumption of a rich kleptocratic elite? This is a question of mechanisms and incentive structures. Unfortunately I think that economists in general have come to view the whole question of foreign aid as a playground rather than a really important issue. On the one hand I see millions of people dying and on the other I see an academic debate that I do not find commensurate with the challenge. Is it really beyond our capabilities to get insecticide-treated bed nets out to the villages to people who really need them? Should we have to argue endlessly about such a proposition? Can't we even try it in a few places?[43] Instead we see this great generalised debate on aid. The way that this debate is handled analytically I also find preposterous. Running endless regressions of aggregate aid as an explanatory variable of aggregate economic performance is the most ridiculous kind of approach to these issues that I can think of.

*Why do you say that?*
Because it involves taking very poorly measured variables that have multiple determinants and trying to find simple correlations in the data. So either you find a relationship or you don't, and you declare your results. Surely this issue deserves a great deal more subtlety than this. Even the simplest partition of aid flows that distinguishes between aid for emergency relief from aid that actually went for investment actually turns out to make a big difference in the regression results.[44]

*How should economists assess the impact of aid flows to developing countries?*
I would say that if someone is really serious about the aid issue they should take a micro perspective and take a detailed look at aid for immunisation

purposes, or aid for the eradication of smallpox or measles, for example. They should ask questions such as: what is the most effective way to get anti-malaria bed nets to the people who need them? What are the incentive structures that need to be put in place to make sure that aid gets to the intended recipients? What we don't need are these gross, over-the-top generalisations that end up saying 'This is good for you or this is bad for you'. I would like economists to take the whole question of aid more seriously, remembering that millions of lives depend on political decisions that are influenced by our research findings. The issue deserves more than intellectual games. We need to deal with practical grounded concerns that address the substantive realities of tropical African circumstances. I know of innumerable successful aid programmes of significant scale. Many diseases have been successfully controlled even in the most desperate of circumstances. Many immunisation campaigns have been successful. The recent campaign to get 900 000 anti-malaria bed nets out to Togo worked because it was linked to a measles immunisation programme and involved free distribution. I believe that we now have all sorts of possibilities that were not available 20 years ago for monitoring and auditing aid distribution using modern information technology. Let me make it quite clear that the last thing that I am advocating is issuing blank cheques and throwing money at problems. A reasonable level of governance in the poor recipient countries is a precondition if increased aid flows are to be effective. So I clearly recognise the need for an accountable approach to aid. What I am saying is let us take seriously specific challenges, such as how do we get soil nutrients to smallholder farmers in Africa whose soils are depleted and cannot afford fertilisers, or how do we get malaria under control, and let us deal with these problems in a hard-headed, systematic, evidence-based manner. It is even more frustrating when I hear from Washington that they are ready to go and spend $300 billion on the Iraq war, supposedly to bring freedom, and yet washes its hands of getting bed nets to help prevent children getting malaria in Africa. How can we take such a position seriously? The same people that brought us a full-scale war costing $80 billion per year in aid that gets blown up, literally, might have the gumption to at least ask how we may initiate a programme of bed-net deliveries to impoverished villages. Surely this is a lot easier than fighting battles in the city of Fallujah! But Washington doesn't want to take on that particular humanitarian challenge.

## TRADE, OPENNESS AND GROWTH

*Your 1995 paper with Andrew Warner, 'Economic Reform and the Process of Global Integration', has been very influential and heavily cited in the recent growth and development literature.*[45] *As in the case of foreign aid there has been an important ongoing debate on the relationship between openness, growth and poverty reduction.*[46] *In* The End of Poverty, *you advocate aid combined with 'enlightened globalisation' as the best way forward for the poorest developing countries. So your central message seems to be that both trade and aid are necessary engines of progress for the poorest countries of the world.*

That's right. First of all I am a firm advocate of trade as an engine of growth. I do not buy the anti-free-trade sentiments of some parts of the anti-globalisation movement.[47] These sentiments make no sense to me as an economist. In our 1995 paper we show that more open economies tend to exhibit faster rates of convergence towards the living standards of rich countries than is the case with closed economies. I also do not believe that 'exploitation' by multinational companies is a major part of the explanation of the distribution of wealth and poverty in the world. The impoverished places that I have been working in have been completely bypassed by globalisation! There is not a factory to be found and no multinationals come to these places to 'exploit' them. I am not saying that there are no important issues relating to multinational companies. Of course many multinational companies sometimes behave very badly. But their questionable behaviour does not explain the phenomenon of extreme poverty. Extreme poverty is not caused by exploitation by multinational companies. It is caused by factors such as isolation, drought, disease, poor infrastructure and bad governance. However, globalisation must not be treated as a panacea. The slogan 'trade not aid' is preposterous because trade does not even reach into the highlands of East Africa, the Andes or the Himalayas, or the drought-stricken Sahel, except in a limited way involving a narrow range of primary commodities that does not lead to development. In these areas we do not see the diversified trade that we know to be the hallmark of successful economic development. The extremes on both sides of this particular debate have it wrong. Being anti-globalisation is no answer. But globalisation, when viewed as a silver bullet for the problems of developing countries, is equally naïve. So the trade not aid view is also completely wrong.[48] Very poor countries clearly need both.

*What exactly do you mean by enlightened globalisation?*
By 'enlightened globalisation' I mean we need to take an honest look at the planet. You cannot trade if you don't have a healthy, connected and skilled population as a base for new industries. That is why investments in health, education and infrastructure are all prerequisites for moving up the development ladder. It also means that you can be pro-trade and in favour of core labour standards. The fact that multinational firms are not the cause

of extreme impoverishment does not eliminate the need for them to behave in a civilised and legal manner. They sometimes pay bribes and behave in an unethical way, but, I repeat, they do not cause fundamental poverty. Enlightened globalisation means that we need to understand the real contours of globalisation and respond appropriately in the places where it cannot solve the crises that we observe. It is also important to promote market forces where they can be important engines of development.

## ODIOUS DEBT

*Throughout your career you have written a great deal about various aspects of the international debt problem, and have also been involved with the Jubilee 2000 campaign to cancel the international debt of the world's poorest countries.[49] In some interesting research, Michael Kremer has been promoting the idea of 'odious debt', that is, sovereign debt incurred by political leaders, usually unelected and unaccountable dictators, who borrowed and wasted vast sums of money.[50] The regimes of Anastasio Somoza in Nicaragua, Mobutu Sese Seko in Zaire and the Marcos regime in the Philippines come to mind. Iraq's debts incurred by Saddam Hussein would also certainly qualify as odious. The basic idea is that such debt should not be transferable to successor governments. Are you enthusiastic about such an idea and do you see 'odious debt' as a workable concept?*

That's a tough question. I am sympathetic to the idea but I have taken a somewhat different view. I of course agree with Michael Kremer that certain debts need to be forgiven, and his view is that certain debts ought not to be enforceable at all. There are two aspects that concern me with his approach. First, even non-odious debt should be forgiven in many circumstances. So I don't think that the answer to sub-Saharan Africa's debt problem depends so much on where the debt came from as opposed to what the current implications are of the accumulated debt. Some countries get themselves into a mess through bad luck or bad governance, and in my view these countries need help. Societies should not be trapped by debt when it is a life-and-death issue. Second, I am not sure that we know, or can define what 'odious' means in a clear-cut, unambiguous way. Tastes vary a lot about what is or what is not good governance. I worry that rich and powerful countries are likely to manipulate decisions on which debts are to be defined as odious. I would not want to see the Pentagon deciding whose debts are odious and whose are not. So the applicability of the concept worries me. However, there is something particularly troubling about a brutal dictatorship that takes on debt by mortgaging national assets and then insisting that the citizens of that country, for decades to come, have to pay for that debt. After all, in most countries private citizens are not responsible for the repayment of debt incurred in their name by fraudsters. So I sympathise with the idea but have a problem seeing how the idea can be put into operation.

## GLOBAL INEQUALITY AND FAILED STATES

*In your paper 2001 paper, 'The Strategic Significance of Global Inequality', you argue that economic failure in poor countries leads to state failure and this in turn creates the 'seedbeds of violence, terrorism, international criminality, mass migration and refugee movements, drug trafficking and disease'.*[51] *Therefore you suggest that it is in the self-interest of the USA to help reduce international inequalities and promote economic development abroad by increasing, and making better use of, its capacity for foreign assistance. There is an important war on poverty to be fought that is complementary to US concerns about terrorism and failed states. While I think that Tony Blair and Gordon Brown in the UK are persuaded by this line of argument, how are you going to sell it to President George Bush in the USA?*[52]

That particular paper was written before September 11 and I think that event makes the analysis in that paper even more relevant. Rhetorically, the same arguments have now been echoed at many levels of US official policy. Many of George Bush's speeches highlight essentially the same idea. The US National Security Doctrine of 2002 says that overseas economic development is a core part of US security for reasons that I cite in that paper. The Congressional Budget justification for the State Department's budget this year has a nice, and I think correct, approach when it says that US national security rests on three pillars: defence, diplomacy and development. My complaint is not with the State Department, USAID, the White House or the CIA in their analysis of the causes of state failure, but rather with the lack of commitment to make the necessary investments to correct the problem. So they have the diagnosis right but are still investing $500 billion in the military pillar of the strategy but only $16 billion in the development pillar. However, when you look more closely at the $16 billion you find that at least half of that is in fact defence investment because it is going to strategic countries and there is little development component to the spending. The actual allocation of spending to real development projects in Africa is under $2 billion per year. To me this is a massive misallocation of resources between these three pillars, and we need to take all three pillars seriously. The hardest thing is to get Washington to do arithmetic. They are very good at slogans and there are a lot of projects waiting on the shelf, but the actions do not match the rhetoric. So my overriding and frequently given advice to Washington these days is: do the arithmetic! The bottom line is this. Economic failure can breed state failure, and failed states, as we have seen, are the breeding ground of political extremism, terrorism, massive refugee movements and international criminality. As I pointed out in that paper, there are numerous historical examples of economic crisis leading to political change that proved to be disastrous for the world. The Bolshevik seizure of power in 1917, Hitler's seizure of power in 1933, the disintegration of Yugoslavia and the situation in Afghanistan come to mind.

## PHILOSOPHICAL APPROACH

*Almost 20 years ago Alan Blinder wrote a book entitled* Hard Heads Soft Hearts: Tough Minded Economics for a Just Society. *Your approach to economics and policy reminds me of Blinder's philosophy, namely that you need to start out your assessment of any significant political-economy problem with solid economic analysis, including a recognition of the power of markets. However, at the same time it is important to combine this with a 'soft-hearted concern for society's underdogs'. You appear to be extending this philosophy to the international sphere. Is this a reasonable summary of your overall philosophy?*

It is. I am certainly hard headed in the sense that I believe in the power and importance of sound economic analysis when it comes to understanding and dealing with important issues of public policy. The soft-hearted aspect has two dimensions. One is the need to recognise that our humanity calls on us to do something about world poverty. Some people express this message in a religious way, others do it in a secular–ethical way. But I feel very strongly about the humanitarian dimension to the whole issue of international poverty. There are about one billion people who on a daily basis have to struggle to exist. To me the objective of ending extreme impoverishment, of achieving the Millennium Development Goals, is a grand moral task, and this challenge can be met by our generation.[53] There are numerous low-cost interventions that can make a profound difference to the lives of the poor of this world. There is also a hard-headed dimension which asks the question: what kind of world will give value to everybody's life, regardless of race or nationality? As an economist I think that if we profoundly devalue life on the margin, by saying that poor people living on the continent of Africa are expendable because to help fix the problems will cost us $1 per person per day, then I have a feeling that there is likely to be an arbitrage relationship that comes into play, namely that the rest of the world won't value the lives of my children. So the kind of violence and horrific treatment of humans by other humans that pervades the world should be challenged by a practical philosophy that says that we should take seriously the value of others' lives and do that on a regular, rigorous and sustained basis. I believe that this philosophy should form the basis of how we organise society so that all our lives are similarly taken seriously. That is the practical side of ethics and I believe in it.

## NOTES

1.  I interviewed professor Sachs in his office at the Earth Institute, Columbia University, New York, on 2 May 2005.
2.  Details of Professor Sachs's publications, many of which are available online, can be found at http://www.earthinstitute.columbia.edu/about/director/index.html.
3.  The Earth Institute is a centre for research into the 'complex issues facing the planet and its inhabitants, with a particular focus on sustainable development and the needs of the world's poor'. Detailed information concerning the research activities of the Earth Institute can be found at http://www.earthinstitute.columbia.edu.
4.  Schumpeter (1942).
5.  See, for example, Eichengreen and Sachs (1985).
6.  Keynes (1936).
7.  See Eichengreen (1984).
8.  See Snowdon (2002a), ch. 4.
9.  See also Sachs and Larrain (1992).
10.  See Sachs (1987, and 2005a, ch. 5).
11.  See Cagan (1956); Friedman, M. (1956); Sargent (1982).
12.  Keynes (1919, 1923).
13.  Smith (1776).
14.  See Sachs (2005a), chs 6 and 7; Sachs (1993, 1996a); Lipton and Sachs (1992); Sachs, Woo and Parker (1997); Lipton and Sachs (1990a).
15.  Sachs (1996b).
16.  See Lipton and Sachs (1990b).
17.  Fischer (1993b). See also Fischer interview.
18.  Sachs (2002a).
19.  See Kornai interview for a discussion of failed reform in Hungary.
20.  See Sachs and Woo (1994).
21.  This type of process was formalised in Arthur Lewis's (1954) seminal paper, 'Economic Development with Unlimited Supplies of Labour'.
22.  See Sachs and Woo (1997).
23.  See Sachs (2000a, 2003a); Bloom and Sachs (1998); Sachs and McArthur (2001); Gallup et al. (1999); World Bank (2002); Acemoglu (2003a); Rodrik and Subramanian (2003); Rodrik, Subramanian and Trebbi (2004); Sachs et al. (2004); IMF (2005).
24.  See Faye et al. (2004).
25.  See Sachs et al. (2002).
26.  See Sachs and Rappaport (2003).
27.  Krugman (1999b); Krugman and Venables (1995).
28.  Myrdal (1957); Kaldor (1970).
29.  Porter (1996).
30.  Gallup et al. (1999).
31.  Rodrik (2003a).
32.  See Sachs and Rodriguez (1999); Sachs and Warner (1999, 2001); Auty (2001); Sala-i-Martin and Subramanian (2003); Bulte et al. (2005); Mehlum et al. (2006).

33. See Easterly and Levine (1997); Sachs and Warner (1997a); Woglin (1997); Collier (1998); Collier and Gunning (1999a, 1999b); Sender (1999); Sachs (2000b, 2001a, 2003b, 2005b, 2005c, 2005d); Bigsten (2002); Artadi and Sala-i-Martin (2003); Easterly, Devarajan and Pack (2003); Sahn and Stifel (2003); Sachs and McArthur (2005).
34. For a discussion of these ideas see Todaro and Smith (2003). See also Easterly (2005).
35. See Snowdon and Vane (2005), ch. 11, for an extensive discussion of growth theory.
36. See Nurkse (1953); Nelson (1956); Leibenstein (1957); Murphy, Shleifer and Vishny (1989); Ben-David (1998).
37. See Snowdon and Vane (2005), for a discussion of the Solow growth model.
38. See Sachs et al. (2004), pp. 124–30.
39. See Friedman, M. (1958); Bauer (1972); Boone (1996); Easterly (2001a, 2003a, 2003b, 2004, 2006a, 2007); Easterly, Levine and Roodman (2004). See also the lively exchange of views on aid between Sachs and Easterly in the *Washington Post*, 13 and 27 March 2005.
40. See Rowley (2000); Svensson (2000).
41. Sachs (2003b).
42. See Snowdon (2001b).
43. Sachs (2002b).
44. See Jamison and Radelet (2005); Radelet et al. (2005).
45. See also Sachs and Warner (1997b).
46. See Dollar and Kraay (2004).
47. Sachs (1995).
48. However, in a *Financial Times* article (24 October 2005), World Bank President Paul Wolfowitz argued that 'It is trade not aid, that holds the key to creating jobs and raising incomes.'
49. See Sachs and Williamson (1986); Sachs (1990, 2002c).
50. Kremer and Jayachandran (2002, 2006). See also Arslanalp and Blair Henry (2006).
51. See also Fukuyama (2004).
52. See Radelet (2003).
53. Sachs (2005e).

# Xavier Sala-i-Martin[1]

Xavier Sala-i-Martin is widely recognised as one of the world's leading economists in the field of economic growth. Since 1990 he has made numerous theoretical and empirical contributions to growth analysis, recognised by many awards, fellowships and research grants. He is also the co-author, with Robert Barro, of *Economic Growth* (2003), *the* leading graduate textbook in the field.[2]

Professor Sala-i-Martin received his undergraduate education at the Universitat Autonoma de Barcelona, and completed his MA and PhD degree in economics at Harvard University in 1987 and 1990 respectively. He was Assistant Professor of Economics (1990–93), then Associate Professor of Economics (1993–96) at Yale University, before joining Columbia University as Professor of Economics in 1996. He was also Visiting Professor at Barcelona's Universitat Pompeu Fabra (1994–2005), and was Visiting Professor at Harvard University in 2003–04.

Among his numerous professional activities, Professor Sala-i-Martin has a been a consultant to the IMF and the World Bank (since 1993), and Senior Economic Advisor to the World Economic Forum (since 2002). In 2002 he founded the 'Umbele Foundation: A Future for Africa'. Professor Sala-i-Martin is a Research Fellow at the Centre for European Policy Research, London, the Institute for Policy Research, Washington, DC, and the National Bureau of Economic Research, Cambridge,

Massachusetts. He is also associate editor of the prestigious *Journal of Economic Growth.*[3]

In the following interview I discuss with Professor Sala-i-Martin several important issues relating to economic growth and development.

## BACKGROUND INFORMATION

*How did you become interested in economics?*
In high school I was unsure what to do so I asked my parents: who is the richest member of our family? It turned out to be one of my uncles, so I then asked: what did he study? He studied economics, so that's how I chose (*laughter*).

*Were there any people who during your student days particularly influenced the development of your thinking?*
Yes, although I have to confess that I was not a very good student as an undergraduate because I did not find many of the subjects that interesting. However, I did very well in those areas that did interest me, in particular microeconomics. At that time I was an undergraduate student at the Universitat Autonoma de Barcelona, and microeconomics was being taught by a visiting professor from the University of California, Davis. His name was Joaquim Silvestre, and he changed my way of thinking and the way that I saw economics. He really aroused my interest in economic theory, first micro, then macro. I also enjoyed the mathematical approach to economic analysis. Because of Joaquim's influence I then went on to Harvard where I met people like Jeff Sachs and Robert Barro and my interest gradually moved towards macroeconomics, development and growth.

## THE RENAISSANCE OF GROWTH RESEARCH

*You have written a large number of influential papers in the field of economic growth[4] as well as a very successful graduate textbook, co-authored with Robert Barro.[5] What is it about economic growth that fascinates you?*
To me the interest comes from the fact that economic growth is potentially so important for improving human welfare. I think that the most important question that an economist can ask is: what is it that makes a country grow? More than anything else it is economic growth that affects human welfare, including the discovery of an AIDS vaccine. Millions more people have died as the result of bad economic policies than have died of AIDS![6] It is also a very old question since it is the one that Adam Smith set out to

answer in his classic *The Wealth of Nations*.[7] This question remains unanswered even though many organisations, such as the World Bank, the IMF, the OECD and the United Nations, and many policy advisers, act as if we economists did know the answer. I don't think that we do know with any certainty what we need to do in sub-Saharan Africa today to turn economic performance around. If you look at poverty eradication, something that also interests me, you find that the countries that are successful in eradicating poverty are the countries that grow and vice versa.[8] So the absence of sustained growth has incredibly important consequences for human welfare and this is why it must remain a major research interest for economists.

*Economic growth is crucially important and yet between the mid-1960s and mid-1980s research into economic growth went into relative decline compared to other areas of macroeconomics.[9] How do you explain this recession in the field, given its importance?*

I think the main reason is that many young economic theorists at American universities are obsessed with mathematics. The beauty of economic modelling is so attractive that some of the best young economists tend to focus on theorising in areas that are not always so important and relevant for the major problems facing the world. During the 1960s the neoclassical revolution made growth theory highly mathematical and abstract. So many beautiful mathematical growth models were created but with results that were essentially irrelevant. The final product of a paper might be that a unique equilibrium for this particular model exists and everybody in the room would be very happy (*laughter*). But the real world demanded answers to important questions and so, beginning in the 1950s, there emerged an alternative, low-tech approach, to providing answers which we call 'development economics'. So interest in growth theory died for 20 years and discussions of growth were mainly confined to the field of development economics. But because development economics was not built on strong theoretical foundations, many of the answers it provided turned out to be wrong.[10] Then, in the early 1970s, new techniques associated with the equilibrium business cycle research of Robert Lucas, Thomas Sargent, Edward Prescott, Robert Barro and others were incredibly influential. This new methodology was very attractive to young economists just out of graduate school.[11] Macroeconomists became obsessed with business cycle theory during the 1970s and early 1980s. However, growth was reborn and today many macroeconomists see long-run growth as *the* major issue, much more important than the analysis of short-run fluctuations. Perhaps the most exciting aspect of the resurgence of interest in growth analysis has been the integration of theoretical and empirical research. In the new wave of research on economic growth, economists have taken economic theory more seriously when it comes to empirical research. A good example is the work on convergence.[12]

## GROWTH AND HISTORY

*You mention the importance of empirical research and obviously such research requires good data. During the last quarter of the twentieth century economists interested in economic growth have also had access to much improved data sets, notably the Heston–Summers Penn World Tables.[13] Angus Maddison has also made some heroic attempts to estimate GDP per capita for a large sample of regions and countries going back 2000 years.[14] How much faith do you have in data sets that go back a long way into history?*

I don't think that the data are very reliable once you go back beyond 1960: data are a luxury good and only rich countries are likely to be able to collect reliable data. Once you start looking at poor countries you need to have a large degree of imagination to collect data. Having said that, some of the lessons we get from these data sets are probably valid, for example the lessons on growing economic inequality (or divergence) between the 1760s and, say, 1980. Basically the whole world was poor until about 1760, with the vast majority of people living on subsistence income. Regional differences in real GDP per capita were very small. The average income of a peasant in China was about the same as that of the average European serf or the average American or African farmer. From the beginning of organised agriculture until the mid-eighteenth century Malthusian dynamics prevailed.[15] And then, around 1760, the Industrial Revolution arrived: initially, a small number of countries managed to take off, allowing them to experience sustained growth of per capita income for the next 250 years. The main distinguishing characteristic of the Industrial Revolution is not that incomes are higher, but that they grow continuously for the first time in human history. Because the spread of the Industrial Revolution was highly uneven, this led to the emergence of growing income inequalities between nations, which continued until about 1980. Fortunately, during the last two and a half decades, the process has been reversing as the majority of the citizens of the world are now experiencing rising incomes, especially as a result of the growth accelerations in China and India, which together contain over 2.3 billion people, about 37 per cent of the world's population.[16] I think these big trends are correct even though we do not have that many reliable data. However, I don't think we can tell with any real precision what the income per capita was in China or the USA, or anywhere else, in 1700, 1750 or 1820, never mind in AD 1100.

*One of the recent trends in the growth literature has been the attempt by many growth theorists to build models that can provide a unified explanation of the historical evolution of income per capita. Such models try to account for the Malthusian, post-Malthusian and modern growth regime periods.[17] Are you sympathetic to this recent work?*

This literature began with Michael Kremer's 1993 paper and the authors of subsequent papers have produced some very innovative theories. But will we gain much from being able to explain from the same theory the stagnation of the pre-Industrial Revolution period, the Industrial Revolution take-off period, and the sustained growth of the post-Industrial Revolution era? I am not so sure.

## GROWTH THEORY AND EMPIRICS

*Greg Mankiw has argued that 'whenever practical macroeconomists have to answer questions about long-run growth they usually begin with a simple neoclassical growth model'.[18] To what extent is the Solow neoclassical growth model[19] still the central idea in the analysis of economic growth?*

The way that I look at theories or models is that they are tools that enable us to address particular questions. Relating back to your previous question, suppose we develop a theory that explains why, at a particular point in human history, income per capita starts to grow and people decide to reduce the number of children that they want. Such a theory is not much use if we want to answer questions such as: how do we get growth started in Malawi? Models address particular questions. The Solow model is an important framework for answering one very important question: is capital accumulation the key to economic growth? We do observe, by and large, that countries with high rates of growth have high investment–GDP ratios. For example, Africa has a poor record of growth, and has investment rates of about 5 per cent, the OECD grows at about 2 per cent with investment rates of about 20 per cent, and East Asia grows at 5, 6 and sometimes 10 per cent and has investment ratios at 30, 40, sometimes even 50 per cent. The Soviet Union also believed that investment would lead to growth. During the 1950s, Rostow's theory relating to the stages of development and 'take-off' into self-sustained growth was also based on increasing investment ratios.[20] Moreover, institutions like the World Bank claim that capital accumulation is the key to economic growth. In fact, the financing gap model, whose central element is that investment is the engine of growth, has guided official development aid for decades. Therefore many economists believe that investment is a key variable in any explanation of economic growth. So the Solow model is an excellent tool for examining the importance of the relationship between capital accumulation and economic growth. The answer to that question is that if there are diminishing returns to capital accumulation, then increasing investment ratios are *not* the key. That is a very important insight.[21] An additional insight of the theory is that it leaves technological progress as the only long-run source of growth. Unfortunately, the Solow model *assumes* that technology is exogenous so it is obviously not a good tool for explaining technological progress. This is why theories of endogenous growth became so popular during the 1980s. The Solow model tells us nothing about why people have fewer children as their incomes increase: declining fertility is a very important phenomenon that occurs as an economy develops, but the Solow model has nothing to say about this.[22] The same applies to questions relating to the role of the financial sector and the importance of institutions in promoting growth. But the fact that the Solow model does not help us answer *all* economic development questions does not mean that it is not very useful for answering the questions for which it was designed. It is also a very simple tool, which means that it is easy to teach undergraduates the basics of growth theory. I suppose that is why it is the classic textbook model!

*What are the most important lessons that economists have learned from the endogenous growth literature?*
There have been various important insights from this literature. First, the endogenous growth literature attempts to deal seriously with important questions relating to technology. One major problem is this. In the classical world of Adam Smith we have classical goods that are both rival and excludable.[23] In this kind of world the invisible hand and perfect competition lead to the best possible outcome. But technology is not a classical good. Once someone invents a formula, everyone can use that formula at the same time and they can all use the formula as many times as they wish. Technology is a non-rival good. Take the example of a vaccine. The formula for the vaccine has to be invented, and this can be a very expensive process because there is a large fixed cost. But once we know the formula, many people can use it. In the case of perfect competition we will not get an optimal outcome because prices converge to marginal cost and, consequently, there is no surplus to pay for the initial research cost. Therefore, in a world of perfect competition, very few things will be invented! Adam Smith's invisible hand does not work in the case of ideas.[24] So we need to think about what kind of institutions we need to create the ideas that lead to technological progress, which is the driving force behind long-run economic growth. That is a very interesting insight. A second important idea is the focus of research on various social interactions and institutions that

allow markets to work. For example, there is now a vibrant literature that investigates the importance for economic growth of trust or the rule of law.[25]

*These are things that Adam Smith emphasised.*
Absolutely. No economy can work in a lawless environment. However, the question of how countries develop and can best improve their legal systems and institutions is complicated. For example, when one country tries to impose the institutions that work in one setting on another country, it does not always work. In fact, it really never works. Take the example of the imposition of institutions by the West in the countries of Africa when they gained independence. Initially these countries began as parliamentary democracies with either British or French rule of law. Five to ten years later the democracies had disappeared and had been largely replaced with auto-cratic dictators. We need to think how we can develop Africa-specific insti-tutions that will allow markets to operate efficiently because we all know that, at the end of the day, the only way out of poverty is growth, and sus-tained growth can be generated only through markets. The solution to Africa's poverty is not debt forgiveness and more aid. Targets for the rich nations to provide assistance to poor nations of 0.7 per cent of GDP are not very useful. None of the rich nations of the world have reached that position because of aid and debt forgiveness. They became rich through being successful market economies.[26]

*But there are many variants of the capitalist market system. For example, China has also developed a unique institutional approach that has been very successful during the last 20 years.*
Yes, and who would have imagined that a capitalist system without a pre-dominance of private property would work? Certainly not Adam Smith. No reasonable economist would have imagined that this would be possi-ble. But it helped China during the first years of their transition from communism. The Chinese developed their own institutions that allow markets to work and reach similar outcomes to a Western-style market economy with private property. Certainly the market systems of Sweden, Hong Kong and the USA are very different; they all have their own pecu-liarities, but they all work in their own way.[27] So we know that for eco-nomic success you need markets, but how you achieve those markets and how those markets are regulated by the state is open for debate. If you try and impose a US, or Chinese or Swedish style of market system in Malawi it will not work. Japanese-style capitalism is not going to work in Zambia. Each country needs to develop its own market-supporting institutions. Every time a new region of the world takes off, it does so with an entirely

different and often surprising set of rules and institutions. For example, compare the growth take-offs of the UK, Japan, the 'Asian Tigers' and China. We as economists could not imagine in advance that the Chinese model of capitalism would work. If Jeff Sachs, Andrei Shleifer, Robert Barro or Adam Smith had been economic advisers to China in 1979 they would not have advocated or advised the institutional path actually chosen by the Chinese leadership. They would have advocated Western-style reforms. Most likely, their advice would have led to failure.[28] The Chinese have come up with a new style of capitalism that surprised everybody and, so far, it works.[29] Even if we learn what are the key differences between Chinese, US, Swedish and Japanese-style capitalism, I do not believe that comparisons, such as the relationship between the origins of the legal system and subsequent economic success, will provide lessons that will help us answer the question of what we need to advise in Africa in order to promote sustained growth.

## GROWTH, GLOBALISATION AND CONVERGENCE

*You mentioned earlier that a good example of the merging of theoretical and empirical work is to be found in the research on growth and convergence. You have made an influential contribution to this literature, especially during the early 1990s.[30] Initially it was thought that the lack of evidence for the 'absolute convergence hypothesis', that poor countries as a whole tend to grow faster than rich countries, was evidence in favour of the new endogenous growth theories and against the traditional neoclassical model.[31] However, your research with Robert Barro, and the paper by Mankiw, Romer and Weil, made it clear that the neoclassical model predicts 'conditional convergence'.[32] Has this hypothesis been confirmed in the data?*

Yes, I think so. There are many studies confirming conditional convergence although the speed of convergence at about 2 per cent per year is slower than predicted by the neoclassical model with a capital share of 0.3. An important feature of the neoclassical growth model is the convergence property. This is the idea that the growth rate of per capita income will be inversely related to some initial level of income per capita. However, Solow's neoclassical growth theory predicts *conditional* convergence; that is, poor countries will tend to grow faster than rich countries only if they approach the same steady state. This requires rich and poor countries to have very similar preferences, population growth rates, and to have access to similar technology. Clearly this is not the case. In our research we found strong evidence for conditional convergence in various data sets providing diminishing returns set in slowly.[33]

*While economists are in general pro-globalisation,[34] we do observe consider-*
*able hostility towards globalisation from other social scientists, politicians*
*and large sections of the general public. To what extent is increasing interna-*
*tional integration a powerful force promoting international convergence of per*
*capita incomes?*

It is unquestionably a powerful force for convergence. There are five important aspects of globalisation, namely, the mobility of goods, capital, labour,
and information, and the diffusion of technology. Look at the countries
that have had a disastrous growth record and compare them with the countries that have experienced sustained steady growth or growth miracles. For
example, compare sub-Saharan Africa's experience with East Asia. The
USA and Europe have sustained steady growth and are doing fairly well,
Latin America has stagnated, and the Arab world is underperforming.[35]
But when it comes to sub-Saharan Africa you need to ask yourself the following question: which of the five globalisation factors has arrived in
Africa? What answer do you get? Is the problem of Africa that there is too
much capital mobility and foreign direct investment? No. Not even
Africans invest in Africa, where private investment is less than 5 per cent of
GDP. Is the problem that there is too much labour mobility? When people
from Africa cross the straits of Gibraltar, Spain does everything it can to
return them to Africa! Spanish people, on the other hand, can work in
Germany, Belgium or Sweden, for example, but Africans cannot freely
move to Spain. Does Africa trade too much? No. If anything the problem
they have is that they are prevented from exporting to Europe and the USA
by our protectionism. In the USA, Europe and Japan we see these obscene
agricultural subsidies that deter consumers in the rich countries from
buying their products. Because of these subsidies it is cheaper for people in
many parts of Africa to buy agricultural products from the rich countries.
This is crazy. So the idea that Africa suffers from too much trade is completely absurd. Does Africa have too much Western technology? No. In the
West we have the anti-retroviral drugs that can help HIV-positive patients.
We have the technology and they cannot apply it because they have too few
doctors and hospitals. Finally, information. Information is, perhaps, the
only one of the five factors that moves easily to Africa. That is the surprising thing when you visit Africa. You see people watching Real Madrid play
Barcelona live on TV (*laughter*). But you must agree with me that, of the
five factors that define globalisation, information, as opposed to capital,
labour, goods and technology, is the least important. Now ask the same
questions about China. Take labour mobility. There are unlimited amounts
of Chinese people working abroad. Moreover, there are numerous Chinese
studying around the world. Take capital mobility. China has enjoyed a huge
inflow of FDI. Take trade in goods. China has experienced export-led

growth. Technology and information pour into China. There should be no doubt that globalisation helps countries to grow faster and catch up. I think that the experience of Africa and Asia over the last three decades has clearly demonstrated that globalisation is good, period. Numerous empirical papers try to estimate econometrically whether growth is positively correlated with openness.[36] Some papers show that openness is good for growth. Others show that this relation is weak. But none of them shows that this relation is negative. Given all of this, I do not think we can blame globalisation for what is going on in Africa. In fact, if you were to ask African political leaders what their opinion is of globalisation they will answer: what globalisation? We do not have globalisation!

## POLITICAL BARRIERS AND THE 'NATURAL-RESOURCE CURSE'

*Given that capital and technology can migrate across political boundaries, the persistence of significant differences in the level of output per worker and lack of convergence suggests the presence of entrenched barriers to growth and development. Daron Acemoglu's recent research highlights the importance of political barriers to development.[37] This work focuses on attitudes to change in hierarchical societies. Political elites deliberately block the adoption of institutions and policies that would help to eliminate economic backwardness. Acemoglu and Robinson argue that superior institutions and technologies are resisted because they may reduce the political power of the elite.[38] Where there are abundant natural-resource revenues to plunder by the politically powerful, this problem is likely to be a serious barrier to development.*

Yes, the political and economic elites in many poor countries certainly oppose the use of new technologies, and they also oppose many reforms. Look at Nigeria, which by almost any measure has been a development disaster. If you look at the distribution of income for countries like Nigeria you will see that 80 per cent of the population are making little or no progress, or even becoming worse off, and 20 per cent are doing very well.[39] In 2000 the richest 2 per cent of Nigeria's population had the same share of income as the poorest 55 per cent. So it is not surprising that the political elites do not want reforms that will threaten their wealth and power. Why change the legal system or the current arrangements for the distribution of oil revenues if it's working in your favour? Why introduce more competition and open up the economy when this will erode your power? Nigeria has had 40 years of mismanagement under military rule. The natural-resource curse in Nigeria's case has worked through the detrimental impact that oil revenues have had on domestic institutions and the consequent corruption and waste that has plagued Nigeria's economic and political history since independence. The oil revenues in Nigeria have fuelled rent-seeking activity, which has adversely affected long-run growth of per capita income. In my paper with Arvind Subramanian we show that Nigeria's per capita income between 1965 and 2000 did not increase even though $350 billion of oil revenues were generated.

*What can be done to reverse this cycle of failure?*
Our proposal focuses on the management of the oil revenues. This should be taken out of the hands of government. We propose that all Nigerians should have a constitutional right to an equal share of the oil revenues. And this proposal would also apply to other countries suffering from a natural-resource-curse-induced deterioration of institutions.


## RELIGION, CULTURE AND GROWTH

*Robert Barro has recently argued that empirical research by economists on the determinants of growth has neglected the influence of religion.*[40] *Do you think that religion and culture have an important influence on economic growth?*
There are very few issues where I disagree with Robert, but this is definitely one of them (*laughter*). My reason for disagreeing is that you cannot explain something that changes rapidly with factors that do not change at all, or change only very slowly. In the nineteenth century the first person to talk about religion and economic performance was Max Weber.[41] He believed that predominantly Protestant countries would have superior economic performance compared to Catholic countries because of differences between the Protestant and Catholic religions. He talked about the 'Protestant ethic'. Obviously he was wrong because now there are many predominantly Catholic countries that are as rich as Protestant countries. There are many other examples that undermine the culture hypothesis. Many people at the beginning of the twentieth century believed that the future major powers in the world would be Argentina and Brazil, not the USA. The reason for this line of argument was that the USA was attracting many migrants who came from a cultural background that was not conducive to the spirit of capitalism. By this time educated northern Europeans were migrating to Argentina. Of course today, Polish and Italian Americans are as rich as other groups. The English used to complain about the Irish. The Irish were characterised as lazy, always drinking, and would never become rich. But look at Ireland now. It is richer in per capita terms than the UK![42] So every time predictions are made on the basis of culture

or religion, they turn out to be wrong. We keep observing countries where all of a sudden income starts to grow even though culture and religion have stayed the same.

*How does the East Asian miracle fit into this debate?*
In the 1950s many sociologists used to say that Asia would always be poor. Buddhism and the Confucian philosophy were supposed to constrain the desire for material goods, and for capitalism to work effectively you need people who are motivated by the desire to accumulate material goods. So the analysis based on religion and culture predicted that Asia would always be poor. But as everybody now knows, during the last 50 years we have witnessed the remarkable 'miracle' growth of Japan, Hong Kong, Taiwan, Singapore, South Korea and, more recently, China. There has been a massive convergence of living standards between East Asia and the rich countries. Some now have a higher per capita income than many countries in Europe and the 'Western offshoots'.[43] Now we hear the counter-argument that this success is also down to culture and religion because Asian people are submissive and non-conflictual, and this allows capitalists to exploit the workforce! This sounds like Monday morning quarterbacking! Clearly there is a problem with these types of argument. Why all of a sudden did South Korea, Hong Kong, Singapore, Taiwan, Thailand or Malaysia start to grow without any change of religion? Why all of a sudden did China start to grow rapidly after 1978? China did not change its culture or religion in 1978, did it? China stagnated for hundreds of years, then suddenly it started to grow. Why? To explain this dramatic change using religious and cultural variables you would have to find some dramatic change in those variables around 1978. And you will fail because nothing happened to religion or culture in China in 1978.

## INTERNATIONAL INEQUALITY

*You have written some widely cited papers on the issue of global poverty and inequality.[44] In discussions outside of academia the concepts of poverty and inequality often become confused. Do you think that inequality matters so long as poverty is being effectively reduced?*
No. In my forthcoming *Quarterly Journal of Economics* paper I state clearly that in most cases I don't think that we should pay much attention to inequality, especially income inequality.[45] Why do I say this? Well, inequality would go up if the rich became richer by 10 per cent and the poor became richer by 5 per cent. Is this a bad situation? No. Surely this is good because the poor have become better off. If inequality goes up because the

rich become richer and the poor become poorer in absolute terms, then this might be something to worry about. Or we could imagine a situation where the rich become poorer and the poor also become poorer, but by an even greater amount. This would certainly be bad. In all three situations inequality has increased but the implications are very different. It follows that it is very important to look carefully at the data to see why inequality increases or falls. I also believe that measuring inequality just by using income is a bad idea. Imagine a situation in which there are two brothers. One brother likes to work hard; the other does not like to work. One brother likes to study in order to improve his employment prospects; the other hates to study. They are both reasonable people. It just so happens that one of the brothers prefers to have as much free time as possible and spend his time walking on the beach, while the other works like crazy, and has a lot of material goods. In fact, they could be equally happy. Then along comes the government and – guess what? It looks at the distribution of income, not happiness. It observes one rich brother and one very poor brother, as measured by income. So the government transfers some income from the rich brother to the poorer brother, who now ends up with leisure time, and similar income! Notice that, because the government cares about income as opposed to happiness, redistribution ends up creating more (not less) inequality.

*Why are you writing papers on inequality if you do not think it to be that important?*
My main objective is to estimate the world distribution of income because many people claim that this is important and because it allows me to study the fraction of the population below certain levels of income, a phenomenon we usually call poverty. Once I have this distribution, it is easy for me to estimate measures of inequality so that people who care about it can have a sensible debate about its evolution.

*There has been a huge output of research on the issue of world poverty and inequality during the last decade.[46] What is your assessment of the current state of economists' knowledge about trends in poverty and inequality? What dose the data tell us?*
The world is moving in the right direction. Poverty is clearly going down. The World Bank did not agree a few years ago but now it also estimates that poverty is falling. Some economists say that it is not all good news because the improvements come mainly from China and India, with 2.3 billion people. But this is not a legitimate criticism: to remove from the data the two largest countries where poverty has declined, and then declare that poverty in the world is increasing is not acceptable.[47] Would it make sense

to remove Africa from the data and declare that poverty is falling even faster? Of course not, and notice that, if we did, we would be ignoring many fewer citizens than if we were to ignore China and India! In assessing trends in world poverty we need to include all countries in the data set. When you do that, the results show that poverty and inequality across the world are falling. Some people say that if you look across *countries*, inequality is increasing. That may be true, but it is not relevant for human welfare because looking at countries, rather than at citizens, would give 700 times more weight to the farmer in Mozambique than to a Chinese peasant simply because the former lives in a smaller country! We need to look at population-weighted measures of poverty and inequality because China has 1.3 billion people and Mozambique has about 19 million people.[48] We are interested in human welfare and we therefore have to look at individual income.[49] The implications for human welfare of rapid growth in India and China are much more important than the effect of rapid growth in poor countries with small populations. This does not mean that all we should be talking about is human welfare. In much of my research I talk about countries because I want to test theories. If we want to know which policies produce growth, then we need to look at countries because each country is an independent experiment and we can compare the outcomes of different strategies. So when you are asking questions about policies you must look at country data. If you want to talk about human welfare you need to look at individual data. Every data set is useful for a particular question. It is a conceptual mistake to assume that because different data sets provide different impressions, this implies that we do not know anything.

*Can the growth tragedy of sub-Saharan Africa be reversed? If we could look at the data on international inequality at the end of the twenty-first century, is there some possibility that lower international inequality will include Africa?*
It is possible. But, as I said earlier, what Africa needs is not more aid and debt relief but better policies, more businesses, more trade, and more domestic and foreign direct investment.[50] The share of public spending in GDP also needs to be reduced.[51] The rich countries can also play a major role by allowing easier access of goods into their markets. Above all, sub-Saharan Africa needs peace and an end to violence and civil wars.

## FOREIGN AID AND GROWTH

*Throughout 2005, Jeffrey Sachs, Tony Blair and Gordon Brown have argued in favour of increasing substantially the aid flows to developing countries, especially to sub-Saharan Africa.[52] From what you have just said you clearly have little sympathy for this strategy as a way of promoting growth and development.*

The plans to increase aid over the next decade might be very dangerous if the recipient governments are corrupt, and lack accountability. By promising billions of dollars in development aid over the next ten years, what you are saying to the leaders of such countries is that they have ten years to enrich themselves. Moreover, you are telling them that after ten years all the money will be gone. The Blair–Brown plan to solve the 'poverty trap' in sub-Saharan Africa by bringing forward future aid allocations for the next 30 years to be allocated during the next decade is, potentially, a recipe for theft on a grand scale.

*So there is no case for agreeing with Jeff Sachs's call for aid to be increased to 0.7 per cent of GDP of the developed nations.*

No, I am not at all sympathetic to calls for more foreign aid until we find better ways to distribute it without causing harm.

*Is this because of the governance problems?*

No. Governance is one important reason, but not the only one. My feeling is that aid also has perverse consequences for the allocation of talent in a developing country.[53] Foreign aid is a very important industry, more than 15 per cent of GDP, in many African countries. The existence of all this money may very well lead potentially productive citizens to move away from productive activities into the international aid industry. In other words, rather than becoming engineers, many kids may find it more economically advantageous to become part of the bureaucratic network that specialises in channelling international aid, with the potential to allocate money to friends and relatives. A third problem is that donors do not know how best to spend aid resources. But whatever the reason, it seems clear to me that over the last 50 years international aid has been largely wasted.[54] While international aid was increasing in Africa, the growth rate of income per capita was declining continuously. I think international aid has, by and large, failed to promote widespread economic development.

*Jeffrey Sachs would probably say that this failure is because we did not give enough in aid.*

Jeff is very articulate and persuasive, and I have often heard him use a very appealing parable to describe this situation: 'the fact that one fireman is unable to put out a big fire does not mean that we should send less firemen to the fire. We should send more!' This sounds very good and very appealing, but a careful reading of the growing evidence is that foreign aid has failed almost everywhere. After some research from the World Bank[55] showed that development assistance was positively related to growth, provided that it was given to governments that follow 'good policies', subsequent research showed that aid does not generate growth even in those countries that follow good policies.[56] One reason is that the aid institutions, like the World Bank, the IMF and the United Nations, are getting it wrong. And they are getting it wrong because we, by which I mean economists, do not know what to do. Given our ignorance on this issue, the Gordon Brown plan, which consists of bringing forward 30 years' worth of international aid to the next ten years may be bit dangerous because there is no guarantee that increasing aid will work. In effect we are going to bet 30 years of resources on the next ten years. This is a huge (and perhaps irresponsible) gamble. An additional problem is that the obsession over the Millennium Development Goals might be counterproductive. The Millennium Development Goals are set for 2015, that is, ten years from now. Devoting all development strategies, which are essentially long-term strategies, to *only* achieve goals by 2015 may end up inducing political and economic leaders of the developing world to follow the wrong development strategies. In other words, it might be that the best strategy is to channel resources into activities that will produce benefits to Africa after 2015 – but this is too late to achieve the Millennium Development Goals, so those activities will never be financed!

*What kind of strategy should the rich countries be following to help Africa?*
I am not sure, but I think that one of the priorities should be the financing of R&D that searches for solutions to the three pandemics: AIDS, malaria and TB. The payoff from this would be huge, although it may well come after 2015. I like Michael Kremer's idea of a research fund to purchase vaccines at prices that exceed marginal cost.[57] Africa cannot do this alone because it does not have the technology, the doctors, and the pharmaceutical industry to carry out the necessary research. The rich world should do this. Other things rich countries should do is to promote business activity in Africa, which does not necessarily mean more financial aid. One way to develop this business activity is to reduce trade barriers, including agricultural subsidies.

## HUMAN CAPITAL AND GROWTH

*In your discussion paper 'Fifteen Years of Growth Economics: What Have We Learnt' you note that the cross-country regression literature, which attempts to identify the empirical determinants of growth, does not find a strong relationship between 'most measures of human capital and growth'.[58] Does that not surprise you?*

The Lucas 1988 paper stimulated a huge literature on the impact of human capital on growth. But when researchers started to measure human capital accumulation they found that very few measures of human capital have a positive sign in regressions.[59] Human capital has been a disappointment. If you actually look at Robert Barro's regression, many human capital measures come with a negative sign! The one measure that does seem to be positively related to growth is investment in primary schooling. Neither university education nor secondary schooling seem to matter. This is important because for a while the World Bank and other institutions spent millions of dollars building schools and promoting investment in human capital. Unfortunately this did not seem to translate into a positive impact on economic growth. Perhaps the wrong investments were made. Perhaps the key ingredient in the process of education is the productive use of students' time, not the school buildings or teachers' salaries. But the main lesson from the human capital growth literature is that the results have been disappointing.

## GEOGRAPHY AND GROWTH

*In recent years several economists, notably Jeffrey Sachs, have revived the idea that geography has an important influence on economic performance.[60] This literature emphasises the direct impact that geography can have through climate, natural resources and topography. Such factors obviously influence the health of a population, agricultural productivity, the economic structure of an economy, transport costs and the diffusion of information and knowledge. Do you agree with Sachs that geography matters for economic growth?* I think that we can all agree that geography matters, but there is disagreement on the channels of causation: how does geography matter? Jeffrey Sachs says that the link is direct: it affects through geographically related diseases, such as malaria, which is a tropical disease, and therefore geographically concentrated or geographically related productivities; for example, tropical weather is less amenable to certain types of high-yield agricultural products. Daron Acemoglu and his co-authors think that geography matters because it created the wrong kind of colonial institutions.[61] The Europeans were reluctant to settle in locations with high malaria incidence. So in those areas the Europeans established extractive institutions that had long-lasting adverse effects. Jeff Sachs believes that there are additional direct effects on technology and the health of populations from adverse geography. But they all agree that geography matters. It is obvious that tropical countries have problems with tropical diseases such as malaria, and that there is a relative lack of research and development relating to their specific health and agricultural problems.

*You argued earlier that increasing international economic integration and globalisation are powerful forces for convergence. Since trade is obviously influenced by transport costs, do you agree with Sachs that in many cases landlocked countries are at a particular disadvantage when it comes to achieving satisfactory economic growth?*[62]

But the highest-growth country in the world in recent decades has been Botswana, which is a landlocked country in sub-Saharan Africa! Switzerland and Austria are two of the richest countries in the world and they are also landlocked. About half of US states are landlocked. Vermont and Ohio are landlocked. Obviously this hypothesis has problems.

*Botswana is landlocked, but how much of its success is down to the discovery of diamonds in the 1960s?*

The diamonds have been important but, as you know, the possession of valuable natural resources does not always lead to economic growth. In fact, most countries that discover natural resources end up going down the tubes. They become victims of the 'natural-resource curse'.[63] In the early 1960s diamonds were discovered in Botswana and King Seretse Khama, who became Botswana's first president in 1965, did not steal the diamonds, as happened in other parts of sub-Saharan Africa, and he also maintained democracy. He made sure that the diamond revenues were diverted to useful investments. The strategy worked and Botswana has not been a victim of the natural-resource curse. Why? I don't really know, but it is a very big exception.[64] It is true that other landlocked countries like Chad, Niger and the Central African Republic have been development disasters. But are they disasters because they are landlocked? The Democratic Republic of the Congo is largely landlocked; it has diamonds and other natural resources, so why has it not been able to grow like Botswana? And of course there are lots of poor countries that are not landlocked. Take the countries of Central America such as Guatemala, El Salvador, Honduras, Costa Rica and Nicaragua. They have oceans on both the east and west sides of the country but they are poor! Somalia is not landlocked and neither are the poor countries of West Africa such as Liberia, Sierra Leone and Guinea. So I think the quality of economic policies, regulations and other factors are far more important explanatory factors of economic performance than whether a country is landlocked or not.

*Perhaps Botswana has been more successful than resource-rich countries like Nigeria because it has had a more accountable democratic government.*

That is true, but it remains to be explained why the government in Botswana did not become kleptocratic and steal the diamond revenues. Why was there no military coup after the diamonds were discovered? The diamond deposits are actually in Seretse Khama's own tribal territory. So the key question is: why did Seretse Khama not behave like Mobutu Sese Seko in the Congo, or Sani Abacha in Nigeria, and transfer vast fortunes into a personal Swiss bank account? Unlike human capital or wages, which are hard to steal, it is relatively easy for dictators of resource-rich countries to enrich themselves. In rich democratic countries, when natural resources are discovered, good things tend to happen. Good examples are Norway and Britain after the discovery of North Sea oil. In poor countries, after the discovery of valuable natural resources, the norm is that terrible things happen.

## GROWTH, AND ECONOMIC AND POLITICAL FREEDOM

*The impact of political institutions on economic performance is another area that has been receiving increasing attention from economists.*[65] *Does the evidence support the idea that democracy is good for economic growth?*
I agree with Robert Barro on this issue. There are lots of political dictatorships that have worked in terms of producing economic growth. China is the most recent example. But Singapore, Chile, Taiwan and South Korea have also had successful growth even though they have been dictatorships for much of their recent history. We also have many examples of successful democracies, including post-war Japan and Germany, which experienced growth miracles during the 1950s and 1960s. There are also many examples of democracies and dictatorships that have been a disaster with respect to economic growth. In fact most dictatorships have been disasters. The main point made in Robert Barro's research, and one that I completely agree with, is that democracy is not a critical factor for achieving growth. Let me be clear: this in no way suggests that dictators are a good idea. Remember, the correlation between growth and democracy is zero, not negative. However, for practical purposes, if you have $10 billion to spend in one country, and many things need to be created from scratch, then if the goal is to promote economic growth, democracy should not be the immediate priority. With a budget constraint, there are other projects that appear to be more important, such as investment in infrastructure, establishing law and order, or creating a vibrant business fabric.

*The modernisation thesis suggests that growth and economic development are prerequisites for the establishment of a sustainable democracy. Do you think that growth promotes democracy?*
This is the other part of Barro's story. Eventually, as people become rich, then they begin to demand democracy.[66] If you impose democracy on poor

countries that are not ready, able or willing to defend democracy, then it will invariably fail. This has happened many times. In the early 1960s, following the decolonisation process, most countries in Africa started out as democracies. By 1975 only one country was democratic! Military coups occurred everywhere, eliminating democracy.

# GROWTH AND COMPETITIVENESS

*The World Economic Forum's annual* Global Competitiveness Report *analyses the competitiveness of nations.*[67] *Until recently the Report used two alternative but complementary approaches to measuring competitiveness. The first approach uses the medium- to long-term macroeconomic-oriented 'Growth Competitiveness Index', developed by John McArthur and Jeffrey Sachs. The second approach to measuring competitiveness utilises the 'Business Competitiveness Index', developed by Michael Porter. In the* Global Competitiveness Report, 2004–05, *a new index of competitiveness, that you developed with Elsa Artadi, made its debut.*[68] *The new 'Global Competitiveness Index' aims to 'consolidate the World Economic Forum's work into a single index' that reflects the growing need to take into account a more comprehensive set of factors that significantly influence a country's growth performance. Michael Porter thinks that 'combining these two measures would suppress useful information',*[69] *while you seem to prefer a single index of global competitiveness. Why do you favour a single index of competitiveness?*

Michael Porter wants to separate static from dynamic influences and micro from macro factors in the construction of competitiveness indices. He thinks of the 'Growth Competitiveness Index' as a macroeconomic dynamic index, whereas he views his 'Business Competitiveness Index' as a static microeconomic index.[70] I think that conceptually it is very hard to distinguish between these influences on competitiveness. Both Porter and I define competitiveness in terms of productivity. There is no doubt that productivity determines the *Wealth of Nations*, as Adam Smith so clearly pointed out in 1776. But productivity also determines the rate of return to investment, and so is a determinant of growth. Hence the same concept, productivity, has both static and dynamic considerations. Also, it is difficult to decide what belongs in the realm of macro and micro. For example, take the rule of law, which at the micro level obviously influences the effectiveness of business operations. But the rule of law is also an important factor in determining economic growth through its influence on institutions and regulations. So for me, it is very hard to distinguish the micro from the macro and the static from the dynamic factors. All macro policies have micro consequences and all the decisions made at the micro level of the firm have macroeconomic consequences. That is why I prefer to use one 'Global Competitiveness Index'.

*In developing your index you argue that the main determinants of productivity can be encompassed within 12 'pillars of competitiveness' and each pillar plays a major role, depending on the stage of development. What led you to that approach?*

I was influenced by Porter on this. He thinks in terms of stages of development. What competitiveness is for poor countries is not the same as competitiveness for rich countries. Porter distinguishes three levels of competitiveness. Poor countries are in the first stage of competitiveness where they compete through prices; you need to make things cheaply. For countries in the intermediate stage of development they compete through quality. That is, you try to make things better than your neighbour rather than cheaper. For the developed countries, the key to competitiveness is innovation. This means that the factors that determine how cheaply you can produce should be given more weight in countries that are poor than in richer countries. The factors that determine efficiency should be given more weight in intermediate countries, and the factors that drive innovation need to be given more weight in rich developed countries. Although the concept of stages of development appears in many of Porter's research papers, in his previous index all these factors are given the same weight. This means that a country like Zambia is penalised for not carrying out innovation. But I think that Porter would agree with me that, today, Zambia should not be pouring resources into innovation. Zambia needs to prioritise other aspects. For example, it should integrate more with the rest of the world, reduce crime and guarantee property rights to produce an environment where enterprises can produce goods cheaply to sell on the world market. In contrast, if a country like Spain, which is quite a bit richer than Zambia, does not have a good record in R&D, it will be in trouble. The reason is that Spain can no longer compete with China by producing cheaper or better goods. Its only chance is, therefore, to do different or new things, that is, to innovate. Therefore, a competitiveness index should penalise Spain if it does not innovate. So all I did was to implement his idea of stages of development and assign weights to the various factors depending on how important they are at each stage of development.

*But how do you choose the weights?*

Using maximum likelihood techniques I tried to find the weights that I would need, using my index, to explain the actual growth experience of countries during recent years.

## GROWTH AND HAPPINESS

*In our earlier discussion relating to inequality you mentioned that what the government should be measuring is happiness inequality, rather than income inequality. What is your view of the recent literature on the economics of happiness?*[71]

I had some interest until I read a paper which persuaded me to drop this literature (*laughter*). In this paper comparisons of happiness were being made across countries. This was done by comparing the level of income per capita plotted against a measure of happiness. The result was a curve showing an increasing but diminishing rate of increase of happiness with higher income per capita. The conclusion was that after you reach a certain level of income, then extra income does not bring much extra happiness. When I looked at the graph I noticed two things. First, happiness was measured on the vertical axis with an index number ranging between one and ten. People were asked how happy they were on a scale of one to ten. This is completely flawed because if you are very happy and answer ten this year, and you are even happier in five years time, you can still only answer ten if you are very happy. You are not allowed to say 11 (*laughter*). So the curve must be flat at the top – by construction! A further problem was that the 15 countries that were very poor, with low levels of happiness, were all former Soviet republics. So I think that such measures do not really reflect happiness but *changes* in happiness relative to previous circumstances (former Soviet republics are countries that have deteriorated substantially over a very short period of time). Another puzzle to me is that it does not seem to matter which type of survey I see; Finland is always at the top. This suggests to me that different countries respond to surveys in different ways. Maybe in Finland it does not matter what is being asked, the answer will always be ten (*laughter*). So the Finns are supposed to be very happy, and yet other evidence clearly conflicts with this. For example, they have one of the highest suicide rates in the world.[72] If they are so happy, why do so many Finns want to kill themselves?

## CURRENT RESEARCH

*What are your current research interests?*
I am still working on problems of growth and development in Africa, trying to find out what the optimal economic policy strategy might be for each country. I am also trying to implement an idea related to the Umbele Foundation[73] that I helped to set up. I am looking at the issue of corporate responsibility and how firms can help Africa develop, not by giving money,

but by actually moving to Africa and becoming associated with a particular town that wants to be helped. I think that we in the developed countries do not really listen to what the people in Africa want or need. But we don't have effective mechanisms for listening to what they say. Bill Easterly puts it brilliantly when he says that the market is generally a good instrument to achieve what people want. If a business wants to make profits it has to satisfy a demand. If you do not produce what people want, the market kills off your business. International aid is exactly the opposite. If the World Bank goes to help a country and the country does not grow and is worse off after the World Bank intervenes, what happens? The World Bank says that the country has 'moved away from the Millennium Development Goals' – and then asks for a bigger budget to solve the problem.

*So how do we devise a responsive system of help to Africa that listens to what the people who live there actually want and also penalises failure?*
One way is to actually encourage firms that have the technology, human capital and other resources to go to Africa. Let these firms find out what the real problems are that the people want solving. What are the priorities in the face of budget constraints? Do the people want a new school, more doctors, or better roads? The World Bank doesn't know, the United Nations doesn't know, Bono doesn't know, and I don't know. Only the people in Africa themselves really know what the priorities should be. We need to find better ways of getting this information and meeting their needs.

## NOTES

1. I interviewed Professor Sala-i-Martin in his office at Columbia University, New York, on 6 May 2005.
2. Details of Professor Sala-i-Martin's publications and professional activities can be found at his personal (and magnificently entertaining!) webpage: http://www.columbia.edu/~xs23/home.html.
3. The *Journal of Economic Growth*, first published in 1997, is designed to serve as the main outlet for theoretical and empirical research in economic growth and dynamic macroeconomics.
4. For example, Sala-i-Martin (1990a, 1990b, 1994, 1997a, 1997b, 2002d, 2006); Barro and Sala-i-Martin (1991, 1992a, 1992b, 1992c, 1997); Mulligan and Sala-i-Martin (1993, 2000); Roubini and Sala-i-Martin (1992, 1995); Barro et al. (1995); Doppelhofer et al. (2004).
5. Barro and Sala-i-Martin (2003).
6. The most extreme examples being the millions of lives lost as a result of policy-induced famines, for example, in the Soviet Union, 1931–34, 1947; China, 1959–61; Ethiopia, 1984–85; and North Korea, 1995–97.
7. Smith (1776).
8. See the evidence presented in Dollar and Kraay (2002a, 2002b).
9. See Laband and Wells (1998).
10. See Krugman (1997).

11.  See Snowdon and Vane (1996).
12.  Barro (1991); Barro and Sala-i-Martin (1991, 1992a).
13.  The Penn World Table provides purchasing power parity and national income accounts converted to international prices for 168 countries for some or all of the years 1950–2000. For details go to http://pwt.econ.upenn.edu/.
14.  Maddison (2001).
15.  See Galor and Weil (2000).
16.  See Sala-i-Martin (2002a, 2002b, 2006).
17.  See, for example, Galor and Weil (2000); Jones, C.I. (2001); Parente and Prescott (2006).
18.  Mankiw (1995, 2003).
19.  Solow (1956, 1957, 2002).
20.  Rostow (1956, 1960, 1990).
21.  Robert Solow, found this insight to be a 'real shocker' and 'not what I expected at all'. See Snowdon and Vane (2005), p. 665.
22.  See Lee (2003).
23.  A rival good is one where one person's use of that good reduces the availability of that good to other people. A non-rival good is one where one person's use of that good does not reduce the availability of that good to other people. A good is excludable if it has the property that people can be prevented from using the good. While all goods are either rival or non-rival, the degree of excludability can vary considerably.
24.  See Jones, C.I. (2005).
25.  See, for example, Zak and Knack (2001); Glaeser and Shleifer (2002), Glaeser et al. (2004); Helpman (2004); Acemoglu and Johnson (2005).
26.  See Barro (1997).
27.  See Dore et al. (1999); Shleifer et al. (2003).
28.  Dani Rodrik takes a similar position. See Rodrik (2003a, 2005b).
29.  See Sachs's interview for comments on China's institutions.
30.  For example, Barro and Sala-i-Martin (1991, 1992a); Sala-i-Martin (1990a, 1990b, 1996a, 1996b).
31.  See Romer (1986); Rebelo (1991).
32.  Barro and Sala-i-Martin (1991, 1992a); Mankiw et al. (1992).
33.  See Barro and Sala-i-Martin (2003), for a survey.
34.  See Sachs and Warner (1995); Milanovic (2003); Bhagwati (2004a); Wolf (2004a).
35.  See Artadi and Sala-i-Martin (2002).
36.  For recent surveys of the literature on the relationship between openness, trade reform and economic performance, see Panagariya (2004a); Winters (2002a, 2002b, 2004); Winters et al. (2004).
37.  See Acemoglu interview.
38.  Acemoglu and Robinson (2000b).
39.  See Sala-i-Martin and Subramanian (2003).
40.  Barro and McCleary (2003, 2005, 2006). See also Guiso et al. (2003, 2006).
41.  Weber (1904).
42.  World Bank data show that Ireland's GNI per capita for 2004 was 33 170 ($PPP) while the UK's GNI per capita was 31 460 ($PPP).
43.  See Maddison (2001).
44.  See Sala-i-Martin (2002a, 2002b, 2002c).
45.  Sala-i-Martin (2006).
46.  See, for example, Bourguignon and Morrisson (2002); Ravallion (2003, 2004).
47.  See Wade (2004a, 2004b).
48.  The population-weighted variance of the log of income per capita represents a better measure of inequality than the variance of the log of per capita income, which gives the same weight to each country, no matter how large or small the population.
49.  The analysis of global inequality is further complicated by changes in inequality over time *within* countries. See Milanovic (2002a, 2002b, 2006).
50.  See Artadi and Sala-i-Martin (2003).
51.  See Doppelholfer et al. (2004).

52. See Sachs interview.
53. See Murphy et al. (1991).
54. See Easterly (2003a, 2003b, 2004).
55. See Burnside and Dollar (2000).
56. See Easterly, Levine, and Roodman (2004).
57. See Kremer (2002); Kremer and Glennerster (2004); Kremer and Snyder (2004).
58. Sala-i-Martin (2002d).
59. See Mulligan and Sala-i-Martin (2000).
60. See Bloom and Sachs (1998); Sachs (2005a). See also Gallup et al. (2003).
61. Acemoglu et al. (2001, 2002). See also Acemoglu (2003a).
62. See Faye et al. (2004).
63. Sala-i-Martin and Subramanian (2003); Sachs and Warner (2001).
64. See Acemoglu et al. (2003b).
65. See Acemoglu and Johnson (2005); Barro (1996, 1997, 1999). See also Mulligan and Sala-i-Martin (2004).
66. This is the so-called 'Lipset hypothesis', named after Seymour Lipset (1959); 'From Aristotle down to the present, men have argued that only in a wealthy society in which relatively few citizens lived in real poverty could a situation exist in which the mass the population could intelligently participate in politics and could develop the self-restraint necessary to avoid succumbing to the appeals of irresponsible demagogues' (Lipset, p. 75). For recent critiques of the Lipset–Barro hypothesis, see Feng (2003), and Acemoglu et al. (2005b).
67. http://www.weforum.org/.
68. McArthur and Sachs (2001); Porter (2001, 2004, 2005); Sala-i-Martin and Artadi (2004).
69. See Snowdon and Stonehouse (2006).
70. See Porter (2005); Blanke et al. (2004); Sala-i-Martin and Artadi (2004).
71. See Easterlin (2001); Kahnemann et al. (2004); Layard (2005), Komlos and Snowdon (2005). See also the discussion by Kahneman et al., of the 'Day Reconstruction Method' of measuring well-being, in the 3 December issue of *Science*.
72. In a recent paper, Helliwell (2004) also notes that 'very high Scandinavian measures of subjective well-being are not matched by equally low suicide rates'. Data from the World Health Organisation (http://www.who.int/topics/suicide/en/) show that the male suicide rate in Finland was 32.3 per 100 000 in 2002. This compares with 80.7 for Lithuania, 69.3 for Russia, 60.3 for Belarus (2001), 52.1 for Ukraine (2000), 17.1 for the USA (2000), and 11.8 for the UK (1999). Limited data for China (1999) indicate that it is one of the very few countries where the female suicide rate exceeds that of males.
73. The Foundation Umbele looks for 'experience, honesty, simplicity, transparency and efficiency' in order to return the future of Africa to its own citizens. See information on the activities of the foundation at www.umbele.org.

# Jeffrey Williamson[1]

Jeffrey Williamson is one of the world's leading authorities on the economic history of the international economy. Professor Williamson studied for his BA in mathematics at Wesleyan University (1957) before completing his MA (1959) and PhD (1961) degrees at Stanford University. He took up his first academic appointment as Assistant Professor of Economics at Vanderbilt University in 1961–63, before moving on to the University of Wisconsin as Assistant (1963–64) then Associate Professor (1964–68) of economics. In 1968 he became Professor of Economics at Wisconsin, where he remained until 1983. Since then, Professor Williamson has been at the Department of Economics, Harvard University, where, since 1984, he has been the Laird Bell Professor of Economics. Since 1991 he has been a research associate at the National Bureau of Economic Research and in 1994–95 he was President of the Economic History Association. Professor Williamson has also been a consultant and visiting research fellow at the World Bank since 1976.[2]

During a long and distinguished academic career Professor Williamson has to date authored/co-authored/edited 25 books and over 150 articles in leading academic journals. His interests cover a wide area within the field of economic history and include research on international economic development, the Industrial Revolution, industrialisation and de-industrialisation, international inequality, tariff policy, factor price convergence, demography and economic development, international labour migration and globalisation in history.

In the interview that follows I discuss with Professor Williamson his more recent research relating to the global economy in historical perspective.

## BACKGROUND INFORMATION

*As an undergraduate student you majored in mathematics. How did you become interested in economics?*
I was an undergraduate at Wesleyan, a small liberal arts college in Connecticut. There were only about five or six hundred undergraduate students, so the Faculty soon got to know everybody. One of them was my father, Kossuth M. Williamson, an academic economist at Wesleyan. That might explain why I stayed away from economics for as long as possible (*laughter*). So I went into mathematics instead. Later, in my fourth year, I felt that it was safe to take an advanced economics course from someone other than my father. I studied economics with Gerald Meier, who was an extraordinarily good economist, well known for his work in development economics. He is now Emeritus Professor at Stanford. Gerry was an excellent teacher and he turned my interest towards economics. So I went to Stanford University as a graduate student in economics on the basis of having studied only one course beyond the standard introduction.

*Who else influenced you early on? Presumably you must have been inspired by economic history at some stage given your later career.*
Absolutely. Moses Abramovitz at Stanford was very influential. But since I was coming from a mathematics background I initially thought that I would specialise in mathematical economics. From there, I drifted towards growth and trade theory. With my mathematics background, these were economic issues with technical dimensions that attracted me early on. This was a golden age for Stanford economics. Hirofumi Uzawa, Kenneth Arrow, Robert Mundell, Moses Abramovitz, Irma Adelman and Hollis Chenery were all there in the late 1950s (two of whom became Nobel Laureates).[3] Initially I wanted to model economic growth. That was until I was exposed to empirical work, especially to the research of Moses Abramovitz. I realised that the questions that really interested me were the ones that had empirical content. This is how I became interested in issues relating to Third World growth and development. The interest in economic history followed directly from this. While I was a graduate student, I wasn't particularly interested in history *per se* until I began to write my thesis. I wanted to write on Third World growth and development but soon became

aware that in 1960 there were few time series data available for developing countries. It was suggested that I think about doing a thesis on economic history instead, and that is how that important side of my career began.

*Your curriculum vitae, as of May 2003, contains a remarkable 22 books and over 150 published academic papers.*[4] *Although you have obviously researched a range of issues, can you identify for me what you consider to be the main theme or themes of your work?*

The Industrial Revolution. That's what got me started back in 1960 as a graduate student at Stanford. I was interested in the economic development of the early industrialisers – their transition to modern economic growth, to use Simon Kuznets's phrase – and I still am. This transition, which transforms backward and traditional agrarian systems into modern commercial and industrial systems, is, for my money, the most important transition that economists can study. That transition has always intrigued me and it is a theme that keeps on recurring in my research whether I am working on contemporary issues at the World Bank or working here at Harvard on economic history. Over the past 45 years I have also spent a lot of time thinking about accumulation, inequality, city growth and globalisation. These issues are all connected in some way to the Industrial Revolution. I have also worked on the interaction of economic and demographic transitions. Again, that interaction leads us back to my central theme of industrial revolutions, then or now. So I don't think that I have deviated much from that initial interest. More recently I have spent a lot more of my time working on globalisation issues, but still with that same set of concerns. How does globalisation connect with inequality? Who gains and who loses? Does globalisation promote growth and development? When and how? I am now also much more interested in political-economy issues as they influence our thinking on all the questions I have just mentioned. This applies to my recent work on tariff and trade policy, as well as on world migration and immigration policy.[5]

*Do you have any sympathy with those economic historians who have suggested that the term 'Industrial Revolution' is outdated because the transition process was much more gradual than originally thought?*[6]

No. I think it is a silly debate. I have never been interested in rhetoric or labels. For me the important thing is to measure what actually happened, then try to explain it. We are now much better informed about the dimensions and timing of the Industrial Revolution and its causes. Collecting that knowledge has been vastly more important than debating what label to give the event. Such debates are a real waste of scarce research time and talent.

# ECONOMICS AND ECONOMIC HISTORY

*In your 1996* Journal of Economic History *paper you argue that 'theory needs history'. What is the role of economic history in the training of an economist and does a knowledge of economic history make for a better-trained economist?*

Absolutely. Of course you can be a theorist without ever being exposed to history. However, you are likely to be a bad economist if you are not exposed to the institutions that interact with economic events and policies. The best place to find evidence of this interaction is in history. The problem is finding economic historians who can teach smart young economists economic history while using the language and agenda of modern economics. It may be a difficult role to play, but we do it here at Harvard today, just like Moses Abramovitz did for my cohort at Stanford nearly 50 years ago. There are two of us in the Harvard Economics Department teaching and doing research in economic history, Claudia Goldin and myself. We are in a constant dialogue with our graduate students so we have no difficulty speaking the same language and exploring the same issues that they are being taught by our colleagues, whether it be pure theory, applied theory, development, growth, international or labour. We pay careful attention to their agenda as well as our own. If economic historians fail to do this, if they only speak to each other, and if they only take their agenda from historians, then they will never have a big impact on our discipline. But where economic history is allowed to interact – indeed directly compete – with the rest of economics, it can and does have a big impact. That fact is evident from the quality of the work produced by a number of economists who pay attention to economic history. For example, here at Harvard the work of Alberto Alesina, Robert Barro, Francesco Caselli, Ed Glaeser, Larry Katz, Michael Kremer and Andrei Shleifer exhibits this quality, as does the work of Daron Acemoglu and Abhijit Banerjee at MIT. Dani Rodrik, at the Kennedy School, and Jeffrey Sachs, previously at Harvard, also pay very close attention to economic history and economic historians, and use both to support their arguments.[7] Berkeley, Chicago, Columbia, LSE, Northwestern, Stanford, UCLA, Yale and other fine economics departments can make the same claim.

*A notable recent trend within the economics profession over the last ten years has been a recovery of interest in economic history and the work of economic historians. Would you attribute that revival to the renaissance of interest in long-run growth?*

That is certainly part of the reason, but I think there is much more to it than that. A second important factor has been the influence of the new

institutional economics, inspired by Nobel Laureate Douglass North.[8] This
research has helped bridge the gap between history and economics. A third
factor has been a decline in the relative importance of pure theory and a
rise in importance of applied theory. As young economists have become
more and more skilled in technique they have become less interested in (and
less intimidated by) pure theory. They are more interested, and more
capable, of doing applied theory. Really good applied theory had been
missing from our profession after pure theory became mathematised in the
1950s and 1960s. When I entered Stanford in the late 1950s, there was pure
theory and empirical work, while the bridge between them was weak and
fragile. Things were not much different when I left Stanford in 1961, or even
in 1971. Today, applied theory is ubiquitous, exciting and extremely powerful. The best minds are doing it, especially in the fields that interest me
most – growth, development and trade. Today, there is a much stronger urge
to connect with social questions that matter and with good evidence that
can confirm or reject sophisticated hypotheses, and economists are discov-
ering that history is an excellent place to look for both the important social
questions and the evidence to answer them.

## GLOBALISATION IN HISTORY

*In your NBER paper, 'Winners and Losers Over Two Centuries of Globali-
sation', you decompose the period since Columbus's voyage of discovery in
1492 into four distinct epochs.[9] Two of those epochs were pro-global and two
were anti-global. Let us discuss the main features of each of these epochs in
turn. Your first epoch is the period 1492–1820. What is distinctive about this
period?*
I think there has been a lot of confusion about the whole question of when
globalisation begins. The error starts in elementary school when we are
taught the conventional wisdom that following the voyages of discovery by
Christopher Columbus and Vasco da Gama et al. the world became a more
open and a more connected place. I suppose one could go back even further
to Marco Polo or to the Romans to find evidence of increased global con-
nectedness, but, in my view, this characterisation is fundamentally mistaken. There certainly were heroes of discovery before 1800, and there were
also spectacular transfers in technology and disease that took place. But if
you apply standard economic analysis to the event, the first thing an
economist looks for to establish 'globalisation' is evidence of greater
market integration. So, is there any evidence of greater world market integration from 1492 up to the early nineteenth century? The answer is, not
much! Why not much? After all, this was a period when mercantilism and

monopoly trading power were dominant, a period when state policy and trading monopolies restricted trade so as to extract higher rents. That is what monopolists do. Therefore, it is not surprising that we see absolutely no evidence of world market integration over those 300 years. The most important piece of evidence confirming greater market integration is price convergence between trading partners, but there is absolutely no evidence of such convergence. On the contrary, we see evidence of price *divergence*. So whatever the glorious tales historians may tell us about trends in technological change in transport, about Chinese imperial junks bringing giraffes back from Zanzibar, or about American silver flowing on stately galleons to the east, such tales do not speak to the question: did globalisation take place or not?

The decades during and after Columbus were certainly ones of discovery, and the three centuries after 1492 were certainly ones when European trade was booming. Indeed, the evidence clearly shows that the share of European trade in GDP increased significantly after 1492. But what drove the growth of European trade? It was *not* the removal of policy-made trade barriers, the destruction of pirate operations, the break-up of monopoly trading, the decline in transport costs and other market-integrating forces that explain the world trade boom after Columbus, as those who support the 'market integration hypothesis' suggest.[10] If this hypothesis were correct, we would observe evidence of commodity price convergence between Europe, Asia and the Americas. We do not find such evidence. We also know that there were forces suppressing trade and this means that trade would have been much greater without those restrictions. Policy and institutions during that period were anti-global and they *restricted* trade. So, if it wasn't 'globalisation' that explained the trade boom, what was it? My research with Kevin O'Rourke suggests that as much as two-thirds of the European trade boom between 1500 and 1800 can be explained by European income growth, and income growth of the landed rich in particular. As you might expect, these conclusions have generated a hostile response from world historians.

*Your next epoch is the period 1820–1913. What major changes happened in the world economy during these years?*
This epoch is so clearly the opposite of the one that preceded it. From the early nineteenth century until the First World War, all the evidence satisfies the conditions one might expect to find during a period of increasing globalisation in the three markets that matter – capital, labour and commodities. There is clear evidence of world commodity price convergence. You can also find evidence of increasing globalisation in world commodity markets by looking at the qualitative history of trade policy, especially that

of the world economic leader. Britain steadily retreated from an anti-global position after overwhelming Napoleon in 1815. It did so by dismantling its whole protectionist system. Tariffs were reduced, embargoes were lifted, and the Navigation Acts that determined who carried what to where were eliminated. Restrictions on the migration of labour and capital were also relaxed, and there was greater cross-border movement of new ideas. This all happens long before the repeal of the Corn Laws in 1846. That is why Kevin O'Rourke and I favour dates like 1820 as representing the real starting date for globalisation as economists understand it. During the nineteenth century, we observe increasing integration of world commodity and capital markets as mercantilism was dismantled and the worldwide transportation revolution led to a sustained decline in transport costs, including the penetration of interior markets by steamboats and railroads. These markets exhibit the same laws of motion that we observe today, and the orders of magnitude were big then, even compared with today. British capital movements were huge relative to the size of the economy. A mass labour migration also took place in the Atlantic economy, as did a 'churning' within what later became known as the 'Third World' – large migrations from labour-abundant India and China to labour-scarce Southeast Asia, to cite just one example – both of which were of equal or greater magnitude than today.[11]

*What was the main destination of British capital flows during this first era of globalisation?*
In recent papers, Michael Clemens and I show that during the first great capital market boom after 1870 only a small proportion of British capital exports went to poor labour-abundant countries.[12] Most of it, about two-thirds, went to the labour-scarce New World. Thus global capital flows in this era were a force for *divergence* rather than convergence. In 1990, Nobel Laureate Robert Lucas asked the question: why doesn't capital flow from rich to poor countries? Orthodox neoclassical growth theory predicts that capital should flow to low-wage, labour-abundant economies where the marginal product of capital should be high. Lucas drew attention to how this was not happening in the period after 1970 when the world's second great capital market boom began. What we call the 'Lucas paradox' refers to the fact that during the period before 1913 a country's GDP per capita had, and after 1970 still has, a powerful positive attraction for the capital exported from rich countries. Lucas may have popularised the paradox for the late twentieth century, but this paradox was alive and well in the late nineteenth century. British capital was attracted to countries with natural resources, educated labour, and young migrant populations. It was not attracted to cheap labour.

*We now come to a very different anti-global epoch. The period 1913–50 witnesses a disintegration of the global world economy. What is driving the anti-global forces during this period?*

First of all, labour migration was shut down, and legislation mainly accounted for this. The collapse of 'free' world labour migration took place long before the Great Depression began. Second, capital markets began to fall apart as countries tried to re-establish control over domestic monetary policy. You cannot have monetary policy independence without first taking control of capital flows across your borders. Third, as the inter-war period unfolded, each country attempted to shift its unemployment burden onto its neighbours by restricting imports, the so-called 'beggar thy neighbour' policies. I think it is fair to say that by 1938 the world economy had probably lost everything in terms of globalisation that had been gained by 1870.

*What about the emergence of an isolationist Soviet Union after the 1917 Bolshevik revolution?*

Yes indeed. Not only did the Soviet Union drop out of the international system in the 1920s, but by doing so it encouraged others to follow. Indeed, the economic success of the controlled Soviet economy after the first two five-year plans helped encourage interventionist and autarkic policies in the Third World after the Second World War.

*Your final epoch is the second half of the twentieth century to the beginning of the twenty-first century, 1950–2003. This is the second great period of globalisation. But would it not make more sense to split this epoch into two parts in order to distinguish between the pre- and post-1989 periods? The fall of communism in Eastern Europe and the Soviet Union surely marks an important turning point for the global economy.*

I think that carving up the long second half of the twentieth century into two parts is useful. However, I would carve it up somewhat differently than you suggest. I would divide the recent half-century into two, the years between 1950 and early 1970s, and the years from the early 1970s to the present. The OPEC shocks of the 1970s certainly did not contribute to the dividing line, since, after all, OPEC is a cartel whose purpose was and is to restrict oil supply and raise price. Instead, here are the three events that suggest that early 1970s dividing line: first, the true beginnings of a global capital market were only apparent in the early 1970s when private lending started its secular boom; second, in the early 1970s Third World policy began to shift from closed to open, led by East Asian success; third, and in the wake of the US Migration Act of 1965, a new surge in world migrations began to enter high-wage OECD labour markets, this time from Asia, Latin America and Africa.[13]

*Does an end to the so-called 'golden age' of growth, 1950–73, act as your demarcation line?*

In one sense, perhaps. The European 'golden age' of growth and catching up with the USA does cover the period 1950–73, and that growth raised world trade shares. But, more importantly, the OECD was playing the integration game, not so much in factor markets, but certainly in trade and commodity markets. Indeed, the Third World was allowed to absent itself from these trade-liberalising conversations: by choice, the Third World forewent participation in the trade boom generated by the European 'golden age'. As I have already suggested, the Third World opted for closed economy strategies. It was, after all, led or at least influenced by the closed Soviet development model up to 1970. Furthermore, their annoyance with their colonial masters persuaded them to adopt an inward-looking strategy of industrialisation via import substitution. These and other forces sent the Third World in an autarkic direction just when the OECD was shedding autarky and going open. So, looking at the period up to the early 1970s, increasing integration and convergence took place within the OECD. After the early 1970s the Third World finally started to come on board. Led by East Asia, others began to follow. In short, the second global century can be split in to two parts. The first, up to the early 1970s, was limited primarily to the OECD. The second, after the early 1970s, involved the Third World and Eastern Europe as well.

*What caused what you call the globalisation 'policy backlash' in the inter-war period?*[14]

Actually, the backlash started earlier, in the late nineteenth century, and we can see it in both trade and immigration policy. In the latter part of the nineteenth century a great debate began in the USA about immigration policy. There had always been latent hostility towards immigrants in the USA going back to the 1830s when the first inflow began to arrive from poorer parts of Europe. But the really big political debate started in the mid-1890s during years of temporary growth slowdown and industrial crisis. Against that background, the House of Representatives voted in 1896 to restrict immigration (using literacy requirements) but the Senate disagreed. To achieve legislative success in the USA, three bodies need to agree – the House, the Senate and the President. On immigration policy, they could not agree. The immigration issue was batted back and forth, and for over 25 years it was the most contentious political issue in America. The problem never went away, and citizens were informed by vigorous public debate involving various commissions and hearings, as well as by reformist journalism. These debates reveal one important American perception about immigration: new immigrants were thought to lower the living standards of the working class already settled in the USA (there were, I must report, also some ugly racist tinges to the debate). Finally, majority opinion in Congress overwhelmed President Woodrow Wilson's veto and the House and Senate approved restrictions. The policy tool being debated then was to impose literacy requirements on potential immigrants to restrict the size and source of immigration. Meanwhile, the First World War caused a sharp decline in US immigration, but when it was over, the policy tool actually implemented was the quota-by-origin. These legislated restrictions lasted from the early 1920s until 1965. In short, there was a backlash already present in America *before* the inter-war period and the Great Depression. Meanwhile, the countries with whom the USA had competed for immigrants, such as Australia, Brazil and Argentina, also restricted immigration. This was partly in response to US policy: these countries expected that many migrants that would previously have gone to the USA would now be deflected to them. But rising inequality in their own countries was also important in stimulating anti-immigration policies everywhere in high-wage labour markets. Australia, for example, did not undergo an improvement in living standards from 1870 to 1910 even though it was the richest country in the world both in per capita income and in real wages at the start of this period. Australians – like most Americans – thought that this was, at least in large part, due to the inflow of migrants, and my research supports that conclusion. There was a definite anti-migration backlash generated by conditions in high-wage labour markets well before the First World War.

*What about tariff policy and protectionism in goods markets?*
Tariff policy also reflects globalisation backlash. Consider Europe. Even in the late nineteenth century, Europe exported manufactures and imported primary products, foodstuffs in particular. Europe got 'invaded' (military rhetoric was used to describe the event then) by grain from the USA and Ukraine. This lowered the price of grain in European markets, hence lowered rents on land producing grain, and hence lowered land values. Who owned the land? Those at the top of the income and wealth distribution, the landed interests with political power. So it did not take long for most of Europe to introduce a restrictive tariff policy to offset the invasion of these imports. There has been much written on this; indeed, our library shelves sag with the weight of such books (*laughter*).

*What is happening in the rest of the world during this period?*
The rise in tariffs in the rest of the world – what some of us call the periphery – was even greater than in Europe, where the tariff increases were modest by comparison.[15] The countries in the periphery were 'invaded' by manufactures, and tariff policy was used in part to ease the pain for the import-competing industries. There is strong evidence that this anti-global

reaction helped mute the impact of globalisation during this period. The policy reaction did not erase the impact of globalisation coming from the worldwide transport revolution, but it did mute it. That's the nature of the world policy environment prior to the First World War.

*There have been several recent papers asking the question: is the world more globalised now than it was in the late nineteenth century?*[16] *What is your interpretation of the evidence on this?*
The world was more globalised then than it is now in the following sense. Remember that we have three markets that are important to this assessment: the markets for labour, capital and commodities. In terms of migration, there was much greater movement of people in the nineteenth century than there was in the twentieth century.[17] Even for the USA, which is the dominant country in terms of modern migrant absorption, it was much bigger relative to the size of the labour market in the nineteenth century. This, then, is an important qualifier because many commentators think only in terms of trade and capital movements when they talk about globalisation. It is clear that mass emigration from Europe and its impact on labour market integration in what we now call the OECD probably mattered more in the nineteenth century than the other two forces. In another sense there is more globalisation now. In terms of technological transfer, and the role of FDI in that process, the world is more globalised now. FDI was a minor share of total foreign investment during the nineteenth-century global capital market boom. Today, FDI is a bigger share and it also involves the developing countries. It is also true that the standard characterisation of the 'periphery' is very different now in one important sense. In the nineteenth century the European countries and their offshoots exported manufactures while the rest exported foodstuffs and intermediate goods processed by manufacturing abroad. That is not the picture today since about 70 per cent of developing-country exports are now manufactures. It can be, and was argued (e.g. by Raul Prebisch and Hans Singer), that trade for the nineteenth-century periphery implied specialisation in primary products, and thus de-industrialisation.[18] Not today, since most developing countries (excluding sub-Saharan Africa) can use trade as an engine of industrialisation and thus (presumably) growth. It appears that globalisation has even more to offer the poor country today than was true a century ago.

## WORLD INEQUALITY

*Angus Maddison has produced some heroic estimates of world income per capita for the last 2000 years.*[19] *His estimates show that there was a gap in living standards clearly visible by the early nineteenth century although that gap was relatively small by contemporary standards. What is your impression about the extent of divergence in living standards across the world circa 1820, your preferred date for the beginning of the first wave of globalisation?*

Given the quality of the data, I find that kind of question to be less useful than asking what happens to those gaps over time. My own research relates mainly to those countries that comprise what we now call the OECD. Here we see living standard gaps of an order ranging from 2–1 to 4–1. For example, Irish real wages just after the potato famine were about half of British real wages, and about a quarter of real wages in the USA. No wonder the poor Irish migrated to Liverpool and Boston. Yet, these gaps *within* the OECD were pretty modest compared to what the ratios were *between* the OECD and poor parts of Africa and Asia.[20] But when we ask the question: when does the big gap between rich and poor countries begin to manifest itself?, I am less persuaded by Angus Maddison's evidence and more persuaded by the kinds of evidence offered by recent wage and price studies. Robert Allen has looked at the dispersion of real wages for European unskilled urban workers from the sixteenth century until the First World War.[21] His work shows very clearly that there is an increasing gap starting around 1600 when the gap was no more than about 20 per cent between high-wage and low-wage Europe. Northwestern Europe then pulled ahead of the rest of continental Europe in the period before the Industrial Revolution. In England and the Low Countries, workers began to get a real edge in terms of living standards, more than twice that of the rest of Europe just before the Industrial Revolution. So there was already a big gap in living standards before the Industrial Revolution within Europe and we need to identify the causes of this emerging gap in the earlier period. That is where the work of economists like Douglass North, Daron Acemoglu, Simon Johnson and James Robinson is contributing so much.[22] Their work on institutions, geography and politics is very important. There is also a lot of evidence being collected by scholars like Kenneth Pomeranz,[23] whose recent claim that China had a similar level of economic development as Western Europe in the eighteenth century has received a lot of attention. But there are many other scholars who have been given less exposure who are trying to establish just when the gap between Western Europe and the rest appeared. I am persuaded by the evidence that says that the gaps had already emerged before the eighteenth century. So if we are looking for explanations of the emergence of living standard gaps across the world, we will have to look well before the Industrial Revolution to find the answers.

*Many neo-Marxists would point to colonialism as an explanation for the 'great divergence'. But from what you have just been saying it would seem that*

*there is strong evidence that these gaps existed well before the major period*
*of European colonialism in the second half of the nineteenth century.*
Yes, these gaps were emerging way before the main colonial period. The evidence is much cruder, but there are those that argue that in the seventeenth
century economic disparities between China, India and Europe are hard to
find. There may be differences, but you have to work very hard to find them.
In contrast, you do not have to work very hard to find them by 1800, and
by 1913 the gaps are abundantly clear to any scholar.[24] So it looks as if there
is living standard parity around the world about the time of Columbus.
This 'fact' doesn't surprise me much given the operation of some demographic regime that must have produced a Malthusian equilibrium, or
steady state, during this era.[25] The argument that globalisation contributes
to the increase in the gap before 1800 is one that I simply don't buy. First,
the timing is wrong. The gaps emerged before colonialism became important. Second, it gives far too much weight to the forces of globalisation.
There were, after all, other forces at work that are likely to have been far
more important. Local and domestic factors even today contribute far
more to economic performance than do globalisation factors, and it seems
plausible to assume than this was even more true before 1800 when the
world was less globally integrated. To attribute the divergence in living standards across the world to globalisation alone is far too simple when
attempting to explain this complex developmental event.

*There has been much recent discussion and controversy in the literature about*
*trends in 'global inequality'.*[26] *What is your impression with respect to the*
*overall trend in global inequality?*
Peter Lindert and I wrote a paper on this issue so I guess that makes us participants in this debate.[27] It turns out that some of the evolution of inequality across time can be explained by changing weights due to the distribution
of population. But most of it is explained by a rise in the size of the income
gaps between countries rather than as a result of a rise in within-country
inequality. In any case, after this literature has provided estimates of the
evolution of world inequality, the reader is often left to infer that globalisation is somehow responsible. The world has undoubtedly become much
more unequal over the last 200 years but this may or may not have had anything to do with globalisation. Peter Lindert and I argue that globalisation
probably mitigated the rise in inequality between countries at least for those
countries that became integrated into the world economy. The income per
capita gaps across the world were not made worse by increasing globalisation, even though it is not clear that globalisation reduced the gaps much.
The evidence shows that the observed rise in world income inequality has
been driven by an increase in the gaps between countries rather than within

countries. However, I am not sure why there is so much interest in this question about what is happening to 'world inequality'. To me, the more interesting and important question relates to the impact of globalisation on income distribution *within* countries, not income gaps between countries or 'world inequality'. Here the effect of globalisation on inequality has gone both ways; there have been both winners and losers.

*Why are you more interested in the distributional effects of globalisation within countries?*
Global economic policy is formed at the country level, and if there is to be anti-global backlash, it will come from policy reaction by the countries themselves. Thus, if I ask how globalisation effects inequality, I think the answer lies with the political response to the perceived impact of globalisation on voting citizens within the domestic economy. Few citizens care what is happening between them and the rest of the world when taking pro-global or anti-global positions.[28] However, they care a great deal about their absolute incomes and their incomes relative to the rest of their compatriots. We are not yet a world nation. Thus, changes in the world income distribution do not get translated into any effective political response and hence any policy response. Only when we have achieved an integrated global political system will global inequality matter. Until then, economists measure it only to get the facts straight.

## TRADE, GLOBALISATION AND ECONOMIC GROWTH

*Another important debate among economists and economic historians relates to the relationship between trade, openness and economic growth. Do more open economies grow faster than more inward-looking economies? The contrasting views of economists such as Jagdish Bhagwati and Dani Rodrik on this issue are well known.[29] Do you go along with the consensus view that openness and increasing integration with the world economy represent the best strategy for ensuring sustained economic growth and development?*
I was with you until the last phrase which contained the word 'best' (*laughter*). Attending to problems at home is the best way to get development. Globalisation will help you, given that proviso. Every economist who has run a regression over the past 15 years, with the exception of Dani Rodrik, has found the correlation we expect for recent historical experience.[30] Controlling for religion, culture, geography and institutions, openness is always correlated with faster growth. Economists have been getting that result ever since the National Bureau of Economic Research did its simple

comparative static studies back in the 1960s and 1970s. Indeed, there has not been a single study that has shown the opposite. That is, no study has shown that openness has been associated with slower growth. So, while some economists may be sceptical about studies that keep reporting the growth–openness correlation, we cannot find the opposite correlation on experience since 1950. I repeat, since 1950. There is, however, one important exception to this rule. Earlier in history, prior to the Second World War, guess what we find? For European countries the classic correlation evaporates. Indeed, not only does it evaporate; it also switches sign: protection was associated with fast growth! This finding has puzzled a lot of scholars. Economists tend to ignore it but economic historians keep reminding them and asking for an explanation. It was first discovered by Paul Bairoch.[31] True, his calculations were not very sophisticated, but he was the first to point out the perverse correlation. More recently, Kevin O'Rourke found the same result in a more sophisticated study.[32] Using the same basic model that Jeffrey Sachs and Andrew Warner and everybody else uses, O'Rourke still gets the result that protection was correlated with faster growth prior to the First World War.[33]

*What about the rest of the world in that earlier period?*
When the same question is asked for the whole world – not just the Atlantic economy – very interesting asymmetries emerge. For Europe, the perverse correlation holds: those who protected grew faster. We need an explanation for this perverse result, and Michael Clemens and I think that we have one.[34] But if you look at the periphery – Latin America, Africa, Asia and the Middle East – the perverse correlation goes away. Indeed, the pre-1940 periphery reports the same correlation as the late twentieth century: countries that grew fast had low levels of protection. I think this standard correlation in the periphery before the Second World War has little to do with the impact of openness on growth. I think the causality goes the other way round, and I said so at the recent Heckscher conference in Stockholm.[35] I argue that countries that had slow economic growth used high tariffs as their main source of revenue to finance social overhead and military spending.[36] Countries with slow growth, and slow growth of their tax base, had an incentive to increase their tariff revenues by imposing high tariffs. Thus we observe an inverse correlation between growth and protection. This is one of the first questions posed of the econometric growth–openness literature exploring the period after 1965: are we sure about the causality? Economists don't worry enough about the world economic environment that may condition their answers. Suppose the world economic environment changed? Would you expect the same answers? Look to history to be sure.

# TRADE THEORY AND ECONOMIC HISTORY

*Has the research of economic historians confirmed the main ideas of economists on trade theory?*
Absolutely. Historical studies have confirmed the predictions of the Heckscher–Ohlin theorem and the Samuelson–Stolper corollary. There is no doubt about this, at least for earlier historical periods.[37] However, we have also learned that economies in the nineteenth century and the centuries before were pretty simple. Those were the centuries being used by Hechscher and Ohlin when they were developing their endowment-driven theories around the First World War. They were looking at a simpler time. Now we live in a more complex time, requiring more complex theories.

*What do you mean by a 'more complex time'?*
Looking at the first global century, you can get away with applying models containing just land and labour. You cannot do that for the second global century. You have to add skills, human capital, technological complexities and so on. The standard Heckscher–Ohlin prediction is rejected when exposed to modern data whereas it survives when exposed to historical data from a century ago. Conditions and economies have changed, and theorists have not yet successfully developed models that can take account of the movement away from competition towards oligopoly and various forms of monopolistic competition. The best minds in international trade theory are currently working on this problem including, for example, Gene Grossman at Princeton and my Harvard colleague Elhanan Helpman.[38] It is hard now to do trade theory without basing it on non-competitive foundations. In the 1890s this was not a problem for theorists because the world was mostly competitive. This is not true today.

# INTERNATIONAL LABOUR MIGRATION

*You have written a great deal on international labour migration issues, in particular your co-authored books and papers with Timothy Hatton. Looking at what you call the 'Atlantic economy', what were the main causes of the massive north–north migrations that took place in the nineteenth century through to 1914?[39]*
The really interesting paradox revealed by European mass emigrations during the nineteenth century is that you get the expected prediction only about half the time. That is, the poorest countries are not the ones that sent migrants to the New World. The poorest labourers are not the ones who left the European labour market for better conditions abroad. Really poor

regions were not a major source of migrants. These facts are puzzling because you would expect the economic return to migration to have been higher the poorer the labourer. The explanation, of course, is that really poor people find it difficult to move because of income constraints. There is capital market failure in the sense that nobody is prepared to invest in the movement of poor people unless there is imposed on them a system of slavery or indentured servitude. Such practices are, of course, now outlawed. But such practices were allowed for some time and they worked by making the migration of poor people to North America and elsewhere possible. In the Americas, the number of free white migrants from Europe exceeded coerced African migrants only by 1880. For centuries only slaves could 'afford' the move, so to speak. That is, free migration was limited to those who could afford it. Europeans either had to be *relatively* rich to make the move to the Americas, or they entered indentured servitude. Given the important income constraints on migration, it is not surprising that individual country emigration experience typically passes through an 'inverted U' life cycle. When economies are pre-industrial and poor, few leave because they cannot afford the move. When the Industrial Revolution begins at home you might think that improving job prospects and incomes at home would deter out-migration. Wrong. More people actually leave!

*Can you expand on the reasons for this?*
As real wages increase at home, even compared to rich countries, more and more people emigrate because the income constraints are gradually released. Real wages rise, so the poor can begin to accumulate savings. There is also the so-called remittance effect, the transfer of income back home from pioneering family members who previously migrated. Those remittances help solve the capital market problem. So it is not surprising that Mexican migration to the USA in the last 30 years has increased as Mexico has undergone substantial development.[40] It *did* come as a surprise to a lot of observers, who thought that economic development at home would suppress Mexican emigration. Many believed that NAFTA would also help reduce the flow of Mexican migrants to the USA but that is not how it has turned out, offering further confirmation of the life-cycle inverted-U pattern of migration. A second force at work is that as countries gradually escape agrarian backwardness and achieve industrialisation, they experience a demographic transition. Child mortality rates decline, fertility rates rise, population grows more rapidly and the age distribution of the population becomes younger, thus generating, after a couple of decades, a glut of young adults who are the first to migrate. These demographic forces mattered in the nineteenth century and they also matter today. One of the

reasons why African emigration has been on the increase in the last 20–30 years is because the region is experiencing a demographic transition and has an increasingly large proportion of young adults. This provides a large pool of potential migrants, both now and in the future, who will try to get across the moat to Europe and the USA. So the release of the income constraints on migration together with these demographic forces can explain a secular surge in emigration. These dynamics take place in an environment of wide wage gaps between labour-scarce and labour-abundant areas and they always create pressures on emigration. Even as the poor countries start to catch up with the rich, huge differentials in living standards still remain, and they continue to act as a strong incentive to emigrate from the poorer countries as the income constraint is released. These forces are captured in the upside of the inverted U of the life cycle of migration. These nineteenth-century laws of motion have been repeated since 1965, when the USA revised its immigration policy. Since then, the US immigration rate has soared, particularly from the poorer parts of the world.

*During the last few years one of the big ongoing debates in the UK has been over inward migration. Does the UK economy need more migrants? Are many of the migrants coming to the UK genuine asylum seekers or are they basically economic migrants posing as asylum seekers to gain entry to the UK economy? This debate was further inflamed by the events of September 11, 2001, and public fears relating to international terrorism. Given that Europe is facing an ageing population structure for the twenty-first century, it would seem that more young migrants from outside Europe will be needed to boost the supply of labour. However, such inflows are likely to cause political controversy.[41] The same problem faces many other rich countries. What are your thoughts on this issue?*

You are right about the demographic trends. During the next 30 years or so we are going to be passing through a demographic event that the nineteenth century did not come close to matching during the age of mass migration: namely, demographic asymmetry between the labour-scarce OECD countries and the labour-abundant developing countries. The OECD has numerous elderly people who are about to withdraw from the labour force and that number is going to get bigger over time as they live longer. Meanwhile the proportion of young people in the population is getting smaller. In the developing countries it is the other way around. The proportion of young to old is increasing. This demographic asymmetry is breathing down the necks of politicians and voters in Europe and North America. The same kind of asymmetry existed in the late nineteenth century as Europe was generating a lot of young adults, many of whom became migrants. But the asymmetry was never as dramatic as it is now. In short, the demographic forces pushing Europe and North America to open their doors are much stronger now than they have been at any other time.

*Do you think that Europe and the USA will be able to resist these forces?*
I don't know. But the forces to open up are much stronger than they were in the nineteenth century.

*Earlier in this interview you talked about the backlash against immigration in the USA that took place between the 1890s until the imposition of immigration quotas some 25 years later. Is another backlash coming?*
I don't think so, at least in America. Still, why is there such a benign attitude towards the invasion of commodities resulting from more open trade policies and hostility towards immigrants, especially in Europe? I would have thought that today there are fewer unskilled workers who potentially could get damaged by the competition coming from unskilled immigrants. And most immigrants are unskilled even if they have a doctorate when they arrive in Boston or London. It is not easy to convert human capital assets immediately upon arrival in a new country. So there are fewer workers to crowd out of the labour market now than was the case in the late nineteenth and early twentieth century. The safety nets are also more extensive now. They were non-existent in 1890. A century ago, if a Sicilian immigrant could not get a job in New York, he returned to Palermo. He did not receive any public support. Another consideration is that there is now political suffrage, and everybody gets to vote. This was not the case in Britain even after the reforms of 1867. Political voices representing those who are adversely affected by immigration are louder now than they were then. Thus there is a variety of forces pushing in different directions. Weighing up the balance of forces – the increasing voice of the unskilled displaced workers versus the existence of safety nets to protect unemployed resident workers – is difficult. However, on balance one might conclude that the impact of immigration should be less destructive now than it was in the USA back in the 1890s. Indeed, recent experience suggests that there is not as much hostility towards immigration as there was in the 1890s, at least in the USA. The USA revised its immigration policy, first in 1965, then a number of times since. The 1965 Amendments to the Immigration Act abolished quotas and replaced them with a system that emphasised the reunification of families, a system that became immigration friendly towards the developing countries.[42] As a result, the USA has undergone an enormous change in the source of its immigrants, just as it did in the late nineteenth century. The rhetoric used then referred to the deterioration in the quality of US immigrants, who were increasingly coming from places that had far lower levels of literacy and other correlates of underdevelopment. Not much has changed in that sense since US

immigrants increasingly come from areas of the world with lower educational standards and lower levels of development. In the short run, this serves to lower the average quality of the US labour force.

*What is the political economy that has allowed this to happen in the USA?*
Oddly, there has not been much debate or complaint. Remarkably, it has not been a big political issue. It just happened. I find this fact amazing. While the World Bank is pulling its hair out worrying about European restrictive immigration policies, the USA has become more open to immigration from poor countries and nobody seems to have noticed. Surely this should have helped erase poverty in the sending countries.

*What do you think of Jagdish Bhagwati's idea that we need an international institution to deal with world migration?*[43] *He suggests that 'the new world order now needs a World Migration Organisation' (WMO) that will stand alongside the other major international institutions such as the World Trade Organisation, the IMF and the World Bank.*
I am amazed that really smart and sophisticated people like Bhagwati and other economists pay so little attention to political-economy considerations when discussing these issues. He has argued so eloquently, over and over again, about the advantages of free trade. Yet many countries reject the arguments for free trade. Why is that? The reason why free trade is often rejected lies with political economy. The same is true of migration. Who wins and who loses from free trade? Who gains and who pays the price for open migration policies? Are the losers compensated? What is the nature of the politics? Until we can provide clear answers to these questions, how can Bhagwati expect that his suggestion for a WMO is likely to be taken seriously and have any impact? I think it makes far more sense to understand and influence the immigration policies that are coming from the immigrant countries that matter, namely, Western Europe and the USA.

*What about Japan? Here is a county that has remained essentially closed to inward migration throughout its history and is now facing an enormous demographic crisis. Forecasts indicate that Japan's population will decline substantially over the next few decades unless it has a more open immigration policy.*
Japan has a history of total restriction on immigration except for Koreans during the Second World War. You are right about the demographics. One of their solutions to this problem seems to be that elderly Japanese citizens should be encouraged to move to Hawaii or to Australia (*laughter*). Sooner or later that demographic problem is going to explode into a huge political debate in Japan. Demographic forces cannot be avoided.

*Are you currently doing more research on migration issues?*
Yes. Much more research needs to be done in the area of international migration, and next fall [2004] Tim Hatton and I are planning to write a book on world migration while I am on leave in Canberra, Australia. We intend to do more on comparing the contemporary scene with the past.


# MODERN GROWTH THEORY, ECONOMIC HISTORY AND GEOGRAPHY

*As an economic historian, to what extent has modern growth theory helped you get a better insight into the past growth experience of countries or are these 'new' ideas simply formalising what economic historians already know?*
Until about 15 years ago there was a wide divide between the way economic historians were talking about growth and the way that growth theorists were talking about growth. Thirty years ago, growth theorists felt that there was no need to talk about institutions, leaving such issues to other social scientists. Growth theorists did not think that institutions could be formalised and therefore little progress could be made along this route. The same attitude was shown to the influence of culture, geography and other fundamentals. Applied theory has made huge progress in recent years, so that these factors can now be formalised. The institutions that matter can be brought into the theoretical models, so much so that these models make precise predictions that can now be tested. That is an amazing change that has taken place within growth theory. So, economic history can now form a happy marriage with this new growth literature. That was not possible even 15 years ago.

*One debate that has received a lot of attention in the literature is the one ignited by Jeffrey Sachs relating to the neglect of geography by economists when explaining economic growth and comparative economic development.[44] Do you agree with Sachs that geography has been neglected by economists?*
I think geography is important. I don't think you will find any development economist or economic historian who would argue that space and geography do not matter. Indeed, when Jeffrey Sachs writes he is the first to cite a long list of previous scholars who have explored the role of geography on economic growth. So geography is not news, but economists need reminders. The difficult problem, however, is trying to formalise such assertions so that we can better understand how geography interacts with institutions, endowments, policy and performance. I like the way that Sachs has engaged in these debates with Daron Acemoglu and others.[45] Of course each of these horses out there on the academic racetrack have their own

view of what is important, whether it be geography, culture, institutions or something else. But growth is too complicated, and the evolution of policy is too complex to expect to have one factor carry the day. Furthermore, the problems associated with establishing causality are well known. Thus there will always be an interesting and rich debate on the interaction between culture, geography, institutions and policy. But geography does matter.

*Can you give me some examples of how geography matters?*
I have been doing a lot of work on Latin America recently, and the impact of geography on development there is spectacular.[46] Take Colombia for example. There is a reason why Colombia has been plagued with problems of violence for 200 years. This is not just a recent problem related to the drug trade. It is a long-standing problem and some of it has to do with geography and the difficulty Colombia has had in creating groups that can function as a coherent political unit as opposed to isolated tribes who are constantly in conflict with each other. What is impressive about the recent literature is how scholars have begun to model these influences to the point that competing hypotheses can be tested in a persuasive way.

*There has also been a rebirth of interest in the relationship between inequality and growth, including your own research.[47] During the 1950s period of 'capital fundamentalism' it was assumed that inequality was good for growth. However, the experience of East Asian economic development has shown that countries can grow rapidly without necessarily experiencing increasing inequality. Is there any kind of clear relationship showing up in the historical data?*
When I teach these issues and compare the modern take on this problem with what economic history has to say, I end up arguing that we do not know the answer to this question and maybe we never will. Looking at the reduced-form equation relating growth to inequality, you can get the causation going either way. In simple theories the relationship is clear. If you believe that the accumulation is carried out by the rich, then you will accept the classical conclusion that inequality will promote growth via higher saving and capital accumulation. As we became more sophisticated in the twentieth century we added on human capital and R&D, but we still had the same story. Don't we need to ask what creates inequality in the first place? Suppose a technological surge is capital-using, thus raising the returns to investment and increasing inequality at the same time. Do higher profits and more inequality account for the increased saving and accumulation? Or is it the technology-driven high rate of return doing all the work? Consider another example. If skills are scarce, it means that there will be wage inequality. This will encourage more schooling and eventually the

skill premium will be erased, producing more equality. Under those conditions, we are certain to see a Kuznets curve in the data.[48] However, economic life gets more complicated when we take the global environment into account. Suppose that you asked me this question in 1936 and I was living in a world where there was virtually no international capital mobility. In this world, if a country wanted to accumulate capital, then it would have to go it alone. Such a country would have been completely constrained by domestic savings when trying to achieve specific accumulation targets. This is what the Soviet Union experienced during the early five-year plans under Stalin. So the models developed during the 1940s and 1950s were those associated with the names of Mahalanobis, Lewis, Harrod and Domar, economists who developed models that focused on capital accumulation from domestic sources.[49] Furthermore, economic life gets even more complicated when we take account of the fact that the country must get its capital goods from some trading partner. If international trade were closed down, then our country would be additionally constrained by the capacity of the domestic capital goods sector. Thus the models that came out of that era – the ones being taught in the late 1950s and 1960s – assumed an economy closed to capital and trade. Domestic savings matter in those models, and if inequality raises domestic savings then it follows that inequality promotes economic growth. Are such models relevant now? No. World capital markets are now integrated. If a country needs more capital it can raise it on the international capital markets. We now live in a very different world where domestic savings don't matter as much. Policy advice and models reflect that new reality of global capital market integration. Now, when modern economists are looking at the data from the past 20 years, they are unlikely to find a positive connection between capital accumulation and domestic savings.

## POLITICS, ECONOMIC DEVELOPMENT AND GLOBALISATION

*An important question that has fascinated economic historians is: why did the Industrial Revolution and modern economic growth first happen in Britain? One answer, following the ideas of Douglass North and Mancur Olson, is that following the 'Glorious Revolution' of 1688, Britain benefited from having a more representative and less predatory government.[50] How important was the establishment of the Constitution in the 1780s to the subsequent economic development of the US economy?*
Reading the Federalist Papers makes one realise how important a few individuals were in creating a Constitution that worked. Still, US revolutionary

experience was unusual. Many revolutions have been successful in getting rid of some dictatorial villain. But it's what happens next that matters. Revolutions are invariably followed by bloodshed and further violence. This was certainly true of France. And it was also true of Latin America, where independence in the 1820s was followed by 50 years of bloodshed, political instability and 'lost decades' of zero growth. The US revolution was exceptional in that it was the only one, to my knowledge, that was not followed by bloodshed. I don't know how the USA was able to dodge that particular bullet. Southerners, who had an export- and slave-oriented economy, persuaded northerners to agree that slavery would not be on the federal political agenda. How on earth was that agreement reached? Of course after the initial period of nation building, the agreement fell apart and we finally had our Civil War in 1861–65. But no other country had such a long period of stability following its revolution for independence. As far as the economy is concerned, the first step occurred in 1783 when the USA formed a loose confederation. The states rejected the formation of a customs union. None of the states wanted to turn over their trade-taxing power to the federal government, and they each maintained their independent authority over tariffs. For six years the British exploited this opportunity. Sixty per cent of British trade was with North America and each state lowered tariffs to attract British goods to their ports, where they would be re-exported to other states. This led to what Dani Rodrik calls a 'race to the bottom', and an economic disaster for the young republics. So in 1789 the states met and agreed to obey a Constitution that created a tighter federation with a customs union. This customs union worked well, well enough to encourage the newly united states to use their collective market power to force Britain to lower its tariffs on US goods by increasing US tariffs on British goods. Starting from very low levels, US tariffs rose over a 20-year period to about 40 per cent. In contrast, Britain started with a tariff rate of about 50 per cent and ended up with a rate of about 10 per cent. In short, the newly united states pursued what economists now call strategic tariff behaviour. The tariff policy was successful, just as the signers of the 1789 document guessed it would be.

*It seems that democracy has been good for US economic development. But is the current wave of globalisation a threat to democracy?*
No. I think globalisation is liberating. In fact, as my colleagues Alberto Alesina and Enrico Spolare have shown, globalisation tends to create (or makes possible) regional fragmentation and autonomy.[51] It is much easier to offer political concessions to regional groups in a globalised economy where the cost imposed on the national economy is modest. Similarly, it could be argued that late nineteenth-century globalisation helped provoke political suffrage in Britain and other parts of Europe before the First

World War. One can only hope that it will do the same in many of today's poor nations.

*Are you an optimist with respect to the prospects for economic progress in the twenty-first century or are we more likely to witness what Samuel Huntington has called a 'clash of civilisations'?*[52]

Yes, I worry about this possibility, especially in terms of world migrations. American and other immigrant countries are used to the clash of cultures given our multicultural immigrant background. We are by no means perfect, but this is at least one thing we have learned to do well over the last 200 years: absorb different cultures with minimum hostility. Most of the world, including Europe, does not have this same experience, inviting a 'clash of cultures'. More to the point, globalisation *does* threaten to reduce cultural diversity. Travelling the world in the 1950s was a very different experience to travelling the world today. It is much easier to travel now, but also much less exciting and enriching. 'Majority' cultures tend to swallow up 'minority' cultures. Local languages and cuisines disappear. Thus there is a cultural price to be paid for increasing globalisation and these changes are often resisted. Furthermore, as we all know so well, it is easier and cheaper for modern dissident groups to resist change with violence. On the other hand, the economic prospects for the poorer parts of the world in the twenty-first century are excellent. Over the last 30 years, a convergence of living standards between rich and poor countries has been in motion. Not everywhere, of course: Africa in particular remains a huge problem. But progress in India and China, with over a third of the world's population, has been tremendous. I think this will continue and even accelerate for these two countries and for the transition economies of Eastern Europe and Russia.

## NOTES

1. I interviewed Professor Williamson in his office at Harvard University on 15 May 2003.
2. Full details of Professor Williamson's curriculum vitae can be found on his webpage at http://www.economics.harvard.edu/~jwilliam/.
3. Kenneth Arrow was awarded the Nobel Prize (jointly with John Hicks) in 1982, and Robert Mundell received his award in 1999.
4. Details of Professor Williamson's publications and working papers can be found on his webpage at http://www.economics.harvard.edu/~jwilliam/. His recent working papers are also available at the National Bureau of Economic Research, www.nber.org.
5. See Hatton and Williamson (1998, 2002a, 2005); Clemens and Williamson (2001, 2004a); Coatsworth and Williamson (2002); Williamson (2002a, 2002b, 2003, 2004).
6. For example Jones, E.L. (1988). See also Lindert and Williamson (1983); Williamson (1984, 1987).
7. See Snowdon (2002a, 2002b).

8. See, for example, North (1990).
9. Williamson (2002a).
10. See O'Rourke and Williamson (1999, 2002a, 2002b, 2004).
11. The 'Atlantic economy' refers to Western and Southern Europe, North America and Australasia. See O'Rourke and Williamson (1999).
12. See Clemens and Williamson (2000, 2004b).
13. See Williamson (2004), and Hatton and Williamson (2005).
14. See Williamson (1998a); Timmer and Williamson (1998); Estevadeordal et al. (2003).
15. See Blattman et al. (2002); Williamson (2003, 2006a).
16. See, for example, Baldwin and Martin (1999); Bordo et al. (1999).
17. See Hatton and Williamson (1998, 2002a, 2002b, 2003, 2004, 2005).
18. See Prebisch (1950); Singer (1950); Williamson and Hadass (2003); Blattman et al. (2007).
19. Maddison (2001).
20. Pritchett (1997a).
21. See Allen (2001).
22. North (1990); Acemoglu et al. (2001, 2002, 2005b).
23. See Pomeranz (2000).
24. See Williamson (1998b, 1998c, 1998d).
25. See Galor and Weil (2000).
26. See, for example, Pritchett (1997a); Melchior (2001); O'Rourke (2001); Bhalla (2002); Bourguignon and Morrisson (2002); Milanovic (2006); Sala-i-Martin (2002a, 2002b, 2006); Fischer (2003); Bordo et al. (2003).
27. Lindert and Williamson (2003).
28. Jeffrey Sachs (2001b) has argued that the USA has a 'strategic interest' in reducing the problem of global inequality. Since growing inequality reflects poor economic performance in many developing countries, it is also likely that growing inequality will herald an increasing risk of state failure. The malfunction of foreign states then has knock-on effects for the rest of the world, including the USA. To quote Sachs, 'Failed states are seedbeds of violence, terrorism, international criminality, mass migration and refugee movements, drug trafficking, and disease.' See also Fukuyama (2004).
29. See Snowdon (2001a), and Dani Rodrik interview.
30. See Rodriguez and Rodrik (2000).
31. Bairoch (1972).
32. O'Rourke (2000).
33. Sachs and Warner (1995).
34. Clemens and Williamson (2004a).
35. Williamson (2006a).
36. See also Irwin (2002b).
37. The Heckscher–Ohlin factor endowment trade theory predicts that countries will tend to export goods that are intensive in the factors of production with which they are abundantly supplied. The Samuelson–Stolper theorem relates to the effects of trade on factor prices and income distribution. The theorem demonstrates that the opening up of trade between two countries will raise the relative price of labour in the labour-abundant economy, and reduce it in the labour-scarce economy. See O'Rourke and Williamson (1994, 1999, 2002c, 2005); Williamson (2006a).
38. See Grossman and Helpman (1991).
39. See Williamson (1988); Hatton and Williamson (1998, 2002a, 2002b, 2003); O'Rourke and Williamson (1999).
40. See also Clark et al. (2002, 2004).
41. See Schieber and Hewitt (2000); Coleman and Harris (2003).
42. See Hatton and Williamson (2005).
43. Bhagwati (1998a).
44. See Bloom and Sachs (1998), Acemoglu et al. (2001, 2002); Easterly and Levine (2003).
45. See Acemoglu (2003a); Rodrik and Subramanian (2003); Sachs (2003a).
46. See Bertola and Williamson (2006).

47. See Alesina and Perotti (1996c); Williamson (1997); Aghion and Williamson (1998); Barro (2000).
48. A Kuznets curve, named after the Nobel Prize winning economist Simon Kuznets, shows a relationship between a country's income per capita and its income distribution. Kuznets research suggested that a country's income distribution may become more unequal during the early stages of economic development before becoming more equal.
49. See Snowdon (2002a); Snowdon and Vane (2005).
50. North (1990); Olson (2000).
51. See Alesina and Spolare (1997, 2003, 2005, 2007).
52. Huntington (1996).

# Bibliography

*Note*: Titles marked with an asterisk are particularly recommended for student reading.

*Abramovitz, M. (1986), 'Catching Up, Forging Ahead, and Falling Behind', *Journal of Economic History*, June.

Acemoglu, D. (2002), 'Technical Change, Inequality and the Labour Market', *Journal of Economic Literature*, March.

*Acemoglu, D. (2003a), 'A Historical Approach to Assessing the Role of Institutions in Economic Development', *Finance and Development*, June.

Acemoglu, D. (2003b), 'Cross Country Inequality Trends', *Economic Journal*, February.

Acemoglu, D. (2003c), 'Why Not a Political Coase Theorem? Social Conflict, Commitment, and Politics', *Journal of Comparative Economics*, December.

*Acemoglu, D. and S. Johnson (2005), 'Unbundling Institutions', *Journal of Political Economy*, October.

Acemoglu, D. and S. Johnson (2006), 'Disease and Development: The Effect of Life Expectancy on Economic Growth', MIT Department of Economics Working Paper, May.

Acemoglu, D. and J. Robinson (2000a), 'Why Did the West Extend the Franchise? Democracy, Inequality and Growth in Historical Perspective', *Quarterly Journal of Economics*, November.

*Acemoglu, D. and J. Robinson (2000b), 'Political Losers as a Barrier to Development', *American Economic Review*, May.

Acemoglu, D. and J. Robinson (2000c), 'Democratization or Repression?', *European Economic Review*, May.

Acemoglu, D. and J. Robinson (2001), 'A Theory of Political Transitions', *American Economic Review*, September.

Acemoglu, D. and J. Robinson (2006a), *Economic Origins of Dictatorship and Democracy*, Cambridge: Cambridge University Press.

Acemoglu, D. and J. Robinson (2006b), 'De Facto Political Power and Institutional Persistence', *American Economic Review*, May.

Acemoglu, D. and J. Ventura (2002), 'The World Income Distribution', *Quarterly Journal of Economics*, May.

Acemoglu, D. and F. Zilibotti (1997), 'Was Prometheus Unbound by Chance? Risk, Diversification, and Growth', *Journal of Political Economy*, August.

Acemoglu, D., P. Aghion and F. Zilibotti (2006), 'Distance to Frontier, Selection, and Economic Growth', *Journal of the European Economic Association*, March.

*Acemoglu, D., S. Johnson and J. Robinson (2001), 'The Colonial Origins of Comparative Development: An Empirical Investigation', *American Economic Review*, September.

*Acemoglu, D., S. Johnson and J. Robinson (2002), 'Reversal of Fortune: Geography and Institutions in the Making of the Modern World Income Distribution', *Quarterly Journal of Economics*, November.

Acemoglu, D., S. Johnson and J. Robinson (2003a), 'Disease and Development in Historical Perspective', *Journal of the European Economics Association: Papers and Proceedings*, April.

Acemoglu, D., S. Johnson and J. Robinson (2003b), 'An African Success Story: Botswana?', in Dani Rodrik (ed.), *In Search of Prosperity: Analytic Narratives on Economic Growth*, Princeton, NJ: Princeton University Press.

*Acemoglu, D., S. Johnson and J. Robinson (2005a), 'The Rise of Europe: Atlantic Trade, Institutional Change, and Growth', *American Economic Review*, June.

Acemoglu, D., S. Johnson and J.A. Robinson (2005b), 'From Education to Democracy', *American Economic Review*, May.

*Acemoglu, D., S. Johnson and J. Robinson (2005c), 'Institutions as the Fundamental Cause of Long-Run Growth', in P. Aghion and S. Durlauf (eds), *Handbook of Economic Growth*, Amsterdam: North-Holland.

Acemoglu, D., S. Johnson and T. Verdier (2004), 'Kleptocracy and Divide and Rule: A Model of Personal Rule', *Journal of the European Economics Association Papers and Proceedings*, April.

Adelman, I. and C.T. Morris (1967), *Society, Politics, and Economic Development*, Baltimore, MD: Johns Hopkins University Press.

Adserà, A., C. Boix and M. Payne (2003), 'Are You Being Served? Political Accountability and the Quality of Government', *Journal of Law, Economics and Organization*, October.

*Agenor, P. (2003), 'Benefits and Costs of International Financial Integration: Theory and Facts', *World Economy*, August.

Aghion, P. and S. Durlauf (eds) (2005), *Handbook of Economic Growth*, Amsterdam: Elsevier.

Aghion, P. and J.G. Williamson (1998), *Growth, Inequality and Globalisation: Theory, History, and Policy*, Cambridge: Cambridge University Press.

Aghion, P., E. Caroli and C. Garcia-Penalosa (1999), 'Inequality and Growth: The Perspective of the New Growth Theories', *Journal of Economic Literature*, September.

Ahluwalia, M. (2002), 'Economic Reforms in India Since 1991: Has Gradualism Worked?', *Journal of Economic Perspectives*, Summer.

Aisbett, E. (2005), 'Why Are The Critics So Convinced That Globalisation is Bad For the Poor?', National Bureau of Economic Research Working Paper, No. 11066, January.

Aizenman, J. (2002), 'Financial Opening: Evidence and Policy Options', in R. Baldwin and A. Winters (eds), *Challenges to Globalisation: Analysing the Economics*, Chicago, IL: Chicago University Press.

Akerlof, G.A., W.T. Dickens and G.L. Perry (1996), 'The Macroeconomics of Low Inflation', *Brookings Papers on Economic Activity*, No. 1.

Alesina, A. (1987), 'Macroeconomic Policy in a Two-Party System as a Repeated Game', *Quarterly Journal of Economics*, August.

Alesina, A. (1988), 'Macroeconomics and Politics', *National Bureau of Economic Research Macroeconomics Annual*.

Alesina, A. (1989), 'Politics and Business Cycles in Industrial Democracies', *Economic Policy*, April.

Alesina, A. (1994), 'Political Models of Macroeconomic Policy and Fiscal Reforms', in S. Haggard and S. Webb (eds), *Voting for Reform*, Oxford: Oxford University Press.

Alesina, A. (1995), 'Elections, Party Structure, and the Economy', in J.S. Banks and E.A. Hanushek (eds), *Modern Political Economy: Old Topics, New Directions*, Cambridge: Cambridge University Press.

Alesina, A. (2000a), 'The Political Business Cycle 25 Years Later: A Comment', *National Bureau of Economic Research Macroeconomics Annual*.

*Alesina, A. (2000b), 'The Political Economy of the Budget Surplus', *Journal of Economic Perspectives*, Summer.

Alesina, A. and S. Ardagna (1998), 'Tales of Fiscal Adjustment', *Economic Policy*, October.

Alesina, A. and R.J. Barro (eds) (2001), *Currency Unions*, Cambridge, MA: MIT Press.

Alesina, A. and R.J. Barro (2002), 'Currency Unions', *Quarterly Journal of Economics*, May.

*Alesina, A. and D. Dollar (2000), 'Who Gives Foreign Aid to Whom and Why?', *Journal of Economic Growth*, March.

Alesina, A. and A. Drazen (1991), 'Why are Stabilisations Delayed?', *American Economic Review*, December.

Alesina, A. and N. Fuchs-Schundeln (2005), 'Goodbye Lenin (or Not?): The Effect of Communism on People's Preferences', National Bureau of Economic Research Working Paper, No. 11700, October.

Alesina, A. and R. Gatti (1995), 'Independent Central Banks: Low Inflation at No Cost?' *American Economic Review*, May.

*Alesina, A. and E.L. Glaeser (2004), *Fighting Poverty in the US and Europe: A World of Difference*, Oxford: Oxford University Press.

Alesina, A. and E. La Ferrara (2002), 'Who Trusts Others?', *Journal of Public Economics*, August.

*Alesina, A. and E. La Ferrara (2005), 'Ethnic Diversity and Economic Performance', *Journal of Economic Literature*, September.

Alesina, A. and R. Perotti (1994), 'The Political Economy of Growth: A Critical Survey of the Recent Literature', *World Bank Economic Review*, September.

*Alesina, A. and R. Perotti (1995), 'The Political Economy of Budget Deficits', *IMF Staff Papers*, March.

Alesina, A. and R. Perotti (1996a), 'Fiscal Discipline and the Budget Process', *American Economic Review*, May.

Alesina, A. and R. Perotti (1996b), 'Reducing Budget Deficits', *Swedish Economic Policy Review*, Spring.

Alesina, A. and R. Perotti (1996c), 'Income Distribution, Political Instability and Investment', *European Economic Review*, June.

Alesina, A. and R. Perotti (1997a), 'Fiscal Adjustments in OECD Countries: Composition and Macroeconomic Effects', *IMF Staff Papers*, June.

Alesina, A. and R. Perotti (1997b), 'The Welfare State and Competitiveness', *American Economic Review*, December.

Alesina, A. and R. Perotti (1998), 'Economic Risk and Political Risk in Fiscal Unions', *Economic Journal*, July.

Alesina, A. and R. Perotti (2004), 'The European Union: A Politically Incorrect View', *Journal of Economic Perspectives*, Winter.

Alesina, A. and D. Rodrik (1994), 'Distributive Politics and Economic Growth', *Quarterly Journal of Economics*, May.

Alesina, A. and H. Rosenthal (1995), *Partisan Politics, Divided Government and the Economy*, Cambridge: Cambridge University Press.

Alesina, A. and N. Roubini (1992), 'Political Cycles in OECD Economies', *Review of Economic Studies*, October.

Alesina, A. and J. Sachs (1988), 'Political Parties and the Business Cycle in the United States, 1914–1984', *Journal of Money, Credit, and Banking*, February.

Alesina, A. and E. Spolare (1997), 'On the Number and Size of Nations', *Quarterly Journal of Economics*, November.

*Alesina, A. and E. Spolare (2003), *The Size of Nations*, Cambridge, MA: MIT Press.

Alesina, A. and E. Spolare (2005), 'War, Peace and the Size of Nations', *Journal of Public Economics*, July.

Alesina, A. and E. Spolare (2007), 'International Conflict, Defence Spending and the Size of Countries', *European Economic Review*, forthcoming.

Alesina, A. and L.H. Summers (1993), 'Central Bank Independence and Macroeconomic Performance: Some Comparative Evidence', *Journal of Money, Credit and Banking*, May.

Alesina, A. and G. Tabellini (1988), 'Credibility and Politics', *European Economic Review*, March.

Alesina, A. and G. Tabellini (2007), 'Bureacrats or Politicians?', *American Economic Review*, March.

*Alesina, A. and B. Weder (2002), 'Do Corrupt Governments Receive Less Foreign Aid?', *American Economic Review*, September.

Alesina, A., I. Angeloni and F. Etro (2005), 'International Unions', *American Economic Review*, June.

Alesina, A., I. Angeloni and L. Shucknecht (2005), 'What Does the European Union Do?', *Public Choice*, June.

Alesina, A., R. Baqir and W. Easterly (1999), 'Public Goods and Ethnic Divisions', *Quarterly Journal of Economics*, November.

*Alesina, A., R.J. Barro and S. Tenreyro (2002), 'Optimal Currency Areas', *National Bureau of Economic Research Macroeconomics Annual*.

Alesina, A., G.D. Cohen and N. Roubini (1992), 'Macroeconomic Policy and Elections in OECD Democracies', *Economics and Politics*, March.

Alesina, A., G.D. Cohen and N. Roubini (1993), 'Electoral Business Cycle in Industrial Democracies', *European Journal of Political Economy*, March.

Alesina, A., R. Di Tella and R. MacCulloch (2001), 'Inequality and Happiness: Are Europeans and Americans Different?', *Journal of Public Economics*, August.

Alesina, A., E.L. Glaeser and B. Sacerdote (2001), 'Why Doesn't the US Have a European-Style Welfare State?', *Brookings Papers on Economic Activity*, Fall.

Alesina, A., R. Perotti and J. Tavares (1998), 'The Political Economy of Fiscal Adjustments', *Brookings Papers on Economic Activity*, No. 1.

*Alesina, A. and N. Roubini, with G.D. Cohen (1997), *Political Cycles and the Macroeconomy: Theory and Evidence*, Cambridge, MA: MIT Press.

Alesina, A., E. Spolare and R. Wacziarg (2000), 'Economic Integration and Political Disintegration', *American Economic Review*, December.

*Alesina, A., E. Spolare and R. Wacziarg (2005), 'Trade, Growth and the Size of Nations', in P. Aghion and S. Durlauf (eds), *Handbook of Economic Growth*, Amsterdam: Elsevier.

*Alesina, A., S. Ozler, N. Roubini and P. Swagel (1996), 'Political Instability and Growth', *Journal of Economic Growth*, June.

*Alesina, A., A. Devleeschauwer, W. Easterly, S. Kurlat and R. Wacziarg (2003), 'Fractionalization', *Journal of Economic Growth*, June.

Alexeev, M., C. Gaddy and J. Leitzel (1992), 'Economics in the Former Soviet Union', *Journal of Economic Perspectives*, Spring.

Allen, R.C. (2001), 'The Great Divergence in European Wages and Prices from the Middle Ages to the First World War', *Explorations in Economic History*, October.

Allen, R.C., T. Bengtsson and M. Dribe (2005), *Living Standards in the Past: New Perspectives on Well-Being in Asia and Europe*, Oxford: Oxford University Press.

Anand, S. and M. Ravillion (1993), 'Human Development in Poor Countries: On the Role of Private Incomes and Public Services', *Journal of Economic Perspectives*, Winter.

Anderson, S. and J. Cavanagh (2000), *Top 2000: The Rise of Corporate Global Power*, Washington, DC: Institute of Policy Studies.

Arrow, K. and G. Debreu (1954), 'Existence of Equilibrium for a Competitive Economy', *Econometrica*, July.

*Arslanalp, S. and P. Blair Henry (2006), 'Debt Relief', *Journal of Economic Perspectives*, Winter.

Artadi, E. and X. Sala-i-Martin (2002), 'Economic Growth and Investment in the Arab World', *The Arab Competitiveness Report*, New York: Oxford University Press.

*Artadi, E. and X. Sala-i-Martin (2003), 'The Economic Tragedy of the Twentieth Century: Growth in Africa', National Bureau of Economic Research Working Paper, No. 9865, July.

Arteta, C., B. Eichengreen and C. Wyplosz (2001), 'On the Growth Effects of Capital Account Liberalisation', March (unpublished).

Aslund, A. (1995), *How Russia Became a Market Economy*, Washington, DC: The Brookings Institution.

Aslund, A. (2001), 'The Myth of Output Collapse After Communism', Carnegie Endowment for International Peace, Working Paper No. 18, March.

*Aslund, A. (2002), *Building Capitalism: The Transformation of the Former Soviet Union*, Cambridge: Cambridge University Press.

Aslund, A. (2005), 'Putin's Decline and America's Response', Policy Brief No. 41, August, Carnegie Endowment for International Peace.

Auty, R.M. (2001), 'The Political Economy of Resource Driven Growth', *European Economic Review*, May.

Azariadis, C. and J. Stachurski (2005), 'Poverty Traps', in P. Aghion and S. Durlauf (eds), *Handbook of Economic Growth*, Amsterdam: Elsevier.

Bairoch, P. (1972), 'Free Trade and European Economic Development in the 19th Century', *European Economic Review*, November.

Balassa, B. (1989), 'Outward Orientation', in H. Chenery and T.N. Srinivasan (eds), *Handbook of Development Economics Vol. II*, Amsterdam: North-Holland.

Balcerowicz, L. (1994a), 'Transition to the Market: Poland, 1989–93, in Comparative Perspective', *Economic Policy*, December.

*Balcerowicz, L. (1994b), 'Common Fallacies in the Debate on the Transition to a Market Economy', *Economic Policy*, December.

Baldwin, R.E. (2000), 'Trade and Growth: Still Disagreement About the Relationships', OECD Economics Department Working Paper No. 264, www.oecd.org/eco/eco.

*Baldwin, R.E. (2003), 'Openness and Growth: What's the Empirical Relationship?', in R.E. Baldwin and A. Winters (eds), *Challenges to Globalisation: Analysing the Economics*, Chicago, IL: Chicago University Press.

*Baldwin, R.E. and P. Martin (1999), 'Two Waves of Globalisation: Superficial Similarities, Fundamental Differences', National Bureau of Economic Research Working Paper No. 6904, January.

*Baldwin, R.E. and L.A Winters (eds) (2004), *Challenges to Globalisation: Analysing the Economics*, Chicago, IL: Chicago University Press.

Banerjee, A. and E. Duflo (2003), 'Inequality and Growth: What Can the Data Say?', *Journal of Economic Growth*, September.

Bardhan, P. (1993), 'Economics of Development and the Development of Economics', *Journal of Economic Perspectives*, Spring.

*Bardhan, P. and J.E. Roemer (1992), 'Market Socialism: A Case for Rejuvenation', *Journal of Economic Perspectives*, Summer.

Bardhan, P. and J.E. Roemer (1993), *Market Socialism: The Current Debate*, New York: Oxford University Press.

Bardhan, P. and J.E. Roemer (1994), 'On the Workability of Market Socialism', *Journal of Economic Perspectives*, Spring.

Barone, E. (1908), 'The Ministry of Production in a Collectivist State', in F.A. Hayek (ed.) (1935), *Collectivist Economic Planning*, London: Routledge and Kegan Paul.

Barro, R.J. (1991), 'Economic Growth in a Cross Section of Countries', *Quarterly Journal of Economics*, May.

Barro, R.J. (1996), 'Democracy and Growth', *Journal of Economic Growth*, March.

*Barro, R.J. (1997), *Determinants of Economic Growth*, Cambridge, MA: MIT Press.

Barro, R.J. (1999), 'Determinants of Democracy', *Journal of Political Economy*, December.

Barro, R.J. (2000), 'Inequality and Growth in a Panel of Countries', *Journal of Economic Growth*, March.

Barro, R.J. and S. Fischer (1976), 'Recent Developments in Monetary Theory', *Journal of Monetary Economics*, April.

Barro, R.J. and D.B. Gordon (1983a), 'Rules, Discretion and Reputation in a Model of Monetary Policy', *Journal of Monetary Economics*, July.

Barro, R.J. and D.B. Gordon (1983b), 'A Positive Theory of Monetary Policy in a Natural Rate Model', *Journal of Political Economy*, July.

Barro, R.J. and R.M. McCleary (2003), 'Religion and Economic Growth', *American Sociological Review*, October.

Barro, R.J. and R.M. McCleary (2005), 'Which Countries Have State Religions?', *Quarterly Journal of Economics*, November.

*Barro, R.J. and R.M. McCleary (2006), 'Religion and Economy', *Journal of Economic Perspectives*, Spring.

*Barro, R.J. and X. Sala-i-Martin (1991), 'Convergence Across States and Regions', *Brookings Papers on Economic Activity*, No. 1.

*Barro, R.J. and X. Sala-i-Martin (1992a), 'Convergence', *Journal of Political Economy*, April.

Barro, R.J. and X. Sala-i-Martin (1992b), 'Regional Growth and Migration: A Japan–US Comparison', *Journal of the Japanese and International Economies*, December.

Barro, R.J. and X. Sala-i-Martin (1992c), 'Public Finance in Models of Economic Growth', *Review of Economic Studies*, November.

Barro, R.J. and X. Sala-i-Martin (1997), 'Technological Diffusion and Convergence', *Journal of Economic Growth*, March.

Barro, R.J. and X. Sala-i-Martin (2003), *Economic Growth*, 2nd edn, Cambridge, MA: MIT Press.

Barro, R.J., G.N. Mankiw and X. Sala-i-Martin (1995), 'Capital Mobility in Neoclassical Models of Economic Growth', *American Economic Review*, March.

Baster, N. (ed.) (1972), *Measuring Development: The Role and Adequacy of Development Indicators*, London: Frank Cass.

Basu, K. (2003), 'Globalisation and the Politics of International Finance: The Stiglitz Verdict', *Journal of Economic Literature*, September.

Bates, R. (1981), *Markets and States in Tropical Africa*, Berkeley, CA: University of California Press.

Bates, R. (1989), *Beyond the Miracle of the Market*, New York: Cambridge University Press.

*Bates, R. (2001), *Prosperity and Violence: The Political Economy of Development*, New York: W.W. Norton.

Bates, R. (2004), 'On the *Politics of Property Rights*, by Haber, Razo and Maurer', *Journal of Economic Literature*, June.

*Bauer, P. (1972), *Dissent on Development*, London: Weidenfeld and Nicolson.

Baumol, W.J. (1965), *Economic Theory and Operations Analysis*, Englewood Cliffs, NJ: Prentice-Hall.

Baumol, W.J. (1986), 'Productivity Growth, Convergence and Welfare: What the Long-Run Data Show', *American Economic Review*, December.

*Baumol, W.J. (1990), 'Entrepreneurship: Productive, Unproductive and Destructive', *Journal of Political Economy*, October.

*Baumol, W.J. (2002), *The Free Market Innovation Machine: Analyzing the Growth Miracle of Capitalism*, Princeton, NJ: Princeton University Press.

Bayoumi, T., G. Fazio, M. Kumar and R. MacDonald (2003), 'Fatal Attraction: A New Measure of Contagion', IMF Working Paper/03/80, April.

Beck, T. and L. Laeven (2006), 'Institution Building and Growth in Transition Economies', *Journal of Economic Growth*, June.

Becker, G., T.J. Philipson and R.R. Soares (2003), 'The Quantity and Quality of Life and the Evolution of World Inequality', *American Economic Review*, March.

Begg, D., S. Fischer and R. Dornbusch (2003), *Economics*, 7th edn, London: McGraw-Hill.

Bellows, J. and E. Miguel (2006), 'War and Institutions: New Evidence from Sierra Leone', *American Economic Review*, May.

Benabou, R. (1996), 'Inequality and Growth', *National Bureau of Economic Research Macroeconomics Annual*.

Ben-David, D. (1998), 'Convergence Clubs in Subsistence Economies', *Journal of Development Economics*, February.

Ben-David, D. and M.B. Loewy (1998), 'Free Trade, Growth and Convergence', *Journal of Economic Growth*, June.

Berger, H. and M. Spoerer (2001), 'Economic Crises and the European Revolutions of 1848', *Journal of Economic History*, June.

Bergson, A. (1967), 'Market Socialism Revisited', *Journal of Political Economy*, October.

Bergson, A. (1978), 'The Soviet Economic Slowdown', *Challenge*, January–February.

Bergson, A. (1991), 'The USSR Before the Fall: How Poor and Why?', *Journal of Economic Perspectives*, Fall.

Berliner, J.S. (1983), 'Managing the USSR Economy: Alternative Models', *Problems of Communism*, January–February.

Bernanke, B.S., T. Laubach, F.S. Mishkin and A.S. Posen (1999), *Inflation Targeting: Lessons from the International Experience*, Princeton, NJ: Princeton University Press.

Bertola, L. and J.G. Williamson (2006), 'Globalisation in Latin America Before 1940', in V. Bulmer-Thomas et al. (eds), *Cambridge Economic History of Latin America*, Cambridge: Cambridge University Press (forthcoming).

Bhagwati, J. (1978), *Foreign Trade Regimes and Economic Development: Anatomy and Consequences of Exchange Control Regimes*, Cambridge, MA: Ballinger.

Bhagwati, J. (1993), *India in Transition: Freeing the Economy*, Oxford: Clarendon Press.

*Bhagwati, J. (1998a), *A Stream of Windows: Unsettling Reflections on Trade, Immigration, and Democracy*, Cambridge, MA: MIT Press.

*Bhagwati, J. (1998b), 'The Capital Myth', *Foreign Affairs*, May.

*Bhagwati, J. (2000), *The Wind of the Hundred Days: How Washington Mismanaged Globalisation*, Cambridge, MA: MIT Press.

*Bhagwati, J. (2002), *Free Trade Today*, Princeton, NJ: Princeton University Press.

*Bhagwati, J. (2004a), *In Defence of Globalization*, Oxford: Oxford University Press.

Bhagwati, J. (2004b), 'Anti-globalisation: Why?', *Journal of Policy Modeling*, **26**(4).

Bhagwati, J. (2005), 'From Seattle to Hong Kong: Are We getting Anywhere?', *Foreign Affairs*, December.

Bhagwati, J. and P. Desai (1970), *India: Planning for Industrialisation*, Oxford: Oxford University Press.

Bhagwati, J. and P. Desai (1975), 'Socialism and Indian Economic Policy', *World Development*, June.

Bhagwati, J. and T.N. Srinivasan (2001), 'Outward Orientation and Development: Are the Revisionists Right?', in D. Lall and R. Snape (eds), *Essays in Honour of Anne O. Krueger*, London: Palgrave.

*Bhagwati, J. and T.N. Srinivasan (2002), 'Trade and Poverty in Poor Countries', *American Economic Review*, May.

Bhagwati, J., A. Panagariya and T.N. Srinivasan (2004), 'The Muddles Over Outsourcing', *Journal of Economic Perspectives*, Fall.

Bhalla, S. (2002), *Imagine There's No Country: Poverty, Inequality and Growth in the Era of Globalisation*, Washington, DC: Institute of International Economics.

Biais, B. and E. Perotti (2002), 'Machiavellian Privatisation', *American Economic Review*, March.

Bigsten, A. (2002), 'Can Africa Catch Up?', *World Economics*, April–June.

*Bird, G. (2000), 'Sins of The Commission: The Meltzer Report on International Financial Institutions', *World Economics*, July–September.

Bird, G. (2001), 'IMF Programmes: Is There a Conditionality Laffer Curve?', *World Economics*, April–June.

Bird, G. (2006), 'Are Mr. Rato's Spectacles Rose Tinted?', *World Economics*, April–June.

Blanchard, O. (1996), 'Theoretical Aspects of Transition', *American Economic Review*, May.

Blanchard, O. and S. Fischer (1989), *Lectures on Macroeconomics*, Cambridge, MA: MIT Press.

Blanchard, O. and M. Kremer (1997), 'Disorganisation', *Quarterly Journal of Economics*, November.

Blanchflower, D.G. and A.J. Oswald (2004), 'Money, Sex and Happiness: An Empirical Study', *Scandinavian Journal of Economics*, **106**(3).

Blanke, J. and E. Loades (2004), 'Capturing the State of Country Competitiveness with the Executive Opinion Survey', in M.E. Porter, K. Schwab, X. Sala-i-Martin and A. Lopez-Claros (eds), *The Global Competitiveness Report 2004–05*, World Economic Forum, New York: Palgrave Macmillan.

Blanke, J. and C. Lopez-Carlos (2004), 'The Growth Competitiveness Index: Assessing Countries' Potential for Sustained Growth', in M.E. Porter, K. Schwab, X. Sala-i-Martin and A. Lopez-Claros (eds), *The Global Competitiveness Report 2004–05*, New York: Palgrave Macmillan.

*Blanke, J, F. Paua and X. Sala-i-Martin (2004), 'The Growth Competitiveness Index: Analyzing Key Underpinnings of Sustained Economic Growth', in M.E. Porter, K. Schwab, X. Sala-i-Martin and A. Lopez-Claros (eds), *The Global Competitiveness Report: 2004–05*, New York: Palgrave Macmillan.

Blattman, C., M.A. Clemens and J.G. Williamson (2002), 'Who Protected and Why? Tariffs Around the World 1870–1938', Working Paper, www.economics.harvard.edu/~jwilliam/.

Blattman, C., J. Hwang and J.G. Williamson (2007), 'The Terms of Trade and Economic Growth in the Periphery 1870–1939', *Journal of Development Economics*, January.

Blaug, M. (1993), 'Review of Steel, *From Marx to Mises*', *Economic Journal*, November.

Blaug, M. (1997), *Economic Theory in Retrospect*, 5th edn, Cambridge: Cambridge University Press.

*Blaug, M. (2001), 'No History of Ideas Please, We're Economists', *Journal of Economic Perspectives*, Winter.

*Blinder, A.S. (1987), *Hard Heads, Soft Hearts: Tough-Minded Economics for a Just Society*, New York: Addison Wesley.

Blinder, A.S. (2006), 'Fear of Offshoring', *Foreign Affairs*, March–April.

*Bloom, D.E. and D. Canning (2006), 'Booms, Busts, and Echoes', *Finance and Development*, September.

*Bloom, D.E. and J.D. Sachs (1998), 'Geography, Demography and Economic Growth in Africa', *Brookings Papers on Economic Activity*, No. 2.

Boone, P. (1996), 'Politics and the Effectiveness of Foreign Aid', *European Economic Review*, **40**(2).

Bordo, M.D. (2004), 'The United States as a Monetary Union and the Euro: A Historical Perspective', *Cato Journal*, Spring/Summer.

*Bordo, M.D., B. Eichengreen and J.D. Irwin (1999), 'Is Globalisation Today Really Different from Globalisation a Hundred Years Ago?', National Bureau of Economic Research Working Paper No. 7195, June.

*Bordo, M.D., A. Taylor and J.G. Williamson (eds) (2003), *Globalisation in Historical Perspective*, Chicago, IL: Chicago University Press.

*Bordo, M., B. Eichengreem, D. Klingebiel and M.S. Martinez-Peria (2001), 'Is the Crisis Problem Becoming More Severe?', *Economic Policy*, April.

*Borjas, G.J. (1995), 'The Economic Benefits from Migration', *Journal of Economic Perspectives*, Spring.

Borjas, G.J. (2003), 'The Labour Demand Curve is Downward Sloping: Re-Examining the Impact of Immigration on the Labour Market, *Quarterly Journal of Economics*, November.

*Bourguignon, F. and C. Morrisson (2002), 'Inequality Among World Citizens: 1820–1992', *American Economic Review*, September.

Boycko, M., A. Shleifer and R. Vishny (1995), *Privatising Russia*, Cambridge, MA: MIT Press.

Boycko, M., A. Shleifer and R. Vishny (1996), 'A Theory of Privatisation', *Economic Journal*, March.

*Boyer, G. (1998), 'The Historical Background of the Communist Manifesto', *Journal of Economic Perspectives*, Fall.

Brainerd, E. and D.M. Cutler (2005), 'Autopsy on an Empire: Understanding Mortality in Russia and the Former Soviet Union', *Journal of Economic Perspectives*, Winter.

Brandt, W. (1980), *North–South: A Program for Survival (The Brandt Report)*, Cambridge, MA: MIT Press.

Branstetter, L. and N. Lardy (2006), 'China's Embrace of Globalisation', National Bureau of Economic Research Working Paper No. 12373, July.

*Brautigam, D.A. and S. Knack (2004), 'Foreign Aid, Institutions, and Governance in Sub-Saharan Africa', *Economic Development and Cultural Change*, January.

Brendon, P. (2000), *The Dark Valley: A Panorama of the 1930s*, London: Jonathan Cape.

Brodsky, D.A. and D. Rodrik (1981), 'Indices of Development and Data Availability: The Case of the PQLI', *World Development*, July.

Bromley, D.W. and Y. Yao (2006), 'Understanding China's Economic Transformation', *World Economics*, April–June.

Brown, G. (1997), 'Letter from the Chancellor to the Governor: 6th May 1997', *Bank of England Quarterly Bulletin*, August.

Brown, G. (2001), 'The Conditions for High and Stable Growth and Employment', *Economic Journal*, May.

Brumm, H.J. (2003), 'Aid Policies and Growth: Bauer was Right', *Cato Journal*, Fall.

Bruni, L. and P.L. Porta (2005), *Economics and Happiness: Framing the Analysis*, Oxford: Oxford University Press.

Bruno, M. (1993), 'Stabilisation and Macroeconomics of Transition: How Different is Eastern Europe?', *Economics of Transition*, 1(1).

Bruno, M. and W. Easterly (1998), 'Inflation Crises and Long-run Growth', *Journal of Monetary Economics*, February.

Bruno, M. and J.D. Sachs (1985), *Economics of World-wide Stagflation*, Cambridge, MA: Harvard University Press.

*Bruton, H.J. (1998), 'A Reconsideration of Import Substitution', *Journal of Economic Literature*, June.

Budd, A. (2004), 'What Do Economists Know?', *World Economics*, July–September.

Bukharin, N.L. and E. Preobrazhensky (1972), 'The ABC of Communism', reprinted in A. Nove and D. Nuti (eds), *Socialist Economics*, Harmondsworth, UK: Penguin.

Bulte, E.H., R. Damania and R.T. Deacon (2005), 'Resource Intensity, Institutions and Development', *World Development*, July.

*Burnside, C. and D. Dollar (2000), 'Aid, Policies and Growth', *American Economic Review*, September.

Burtless, G., R.Z. Lawrence, R.E. Litan and R.J. Shapiro (1998), *Globaphobia: Confronting Fears About Open Trade*, Washington, DC: Brookings Institution.

Caballero, R. (2003), 'The Future of the IMF', *American Economic Review*, May.

Cagan, P. (1956), 'The Monetary Dynamics of Hyperinflation', in M. Friedman (ed.), *Studies in the Quantity Theory of Money*, Chicago, IL: University of Chicago Press.

Cahill, M.B. (2005), 'Is the Human Development Index Redundant?', *Eastern Economic Journal*, Winter.

*Caldwell, B. (1997), 'Hayek and Socialism', *Journal of Economic Literature*, December.

*Calomiris, C. (2002), *A Globalist Manifesto for Public Policy*, London: Institute of Economic Affairs.

Calvo, G.A. (2006), *Emerging Capital Markets in Turmoil: Bad Luck or Bad Policy?* Cambridge, MA: MIT Press.

*Campos, N.F. and F. Coricelli (2002), 'Growth in Transition: What We Know, What We Don't Know and What We Should Know', *Journal of Economic Literature*, September.

Cardwell, D.S.L. (1972), *Turning Points in Western Technology*, New York: Neale Watson.

Cassen, R. et al. (1994), *Does Aid Work?*, 2nd edn, Oxford: Clarendon Press.

Castles, I. and D. Henderson (2005), 'International Comparisons of GDP', *World Economics*, January–March.

Cawley, J. and R.V. Burkhauser (2006), 'Beyond BMI: The Value of More Accurate Measures of Fatness and Obesity in Social Science Research', National Bureau of Economic Research Working Paper No. 12291, June.

*Chang, H. (2002), 'Kicking Away the Ladder: An Unofficial History of Capitalism, Especially in Britain and the United States', *Challenge*, September–October.

Chenery, H. (1964), 'Objectives and Criteria of Foreign Assistance', in G. Ranis (ed.), *The United Nations and the Developing Economies*, New York: W.W. Norton.

Chenery. H.B. and A.M. Strout (1966), 'Foreign Assistance and Economic Development', *American Economic Review*, September.

Chou, S., M. Grossman and H. Saffer (2004), 'An Economic Analysis of Adult Obesity: Results from The Behavioural Risk Factor Surveillance System', *Journal of Health Economics*, **23**(3).

Choudhury, A. and G. Mavrotas (2006), FDI and Growth: What Causes What?', *World Economy*, January.

Citrin, D. and S. Fischer (2000), 'Strengthening the International Financial System', *World Development*, June.

Clark, A.E. and A. Oswald (1994), 'Unhappiness and Unemployment', *Economic Journal*, May.

Clark, G. (2003), 'The Great Escape: The Industrial Revolution in Theory and History', University of California, Davis, Working Paper, September.

*Clark, G. (2005), 'The Condition of the Working Class in England, 1209–2004', *Journal of Political Economy*, December.

Clark, G. and S. Wolcott (1999), 'Why Nations Fail: Managerial Decisions and Performance in Indian Cotton Textiles, 1890–1938', *Journal of Economic History*, June.

Clark, X., T.J. Hatton and J.G. Williamson (2002), 'Where Do US Immigrants Come From, and Why?', National Bureau of Economic Research Working Paper No. 8998, June.

Clark, X., T.J. Hatton and J.G. Williamson (2004), 'What Explains Emigration Out of Latin America?', *World Development*, November.

Clemens, M.A. and J.G. Williamson (2000), 'Where Did British Foreign Capital Go? Fundamentals, Failures and the Lucas Paradox', National Bureau of Economic Research Working Paper No. 8028, December.

Clemens, M.A. and J.G. Williamson (2001), 'A Tariff–Growth Paradox? Protectionism's Impact on the World Around 1875–1997', National Bureau of Economic Research Working Paper No. 8459, September.

Clemens, M.A. and J.G. Williamson (2004a), 'Why Did the Tariff–Growth Correlation Reverse After 1950?', *Journal of Economic Growth*, March.

Clemens, M.A. and J.G. Williamson (2004b), 'Wealth Bias in the First Global Capital Market Boom 1870–1913', *Economic Journal*, April.

Coale, A.J. and E.M. Hoover (1958), *Population Growth and Economic Development in Low Income Countries*, Princeton, NJ: Princeton University Press.

Coatsworth, J.H. and J.G. Williamson (2002), 'The Roots of Latin American Protectionism: Looking Before the Great Depression', National Bureau of Economic Research Working Paper No. 8999, June.

*Coleman, D. and N. Harris (2003), 'Does Britain Need More Immigrants?: A Debate', *World Economics*, April–June.

Collier, P. (1998), *Living Down the Past: How Europe can Help Africa to Grow*, London: IEA.

*Collier, P. (2001), 'Implications of Ethnic Diversity', *Economic Policy*, April.

Collier, P. (2003), 'Natural Resources, Development and Conflict: Channels of Causation and Policy Intervention', www.worldbank.org, April.

Collier, P. and D. Dollar (2002), *Globalisation, Growth and Poverty: Building an Inclusive World Economy*, Oxford: World Bank and Oxford University Press.

*Collier, P. and J. Gunning (1999a), 'Explaining African Economic Performance', *Journal of Economic Literature*, March.

*Collier, P. and J. Gunning (1999b), 'Why has Africa Grown So Slowly?', *Journal of Economic Perspectives*, Summer.

Colton, T.J. (1986), *The Dilemma of Reform in the Soviet Union*, New York: Council of Foreign Relations.

Commander, S., M. Kangasniemi and L.A. Winters (2003), 'Brian Drain: Curse or Boom?', IZA Discussion Paper No. 809, June.

Commission for Africa (2005), *Our Common Interest: Report of the Commission for Africa*, Harmondsworth, UK.

Compte, A. (1896), *The Positive Philosophy*, London: George Bell and Son.

Cooper, J. and S. Fischer (1973), 'Stabilisation Policy and Lags', *Journal of Political Economy*, July–August.

*Corbett, J. and D. Vines (1999), 'Asian Currency and Financial Crises: Lessons from Vulnerability, Crisis and Collapse', *The World Economy*, March.

Crafts, N.F.R. (1999), 'Economic Growth in the Twentieth Century', *Oxford Economic Review of Economic Policy*, December.

Crafts, N.F.R. (2000), 'Globalisation and Growth', IMF Working Paper No. 00/44, March.

Crafts, N.C.R. (2002), 'The Human Development Index, 1870–1999: Some Revised Estimates', *European Review of Economic History*, **6**(3).

*Crafts, N.C.R. (2003), 'Is Economic Growth Good For Us?', *World Economics*, July–September.

*Crafts, N.C.R. (2004a), 'Globalisation and Economic Growth: A Historical Perspective', *World Economy*, January.

Crafts, N.C.R. (2004b), 'Fifty Years of Economic Growth In Western Europe: No Longer Catching Up but Falling Behind', *World Economics*, April–June.

*Crafts, N.C.R. (2005), 'The Death of Distance: What Does it Mean for Economic Development?', *World Economics*, July–September.

Crafts, N.F.R. and G. Toniolo (eds) (1996), *Economic Growth in Post-war Europe*, Cambridge: Cambridge University Press.

Crafts, N.F.R. and A. Venables (2002), 'Globalisation and Geography: An Historical Perspective', in M. Bordo, A. Taylor and J.G. Williamson (eds), *Globalisation in Historical Perspective*, Chicago, IL: University of Chicago Press.

Craven, B., C. Fiala, E. De Harven and G. Stewart (2005), 'The Anomalous Case of HIV/AIDS', *World Economics*, January–March.

Curtois, S. et al. (1999), *The Black Book of Communism: Crimes, Terror, Repression*, Cambridge, MA: Harvard University Press.

*Cutler, D.M., E.L. Glaeser and J. Shapiro (2003), 'Why Have Americans Become More Obese?', *Journal of Economic Perspectives*, Summer.

Dasgupta, P. (1995), *An Enquiry into Well-Being and Destitution*, Oxford: Oxford University Press.

Dasgupta, P. and I. Serageldin (2000), *Social Capital: A Multifaceted Approach*, Washington, DC: The World Bank.

Davies, R.W. (1998), *Soviet Economic Development: From Lenin to Krushchev*, Cambridge: Cambridge University Press.

Dawson, T. and G. Bhatt (2001), 'The IMF and CSO Organisations: Striking a Balance', IMF Working Paper/01/02, September.

De Grauwe, P. and F. Camerman (2003), 'Are Multinationals Really Bigger than Nations?', *World Economics*, April–June.

*De Soto, H. (2000), *The Mystery of Capital: Why Capitalism Succeeds in the West and Fails Everywhere Else*, New York: Basic Books.

*Deardorff, A.V. (2003), 'What Might Globalisation's Critics Believe?', *World Economy*, May.

Deininger, K. and L. Squire (1996), 'New Data Set Measuring Income Inequality', *World Bank Economic Review*, September.

DeLong, J.B. (1992), 'Growth in the World Economy, ca. 1870–1990', in H. Siebert (ed.), *Economic Growth in the World Economy*, Tübingen: Mohr/Siebeck.

DeLong, J.B. (1999), 'Why We Should Fear Deflation', *Brookings Papers on Economic Activity*, Spring.

*DeLong, J. (2000a), 'The Shape of Twentieth Century Economic History', National Bureau of Economic Research Working Paper No. 7569, February.

*DeLong, B. (2000b), 'Cornucopia: The Pace of Economic Growth in the Twentieth Century', National Bureau of Economic Research Working Paper No. 7602, March.

DeLong, B. (2003), 'India Since Independence: An Analytical Growth Narrative', in D. Rodrik (ed.), *In Search of Prosperity: Analytic Narratives on Economic Growth*, Princeton, NJ: Princeton University Press.

DeLong, J. and B. Eichengreen (1993), 'The Marshall Plan: History's Most Successful Structural Adjustment Programme', in Rudiger Dornbusch, Willem Nolling and Richard Layard (eds), *Post-War Reconstruction and Lessons for the East Today*, Cambridge, MA: MIT Press.

DeLong, J. and A. Shleifer (1993), 'Princes and Merchants: City Growth Before the Industrial Revolution', *Journal of Law and Economics*, October.

DeLong, J.B. and L.H. Summers (1993), 'How Strongly Do Developing Countries Benefit from Equipment Investment?', *Journal of Monetary Economics*, December.

Demirbas, D. (2002), 'Optimal Currency Area', in B. Snowdon and H.R. Vane (eds), *An Encyclopedia of Macroeconomics*, Cheltenham, UK and Northampton, MA, USA: Edward Elgar.

Desai, P. (1961), 'A Short-term Planning Model for the Indian Economy', *Review of Economics and Statistics*, June.

Desai, P. (1963), 'The Development of the Indian Economy – An Exercise in Economic Planning', *Oxford Economic Papers*, November.

Desai, P. (1969), 'Alternative Measures of Import Substitution', *Oxford Economic Papers*, November.

Desai, P. (1973), 'Soviet Industrial Production: Estimates of Gross Outputs by Branches and Groups', *Oxford Bulletin of Economics and Statistics*, Summer.

Desai, P. (1975a), 'China and India: Development During the Last 25 Years: Discussion', *American Economic Review*, May.

Desai, P. (1975b), 'The Total Factor Productivity of Post-war Soviet Industry and its Branches', *Journal of Comparative Economics*, March.

Desai, P. (1976), 'The Production Function and Technical Change in Post-war Soviet Industry: A Re-examination', *American Economic Review*, June.

Desai, P. (1979), 'The Productivity of Resource Inflow to the Soviet Economy', *American Economic Review*, May.

Desai, P. (ed.) (1983), *Marxism, Central Planning, and the Soviet Economy: Economic Essays in Honour of Alexander Erlich*, Cambridge, MA: MIT Press.

*Desai, P. (1986), 'Soviet Growth Retardation', *American Economic Review*, May.

Desai, P. (1987), *The Soviet Economy: Problems and Prospects*, Oxford: Basil Blackwell.

Desai, P. (1990), *Perestroika in Perspective: The Design and Dilemmas of Soviet Reform*, Princeton, NJ: Princeton University Press.

Desai, P. (1994a), 'Confused Thinking About Russian Gradualism', *Financial Times*, 19 April.

Desai, P. (1994b), 'Aftershock in Russia's Economy', *Current History*, October.

*Desai, P. (1995a), 'Russian Privatisation: A Comparative Perspective', *Harriman Review*, August.

*Desai, P. (1995b), 'Beyond Shock Therapy', *Journal of Democracy*, April.

Desai, P. (1996), 'Shock Therapy and After', in M. Kraus and R.D. Liebowitz (eds), *Russia & Eastern Europe after Communism: The Search for New Political, Economic, and Security Systems*, Boulder, CO: Westview Press.

Desai, P. (1997a), 'The Soviet Bloc and the Soviet Union: Why Did They Fall Apart?', *Harriman Review*, Summer.

Desai, P. (1997b), 'Shock Therapy is an Unwise Choice', Letters to the Editor: *Financial Times*, 20 March.

Desai, P. (1998), 'Macroeconomic Fragility and Exchange Rate Vulnerability: A Cautionary Tale of Transition Economies', *Journal of Comparative Economies*, December.

Desai, P. (1999a), 'Russian Reform: What Went Wrong?', *Harriman Review*, June.

Desai, P. (1999b), *Going Global: Transition from Plan to Market in the World Economy*, Cambridge, MA: MIT Press.

Desai, P. (2000), 'Russia: Why Did the Rouble Collapse in August 1998?', *American Economic Review*, May.

Desai, P. (2003), *Financial Crisis, Contagion, and Containment: From Asia to Argentina*, Princeton, NJ: Princeton University Press.

*Desai, P. (2005a), 'Russian Retrospectives on Reforms from Yeltsin to Putin', *Journal of Economic Perspectives*, Winter.

Desai, P. (2005b), 'Abram Bergson, 1914–2003', *Journal of the American Philosophical Society*, September.

Desai, P. (2005c), 'Give Putin a Break', *The Wall Street Journal*, 17 February.

*Desai, P. (2006a), *Conversations on Russia: Reform from Yeltsin to Putin*, Oxford: Oxford University Press.

Desai, P. (2006b), 'Why Is Russian GDP Growth Slowing?', *American Economic Review*, May.

Desai, P. and T. Idson (2000), *Work Without Wages: Russia's Non-payment Crisis*, Cambridge, MA: MIT Press.

Desai, P. and R. Martin (1983), 'The Efficiency Loss from Resource Misallocation in Soviet Industry, *Quarterly Journal of Economics*, August.

Dewatripont, M. and E. Maskin (1995), 'Credit and Efficiency in Centralized and Decentralized Economies', *Review of Economic Studies*, **62**(4).

Dewatripont, M. and G. Roland (1992), 'The Virtues of Gradualism and Legitimacy in the Transition to a Market Economy', *Economic Journal*, March.

Dewatripont, M. and G. Roland (1995), 'The Design of Reform Packages Under Uncertainty', *American Economic Review*, December.

Di Tella, R. and R. McCulloch (2006), 'Some Uses of Happiness Data in Economics', *Journal of Economic Perspectives*, Winter.

*Diamond, J. (1998), *Guns, Germs and Steel*, London: Vintage.

Dickinson, H.D. (1933), 'Price Formation in a Socialist Community', *Economic Journal*, June.

Dillon, P. and F.C. Wykoff (2002), *Creating Capitalism: Transitions and Growth in Post Soviet Europe*, Cheltenham, UK and Northampton, MA, USA: Edward Elgar.

*Dixon, W. (1994), 'Democracy and the Peaceful Settlement of International Conflict', *American Political Science Review*, March.

Djankov, S. and P. Murrell (2002), 'Enterprise Restructuring in Transition: A Quantitative Survey', *Journal of Economic Literature*, September.

Djankov, S., J.G. Montalvo and M. Reynal-Querol (2006), 'Does Foreign Aid Help?', *The Cato Journal*, Winter.

Djankov, S., R. La Porta, F. Lopez-de-Silanes and A. Shleifer (2002), 'The Regulation of Entry', *Quarterly Journal of Economics*, February.

Dobb, M. (1933), 'Economic Theory and Problems of a Socialist Economy', *Economic Journal*, December.

Dobb, M. (1940), *Political Economy and Capitalism*, New York: International.

Dollar, D. (1992), 'Outward-Oriented Developing Countries Really Do Grow More Rapidly: Evidence from 95 LDCs, 1976–1985', *Economic Development and Cultural Change*, **40**(3).

*Dollar, D. and A. Kraay (2002a), 'Spreading the Wealth', *Foreign Affairs*, February.

*Dollar, D. and A. Kraay (2002b), 'Growth is Good for the Poor', *Journal of Economic Growth*, September.

*Dollar, D. and A. Kraay (2004), 'Trade, Growth, and Poverty', *Economic Journal*, February.

Domar, E.D. (1946), 'Capital Expansion, Rate of Growth and Employment', *Econometrica*, April.

Domar, E.D. (1947), 'Expansion and Employment', *American Economic Review*, March.

Donovan, N. and D. Halpern (2002), 'Life Satisfaction: The State of Knowledge and Implications for Government', Prime Minister's Strategy Unit, http://www.strategy.gov.uk/publications/.

Doppelholfer, G., R. Miller and X. Sala-i-Martin (2004), 'Determinants of Long-Term Growth: A Bayesian Averaging of Classical Estimates Approach', *American Economic Review*, September.

Dore, R., W. Lazonick and M. O'Sullivan (1999), 'Varieties of Capitalism in the Twentieth Century', *Oxford Review of Economic Policy*, **15**(4).

Dorfman, R., P.A. Samuelson and R.M. Solow (1958), *Linear Programming and Economic Analysis*, New York: McGraw-Hill.

Dornbusch, R., S. Fischer and R. Startz (2004), *Macroeconomics*, 9th edn, New York: McGraw-Hill.

*Dowrick, S. and J. Golley (2004), 'Trade Openness and Growth: Who Benefits?', *Oxford Review of Economic Policy*, **20**(1).

Drazen, A. (2000a), *Political Economy in Macroeconomics*, Princeton, NJ: Princeton University Press.

Drazen, A. (2000b), 'The Political Business Cycle After Twenty Five Years', *National Bureau of Economics Research Macroeconomics Annual*.

Easterlin, R. (1974), 'Does Economic Growth Improve the Human Lot?', in P.A. David and M.W. Reder (eds), *Nations and Households in Economic Growth: Essays in Honour of Moses Abramovitz*, New York: Academic Press.

*Easterlin, R.A. (1996), *Growth Triumphant: The Twenty-First Century in Historical Perspective*, Ann Arbor, MI: University of Michigan Press.

Easterlin, R.A. (1999), 'How Beneficent is the Market? A Look at the Modern History of Mortality', *European Review of Economic History*, December.

*Easterlin, R.A. (2000), 'The World-Wide Standard of Living', *Journal of Economic Perspectives*, Winter.

*Easterlin, R.A. (2001), 'Income and Happiness: Toward a Unified Theory', *Economic Journal*, July.

Easterly, W. (1999), 'The Ghost of the Financing Gap: Testing the Growth Model Used in International Financial Institutions', *Journal of Development Economics*, December.

\*Easterly, W. (2001a), *The Elusive Quest for Growth: Economists' Adventures and Misadventures in the Tropics*, Cambridge, MA: MIT Press.

Easterly, W. (2001b), 'The Lost Decades: Developing Countries' Stagnation in Spite of Policy Reform', *Journal of Economic Growth*, June.

Easterly, W. (2001c), 'Can Institutions Resolve Ethnic Conflict?', *Economic Development and Cultural Change*, July.

Easterly, W. (2001d), 'The Middle Class Consensus and Economic Development', *Journal of Economic Growth*, December.

Easterly, W. (2002a), 'How Did the Heavily Indebted Countries Become Heavily Indebted? A Review of Two Decades of Debt Relief', *World Development*, October.

Easterly, W. (2002b), 'Inequality Does Cause Underdevelopment: New Evidence', Centre for Global Development Working Paper No. 1, June.

\*Easterly, W. (2003a), 'Can Foreign Aid Buy Growth?', *Journal of Economic Perspectives*, Summer.

\*Easterly, W. (2003b), 'A Cartel of Good Intentions: The Problem of Bureaucracy in Foreign Aid', *Policy Reform*, 5(4).

\*Easterly, W. (2004), 'Can Foreign Aid Make Poor Countries More Competitive?', in M. Porter, K. Schwab, X. Sala-i-Martin and A. Lopez-Claros (eds), *The Global Competitiveness Report 2004–05*, New York: Palgrave Macmillan.

Easterly, W. (2005), 'Reliving the 50s: The Big Push, Poverty Traps, and Takeoffs in Economic Development', Working Paper, Department of Economics, New York University.

\*Easterly, W. (2006a), *The White Man's Burden: Why the West's Efforts to Aid the Rest Have Done So Much Ill and So Little Good*, New York: Penguin.

\*Easterly, W. (2006b), 'Big Push Deja Vu: A Review of Jeffrey Sachs, *The End of Poverty: Economic Possibilities for Our Time*', *Journal of Economic Literature*, March.

\*Easterly, W. (ed.) (2007), *Reinventing Foreign Aid*, Cambridge, MA: MIT Press.

Easterly, W. and S. Fischer (1995), 'The Soviet Economic Decline', *World Bank Economic Review*, September.

Easterly, W. and S. Fischer (2001), 'Inflation and the Poor', *Journal of Money, Credit, and Banking*, May.

\*Easterly, W. and R. Levine (1997), 'Africa's Growth Tragedy: Policies and Ethnic Divisions', *Quarterly Journal of Economics*, November.

Easterly, W. and R. Levine (2001), 'It's Not Factor Accumulation: Stylised Facts and Growth Models', *World Bank Economic Review*, 15(2).

Easterly, W. and R. Levine (2003), 'Tropics, Germs, and Crops: The Role of Endowments in Economic Development', *Journal of Monetary Economics*, January.

Easterly, W., S. Devarajan and H. Pack (2003), 'Low Investment is Not the Constraint on African Development', *Economic Development and Cultural Change*, April.

Easterly, W., R. Gatti and S. Kurlat (2006), 'Development, Democracy and Mass Killings', *Journal of Economic Growth*, June.

Easterly, W., R. Levine and D. Roodman (2004), 'New Data, New Doubts: A Comment on Burnside and Dollar's "Aid, Policies and Growth"', *American Economic Review*, June.

Easterly, W., J. Ritzen and M. Woolcock (2006), Social Cohesion, Institutions, and Growth', *Economics and Politics*, July.

Edwards, S. (1993), 'Openness, Trade Liberalisation and Growth in Developing Countries', *Journal of Economic Literature*, September.

Edwards, S. (1994), 'The Political Economy of Inflation and Stabilization in Developing Countries', *Economic Development and Cultural Change*, January.

*Edwards, S. (1998), 'Openness, Productivity and Growth: What Do We Really Know?', *Economic Journal*, March.

Ehrlich, P.R. (1968), *The Population Bomb*, New York: Ballantine Books.

Eichengreen, B. (1984), 'Keynes and Protection', *Journal of Economic History*, June.

Eichengreen, B. (1992), *Golden Fetters: The Gold Standard and the Great Depression, 1919–1939*, New York: Oxford University Press.

Eichengreen, B. (1996), 'Institutions and Economic Growth: Europe After World War II', in N.C.R. Crafts and G. Toniolo (eds), *Economic Growth in Europe Since 1945*, Cambridge: Cambridge University Press.

Eichengreen, B. (1999), *Toward a New International Financial Architecture: A Practical Post-Asia Agenda*, Washington, DC: Institute for International Economics Press.

Eichengreen, B. (2001), 'Capital Account Liberalisation: What Do Cross-Country Studies Tell Us?', *World Bank Economic Review*, October.

*Eichengreen, B. (2002), *Financial Crises and What to do About Them*, New York: Oxford University Press.

Eichengreen, B. and J.D. Sachs (1985), 'Exchange Rates and Economic Recovery in the 1930s', *Journal of Economic History*, December.

Eichengreen, B. et al. (1999), 'Liberalising Capital Movements: Some Analytical Issues', *Economic Issues*, No. 17, IMF.

Eifert. B. et al. (2003), 'Managing Oil Wealth', *Finance and Development*, March.

Eijffinger, S.C.W. (2002a), 'Central Bank Independence', in B. Snowdon and H.R. Vane (eds), *An Encyclopedia of Macroeconomics*, Cheltenham, UK and Northampton, MA, USA: Edward Elgar.

Eijffinger, S.C.W. (2002b), 'Central Bank Accountability and Transparency', in B. Snowdon and H.R. Vane (eds), *An Encyclopedia of Macroeconomics*, Cheltenham, UK and Northampton, MA, USA: Edward Elgar.

Elbadawi, I. (2005), 'Reviving Growth in the Arab World', *Economic Development and Cultural Change*, January.

*Ellerman, D. (2003), 'On the Russian Privatisation Debate', *Challenge*, May–June.

Ellman, M. (1989), *Socialist Planning*, Cambridge: Cambridge University Press.

Ellman, M. (1994), 'Transformation, Depression, and Economics: Some Lessons', *Journal of Comparative Economics*, June.

Ellman, M. (2000), 'The 1947 Soviet Famine and the Entitlements Approach to Famines', *Cambridge Journal of Economics*, **24**.

Ellman, M. and V. Kontorovich (1992), *The Disintegration of the Soviet Economic System*, London: Routledge.

*Ellman, M. and V. Kontorovich (eds) (1998), *The Destruction of the Soviet Economic System: An Insider's History*, Armonk, NY: M.E. Sharpe.

*Elson, A. (2006), 'The Economic Growth of East Asia and Latin America in Comparative Perspective', *World Economics*, April–June.

Engerman, S. (1976), 'The Height of Slaves', *Local Population Studies*, 16(1).

Engerman, S. (1994), 'The Big Picture: How (and When and Why) the West Grew Rich', *Research Policy*, September.

*Engerman, S. and K Sokoloff (2000), 'Institutions, Factor Endowments, and Paths of Development in the New World', *Journal of Economic Perspectives*, Fall.

Enke, S. (1966), 'The Economic Aspects of Slowing Population Growth', *Economic Journal*, March.

Eremin, A. (1970), 'On the Concept of Market Socialism', *Problems of Economics*, August.

*Ericson, R. (1991), 'The Classical Soviet-Type Economy: Nature of the System and Implications for Reform', *Journal of Economic Perspectives*, Fall.

Erlich, A. (1960), *The Soviet Industrialisation Debate, 1924–28*, Cambridge, MA: Harvard University Press.

Estevadeordal, A., B. Frantz and A.M. Taylor (2003), 'The Rise and Fall of World Trade, 1870–1939', *Quarterly Journal of Economics*, May.

Faye, M.L., J.W. McArthur, J.D. Sachs and T. Snow (2004), 'The Challenges Facing Landlocked Developing Countries', *Journal of Human Development*, March.

*Feinstein, C.H. (1998), 'Pessimism Perpetuated: Real Wages and the Standard of Living in Britain During and After the Industrial Revolution', *Journal of Economic History*, September.

*Feldstein, M. (1998), 'Refocusing the IMF', *Foreign Affairs*, March/April.

*Feldstein, M. (2002), 'Economic and Financial Crises in Emerging Market Economies: Overview of Prevention and Management', National Bureau of Economic Research Working Paper No. 8837, March.

Feng, Y. (2003), *Democracy, Government, and Economic Performance*, Cambridge: MIT Press.

Findlay, R. and K. O'Rourke (2003), 'Commodity Market Integration, 1500–2000', in M.D. Bordo, A. Taylor and J.G. Williamson (eds) (2002), *Globalisation in Historical Perspective*, Chicago, IL: Chicago University Press.

Fischer, S. (1977), 'Long-Term Contracts, Rational Expectations, and the Optimal Money Supply Rule', *Journal of Political Economy*, February.

Fischer, S. (ed.) (1980), *Rational Expectations and Economic Policy*, Chicago, IL: Chicago University Press.

Fischer, S. (1988), 'Recent Developments in Macroeconomics', *Economic Journal*, June.

Fischer, S. (1990), 'Rules Versus Discretion in Monetary Policy', in B.M. Friedman and F.H. Hahn (eds), *Handbook of Monetary Economics Vol. II*, Amsterdam: North-Holland.

Fischer, S. (1991), 'Growth, Macroeconomics and Development', *National Bureau of Economic Research Macroeconomics Annual*.

*Fischer, S. (1993a), 'The Role of Macroeconomic Factors in Growth', *Journal of Monetary Economics*, December.

Fischer, S. (1993b), 'Socialist Economy Reform: Lessons of the First Three Years', *American Economic Review*, May.

Fischer, S. (1994), 'Interview with Stanley Fischer', in B. Snowdon, H.R. Vane and P. Wynarczyk (eds), *A Modern Guide to Macroeconomics: An Introduction to Competing Schools of Thought*, Aldershot, UK and Brookfield, VT, USA: Edward Elgar.

Fischer, S. (1995a), 'Central Bank Independence Revisited', *American Economic Review*, May.

Fischer, S. (1995b), 'The Unending Search for Monetary Salvation', *National Bureau of Economic Research Macroeconomics Annual*.

Fischer, S. (1996a), 'Why are Central Banks Pursuing Long-Run Price Stability?', in *Achieving Price Stability*, Federal Reserve Bank of Kansas.

Fischer, S. (1996c), 'Economies in Transition: The Beginnings of Growth', *American Economic Review*, May.

Fischer, S. (1997a), 'Capital Account Liberalisation and the Role of the IMF', www.imf.org/external/speeches/.

Fischer, S. (1997b), 'How to Avoid International Financial Crises and the Role of the IMF', www.imf.org/external/speeches/.

Fischer, S. (1998a), *Capital Account Liberalisation and the IMF*, Princeton, NJ: Princeton Essays in International Finance.

*Fischer, S. (1998b), 'In Defence of the IMF: Specialised Tools for a Specialised Task', *Foreign Affairs*, July/August.

*Fischer, S. (1999a), 'Reforming the International Financial System', *Economic Journal*, November.

*Fischer, S. (1999b), 'On the Need for an International Lender of Last Resort', *Journal of Economic Perspectives*, Fall.

Fischer, S. (1999c), 'Ten Tentative Conclusions of the Past Three Years', www.imf.org.

*Fischer, S. (2001a), 'Exchange Rate Regimes: Is the Bi-Polar View Correct?', *Journal of Economic Perspectives*, Spring; and *Finance and Development*, June.

Fischer, S. (2001b), 'Beyond the Ivory Tower: The Role of the Economist in Society', Citigroup, May.

*Fischer, S. (2001c), 'Ten Years of Transition: Looking Back and Looking Forward', *IMF Staff Papers*, **48**, Special Issue.

Fischer, S. (2001d), 'The Russian Economy: Prospects and Retrospect', www.omf.org/external/ speeches/.

Fischer, S. (2002), 'Financial Crises and Reform of the International Financial System', National Bureau of Economic Research Working Paper No. 9297.

*Fischer, S. (2003), 'Globalisation and its Challenges', *American Economic Review*, May.

Fischer, S. (2004), *IMF Essays From a Time of Crisis*, Cambridge, MA: MIT Press.

Fischer, S. (2006), 'Reflections on One Year at the Bank of Israel', National Bureau of Economic Research Working Paper No. 12426, August.

*Fischer, S. and A. Gelb (1991), 'The Process of Socialist Economic Transformation', *Journal of Economic Perspectives*, Fall.

Fischer, S. and F. Modigliani (1978), 'Towards an Understanding of the Real Effects and Costs of Inflation', *Weltwirtschaftliches Archiv*, **114**(4).

Fischer, S. and R. Sahay (2000a), 'Taking Stock', *Finance and Development*, September.

*Fischer, S. and R. Sahay (2000b), 'The Transition Economies After Ten Years', IMF Working Paper 00/30.

Fischer, S., M.S. Khan and E. Hernandez-Cata (1998), 'Africa: Is This the Turning Point?' IMF Paper on Policy Analysis and Assessment, Washington, DC.

Fischer, S., R. Sahay and C. Vegh (1996), 'Stabilisation and Growth in Transition Economies: The Early Experiences', *Journal of Economic Perspectives*, Spring.

*Fischer, S., R. Sahay and C. Vegh (2002), 'Modern Hyper- and High Inflations', *Journal of Economic Literature*, September.

Fischer, S. et al. (1988), 'Symposium on the Slowdown in Productivity Growth', *Journal of Economic Perspectives*, Fall.

Fischer, S. et al. (1998), 'Capital Account Liberalisation and the Role of the IMF', in S. Fischer et al. (eds), *Should the IMF Pursue Capital Account Convertibility?*', Princeton Essays in International Finance No. 207, Princeton University.

Fischer, S. et al. (2003), 'The Future of the IMF and World Bank: Comments', *American Economic Review*, May.

Flegal, K.M. et al. (2005), 'Excess Deaths Associated with Underweight, Overweight and Obesity', *Journal of the American Medical Association*, April.

*Fogel, R.W. (1994), 'Economic Growth, Population Theory, and Physiology: The Bearing of Long-Term Growth Processes on the Making of Economic Policy', *American Economic Review*, June.

*Fogel, R.W. (1999), 'Catching Up With the Economy', *American Economic Review*, March.

*Fogel, R.W. (2004a), 'Health, Nutrition and Economic Growth', *Economic Development and Cultural Change*, April.

Fogel, R.W. (2004b), *The Escape from Hunger and Premature Death, 1700–2100*, Cambridge: Cambridge University Press.

Fogel, R.W. (2005), 'Reconsidering Expectations of Economic Growth After World War II from the Perspective of 2004', *IMF Staff Papers*, **52**, Special issue.

Fogel, R.W. (2006), 'Why China is Likely to Achieve its Growth Objectives', National Bureau of Economic Research Working Paper No. 12122, March.

Fogel, R.W. and S.L. Engerman (1974), *Time on the Cross: The Economics of American Negro Slavery*, Boston, MA: Little, Brown and Co.

Foote, C., W. Block, K. Crane and S. Gray (2004), 'Economic Policy and Prospects in Iraq', *Journal of Economic Perspectives*, Summer.

Forbes, K. (2000), 'A Reassessment of the Relationship between Inequality and Growth', *American Economic Review*, September.

Frank, A.G. (1978), *Dependent Accumulation and Underdevelopment*, London: Macmillan.

Frank, A.G. (1998), *Reorient: Global Economy in the Asian Age*, Berkeley, CA: University of California Press.

Frank, R.H. (1997), 'The Frame of Reference as a Public Good', *Economic Journal*, November.

Frankel, J. (1999), 'No Single Currency Regime is Right for All Countries or at All Times', National Bureau of Economic Research Working Paper No. 7338, September.

Frankel, J. and D. Romer (1999), 'Does Trade Cause Growth?', *American Economic Review*, June.

Frankel, J. and A. Rose (1998), 'The Endogeneity of the Optimal Currency Area Criteria', *Economic Journal*, July.

Frankel, J. and A. Rose (2002), 'An Estimate of the Effect of Currency Unions on Trade and Income', *Quarterly Journal of Economics*, May.

Freedom House (2005), *Countries at the Crossroads 2005: A Survey of Democratic Governance*, Lanham, MD: Rowan and Littlefield.

*Freeman, R.B. (2006), 'People Flows in Globalisation', *Journal of Economic Perspectives*, Spring.

Frey, B.S. and A. Stutzer (2002a), 'The Economics of Happiness', *World Economics*, January–March.

Frey, B.S. and A. Stutzer (2002b), *Happiness and Economics: How the Economy and Institutions Affect Human Well-Being*, Princeton, NJ: Princeton University Press.

*Frey, B. and A. Stutzer (2002c), 'What Can Economists Learn From Happiness Research?', *Journal of Economic Literature*, June.

*Friedberg, R.M. and J. Hunt (1995), 'The Impact of Immigrants on Host Country Wages, Employment and Growth', *Journal of Economic Perspectives*, Spring.

Frieden, J.A. (2006), *Global Capitalism: Its Rise and Fall in the Twentieth Century*, New York: W.W. Norton.

*Friedman, B.M. (2005), *The Moral Consequences of Economic Growth*, New York: Alfred A. Knopf.

Friedman, M. (1956), 'The Quantity Theory of Money, A Restatement', in M. Friedman (ed.), *Studies in the Quantity Theory of Money*, Chicago, IL: University of Chicago Press.

Friedman, M. (1958), 'Foreign Economic Aid: Means and Objectives', *Yale Review*, **47**.

*Friedman, M. (1962), *Capitalism and Freedom*, Chicago, IL: University of Chicago Press.

Friedman, T.L. (1999), *The Lexus and the Oak Tree: Understanding Globalisation*, New York: Farrar, Straus and Giroux.

Frijters, P., J.P. Haisken-Denew and M.A. Sheilds (2004), 'Money Does Matter! Evidence from Increasing Real Income and Life Satisfaction in East Germany Following Reunification', *American Economic Review*, June.

Fukuyama, F. (1989), 'The End of History?', *National Interest*, No. 16, Summer.

Fukuyama, F. (1992), *The End of History and the Last Man*, New York: The Free Press.

Fukuyama, F. (1995), *Trust: The Social Virtues and the Creation of Prosperity*, New York: The Free Press.

*Fukuyama, F. (2004), *State Building: Governance and World Order in the Twenty-First Century*, London: Profile Books.

*Furman, J. and J.E. Stiglitz (1998), 'Economic Crises: Evidence and Insights from East Asia', *Brookings Papers on Economic Activity*, No. 2.

Fusfeld, D.R. (1982), *The Age of the Economist*, 4th edn, London: Scott, Foresman and Company.

Gallup, J.L., A. Gaviria and E. Lora (2003), *Is Geography Destiny? Lessons From South America*, Washington, DC: The World Bank and Stanford University Press.

*Gallup, J., J.D. Sachs and A. Mellinger (1999), 'Geography and Economic Development', *International Regional Science Review*, August.

Galor, O. and O. Moav (2002), 'Natural Selection and the Origin of Economic Growth', *Quarterly Journal of Economics*, November.

Galor, O. and O. Moav (2006), 'Das Human Kapital: A Theory of the Demise of the Class Structure', *Review of Economic Studies*, January.

Galor, O. and A. Mountford (2006), 'Trade and the Great Divergence: The Family Connection', *American Economic Review*, May.

Galor, O. and M. Omer (2002), 'From Physical to Human Capital Accumulation: Inequality in the Process of Development', Brown University Working Paper No. 99-27, February.

Galor, O. and D.N. Weil (2000), 'Population, Technology, and Growth: From Malthusian Stagnation to the Demographic Transition and Beyond', *American Economic Review*, September.

Gärtner, M. (2000), 'Political Macroeconomics: A Survey of Recent Developments', *Journal of Economic Surveys*, December.

*Gilpin, R. (2000), *The Challenge of Global Capitalism: The World Economy in the Twenty-First Century*, Princeton, NJ: Princeton University Press.

Glaeser, E. (2005), 'The Political Economy of Hatred', *Quarterly Journal of Economics*, February.

Glaeser, E. and A. Shleifer (2002), 'Legal Origins', *Quarterly Journal of Economics*, November.

*Glaeser, E. et al. (2004), 'Do Institutions Cause Growth?', *Journal of Economic Growth*, September.

*Glaeser, E., J. Scheinkman and A. Shleifer (2003), 'The Injustice of Inequality', *Journal of Monetary Economics*, January.

\*Glyn, A. (2004), 'The Assessment: How Far Has Globalisation Gone?', *Oxford Review of Economic Policy*, **20**(1).

Godoy, S. and J.E. Stiglitz (2006), 'Growth, Initial Conditions, Law and Speed of Privatisation in Transition Countries: Eleven Years Later', National Bureau of Economic Research Working Paper No. 11992, January.

\*Goldin, C. (1995), 'Cliometrics and the Nobel', *Journal of Economic Perspectives*, Spring.

Goldin, C. (2001), 'The Human Capital Century and American Leadership: Virtues of the Past', *Journal of Economic History*, June.

Goldman, M. (2003), *The Piratisation of Russia: Russian Reform Goes Awry*, London: Routledge.

Goldstein, M. and N. Lardy (2006), 'China's Exchange Rate Policy Dilemma', *American Economic Review*, May.

Gomory, R.E. and W.J. Baumol (2004), 'Globalisation: Prospects, Promise, and Problems', *Journal of Policy Modeling*, **26**(4).

Gorbachev, M.S. (1987), *Perestroika: New Thinking for Our Country and the World*, New York: Harper & Row.

Gordon, R.J. (1998), 'Foundations of the Goldilocks Economy: Supply Shocks and the Time-Varying Nairu', *Brookings Papers on Economic Activity*, No. 2.

Graham, B.S. and J.R.W. Temple (2006), 'Rich Nations, Poor Nations: How Much Can Multiple Equilibria Explain?', *Journal of Economic Growth*, March.

Greenwald, B. and J.E. Stiglitz (2006), 'Helping Infant Economies Grow: Foundations of Trade Policies for Developing Countries', *American Economic Review*, May.

\*Gregory, P. and M. Harrison (2005), 'Allocation Under Dictatorship: Research in Stalin's Archives', *Journal of Economic Literature*, September.

\*Grief, A. (2006), *Institutions: Theory and History: Lessons from Medieval Trade*, Cambridge: Cambridge University Press.

Griffin, K. (1970), 'Foreign Capital, Domestic Savings and Economic Development', *Bulletin of the Oxford University Institute of Economics and Statistics*, May.

Griffin, K. and J.L. Enos (1970), 'Foreign Assistance: Objectives and Consequences', *Economic Development and Cultural Change*, April.

Grossman, G. and E. Helpman (1991), *Innovation and Growth in the Global Economy*, Cambridge, MA: MIT Press.

Guiso, L., P. Sapienza and L. Zingales (2003), 'People's Opium? Religion and Economic Attitudes', *Journal of Monetary Economics*, January.

\*Guiso, L., P. Sapienza and L. Zingales (2006), 'Does Culture Affect Economic Outcomes?', *Journal of Economic Perspectives*, Spring.

Gupta, S., C. Patillo and S. Wagh (2006), 'Are Donor Countries Giving More or Less Aid?', *Review of Development Economics*, **10**(3).

Guriev, S. and W. Meggison (2006), 'Privatisation: What Have We Learned?', World Bank ABCDE Conference Paper, St Petersburg, January.

*Guriev, S. and A. Rachinsky (2005), 'The Role of the Oligarchs in Russian Capitalism', *Journal of Economic Perspectives*, Winter.

*Gwartney, J. and R. Lawson (2003), 'The Concept and Measurement of Economic Freedom', *European Journal of Political Economy*, September.

Haberler, G. (1936), *The Theory of International Trade*, New York: A.M. Kelley, 1968.

*Hamilton, C.B. (2004), 'Globalisation and Democracy', in R.E. Baldwin and L.A. Winters (eds), *Challenges to Globalisation*, Chicago, IL: Chicago University Press.

*Hanke, S.H. and S.K. Walters (1997), 'Economic Freedom, Prosperity, and Equality: A Survey', *The Cato Journal*, Fall–Winter.

Hansen, A.H. (1939), 'Economic Progress and Declining Population', *American Economic Review*, March.

Hansen, H. and J. Rand (2006), 'On the Causal Links between FDI and Growth in Developing Countries', *The World Economy*, January.

Haq, M. (1995), *Reflections of Human Development*, New York: Oxford University Press.

Harrison, A. (1996), 'Openness and Growth: A Time Series Cross Country Analysis for Developing Countries', *Journal of Development Economics*, March.

Harrison, M. (2002), 'Coercion, Compliances, and the Collapse of the Soviet Command Economy', *Economic History Review*, **LV**(3).

Harrod, R. (1939), 'An Essay in Dynamic Theory', *Economic Journal*, March.

Harrod, R.F. (1948), *Towards a Dynamic Economics*, London: Macmillan.

*Hatton, T.J. and J.G. Williamson (1998), *The Age of Mass Migration: Causes and Economic Impact*, Oxford: Oxford University Press.

Hatton, T.J. and J.G. Williamson (2002a), 'What Fundamentals Drive World Migration?', National Bureau of Economic Research Working Paper No. 9159, September.

Hatton, T.J. and J.G. Williamson (2002b), 'Out of Africa: Using the Past to Project African Emigration Pressure in the Future', *Review of International Economics*, **10**(2).

Hatton, T.J. and J.G. Williamson (2003), 'Demographic and Economic Pressures on Emigration out of Africa', *Scandinavian Journal of Economics*, September.

Hatton, T.J. and J.G. Williamson (2004), 'International Migration in the Long Run: Positive Selection, Negative Selection and Policy', National Bureau of Economic Research Working Paper No. 10529, May.

\*Hatton, T.J. and J.G. Williamson (2005), *Global Migration and the World Economy, Two Centuries of Policy Performance*, Cambridge, MA: MIT Press.

\*Hatton, T.J. and J.G. Williamson (2006), 'What Determines Immigration's Impact: Comparing Two Global Centuries', National Bureau of Economic Research Working Paper No. 12414, July.

\*Havrylyshyn, O. (2001), 'Recovery and Growth in Transition: A Decade of Evidence', *IMF Staff Papers*, December.

\*Hayek, F.A. (ed.) (1935), *Collectivist Economic Planning*, London: Routledge and Kegan Paul.

Hayek, F.A. (1940), 'Socialist Calculation: The Competitive Solution', *Economica*, May.

\*Hayek, F.A. (1944), *Road to Serfdom*, London: Routledge and Kegan Paul.

Hayek, F.A. (1945), 'The Use of Knowledge in Society', *American Economic Review*, September.

Hayek, F.A. (1988), *The Fatal Conceit: The Errors of Socialism*, London: Routledge.

Hayter, T. (1971), *Aid as Imperialism*, Harmondsworth, UK: Penguin.

Heller, F. (1943), *A Közgazdasági Elméletek Története (A History of Economic Thought)*, Budapest: Gergely R. Könyvkereskedése.

Helliwell, J. (2004), 'Well-being and Social Capital: Does Suicide Pose a Puzzle?', National Bureau of Economic Research Working Paper No. 10896, November.

\*Helpman, E. (2004), *The Mystery of Economic Growth*, Cambridge, MA: Harvard University Press.

Henderson, D. (1998), *The Changing Fortunes of Economic Liberalism: Yesterday, Today and Tomorrow*, Occasional Paper, London: Institute of Economic Affairs.

Henderson, D. (2001), *Anti-Liberalism 2000: The Rise of New Millennium Collectivism*, Occasional Paper, London: Institute of Economic Affairs.

\*Henderson, D. (2004), 'Globalisation, Economic Progress and the New Millennium Collectivism', *World Economics*, July–September.

\*Herbst, J. (2000), *States and Power in Africa: Comparative Lessons in Authority and Control*, Princeton, NJ: Princeton University Press.

Hernandez, Z. (2004), 'Industrial Policy in East Asia: In Search of Lessons', *World Development Report, 2005, Background Paper*, 1–33, www.worldbank.org.

\*Hibbs, D.A. (2001), 'The Politicisation of Growth Theory', *Kyklos*, **54**(2/3).

\*Hibbs, D.A. and O. Olsson (2005), 'Biogeography and Long-Run Economic Development', *European Economic Review*, May.

Hicks, N. and P. Streeten (1979), 'Indicators of Development: The Search for a Basic Needs Yardstick', *World Development*, **7**(6).

Hirsch, F. (1977), *The Social Limits to Growth*, London: Routledge and Kegan Paul.

Hirschman, A.O. (1958), *The Strategy of Economic Development*. New Haven, CT: Yale University Press.

Hirschman, A.O. (1970), *Exit, Voice and Loyalty: Responses to Decline in Firms, Organisations, and States*, Cambridge, MA: Harvard University Press.

Hoff, K. and J.E. Stiglitz (2004), 'After the Big Bang? Obstacles to the Emergence of Law in Post-Communist Societies', *American Economic Review*, June.

*Horrell, S. (2003), 'The Wonderful Usefulness of History', *Economic Journal*, February.

Hoynes, H., M.E. Page and A.H. Stevens (2006), 'Poverty in America: Trends and Explanations', *Journal of Economic Perspectives*, Winter.

Hsieh, C. (1999), 'Productivity Growth and Factor Prices in East Asia', *American Economic Review*, May.

*Hudson, J. et al. (2004), 'Aid and Development', *Economic Journal*, June.

*Hunt, D. (1989), *Economic Theories of Development: An Analysis of Competing Paradigms*, London: Harvester Wheatsheaf.

Huntington, S. (1996), *The Clash of Civilisations and the Remaking of World Order*, London: Simon and Schuster.

Inada, K. (1963), 'On a Two Sector Model of Economic Growth', *Review of Economic Studies*, June.

International Monetary Fund (2003), 'Growth and Institutions', in *World Economic Outlook*, Washington, DC, April.

International Monetary Fund (2005), *World Economic Outlook*, www.imf.org.

Irwin, D. (1996), *Against the Tide: An Intellectual History of Free Trade*, Princeton, NJ: Princeton University Press.

*Irwin, D. (2002a), *Free Trade Under Fire*, Princeton, NJ: Princeton University Press.

Irwin, D. (2002b), 'Interpreting the Tariff–Growth Correlation of the Late 19th Century', *American Economic Review*, May.

Isard, P. (2005), *Globalization and the International Financial System: What's Wrong and What Can Be Done?*, Cambridge: Cambridge University Press.

James, H. (1999), 'Is Liberalisation Reversible?', *Finance and Development*, December.

*James, H. (2001), *The End of Globalisation: Lessons from the Great Depression*, Cambridge, MA: Harvard University Press.

*Jamison, D.T. and S. Radelet (2005), 'Making Aid Smarter', *Finance and Development*, June.

Johnson, C. (1982), *MITI and the Japanese Miracle: The Growth of Industrial Policy, 1925–75*, Stanford, CA: Stanford University Press.

*Johnson, D.G. (1997), 'Agriculture and the Wealth of Nations', *American Economic Review*, May.

*Johnson, D.G. (2000), 'Population, Food and Knowledge', *American Economic Review*, March.

Jones, B.F. and B.A. Olken (2005), 'The Anatomy of Start–Stop Growth', National Bureau of Economic Research Working Paper No. 11528, July.

*Jones, C.I. (2001), 'Was an Industrial Revolution Inevitable? Economic Growth Over the Very Long Run', *Advances in Macroeconomics*, August.

Jones, C.I. (2002), *Introduction to Economic Growth*, 2nd edn, New York: W.W. Norton.

Jones, C.I. (2005), 'Growth and Ideas', in P. Aghion and S. Durlauf (eds), *Handbook of Economic Growth*, Amsterdam: Elsevier.

*Jones, E.L. (1988), *Growth Recurring: Economic Change in World History*, Ann Arbor, MI: University of Michigan Press.

Jones, E.L. (2002), *The Record of Global Economic Development*, Cheltenham, UK and Northampton, MA, USA: Edward Elgar.

Jütting, J. (2003), 'Institutions and Development: A Critical Review', OECD Development Centre Technical Papers No. 210, July.

Kahneman, D. et al. (2004), 'Toward National Well-Being Accounts', *American Economic Review*, May.

Kahneman, D. and A.B. Krueger (2006), 'Developments in the Measurement of Well-Being', *Journal of Economic Perspectives*, Winter.

Kahneman, D., E. Diener and N. Schwarz (eds) (1999), *Well-Being: The Foundations of Hedonic Psychology*, New York: Russell Sage Foundation.

Kaldor, N. (1970), 'The Case for Regional Policies', *Scottish Journal of Political Economy*, November.

Kalecki, M. (1943), 'Political Aspects of Full Employment', *Political Quarterly*, October/December.

Kaminsky, G. and S. Schmukler (2003), 'Short-Run Pain, Long-Run Gain: The Effects of Financial Liberalisation', National Bureau of Economic Research Working Paper No. 9787, June.

Kaminsky, G.L. and C.M. Reinhart (2000), 'On Crises, Contagion and Confusion', *Journal of International Economics*, June.

Kantorovich, L.V. (1965), *The Best Use of Economic Resources*, Cambridge, MA: Harvard University Press.

Kaplan, E. and D. Rodrik (2001), 'Did the Malaysian Capital Controls Work?', www.ksg.harvard.edu/rodrik/.

*Keller, W. (2004), 'International Technology Diffusion', *Journal of Economic Literature*, September.

*Kenny, C. (2005), 'Why Are We Worried About Income? Nearly Everything that Matters is Converging', *World Development*, January.

Keynes, J.M. (1919), *The Economic Consequences of the Peace*, London: Macmillan.

Keynes, J.M. (1923), *A Tract on Monetary Reform*, London: Macmillan.

Keynes, J.M. (1926), 'The End of Laissez-Faire', reprinted in *Essays in Persuasion* (1963), New York: W.W. Norton.

Keynes, J.M. (1930), 'The Economic Possibilities of Our Grandchildren', *Nation and Athenaeum*, October; reprinted in *Essays in Persuasion* (1963), New York: W.W. Norton.

Keynes, J.M. (1933), 'National Self Sufficiency', *The Yale Review*, **22**.

Keynes, J.M. (1936), *The General Theory of Employment, Interest and Money*, London: Macmillan.

Kindleberger, C. (1978), *Manias, Panics and Crashes*, New York: Basic Books.

King, M. (1997a), 'The Inflation Target Five Years On', *Bank of England Quarterly Bulletin*, November.

King, M. (1997b), 'Changes in UK Monetary Policy: Rules and Discretion in Practice', *Journal of Monetary Economics*, June.

King, R.G. and R. Levine (1994), 'Capital Fundamentalism, Economic Development and Economic Growth', *Carnegie–Rochester Conference Series on Public Policy*, **40**.

Kirshner, J. (2001), 'The Political Economy of Low Inflation', *Journal of Economic Surveys*, January.

Knack, S. and P. Keefer (1995), 'Institutions and Economic Performance: Cross Country Tests Using Alternative Institutional Measures', *Economics and Politics*, November.

*Knack, S. and P. Keefer (1997), 'Why Don't Poor Countries Catch Up? A Cross-National Test of an Institutional Explanation', *Economic Inquiry*, July.

Kochhar, K., U. Kumar, R. Rajan, A. Subramanian and I. Tokatlidis (2006), 'India's Pattern of Development: What Happened, What Follows', IMF Working Paper WP/06/22.

Koepke, N. and J. Baten (2005), 'The Biological Standard of Living in Europe During the Last Two Millennia', *European Review of Economic History*, **9**(1).

Komlos, J. (1987), 'The Height of West Point Cadets: Dietary Change in Antebellum America', *Journal of Economic History*, December.

Komlos, J. (1996), 'Anomalies in Economic History: Towards a Resolution of the "Antebellum" Puzzle', *Journal of Economic History*, March.

*Komlos, J. (1998), 'Shrinking in a Growing Economy? The Mystery of Physical Stature During the Industrial Revolution', *Journal of Economic History*, September.

Komlos, J. and M. Baur (2004), 'From the Tallest in the World to (One of) the Fattest: The Enigmatic Fate of the American Population in the Twentieth Century', Working Paper, University of Munich.

Komlos, J. and P. Coclanis (1997), 'On the Puzzling Cycle in the Biological Standard of Living: the Case of the Antebellum Georgia', *Explorations in Economic History*, October.

Komlos, J. and B. Snowdon (2005), 'Measures of Progress and Other Tall Stories: From Income to Anthropometrics', *World Economics*, April–June.

Komlos, J., P.K. Smith and B. Bogin (2004), 'Obesity and the Rate of Time Preference: Is There a Connection?', *Journal of Biosocial Science*, March.

Kornai, J. (1957), *Overcentralisation in Economic Administration: A Critical Analysis Based on Experience in Hungarian Light Industry*, English translation, London: Oxford University Press (1959).

Kornai, J. (1965), 'Mathematical Programming as a Tool in Drawing Up the Five Year Economic Plan', *Economics of Planning*, **5**(3).

Kornai, J. (1967), *Mathematical Planning of Structural Decisions*, Amsterdam: North-Holland.

Kornai, J. (1969), 'Multi-level Programming: A First Report on the Model and on Experimental Computations', *European Economic Review*, **1**(1).

Kornai, J. (1970), 'A General Descriptive Model of the Planning Processes', *Economics of Planning*, **10**(1–2).

Kornai, J. (1971), *Anti-Equilibrium*, Amsterdam: North-Holland.

Kornai, J. (1976), 'The Measurement of Shortage', *Acta Oeconomica*, **16**(3–4).

Kornai, J. (1979), 'Resource Constrained Versus Demand Constrained Systems', *Econometrica*, July.

*Kornai, J. (1980), *Economics of Shortage*, Amsterdam: North-Holland.

Kornai, J. (1981), 'The Dilemmas of a Socialist Country: The Hungarian Experiment', *Cambridge Journal of Economics*, **4**(2).

Kornai, J. (1982), *Growth, Shortage and Efficiency*, Oxford: Blackwell.

*Kornai, J. (1986a), 'The Soft Budget Constraint', *Kyklos*, **39**(1).

Kornai, J. (1986b), 'The Hungarian Reform Process: Visions, Hopes, and Reality', *Journal of Economic Literature*, **24**(4).

Kornai, J. (1988), 'Individual Freedom and Reform of the Socialist Economy', *European Economic Review*, **32**(2–3).

Kornai, J. (1990a), *The Road to a Free Economy, Shifting from the Socialist System: The Example of Hungary*, New York: W.W. Norton.

Kornai, J. (1990b), 'The Affinity Between Ownership Forms and Coordination Mechanisms: The Common Experience of Reform in Socialist Countries', *Journal of Economic Perspectives*, 4(3).

Kornai, J. (1990c), 'Comment on Sachs and Lipton', *Brookings Papers on Economic Activity*, No. 1.

*Kornai, J. (1992a), *The Socialist System: The Political Economy of Communism*, Oxford: Clarendon Press.

Kornai, J. (1992b), 'The Principles of Privatisation in Eastern Europe', *De Economist*, **140**(2).

Kornai, J. (1992c), 'The Postsocialist Transition and the State: Reflections in the Light of Hungarian Fiscal Problems', *American Economic Review*, May.

Kornai, J. (1992d), 'Transformational Recession: A General Phenomenon Examined Through the Example of Hungary's Development', *Economie Appliquée*, **46**(2).

Kornai, J. (1993), 'The Evolution of Financial Discipline Under the Postsocialist System', *Kyklos*, Fall.

*Kornai, J. (1994), 'Transformational Recession: The Main Causes', *Journal of Comparative Economics*, **19**(3).

Kornai, J. (1995), 'Eliminating the Shortage Economy: A General Analysis and Examination of the Developments in Hungary', Part I–II. *Economics of Transition*, **3**(1–2).

Kornai, J. (1997a), *Struggle and Hope: Essays on Stabilisation and Reform in a Post-Socialist Economy*, Cheltenham, UK and Lyme, USA: Edward Elgar.

Kornai, J. (1997b), 'Editorial: Reforming the Welfare State in Post-Socialist Societies', *World Development*, August.

Kornai, J. (1997c), 'The Reform of the Welfare State and Public Opinion', *American Economic Review*, May.

Kornai, J. (1998a), 'Legal Obligation, Non-Compliance and Soft Budget Constraints', in P. Newman (ed.), *New Palgrave Dictionary of Economics and the Law*, New York: Macmillan.

*Kornai, J. (1998b), 'The Concept of the Soft Budget Constraint Syndrome in Economic Theory', *Journal of Comparative Economics*, **26**(1).

*Kornai, J (2000a), 'What the Change of System from Socialism to Capitalism Does and Does Not Mean', *Journal of Economic Perspectives*, Winter.

Kornai, J. (2000b), 'Ten Years After "The Road to a Free Economy": The Author's Self Evaluation', in Boris Pleskovic and Nicolas Stern (eds), *Annual Bank Conference on Development Economics 2000*, Washington, DC: The World Bank.

Kornai, J. (2000c), 'Making the Transition to Private Ownership', *Finance and Development*, September.

*Kornai, J. (2001), 'Hardening of the Budget Constraint: The Experience of the Post-Socialist Countries', *European Economic Review*, 45(9).

*Kornai, J. (2006), 'The Great Transformation of Central Eastern Europe: Success and Disappointment', *Economics of Transition*, July.

Kornai, J. and T. Lipták (1962), 'Mathematical Investigation of Some Economic Effects of Profit Sharing in Socialist Firms', *Econometrica*, 30(l).

Kornai, J. and T. Lipták (1965), 'Two-Level Planning', *Econometrica*, 33(1).

Kornai, J. and B. Martos (1973), 'Autonomous Control of the Economic System', *Econometrica*, 41(3).

Kornai, J. and A. Simonovits (1977), 'Decentralised Control Problems in von Neumann Economies', *Journal of Economic Theory*, 14(1).

Kornai, J. and J.W. Weibull (1978), 'The Normal State of the Market in a Shortage Economy: A Queue Model', *Scandinavian Journal of Economics*, 80(4).

Kornai, J. and J.W. Weibull (1983), 'Paternalism, Buyers' and Sellers' Market', *Mathematical Social Sciences*, 6(2).

*Kornai, J., E. Maskin and G. Roland (2003), 'Understanding the Soft Budget Constraint', *Journal of Economic Literature*, December.

Kose, M.A., E.S. Prasad and M.E. Terrones (2005), 'Growth and Volatility in a Era of Globalisation', *IMF Staff Papers*, **52**, Special Issue.

Kose, M.A., E.S. Prasad, K. Rogoff and S. Wei (2006), 'Financial Globalisation', National Bureau of Economic Research Working Paper No. 12484, August.

Kraay, A. and C. Raddatz (2005), 'Poverty Traps, Aid and Growth', World Bank Policy Research Working Paper No. WPS3631, June.

Kravis, I.B., A. Heston and R. Summers (1982), *World Product and Income: International Comparisons of Real Gross Product*, Baltimore, MD: Johns Hopkins Press.

Kravis, I.B., Z. Kenessey, A. Heston and R. Summers (1975), *A System of International Comparisons of Gross Product and Purchasing Power*, Baltimore, MD: Johns Hopkins University Press.

Kremer, M. (1993), 'Population Growth and Technological Change: One Million B.C. to 1990', *Quarterly Journal of Economics*, August.

Kremer, M. (2002), 'Pharmaceuticals and the Developing World', *Journal of Economic Perspectives*, Fall.

Kremer, M. and R. Glennerster (2004), *Strong Medicine: Creating Incentives for Pharmaceutical Research on Neglected Diseases*, Princeton, NJ: Princeton University Press.

*Kremer, M. and S. Jayachandran (2002), 'Odious Debt', *Finance and Development*, June.

Kremer, M. and S. Jayachandran (2006), 'Odious Debt', *American Economic Review*, March.

Kremer, M. and C. Snyder (2004), 'Why is There No AIDS Vaccine?', Harvard Centre for International Development Working Paper No. 111.

Krueger, A.O. (1978), *Foreign Trade Regimes and Economic Development: Liberalisation Attempts and Consequences*, Cambridge, MA: Ballinger.

*Krueger, A.O. (1990), 'Government Failures in Development', *Journal of Economic Perspectives*, Summer.

*Kreuger, A.O. (1997), 'Trade Policy and Economic Development: How we Learn', *American Economic Review*, March.

*Krueger, A.O. (1998), 'Why Trade Liberalisation is Good for Growth', *Economic Journal*, September.

*Krueger, A.O. (1998), 'Whither the World Bank and IMF?', *Journal of Economic Literature*, December.

*Krueger, A.O. (2000), 'Conflicting Demands on the International Monetary Fund', *American Economic Review*, May.

Krueger, A.O. (2005), 'De Tocqueville's Dangerous Moment: The Importance of Getting Reforms Right', *World Economy*, June.

Krugman, P. (1992), 'Towards a Counter-Revolution in Development Theory', *Proceedings of the World Bank Conference on Development Economics*, Washington, DC: World Bank.

Krugman, P. (1993a), 'The Narrow and Broad Arguments for Free Trade', *American Economic Review*, May.

Krugman, P. (1993b), 'What Do Undergrads Need to Know About Trade?', *American Economic Review*, May.

*Krugman, P. (1994a), 'Competitiveness: A Dangerous Obsession', *Foreign Affairs*, March–April.

*Krugman, P. (1994b), 'The Myth of Asia's Miracle', *Foreign Affairs*, November/December.

Krugman, P. (1995), *Development, Geography and Economic Theory*, Cambridge, MA: MIT Press.

*Krugman, P. (1996), *Pop Internationalism*, Cambridge, MA: MIT Press.

Krugman, P. (1997), *Development, Geography and Economic Theory*, Cambridge, MA: MIT Press.

Krugman, P. (1998), 'Its Baaack! Japan's Slump and the Return of the Liquidity Trap', *Brookings Papers on Economic Activity*, No. 2.

Krugman, P. (1999a), *The Return of Depression Economics*, New York: W.W. Norton.

Krugman, P. (1999b), 'The Role of Geography in Development', *International Regional Science Review*, August.

Krugman, P. (1999c), 'Enemies of the WTO: Bogus Arguments Against the World Trade Organisation', *Slate Magazine*, 24 November.

Krugman, P. and A. Venables (1995), 'Globalisation and the Inequality of Nations', *Quarterly Journal of Economics*, November.

*Kuczynski, P. and J. Williamson (2003), *After the Washington Consensus: Restarting Growth and Reform in Latin America*, Washington, DC: Institute of International Economics.

Kumar, M.S. (2003), 'Deflation: The New Threat?', *Finance and Development*, June.

Kumar, S. and R.R. Russell (2002), 'Technological Change, Technological Catch-Up, and Capital Deepening: Relative Contributions to Growth and Convergence', *American Economic Review*, June.

*Kunz, D.B. et al. (1997), 'The Marshall Plan and Its Legacy', *Foreign Affairs*, May/June.

Kuran, T. (2004), 'Why the Middle East is Economically Underdeveloped: Historical Mechanisms of Institutional Stagnation', *Journal of Economic Perspectives*, Summer.

Kuznets, S. (1955), 'Economic Growth and Income Inequality', *American Economic Review*, March.

Kuznets, S. (1973), 'Modern Economic Growth: Findings and Reflections', *American Economic Review*, June.

Kydland, F.E. and E.C. Prescott (1977), 'Rules Rather Than Discretion: The Inconsistency of Optimal Plans', *Journal of Political Economy*, June.

*La Porta, R. et al. (1999), 'The Quality of Government', *Journal of Law, Economics and Organisation*, March.

Laband, D. and J. Wells (1998), 'The Scholarly Journal Literature of Economics: An Historical Profile of the AER, JPE and QJE', *American Economist*, Fall.

*Lackner, K.S. and J.D. Sachs (2005), 'A Robust Strategy for Sustainable Energy', *Brookings Papers on Economic Activity*, No. 2.

Lakdawalla, D., T. Philipson and J. Bhattacharya (2005), 'Welfare Enhancing Technological Change and the Growth of Obesity', paper presented at the American Economics Association Annual Meeting, Philadelphia, January.

*Lake, D. (1992), 'Powerful Pacifists: Democratic States and War', *American Political Science Review*, March.

*Lal, D. (1999), *Unintended Consequences: The Impact of Factor Endowments, Culture, and Politics on Long-Run Economic Performance*, Cambridge, MA: MIT Press.

Lal, D. (2005), 'The Hare and the Tortoise', *Business Standard*, New Delhi, 15 March.

*Landau, D. (2003), 'A Simple Theory of Economic Growth', *Economic Development and Cultural Change*, October.

Landes, D.S. (1969), *The Unbound Prometheus: Technological Change and Development in Western Europe from 1750 to the Present*, Cambridge: Cambridge University Press.

*Landes, D.S. (1998), *The Wealth and Poverty of Nations: Why Some Are So Rich and Some So Poor*, New York: W.W. Norton.

*Landes, D.S. (2006), 'Why Europe and the West? Why Not China?', *Journal of Economic Perspectives*, Spring.

Lane, T. and S. Phillips (2002), 'Moral Hazard: Does IMF Financing Encourage the Imprudence of Borrowers and Lenders?', *Economic Issues*, No. 28, IMF.

Lange, O. (1936), 'On the Economic Theory of Socialism', *Review of Economic Studies*, October.

Lange, O. (1937), 'On the Economic Theory of Socialism', *Review of Economic Studies*, February.

*Lange, O. and F.M. Taylor (1938), *On the Economic Theory of Socialism*, New York: McGraw-Hill.

Larson, D.A. and W.T. Wilford (1979), 'The Physical Quality of Life Index: A Useful Social Indicator?', *World Development*, June.

Lau, L.J., Y. Qian and G. Roland (2000), 'Reform Without Losers: An Interpretation of China's Dual-Track Approach to Transition', *Journal of Political Economy*, February.

Lavigne, M. (1995), *The Economics of Transition: From Socialist Economy to Market Economy*, Basingstoke, UK: Macmillan.

Lavoie, D. (1985), *Rivalry and Central Planning: The Socialist Calculation Debate Reconsidered*, Cambridge: Cambridge University Press.

Lawrence, R. and D. Weinstein (2001), 'Trade and Growth: Import-Led or Export-Led? Evidence from Japan and Korea', in J.E. Stiglitz and S. Yusuf (eds), *Rethinking the East Asian Miracle*, Oxford: Oxford University Press.

*Layard, R. (2005), *Happiness: Lessons from a New Science*, London: Penguin.

*Lee, R. (2003), 'The Demographic Transition: Three Centuries of Fundamental Change', *Journal of Economic Perspectives*, Fall.

Leibenstein, H. (1957), *Economic Backwardness and Economic Growth*, New York: Wiley.

Leibenstein, H. (1966), 'Allocative Efficiency v X-Efficiency', *American Economic Review*, June.

Leibenstein, H. (1974), 'An Interpretation of the Economic Theory of Fertility: Promising Path or Blind Alley', *Journal of Economic Literature*, **12**(2).

Leibenstein, H. (1979), 'A Branch of Economics Is Missing: Micro–Micro Theory', *Journal of Economic Literature*, June.

Lerner, A. (1934), 'Economic Theory and Socialist Economy', *Review of Economic Studies*, October.

*Levine, R. (1997), 'Financial Development and Economic Growth: Views and Agenda', *Journal of Economic Literature*, June.

Levitt, T. (1983), 'The Globalization of Markets', *Harvard Business Review*, May–June.

*Lewis, W.A. (1954), 'Economic Development with Unlimited Supplies of Labour', *Manchester School of Economic and Social Studies*, May.

Lewis, W.A. (1955), *Theory of Economic Growth*, London: Allen and Unwin.

Lewis, W.W. (2004), *The Power of Productivity*, Chicago, IL: Chicago University Press.

*Lindert, P. (2003), 'Voice and Growth: Was Churchill Right?', National Bureau of Economic Research Working Paper No. 9749.

Lindert, P. (2004), *Growing Public: Social Spending and Economic Growth Since the Eighteenth Century*, Cambridge: Cambridge University Press.

Lindert, P.H. and J.G. Williamson (1983), 'Reinterpreting England's Social Tables, 1688–1812', *Explorations in Economic History*, January.

Lindert, P.H. and J.G. Williamson (2003), 'Does Globalisation Make the World More Unequal?', in M. Bordo, A.M. Taylor and J.G. Williamson (eds), *Globalisation in Historical Perspective*, Chicago, IL: Chicago University Press.

*Lipset, S.M. (1959), 'Some Social Requisites of Democracy: Economic Development and Political Legitimacy', *American Political Science Review*, March.

Lipset, S.M. and G. Marks (2000), *It Didn't Happen Here: Why Socialism Failed in the United States*, New York: W.W. Norton.

*Lipton, D. and J.D. Sachs (1990a), 'Creating a Market Economy in Eastern Europe: The Case of Poland', *Brookings Papers on Economic Activity*, No. 1.

Lipton, D. and J.D. Sachs (1990b), 'Privatisation in Eastern Europe: The Case of Poland', *Brookings Papers on Economic Activity*, No. 2.

Lipton, D. and J.D. Sachs (1992), 'Prospects for Russia's Economic Reforms', *Brookings Papers on Economic Activity*, No. 2.

Little, I.M.D., T. Scitovsky and M.F.G. Scott (1970), *Industry and Trade in Some Developing Countries*, Oxford: Oxford University Press.

Lockwood, B. (2004), 'How Robust is the Kearney/Foreign Policy Globalisation Index?', *World Economy*, April.

Lopez-Claros, A. (2005), 'Russia: Competitiveness, Growth, and the Next Stage of Development', in A. Lopez-Claros, M.E. Porter and K. Schwab (eds) (2005), *The Global Competitiveness Report, 2005–2006*, Basingstoke: Palgrave Macmillan.

*Lopez-Claros, A., J. Blanke, M. Drzeniek, I. Mia and S. Zahidi (2005), 'Policies and Institutions Underpinning Economic Growth: Results from the Competitiveness Indexes', in A. Lopez-Claros, M.E. Porter and K. Schwab (eds) (2005), *The Global Competitiveness Report, 2005–2006*, Basingstoke: Palgrave Macmillan.

Lucas, R.E. Jr (1988), 'On the Mechanics of Economic Development', *Journal of Monetary Economics*, July.

Lucas, R.E. Jr (1990), 'Why Doesn't Capital Flow from Rich to Poor Countries?', *American Economic Review*, May.

*Lucas, R. (2000), 'Some Macroeconomics for the 21st Century', *Journal of Economic Perspectives*, Winter.

Maddison, A. (1995), *Explaining the Economic Performance of Nations*, Aldershot, UK and Brookfield, US: Edward Elgar.

*Maddison, A. (2001), *The World Economy in Millennial Perspective*, Paris: OECD.

Maddison, A. (2004), 'Macromeasurement Before and After Colin Clark', *Australian Economic History Review*, March.

Malthus, T.R. (1798/1909), *An Essay on the Principle of Population*, London: Macmillan.

*Mankiw, N.G. (1995), 'The Growth of Nations', *Brookings Papers on Economic Activity*, No. 1.

Mankiw, N.G. (2003), *Macroeconomics*, 3rd edn, New York: Worth.

*Mankiw, N.G. and P. Swagel (2006), 'The Politics and Economics of Offshore Outsourcing', National Bureau of Economic Research Working Paper No. 12398, July.

Mankiw, N.G., D. Romer and D.N. Weil (1992), 'A Contribution to the Empirics of Economic Growth', *Quarterly Journal of Economics*, May.

*Marangos, J. (2002), 'The Political Economy of Shock Therapy', *Journal of Economic Surveys*, **16**(1).

*Marangos, J. (2005), 'A Political Economy Approach to the Neoclassical Gradualist Model of Transition', *Journal of Economic Surveys*, **19**(2).

Marks, L.A., N. Kalaitzandonakes and S. Konduru (2006), 'Images of Globalisation in the Mass Media', *World Economy*, May.

Marshall, A. (1890), *Principles of Economics*, 8th edn, 1920, London: Macmillan.

Marshall, A. (1907), 'The Social Possibilities of Economic Chivalry', *Economic Journal*, March.

Marshall, M. and K. Jaggers (2000), 'Polity IV Project, Political Regime Characteristics and Transitions 1800–1999, Dataset Users' Manual', Center for International Development and Conflict Management, University of Maryland.

Marx, K. (1867), *Capital*, Vols I (1990) and II (1992), Harmondsworth, UK: Penguin.

*Marx, K. and F. Engels (1848), *The Communist Manifesto*, Oxford: Oxford University Press (1992).

Matlock, J. (2005), *Reagan and Gorbachev: How the Cold War Ended*, New York: Random House.

*Mauro, P. (1995), 'Corruption and Growth', *Quarterly Journal of Economics*, August.

Mazower, M. (1998), *Dark Continent: Europe's Twentieth Century*, Harmondsworth, UK: Allen Lane Penguin.

McArthur, J.W. and J.D. Sachs (2001), 'The Growth Competitiveness Index: Measuring Technological Advancement and Stages of Development', in *The Global Competitiveness Report 2001–02*, New York: Oxford University Press.

McCallum, J. (1995), 'National Borders Matter: Canadian–US Regional Trade Patterns', *American Economic Review*, June.

McCloskey, D.N. (1994), '1780–1860: A Survey', in R. Floud and D.N. McCloskey (eds), *The Economic History of Britain Since 1700, Vol. I*, 2nd edn, Cambridge: Cambridge University Press.

Meadows, D. et al. (1972), *The Limits to Growth*, London: Earth Island.

*Meggison, W.L. and J.M. Netter (2001), 'From State to Market: A Survey of Empirical Studies on Privatisation', *Journal of Economic Literature*, June.

Mehlum, H., K. Moene and R. Torvik (2006), 'Cursed By Resources or Institutions', *World Economy*, August.

Meier, G.M. (1994), 'Review of Development Research in the UK: Report to the Development Studies Association', *Journal of International Development*, **6**(5).

*Meier, G.M. and J.E. Rauch (eds) (2005), *Leading Issues in Economic Development*, 8th edn, Oxford: Oxford University Press.

Meier, G.M. and D. Seers (eds) (1984), *Pioneers in Development*, Oxford: Oxford University Press.

*Meier, G.M. and J.E. Stiglitz (eds) (2001), *Frontiers of Development Economics: The Future in Perspective*, Oxford: Oxford University Press.

Melchior, A. (2001), 'Global Income Inequality: Beliefs, Facts and Unresolved Issues', *World Economics*, July–September.

Meltzer, A.H. (2000), 'Response to Professor Bird', *World Economics*, July–September.

*Meltzer, A.H. et al. (2000), *Report of the International Financial Advisory Commission*, Washington, DC: Government Printing Office.

Mendoza, R. and C. Bahadur (2002), 'Toward Free and Fair Trade: A Global Public Good Perspective', *Challenge*, September–October.

Milanovic, B. (2002a), *Worlds Apart: Inter-National and World Inequality, 1950–2000*, Washington, DC: World Bank.

Milanovic, B. (2002b), 'True World Income Distribution, 1988 and 1993: First Calculation Based on Household Surveys Alone', *Economic Journal*, January.

*Milanovic, B. (2003), 'The Two Faces of Globalisation: Against Globalisation as We Know it', *World Development*, April.

*Milanovic, B. (2006), 'Global Income Inequality: A Review', *World Economics*, January–March.

Mill, J.S. (1848), *Principles of Political Economy*, Harmondsworth, UK: Pelican (1970).

Mises, L. von (1920), 'Economic Calculation in a Socialist Commonwealth', reprinted in F. von Hayek (ed.), *Collectivist Economic Planning*, London: Routledge and Kegan Paul.

*Mishkin, F.S. (1999a), 'Global Financial Instability: Framework, Events, Issues', *Journal of Economic Perspectives*, Fall.

*Mishkin, F.S. (1999b), 'International Experiences with Different Monetary Regimes', *Journal of Monetary Economics*, June.

*Mishkin, F. (2001), 'Financial Policies and the Prevention of Financial Crises in Emerging Market Economies', National Bureau of Economic Research Working Paper No. 8087.

*Mishkin, F.S. (2005), 'Is Financial Globalisation Beneficial?', National Bureau of Economic Research Working Paper No. 11891, December.

Mokyr, J. (1990), *The Lever of Riches: Technological Creativity and Economic Change*, Oxford: Oxford University Press.

Mokyr, J. (1994), 'Cardwell's Law and the Political Economy of Technological Progress', *Research Policy*, September.

Mokyr, J. (1998), *The British Industrial Revolution: An Economic Perspective*, Boulder, CO: Westview Press.

*Mokyr, J. (2002), *The Gifts of Athena*, Princeton, NJ: Princeton University Press.

*Mokyr, J. (2005a), 'Long-Term Economic Growth and the History of Technology', in P. Aghion and S. Durlauf (eds), *Handbook of Economic Growth*, Amsterdam: Elsevier.

*Mokyr, J. (2005b), 'The Intellectual Origins of Modern Economic Growth', *Journal of Economic History*, June.

Morgan, P.S. (2003), 'Is Low Fertility a Twenty-First-Century Demographic Crisis?', *Demography*, November.

Morris, M.D. (1979), *Measuring the Condition of the World's Poor, The Physical Quality of Life Index*, London: Frank Cass.

Mulligan, C. and X. Sala-i-Martin (1993), 'Transitional Dynamics in Two-Sector Models of Endogenous Growth', *Quarterly Journal of Economics*, August.

Mulligan, C. and X. Sala-i-Martin (2000), 'Measuring Aggregate Human Capital', *Journal of Economic Growth*, September.

Mulligan, C. and X. Sala-i-Martin (2004), 'Do Democracies Have Different Public Policies Than Non-Democracies?', *Journal of Economic Perspectives*, Winter.

Mundell, R.A. (1961), 'A Theory of Optimum Currency Areas', *American Economic Review*, November.

Murphy, K.M., A. Shleifer and R.W. Vishny (1989), 'Industrialisation and the Big Push', *Quarterly Journal of Economics*, May.

Murphy, K.M., A. Shleifer and R.W. Vishny (1991), 'The Allocation of Talent: Implications for Growth', *Quarterly Journal of Economics*, May.

Murphy, K.M., A. Shleifer and R.W. Vishny (1992), 'The Transition to a Market Economy: Pitfalls of Partial Reform', *Quarterly Journal of Economics*, August.

*Murphy, K.M., A. Shleifer and R.W. Vishny (1993), 'Why is Rent Seeking so Costly for Growth?', *American Economic Review*, May.

Murrell, P. (1991), 'Can Neoclassical Economics Underpin the Reform of Centrally Planned Economies?', *Journal of Economic Perspectives*, Fall.

Murrell, P. (1993), 'What is Shock Therapy? What Did it Do in Poland and Russia?', *Post-Soviet Affairs*, 9(2).

*Murrell, P. (1995), 'The Transition According to Cambridge Mass', *Journal of Economic Literature*, March.

Murrell, P. (2006), 'Institutions and Transition', in L. Blume and S. Durlauf (eds), *The New Palgrave Dictionary of Economics*, 2nd edn, Basingstoke: Palgrave Macmillan.

Mussa, M. (2000), 'Factors Driving Global Integration', www.imf.org.

Myrdal, G. (1957), *Economic Theory and Underdeveloped Regions*, London: Methuen.

Nelson, R.R. (1956), 'A Theory of the Low Level Equilibrium Trap', *American Economic Review*, 46(5).

Neumayer, E. and I. De Soysa (2004), 'Trade Openness, Foreign Direct Investment, and Child Labour', *World Development*, January.

Ng, Y. (1997), 'A Case for Happiness, Cardinalism, and Interpersonal Comparability', *Economic Journal*, November.

*Nixon, F., B. Walters et al. (1999), 'The Asian Crisis: Causes and Consequences', *Manchester School*, special issue.

Noland, M. (2003), 'Religion, Culture, and Economic Development', Institute for International Economics Working Paper No. 03-8, September.

Noland, M., S. Robinson and T. Wang (2001), 'Famine in North Korea: Causes and Cures', *Economic Development and Cultural Change*, July.

Nordhaus, W.D. (1975), 'The Political Business Cycle', *Review of Economic Studies*, April.

Nordhaus, W.D. (2001), 'New Directions in National Economic Accounting', *American Economic Review*, May.

*Nordhaus, W.D. (2002), 'The Health of Nations: The Contribution of Improved Health to Living Standards', National Bureau of Economic Research Working Paper No. 8818, March.

Nordhaus, W.D. (2006), 'The "Stern Review" on the Economics of Climate Change', National Bureau of Economic Research Working Paper No. 12741, December.

North, D.C. (1989), 'Institutions and Economic Growth: An Historical Approach', *World Development*, September.

*North, D.C. (1990), *Institutions, Institutional Change and Economic Performance*, Cambridge: Cambridge University Press.

*North, D.C. (1991), 'Institutions', *Journal of Economic Perspectives*, Winter.

*North, D.C. (1994), 'Economic Performance Through Time', *American Economic Review*, June.

*North, D.C. (2004), *Understanding the Process of Economic Change*, Princeton, NJ: Princeton University Press.

North, D.C. and R. Thomas (1973), *The Rise of the Western World: A New Economic History*, Cambridge: Cambridge University Press.

North, D.C. and B. Weingast (1989), 'Constitutions and Commitment: The Evolution of Institutions Governing Public Choice in Seventeenth-Century England', *Journal of Economic History*, December.

*Nove, A. (1983), *The Economics of Feasible Socialism*, London: George Allen and Unwin.

Nove, A. and D.M. Nuti (eds) (1972), *Socialist Economics*, Harmondsworth, UK: Penguin.

Nuti, D.M. (1988), 'Perestroika: Transition from Central Planning to Market Socialism', *Economic Policy*, October.

Nurkse, R. (1953), *Problems of Capital Formation in Underdeveloped Countries*, New York: Oxford University Press.

Oates, W. (1999), 'An Essay on Fiscal Federalism', *Journal of Economic Literature*, September.

*Obstfeld, M. (1998), 'The Global Capital Market: Benefactor or Menace?', *Journal of Economic Perspectives*, Fall.

Obstfeld, M. and A. Taylor (2003), 'Globalisation in Capital Markets', in M. Bordo, A. Taylor and J.G. Williamson (eds), *Globalisation in Historical Perspective*, Chicago, IL: University of Chicago Press.

*Obstfeld, M. and A.M. Taylor (2004), *Global Capital Markets: Integration, Crisis and Growth*, Cambridge: Cambridge University Press.

OECD (2004), *Understanding Economic Growth: Macro Level, Industry Level, Firm Level*, Basingstoke: Palgrave Macmillan.

OECD (2005), *Measuring Globalisation: OECD Economic Globalisation Statistics*, Paris: OECD.

Ofer, G. (1987), 'Soviet Economic Growth: 1928–1985', *Journal of Economic Literature*, December.

*Olson, M. (1993), 'Dictatorship, Democracy and Development', *American Political Science Review*, September.

*Olson, M. (1996), 'Distinguished Lecture on Economics in Government: Big Bills Left on the Sidewalk: Why Some Nations are Rich, and Others Poor', *Journal of Economic Perspectives*, Spring.

*Olson, M. (2000), *Power and Prosperity: Outgrowing Communist and Capitalist Dictatorships*, New York: Basic Books.

Olsson, O. (2006), 'Diamonds are a Rebel's Best Friend', *The World Economy*, August.

O'Rourke, K.H. (2000), 'Tariffs and Growth in the Late 19th Century', *Economic Journal*, April.

O'Rourke, K.H. (2001), 'Globalisation and Inequality: Historical Trends', National Bureau of Economic Research Working Paper No. 8339, June.

O'Rourke, K.H. (2002), 'Europe and the Causes of Globalisation: 1790–2000', in H. Kierzkowski (ed.), *From Europeanisation of the Globe to the Globalisation of Europe*, London: Palgrave.

O'Rourke, K.H. (2005), 'The World-wide Economic Impact of the Revolutionary and Napoleonic Wars', National Bureau of Economic Research Working Paper No. 11344, May.

O'Rourke, K.H. and J.G. Williamson (1994), 'Late Nineteenth Century Anglo-American Factor Price Convergence: Were Heckscher and Ohlin Right?', *Journal of Economic History*, December.

*O'Rourke, K.H. and J.G. Williamson (1999), *Globalisation and History: Evolution of the Nineteenth Century Atlantic Economy*, Cambridge, MA: MIT Press.

O'Rourke, K.H. and J.G. Williamson (2002a), 'After Columbus: Explaining Europe's Overseas Trade Boom', *Journal of Economic History*, June.

*O'Rourke, K.H. and J.G. Williamson (2002b), 'When did Globalisation Begin?', *European Review of Economic History*, June.

O'Rourke, K.H. and J.G. Williamson (2002c), 'The Heckscher–Ohlin Model Between 1400 and 2000: When it Explained Factor Price Convergence, When it Did Not, and Why', in R. Findlay, L. Jonung and M. Lundahl (eds), *Bertil Ohlin: A Centennial Celebration*, Cambridge, MA: MIT Press.

O'Rourke, K.H. and J.G. Williamson (2004), 'Once More: When Did Globalisation Begin?', *European Review of Economic History*, April.

O'Rourke, K.H. and J.G. Williamson (2005), 'From Malthus to Ohlin: Trade, Growth and Distribution Since 1500', *Journal of Economic Growth*, January.

Oswald, A. (1997), 'Happiness and Economic Performance', *Economic Journal*, November.

Overseas Development Council (1977), *The United States and World Development: Agenda for 1977*, New York: Praeger.

Palazzi, P. and A. Lauri (1998), 'The Human Development Index: Suggested Corrections', *Banca Nazionale del Lavoro Quarterly Review*, June.

*Paldam, M. (2003), 'Economic Freedom and Success of the East Asian Tigers: An Essay in Controversy', *European Journal of Political Economy*, September.

Panagariya, A. (2002), 'The Costs of Protection: Where Do We Stand?', *American Economic Review*, May.

*Panagariya, A. (2004a), 'Miracles and Debacles: In Defence of Trade Openness', *The World Economy*, August.

Panagariya, A. (2004b), 'India in the 1980s and 1990s: A Triumph of Reforms', IMF Working Paper No. 04/43: 1–38; reprinted in W. Tseng and D. Cowan (eds), (2005), *India's and China's Experience with Reform and Growth*, New York: Palgrave.

*Parente, S.L. and E.C. Prescott (2000), *Barriers to Riches*, Cambridge, MA: MIT Press.

Parente, S.L. and E.C. Prescott (2005), 'A Unified Theory of the Evolution of International Income Levels', in P. Aghion and S. Durlauf (eds), *Handbook of Economic Growth*, Amsterdam: Elsevier.

Pearson, L.B. (1969), *Partners in Development: Report of the UN Commission on International Development (Pearson Report)*, New York: Praeger.

Persky, J. (1991), 'Lange and von Mises, Large Scale Enterprises, and the Economic Case for Socialism', *Journal of Economic Perspectives*, Fall.

Persson, T. and G. Tabellini (1994), 'Is Inequality Harmful to Growth?', *American Economic Review*, June.

Pipes, R. (1954), *The Formation of the Soviet Union*, Cambridge, MA: Harvard University Press.

Pipes, R. (2004), 'Fright from Freedom: What Russians Think and Want', *Foreign Affairs*, May–June.

*Pomeranz, K. (2000), *The Great Divergence: China, Europe and the Making of the Modern World Economy*. Princeton, NJ: Princeton University Press.

Philipson, T. (2001), 'The World-wide Growth in Obesity: An Economic Research Agenda', *Health Economics*, **10**(1).

Popkin, B. and C. Doak (1998), 'The Obesity Epidemic is a Worldwide Phenomenon', *Nutrition Review*, **56**(4).

Popper, K. (1971), *The Open Society and Its Enemies*, Princeton, NJ: Princeton University Press.

Porter, M.E. (1980), *Competitive Strategy: Techniques for Analyzing Industries and Competitors*, New York: The Free Press.
*Porter, M.E. (1990), *The Competitive Advantage of Nations*, New York: The Free Press.
Porter, M.E. (1994), 'The Role of Location in Competition', *Journal of the Economics of Business*, **1**(1).
Porter, M. (1995), 'The Competitive Advantage of the Inner City', *Harvard Business Review*, May–June.
Porter, M.E. (1996), 'Competitive Advantage, Agglomeration Economies, and Regional Policy', *International Regional Science Review*, **19**(1–2).
*Porter, M.E. (1998), 'Clusters and the New Economics of Competition', *Harvard Business Review*, November–December.
*Porter, M.E. (2000), 'Attitudes, Values, Beliefs, and the Microeconomics of Prosperity', in L.E. Harrison and S.P. Huntington (eds), *Culture Matters: How Values Shape Human Progress*, New York: Basic Books.
Porter, M.E. (2001), 'Enhancing the Microeconomic Foundations of Prosperity: The Current Competitiveness Index', in M.E. Porter et al. (eds), *The Global Competitiveness Report, 2001–02*, New York: Oxford University Press.
Porter, M.E. (2003), 'The Economic Performance of Regions', *Regional Studies*, August–October.
Porter, M.E. (2004), 'Building the Microeconomic Foundations of Prosperity: Findings from the Business Competitiveness Index', in M.E. Porter, K. Schwab, X. Sala-i-Martin and A. Lopez-Claros (eds), *The Global Competitiveness Report 2004–2005*, World Economic Forum, New York: Palgrave Macmillan.
*Porter, M.E. (2005), 'Building the Microeconomic Foundations of Prosperity: Findings from the Business Competitiveness Index', in M.E. Porter, K. Schwab and A. Lopez-Claros (eds), *The Global Competitiveness Report 2005–2006*, World Economic Forum, New York: Palgrave Macmillan.
Porter, M.E. and C.H.M. Ketels (2003), *UK Competitiveness: Moving to the Next Stage*, DTI Economics Paper, No. 3.
Porter, M.E. and C. van der Linde (1995), 'Green and Competitive: Ending the Stalemate', *Harvard Business Review*, September–October.
Porter, M.E. and M. Sakakibara (2001), 'Competing at Home to Win Abroad: Evidence from Japanese Industry', *Review of Economics and Statistics*, May.
*Porter, M.E. and M. Sakakibara (2004), 'Competition in Japan', *Journal of Economic Perspectives*, Winter.
Porter, M.E. and Ö. Sölvell (1998), 'The Role of Geography in the Process of Innovation and Sustainable Competitive Advantage of Firms', in

A.D. Chandler, Jr, P. Hagström and Ö. Sölvell (eds), *The Dynamic Firm*, Oxford: Oxford University Press.

*Porter, M.E. and H. Takeuchi (1999), 'Fixing What Really Ails Japan', *Foreign Affairs*, May–June.

Porter, M.E. and E.O. Teisberg (2006), *Redefining Health Care: Creating Value-Based Competition on Results*, Cambridge, MA: Harvard Business School Press.

Porter, M.E., S. Stern and J.L. Furman (2002), 'The Determinants of National Innovative Capacity', *Research Policy*, 31(6).

Porter, M.E., H. Takeuchi and M. Sakakibara (2000), *Can Japan Compete?*, Basingstoke, UK: Macmillan.

Porter, M.E., P.K. Cornelius, M. Levinson and J.D. Sachs (eds) (2000), *The Global Competitiveness Report 2000*, New York: Oxford University Press.

Porter, M.E., P.K. Cornelius, J. McArthur, J.D. Sachs and K. Schwab (eds) (2001), *The Global Competitiveness Report 2001–02*, New York: Oxford University Press.

Porter, M.E., K. Schwab, X. Sala-i-Martin and A. Lopez-Claros (eds) (2004), *The Global Competitiveness Report 2004–05*, New York: Palgrave Macmillan.

*Porter, M.E., K. Schwab and A. Lopez-Claros (eds) (2005), *The Global Competitiveness Report 2005–06*, New York: Palgrave Macmillan.

Prakash, A. (2001), 'Grappling with Globalisation: Challenges for Economic Governance', *World Economy*, April.

Prasad, E.S. and R.G. Rajan (2006), 'Modernising China's Growth Paradigm', *American Economic Review*, May.

Prebisch, R. (1950), *The Economic Development of Latin America and its Principal Problems*, New York: United Nations.

Preobrazhensky, E. (1926), 'Socialist Primitive Accumulation', reprinted in A. Nove and D.M. Nuti (eds) (1972), *Socialist Economics*, Harmondsworth, UK: Penguin.

Prescott, E. (2006), 'The Transformation of Macroeconomic Policy and Research', *Journal of Political Economy*, April.

*Pritchett, L. (1997a), 'Divergence, Big Time', *Journal of Economic Perspectives*, Summer.

Pritchett, L. (1997b), 'Where has All the Education Gone?', World Bank Policy Research Working Paper No. 1581, June.

Pritchett, L. (2000), 'Understanding Patterns of Economic Growth: Searching for Hills, Plateaus, Mountains and Plains', *The World Bank Economic Review*, 14(2).

Pritchett, L. and D.I. Lindauer (2002), 'What's the Big Idea? The Third Generation of Policies for Economic Growth', *Economia*, Fall.

Quibria, M.G. (2005), 'Rethinking Development Effectiveness', *World Economics*, January–March.

Radelet, S. (2003), 'Bush and Foreign Aid', *Foreign Affairs*, September–October.

*Radelet, S. and J.D. Sachs (1998), 'The East Asian Financial Crisis: Diagnosis, Remedies, Prospects', *Brookings Papers on Economic Activity*, No. 1.

*Radelet, S., M. Clemens and R. Bhavnani (2005), 'Aid and Growth', *Finance and Development*, September.

Radelet, S., J.D. Sachs and J. Lee (1997), 'Economic Growth in Asia', Development Discussion Paper No. 609, Harvard Institute for International Development.

*Rajan, R. and G. Bird (2001), 'Economic Globalisation: How Far and How Much Further?', *World Economics*, July–September.

Rajan, R.G. and A. Subramanian (2005a), 'What Undermines Aid's Impact on Growth?', International Monetary Fund Working Paper No. 05/126, June.

Rajan, R.G. and A. Subramanian (2005b), 'Aid and Growth: What Does the Cross-Country Evidence Really Show?', International Monetary Fund Working Paper No. 05/127, June.

Rajan, R. and L. Zingales (2003a), 'The Great Reversals: The Politics of Financial Development in the Twentieth Century', *Journal of Financial Economics*, July.

*Rajan, R. and L. Zingales (2003b), *Saving Capitalism from the Capitalists: Unleashing the Power of Financial Markets to Create Wealth and Spread Opportunity*, New York: Crown Business.

Rajan, R.G. and L. Zingales (2006), 'Making Capitalism Work for Everyone', *World Economics*, January–March.

Ranis, G., F. Stewart and A Ramirez (2000), 'Economic Growth and Human Devlopment', *World Development*, February.

Ravallion, M. (2003), 'The Debate on Globalisation, Poverty and Inequality: Why Measurement Matters', World Bank Policy Research Paper No. 3038, April.

*Ravallion, M. (2004), 'Competing Concepts of Inequality in the Globalisation Debate', World Bank Policy Research Paper No. 3243, March.

Rebelo, S. (1991), 'Long-Run Policy Analysis and Long-Run Growth', *Journal of Political Economy*, June.

Reddaway, P. and D. Glinsky (2001), *Russia's Decade of Tragedy, Market Bolshevism Against Democracy*, Washington, DC: United States Institute of Peace Press.

*Reinhart, C. and K. Rogoff (2004), 'The Modern History of Exchange Rate Regimes: A Reinterpretation', *Quarterly Journal of Economics*, February.

Ricardo, D. (1817), *On the Principles of Political Economy and Taxation*, edited by R.M. Hartwell (1971), Harmondsworth, UK: Penguin.

Riddell, R.C. (1987), *Foreign Aid Reconsidered*, Baltimore, MD: Johns Hopkins University Press.

*Riddell, R. (2007), *Does Foreign Aid Really Work?*, Oxford: Oxford University Press.

Riley, J. (2001), *Rising Life Expectancy: A Global History*, New York: Cambridge University Press.

Rima, I. (1986), *Development of Economic Analysis*, Homewood, IL: Irwin.

Rivera-Batiz, L. and P.M. Romer (1991a), 'Economic Integration and Endogenous Growth', *Quarterly Journal of Economics*, May.

Rivera-Batiz, L. and P.M. Romer (1991b), 'International Trade with Endogenous Technological Change', *European Economic Review*, May.

Robbins, L. (1933), *The Great Depression*, London: Macmillan.

*Roberts, P.C. (1971), 'Oskar Lange's Theory of Socialist Planning', *Journal of Political Economy*, May–June.

Robinson, J.V. (1975), 'Marx, Marshall and Keynes', in *Collected Economic Papers*, Vol. II, Oxford: Basil Blackwell.

Robinson, J.V. (1975), 'Korea, 1964: Economic Miracle', *Monthly Review*, January 1965, reprinted in J. Robinson, *Collected Economic Papers*: Volume III, 2nd edn 1975, Oxford: Basil Blackwell.

Robinson, J. (2002), '*States and Power in Africa* by Jeffrey I Herbst: A Review Essay', *Journal of Economic Literature*, June.

Rockoff, H. (2000), 'How Long Did it Take the US to Become an Optimal Currency Area?', National Bureau of Economic Research Historical Paper No. 124.

Rodriguez, F. and D. Rodrik (2000), 'Trade Policy and Economic Growth: A Sceptics Guide to Cross-National Data', *NBER Macroeconomics Annual*.

Rodrik, D. (1993), 'The Positive Economics of Policy Reform', *American Economic Review*, May.

Rodrik, D. (1994), 'The Rush to Free Trade in the Developing World: Why So Late? Why Now? Will it Last?', in S. Haggard and S. Webb (eds), *Voting for Reform: Democracy, Political Liberalisation, and Economic Adjustment*, Oxford: Oxford University Press.

*Rodrik, D. (1995), 'Getting Interventions Right: How South Korea and Taiwan Grew Rich', *Economic Policy*, April.

*Rodrik, D. (1996), 'Understanding Economic Policy Reform', *Journal of Economic Literature*, March.

Rodrik, D. (1997), *Has Globalisation Gone Too Far?*, Washington, DC: Institute for International Economics.

Rodrik, D. (1998a), 'Symposium on Globalisation in Perspective: An Introduction', *Journal of Economic Perspectives*, Fall.

Rodrik, D. (1998b), 'Who Needs Capital Account Convertibility?', in P. Kenen (ed.), *Should the IMF Pursue Capital Account Convertibility?*, Essays in International Finance No. 207, Princeton: Princeton University Press.

Rodrik, D. (1998c), 'Globalisation, Social Conflict and Economic Growth', *World Economy*, March.

Rodrik, D. (1998d), 'Why Do More Open Economies Have Bigger Governments?', *Journal of Political Economy*, October.

*Rodrik, D. (1999a), *The New Global Economy and Developing Countries: Making Openness Work*, Washington, DC: Overseas Development Council.

Rodrik, D. (1999b), 'Where Did All the Growth Go? External Shocks, Social Conflict and Growth Collapses', *Journal of Economic Growth*, December.

Rodrik, D. (1999c), 'The Asian Financial Crisis and the Virtues of Democracy', *Challenge*, July–August.

Rodrik, D. (1999d), 'Democracies Pay Higher Wages', *Quarterly Journal of Economics*, August.

*Rodrik, D. (2000a), 'How Far Will International Integration Go?', *Journal of Economic Perspectives*, Winter.

Rodrik, D. (2000b), 'Institutions for High-Quality Growth: What are They and How to Acquire Them', *Studies in International Development*, Fall.

Rodrik, D. (2000c), 'Participatory Politics, Social Co-operation and Economic Stability', *American Economic Review*, May.

Rodrik, D. (2001a), 'Development Strategies for the Twenty-first Century', *Annual World Bank Conference on Development*, April, www.ksg.harvard.edu/rodrik/.

Rodrik, D. (2001b), 'Trading in Illusions', *Foreign Policy*, March–April.

Rodrik, D. (2001c), 'The Developing Countries Hazardous Obsession with Global Integration', www.ksg.harvard.edu/rodrik/.

*Rodrik, D. (ed.) (2003a), *In Search of Prosperity: Analytic Narratives on Economic Growth*, Princeton, NJ: Princeton University Press.

Rodrik, D. (2003b), 'Institutions, Integration and Geography: In Search of the Deep Determinants of Economic Growth', in D. Rodrik (ed.), *In Search of Prosperity: Analytic Narratives on Economic Growth*, Princeton, NJ: Princeton University Press.

Rodrik, D. (2004), 'Globalisation and Growth: Looking in the Wrong Places', *Journal of Policy Modeling*, **26**(4).

Rodrik, D. (2005a), 'Feasible Globalizations', in M. Weinstein (ed.), *Globalization: What's New?*, New York: Columbia University Press.

*Rodrik, D. (2005b), 'Growth Strategies', in P. Aghion and S. Durlauf (eds), *Handbook of Economic Growth*, Amsterdam: Elsevier.

Rodrik, D. (2006), 'Goodbye Washington Consensus, Hello Washington Confusion?', *Journal of Economic Literature*, December.

*Rodrik, D. and R. Hausmann (2003), 'Economic Development as Self-Discovery', *Journal of Development Economics*, December.

Rodrik, D. and A. Mayda (2005), 'Why Are Some Individuals (and Countries) More Protectionist than Others?', *European Economic Review*, August.

Rodrik, D. and S. Mukland (2005), 'In Search of the Holy Grail: Policy Convergence, Experimentation, and Economic Performance', *American Economic Review*, March.

*Rodrik, D. and A. Subramanian (2003), 'The Primacy of Institutions', *Finance and Development*, June.

Rodrik, D. and A. Subramanian (2006), 'From "Hindu Growth" to Productivity Surge: The Mystery of the Indian Growth Transition', *IMF Staff Papers*, Vol. 52, No. 2.

Rodrik, D. and A. Velasco (1999), 'Short-term Capital Flows', *Annual World Bank Conference on Development*, www.ksg.harvard.edu/rodrik/.

Rodrik, R. and R. Wacziarg (2005), 'Do Democratic Transitions Produce Bad Economic Outcomes?', *American Economic Review*, May.

*Rodrik, D., R. Hausmann and L. Pritchett (2005), 'Growth Accelerations', *Journal of Economic Growth*, December.

Rodrik, D., R. Hausmann and A. Velasco (2007), 'Growth Diagnostics', in J.E. Stiglitz and N. Serra (eds), *The Washington Consensus Reconsidered: Towards a New Global Governance*, New York: Oxford University Press.

Rodrik, D., A. Subramanian and F. Trebbi (2004), 'Institutions Rule: The Primacy of Institutions over Geography and Integration in Economic Development', *Journal of Economic Growth*, June.

Rogoff, K. (2002), 'An Open Letter to Joseph Stiglitz', www.imf.org.

*Rogoff, K. (2003), 'In Defence of the IMF', *Foreign Policy*, January–February.

*Rogoff, K. (2004), 'Extending the Limits of Global Financial Integration', *Journal of Policy Modeling*, 26(4).

Roland, G. (1994), 'On the Speed and Sequencing of Privatisation and Restructuring', *Economic Journal*, September.

*Roland, G. (2001), 'Ten Years After: Transition and Economics', *IMF Staff Papers*, **48**, special issue.

*Roland, G. (2002), 'The Political Economy of Transition', *Journal of Economic Perspectives*, Winter.

Roland, G. (2005), 'The Russian Economy in 2005', http://www.econ.berkeley.edu/~groland/index.html.

Rolnick, A. (1999), 'Interview with Stanley Fischer', *The Region*, December.

Romer, P.M. (1986), 'Increasing Returns and Long-Run Growth', *Journal of Political Economy*, October.

Romer, P.M. (1990), 'Endogenous Technological Change', *Journal of Political Economy*, October.

Romer, P.M. (1993), 'Idea Gaps and Object Gaps in Economic Development', *Journal of Monetary Economics*, December.

*Romer, P.M. (1994), 'The Origins of Endogenous Growth', *Journal of Economic Perspectives*, Winter.

Romer, P.M. (1999), 'Interview with Paul M. Romer', in B. Snowdon and H.R. Vane (eds), *Conversations with Leading Economists: Interpreting Modern Macroeconomics*, Cheltenham, UK and Northampton, MA, USA: Edward Elgar.

Rose-Ackerman, S. (2001), 'Trust and Honesty in Post-Socialist Societies', *Kyklos*, **54**(2–3).

Rosenstein-Rodan, P. (1943), 'Problems of Industrialization of Eastern and South- Eastern Europe', *Economic Journal*, June–September.

Rosser, J.B. and M.V. Rosser (2004), *Comparative Economics in a Transforming World Economy*, Cambridge, MA: MIT Press.

Rostow, W.W. (1956), 'The Take-off Into Self-Sustained Growth', *Economic Journal*, March.

Rostow, W.W. (1960), *The Stages of Economic Growth*, Cambridge: Cambridge University Press.

*Rostow, W. (1990), *Theories of Economic Growth from David Hume to the Present*, Oxford: Oxford University Press.

Roubini, N. and X. Sala-i-Martin (1992), 'Financial Repression and Economic Growth', *Journal of Development Economics*, July.

Roubini, N. and X. Sala-i-Martin (1995), 'A Growth Model of Inflation, Tax Evasion, and Financial Repression', *Journal of Monetary Economics*, April.

*Rowley, C.K. (2000), 'Political Culture and Economic Performance in Sub-Saharan Africa', *European Journal of Political Economy*, March.

Sachs, J.D. (1987), 'The Bolivian Hyperinflation and Stabilisation', *American Economic Review*, May.

Sachs, J.D. (1990), 'A Strategy for Efficient Debt Reduction', *Journal of Economic Perspectives*, Winter.

Sachs, J.D. (1993), *Poland's Jump to the Market Economy*, Cambridge, MA: MIT Press.

Sachs, J.D. (1995), 'The Age of Global Capitalism', *Foreign Policy*, Spring.

Sachs, J.D. (1996a), 'The Transition at Mid Decade', *American Economic Review*, May.

Sachs, J.D. (1996b), 'Economic Transition and Exchange Rate Regime', *American Economic Review*, May.

*Sachs, J.D. (1999), 'Twentieth-Century Political Economy: A Brief History of Global Capitalism', *Oxford Review of Economic Policy*, December.

*Sachs, J.D. (2000a), 'Notes on a New Sociology of Economic Development', in L.E. Harrison and S.P. Huntington (eds), *Culture Matters: How Values Shape Human Progress*, New York: Basic Books.

Sachs, J.D. (2000b), 'A New Map of the World', *The Economist*, 24 June.

Sachs, J.D. (2001a), 'The Geography and Poverty of Wealth', *Scientific American*, March.

Sachs, J.D. (2001b), 'The Strategic Significance of Global Inequality', *The Washington Quarterly*, Summer.

Sachs, J.D. (2002a), 'A New Global Effort to Control Malaria', *Science*, October.

Sachs, J.D. (2002b), 'Weapons of Mass Salvation', *The Economist*, 26 October.

*Sachs, J.D. (2002c), 'Resolving the Debt Crisis in Low-Income Countries', *Brookings Papers on Economic Activity*, No. 1.

Sachs, J.D. (2003a), 'Institutions Matter, But Not For Everything', *Finance and Development*, June.

*Sachs, J.D. (ed.) (2003b), *Millennium Development Goals: A Compact Among Nations to End Poverty: Human Development Report 2003*, New York: United Nations.

*Sachs, J.D. (2005a), *The End of Poverty: How We Can Make It Happen In Our Lifetime?*, New York: Penguin.

Sachs, J.D. (2005b), 'The End of Poverty', *Time Magazine*, 14 March.

Sachs, J.D. (2005c), 'The Development Challenge', *Foreign Affairs*, March/April.

Sachs, J.D. (2005d), 'The Mission: To Free Africa from War, Poverty and Disease', *Sunday Times Magazine*, 3 July.

Sachs, J.D. (2005e), 'Can Extreme Poverty Be Eliminated?', *Scientific American*, September.

Sachs, J.D. and N. Bajpai (2001), 'The Decade of Development: Goal Setting and Policy Challenges in India', Harvard University Centre for International Development Working Paper No. 62, February.

Sachs, J.D. and P. Larrain (1992), *Macroeconomics in the Global Economy*, New York: Prentice-Hall.

Sachs, J. and J.W. McArthur (2001), 'Institutions and Geography: Comment on Acemoglu, Johnson and Robinson', National Bureau of Economic Research Working Paper No. 8114, February.

Sachs, J.D. and J.W. McArthur (2005), 'A Plan for Meeting the Millennium Development Goals', *The Lancet*, 22 January.

Sachs, J.D. and J. Rappaport (2003), 'The United States as a Coastal Nation', *Journal of Economic Growth*, March.

Sachs, J.D. and F. Rodriguez (1999), 'Why Do Resource-Abundant Economies Grow More Slowly?', *Journal for Economic Growth*, September.

Sachs, J.D. and A.M. Warner (1995), 'Economic Reform and the Process of Global Integration', *Brookings Papers on Economic Activity*, No. 1.

Sachs, J.D. and A.M. Warner (1997a), 'Sources of Slow Growth in African Economies', *Journal of African Economies*, **6**(3).

Sachs, J.D. and A.M. Warner (1997b), 'Fundamental Sources of Long-Run Growth', *American Economic Review*, May.

Sachs, J.D. and A.M. Warner (1999), 'The Big Push, Natural Resource Booms and Growth', *Journal of Development Economics*, June.

*Sachs, J.D. and A.M. Warner (2001), 'The Curse of Natural Resources', *European Economic Review*, May.

Sachs, J.D. and J. Williamson (1986), 'Managing the LDC Debt Crisis', *Brookings Papers on Economic Activity*, No. 2.

*Sachs, J.D. and W.T. Woo (1994), 'Structural Factors in the Economic Reforms of China, Eastern Europe, and the Former Soviet Union', *Economic Policy*, April.

Sachs, J.D. and W.T. Woo (1997), 'Understanding China's Economic Performance', Development Discussion Paper, No. 575, Harvard Institute for International Development, March.

Sachs, J.D., W.T. Woo and S. Parker (eds) (1997), *Economies in Transition*, Cambridge, MA: MIT Press.

Sachs, J.D. et al. (2002), 'Geography, Economic Policy, and Regional Development in China', *Asian Economic Papers*, Winter.

*Sachs, J.D. et al. (2004), 'Ending Africa's Poverty Trap', *Brookings Papers on Economic Activity*, No. 1.

*Sachs, J.D. et al. (2005), *Investing in Development: A Practical Plan to Achieve the Millennium Development Goals*, United Nations Millennium Project, New York: Earthscan.

Sahn, D. and D. Stifel (2003), 'Progress Towards the Millennium Development Goals in Africa', *World Development*, January.

Sala-i-Martin, X. (1990a), 'Lecture Notes on Economic Growth (I): Introduction to the Literature and the Neoclassical Growth Model', National Bureau of Economic Research Working Paper No. 3563, December.

Sala-i-Martin, X. (1990b), 'Lecture Notes on Economic Growth (II): Five Prototype Models of Endogenous Growth', National Bureau of Economic Research Working Paper No. 3564, December.

Sala-i-Martin, X. (1994), 'Cross Sectional Regressions and the Empirics of Economic Growth', *European Economic Review*, April.

Sala-i-Martin, X. (1996a), 'The Classical Approach to Convergence Analysis', *Economic Journal*, July.

Sala-i-Martin, X. (1996b), 'Regional Cohesion: Evidence of Regional Growth and Convergence', *European Economic Review*, June.

Sala-i-Martin, X. (1997a), 'I Just Ran 2 Million Regressions', *American Economic Review*, May.

Sala-i-Martin, X. (1997b), 'Transfers, Social Safety Nets, and Growth', *IMF Staff Papers*, **44**(1).

*Sala-i-Martin, X. (2002a), 'The Disturbing "Rise" of Global Inequality', National Bureau of Economic Research Working Paper No. 8904, April.

*Sala-i-Martin, X. (2002b), 'The World Distribution of Income', National Bureau of Economic Research Working Paper No. 8933, May.

Sala-i-Martin, X. (2002c), 'The Myth of Exploding Income Inequality in Europe and the World', in H. Kierzkowski (ed.), *Europe and Globalisation*, London: Palgrave Macmillan.

Sala-i-Martin, X. (2002d), 'Fifteen Years of Growth Economics: What Have We Learnt?', Department of Economics Discussion Paper No. 0102-47, Columbia University, April.

*Sala-i-Martin, X. (2006), 'The World Distribution of Income: Falling Poverty and . . . Convergence, Period', *Quarterly Journal of Economics*, May.

*Sala-i-Martin, X. and E. Artadi (2004), 'The Global Competitiveness Index', in M. Porter et al. (eds), *The Global Competitiveness Report, 2004–05*, Oxford: Oxford University Press.

*Sala-i-Martin, X. and A. Subramanian (2003), 'Addressing the Natural Resource Curse: An Illustration From Nigeria', National Bureau of Economic Research Working Paper No. 9804, June.

Samuelson, P.A. (1947), *Foundations of Economic Analysis*, Cambridge, MA: Harvard University Press.

Samuelson, P.A. (1948), *Economics*, New York: McGraw-Hill.

Sargent, T.J. (1982), 'The Ends of Four Big Inflations', in R.H. Hall (ed.), *Inflation: Causes and Effects*, Chicago, IL: University of Chicago Press.

Schieber, S. and P. Hewitt (2000), 'Demographic Risk in Industrial Societies', *World Economics*, October–December.

Schneider, E. (1956), *Einführung in die Wirtschaftstheorie*, Tübingen: J.C.B. Mohr (Paul Siebeck).

Schroeder, G.E. (1991), 'The Dismal Fate of Soviet-Type Economies: Mises was Right', *Cato Journal*, Spring–Summer.

Schultz, G.G. and H.J.W. Ursprung (1999), 'Globalisation of the Economy and the Nation State', *World Economy*, May.

Schumpeter, J.A. (1912), *Theory of Economic Development*, Cambridge, MA: Harvard University Press.

Schumpeter, J.A. (1942), *Capitalism, Socialism, and Democracy*, New York: Harper & Row.

*Scully, G.W. (1988), 'The Institutional Framework of Economic Development', *Journal of Political Economy*, June.

*Seabright, P. (2004), *The Company of Strangers: A Natural History of Economic Life*, Princeton, NJ: Princeton University Press.

Seers, D. (1972), 'What Are We Trying To Measure?', *Journal of Development Studies*, April.

Sen, A.K. (1981), *Poverty and Famines: An Essay on Entitlements and Deprivation*, Oxford: Clarendon Press.

Sen, A. (1987), *The Standard of Living*, Cambridge: Cambridge University Press.

Sen, A.K. (1997), 'Population Policy: Authoritarianism Versus Cooperation', *Journal of Population Economics*, Spring.

*Sen, A.K. (1998), 'Mortality as an Indicator of Economic Success and Failure', *Economic Journal*, January.

*Sen, A.K. (1999a), *Development as Freedom*, Oxford: Oxford University Press.

Sen, A.K. (1999b), 'Democracy as a Universal Value', *Journal of Democracy*, **10**(3).

Sen, A.K. (2000), 'A Decade of Human Development', *Journal of Human Development*, February.

Sen, A.K. (2001), 'What is Development About?', in G. Meier and J.E. Stiglitz (eds), *Frontiers of Development Economics: The Future in Perspective*, Oxford: Oxford University Press.

Sen, A. (2006), 'The Man Without Pain', *Foreign Affairs*, March–April.

Sena, V. (2004), 'The Return of the Prince of Denmark: A Survey of Recent Developments in the Economics of Innovation', *Economic Journal*, June.

Sender, J. (1999), 'Africa's Economic Performance: Limitations of the Current Consensus', *Journal of Economic Perspectives*, Summer.

Shaw, G.K. (1992), 'Policy Implications of Endogenous Growth Theory', *Economic Journal*, May.

Shiller, R., M. Boycko and V. Korobov (1991), 'Popular Attitudes Towards Free Markets: The Soviet Union and the United States Compared', *American Economic Review*, June.

Shiller, R.J., M. Boycko and V. Korobov (1992), 'Hunting for Homo Sovieticus: Situational versus Attitudinal Factors in Economic Behaviour', *Brookings Papers on Economic Activity*, No. 1.

*Shleifer, A. (1998), 'State Versus Private Ownership', *Journal of Economic Perspectives*, Fall.

*Shleifer, A. and D. Treisman (2005), 'A Normal Country: Russia After Communism', *Journal of Economic Perspectives*, Winter.

Shleifer, A. and R. Vishny (1994), 'The Politics of Market Socialism', *Journal of Economic Perspectives*, Spring.

Shleifer, A. et al. (2003), 'The New Comparative Economics: A First Look', *Journal of Comparative Economics*, December.

Singer, H.W. (1950), 'The Distribution of Gains Between Borrowing and Investing Countries', *American Economic Review*, May.

Skidelsky, R. (1992), *John Maynard Keynes: The Economist As Saviour 1920–1937*, London: Macmillan.

Skidelsky, R. (2000), *John Maynard Keynes: Fighting for Britain*, London: Macmillan.

Skidelsky, R. (2005), 'Keynes and Globalisation', *World Economics*, January–March.

Slaughter, M.J. (1999), 'Globalisation and Wages: A Tale of Two Perspectives', *World Economy*, July.

Smeeding, T. (2006), 'Poor People in Rich Nations: The United States in Comparative Perspective', *Journal of Economic Perspectives*, Winter.

Smith, A. (1776), *An Inquiry into the Nature and Causes of the Wealth of Nations*, edited by R.H. Campbell and A.S. Skinner (1976), Oxford: Clarendon.

Snowdon, B. (1985), 'The Political Economy of the Ethiopian Famine', *National Westminster Bank Review*, November.

Snowdon, B. (1997), 'Politics and the Business Cycle', *Political Quarterly*, July.

Snowdon, B. (2000), 'The International Economic System in the Twentieth Century: An Interview with Barry Eichengreen', *World Economics*, July–September.

Snowdon, B. (2001a), 'Jagdish Bhagwati on Trade, Democracy and Growth: Championing Free Trade in the Second Age of Globalisation', *World Economics*, October–December.

Snowdon, B. (2001b), 'Redefining the Role of the State: Stiglitz on Building a Post-Washington Consensus', *World Economics*, July– September.

Snowdon, B. (2002a), *Conversations on Growth, Stability and Trade*, Cheltenham, UK and Northampton, MA, USA: Edward Elgar.

Snowdon, B. (2002b), 'In Praise of Historical Economics: Bradford DeLong on Growth, Development and Instability', *World Economics*, January–March.

Snowdon, B. and G. Stonehouse (2006), 'Competitiveness in a Globalised World: Michael Porter on the Microeconomic Foundations of the Competitiveness of Nations, Regions, and Firms', *Journal of International Business Studies*, March.

Snowdon, B. and H.R. Vane (1996), 'The Development of Modern Macroeconomics: Reflections in the Light of Johnson's Analysis After Twenty-Five Years', *Journal of Macroeconomics*, Summer.

Snowdon, B. and H.R. Vane (1999), *Conversations with Leading Economists: Interpreting Modern Macroeconomics*, Cheltenham, UK and Northampton, MA, USA: Edward Elgar.

Snowdon, B. and H.R. Vane (2005), *Modern Macroeconomics: Its Origins, Development and Current State*, Cheltenham, UK and Northampton, MA, USA: Edward Elgar.

Snower, D. and C. Merkl (2006), 'The Caring Hand that Cripples: The East German Labour Market after Reunification', *American Economic Review*, May.

*Sokoloff, K. and S. Engerman (2000), 'Institutions, Factor Endowments, and Paths of Development in the New World', *Journal of Economic Perspectives*, Summer.

Solow, R.M. (1956), 'A Contribution to the Theory of Economic Growth', *Quarterly Journal of Economics*, February.

Solow, R.M. (1957), 'Technical Change and the Aggregate Production Function', *Review of Economics and Statistics*, August.

Solow, R.M. (2002), 'Neoclassical Growth Model', in B. Snowdon and H.R. Vane (eds), *An Encyclopedia of Macroeconomics*, Cheltenham, UK and Northampton, MA, USA: Edward Elgar.

Solow, R. (2002), 'Interview with Robert Solow', *The Region*, September.

Spolare, E. and R. Wacziarg (2005), 'Borders and Growth', *Journal of Economic Growth*, December.

Srinivasan, T.N. (1994), 'Human Development: A New Paradigm or Reinvention of the Wheel', *American Economic Review*, May.

Srinivasan, T.N. (1999), 'Developing Countries in the World Trading System: From GATT, 1947, to the Third Ministerial Meeting of the WTO, 1999', *World Economy*, November.

Sriskandarajah, D. (2005), 'Migration and Development: New Research and Policy Agenda', *World Economics*, April–June.

Stark, O. (2005), 'The New Economics of the Brian Drain', *World Economics*, April–June.

Steckel, R.H. (1979), 'Slave Height Profiles from Coastwise Manifests', *Explorations in Economic History*, **16**(4).

*Steckel, R.H. (1995), 'Stature and the Standard of Living', *Journal of Economic Literature*, December.

*Steckel, R.H. (1998), 'Strategic Ideas in the Rise of the New Anthropometric History and Their Implications for Interdisciplinary Research', *Journal of Economic Literature*, September.

Steckel, R.H. and J.C. Rose (2002), *The Backbone of History: Health and Nutrition in the Western Hemisphere*, Cambridge: Cambridge University Press.

Steel, D.R. (1992), *From Marx to Mises: Post Capitalist Society and the*

*Challenges of Economic Calculation*, La Salle, IL: Open Court.

Stern, N. (2006), 'What is the Economics of Climate Change', *World Economics*, April–June.

Stern, N., J. Dethier and F. Rogers (2005), *Growth and Empowerment: Making Development Happen*, Cambridge, MA: MIT Press.

Stiglitz, J.E. (1986), 'The New Development Economics', *World Development*, February.

Stiglitz, J.E. (1994), *Whither Socialism*, Cambridge, MA: MIT Press.

Stiglitz, J.E. (1996), 'Some Lessons from the East Asian Miracle', *World Bank Research Observer*, August.

Stiglitz, J.E. (1998), 'More Instruments and Broader Goals: Moving Toward the Post-Washington Consensus', The 1998 WIDER Annual Lecture, Helsinki, January, www.worldbank.org.

*Stiglitz, J.E. (1999), 'The World Bank at the Millennium', *Economic Journal*, November.

Stiglitz, J.E. (2000a), 'Capital Market Liberalisation, Economic Growth and Instability', *World Development*, June.

Stiglitz, J.E. (2000b), 'Whither Reform: Ten Years of the Transition', in B. Pleskovic and J.E. Stglitz (eds), *Annual World Bank Conference on Economic Development*, Washington, DC: World Bank.

*Stiglitz, J.E. (2002a), *Globalisation and its Discontents*, London: Allen Lane, The Penguin Press.

Stiglitz, J.E. (2002b), 'Information and the Change of Paradigm in Economics', *American Economic Review*, June.

Stiglitz, J.E. (2004a), 'Globalisation and Growth in Emerging Markets', *Journal of Policy Modeling*, **26**(4).

Stiglitz, J.E. (2004b), 'Capital Market Liberalisation, and the IMF', *Oxford Review of Economic Policy*, **20**(2).

*Stiglitz, J.E. (2006), *Making Globalisation Work: The Next Steps to Global Justice*, London: Penguin Allen Lane.

*Stiglitz, J.E. and A. Charlton (2005), *Fair Trade for All: How Trade Can Promote Development*, Oxford: Oxford University Press.

Stiglitz, J.E. and K. Hoff (2005), 'The Creation of the Rule of Law and the Legitimacy of Property Rights: The Political and Economic Consequences of a Corrupt Privatisation', National Bureau of Economic Research Working Paper No. 11772, November.

*Stiglitz, J.E. and S. Yusuf (eds) (2001), *Rethinking the East Asian Miracle*, Oxford: Oxford University Press.

Stone, R. (1986), 'Nobel Memorial Lecture 1984: The Accounts of Society', *Journal of Applied Econometrics*, January.

Strauss, J. and D. Thomas (1998), 'Health, Nutrition, and Economic Development', *Journal of Economic Literature*, June.

Such, G. and I.J. Tóth (1989), 'A Magyar Közgazdaságtudomány a Közgazdasági Szemle Tudománymetriai Vizsgálatainak Tükrében', *Közgazdasági Szemle*, 36(10).

*Summers, L.H. (1999), 'Reflections on Managed Global Integration', *Journal of Economic Perspectives*, Spring.

*Summers, L.H. (2000), 'International Financial Crises: Causes, Prevention and Cures', *American Economic Review*, May.

Summers, R. and A. Heston (1991), 'The Penn World Table (Mark 5): An Expanded Set of International Comparisons, 1950–88', *Quarterly Journal of Economics*, May.

Summers, R. and A. Heston (1996), 'International Price and Quantity Comparisons: Potentials and Pitfalls', *American Economic Review*, May.

Sunder, M. (2003), 'The Making of Giants in a Welfare State: The Norwegian Experience in the Twentieth Century', *Economics and Biology*, June.

*Sutcliffe, B. (2004), 'World Inequality and Globalisation', *Oxford Review of Economic Policy*, 20(1).

Svejnar, J. (2002), 'Transition Economies: Performance and Challenges', *Journal of Economic Perspectives*, Winter.

Svensson, J. (2000), 'Foreign Aid and Rent Seeking', *Journal of International Economics*, August.

Swan, T.W. (1956), 'Economic Growth and Capital Accumulation', *Economic Record*, November.

*Tanzi, V. (1998), 'Corruption Around the World: Causes, Consequences, Scope and Cures', *IMF Staff Papers*, December.

Tanzi, V. (2002), 'Globalisation and the Future of Social Protection', *Scottish Journal of Political Economy*, February.

Tanzi, V. (2004), 'Globalisation and the need for Fiscal Reform in Developing Countries', *Journal of Policy Modeling*, 26(4).

*Tanzi, V. (2005), 'The Economic Role of the State in the Twenty-first Century', *Cato Journal*, Fall.

*Tavlas, G.S. (2003), 'The Economics of Exchange Rate Regimes: A Review Essay', *World Economy*, August.

Taylor, F.M. (1929), 'The Guidance of Production in a Socialist State', *American Economic Review*, March.

Temin, P. (1997), 'Is it Kosher to Talk About Culture?', *Journal of Economic History*, June.

Temin, P. (1999), 'Globalisation', *Oxford Review of Economic Policy*, December.

Temin, P. (2006), 'The Economy of the Early Roman Empire', *Journal of Economic Perspectives*, Winter.

Temple, J. (1999), 'The New Growth Evidence', *Journal of Economic Literature*, March.

Temple, J. (2000), 'Inflation and Growth: Stories Short and Tall', *Journal of Economic Surveys*, September.

Thacker, S.C. (1999), 'The High Politics of IMF Lending', *World Politics*, **52**.

Thurow, L. (1992), *Head to Head*, New York: Morrow.

Timmer, A. and J.G. Williamson (1998), 'Immigration Policy Prior to the Thirties: Labour Markets, Policy Interaction, and Globalisation Backlash', *Population and Development Review*, December.

Todaro, M.P. (1969), 'A Model of Labour Migration and Urban Unemployment in Less Developed Economies', *American Economic Review*, March.

*Todaro, M. and S. Smith (2003), *Economic Development*, New York: Addison Wesley.

Toniolo, G. (1998), 'Europe's Golden Age, 1950–73: Speculations from a Long-Run Perspective', *Economic History Review*, May.

Tseng, W. and D. Cowan (eds) (2005), *India's and China's Experience with Reform and Growth*, New York: Palgrave.

UK Treasury (2004), *Trade and the Global Economy: The Role of International Trade in Productivity, Economic Reform and Growth*, London: Department of Trade and Industry, www.dti.gov.uk.

United Nations (2005), *The Millennium Development Goals Report 2005*, New York: United Nations.

United Nations Development Programme (2002), *Human Development Report: Deepening Democracy in a Fragmented World*, New York: Oxford University Press.

United Nations Development Programme (2005), *Human Development Report 2005: International Cooperation at the Crossroads: Aid, Trade and Security in an Unequal World*, New York: Oxford University Press.

Vanoli, A. (2005), *A History of National Accounting*, Amsterdam: IOS Press.

*Vaughn, K. (1980), 'Economic Calculation Under Socialism: The Austrian Critique', *Economic Inquiry*, October.

*Wacziarg, R. (2002), 'Review of Easterly's *The Elusive Quest for Growth*', *Journal of Economic Literature*, September.

*Wade, R. (2004a), 'Is Globalization Reducing Poverty and Inequality?', *World Development*, April.

Wade, R (2004b), 'On the Causes of Widening World Income Inequality, or Why the Matthew Effect Prevails', *New Political Economy*, **9**(2).

Webb, B. and S. Webb (1935), *Soviet Communism: A New Civilisation?*, London: Longmans and Co.

Weber, M. (1904/1930), *The Protestant Ethic and the Spirit of Capitalism*, translated by Talcott Parsons, New York: Charles Scribner's Sons.

Weil, D. (2005), *Economic Growth*, London: Pearson Addison Wesley.

White, H. (1992), 'The Macroeconomic Impact of Development Aid: A Critical Survey', *Journal of Development Studies*, January.

Williamson, J. (1990), 'What Washington Means by Policy Reform', in J. Williamson, *Latin American Adjustment: How Much has Happened?*, Washington, DC: Institute of International Economics.

*Williamson, J. (2000a), 'What Should the World Bank Think About the Washington Consensus?', *World Bank Research Observer*, August.

Williamson, J. (2000b), *Exchange Rate Regimes for Emerging Markets: Reviving the Intermediate Option*, Washington, DC: Institute for International Economics.

Williamson, J. (2003), 'From Reform Agenda to Damaged Brand Name', *Finance and Development*, September.

*Williamson, J. (2005), 'Should There be a Development Consensus?', in A. Lopez-Carlos, M.E. Porter and K. Schwab (eds), *The Global Competitiveness Report, 2005–2006*, London: Palgrave Macmillan.

Williamson, J.G. (1984), 'Why Was British Growth So Slow During the Industrial Revolution?', *Journal of Economic History*, September.

Williamson, J.G. (1987), 'Debating the British Industrial Revolution', *Explorations in Economic History*, July.

Williamson, J.G. (1988), 'Migration and Urbanisation', in H. Chenery and T.N. Srinivasan (eds), *Handbook of Development Economics*, Amsterdam: North-Holland.

*Williamson, J.G. (1996), 'Globalisation, Convergence and History', *Journal of Economic History*, June.

Williamson, J.G. (1997), 'Globalisation and Inequality: Past and Present', *World Bank Research Observer*, August.

*Williamson, J.G. (1998a), 'Globalisation, Labour Markets and Policy Backlash in the Past', *Journal of Economic Perspectives*, Fall.

Williamson, J.G. (1998b), 'Real Wages and Relative Factor Prices in the Third World 1820–1940: The Mediterranean Basin', Harvard Institute for Economic Research Discussion Paper No. 1842, July.

Williamson, J.G. (1998c), 'Real Wages and Relative Factor Prices in the Third World 1820–1940: Asia', Harvard Institute for Economic Research Discussion Paper No. 1844, August.

Williamson, J.G. (1998d), 'Real Wages and Relative Factor Prices in the Third World 1820–1940: Latin America', Harvard Institute for Economic Research Discussion Paper No. 1853, November.

Williamson, J.G. (2002a), 'Winners and Losers Over Two Centuries of Globalisation', National Bureau of Economic Research Working Paper No. 9161, September.

Williamson, J.G. (2002b), 'Is Protection Bad For Growth? Will Globalisation Last? Looking For Answers in History', www.economics. harvard.edu/~jwilliam/.

Williamson, J.G. (2003), 'Was it Stolper–Samuelson, Infant Industry or Something Else? World Tariffs 1789–1938', National Bureau of Economic Research Working Paper No. 9656, April.

*Williamson, J.G. (2004), *The Political Economy of World Mass Migration: Comparing Two Global Centuries*, Washington, DC: American Enterprise Institute Press.

*Williamson, J.G. (2005), *Globalisation and the Poor Periphery Before the Modern Era: The Ohlin Lectures*, Cambridge, MA: MIT Press.

Williamson, J.G. (2006a), Explaining World Tariffs 1870–1938: Stolper–Samuelson, Strategic Tariffs and State Revenues', in R. Findlay et al. (eds), *Eli F. Heckscher, 1879–1952: A Celebratory Symposium*, Cambridge, MA: MIT Press.

*Williamson, J.G. (2006b), 'Global Migration', *Finance and Development*, September.

*Williamson, J.G. (2006c), 'Poverty Traps, Distance and Diversity: The Migration Connection', Working Paper, Department of Economics, Harvard University.

Williamson, J.G. and Y. Hadass (2003), 'Terms of Trade Shocks and Economic Performance. 1870–1940: Prebisch and Singer Revisited', *Economic Development and Cultural Change*, April.

Winters, A.L. (2002a), 'Making the Case for Free Trade', *International Finance*, **5**(3).

*Winters, L. (2002b), 'Trade Liberalisation and Poverty: What are the Issues?', *World Economy*, September.

*Winters, A. (2004), 'Trade Performance and Economic Performance: An Overview', *Economic Journal*, February.

*Winters, A., N. McCulloch and A. McKay (2004), 'Trade Liberalization and Poverty: The Evidence So Far', *Journal of Economic Literature*, March.

Woglin, J.M. (1997), 'The Evolution of Economic Policymaking in Africa', *American Economic Review*, May.

Wolf, M. (2003), 'Is Globalisation in Danger?', *World Economy*, April.

*Wolf, M. (2004a), *Why Globalization Works: The Case For the Global Market Economy*, New Haven, CT: Princeton University Press.

Wolf, M. (2004b), 'Globalisation and Global Economic Governance', *Oxford Review of Economic Policy*, **20**(1).

*Wolf, M. (2005), 'Will Globalisation Survive?', *World Economics*, October–December.

*Woo, W.T. (1994), 'The Art of Reforming Centrally Planned Economies: Comparing China, Poland, and Russia', *Journal of Comparative Economics*, June.

World Bank (1993), *The East Asian Miracle: Economic Growth and Public Policy*, Oxford: Oxford University Press.

World Bank (1996), *From Plan to Market*, Oxford: Oxford University Press.

*World Bank (1997), *The State in a Changing World*, Oxford: Oxford University Press.

World Bank (1998), *Assessing Aid: What Works, What Doesn't and Why*, Oxford: Oxford University Press.

World Bank (2001–02), *World Development Report: Attacking Poverty*, Oxford: Oxford University Press.

*World Bank (2002), *Building Institutions for Markets*, Oxford: Oxford University Press.

*World Bank (2005), *World Development Report: A Better Investment Climate for Everyone*, Oxford: Oxford University Press.

Wrigley, E. and R. Schofield (1981), *The Population History of England 1541–1871*, Cambridge: Cambridge University Press.

Yang, X. (2003), *Economic Development and the Division of Labour*, Oxford: Blackwell.

*Yergin, D. and J. Stanislaw (1999), *The Commanding Heights: The Battle Between Government and the Market Place that is Remaking the Modern World*, New York: Simon & Schuster.

Yevstigneyeva, I.V. and R. Yevstigneyeva (1990), 'The Socioeconomic Crisis as a Crisis of State Socialist Property', *Voprosy Ekonomiki*, February.

Young, A. (1995), 'The Tyranny of Numbers: Confronting the Statistical Realities of the East Asian Growth Experience', *Quarterly Journal of Economics*, August.

Yousef, T.M. (2004), 'Development Growth and Policy Reform in the Middle East and North Africa Since 1950', *Journal of Economic Perspectives*, Summer.

Zak, P.J. and S. Knack (2001), 'Trust and Growth', *Economic Journal*, April.

Zinnes, C., Y. Eilat and J. Sachs (2001), 'The Gains from Privatisation in Transition Economies: Is "Change of Ownership" Enough?', *IMF Staff Papers*, December.

# Index